WANEELLA
PIXELSCAPES

On the cover: *Dream*, 17/03/2022, 300 × 480px
Page 97: *Untitled*, 01/10/2020, 270 × 480px
Page 161: *Untitled*, 14/10/2020, 270 × 480px

First published in the United Kingdom in 2024 by under the title *Waneella: Decade* by Read-Only Memory, an imprint of Thames & Hudson Ltd

This edition published in the United Kingdom in 2024 by Thames & Hudson Ltd, 181A High Holborn, London WC1V 7QX

First published in the United States of America in 2024 by Thames & Hudson Inc., 500 Fifth Avenue, New York, New York 10110

British Library Cataloguing-in-Publication Data
A catalogue record for this book is available from the British Library

ISBN 978-0-500-02845-2

Printed in China, by Artron Art (Group) Co., Ltd.

MIX
Paper | Supporting responsible forestry
FSC® C019910

Waneella, also known as Valeriya Sanchilo, is a prolific pixel artist who began her creative journey in multimedia animation at the Gerasimov Institute of Cinematography in Russia. In 2013, halfway through her studies, Waneella began to create pixel art – a change in direction she attributes to her fascination with the 2011 videogame *Superbrothers: Sword & Sworcery EP*. Since then, building upon a dedicated fanbase grown on Tumblr, she has become an established artist. Waneella's captivating urban scenes, with their meticulous detail and 16-bit videogame charm, ambient YouTube animations with music by e.sanchillo and covetable prints have carved out a unique space for her in the universe of pixel art.

Ikumi Nakamura is a Creative Director, Art Director, Concept Artist and the CEO of UNSEEN Inc., as well as an urban explorer. After working at Capcom, Platinum Games and Tango Gameworks, and being involved in the development of games such as *Okami*, *Bayonetta*, *Psycho Break* and *Ghostwire: Tokyo*, she started working independently in 2018. Three years later, Ikumi went on to establish her own game-development studio, UNSEEN, where she serves as both Representative Director and Creative Director. In 2023, the studio announced its first project, *KEMURI*. That same year, she published her own book, an urban-exploration diary called *Project UrbEx*.

WANEELLA
PIXELSCAPES

Foreword by Ikumi Nakamura

With
565 illustrations

T&H

CONTENTS

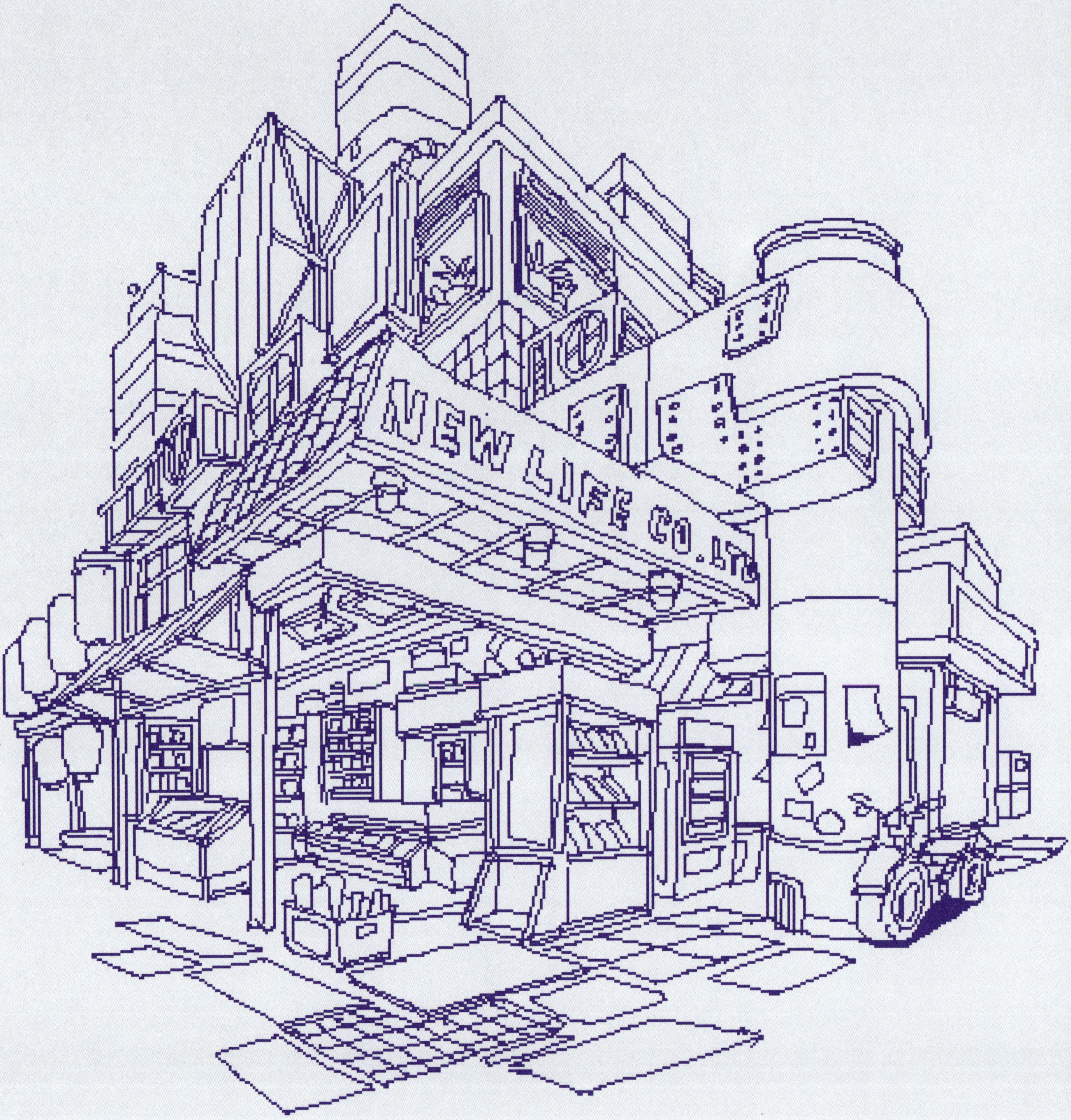

End Of Summer (sketch), 15/08/2019, 450×450px

FOREWORD

In 2013, an artist–sorcerer of pixels emerged on to the expansive digital canvas. It was the year that waneella unveiled her first pixel artwork on Tumblr, marking the commencement of an artistic odyssey that is celebrated in the pages of this book.

As a teenage student, waneella navigated an animation course at Moscow's prestigious Gerasimov Institute of Cinematography while concurrently crafting her unique pixel universe. In this intersection of youth and intellect, her on-screen beauty transcended mere pixels, transforming them into a timeless artistic realm of her own imagination.

She embodies the beauty and philosophy of her Russian homeland, yet her profound understanding of Japanese culture continually echoes throughout her work. This is all the more remarkable because in those early days, waneella embarked on her digital exploration of Japanese streets through Google Street View alone, without ever setting foot on Japanese soil. It was years before she travelled there, yet her Japanese cityscapes have always emerged from within the pixels – a testament to her deep appreciation of and affection for a distant culture. This digital adventure lends an air of mystery and allure to her art, capturing a world swaying between the digital and the tangible.

Waneella's pixel art unfolds as a dance of colour and points, constructing an on-screen universe. Her art is a miraculous display of creativity born from restriction, since pixels, while harbouring boundless potential, simultaneously pose unique challenges to artists by their constraints.

By connecting dot to carefully placed dot, with exquisite colour palettes conveying a breath of passion, her pixel art gives birth to a vast world of profound emotions.

Waneella's journey invites us to witness these urban landscapes through her eyes, pulsating from within the pixels and speaking to us of their beauty and depth. Emerging from the Russian soil and resonating with the Japanese soul, this book celebrates a decade of artistry.

Pixel art, with its beauty extrapolated from tiny dots, imbues our hearts with happiness and gives us all hope for the future. From these minuscule points of pixels spin grand passions. Reminiscent of bright stars lighting the digital darkness, they guide us towards a new dawn.

Tokyo
Winter 2023

IKUMI NAKAMURA

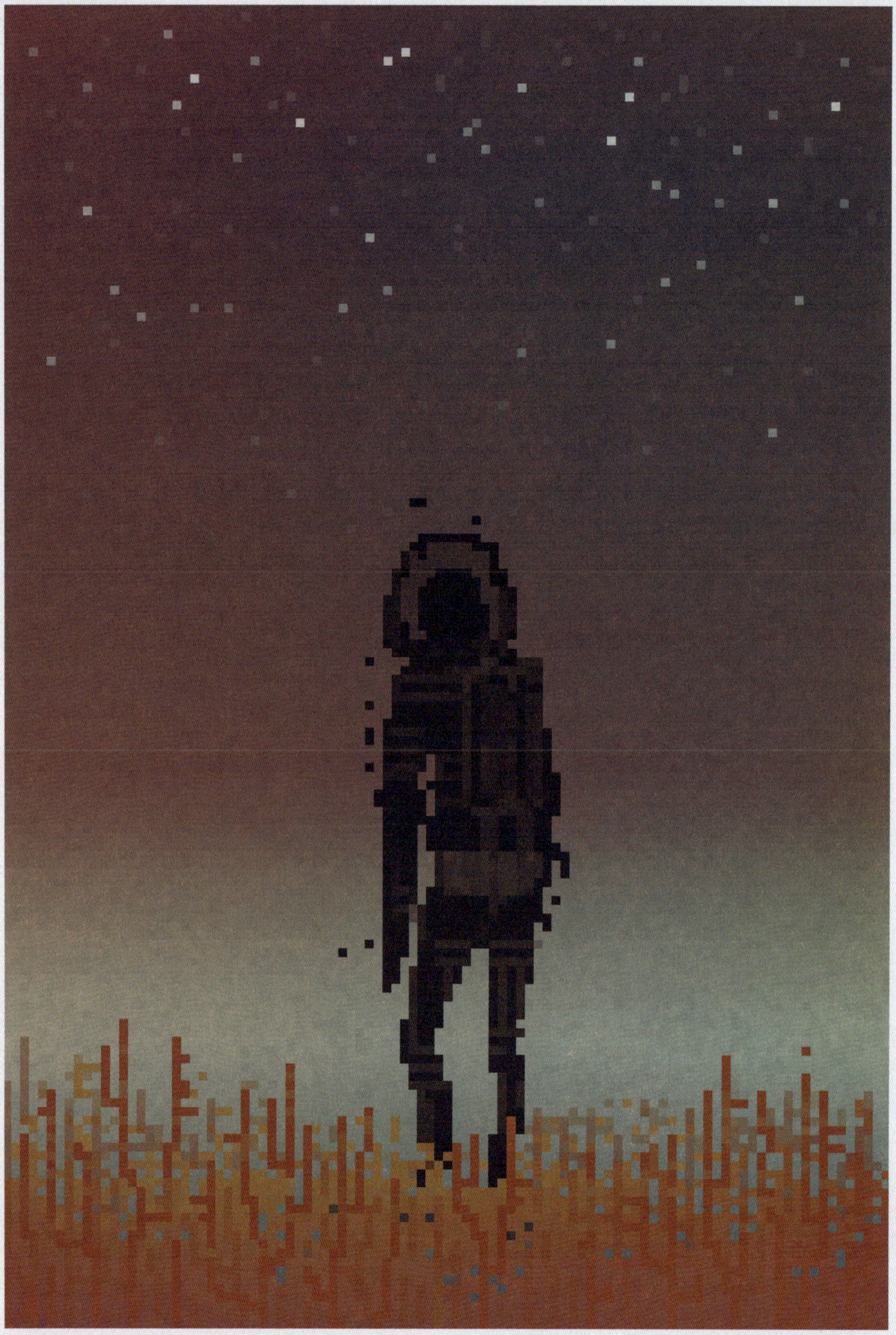

csmnvt, 10/04/2013, 100×150px

Even if you've just bought this book, my name might not be a familiar one. That's because I'm mostly known as 'waneella' – a pixel artist with an online following on Tumblr, Patreon and YouTube. For most of my life, I didn't think it would ever be possible for me to make pixel art full time.

I created 'waneella' to keep myself out of the spotlight; I'm a really quiet person. It's actually 'vanilla', written in a way that felt odd and trendy in my little circle of friends. Back then, when I was starting out, I picked the name because I wanted a soft, friendly pseudonym that might deflect the harshest online comments. While it's succeeded surprisingly well in that respect, I've never been sure that it conveys my image correctly. A lot of people assume it's a contracted version of 'Wayne Ella'. When I first participated in the #VisibleWoman event on Twitter (now 'X'), many were surprised that 'Wane' wasn't a man at all.

As Valeriya, when I meet new people, I normally tell them I draw pixel art. They usually smile and nod politely because they don't really understand what that means. On the rare occasion I'm required to elaborate, I say I draw for videogames or advertising campaigns and that digital pixel art is my chosen style and medium.

I've been creating pixel art for a decade now, having posted my first piece on Tumblr in 2013. I was nineteen back then, and when a picture gained five reactions, I was delighted. It was such an exciting moment and I immediately ran to tell my mother. At the time, I didn't have the slightest idea of what this would become. The ten years since have been filled with so many other amazing moments. I remember clearly reaching 60,000 followers on Tumblr, then 100,000, then 150,000. Each time I passed a milestone, I was amazed there were so many people eager to see each new post. And when I joined Patreon in 2017, people started to back me. It wasn't much at first – perhaps just $50 (£40) each month – but as the number of supporters slowly grew, it was eventually enough to make a living.

What do these people like about my artwork? My hunch is that the Japanese and futuristic settings are instantly appealing to a wide audience – that this vaguely cyberpunk, anime-inspired ambiance draws people in when they see my work for the first time. To others – especially older viewers – I think the pixel-art style harks back to the 16-bit games of their childhood, adding a retro appeal. Of course, pixel art at the time was a technical necessity. While I never intended to use pixel art for its retro appearance, I'm glad my work has the power to unlock old memories. It also turns out there are plenty of people who are intrigued by 'liminal spaces' and views of deserted streets and interiors. Corridors, lobbies, streets and plazas are frequently designed as transitional places – connecting one urban destination to another – but I wonder if they have more of a visual significance than that. I think some of my audience certainly feels this way. These are just my guesses. Perhaps people are drawn to my art for only one of these reasons; maybe it's a combination of all three. Personally, I like to observe beauty in ordinary places because I find them much more eloquent and moving than those intended to be beautiful and meaningful by design. While I can appreciate a wonderful monument or artwork, I feel so much more when I see a corridor flooded with sunlight – or a darkened room illuminated by the streetlights outside through an open window. For me it is these sights, closer to actual life, that reveal everyday beauty.

This book covers the first decade of my life as a pixel artist. Some of it is the story of how I started out; the details of my stumbling progress might inspire some of you to do the same. Other sections offer step-by-step breakdowns of how I create my images, in the hope that I can help other artists or anyone interested in the process behind creating pixel art. The images themselves document my artistic output and development since I began my journey.

As for what comes next, I can't say. I still have plans for my pixel art. I've always wanted to make my own videogame, as well as spending more time on pixel animation. But in a world where there's very little stability, I know I have to be open to change with it. I hope the years ahead will be even more interesting than the ones I've just lived through. It's been an incredible decade.

Moscow
Winter 2023

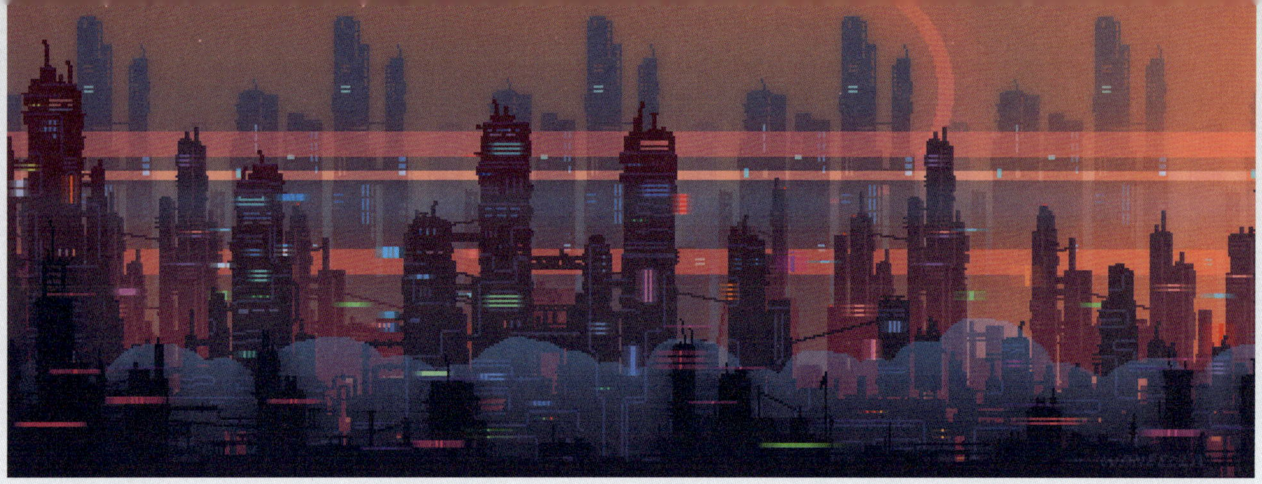

1

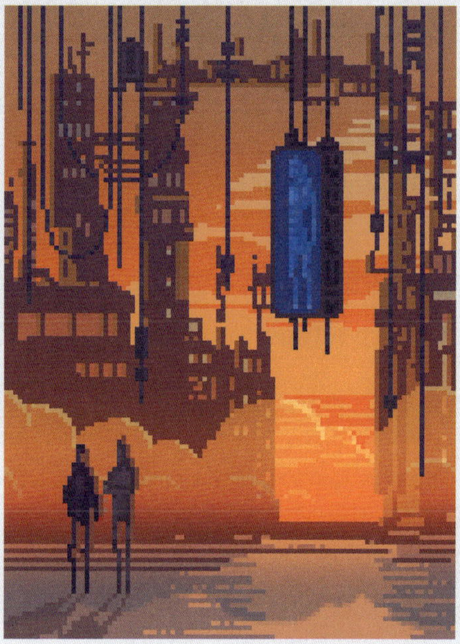

2

3

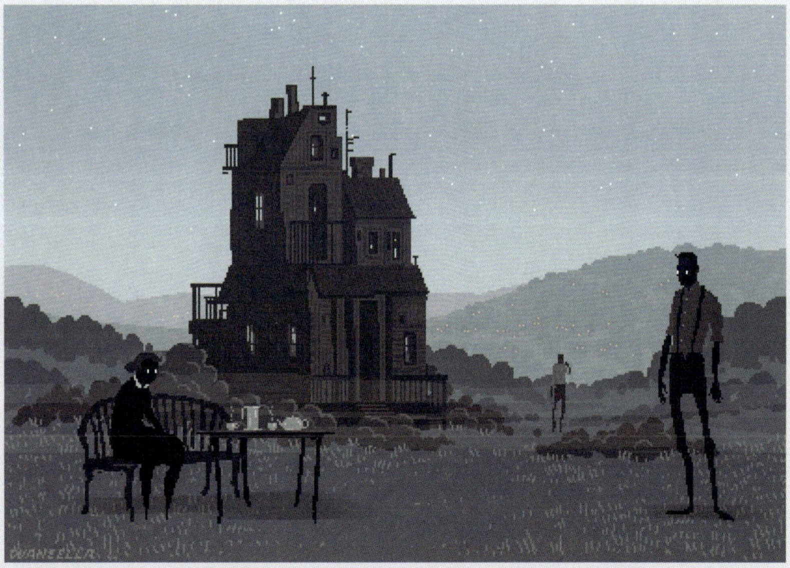

1 *Vozvrashenie*, 10/02/2015, 540×225px
2 *Untitled*, 05/06/2013, 100×140px
3 *Untitled*, 18/08/2014, 420×300px
4 *Untitled*, 04/07/2014, 105×170px
5 *Untitled*, 19/09/2015, 270×480px

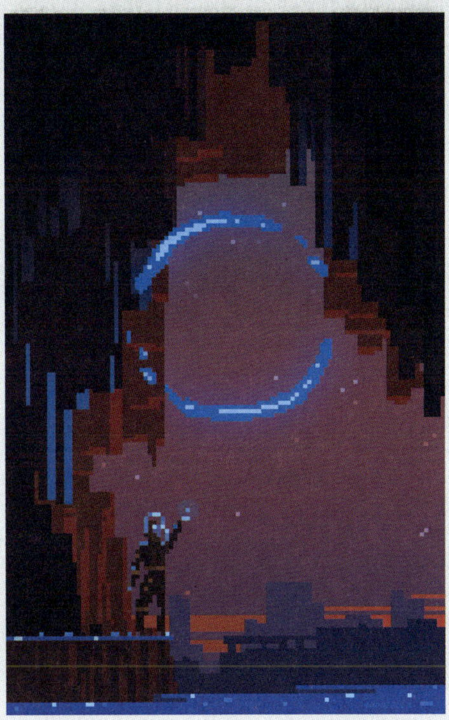

4

5

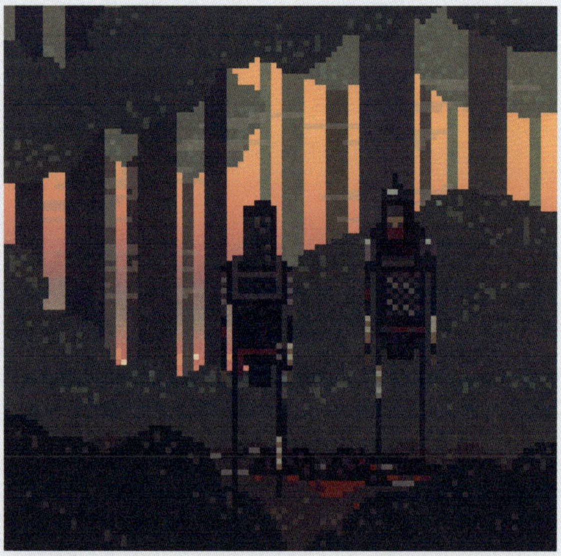

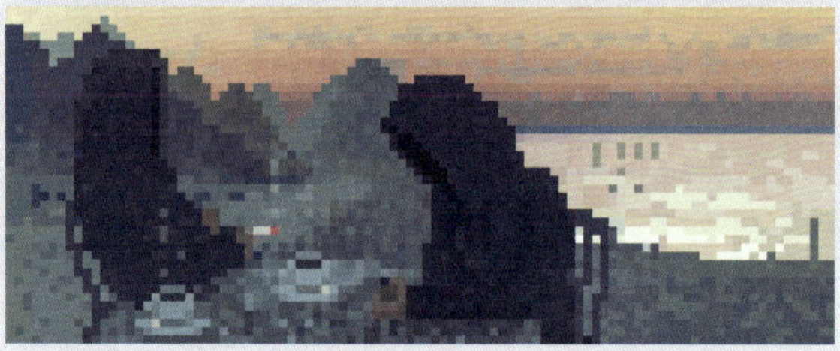

1
2

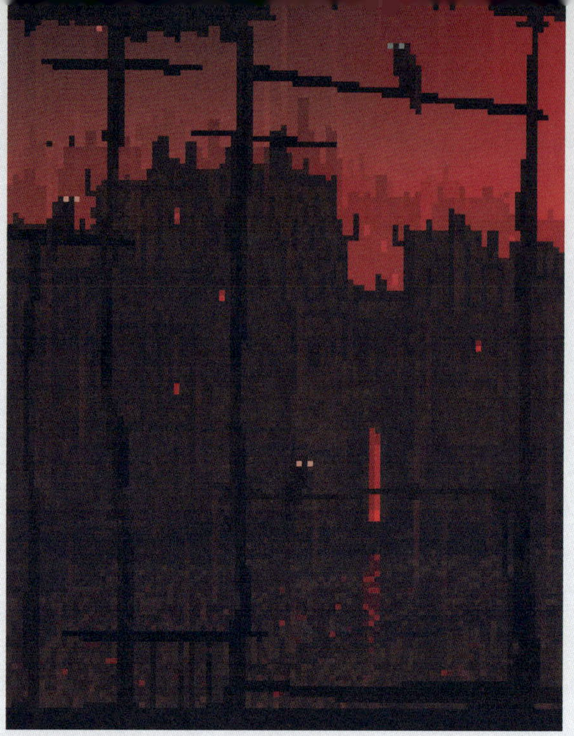

3

4

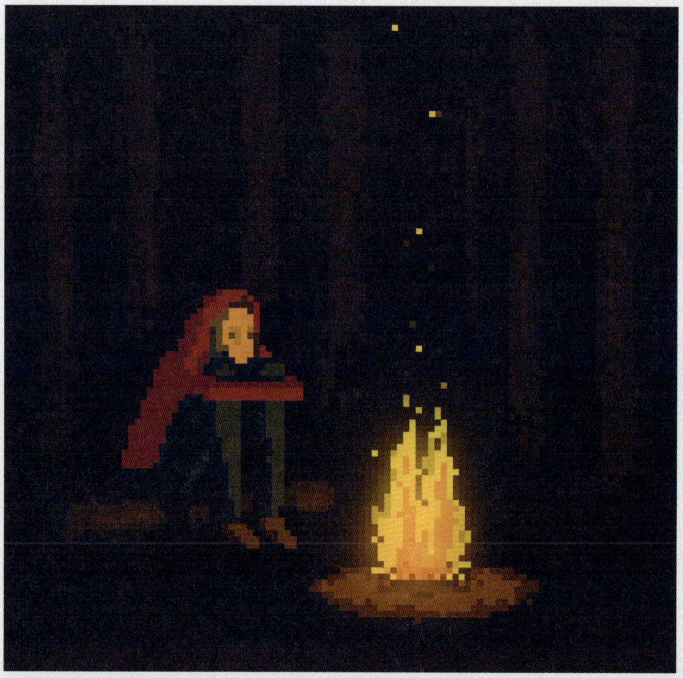

1 *Untitled*, 16/03/2013, 105×105px
2 *Untitled*, 10/03/2013, 100×41px
3 *Untitled*, 23/07/2013, 100×140px
4 *Untitled*, 11/02/2013, 100×100px

Life on the seventh floor

I was born in Moscow in 1993 and raised in a seventh-floor flat owned by my great grandmother in a beautiful brick block built during Stalin's rule. Even though Moscow is regarded as a wealthy city, naturally not everyone who lives there is rich. Among Russians, Moscow has a reputation for being 'another country' due to its bright lights and completely different way of life compared to other cities. It's certainly a massive, industrialized metropolis, with a large, historical centre similar to many European capitals, along with sprawling outskirts of social housing blocks called панелька – 'panelka'.

The Soviet Union broke apart at the end of 1991 and I was born into an era of such deep uncertainty that few Russians wanted to risk having children. This feeling was so widespread that even today, the country suffers from an ageing population, with not enough young people to support various workforce sectors – or its older citizens. As far as I know, my parents didn't have the means or the desire to raise a baby, so I was conceived by accident. Along with my parents, we lived with my great grandmother, the four of us sharing a two-room flat.

Winters in Moscow are long, with the first snow falling at the end of October and spring starting in April. They are intensely cold too, which is perhaps why I remember winters so vividly from an early age – though it could simply be that there was so much fun to be had. Sliding down slopes, building snow castles, having snowball fights – the freezing days definitely imparted plenty of magical memories.

Overall, however, I look back on my childhood as a difficult time that left me as quite an anxious adult. There were perverts and kidnappers around, and the streets weren't a safe place for a small child. The TV news reported a number of terrorist attacks in Moscow during my early years, which made me scared that our house might get blown up. Since our flat was on the corner of the building, I comforted myself with the fact that corners tend to be strong and more stable, so we might survive a blast. But I also worried endlessly about the fate and safety of the family parrot and fish, unsure about how I might evacuate them in an emergency. I could run out with the parrot cage, but how would I ever carry the heavy glass aquarium, filled with water, down from the seventh floor?

The 1990s were a desperate time for many Russians. We sometimes ran out of basic items including clothes, toys and certain kinds of food. But living with constraints makes people more creative: my mother knitted and sewed dresses for me and made me puppets and toys. Even though we didn't have a lot of ordinary things, we had our own, special ones. We learned to create everything we needed with the items that were available to us. My mother once brought home a Barbie doll, only this one was a bit unusual: it was a 'substandard-quality' Barbie, without a painted face. I so wanted to have a Barbie back then, but we didn't have the money spare.

At the time, my mother was painting матрёшка 'matryoshka' dolls and other decorative items to sell at markets, so she painted a new, custom face for my doll. I think it was the most beautiful Barbie I've ever seen.

As well as painting items to sell, my mum also worked long hours as a cook in a local shop.

My father is a musician and played in different Moscow clubs. He would invite his musician friends round to rehearse at our home, so our little flat was often filled with music and talented artists. He even travelled to Europe on several occasions to busk on the streets and see if he could find a better life for us. One time, my father returned with a bag of coins, all from different places. This was before the Euro went into circulation, so each European country had its own currency, which made the coins so exciting and exotic that I often used to take them out of my money box to play with. Later, during a particularly hard period, I remember my parents asking me to check if there was any Russian money in my box to buy food.

Childish things

Life may have been tough, but it was the only childhood I had known. So, like any child, I still enjoyed childish things. There were cartoons and TV programmes on the weekends and after school, and I can remember watching shows like *Teenage Mutant Ninja Turtles*, *Batman*, *Rugrats*, *DuckTales* and *Chip 'n' Dale*. When I was very small, I can even remember my father watching *Beavis and Butt-Head* and *Celebrity Deathmatch* on MTV after he thought I'd gone to bed. Of course, I sneaked in to watch them – they were cartoons, after all.

I also liked Soviet cartoons, which aren't really known outside Russia. It's a shame, because Russian animation has its own distinctive style and some of the shows are truly fantastic. One programme, Спокойной ночи, малыши – '*Good Night, Little Ones!*' – was on TV every evening and, after a small talking segment, it used to showcase a series of short Soviet cartoons from different animation series. I loved it and eagerly awaited every episode.

My older cousin's family had a lot more money than mine; they not only had satellite TV, but such rare and pricey treats as Nesquik, Corn Flakes, Wagon Wheels and Choco Pie! Even though I started learning English at the age of four, the shows on Nickelodeon and Cartoon Network were still very difficult to understand. Nevertheless, I was impressed with the way programmes such as *The Ren & Stimpy Show* had their own crazy style.

I was fascinated by computers and videogames from the moment I saw them. We had an MS-DOS computer with a racing game called *Street Rod*; later on, my mother's friend gave us an old Super Nintendo console with *The Legend of Zelda: A Link to the Past*, *The Lost Vikings*, *F-Zero* and *Illusion of Time*. For some reason, most of the games were in German, but I was so keen to play them, I just pushed the buttons without knowing what I was choosing or what the storyline was.

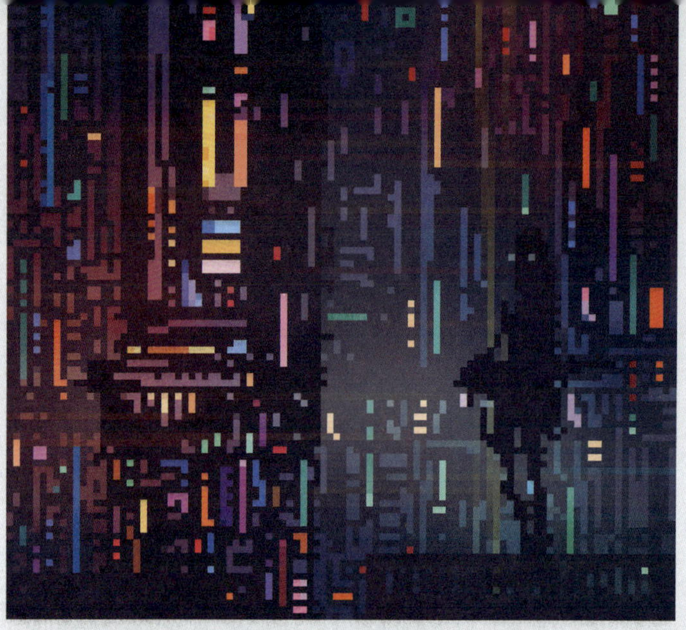

1
2

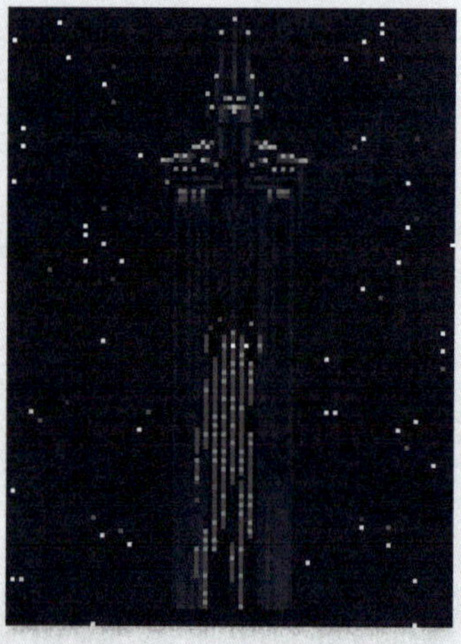

3

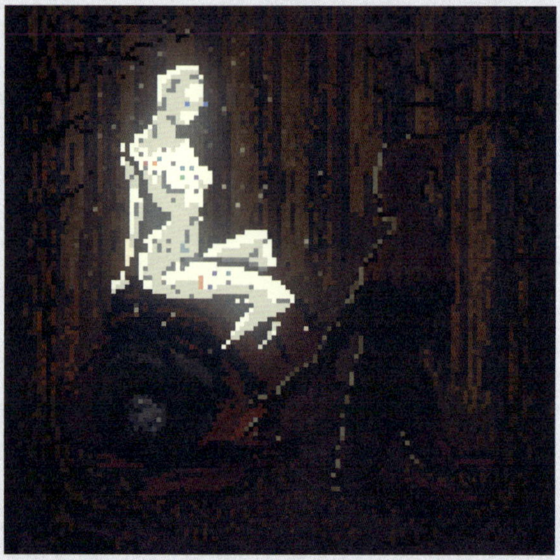

4

5

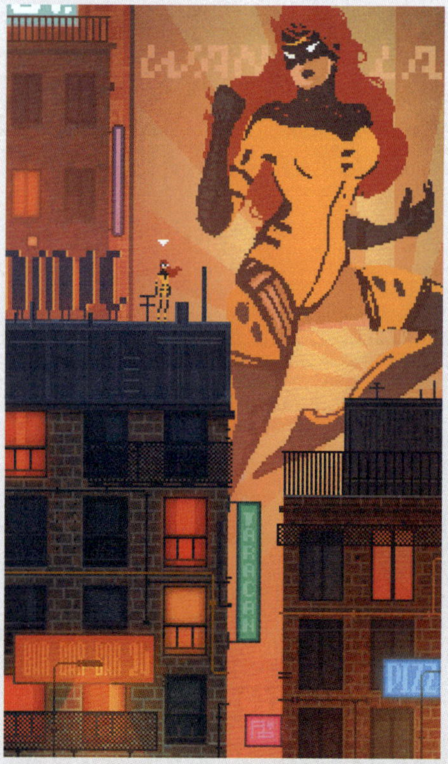

1 *Untitled*, 07/05/2013, 100×100px
2 *Untitled*, 06/06/2013, 250×100px
3 *Untitled*, 15/06/2013, 100×140px
4 *Untitled*, 03/05/2013, 120×120px
5 *Untitled*, 19/10/2013, 196×340px

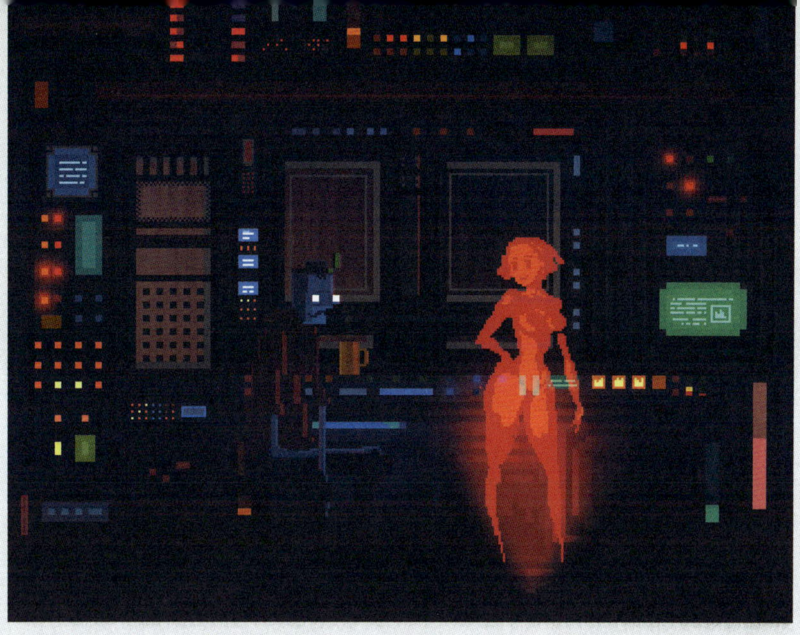

7

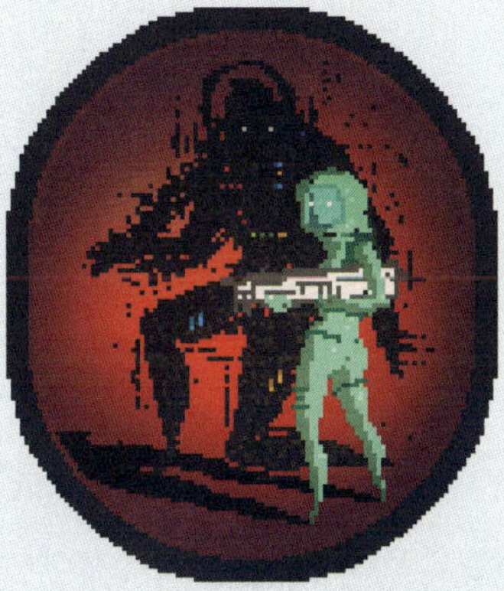

6

8

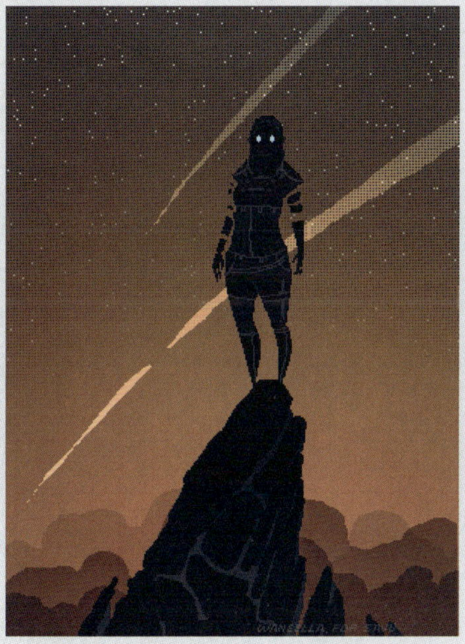

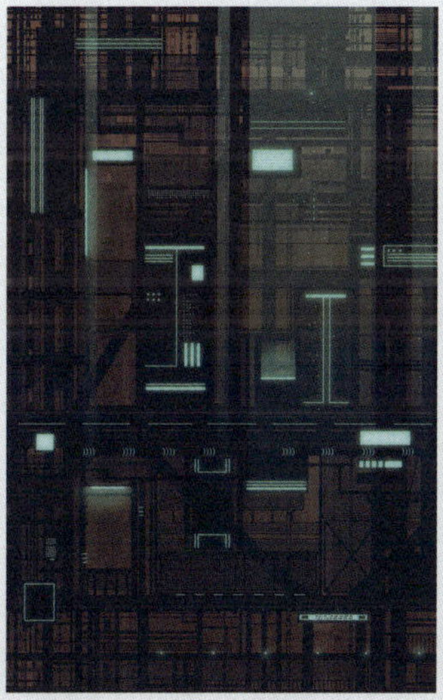

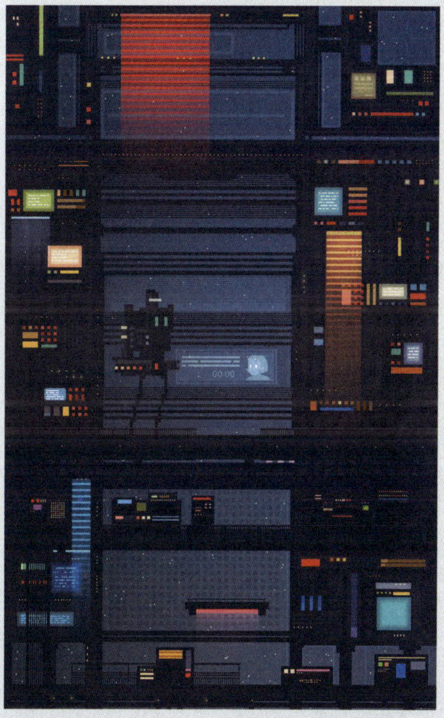

9
10

6 *Untitled*, 01/05/2013, 110×130px
7 *Untitled*, 12/08/2013, 351×300px
8 *Untitled*, 12/08/2013, 300×420px
9 *Moths*, 01/09/2013, 400×642px
10 *Untitled*, 07/09/2013, 420×682px

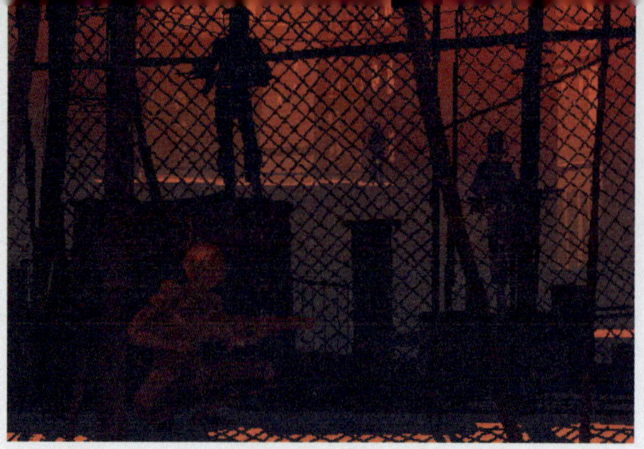

2

3
4

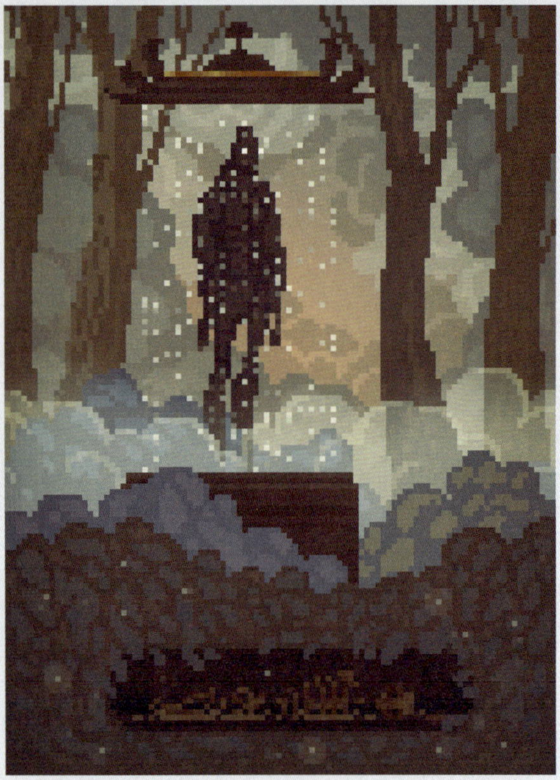

1

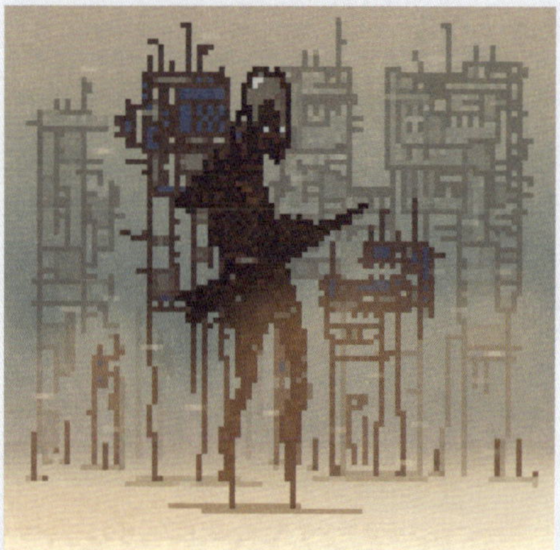

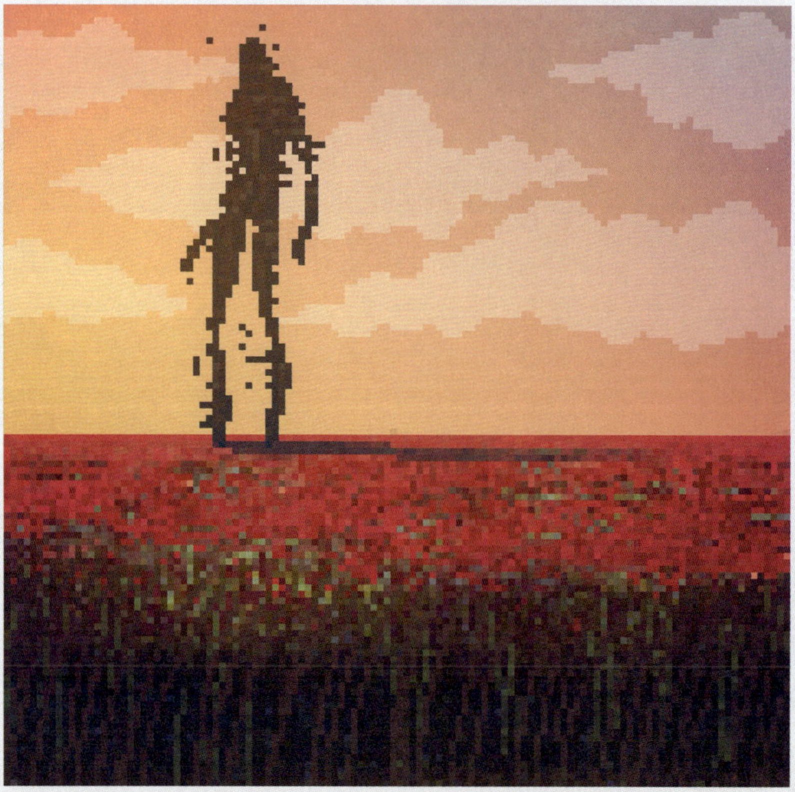

1 *Untitled*, 13/06/2013, 100×140px
2 *Untitled*, 03/09/2013, 500×400px
3 *Untitled*, 06/05/2013, 100×100px
4 *Untitled*, 12/05/2013, 120×120px

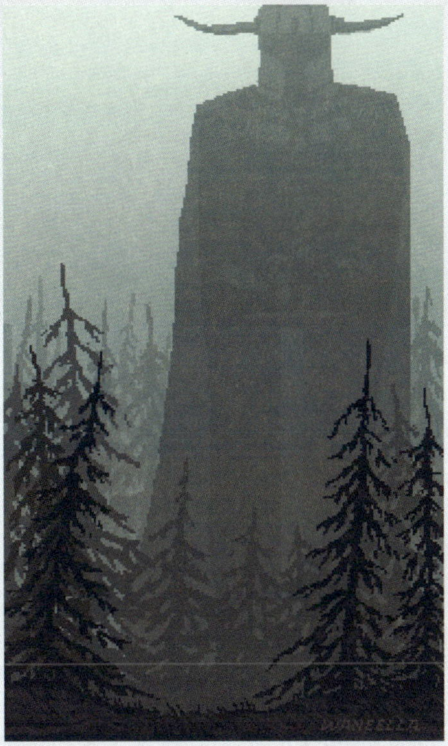

5

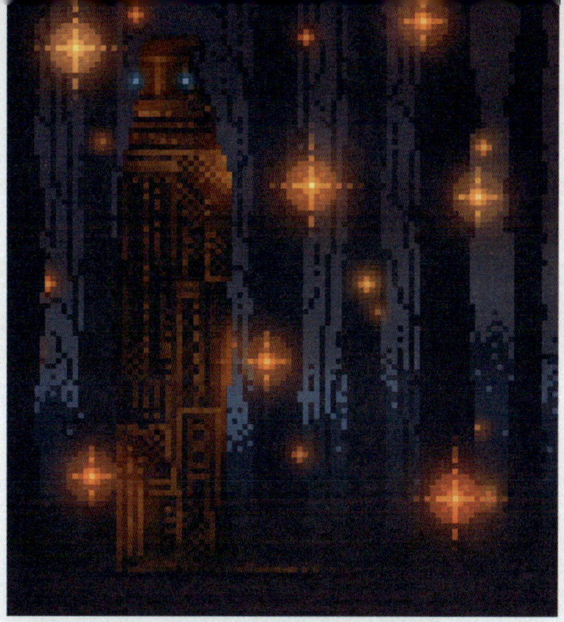

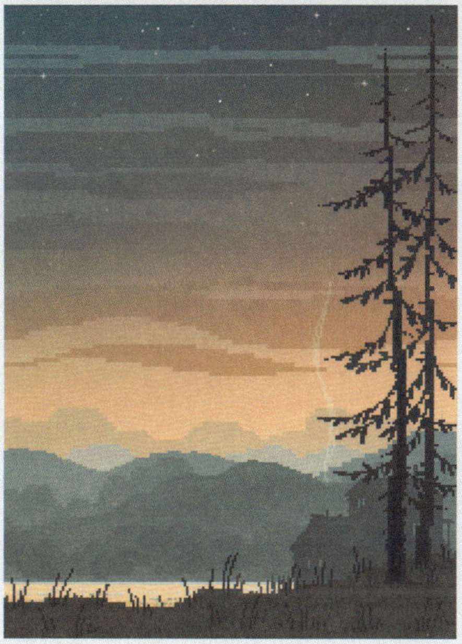

7
8

6

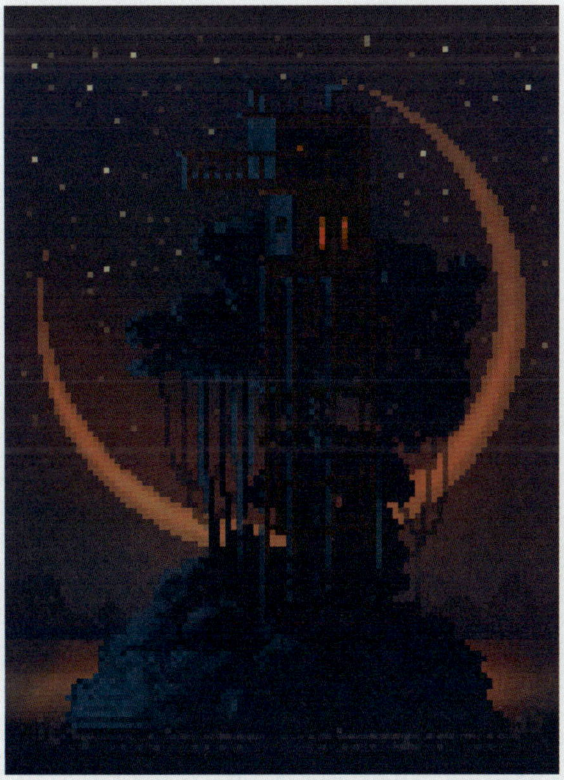

5	*Untitled*, 23/09/2013, 200×340px
6	*Untitled*, 25/04/2013, 100×135px
7	*Untitled*, 30/08/2013, 100×120px
8	*Untitled*, 01/08/2013, 200×280px

The language barriers that existed with US cartoons and German-language games weren't entirely bad experiences. Consuming so much visual media as a child without fully understanding the plots and jokes, which were in foreign languages, led me to concentrate more on the visuals than on the story and narration.

Finding the right path

With an artist for a mother and a musician for a father – and creativity and expression always on show at home – perhaps I was always going to be an artist. My parents certainly think so. They always encouraged my desire to paint; we had brushes and paints in our house and sometimes went to the park to paint the trees together in autumn. I always loved art, in one form or another.

What I drew wasn't genius, but I enjoyed the process and always felt the need to keep trying and to improve. When I decided I wasn't good enough at drawing faces, I asked my father to help me. Both my parents were very supportive, but even though my father drew some wonderful faces for me, I understood that I needed to do it myself – even if I wasn't happy with the results this time, or the next, or the next. But it was a bitter truth about what I needed to do next.

My parents' belief in my art wasn't often shared by my teachers. They not only criticized my work, but even suggested that I was somehow expressing the 'wrong' kind of creativity.

This started as far back as nursery, when I took sticks of coloured plasticine and smudged them on to paper, almost as though they were really thick oil paints. It was an abstract but vivid and interesting drawing – a pure expression of my love for art. But while I was proud of my 'work' and my mother was impressed, the only comment the teachers made was that I'd ruined all their plasticine. Looking back, this seems to be the start of a lifelong pattern. I would get excited by something new and throw myself into it, only to show little obvious talent. But as I kept going, I would learn and develop the skills to succeed. This cycle has been repeated throughout my life.

Before I settled on art, there were definitely a few false starts. I studied piano in music school for two or three years and, for a time, thought that perhaps I would become a musician like my father. I left after my teacher shouted at me for not bringing her flowers on Teacher's Day, which turned out to be quite a big deal for her. But what did I know? I was only six or seven.

I also attended dance classes for a while and even studied karate for two years. I thought karate was great fun, but when the only other girl in the group left, I realized the boys didn't want to be my friend. Eventually, I stopped too.

On it went. Almost every time I started an art-related course, the teachers told my parents that I was drawing at a low level and should consider another activity. My mother stood up for me, telling them they should at least *try* to teach me before they gave up. It's quite possible that I wouldn't have become an artist without her endless faith in me.

I'm glad I stuck at it, because I learnt something valuable in each class. Eventually, even the teachers reluctantly conceded that while I might not be the best, I definitely had a spark. Adding new skills to my arsenal moved me one step closer towards my career as an artist, and I eventually enrolled in university. It's been a complicated, winding path, full of setbacks, 'wasted' plasticine and grumpy karate training partners. It's hard to imagine where I might be now if my life had been easier back then.

The oldest film school in the world

The Gerasimov Institute of Cinematography was founded as the Moscow Film School in 1919, making it the first and oldest in the world. In Russian, it's known as 'Vserossiyskiy gosudarstvyennyy institut kinematografiI imyenI S. A. Gerasimova', so I'll refer to it as 'VGIK' from now on. In the Soviet era, the school was at the very centre of the industry; several prominent filmmakers taught at VGIK, fostering future talents. Sergei Eisenstein, director of *Battleship Potemkin*, lectured there, as did Soviet animation-pioneer Ivan Ivanov-Vano. When *Solaris* director Andrei Tarkovsky studied at VGIK in the 1950s, he shared classes with his future-wife Irma Raush, who acted in some of his films before subsequently becoming a director herself. Incredibly, in 2010, I was accepted to study animation at VGIK for six years. The pressure was palpable.

As my school years drew to a close, I started thinking about what an interesting profession might be. Since making cartoons or videogames sounded fun, that was that – I would aim to become an artist, working in animation or game development. There were only a few schools in Moscow that taught animation, and because I didn't do much research on the topic, I simply chose the best-known and most obvious one – VGIK. But wanting to go there was one thing; being accepted there was an entirely different matter. Cost was always a huge consideration, as my family couldn't afford the fees. However, my close family and friends were insistent that a higher education would get my career off to the best possible start, and the reputation of VGIK persuaded some generous older friends to help out financially.

Russian state universities also offer a few scholarships for the most talented applicants, so that was a possibility too. I passed VGIK's first round of selection on the merit of some oil paintings I had made during my art-school days. But in a repeat of my now-familiar pattern, the next two rounds were so catastrophically bad that out of all the candidates, I wound up with the lowest exam score. Yet amazingly, my elderly friends stuck to their promises, paying my fees for the first academic year. With my future still vague and uncertain, I enrolled – eternally grateful for the chance to study at such a prestigious university, even if only for a short period.

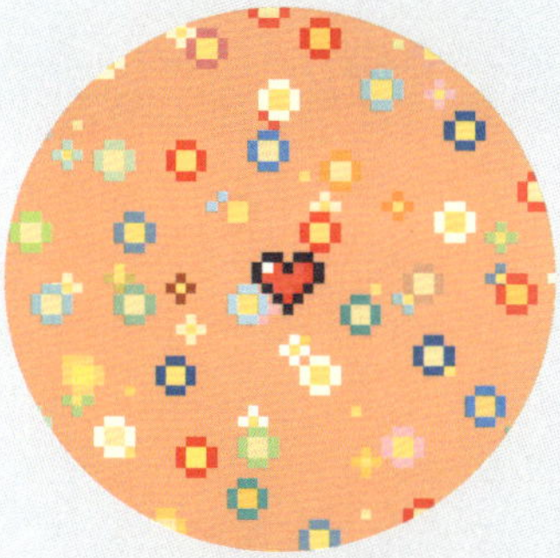

1

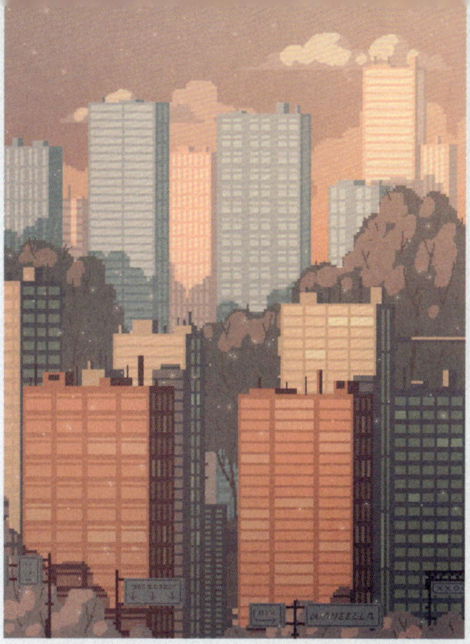

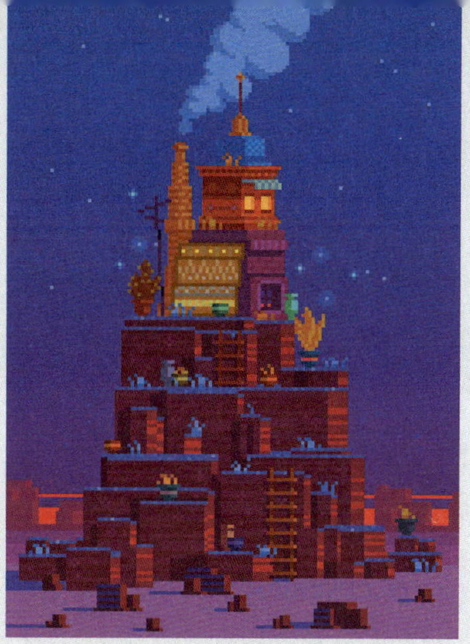

2
3

4

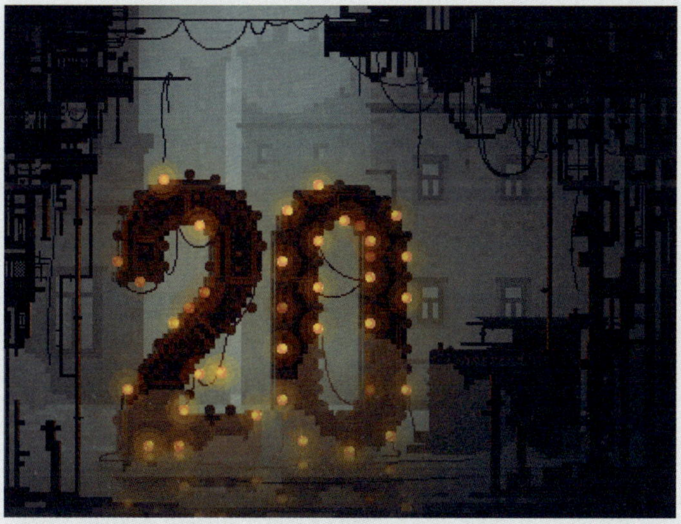

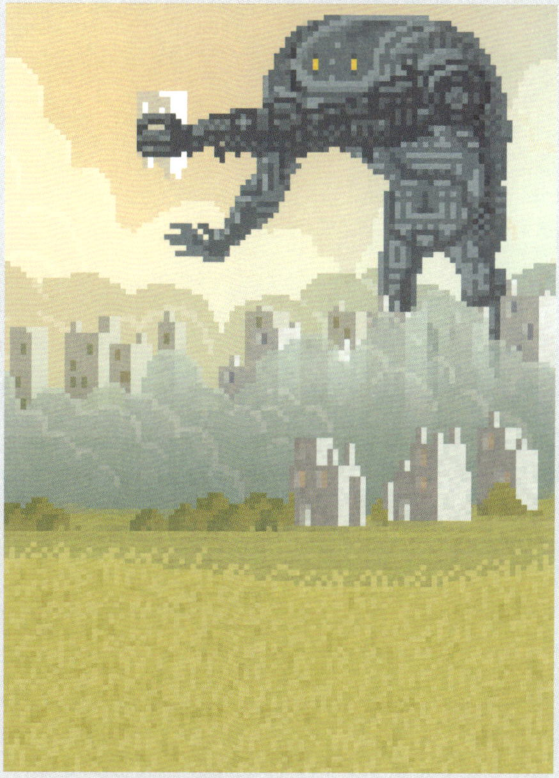

5

1 *Untitled*, 14/02/2013, 59×60px
2 *Outside*, 30/10/2015, 165×255px
3 *Untitled*, 29/11/2015, 135×202px
4 *Untitled*, 26/07/2013, 390×300px
5 *Untitled*, 31/05/2013, 100×140px

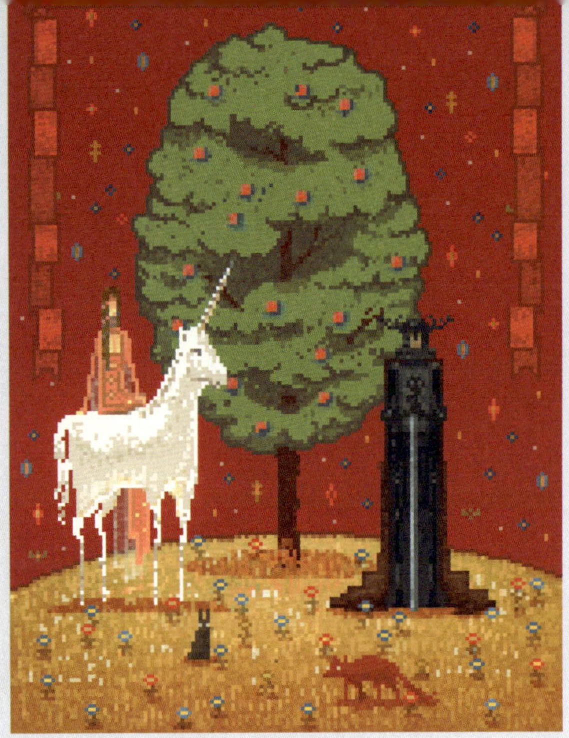

1

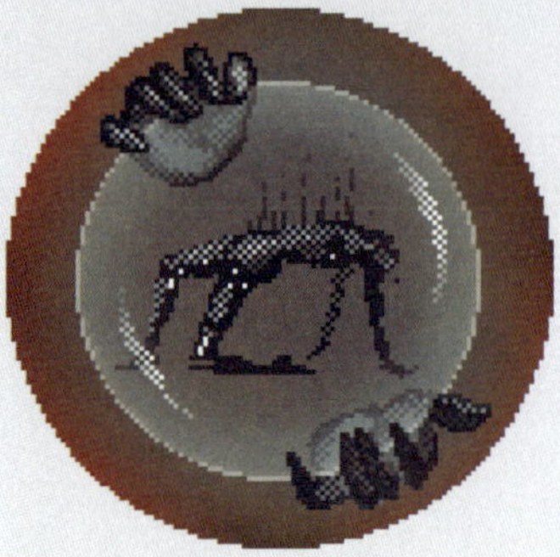

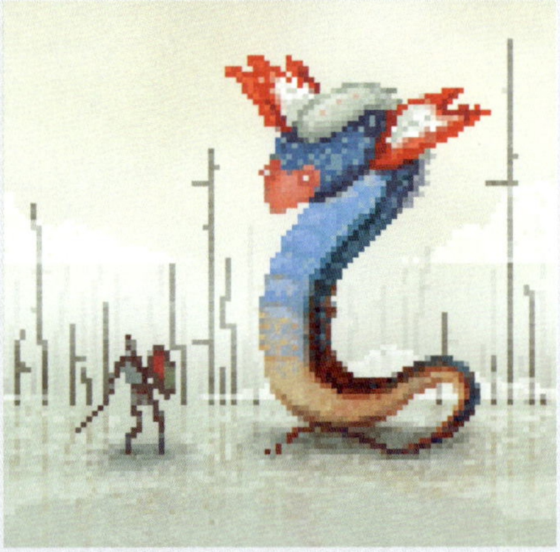

2
3

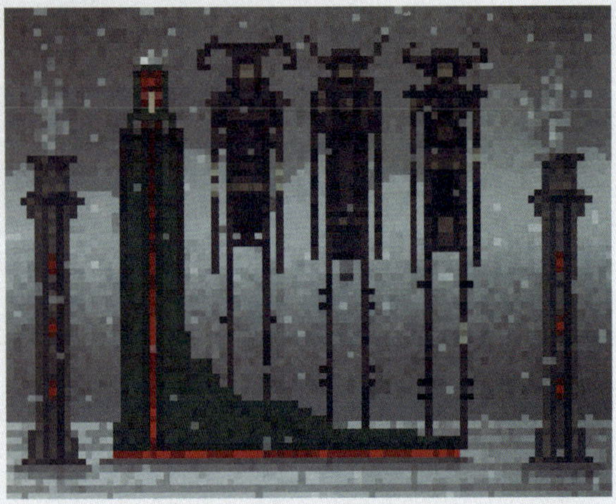

4

5

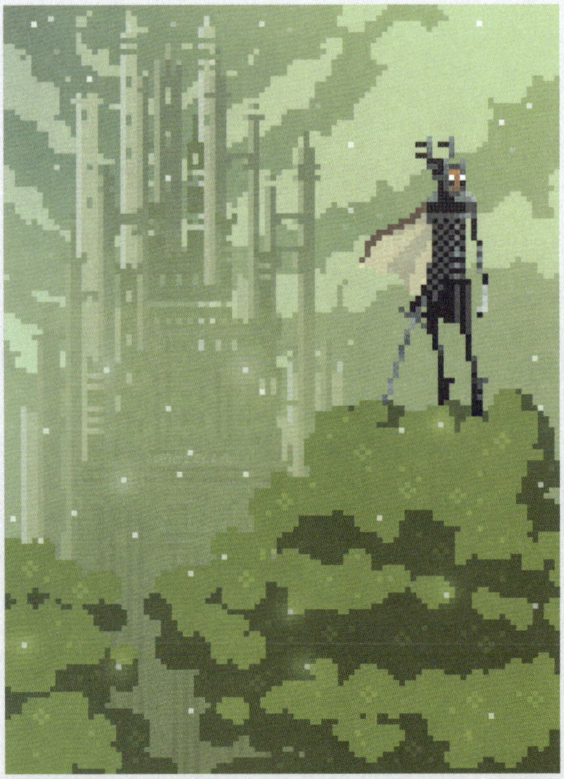

1 *Untitled*, 13/04/2013, 150×210px
2 *Untitled*, 30/04/2013, 112×112px
3 *Untitled*, 22/04/2013, 72×72px
4 *Untitled*, 29/03/2013, 86×70px
5 *Untitled*, 14/08/2013, 100×140px

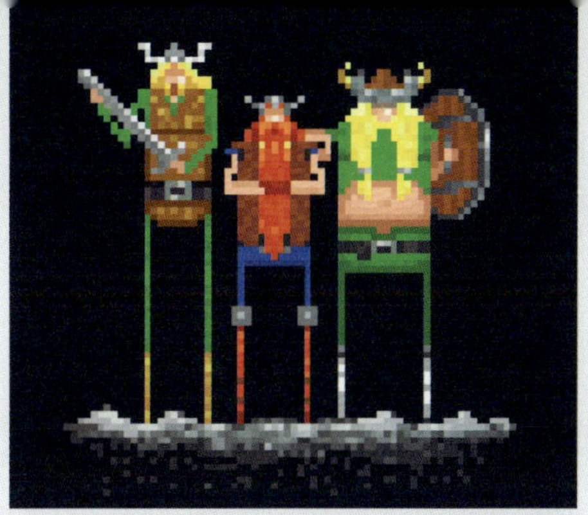

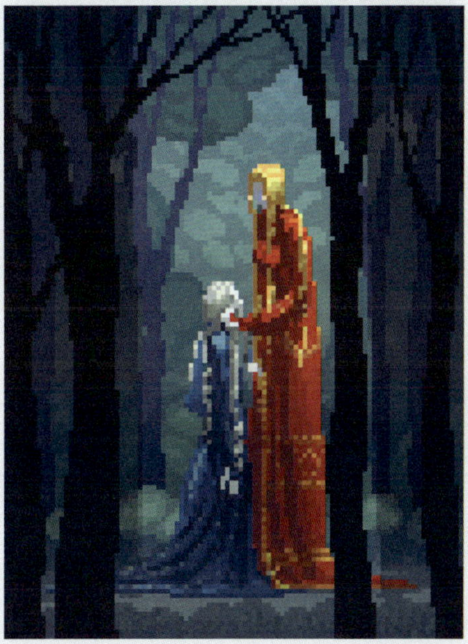

6
7

9

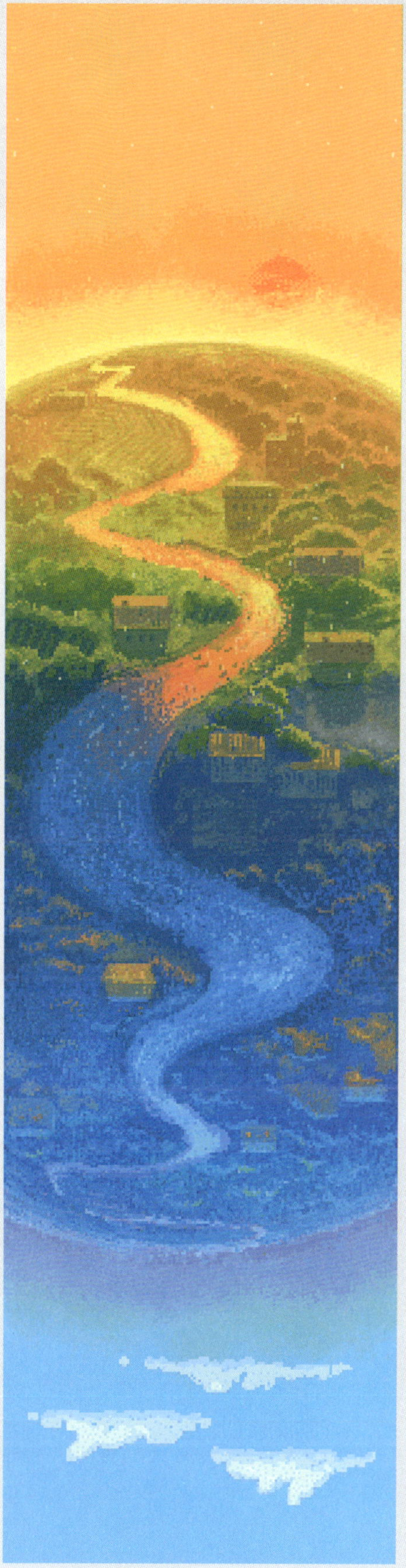

8

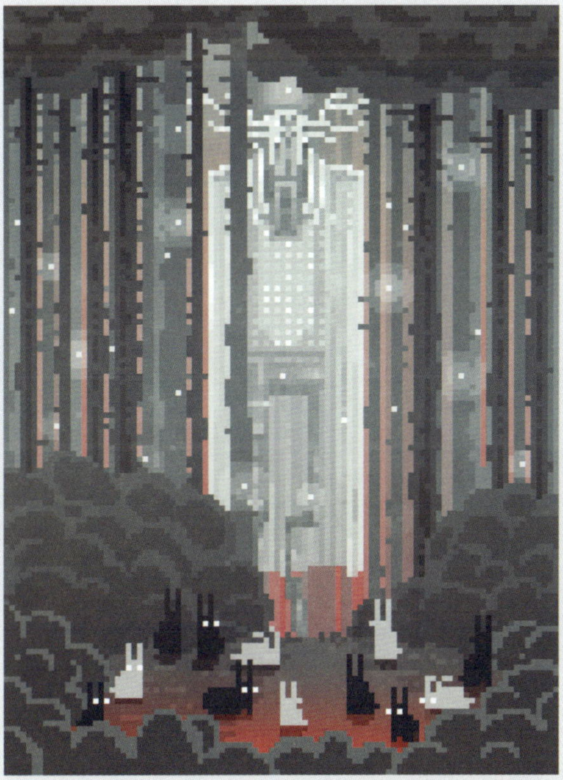

6 *Untitled*, 18/03/2013, 85×85px
7 *Untitled*, 03/06/2013, 100×140px
8 *Untitled*, 07/06/2013, 200×280px
9 *Untitled*, 31/03/2013, 154×611px

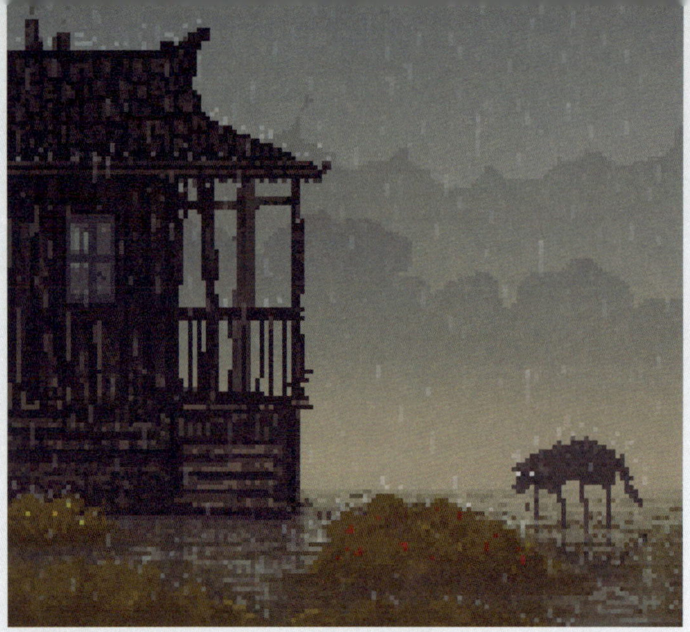

1

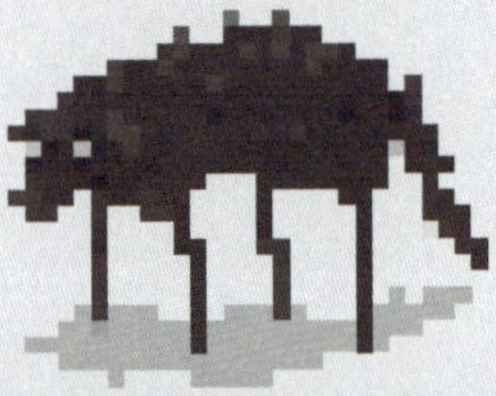

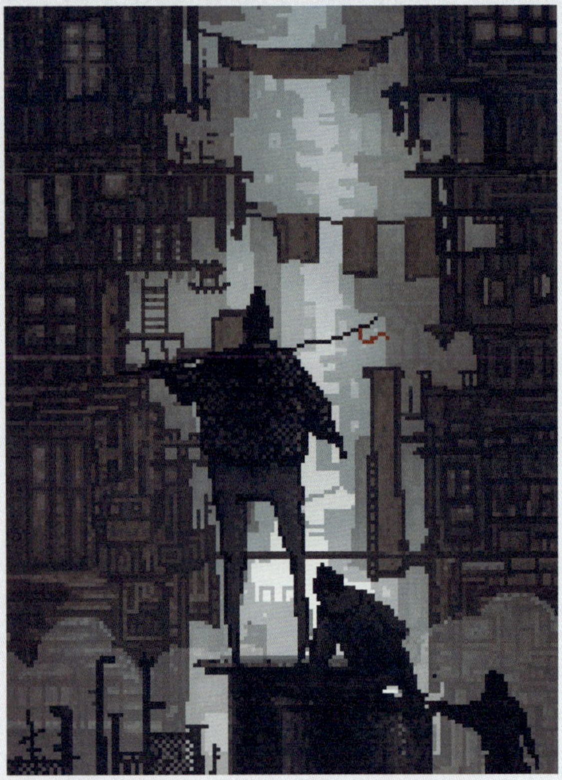

2
3

4
5

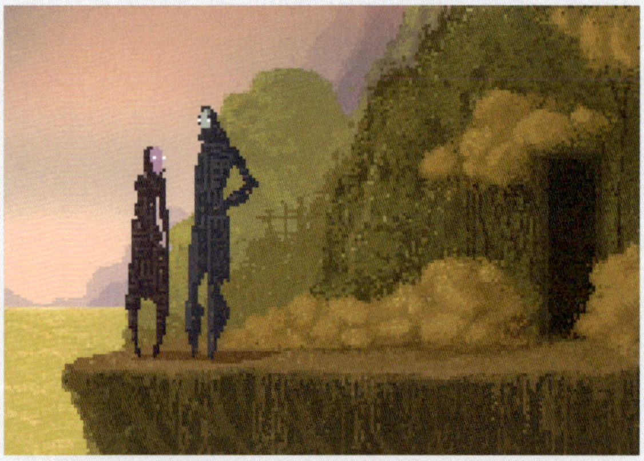

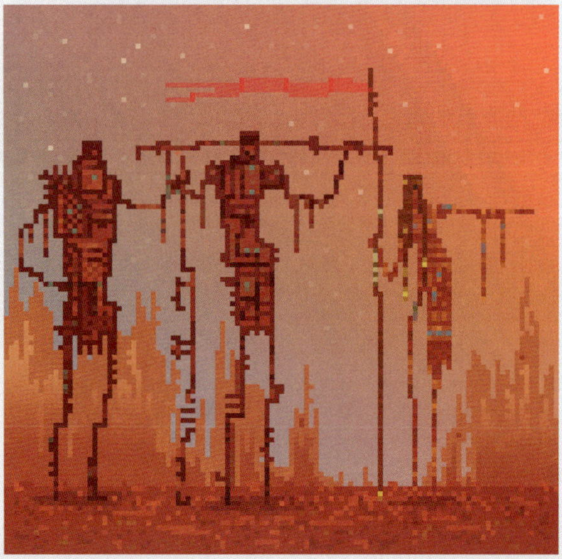

1 *Untitled*, 11/04/2013, 150×150px
2 *Untitled*, 13/04/2013, 39×39px
3 *Untitled*, 19/04/2013, 143×200px
4 *Untitled*, 17/04/2013, 200×143px
5 *Untitled*, 05/04/2013, 113×113px

Student life

VGIK was surprisingly close to my house, its closest buildings just a twenty-five-minute walk away. Every morning, I walked there, through a lovely park with a historical aqueduct; it was a great way to start the day. Aware that the clock was ticking and my fees would run out, I was determined to pack as much into that first year as possible, and I took the whole thing very seriously – perhaps too seriously. After the first semester, I was shocked when a talented scholarship student in my cohort didn't return to classes. Despite having six years of free education ahead of them, they'd decided it wasn't something they wanted to pursue. I was even more shocked when my tutors told me they had recommended me for the spare scholarship. In that one moment, in a strange but wonderful stroke of luck, my single year at university was extended to an entire degree course, just because I was in the same group as someone who had left.
Though I'd enrolled on an animation course, the programme was wide-ranging, and built a strong foundation by exploring many different types of art. Each week, we would spend hours drawing and painting still lifes and nudes, as well as heading outside for plein-air sessions. Each semester, our specialist tutor picked a different literary work as inspiration and we were tasked with making our own visual interpretation of it. There was no prescribed medium for this, so some of us created digital art; some used paint; while others favoured charcoal or inks.
Despite having so much artistic freedom, more financial stability and the advantage of being able to concentrate on my art full time, I still found university stressful. Perhaps it was because I'd been told I wasn't good enough so many times growing up, or because I worried that the scholarship, which had been awarded so suddenly, might be taken away just as quickly. Whatever the case, I was so determined to draw better, to learn quickly and to discover new skills that I rarely found any space for relaxation and fun. Some semesters were good, others less so, as I resolved to never give up, to keep making art and always, to improve.

A (pixellated) light ahead

During the winter break of my third year at VGIK, I discovered a videogame that would unexpectedly change my life and define my career. While I'm not an avid gamer, videogames played a significant role in my childhood. The time I spent at my cousin's house was formative: he not only had a fast, modern PC, but he also bought games magazines that introduced me to the wider world of gaming culture. I remember watching him play and imagining how cool it would be to have so many different games available all day, every day. When I played *Superbrothers: Sword & Sworcery EP*, everything about it was unusual and slightly confusing. I wasn't yet familiar with the world of indie developers and assumed that every game was a triple-A title – with the biggest development teams and the most realistic 3D graphics – and had to be played on a powerful PC.
Yet this was at the other end of the spectrum: anindependently produced game that took pride in its small team, low-tech, low-resolution aesthetic. I was instantly hooked.
I was in awe of the amount of information and beauty that *Superbrothers: Sword & Sworcery EP* packed into so few pixels. Until then, I wasn't aware that pixel art was something you could even make using modern art software, which I had always considered in terms of how well it smoothed out colour gradients and removed pixelization. How was it possible to flip that entirely and use modern applications to produce such a jagged, retro look? Was that even allowed?
There was also something fascinating about the way the game totally embraced its aesthetic. The colours were so obviously picked with great deliberation, while the static backgrounds immersed gamers in the world – as did the music and animation. When I was playing it, I didn't really know what the goal was or why I was doing anything. I wasn't even sure I was playing the game correctly, but somehow it still felt good. And while I'm sure that *Superbrothers: Sword & Sworcery EP* disorientated every player, it made me feel something else too. It made me want to try and recreate its amazing pixellated look.

Waneella – the earliest works

It's often said that the path to success is paved with failure – a truth I know all too well. But there was something about pixel art that compelled me to try... even if it meant failing. Like so many digital artists before me, I opened Adobe Photoshop and tried to work out how to create in this medium, one coloured square at a time. I knew I wouldn't be able to replicate a scene from the game immediately, so I started simply. I drew one vending machine serving up burgers [→ page 24], then another one full of cakes [→ page 24].
Why these subjects? I thought it would be fairly simple to draw food and that vending machines would be easy to animate. That was another fascinating aspect of pixel art – the idea that seemingly static images could flicker or move. When I first looked up how to make a GIF in Photoshop, I realized I could just tick a menu box that would loop the animation endlessly. Even today, this simple concept blows my mind: a GIF can run forever. Since I wanted to create an entire scene rather than an isolated object, after the cake machine, I drew a character next to a campfire [→ page 12]. Next, I made some forever-falling flowers [→ page 19] to make the most of the looping GIF, then some hooded figures on a cigarette break [→ page 12].
Only then was I ready to attempt something that resembled a scene from *Superbrothers: Sword & Sworcery EP*. My previous two attempts included very different characters, so I decided to analyze the game's style by counting the size of each character, the width of the canvas and even the number of pixels that each picture used. The result was an image of two knights

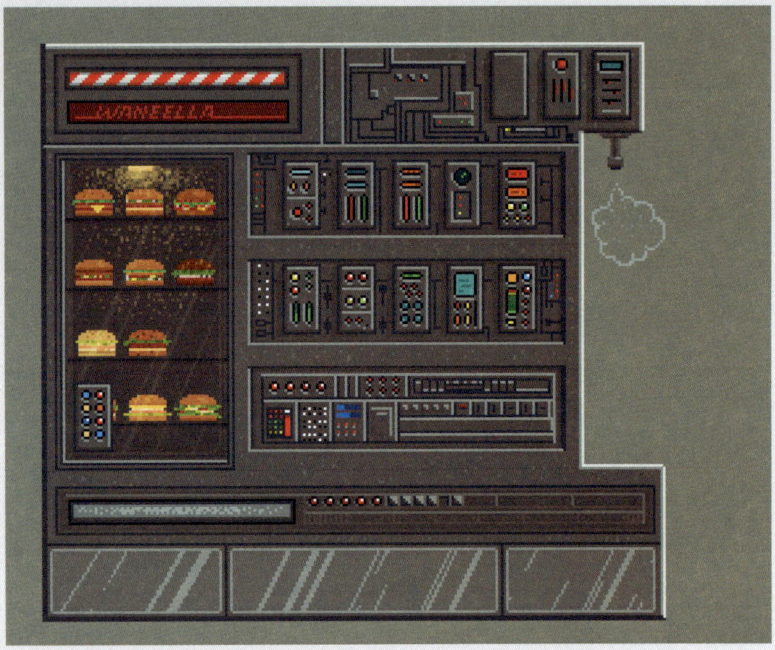

1

3
4

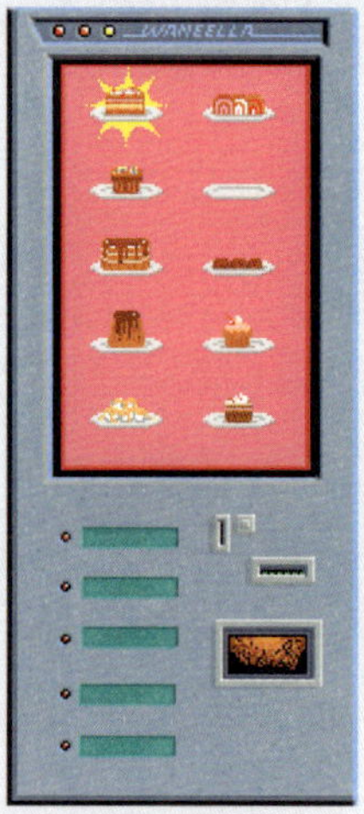

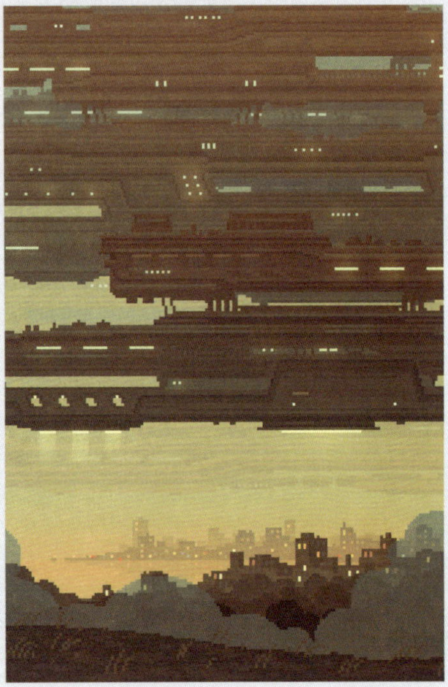

2

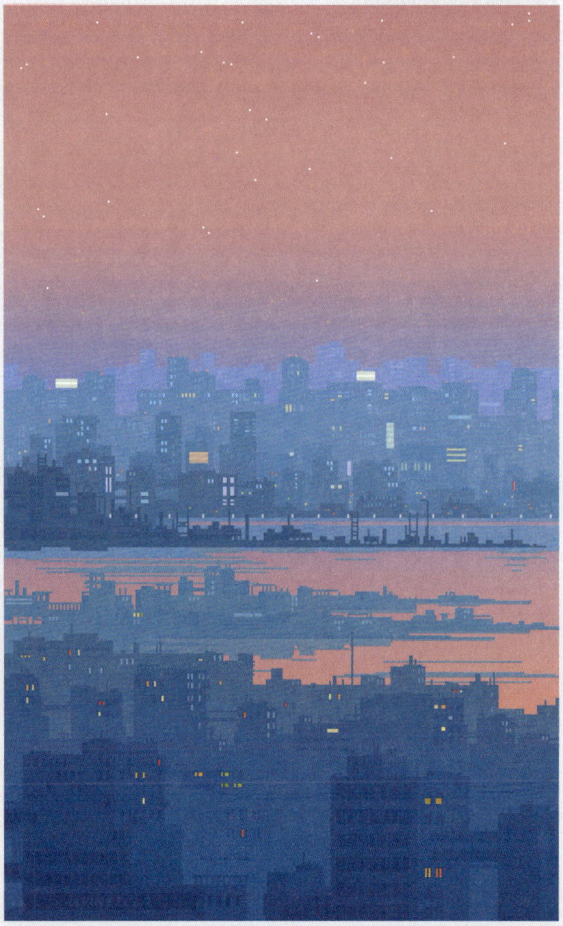

1 *Untitled*, 10/02/2013, 300×245px
2 *Untitled*, 16/03/2014, 175×250px
3 *Untitled*, 10/02/2013, 140×321px
4 *9:15*, 31/08/2014, 300×500px

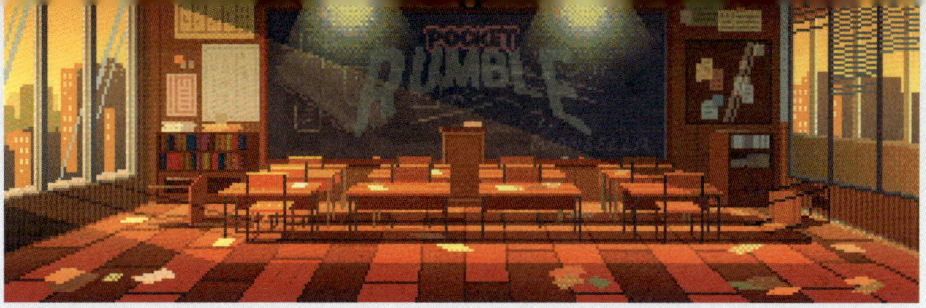

5

6
7

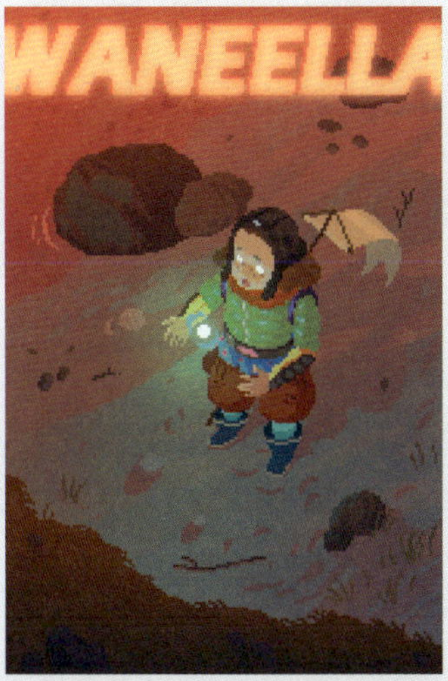

8

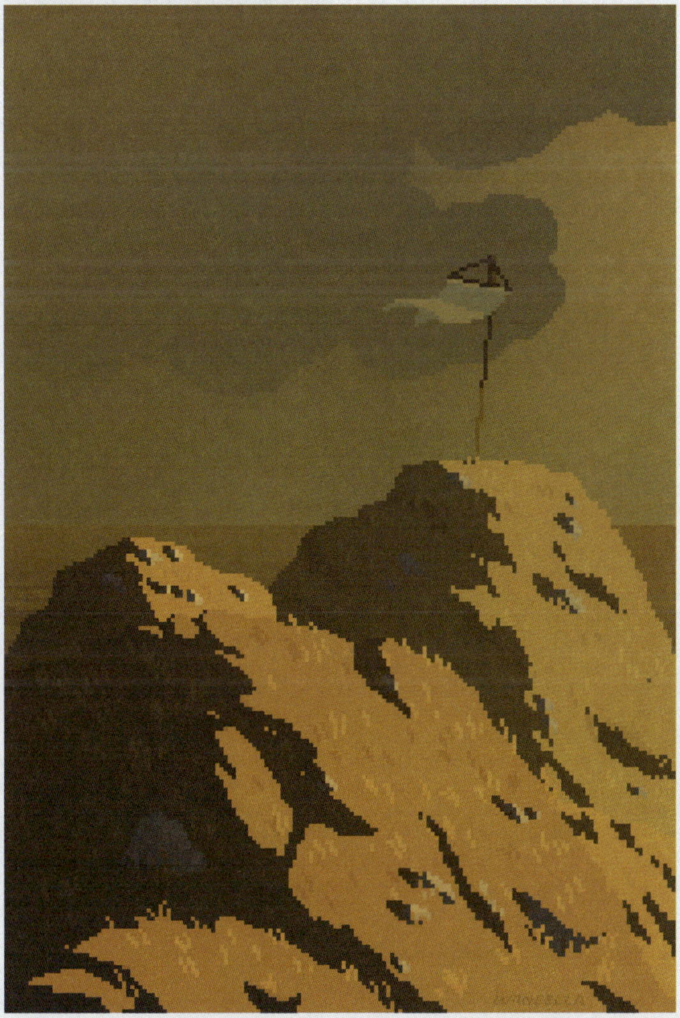

5 Background art for *Pocket Ramble* videogame by Cardboard Robot Games, 2013
6 *Untitled*, 05/05/2014, 160×248px
7 *Untitled*, 30/03/2014, 330×500px
8 *Untitled*, 19/02/2014, 352×500px

in the woods [→ page 12], and while it was a technical improvement, this exercise revealed that I wasn't actually interested in copying someone else's work. *Superbrothers: Sword & Sworcery EP* had fired my imagination, but now I wanted to draw my own scenes and use my own methods – to search and discover for myself. So I moved on.

Graduation and beyond

While I was excited by the possibilities of pixel art, I was yet to develop a style, and I definitely couldn't see any future where I could make a living out of it. I was also only half-way through my course, so I split my time between completing university assignments during the day and drawing pixels at night.
At the end of my fourth year, I found some work experience at an animation studio called Soyuzmultfilm, where I learned a lot about the industry. I realized I needed to make more contacts in the field in order to secure a good job after graduation. Despite my natural quietness, I reached out to various people and made some important connections during my university years. For my final year – my sixth at VGIK – we were required to create a short animation film, which my fellow students and I found an almost impossible task. While we all wrote scripts and created storyboards, most of us only drew and animated parts of it, submitting just a few finished sequences or a rough version. I was no different, since the competing demands of the course, occasional work assignments and my own pixel art proved too much. By the time I graduated, waneella's online following had started to grow, although – partly because most of my followers lived outside Russia – I still thought of my pixel art as a hobby. I wasn't too worried, because I'd been asked to work on a full-length animated project that started just two days after graduation. Just like that, I was an environment artist working in the animation industry. It was an amazing start. Even if I'd given up on the pixel art at that moment, I think I'd have had a rewarding and enjoyable career creating backgrounds.

Into the workplace... occasionally

Truthfully, I've always tried to avoid working in an office: I get easily distracted, find crowds quite tiring and work much more effectively on my own. It isn't all that surprising, then, that being an online artist is a much better fit for me than working in a big organization. Thankfully, remote working has become the norm these days, so it no longer seems odd that I work from home. Though this set-up suits me, I'm grateful for the period I spent working in traditional animation after graduation. It kept me busy and allowed me to gain experience on the other side of the fence.
Throughout 2016, I worked at a Moscow studio and almost stopped drawing pixel art entirely, since I couldn't see how it would ever feed me and my family. However, I picked up a couple of pixel-art commissions that year, so occasionally practiced my skills to keep them sharp.
Russian New Year holidays are long – ten days or so – and during the 2017 break, I decided to focus on my pixel-art cityscapes more seriously, initially by creating new scenes in perspective.
I also became more active on Twitter (X). While my first attempts at generating pictures and tweets weren't great, these steps signalled the next stage of my journey.

Going viral

There's a moment every day when the sun has just set but it's still not dark: the sky is dark blue, shot through with greens and yellows, while the light on the buildings is soft and beautiful. This time captivates me, so I decided to create a twilight scene and was really pleased with the result [→ below & page 51]. I filled the work with detail and animations – the train, TV and trees – then posted it online. Since it was already the middle of the night, I went to bed, only to wake up to so many notifications that I thought my phone might break. My post had gone viral! Someone called Tyler Joseph, who I later discovered was the frontman of a band called Twenty One Pilots, had reposted my picture and suddenly, it was all over the internet.
It was both hilarious and embarrassing, because I didn't immediately know his name. But Tyler's retweet got me so much attention and so many new followers that I quickly started to recognize the special letters that Twenty One Pilots' fans use in their nicknames. There was even some theory that Tyler and I knew each other... we don't.

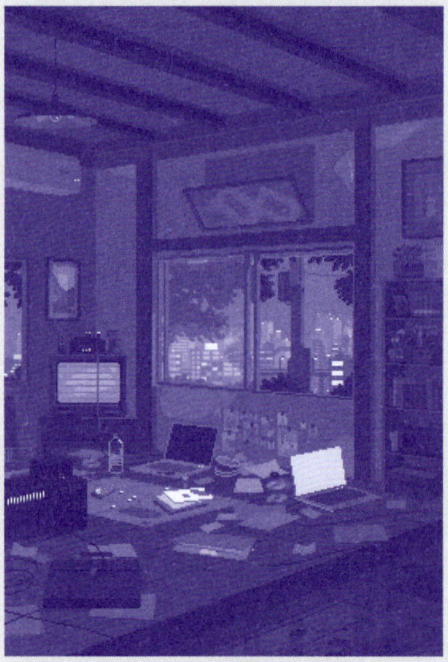

[→ page 51]

The boost caused by this unexpected retweet also landed me some work drawing concept art for Nickelodeon. Surprisingly, it wasn't pixel art, which is why I think it didn't work out in the long-term. I regard myself as a very average traditional illustrator, yet when companies see my pixel art, they assume all my output will

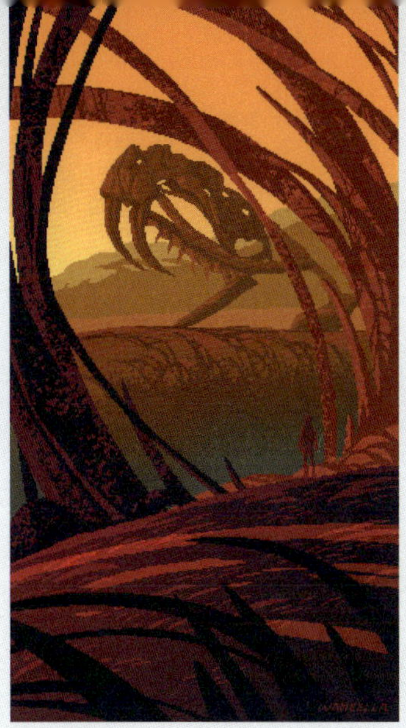
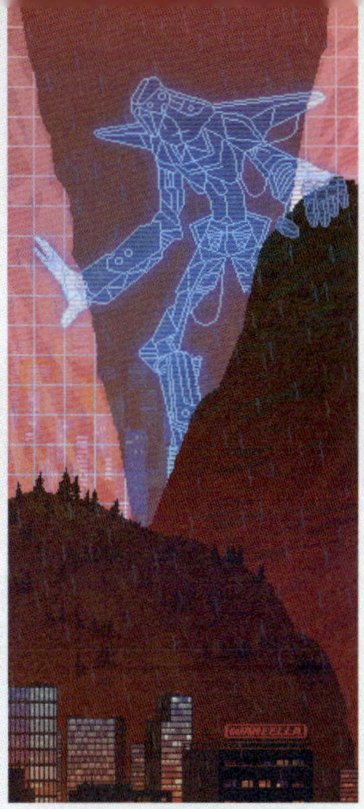

1
2

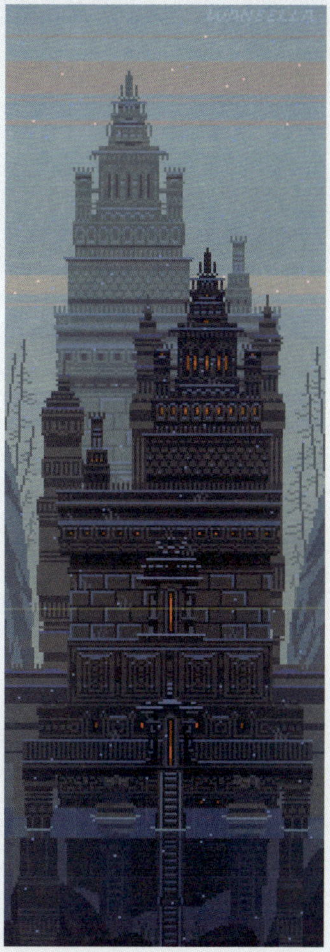

5

3
4

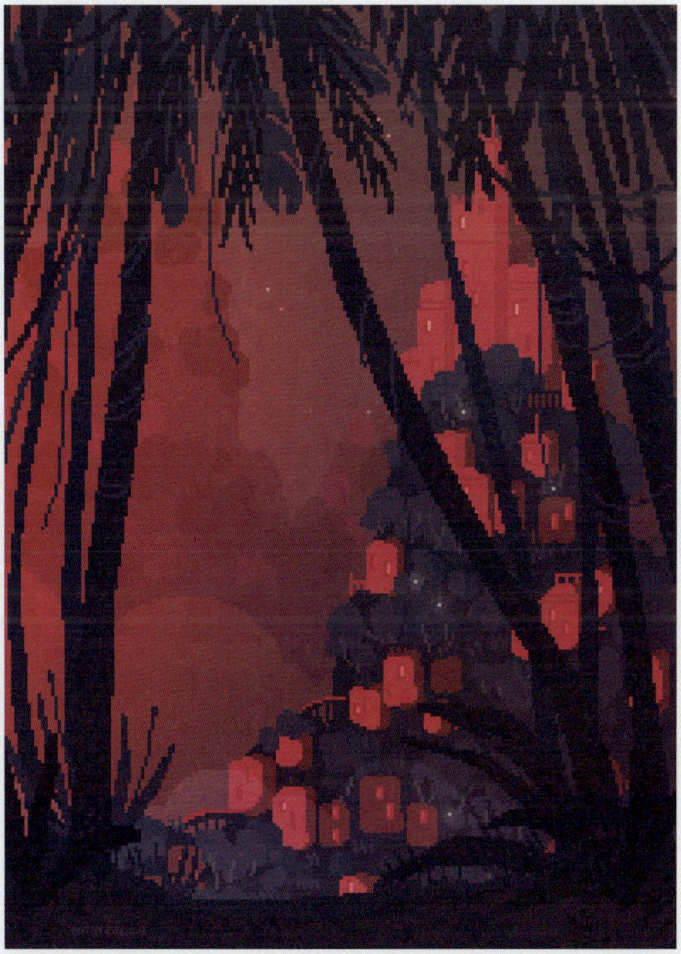
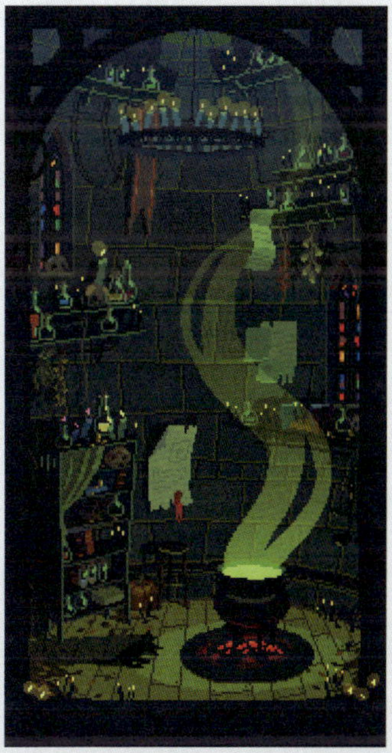

1 *Untitled*, 25/10/2015, 250×500px
2 *Untitled*, 12/06/2015, 220×549px
3 *Untitled*, 22/02/2014, 200×284px
4 *Untitled*, 31/10/2015, 180×350px
5 *Untitled*, 12/09/2015, 135×400px

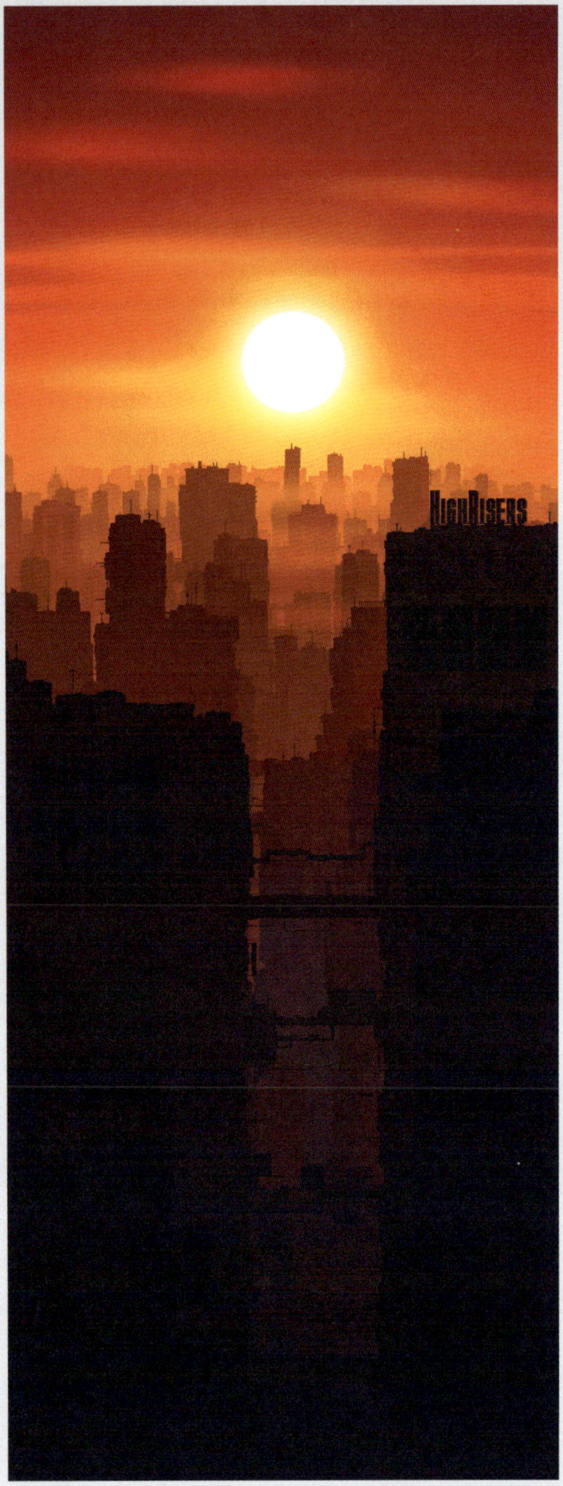

1

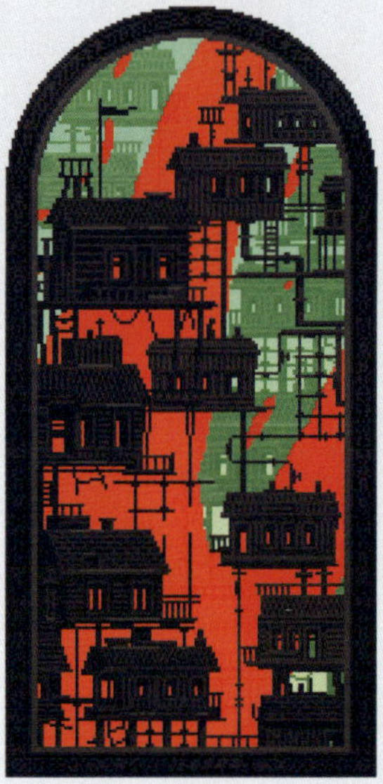

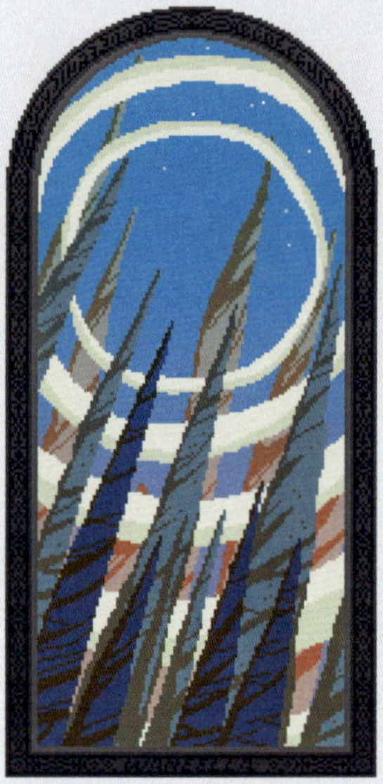

2
3

4
5

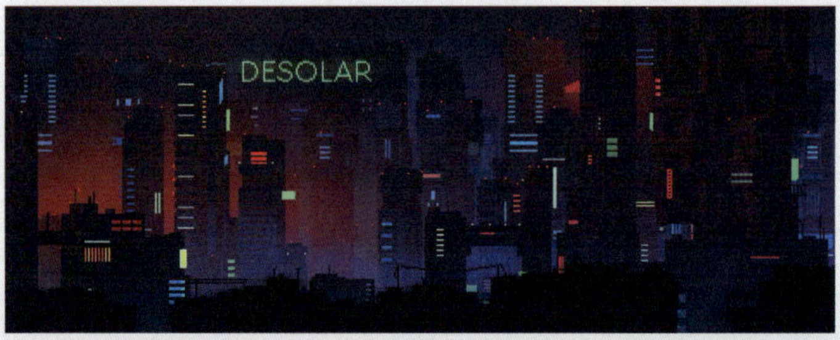

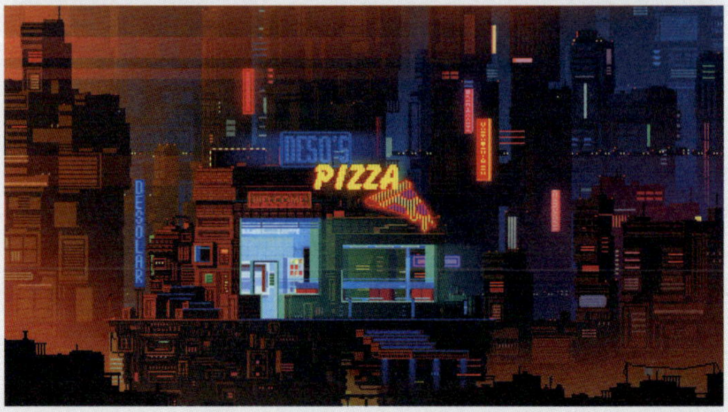

1 Background art for *Highrisers* videogame by Solar Powered Games, 2016
2 *Untitled*, 16/06/2015, 128×270px
3 *Untitled*, 16/06/2015, 128×270px
4 Illustration for *Desolar* twitch.tv / desolar youtube.com / desolarTV, 2015
5 Illustration for *Desolar* twitch.tv / desolar youtube.com / desolarTV, 2016

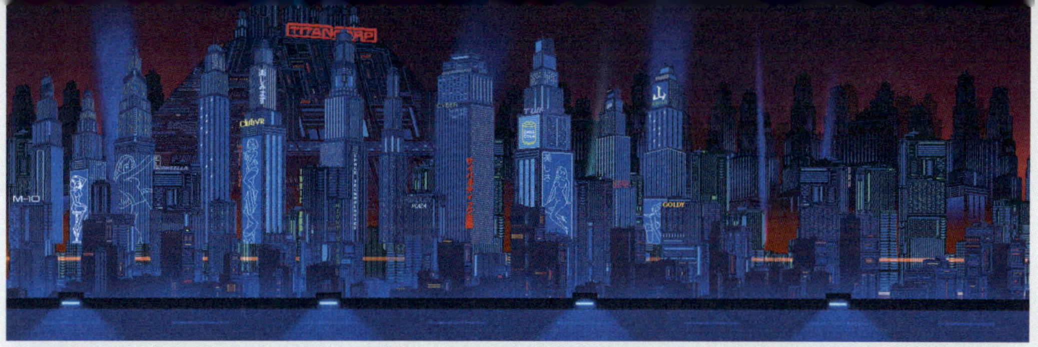

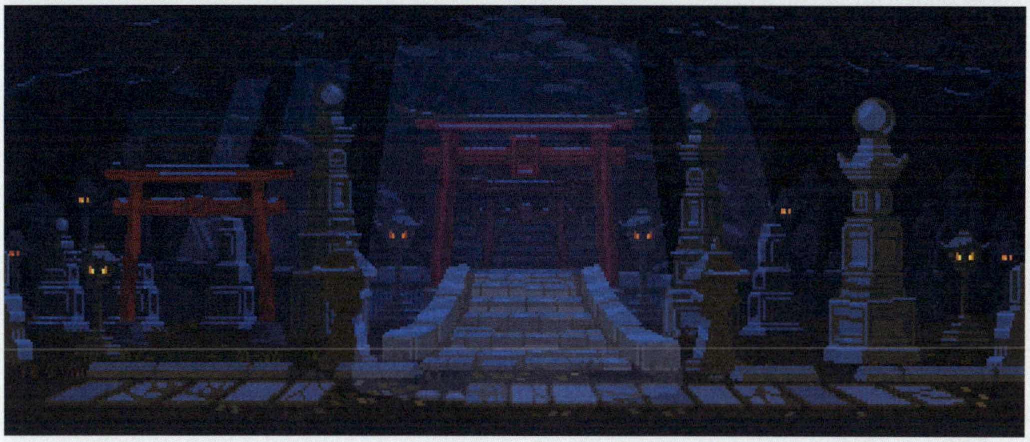

6
7

8
9

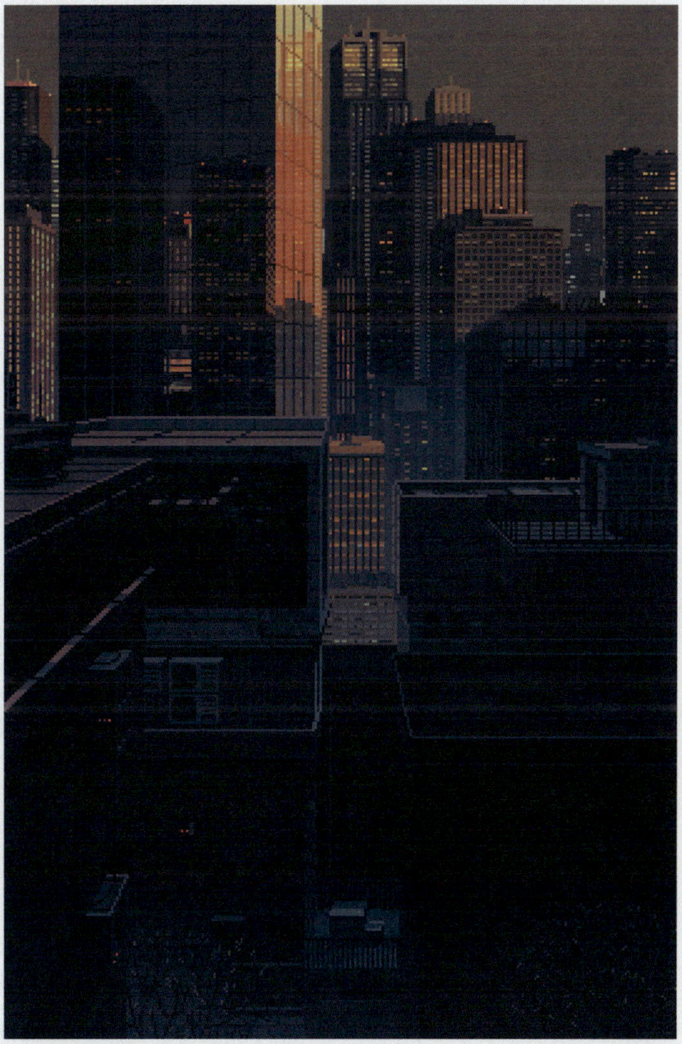

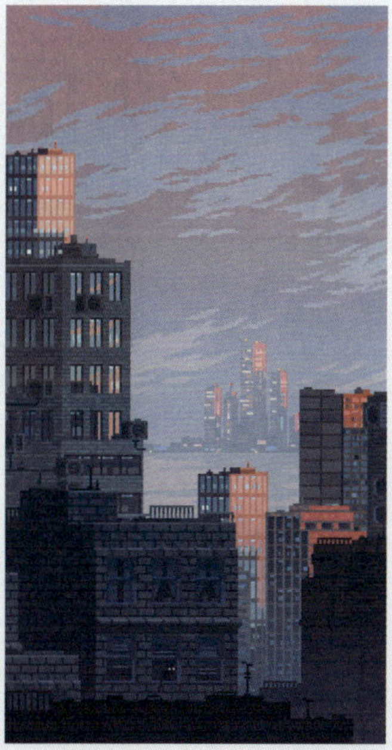

6 Concept art for an untitled game, 2016
7 Background art for *Pocket Ramble* videogame by Cardboard Robot Games, 2016
8 *Long Time No See*, 29/10/2016, 270×420px
9 *60K*, 31/07/2016, 180×350px

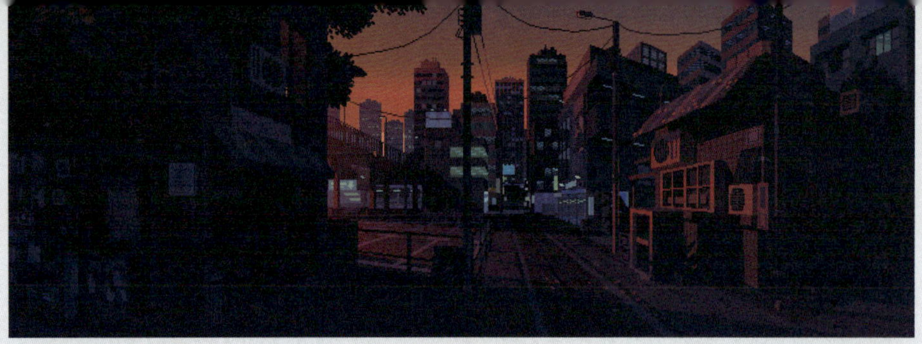

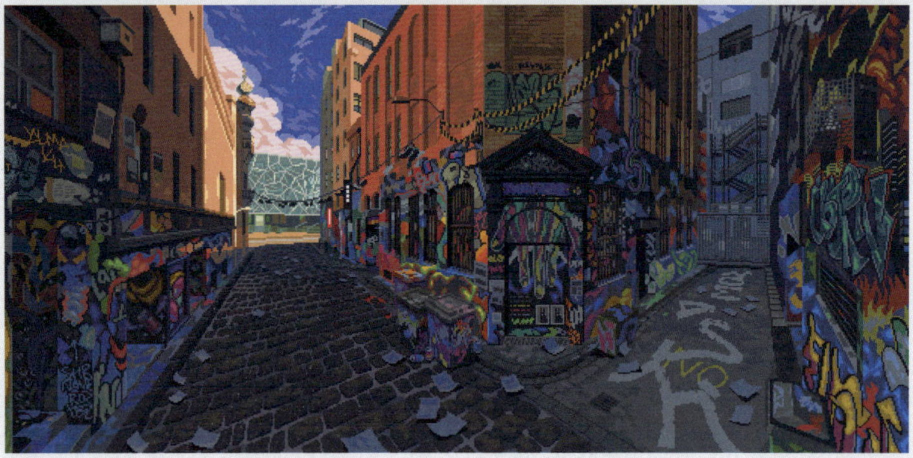

1
2

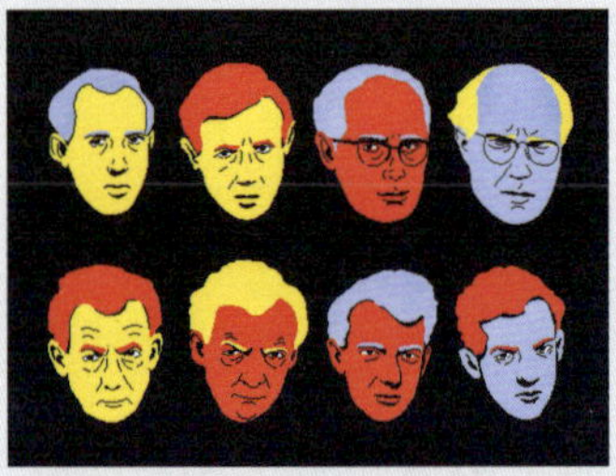

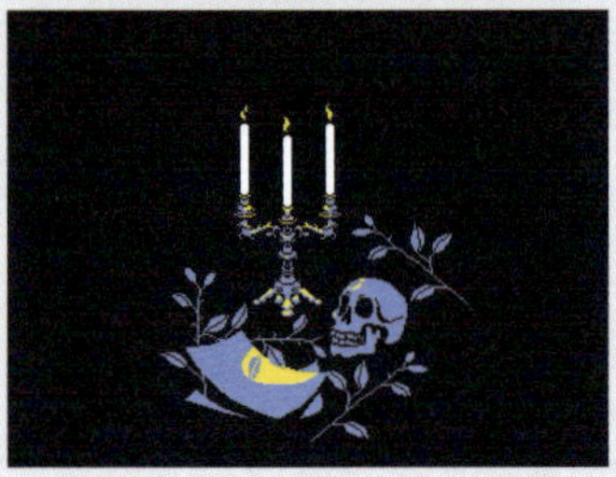

3
4

5
6
7
8

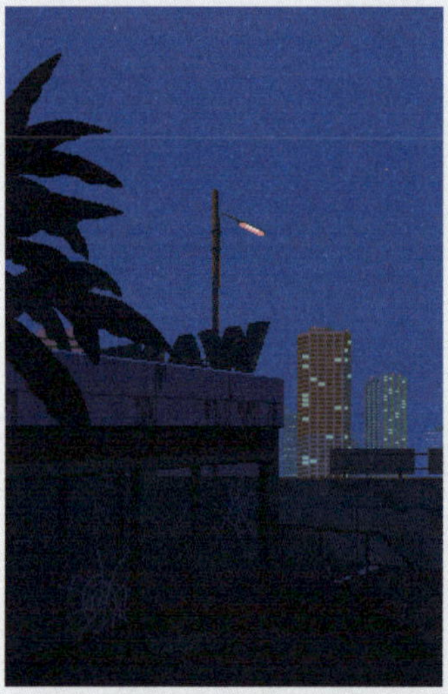

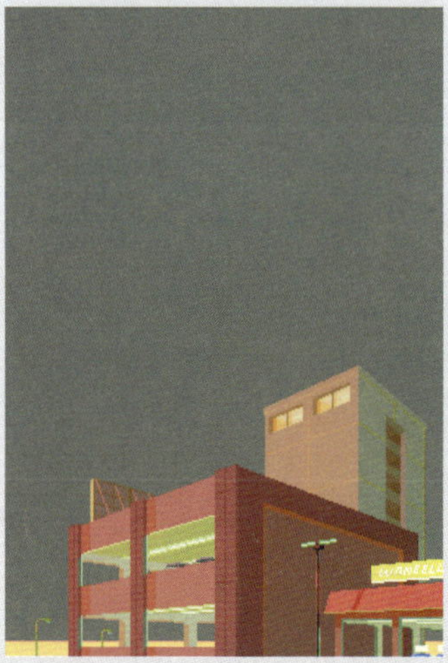

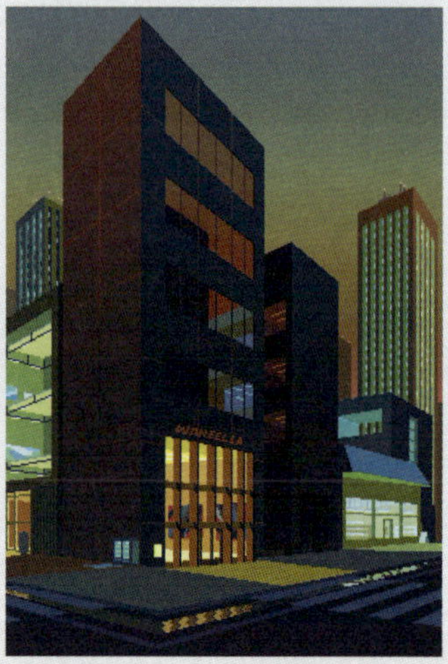

1 *mbRtfWLicq*, 19/09/2017, 688×288px
2 *Hosier Lane*, commissioned by Paul Arden, 2019
3–4 Background art for classical music concert *Britain* by Škola Crew, 2017
5 *zz4xP3UdIN*, 06/06/2017, 270×405px
6 *Untitled*, 30/01/2017, 270×405px
7 *Untitled*, 23/01/2017, 270×405px
8 *Untitled*, 24/01/2017, 270×405px

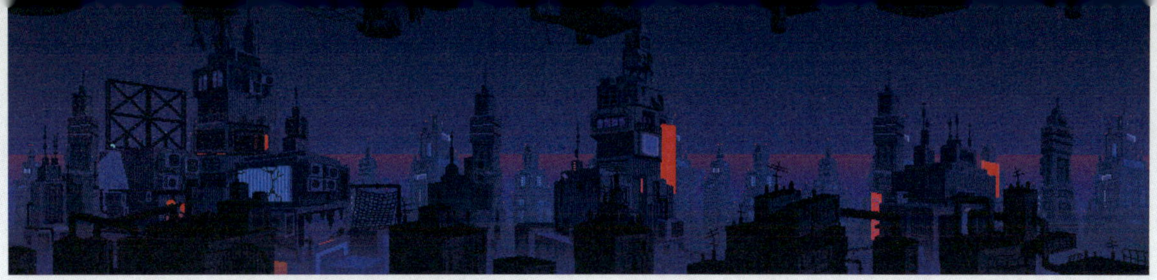

9

10

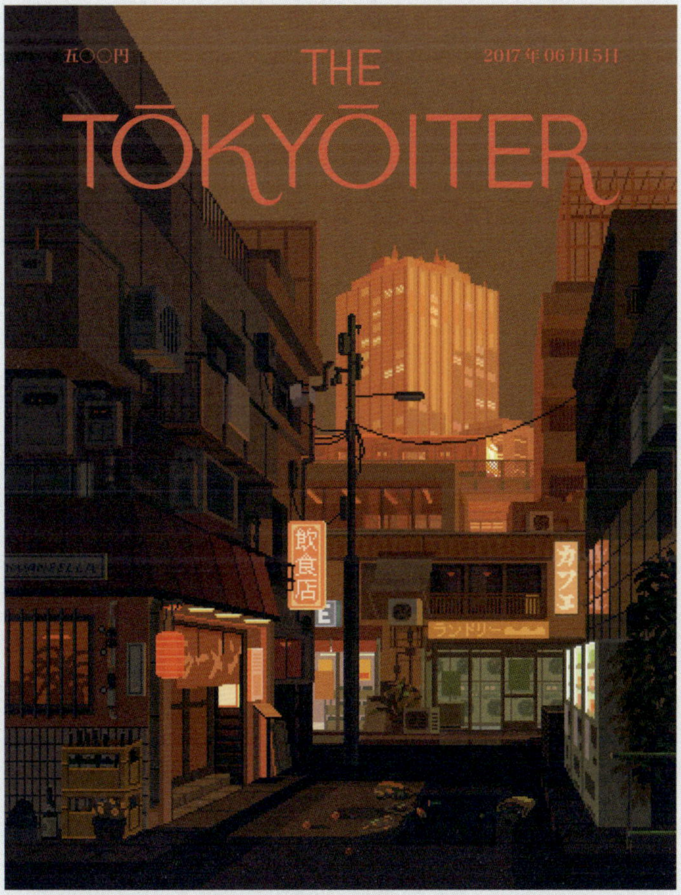

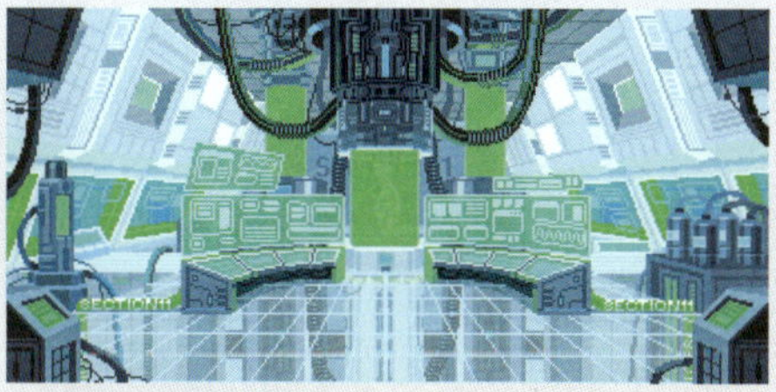

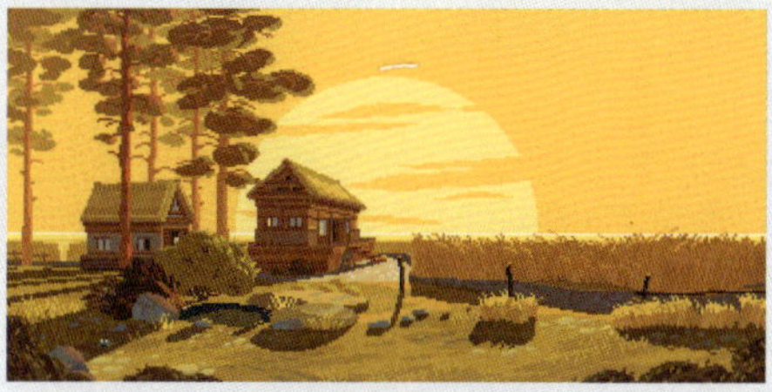

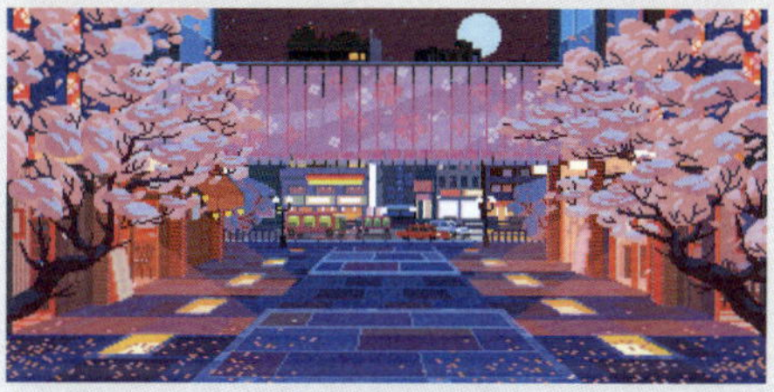

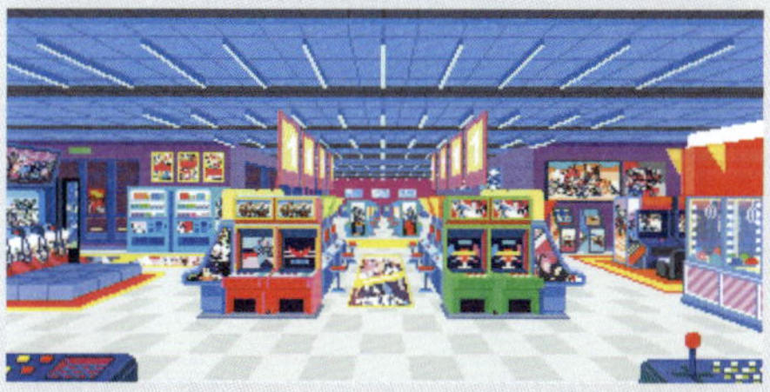

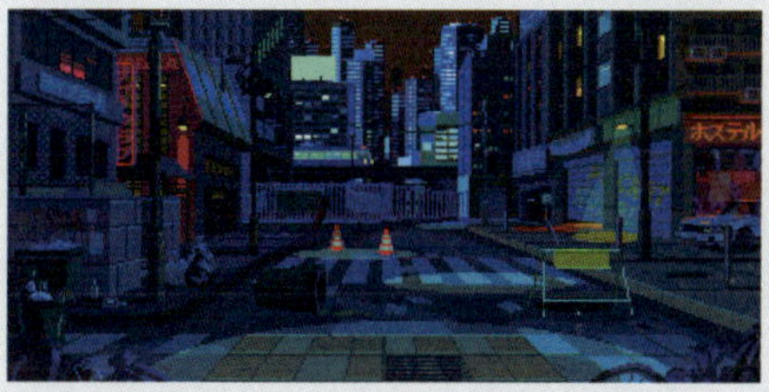

11
12
13
14
15

9 Illustration for *Gunship* music video, 2017
10 Illustration for *The Tokyoiter* project thetokyoiter.com, 2017
11–15 Background art for *Pocket Ramble* videogame by Cardboard Robot Games, 2017

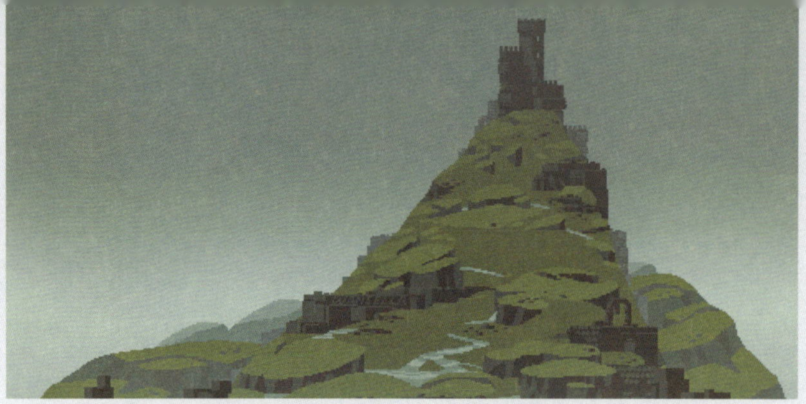

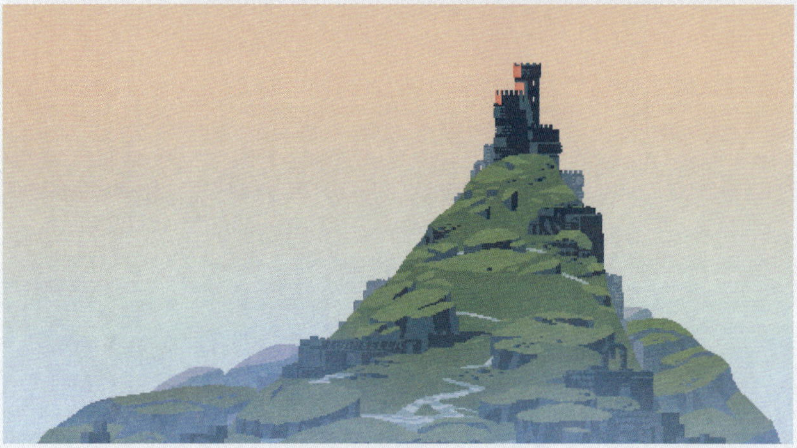

1
2

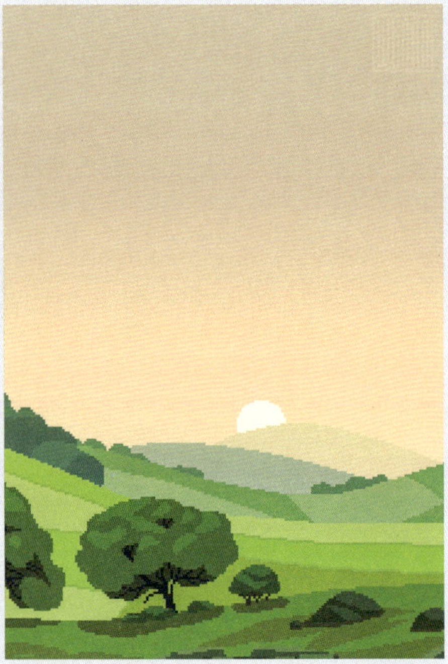

3

4
5

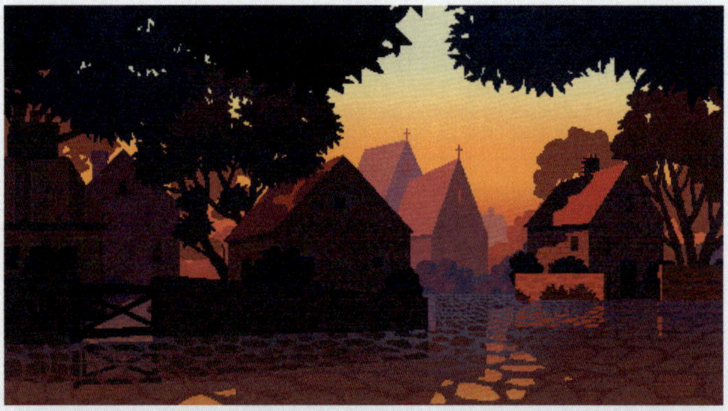

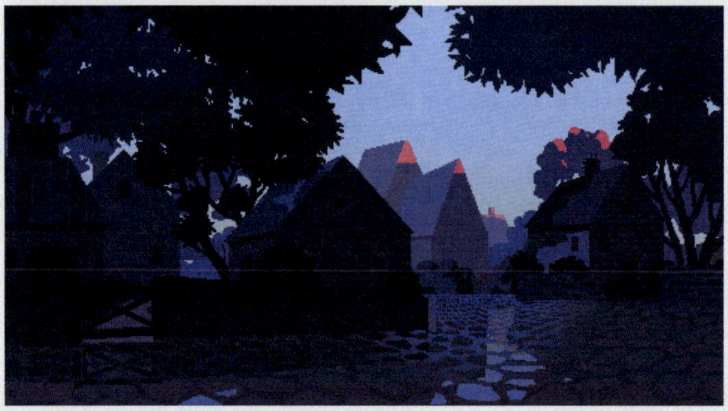

1–2 Background art for classical music concert *Britain* by Škola Crew, 2017
3 Promotional illustration for classical music concert *Britain* by Škola Crew, 2017
4–5 Background art for classical music concert *Britain* by Škola Crew, 2017

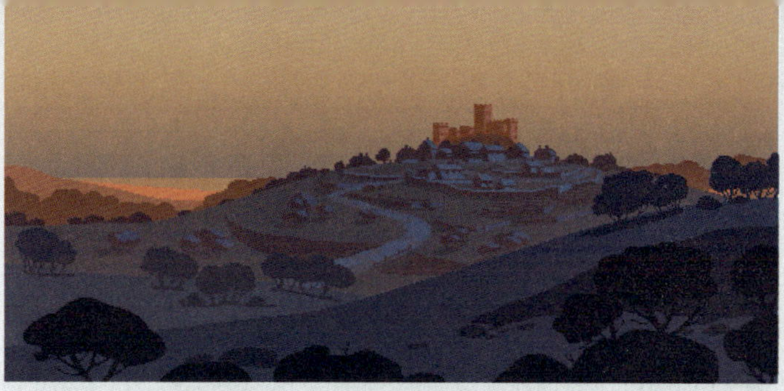

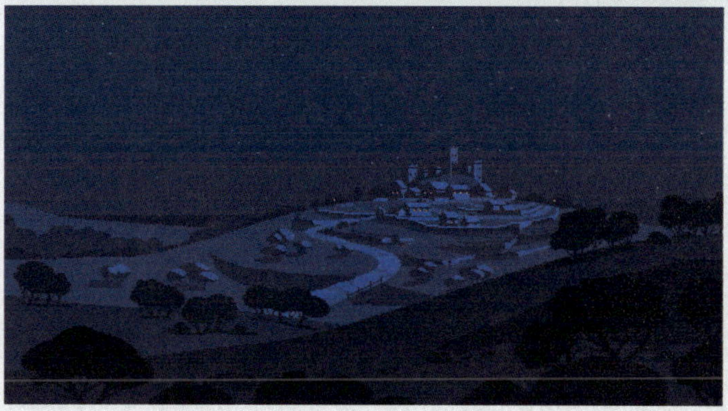

6
7

8
9
10

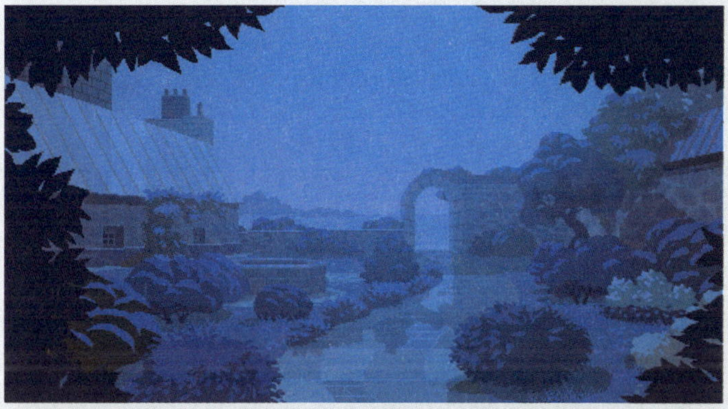

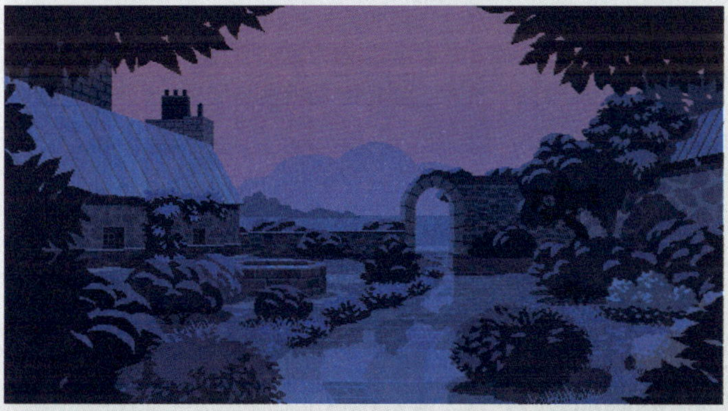

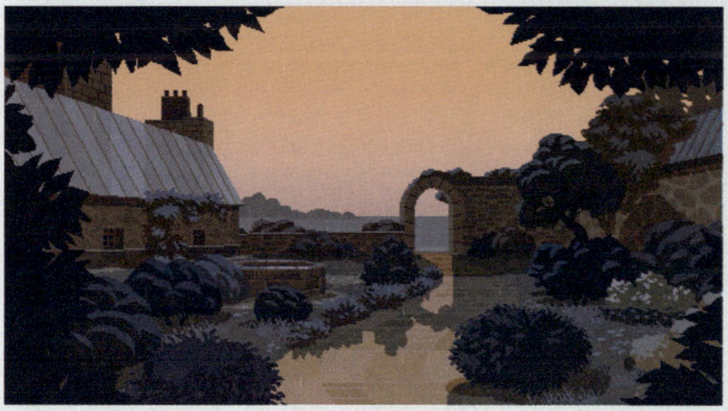

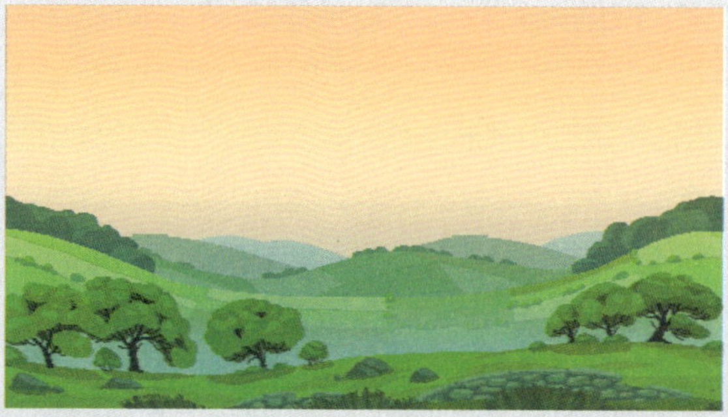

11

6–11 Background art for classical music concert *Britain* by Škola Crew, 2017 be at the same level. But who has the time to practice all styles of art, all the time? That said, I still draw in a number of different styles in my work for Škola Crew, with whom I have a long-standing connection. They're a group of musicians and contemporary artists who combine lectures, classical music and video art projections into wonderful and beautiful projects and concerts. Sadly, classical music is not easy to promote in a way that appeals to all age groups, so I feel that their ongoing project has always been very much underrated.

World tour, waneella edition

In 2018, I received an invitation to take part in the Pixel Art Park 5 (PAP5) event in Tokyo. PAP5 was the first time I travelled abroad on my own, the first time I participated in a festival *and* the first time I met my fans to face.
It was an honour that people were willing to stand in line for two hours to buy my small custom-made art book which, fittingly, I had titled *MOTIONLESS*. I also sold prints of my art and while my mother had wanted me to take some framed posters – she ran a small picture-framing studio at the time – there was no way I could carry that much on the flight from Russia to Japan. After a stunning trip to Japan, at the start of 2019 I felt ready and able to do absolutely anything. I realized that growing my online presence was the way forwards and that posting on YouTube would play a major part. Since videos of my animated pixel art on YouTube required professional musical scores, I asked my father if he would like the job. He'd never had any reason to experiment with electronic music but had always wanted to try, so he jumped at the chance. It turns out that my dad is capable of writing any kind of music – traditional or electronic. Under the credit of 'e.sanchillo' he's now written more than seventy compositions that have been compiled into three albums of '*waneella tunes*'. I think we're creating great work together and while I wish he'd blow up enough to make a living from it, it's still pretty cool to have a dad who's also an underground electronic composer.

The end of the world (as we know it)

I was invited back to the Pixel Art Park event in Tokyo, with PAP6 taking place at the end of 2019 and coinciding with Steam releasing artwork I'd made for its Autumn Sale event. This assignment was such a boost for me that even though I've since produced other artwork for Steam, I still think of this as the peak of my career. The whole situation felt so magical – being back in Japan, receiving so much press and seeing my artwork on the main page of one of the world's most important digital spaces. In that moment, it seemed as though life could only get better.
So when the Covid-19 pandemic hit, it was a huge blow – not only for me, but for millions of people around the globe. Other events I was looking forward to were cancelled, along with travel and then, for most of the world, even normal life. With live events on hold, I had a lot of free time during 2020 – many of us did – so I drew a lot over lockdown.
I also got a grant from the Goethe Institute to create an exhibition as part of the VII Moscow International Biennale of Young Art. Its title translated to *Moscow–Tokyo Train* and the exhibition envisaged a future of peace and stability in which electric trains link Europe to Japan via a transportation hub in Moscow. Of course, at that stage we didn't know what was to come.
Waneella has far better online recognition from a global fanbase than Valeriya Sanchillo does as an artist within Russia. This fact, combined with ongoing strict Covid-19 restrictions, meant that the exhibition, under my full name, came and went rather unnoticed. It was my first and, to date, my only personal exhibition in the 'real' world.

Figuring out the process

When I started making pixel art, I did so because I thought it would be a fast, easy and fun alternative to the traditional ink-and-paint artwork that I'd previously created. Ten years on, I see how young, naive and flat-out wrong I was. Even though making pixel art is now my job, I'm forever trying to figure out the best ways to translate my feelings into digital imagery.
It's turned out to be such a difficult medium precisely because of the limitations it imposes. I had assumed that strict limits on canvas and pixel size would translate into every image taking roughly the same amount of time, but that's not how it works. Many of the tools available in digital art packages such as Photoshop just don't apply to pixel art. I can't use effects or filters, for example. And while I theoretically could use aquarelle brushes, I would have to then correct each stroke so much that it's actually more effective to create the look of a paint stroke pixel-by-pixel. Similarly, surface textures, colour gradients and lighting can't be applied by clicking on a menu item – they all have to be created manually. At the core of pixel art, the artist must add one pixel at a time, without relying on shortcuts. It takes a lot of time and a lot of practice. While I don't think I have 'mastered' pixel art and don't think that I ever will, I do acknowledge that I have honed my skills and created my own distinctive style. Part of this is, without doubt, the settings of my pictures. Up until 2016, I drew on inspiration from many different themes. Gradually, the cityscape started to prevail and then, for some reason, I started drawing Japanese-themed street views.
I can't recall my initial source for reference images but do remember that, at some point, I realized I could use Google Maps – and specifically Street View – to 'tour' Japanese cities. This was back when I had never been to Japan and it didn't seem likely that I would ever go, so I spent long Moscow evenings just virtually 'walking' through beautiful

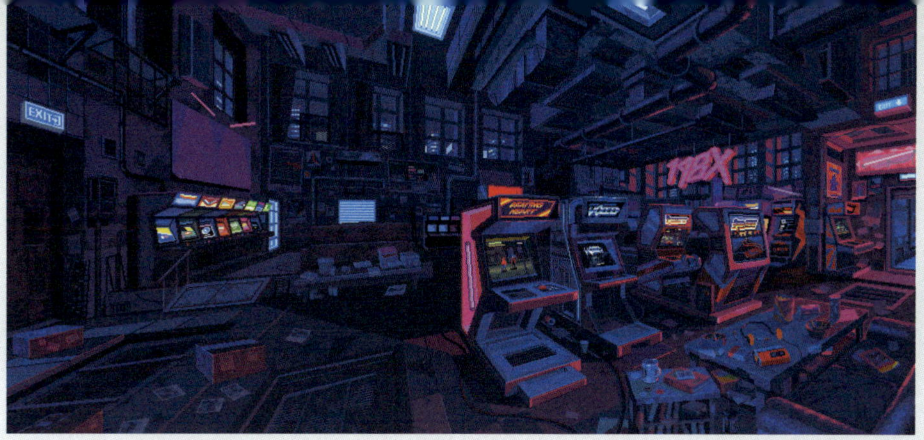

1

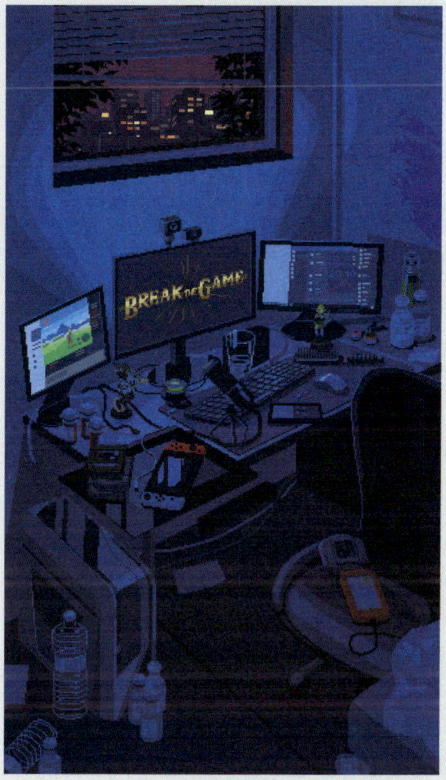

2

3
4
5
6

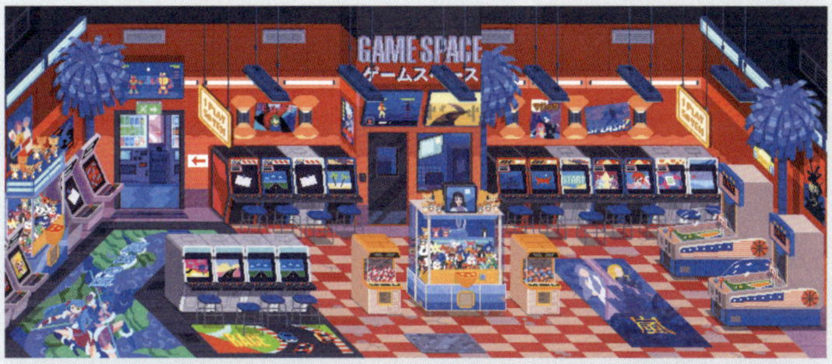

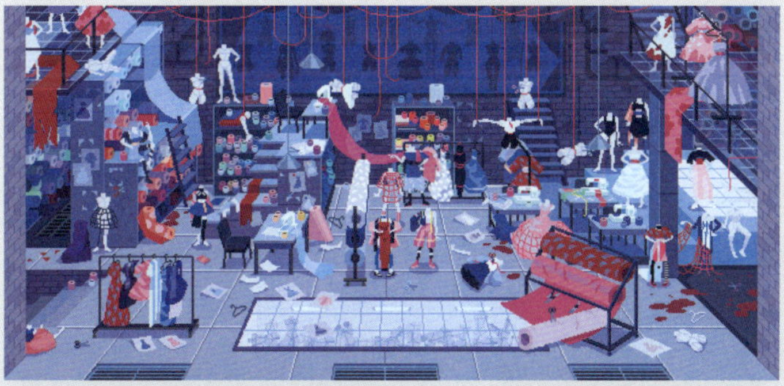

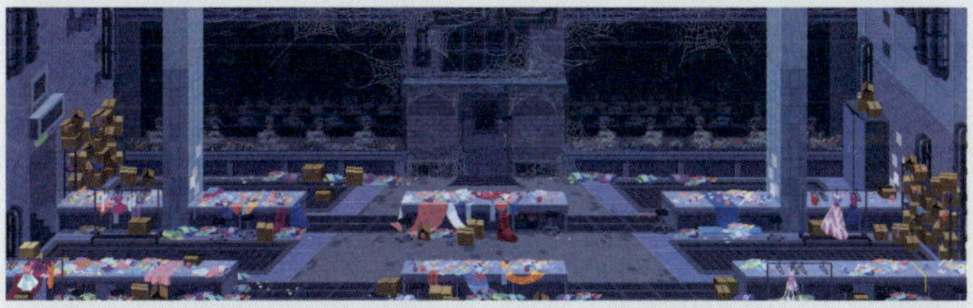

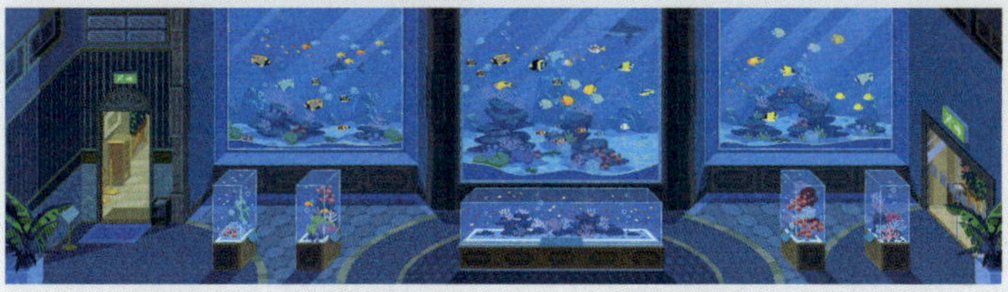

1 Illustration for *198X* videogame by Hi-Bit Studios, 2019
2 Illustration for *Break The Game* project, courtesy of BREAK THE GAME LLC, 2020
3–6 Background art for *River City Girls* videogame, 2018 & 2019, courtesy of WayForward © ARC SYSTEM WORKS

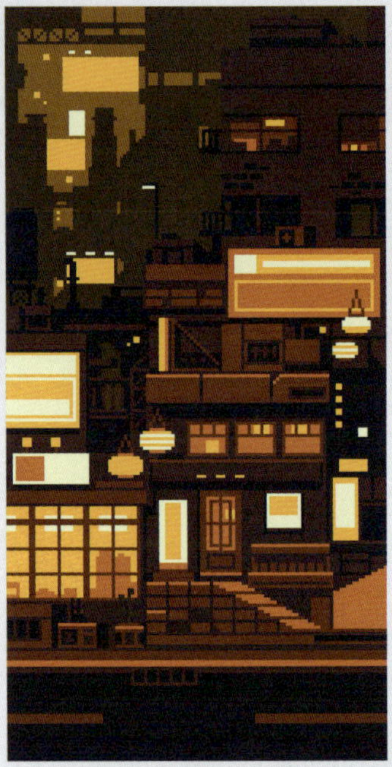

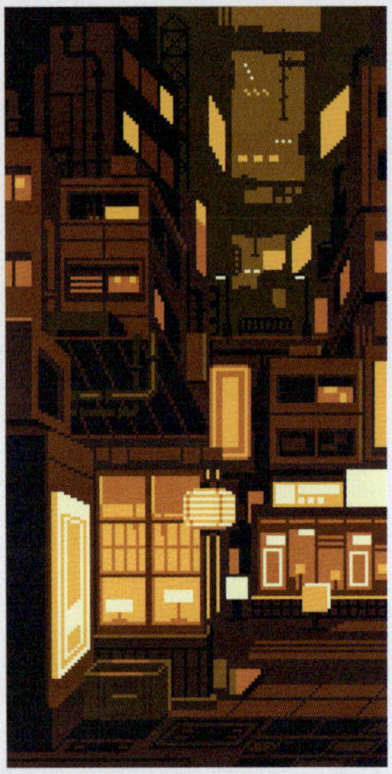

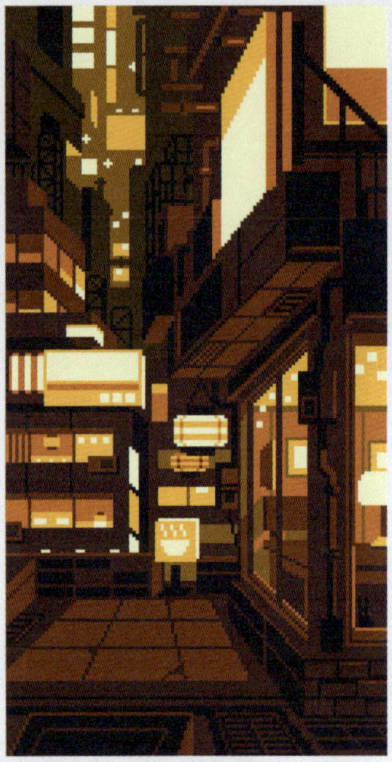

1
2
3

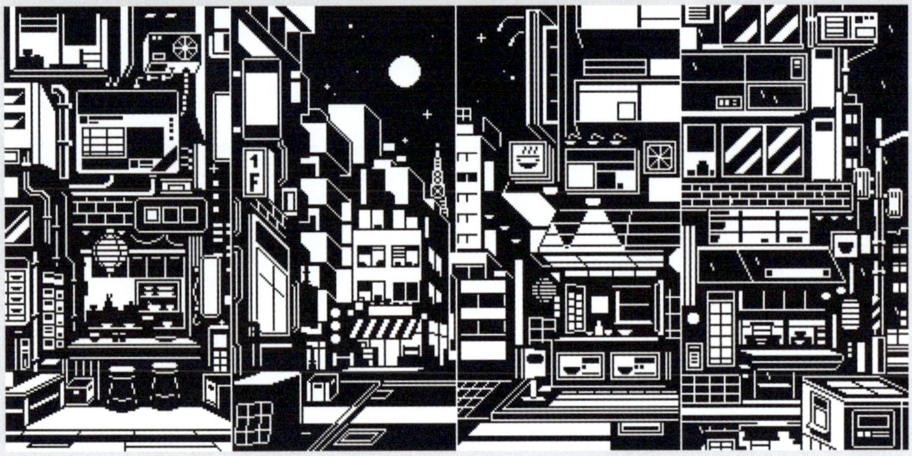

4

5
6

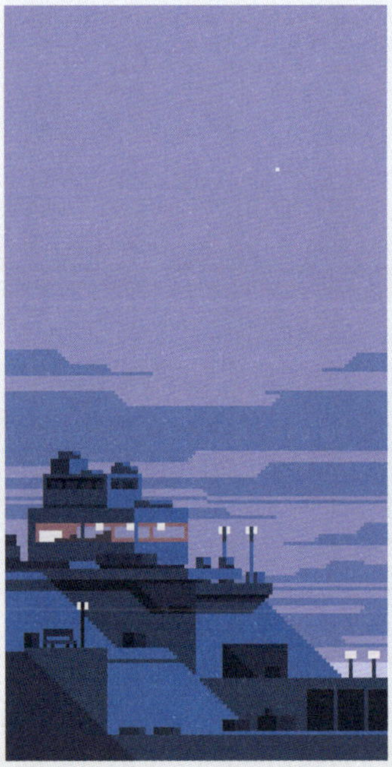

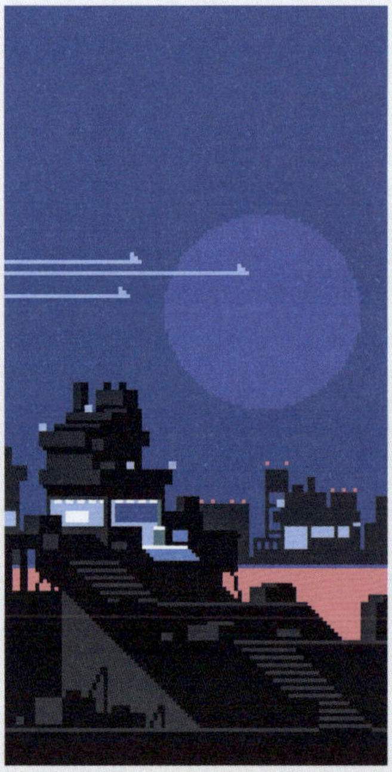

1 *Untitled*, 18/10/2019, 120×240px
2 *Untitled*, 30/10/2019, 120×240px
3 *Untitled*, 30/10/2019, 120×240px
4 *Untitled*, 06/10/2019, 483×240px
5 *Untitled*, 08/08/2019, 100×200px
6 *Untitled*, 09/08/2019, 100×200px

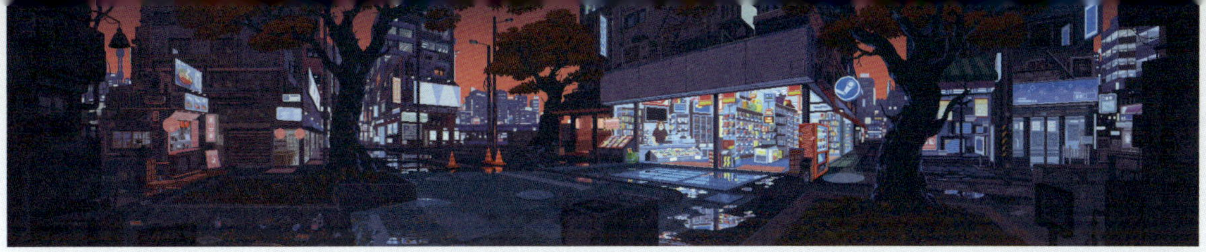

7

9
10
11

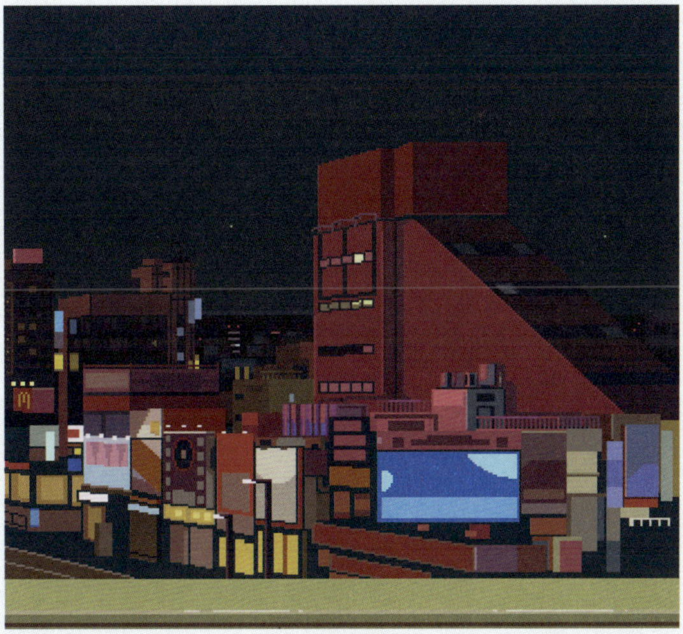

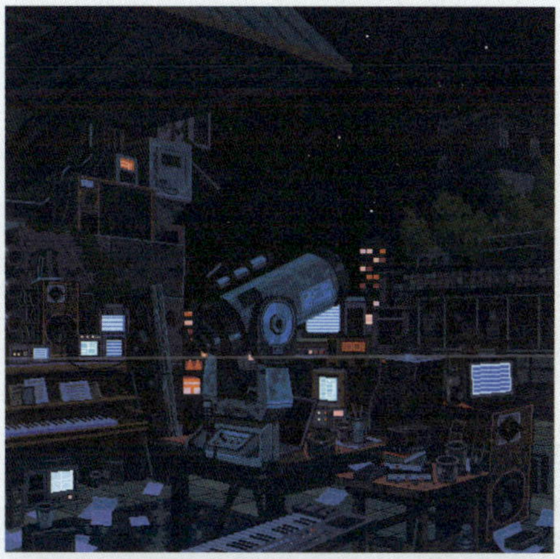

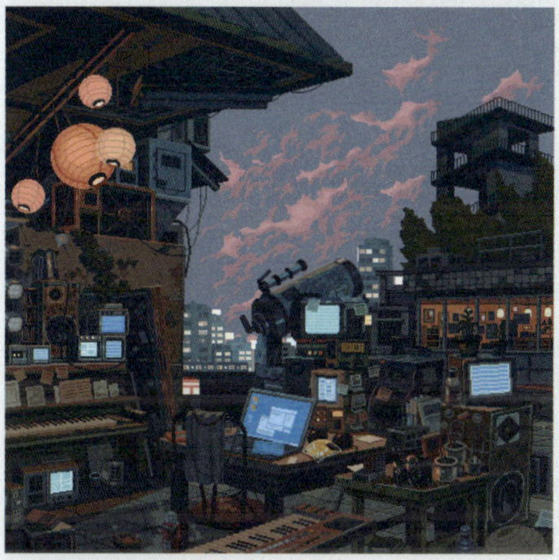

8

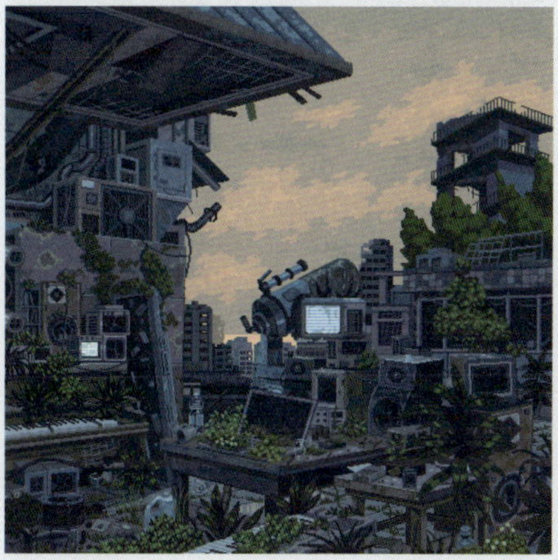

12
13

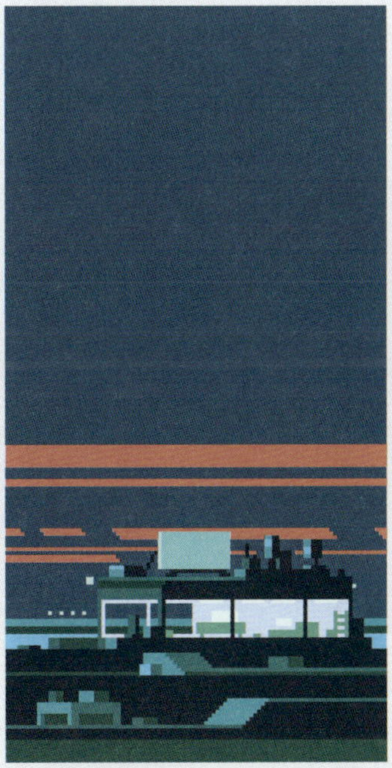

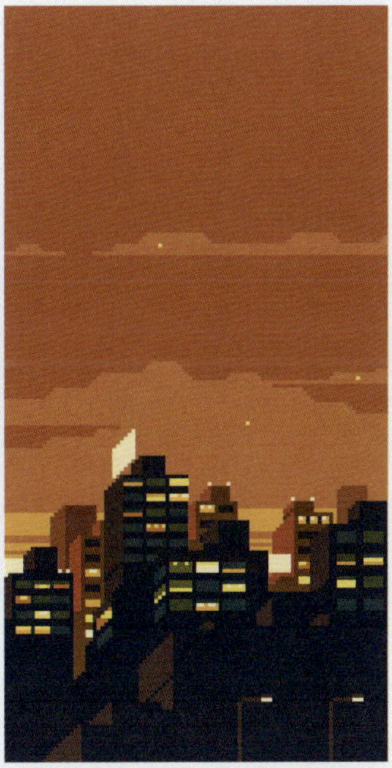

7 Illustration for Valve's Steam Autumn Sale © Valve Corporation, 2019
8 *Untitled*, 09/12/2019, 300×300px
9 Illustration for *Telescope* single by Tennyson for Ninja Tune, 2019
10 Illustration for *Telescope* EP by Tennyson for Ninja Tune, 2019
11 Illustration for *Collapse* single by Tennyson for Ninja Tune, 2019
12 *Untitled*, 08/08/2019, 100×200px
13 *Untitled*, 10/08/2019, 100×200px

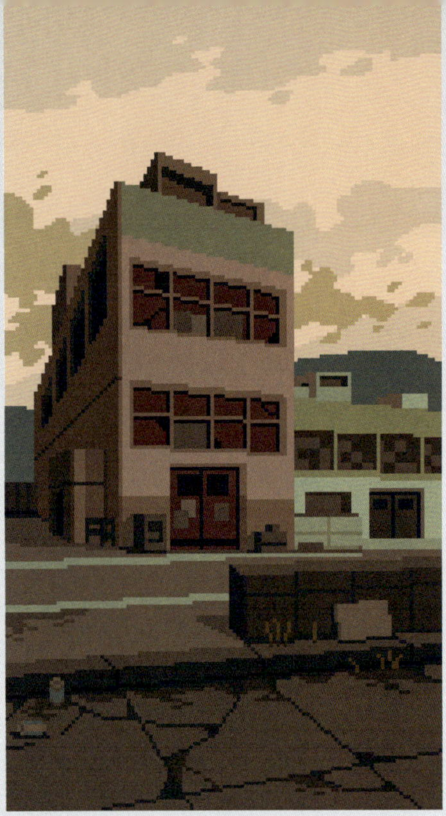

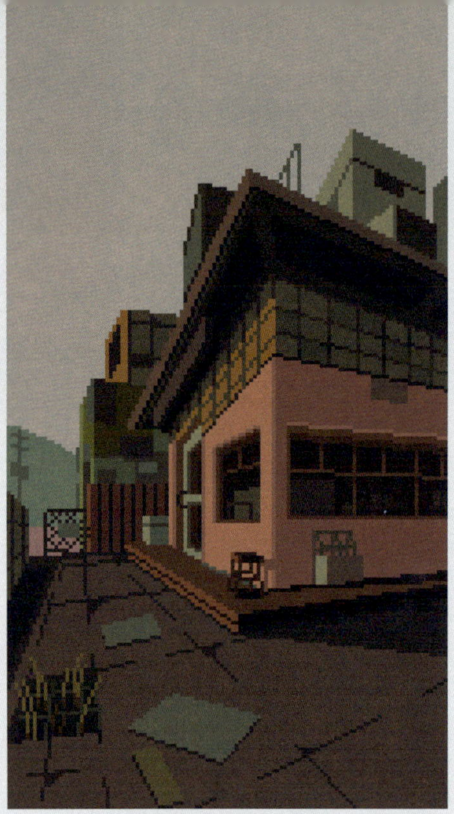

1
2

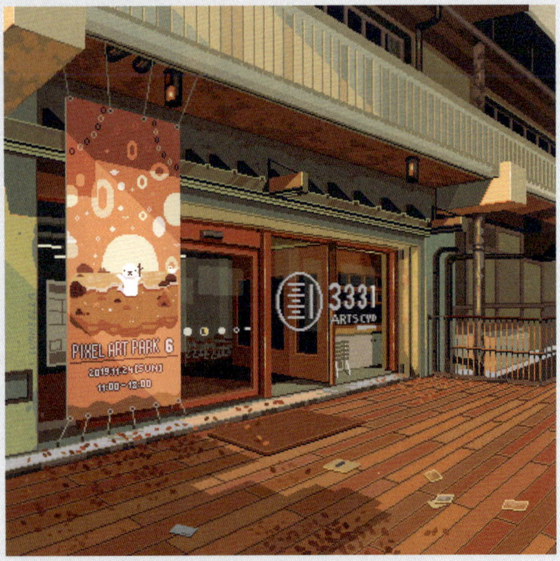

3

4
5

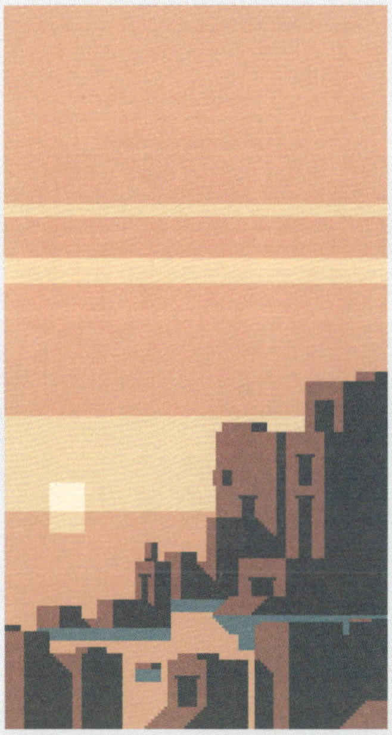

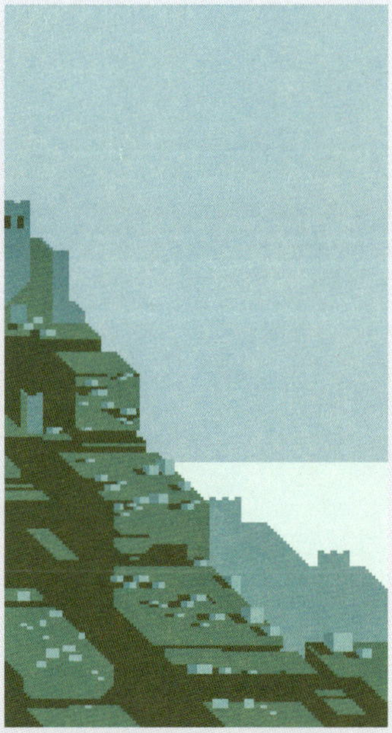

1 *Untitled*, 23/09/2019, 120×240px
2 *Untitled*, 22/09/2019, 120×240px
3 *PAP6xwaneella*, illustration for Pixel Art Park event in Tokyo, 2019
4 *Untitled*, 22/08/2019, 120×240px
5 *Untitled*, 22/08/2019, 120×240px

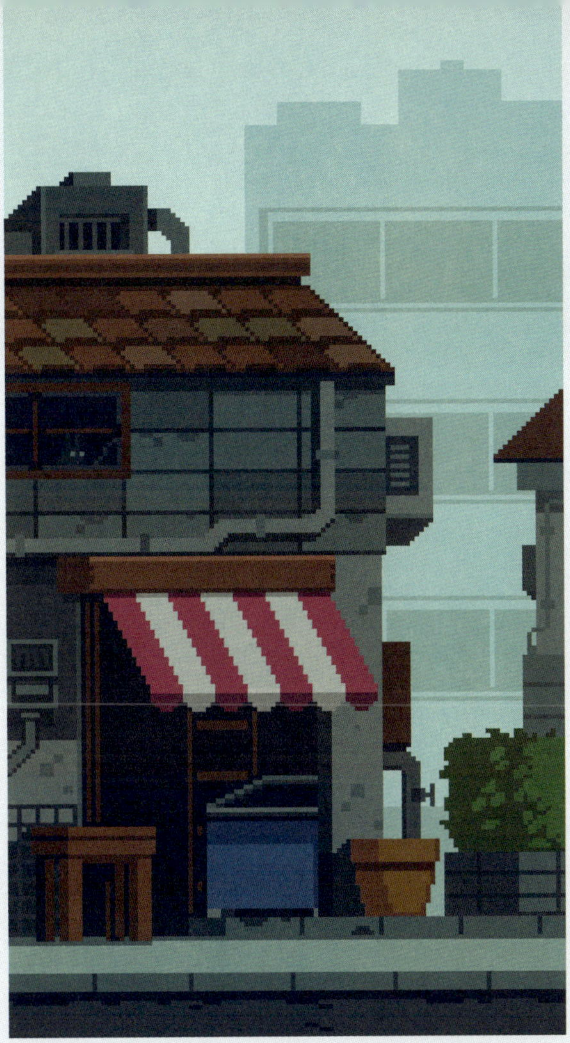

6

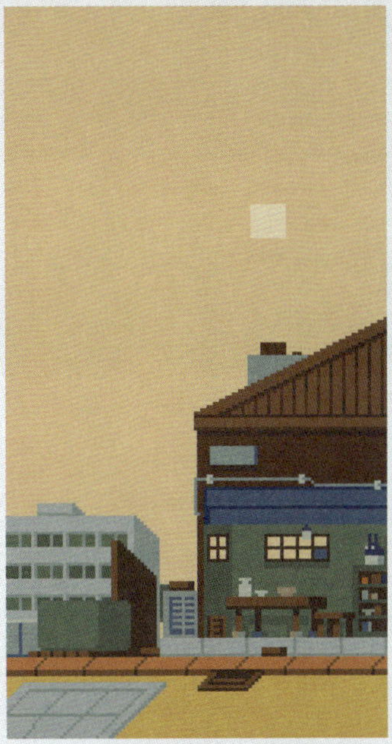

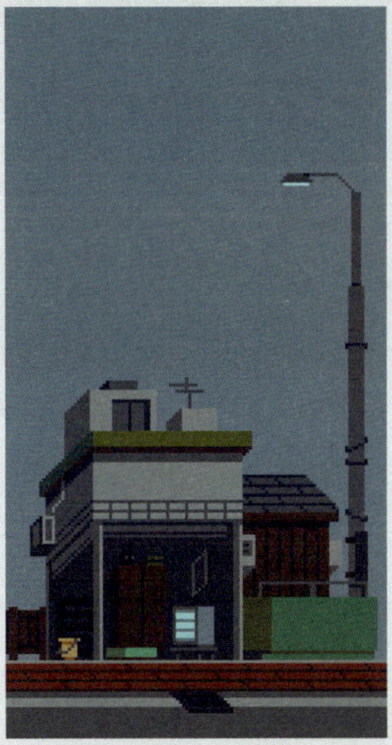

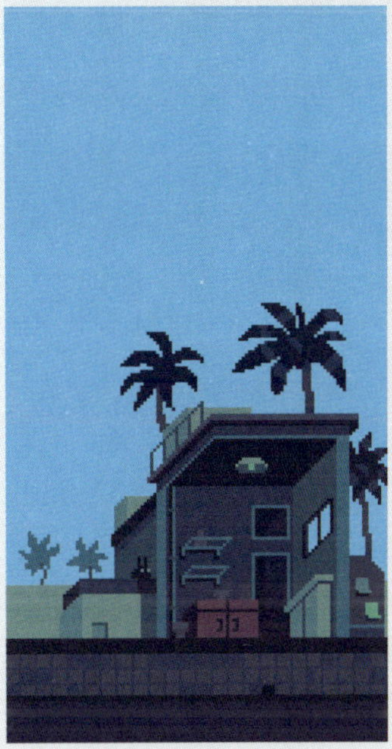

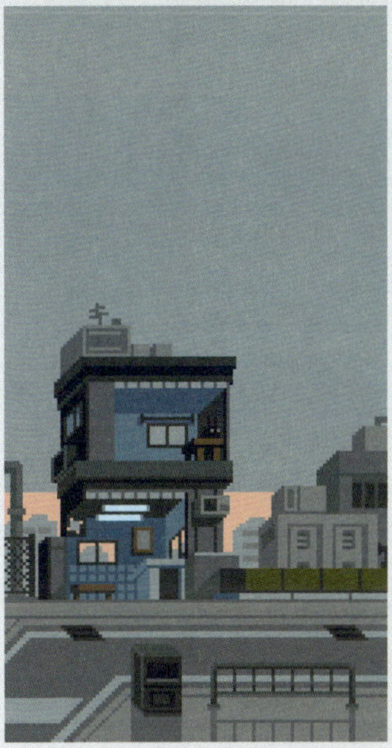

7
8
9
10

11
12

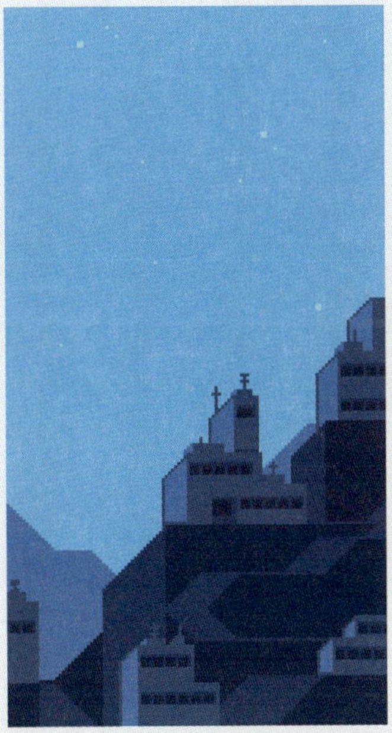

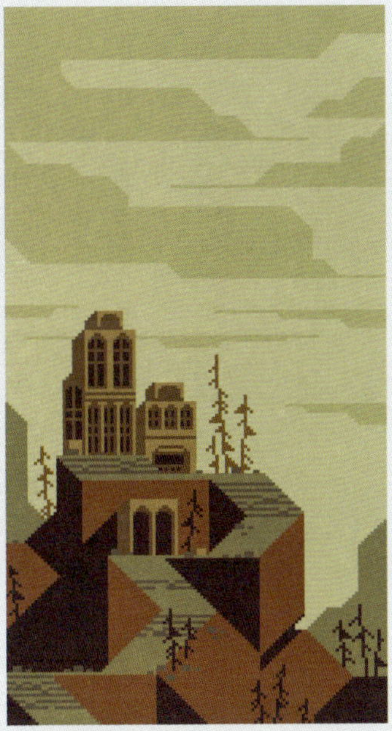

6 *Untitled*, 12/09/2019, 120×240px
7 *Untitled*, 23/08/2019, 120×240px
8 *Untitled*, 23/08/2019, 120×240px
9 *Untitled*, 24/08/2019, 120×240px
10 *Untitled*, 23/08/2019, 120×240px
11 *Untitled*, 22/08/2019, 120×240px
12 *Untitled*, 22/08/2019, 120×240px

Japanese towns and cities. Of course, there are many different cultural and pop-culture sources for Japanese inspiration, from people's Instagram photos to paintings hung in museums, anime features and any number of feature films. I believe that every artist banks numerous visual cues before unconsciously sorting them into their own personal visual database. I certainly can't zoom in on any single image and say that was the main influence for a certain picture.

In addition, while it might be more convenient for me to base each street scene on a tangible, real-world reference, such an approach has always bored me. I've never wanted to be locked into simply recreating something that already exists because what do I do if I know that an additional window here or a background tower block there would improve the composition? Recently, I was looking at the photos I took during my trips to Japan and South Korea and I thought once again about using them as artistic references. I still haven't tried it, though.

While I've never been able to make too many decisions about each setting in advance, once I'm working on a picture, I do think about how to enrich each one with signs of life, especially since I rarely add human characters to my scenes. For me, while it's mostly about the colour and composition of each image, I think about logical and practical reasons to add street furniture, signage, benches and so on. So there's always a number of approaches to take; if I ever settled on some sort of 'perfect' formula, all waneella artworks would look the same, wouldn't they?

Online 'fame'... whatever that means

I've been working from home for six years now. I'm very happy with my set-up, since I've never been the most sociable person. The fact that I've managed to establish myself as an artist in that time is due, almost exclusively, to social media. I find it fascinating that YouTubers can broadcast from their homes, that Etsy designers can sell their ceramics around the world and that I can reach a global audience. What a time to be alive! It's not that I don't like people, just that I get exhausted and overwhelmed so easily that I have to limit my contact with the 'outside world'. When I appeared at the 2018 PAP5 festival in Tokyo, for instance, it was incredible to witness the enthusiasm for my work as people queued for hours to make purchases, but it did stress me out. Thank goodness it was only for one evening – I think my exposure to crowds needs to be rationed. I do feel sorry that I've never even been very active online, though. I rarely engage with people on Tumblr by responding to their comments or keeping conversation threads going but then again, I don't have a huge circle of friends in the 'real' world either.

I'm very aware that my first decade as waneella has coincided with the huge advances of the smartphone, social media and almost universal internet access. I've often wondered what impact being a first-generation 'digital native' has had on my career, but there's nothing to suggest this has been some sort of unique golden age of internet exposure. I can already see how the internet has evolved and how this is affecting the ways that newer artists pitch themselves.

Over the years, I've seen other pixel artists struggle for years to find an audience only, like me, to suddenly blow up. Yet I've also seen new talent get big almost overnight. I'm happy whenever any artist finds success, although it is impossible to predict and, once gained, difficult to hold on to.

Of course, it warms my heart when the art that I make is well received; it also makes me less anxious about my future as an artist. I think it's important for every artist to know that there are people who like them, and I personally don't know anyone who doesn't care about negative reviews. It's also always been essential that I am able to make what I want to make, discovering something new about myself during the process, instead of trying to second-guess what the next trend will be.

That my art has become recognized and that it's found an audience has been like winning the lottery. I don't know why my pixel art became popular enough to sustain a career, but I'm delighted that it did. At the same time, I have accepted that people will, at some point, stop liking my art quite so much and that I'll have to start doing something else to pay the bills. Until that happens, I'm content to remain relevant and be thankful for the decade that I've spent as waneella. I find the fact that nothing is eternal and that everything changes both sad and exciting. I hope that you all do too.

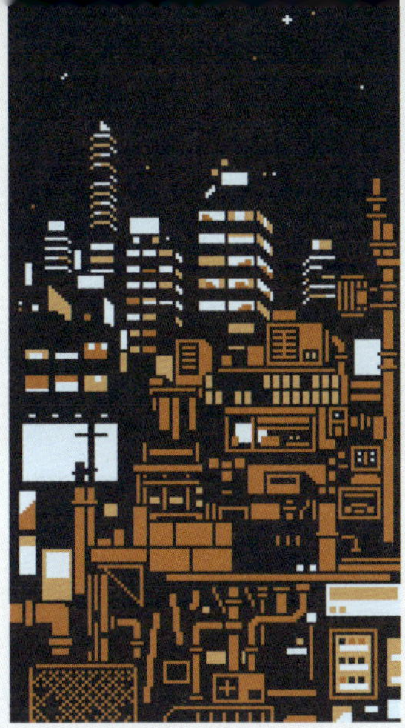

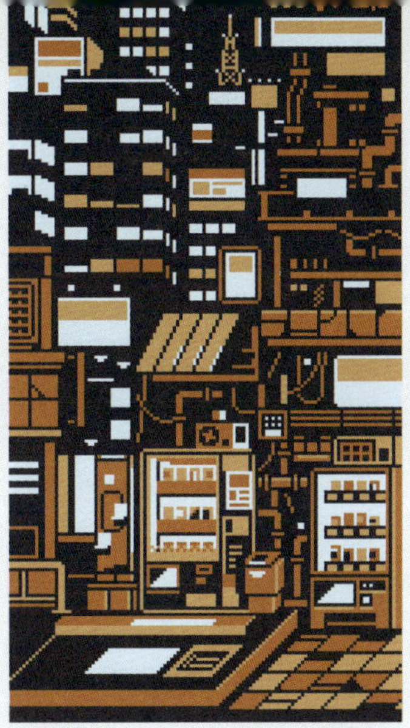

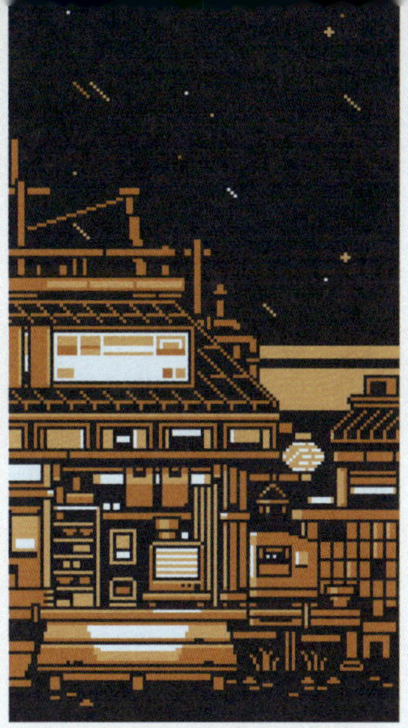

1
2
3

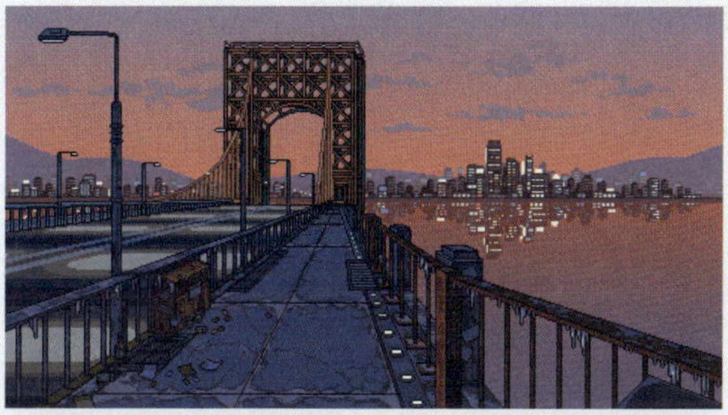

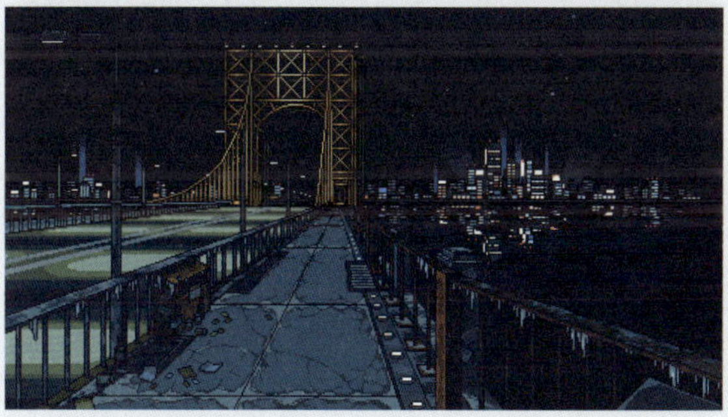

6
7

4
5

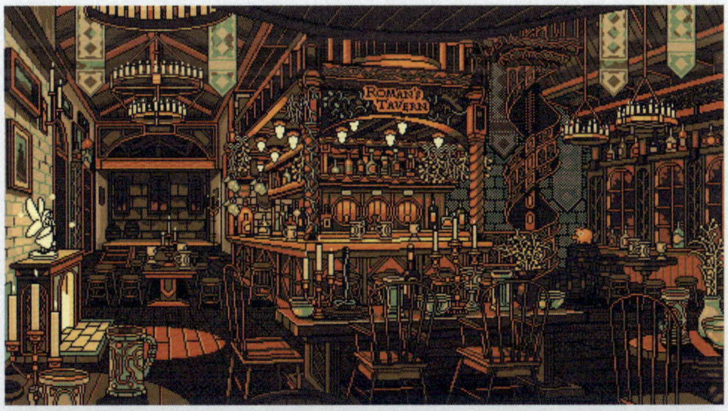

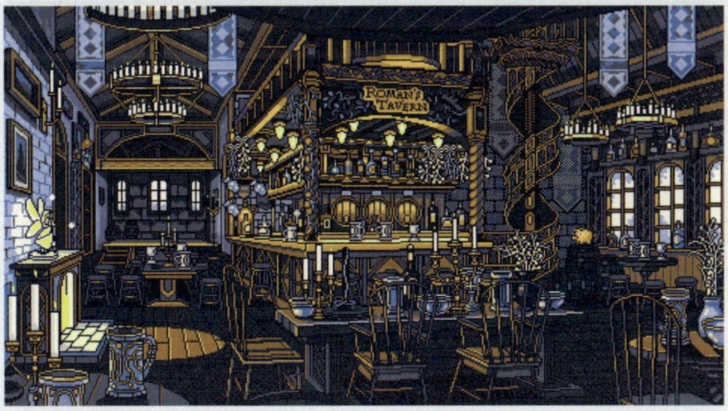

1 *Untitled*, 06/12/2019, 120×240px
2 *Untitled*, 04/12/2019, 120×240px
3 *Untitled*, 04/12/2019, 120×240px
4–7 Commissioned by Havana for a cancelled game project, 2019

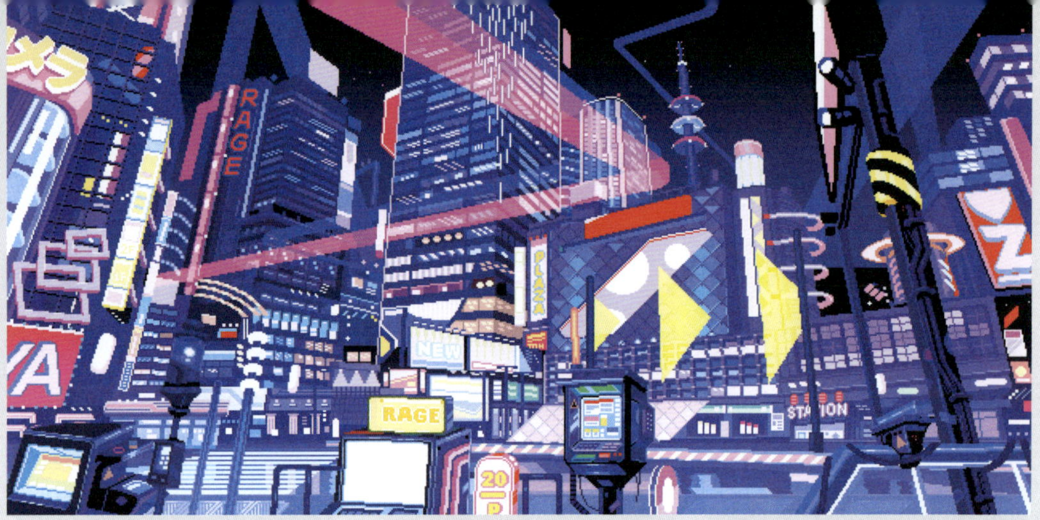

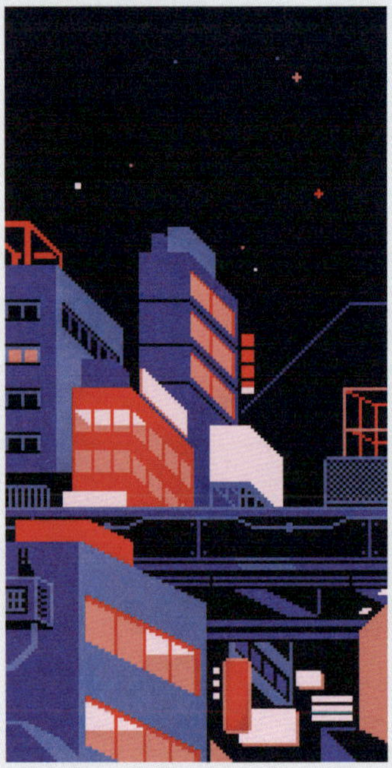

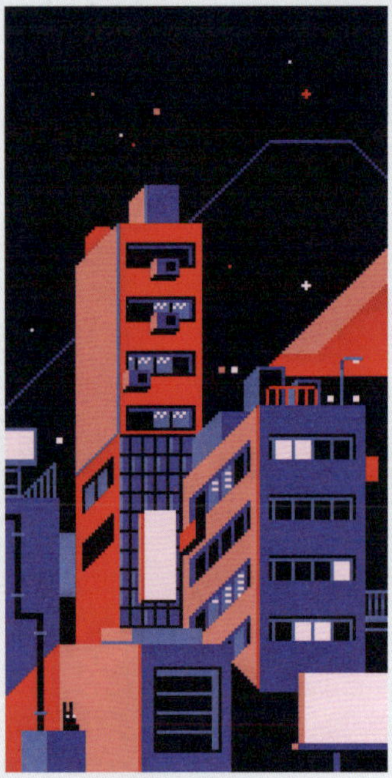

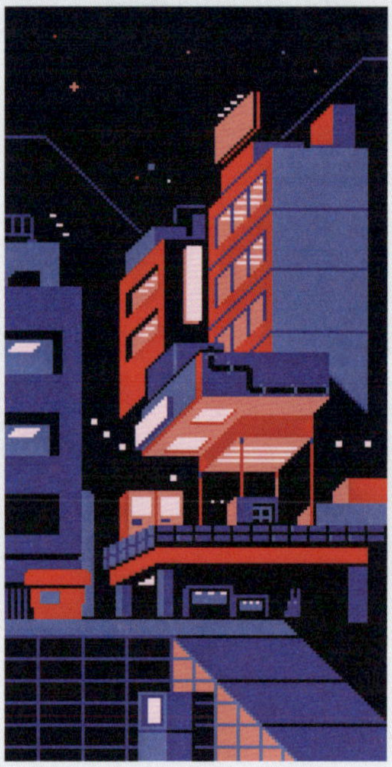

1
2
3
4

5
6

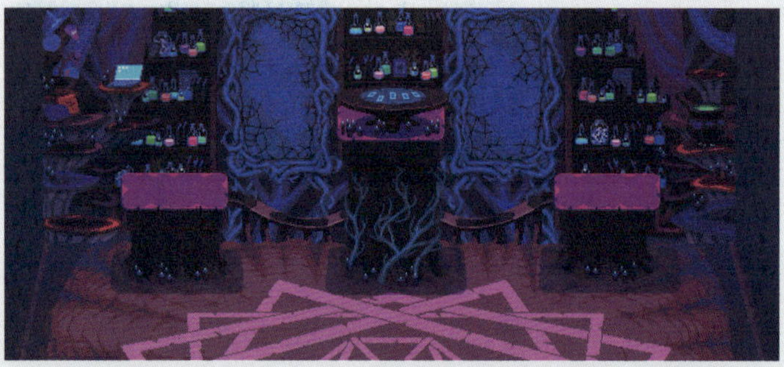

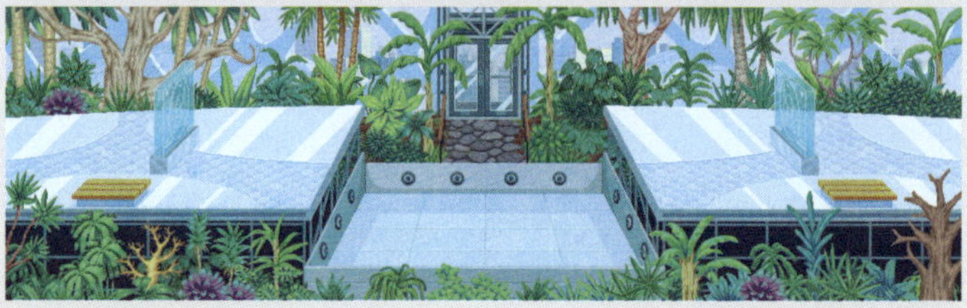

1 Illustration for Rage event by ELEFANT Inc, 2020
2–4 *Untitled*, 12/08/2020, 120×240px
5–6 Background art from *River City Girls 2* videogame, 2021, courtesy of WayForward
© ARC SYSTEMS WORKS

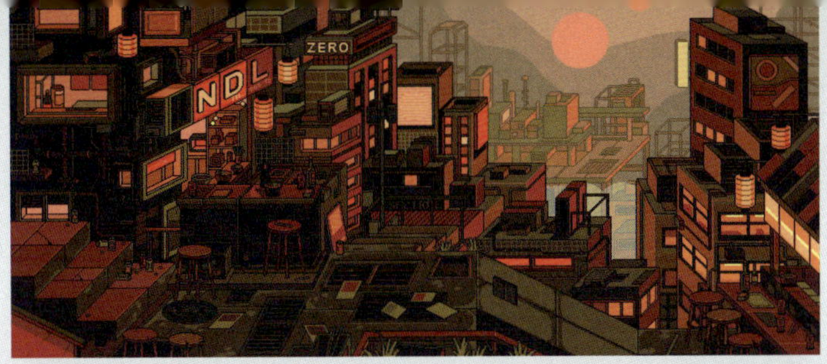

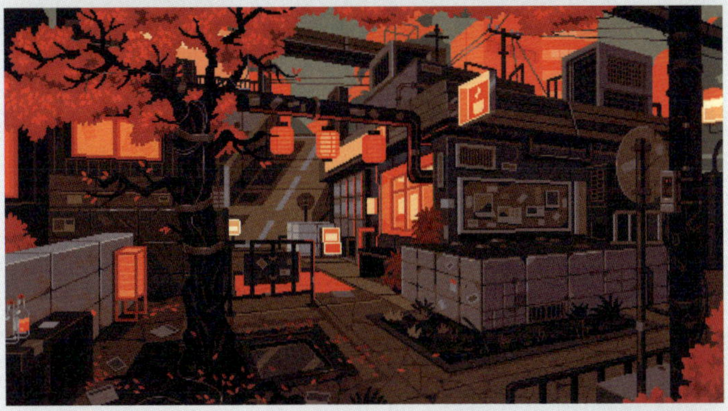

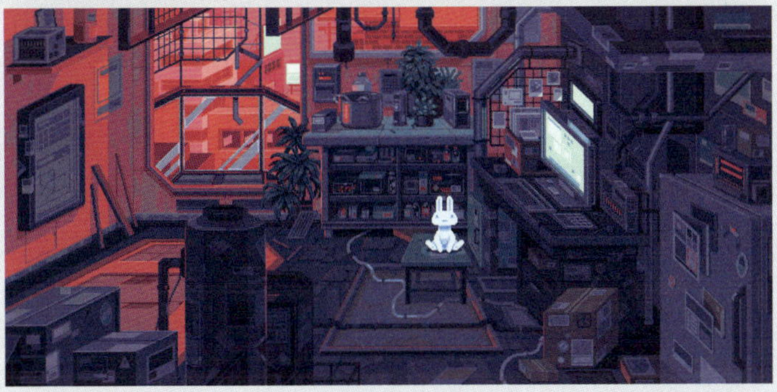

7
8
9

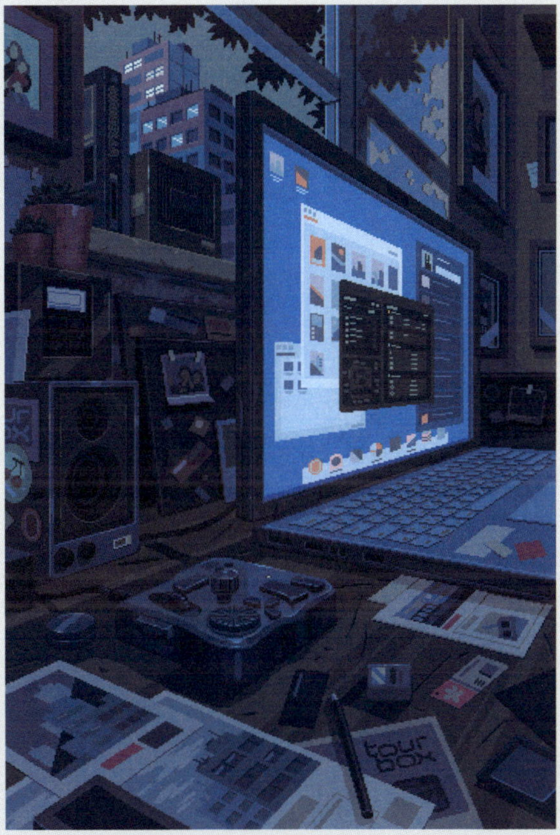

10

11
12

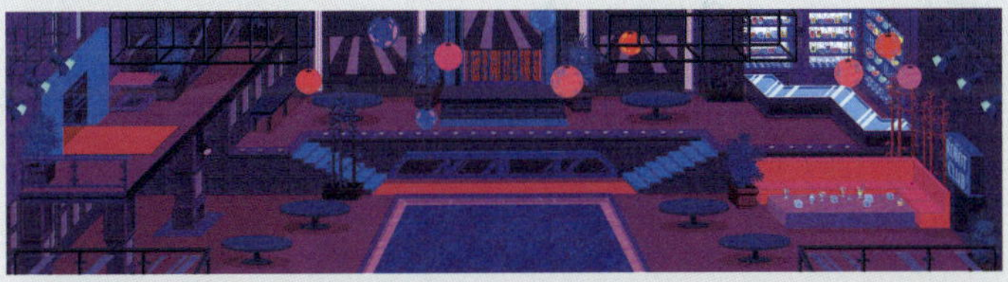

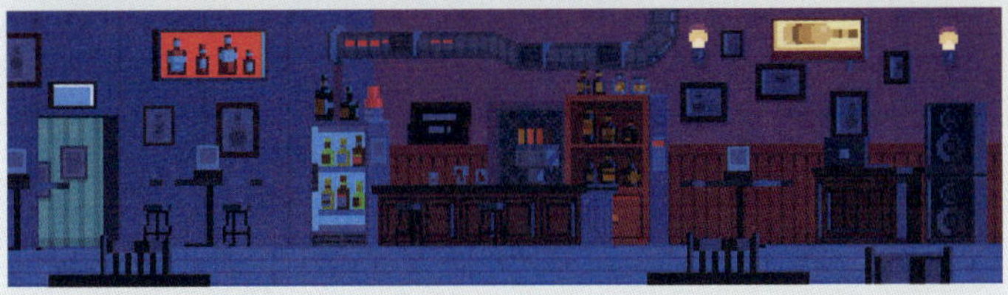

7 *Haze*, 01/11/2020, 800×400px
8 Illustration for XPPen by Hanvon Ugee Technology Co Ltd, 2020
9 *PAP7xwaneella*, illustration for Pixel Art Park event in Tokyo, 2020
10 Illustration for TourBox by Tourbox Tech Inc, 2021
11 Background art from *River City Girls 2* videogame, 2021, courtesy of WayForward © ARC SYSTEMS WORKS
12 Background art from *Super IT Friends* by Mike Manor, 2021

Early milestones

The rush of endorphins that come from people 'Liking' or sharing your work online is uplifting and addictive. These feelings, now familiar to all social-media users, were new to me when I posted a picture on Tumblr and got five reactions overnight. There I was, a nineteen-year-old living with my parents in Moscow, getting noticed by people from five different places on Earth. Knowing there were people out there who appreciated my work was enough to ignite my obsession with pixel art. I felt vindicated. I found the time to create, even if that meant staying awake all night.
My burger vending-machine image was the first of many milestones on the waneella journey. Here are some other artworks that, for various reasons, felt like landmarks in my early career.

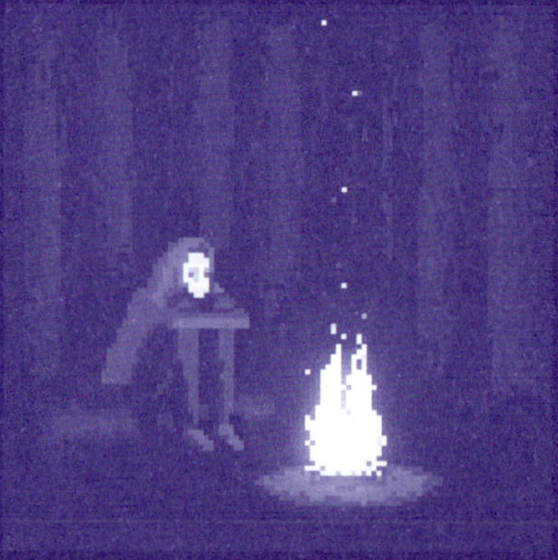

[→ page 12]

Untitled, 2013
This was my third attempt at creating pixel art and it's still out there in the wilds of the World Wide Web. It remains popular on Tumblr for some reason, suggesting that even now, 2013 waneella is still relevant. It looks like a miraculous little time capsule now. With my ever-changing style and application, I'm not sure if I could ever recreate it.

[→ page 8]

Untitled, 2013
I've paired these illustrations because they are two different results of the same creative process. I'd reached a point where I realized that drawing accurate pixel art was too time-consuming and that I just wanted to express myself in a more fluid way. So even though I didn't agonize over every single pixel, both pictures still received recognition, which was very heartening.

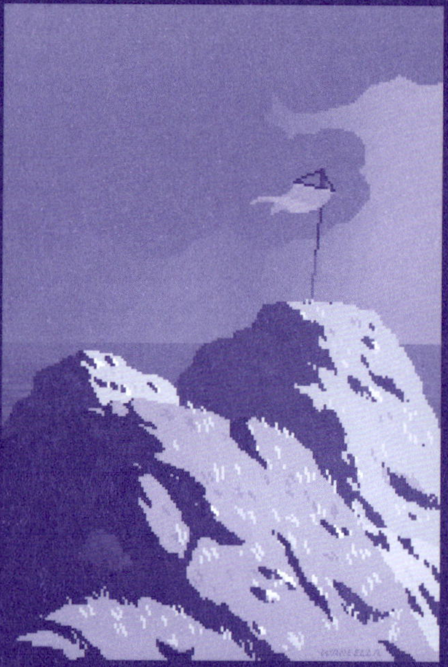

[→ page 25]

Untitled, 2014
Both of these images show depth and shading, space and volume. While for me, this ability to express myself was a huge step forwards, neither one attracted many comments from viewers back in 2014. I remember feeling deflated about this, although perhaps I'd just burned myself out from doing a pixel-art marathon. I made more than fifty artworks during 2013, but only nine in 2014.

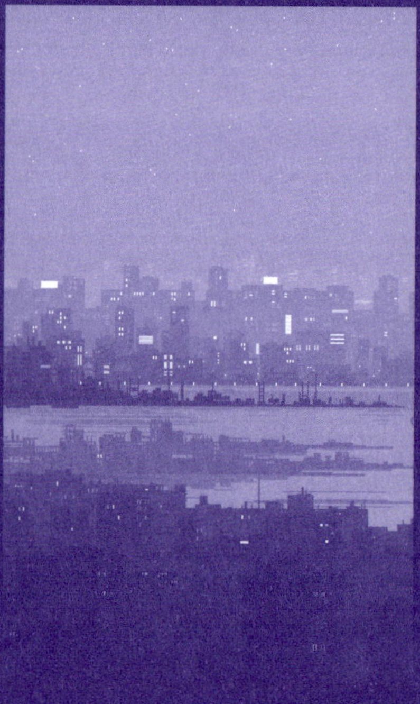

[→ page 24]

Untitled, 2014
This artwork has gained more than 100,000 'Likes', which was strange and unexpected, especially since I drew so little pixel art that year. Through

this image, I finally discovered my love for drawing cityscapes and, crucially, I also found that viewers like them too. In many ways, this created the template for what was to follow.

[→ page 10]

Vozvrashenie, 2015
After the success of my initial drawing, I continued to experiment with cityscapes by adding more animation. This is called *Vozvrashenie* ('Return') because at the time, I hadn't posted on Tumblr for a while and finally felt ready to come back to pixel art. This image took a lot of time to create and when I recently re-opened the file, I saw why. I was both surprised and impressed by the number of layers and tricks I had employed to make it work.

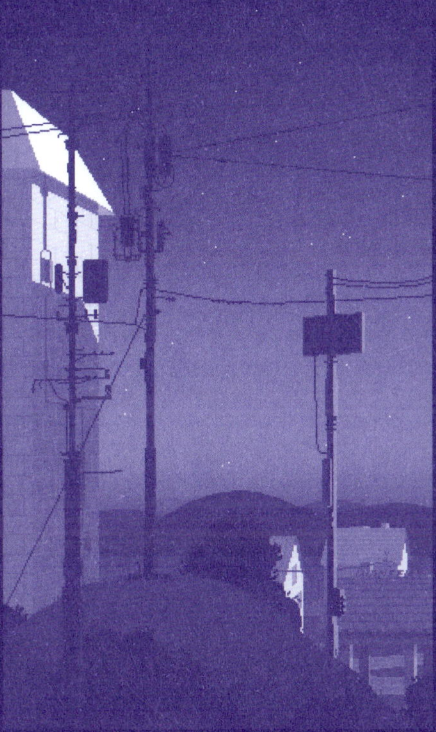

[→ page 11]

Untitled, 2015
This nighttime scene is important to me from an artistic point of view, because it's one of my earliest works that's closest stylistically to a 'modern' waneella. It's an urban scene, tightly framed and on a big canvas, allowing lots of small details. I definitely felt that I'd created something new, although I couldn't quite recognize what the shift was. Also, this might be the first time that I used one-point perspective in my pixel art.

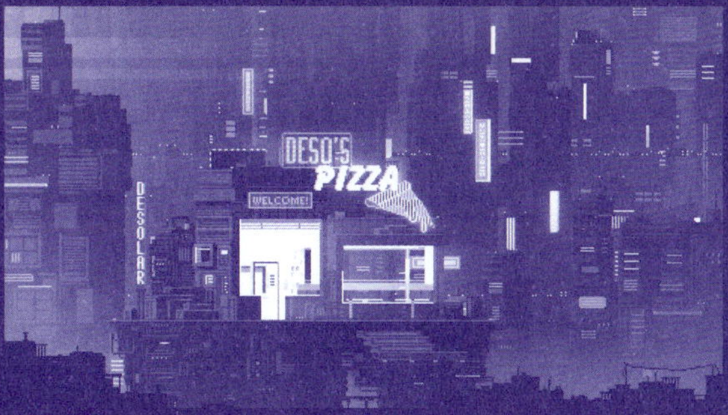

[→ page 28]

Untitled, 2016
This was the second commission I made for Desolar, a videogame streamer. It turned out so much better than the first that I still don't understand how I managed it. Despite being quite minimalistic, it's vibrant and features gradients and blurring, yet it also looks organic and accurate. I think maybe I could have stuck with this art style and still had a career as a relevant pixel artist.

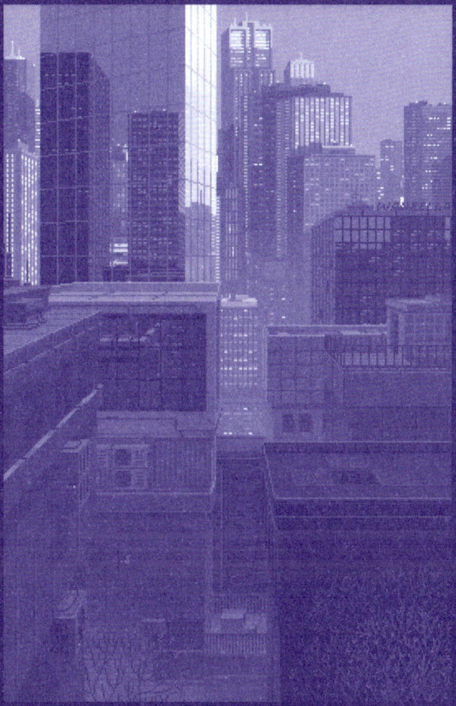

[→ page 29]

Long Time No See, 2016
This is the turning point after which I switched exclusively to cityscapes. I had just graduated from university and didn't have much free time, so this came together slowly over several months. But as the image came together, pixel by pixel, it exceeded all my expectations and I could see the potential of these scenes. Nevertheless, it still took a few more years, alongside the continuing encouragement of my friends, for a steady stream of waneella art to eventually emerge.

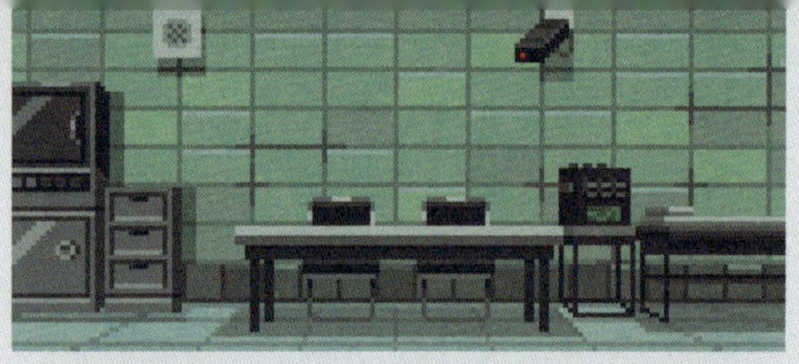

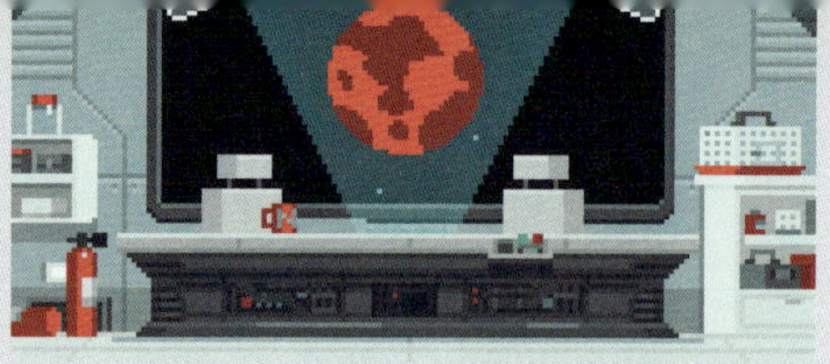

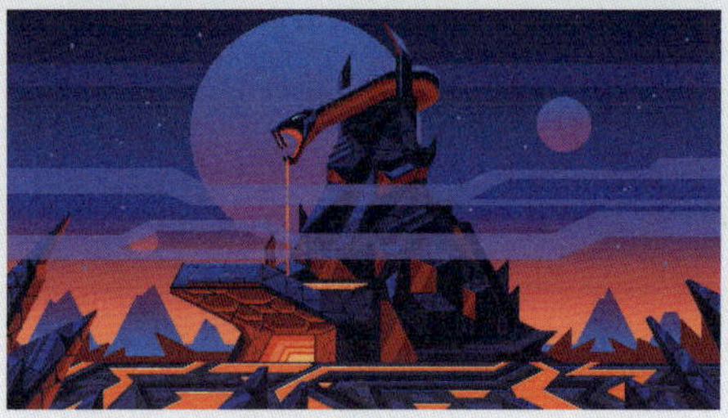

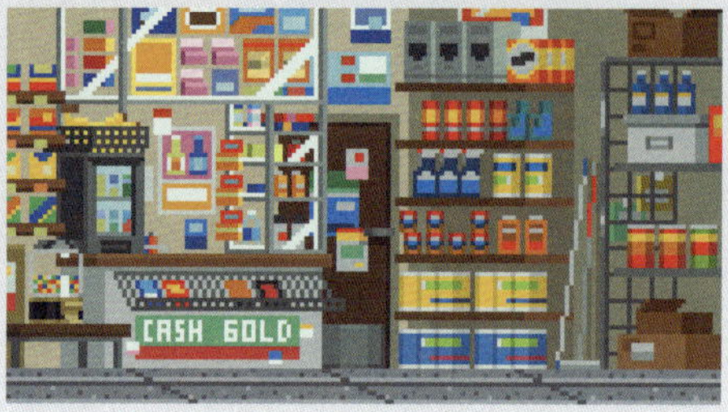

1
2
3
4

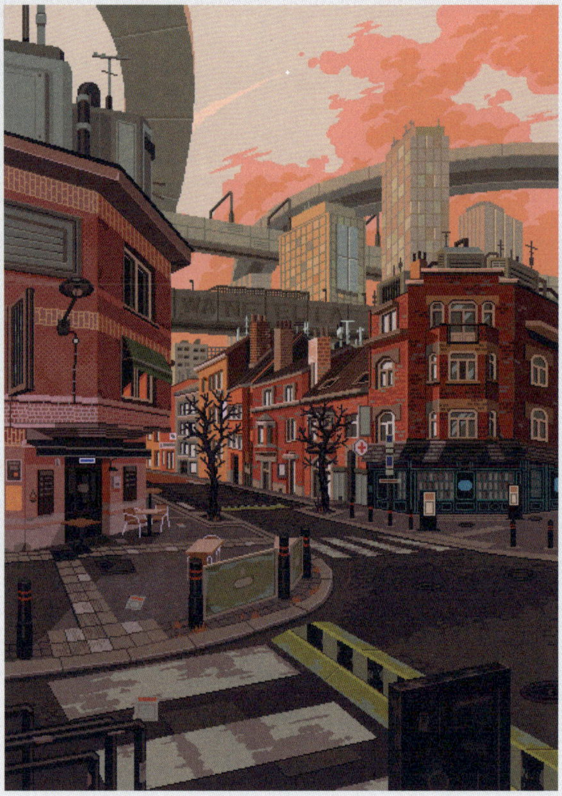

5

6
7

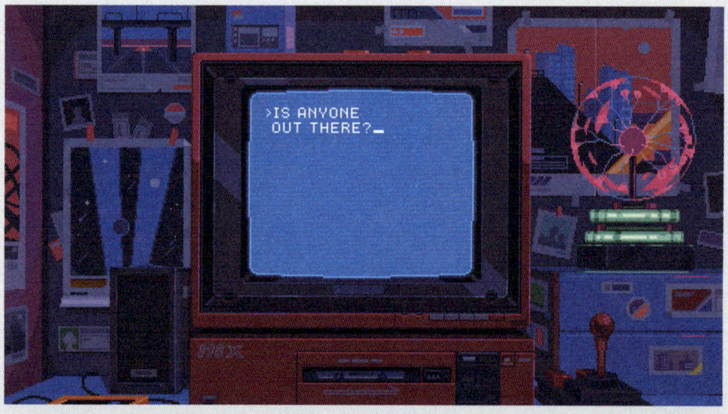

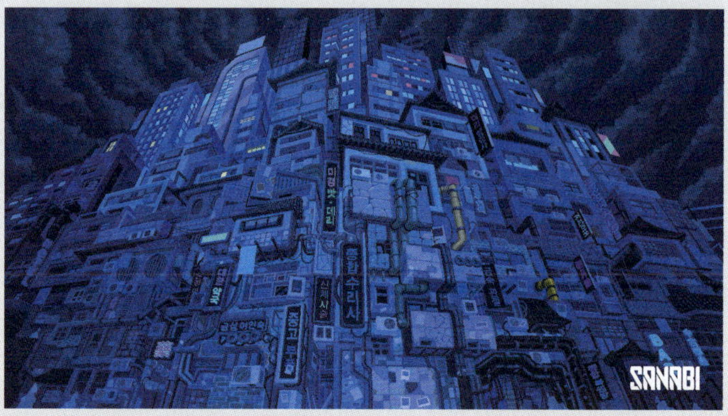

1–4 Background art for *Skeletor Vs Eleven* episode of *GEEKED Title Fights*, 2021
5 Illustration for *The Brusseler* project, 2021
6 Illustration for *198X* videogame by Hi-Bit Studios, 2021
7 Illustration for *SANABI* videogame by Wonder Potion, 2021

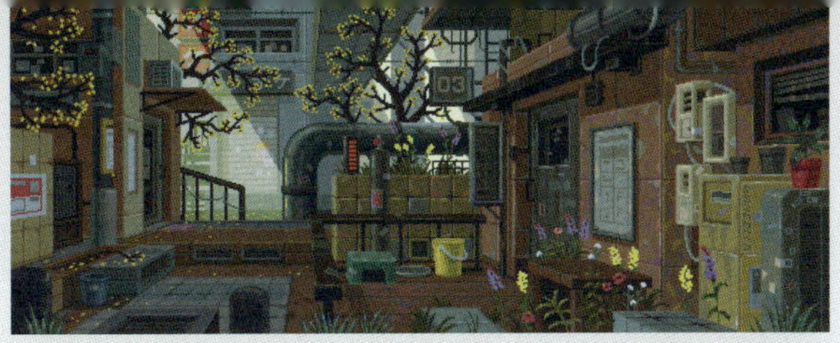

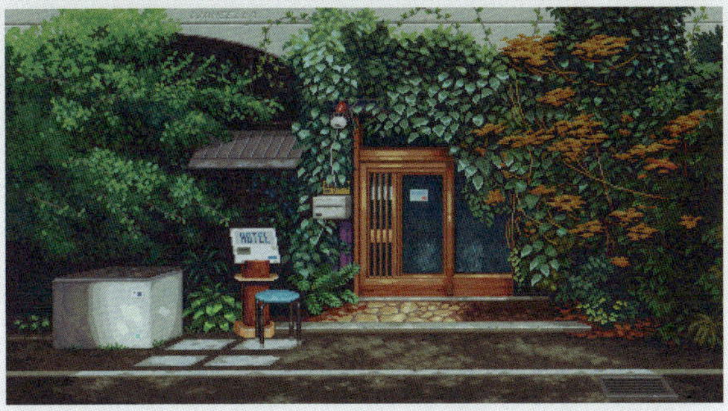

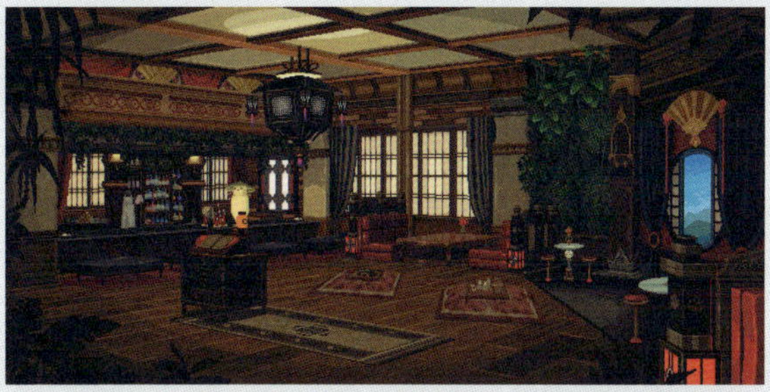

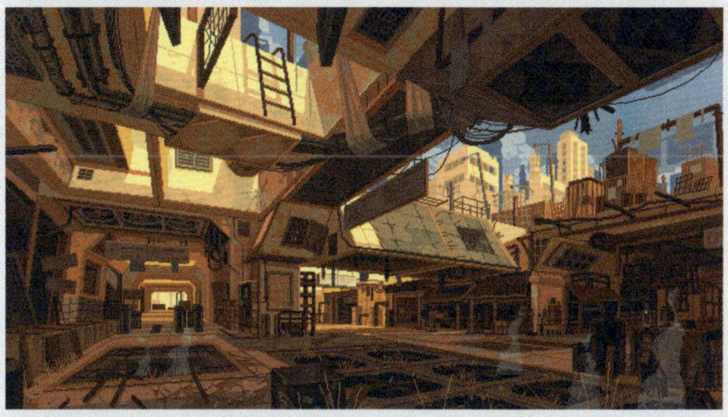

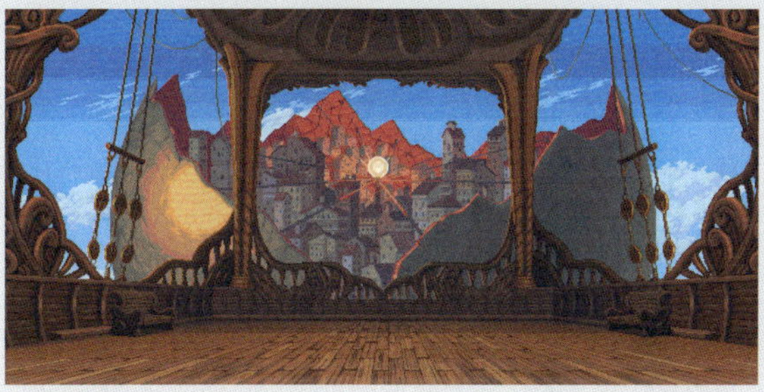

8
9

11
12
13

10

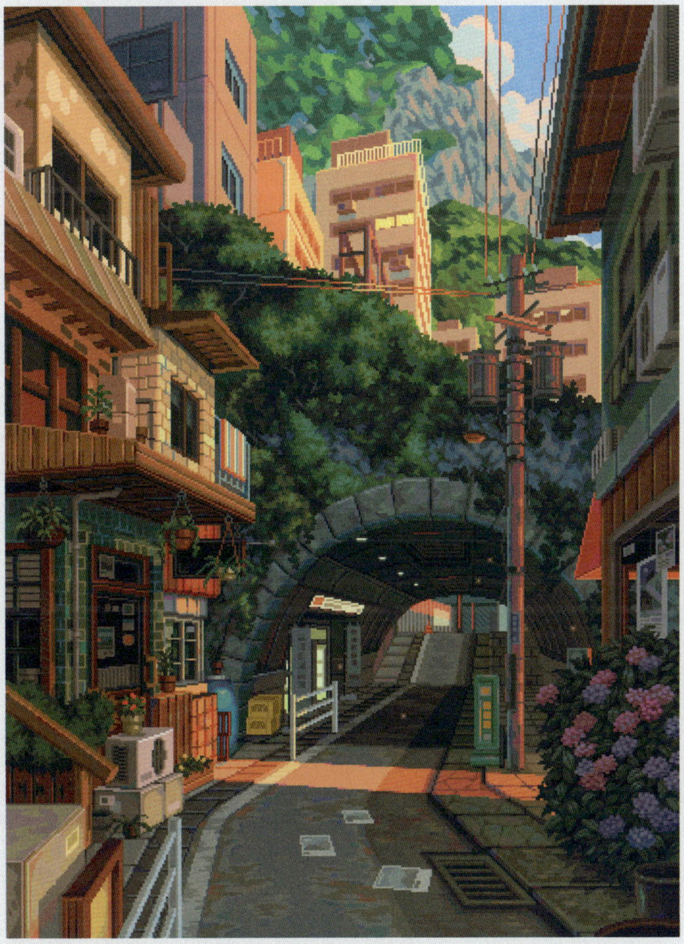

8 *Sunshine*, 01/04/2021, 560x280px
9 Commissioned by Mattymattykk, 2021
10 *Days Are Getting Shorter*, produced for the Harugo No Mayu Summer Collection, 20/07/2021, 350×490px
11 *The Jewelled Cypress*, commissioned by Illeos as a gift to trashi3st and Chimera, an FFXIV Free Company, 2022
12 Illustration for *One More Multiverse* project, 2020
13 Background art for *Shattered* videogame by Team18K, 2022

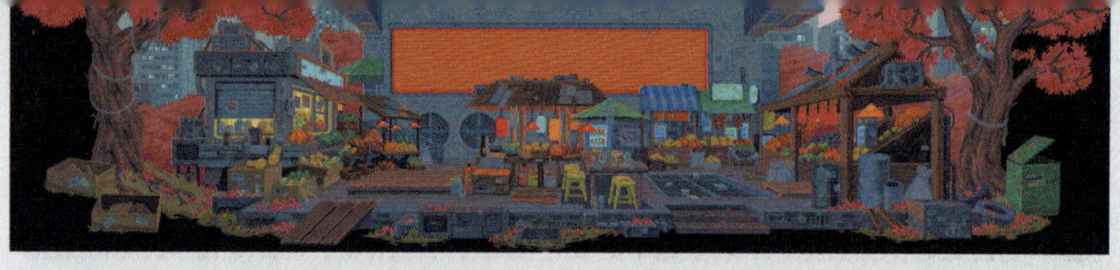

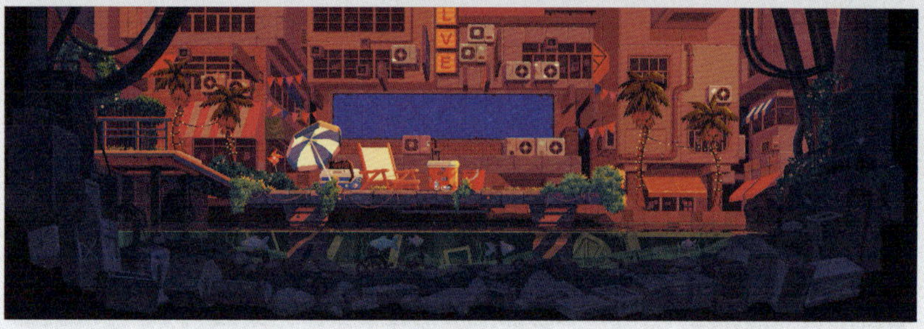

1
2

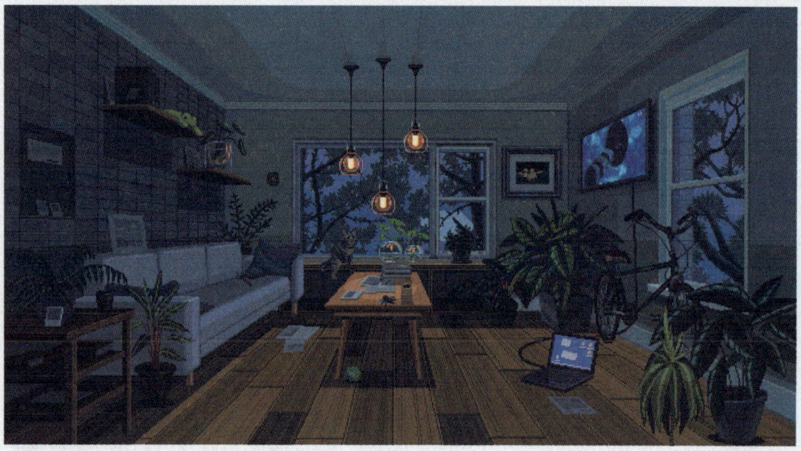

3

4

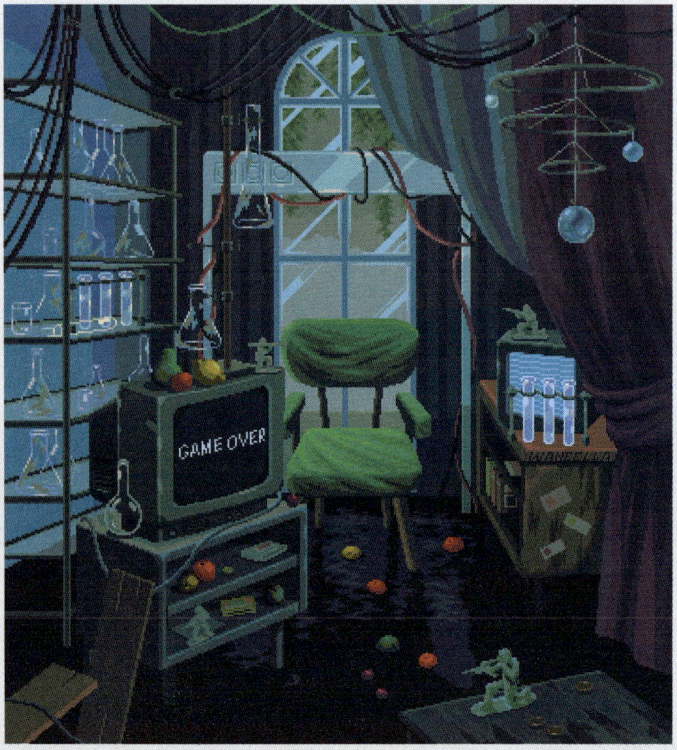

1 Illustration for Valve's Steam Autumn Sale © Valve Corporation, 2023
2 Illustration for Valve's Steam Summer Sale © Valve Corporation, 2023
3 Commissioned by Doreen Lin, 2021
4 *Miracles*, illustration for Shanshui Pixel Scenes 山水像素场景, 2023

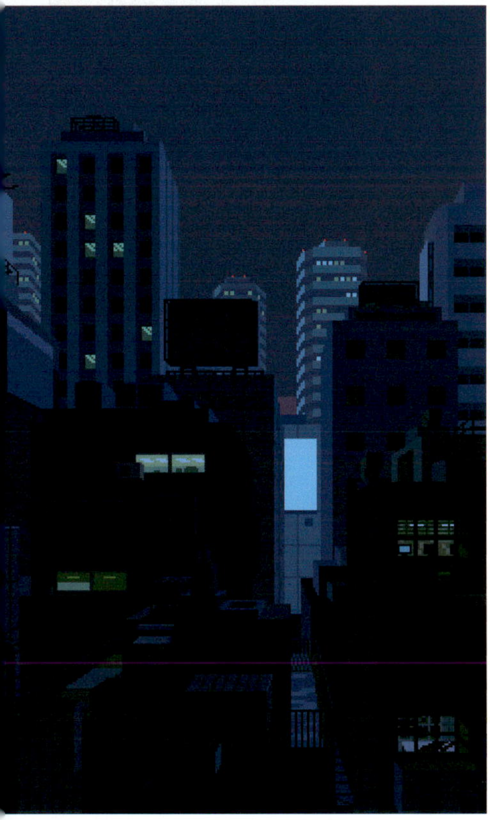

ARTWORKS

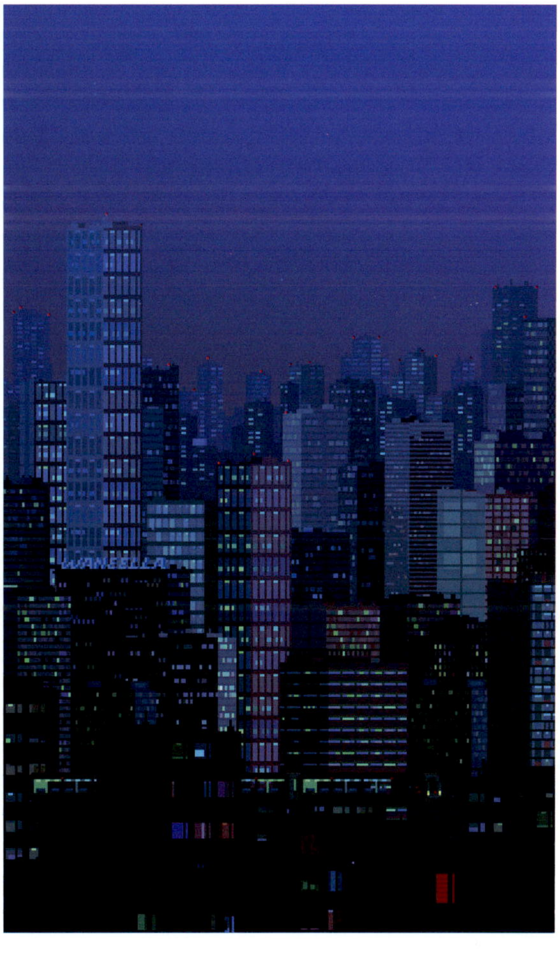

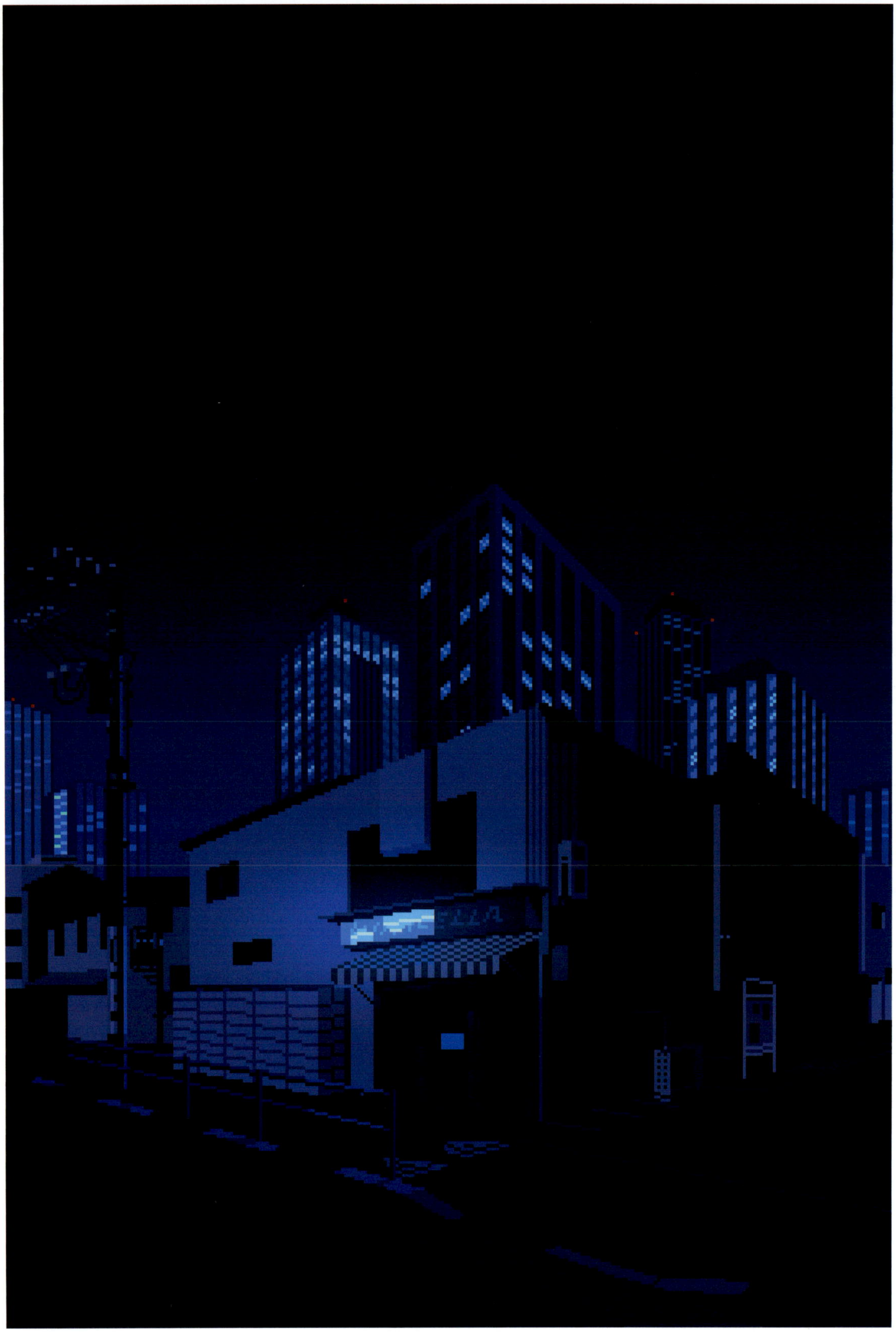

Page 49 top: *VBbVLbGgy7,* 05/10/2017, 270×405px
Page 49 bottom: *17:15,* 06/01/2016, 120×203px
Above: *JmDPgfz5vO,* 20/06/2017, 270×405px
Right: *21:10,* 01/03/2017, 270×405px

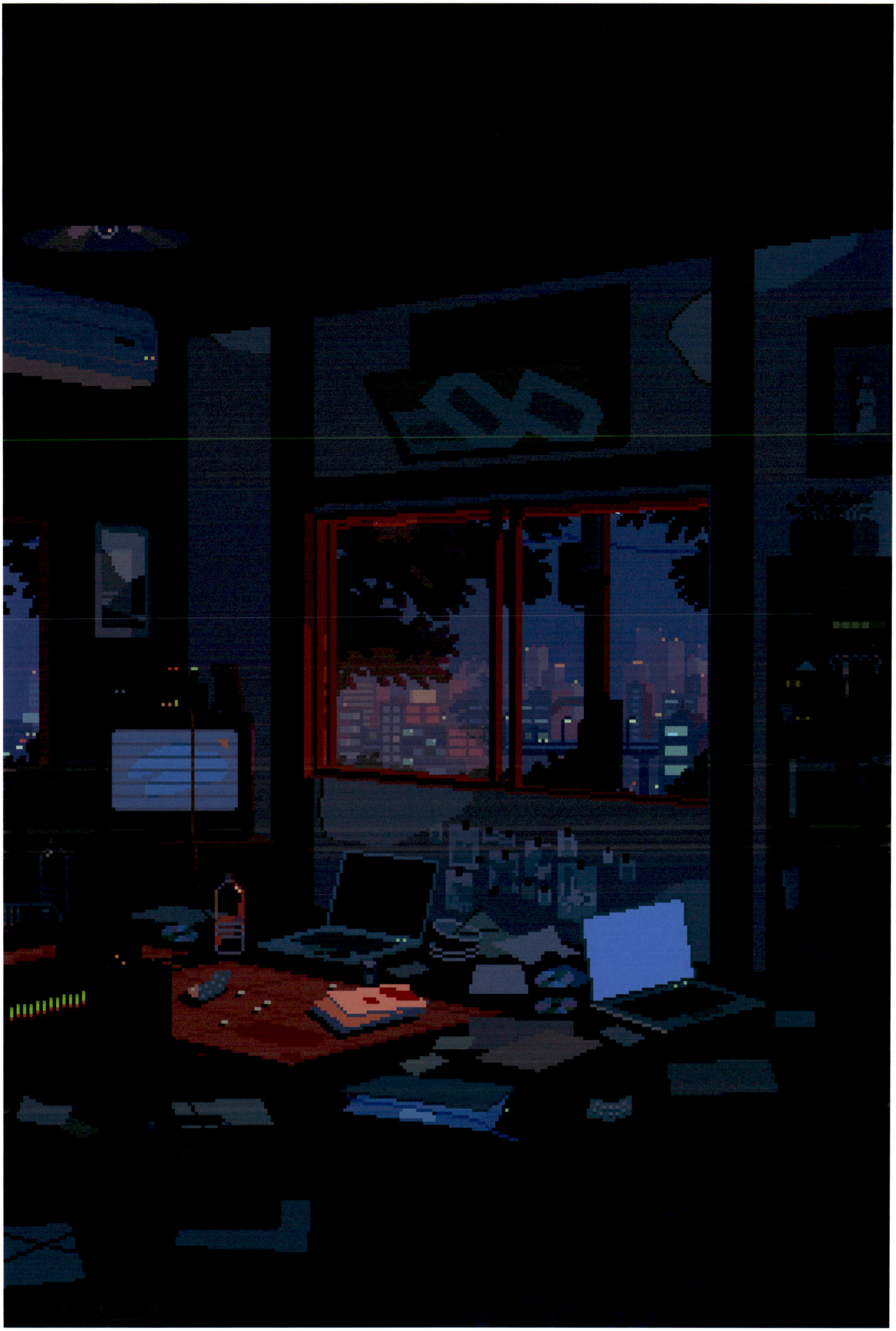

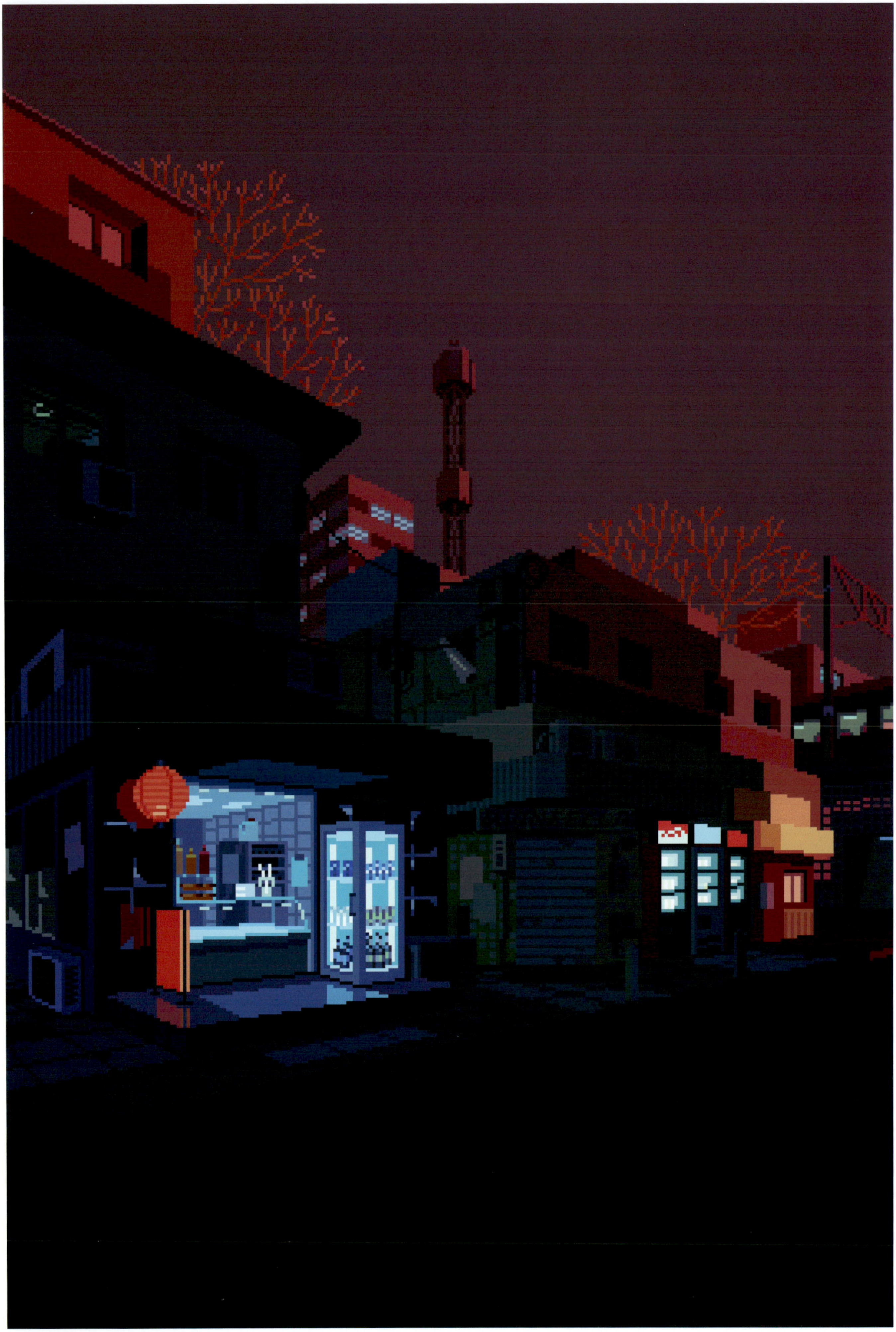

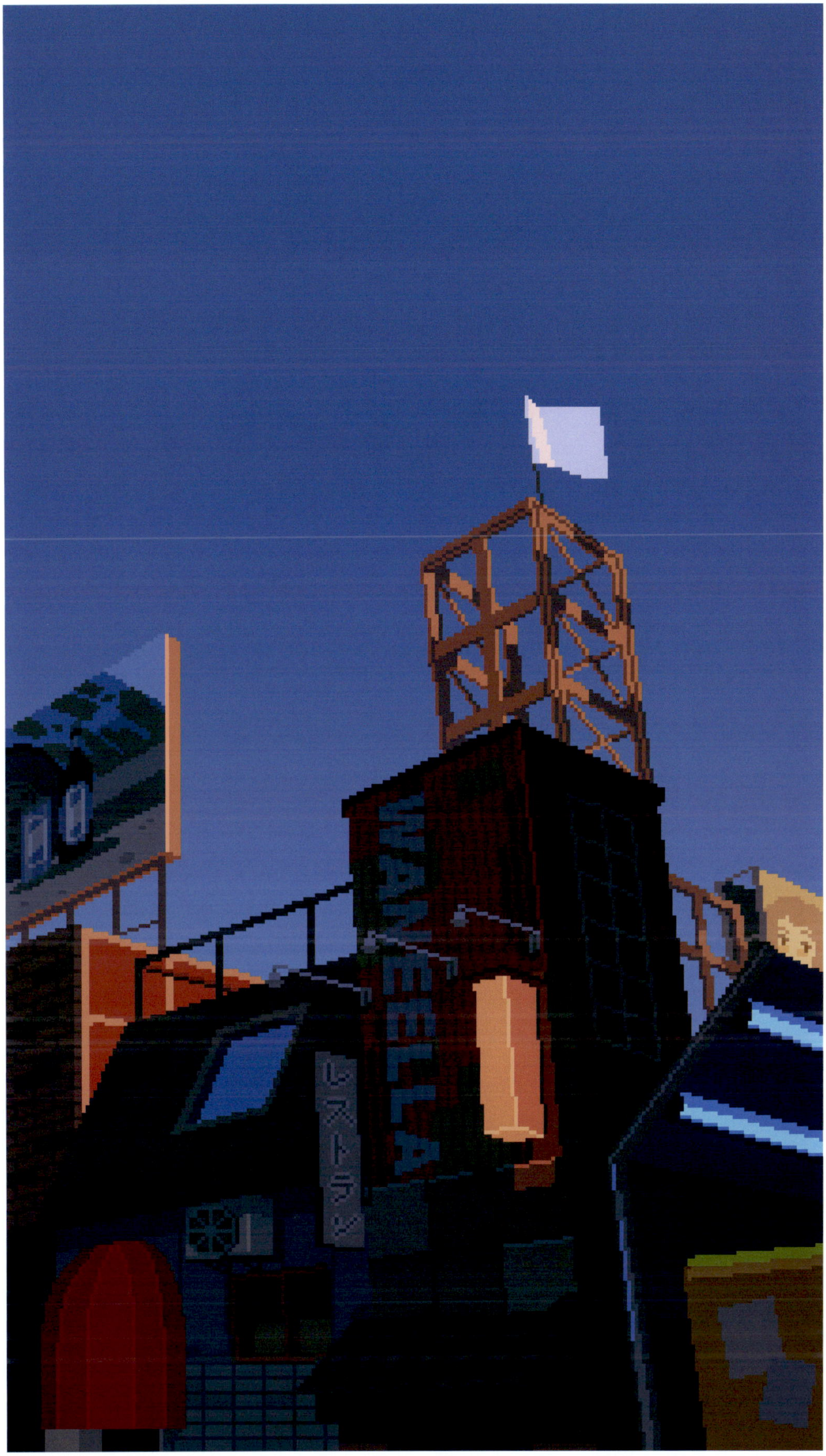

Left: *u60ye58222*, 16/11/2017, 270×405px
Above: *W7WuH84mhR*, 05/05/2018, 216×384px

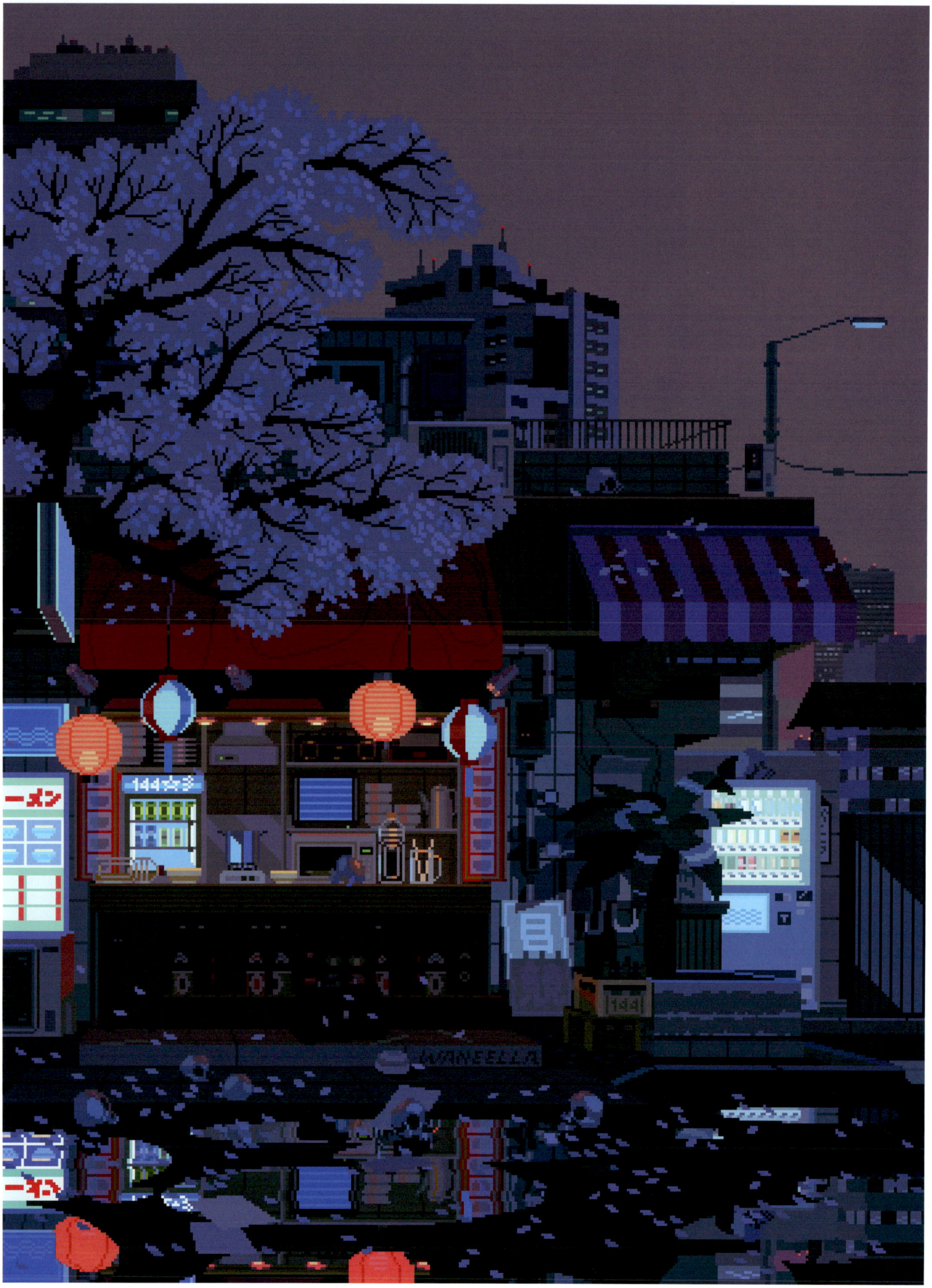

目競, 31/10/2017, 347×484px

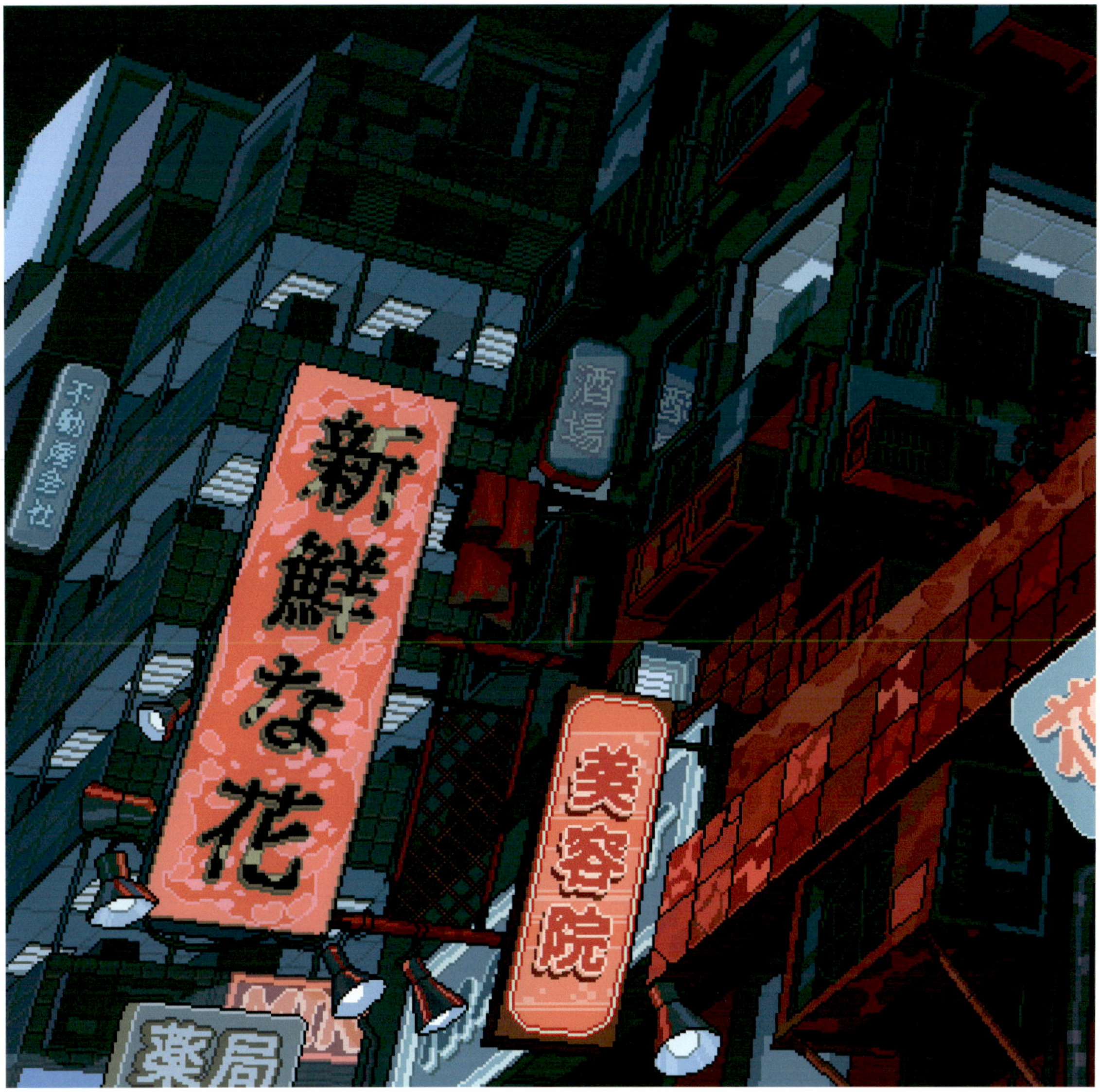

19:23, 23/09/2018, 384×384px

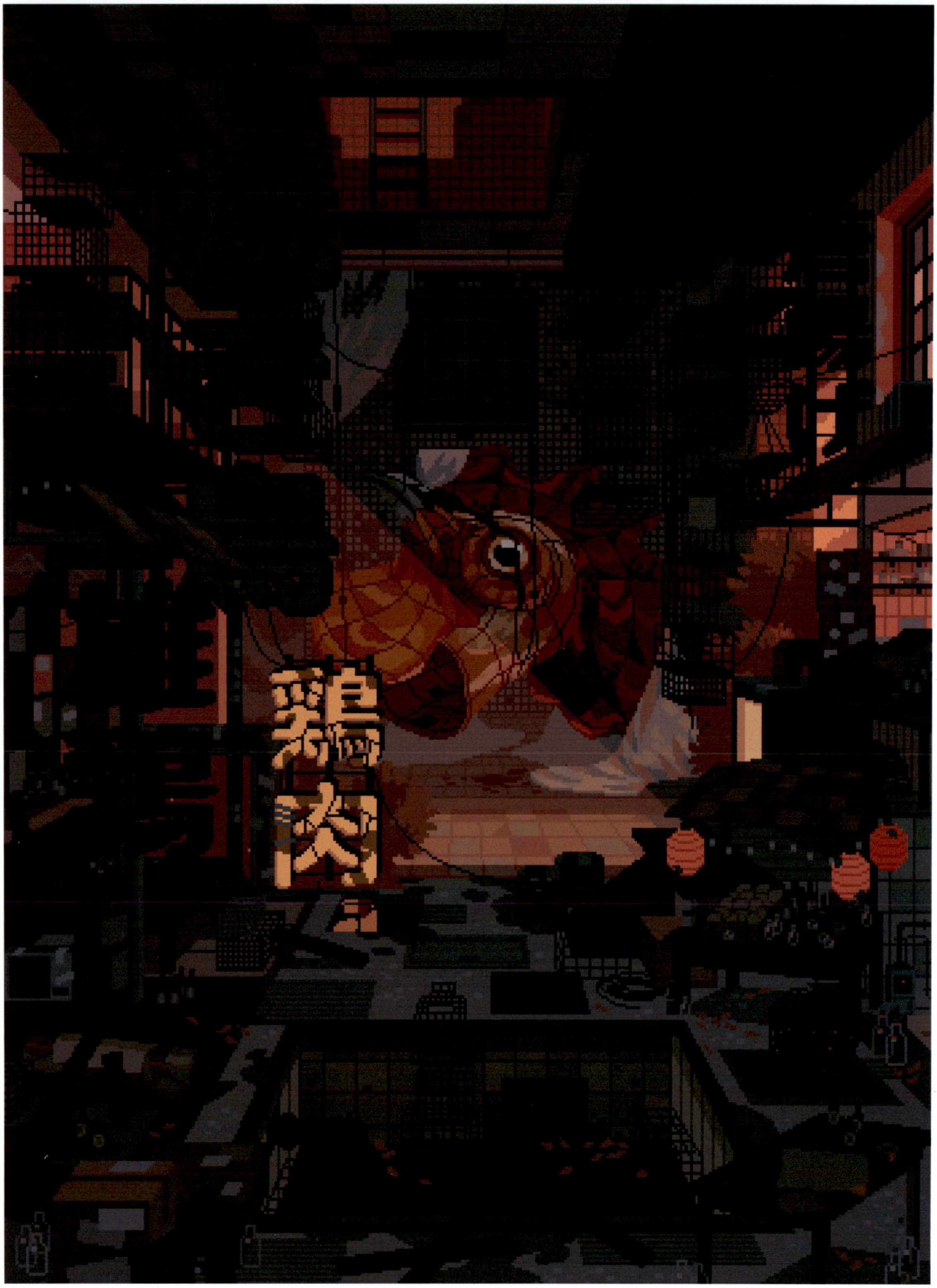

Above: 波山, 22/10/2018, 346×480px
Right: *1xYzhXW3Qs*, 06/01/2018, 270×405px

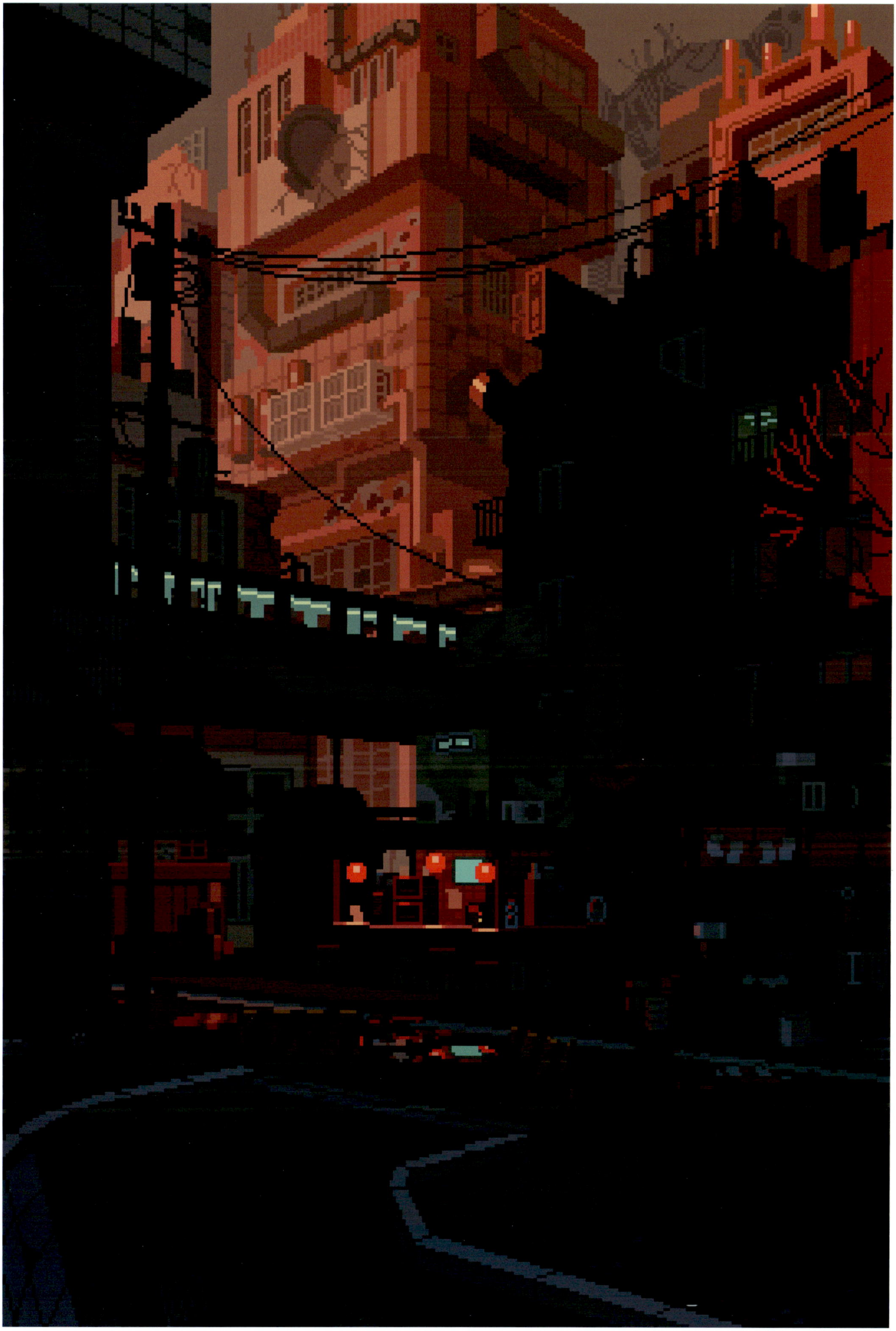

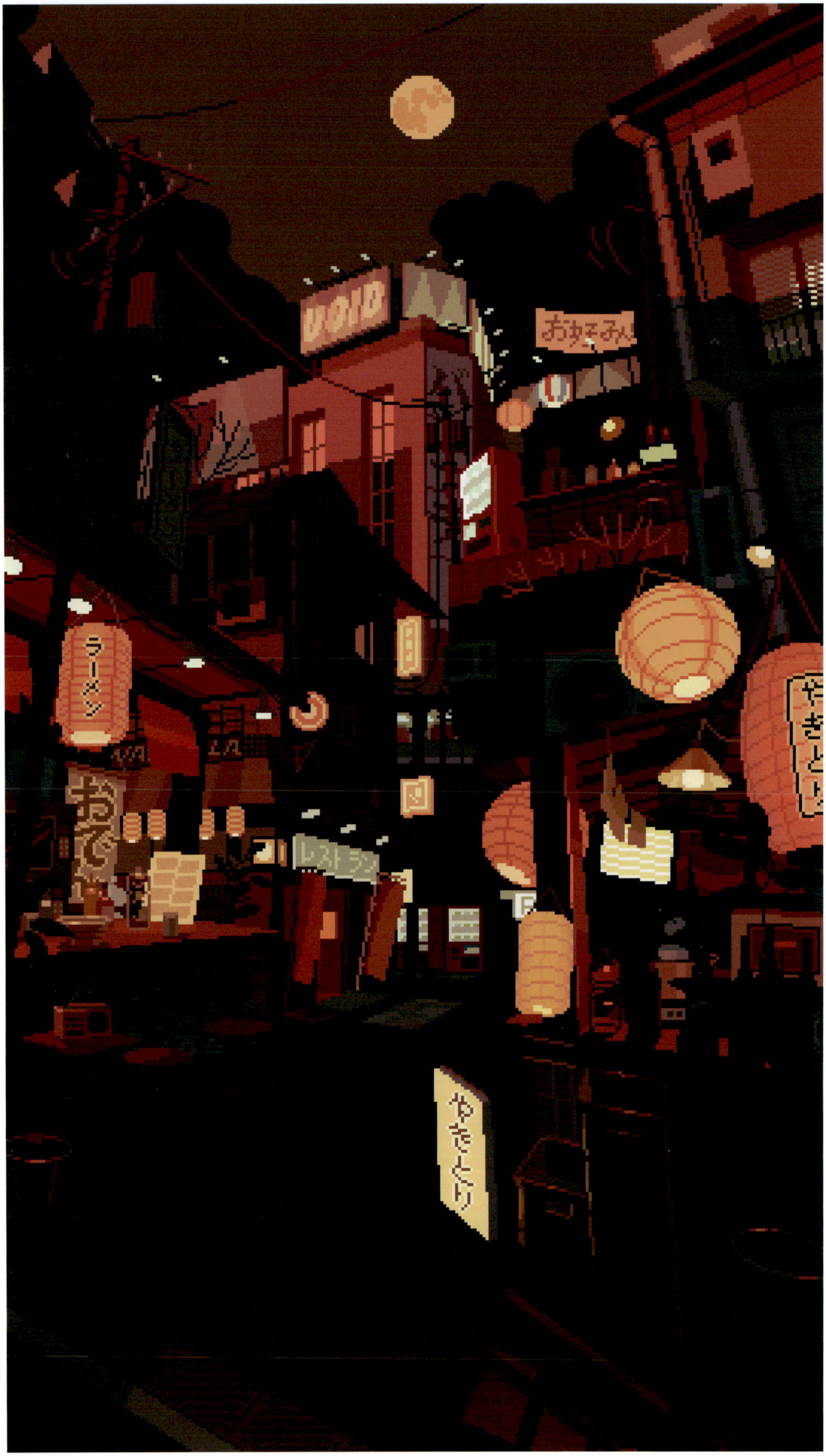
VOID
ラーメン
やきとり

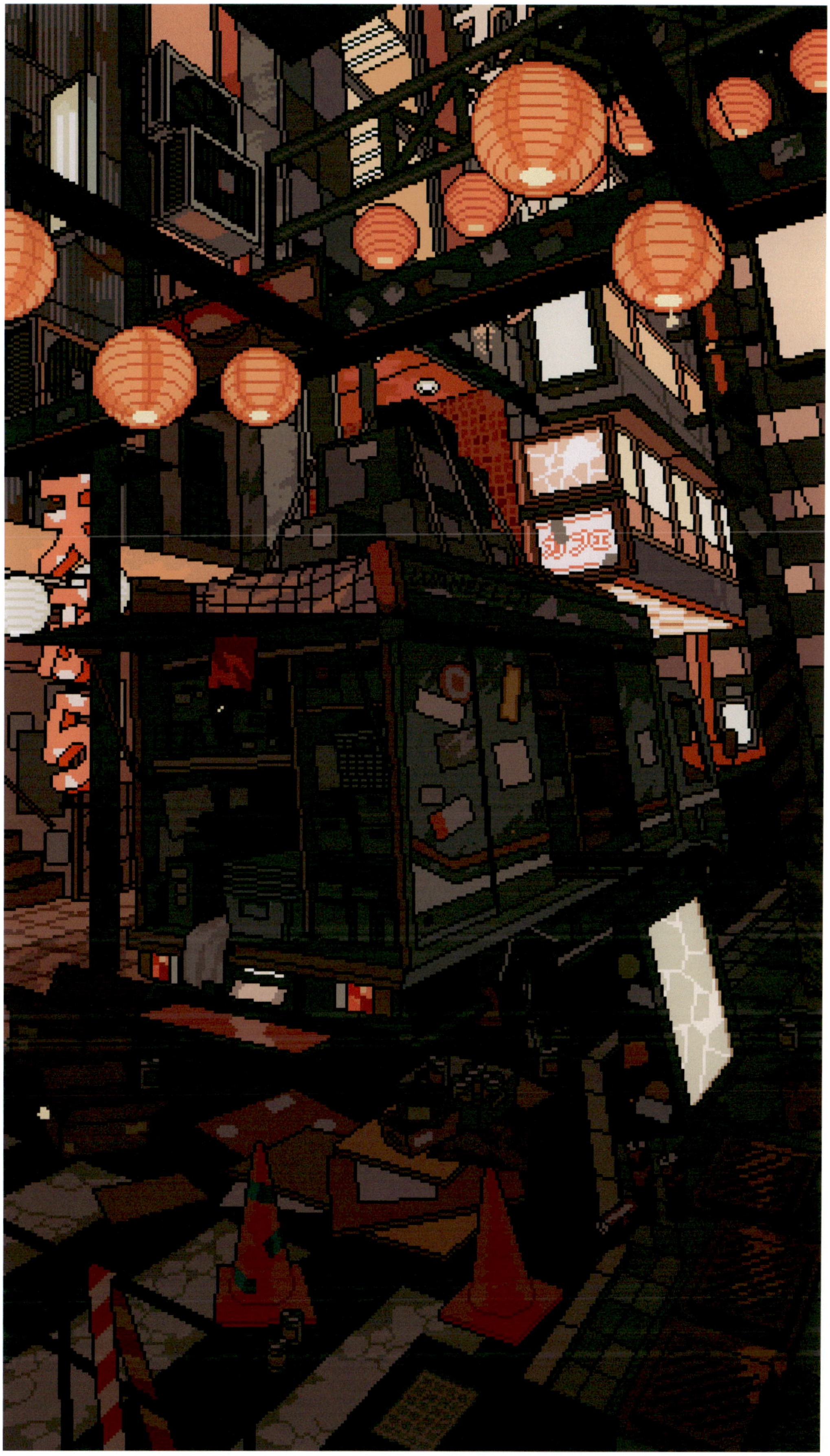

Left: *pRKkeKRqx0*, 06/02/2018, 540×960px
Above: *BOiTCkPa4B*, 26/07/2018, 270×480px

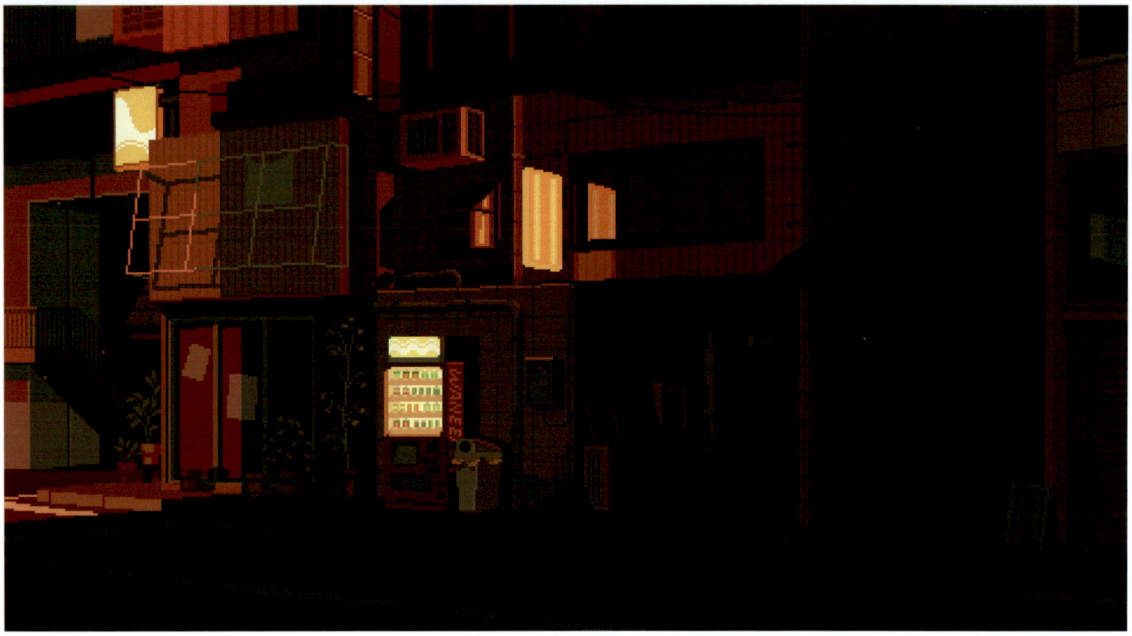

Above: *j0P563I4ZE*, 18/12/2017, 480×270px
Right: *YL58drC0GG*, 10/07/2017, 270×405px

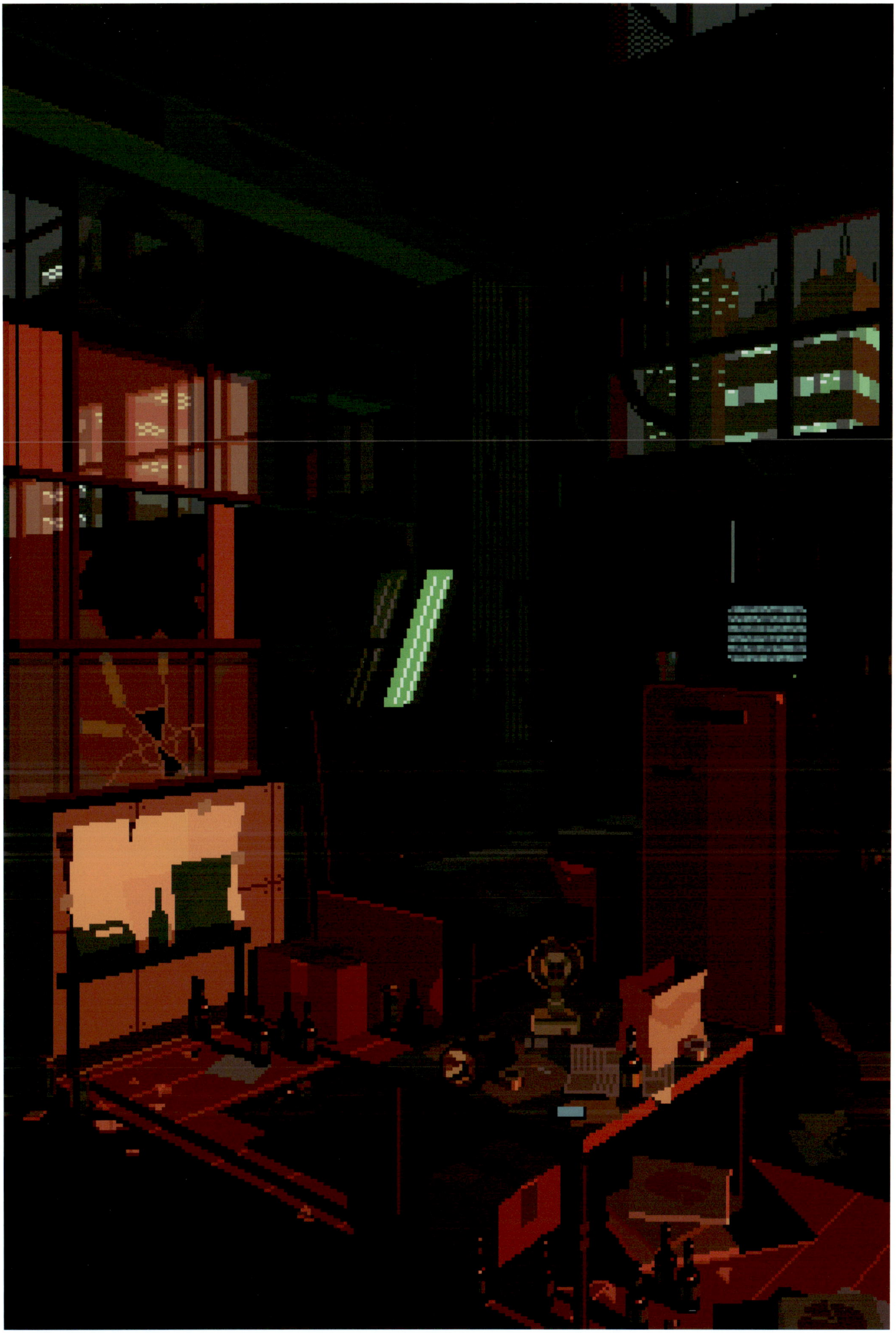

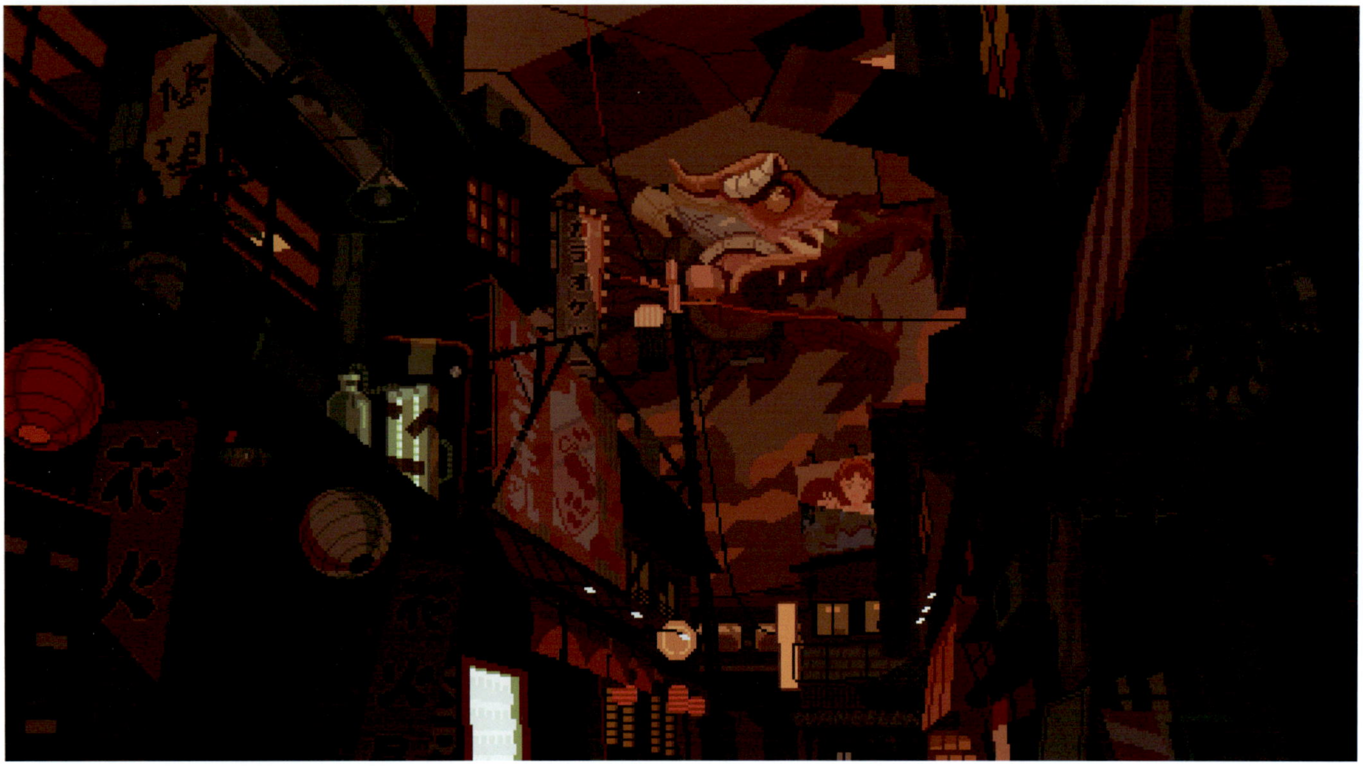

218AFPIJH6, 28/02/2018, 480×270px

63

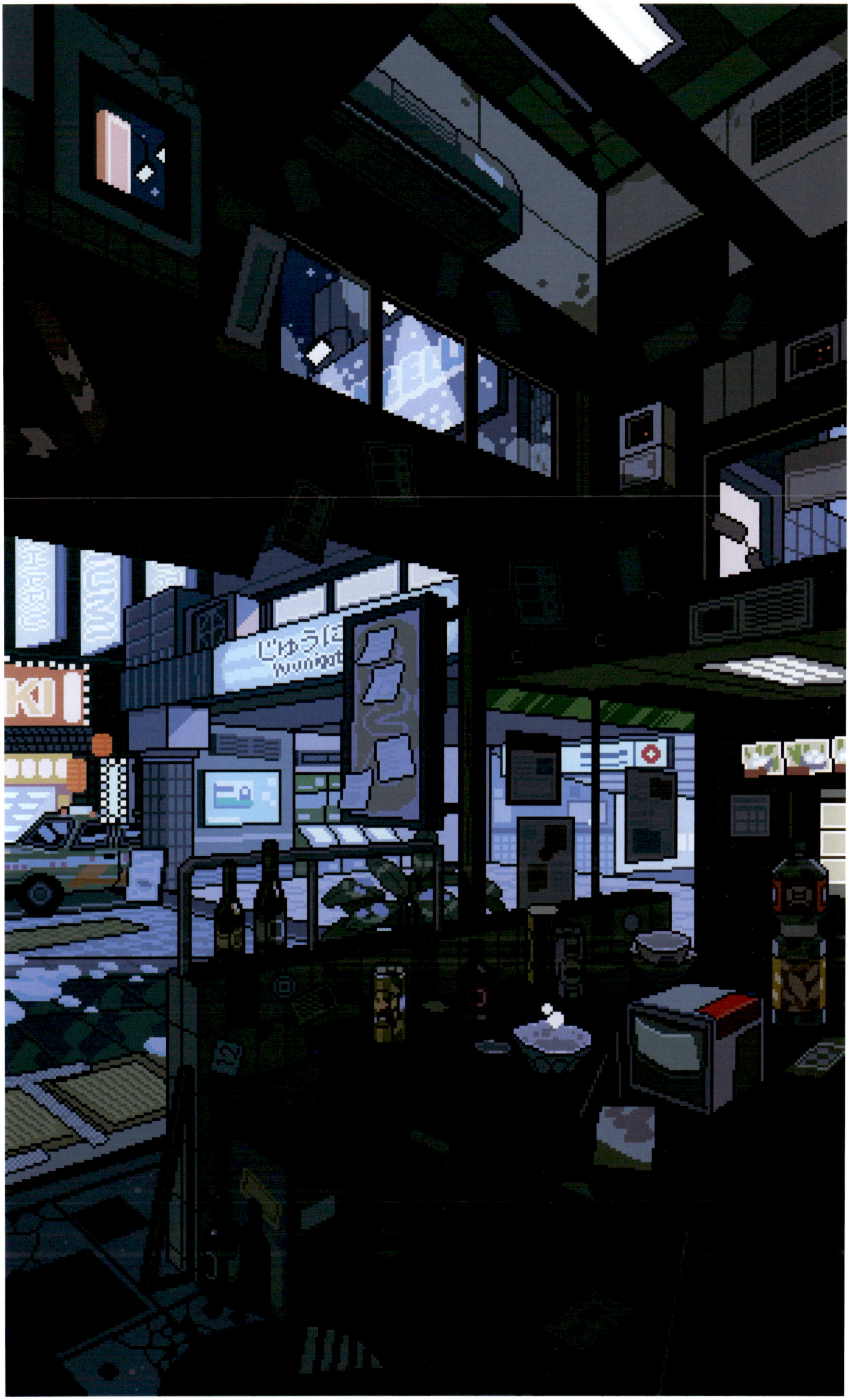

19:25, 21/12/2018, 300×500px

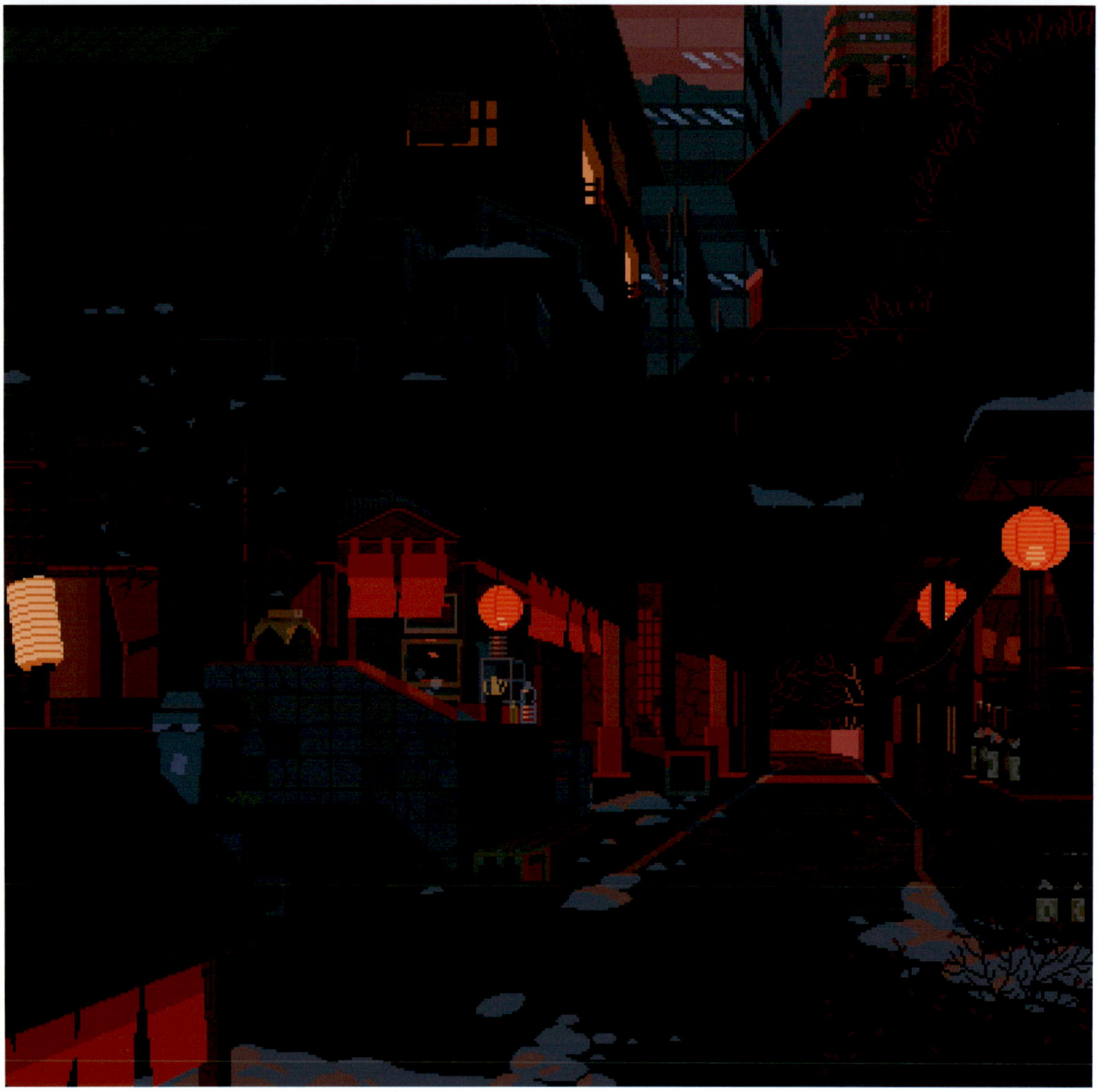

3qnupLBQym, 04/12/2017, 406×406px

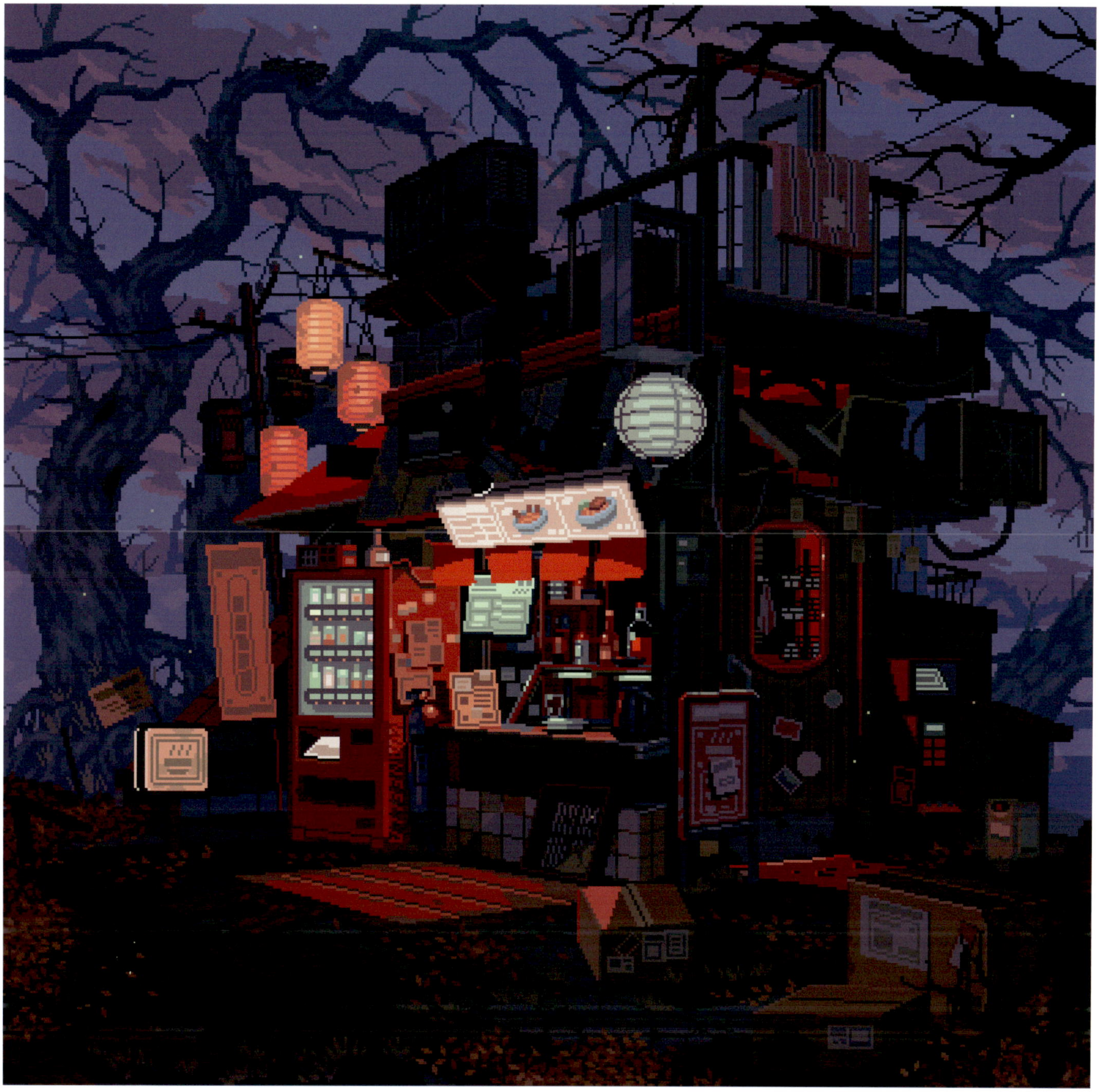

Dusk, 11/10/2019, 400×400px

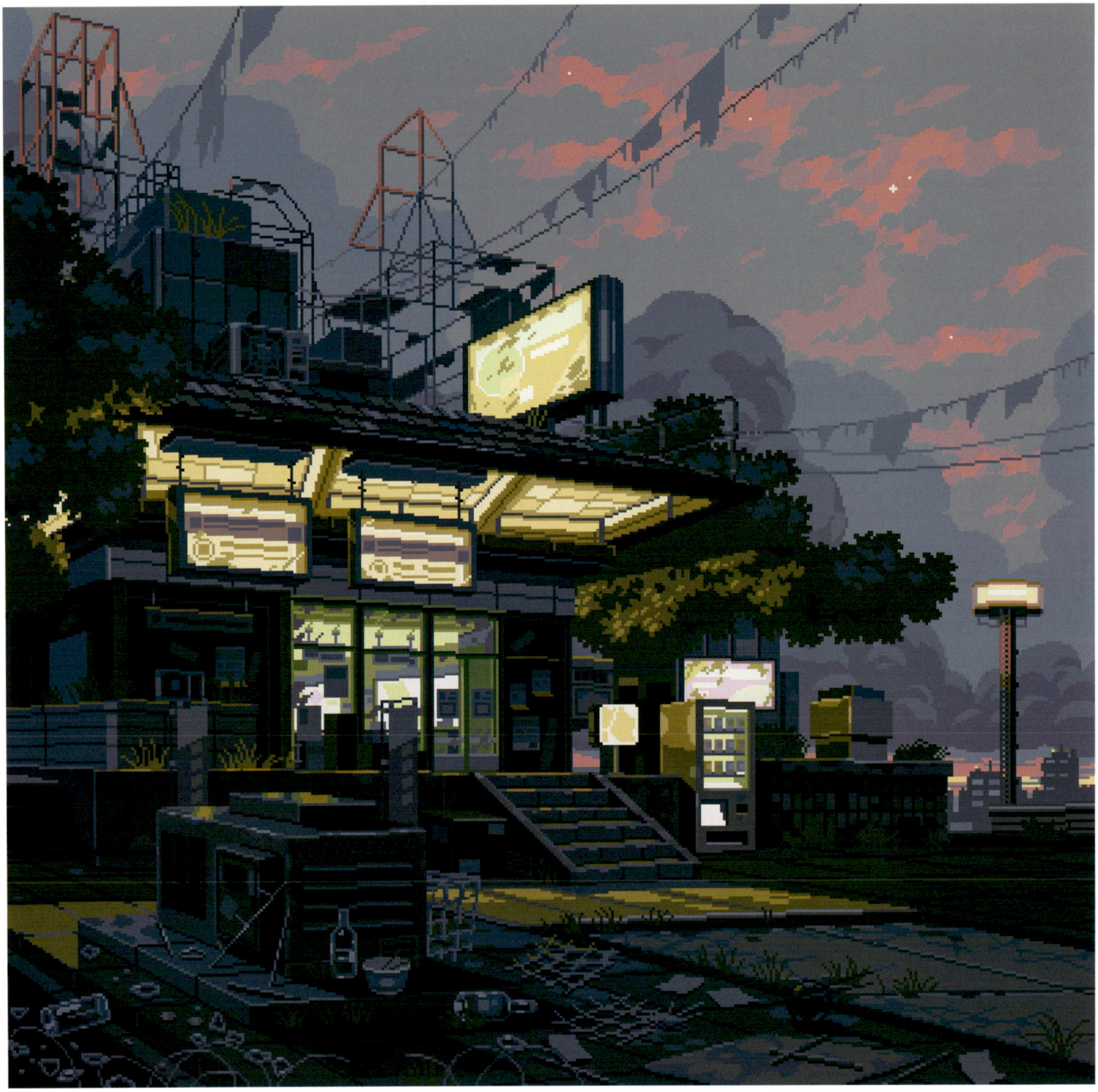

Above: *Terminal E*, 27/06/2019, 400×400px
Right: *35.6534205, 139.6990352*, 04/11/2018, 270×480px

67

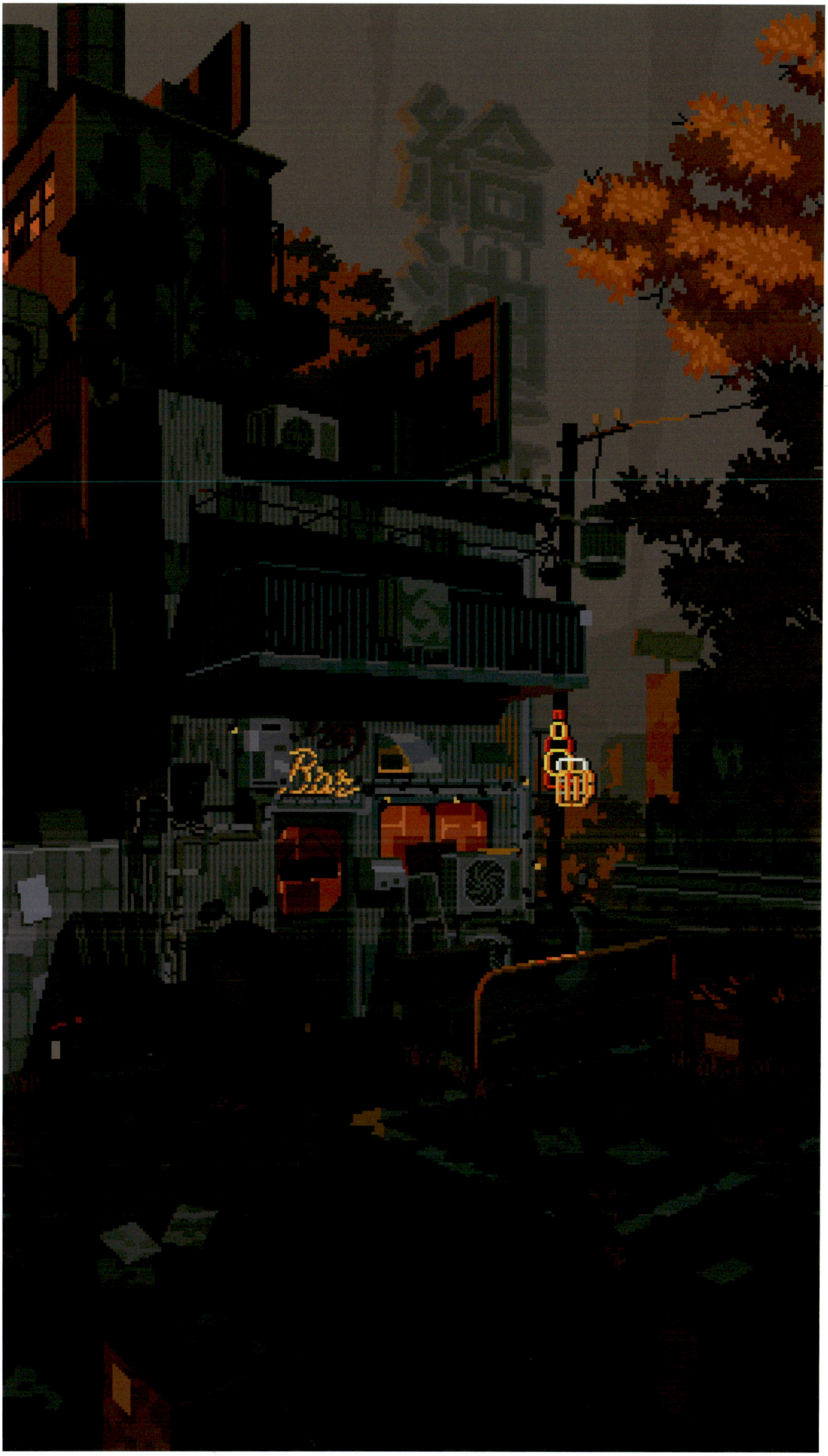

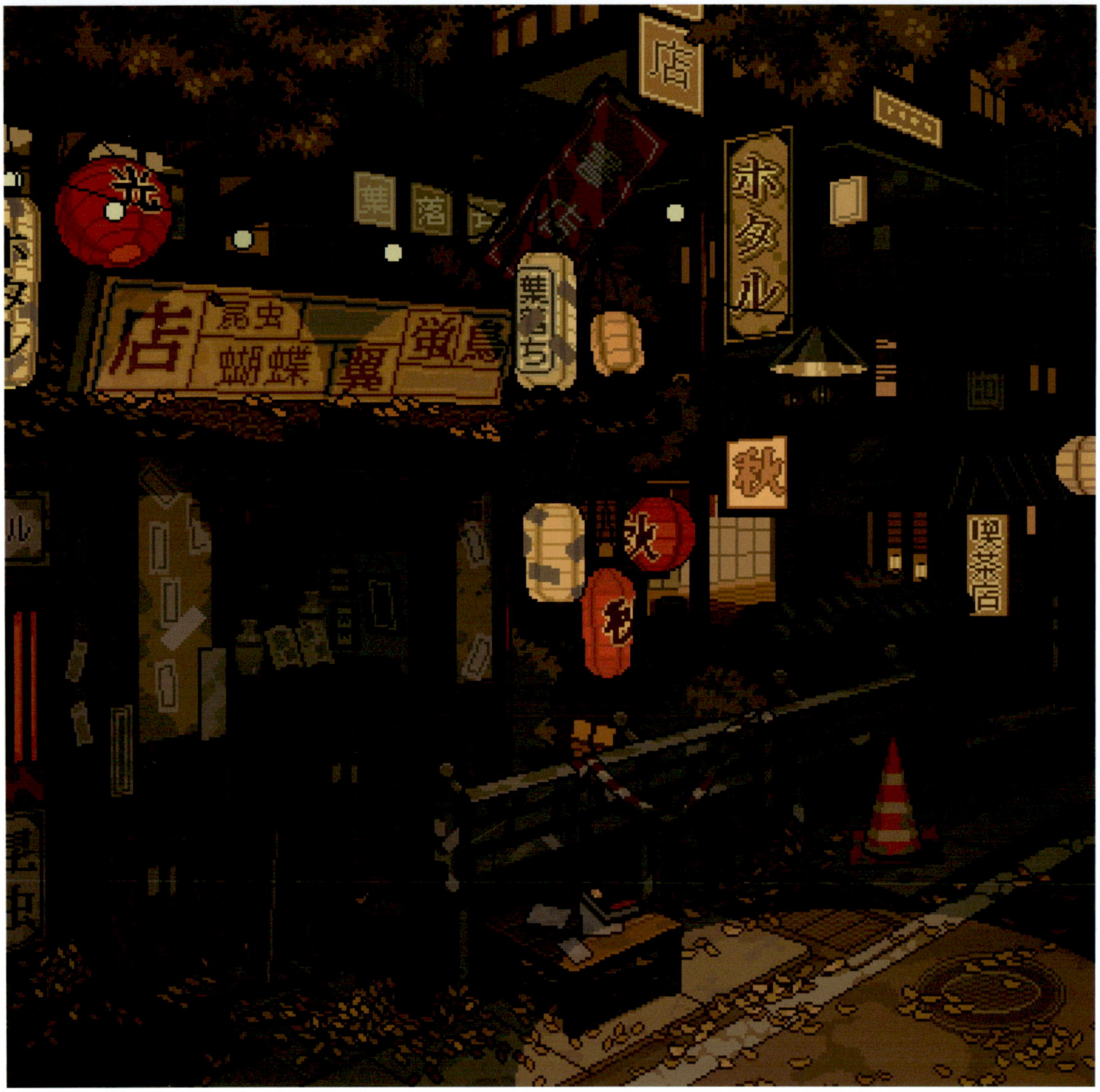

Above: *20:48*, 12/10/2018, 400×400px
Top right: *18:35*, 16/09/2018, 384×384px
Right: *35.6972756, 139.7588493*, 30/08/2018, 480×480px

69

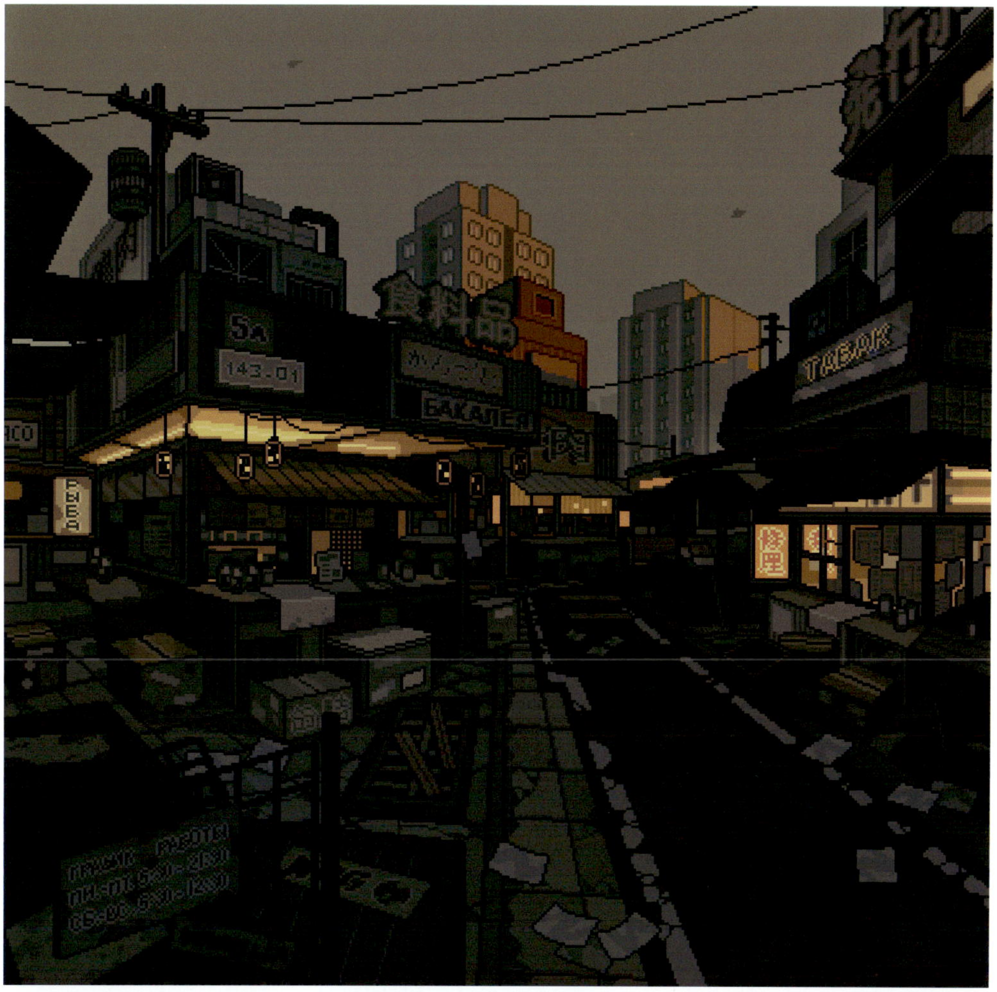

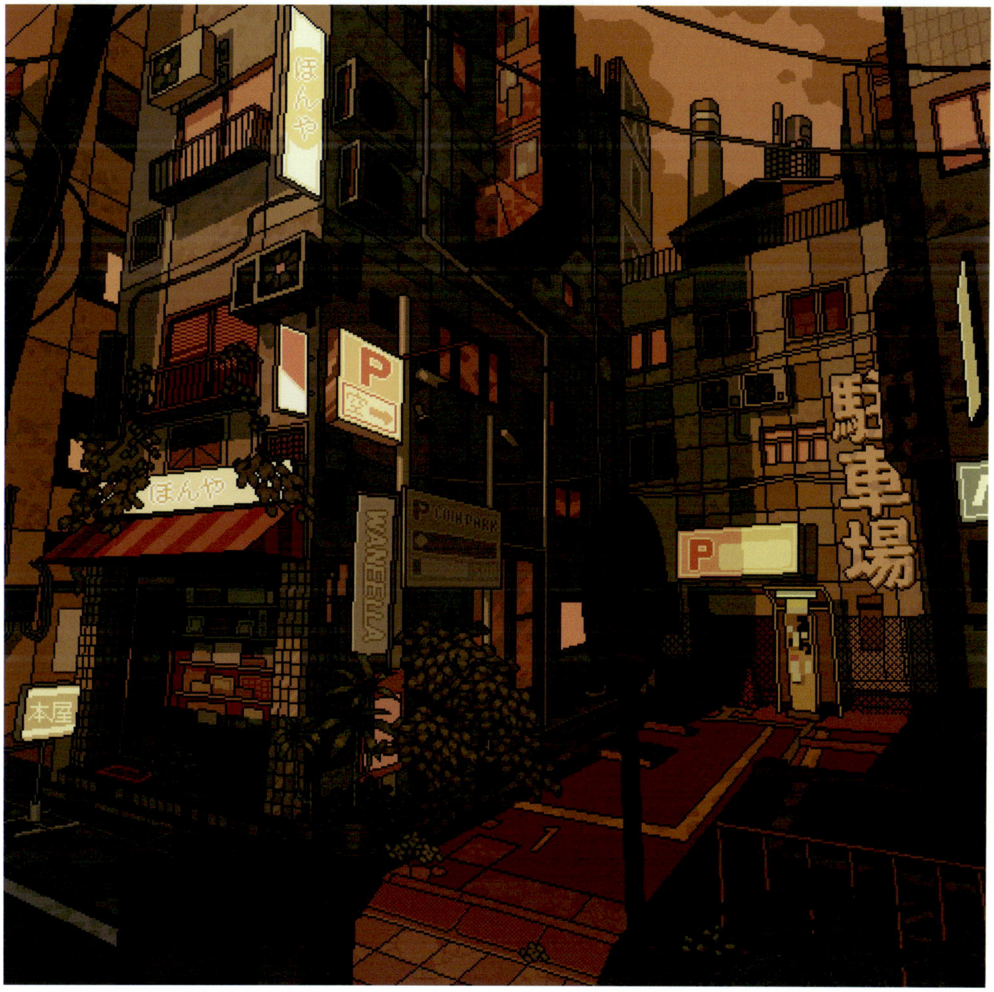

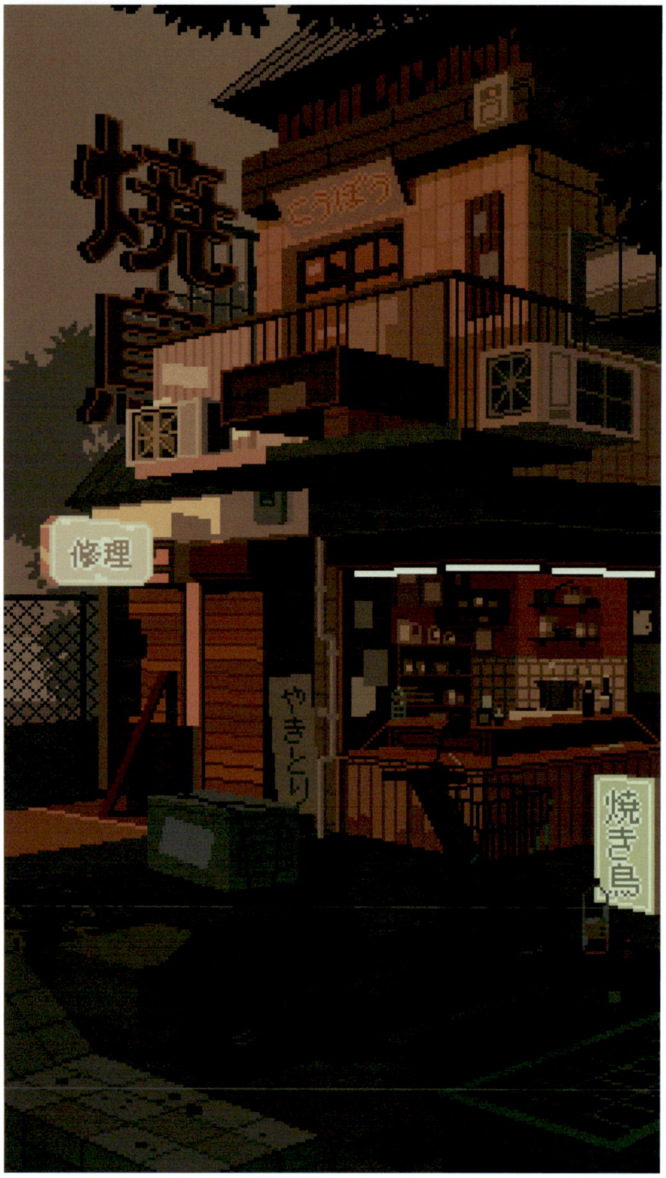

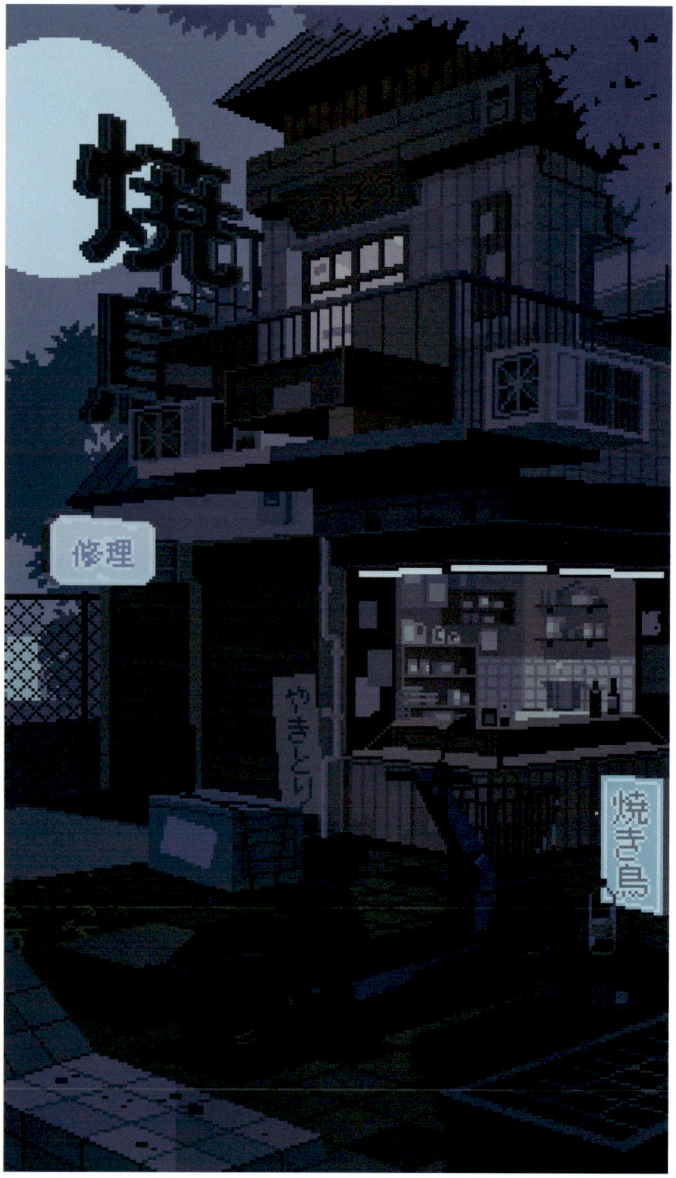

Above left: *6MpSRPxYx8*, 23/06/2018, 216×384px
Above right: *Ja5Z8RB7vU*, 26/06/2018, 216×384px
Right: *VUo6ou5bYS*, 30/04/2018, 270×480px

71

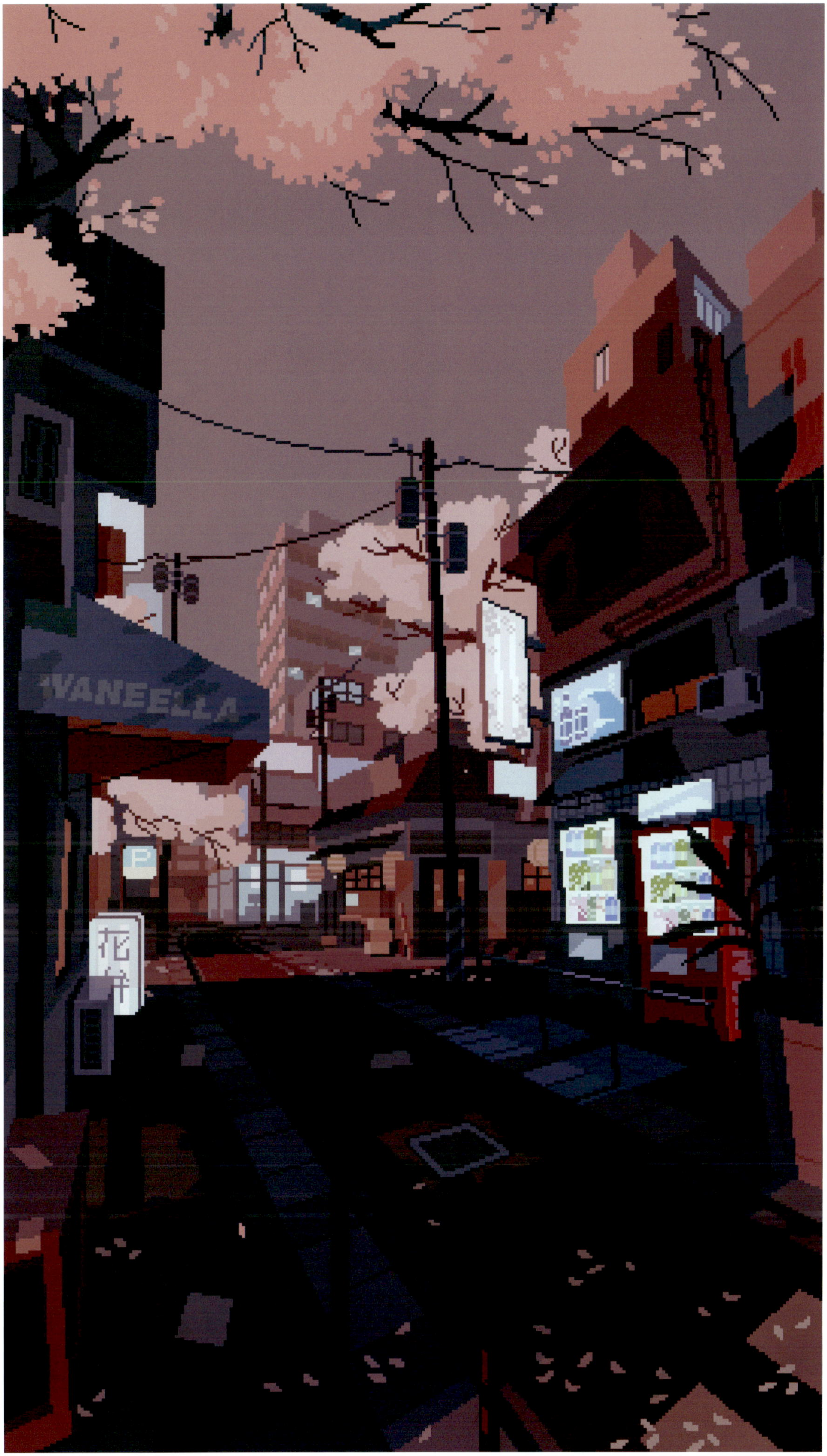

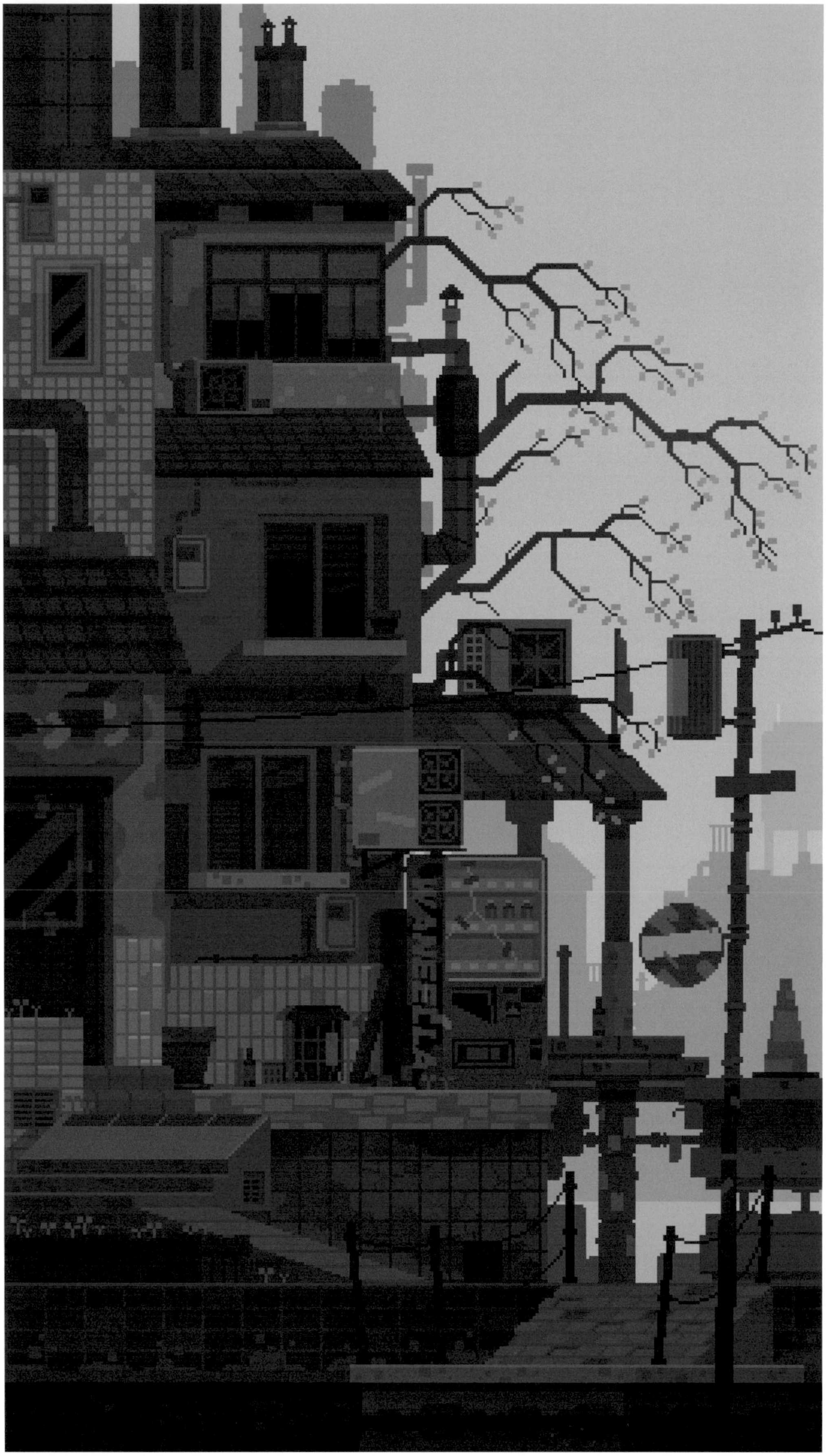

Above: *BluaCV1c7a,* 04/05/2018, 270×480px
Right: *cPPtQQau5z,* 20/05/2018, 270×480px

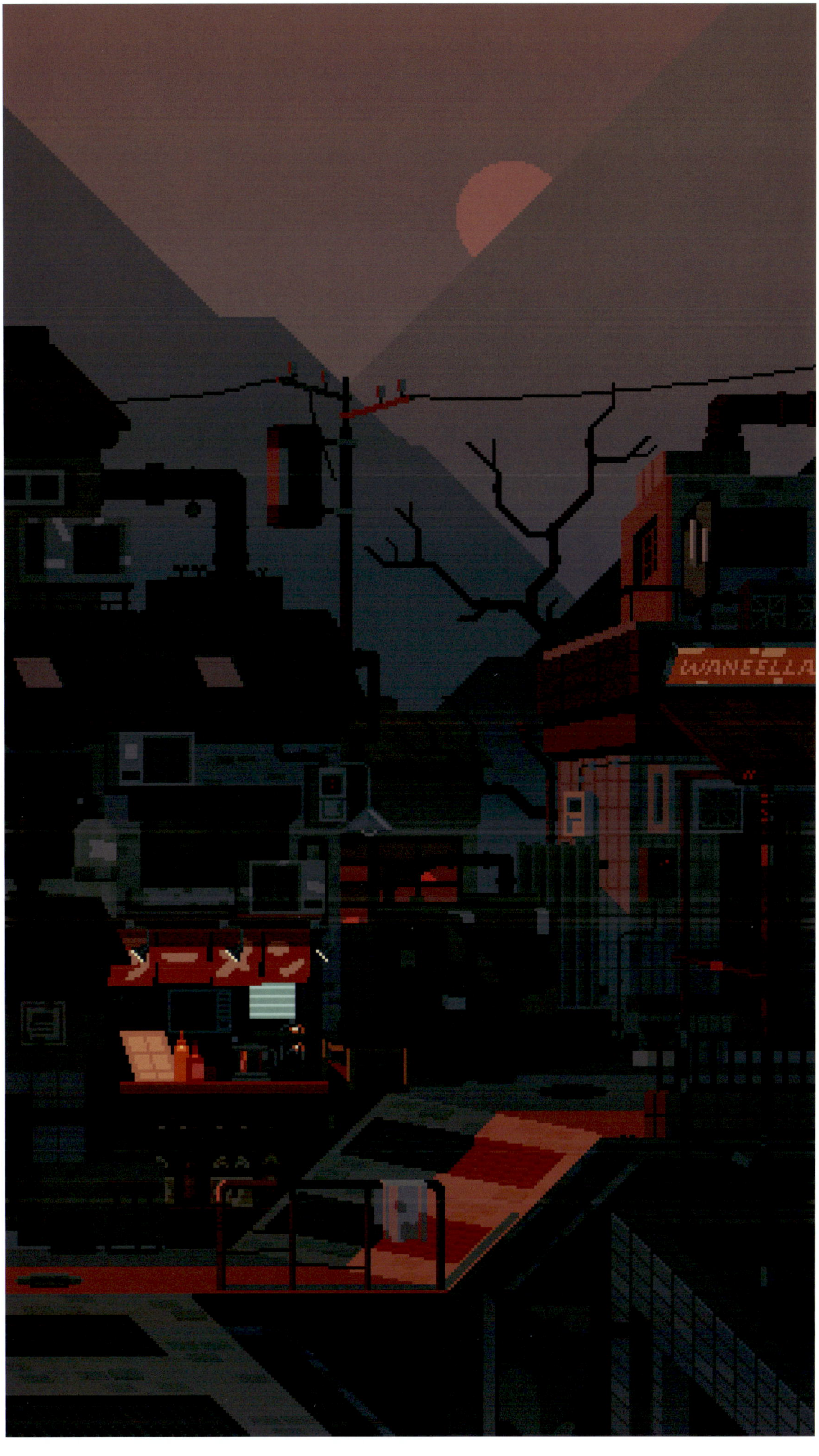
WANEELLA

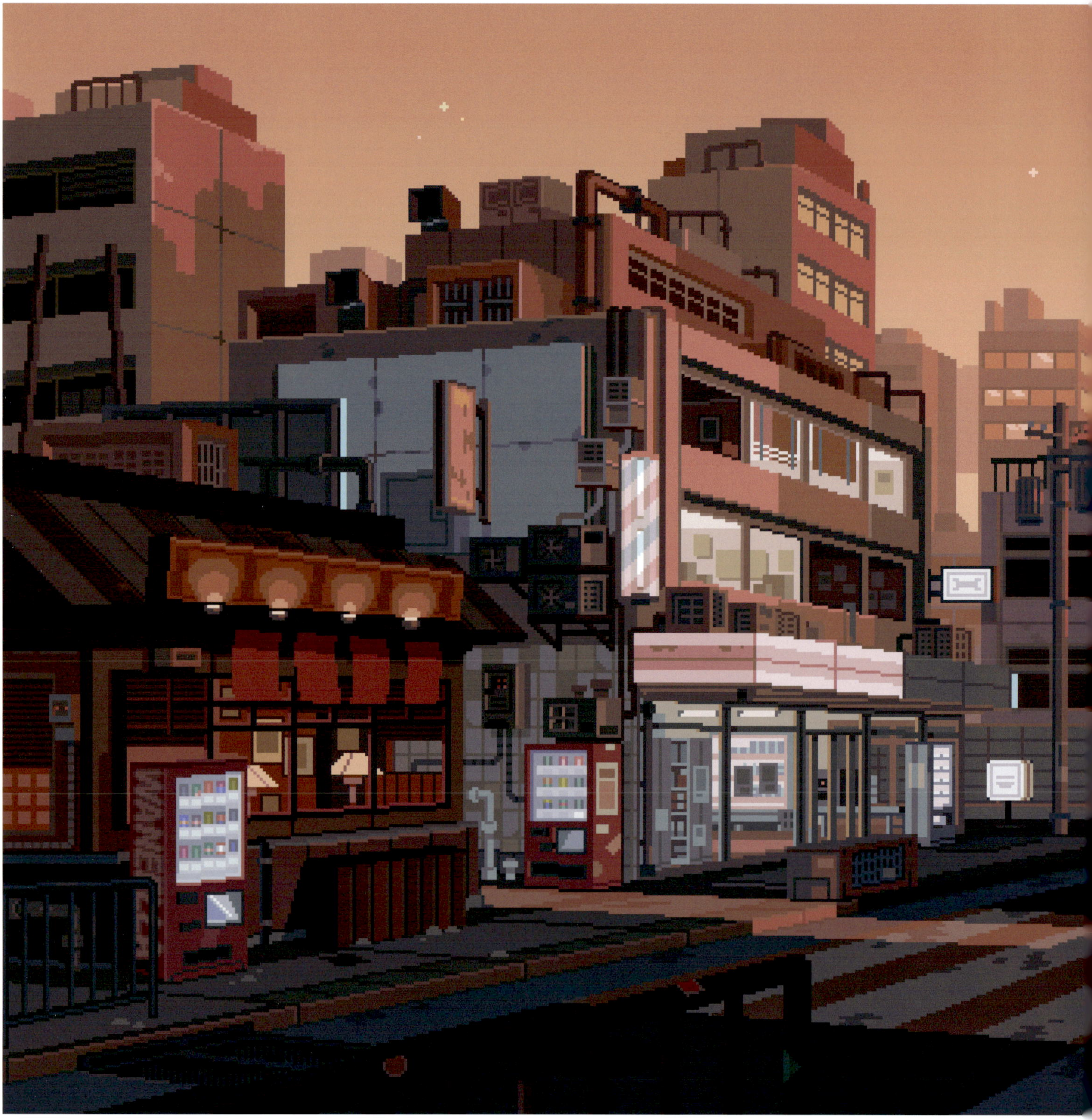

Shadow, 24/04/2020, 720×360px

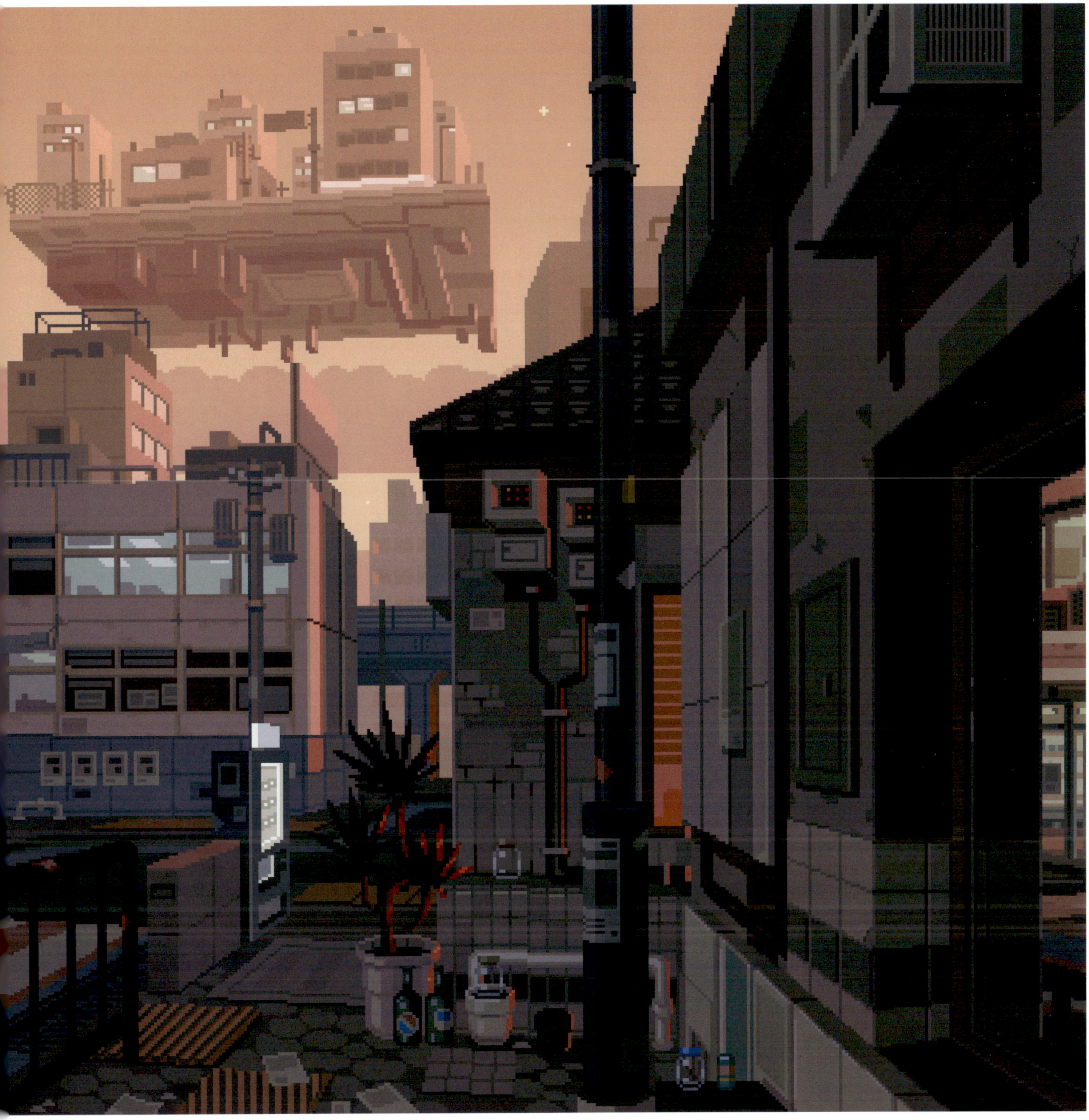

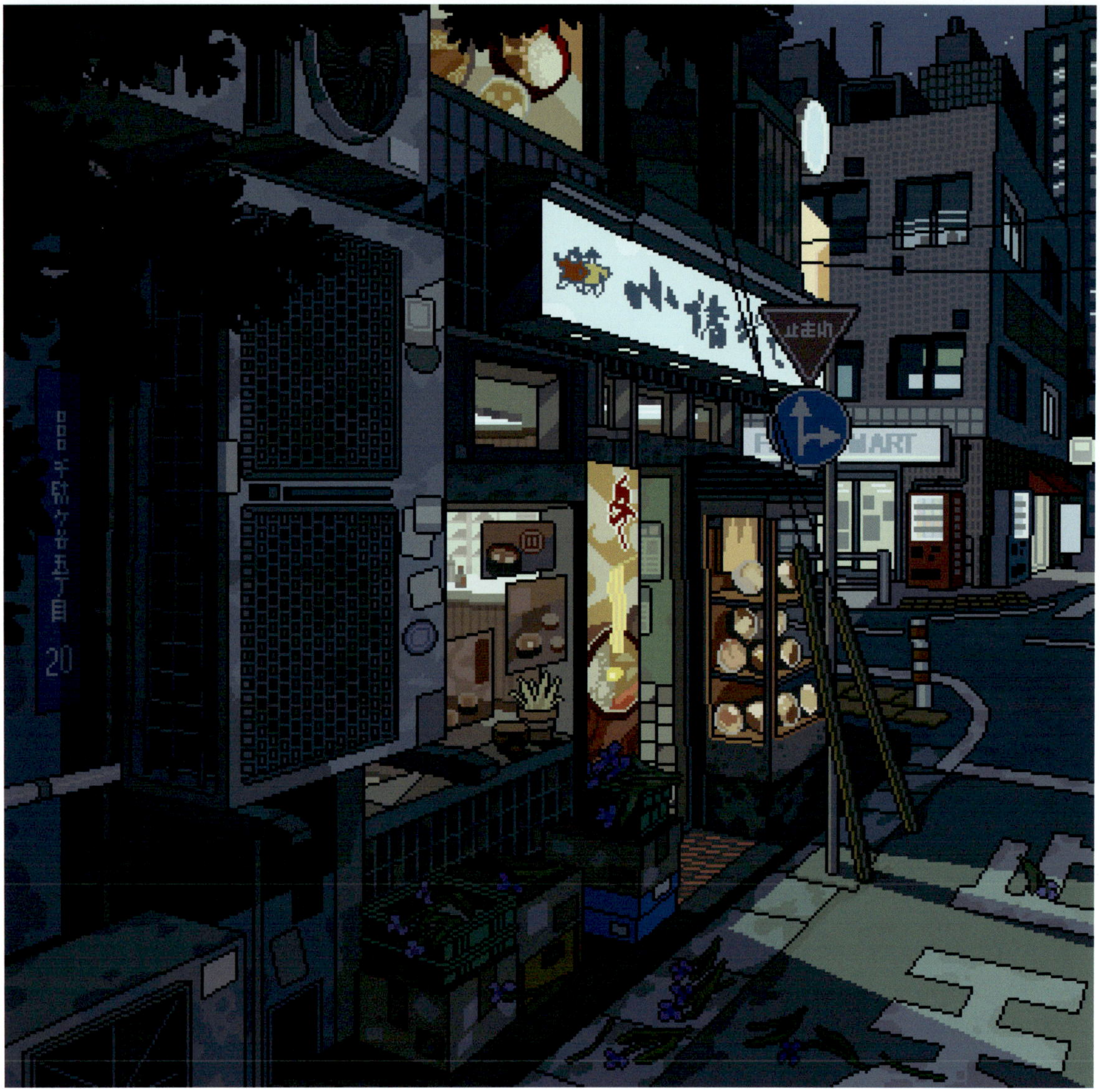

35.6835709, *139.7030749*, 16/08/2018, 384×384px

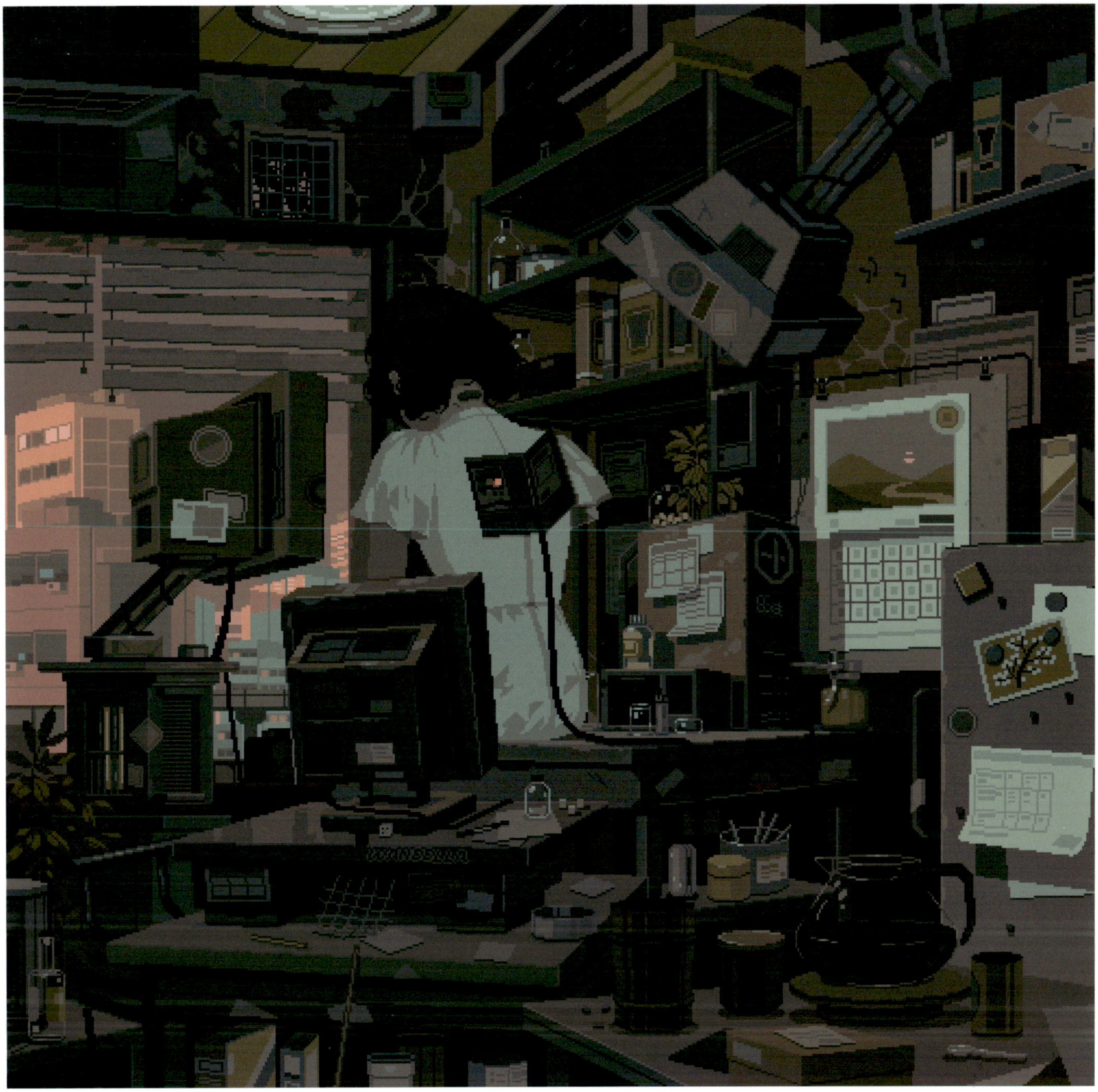

Mist, 19/09/2019, 500×500px

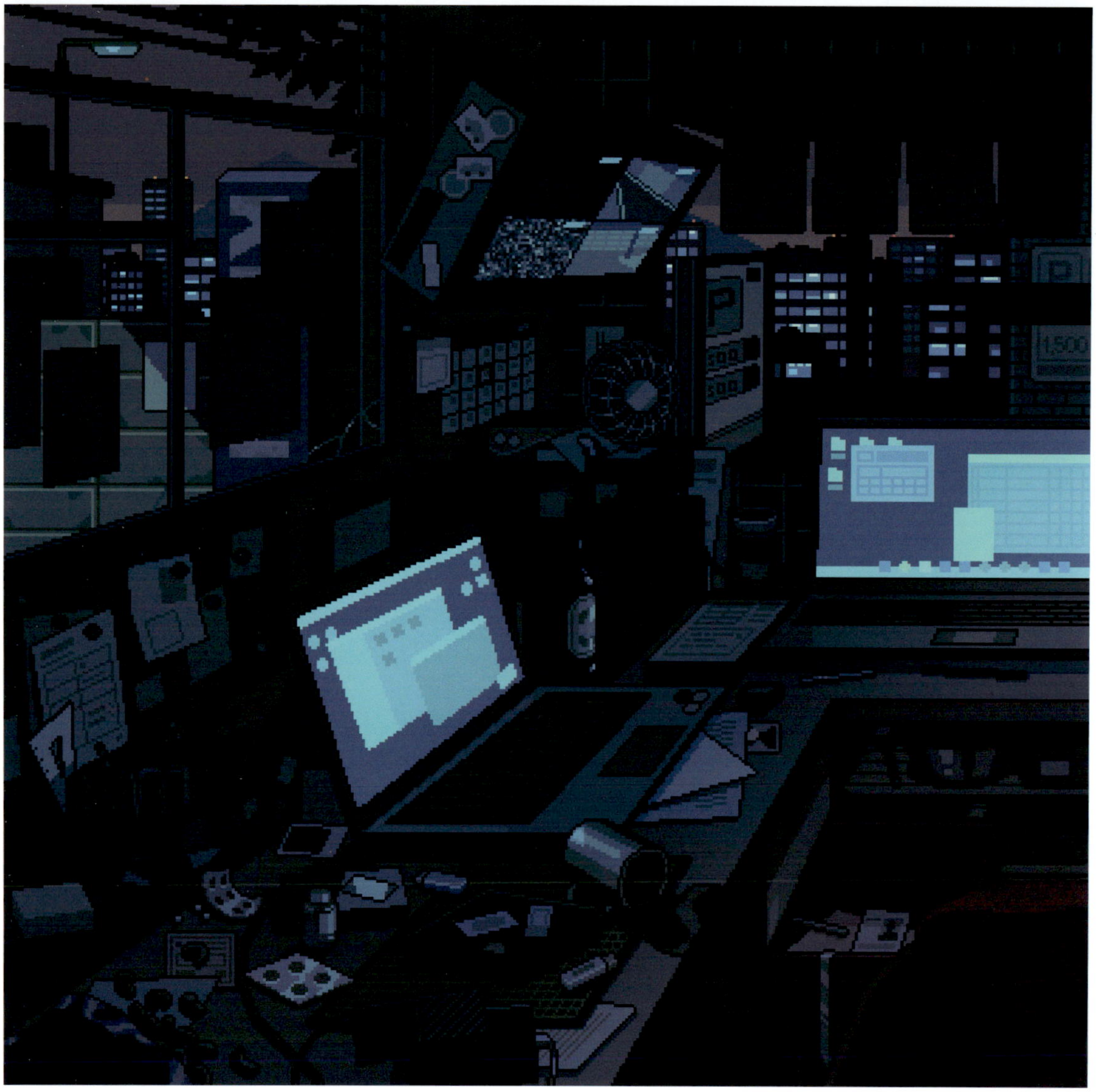

Above: *23:37*, 08/09/2018, 384×384px
Right: *kQly7peTNR*, 04/08/2018, 270×480px

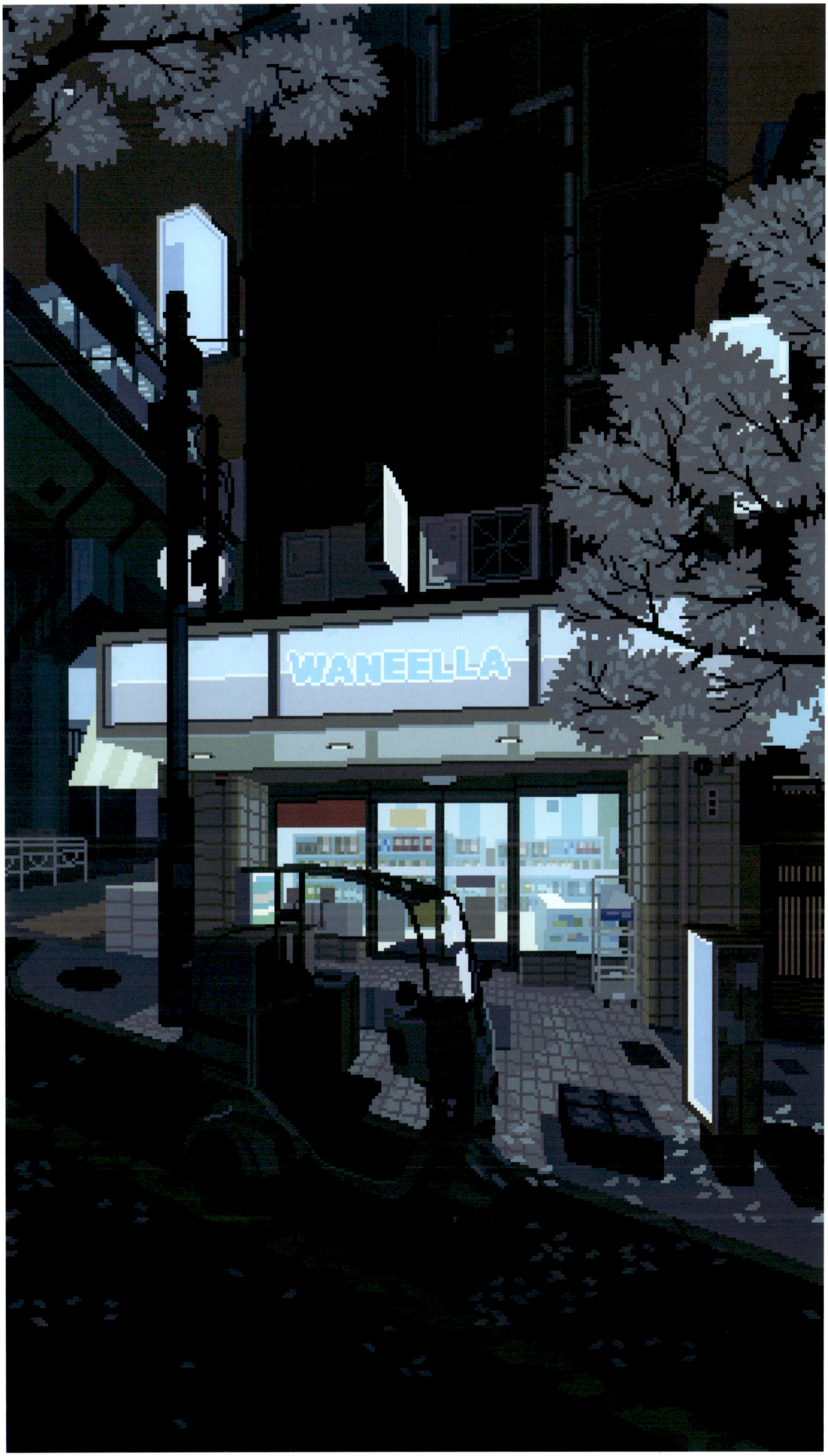
WANEELLA

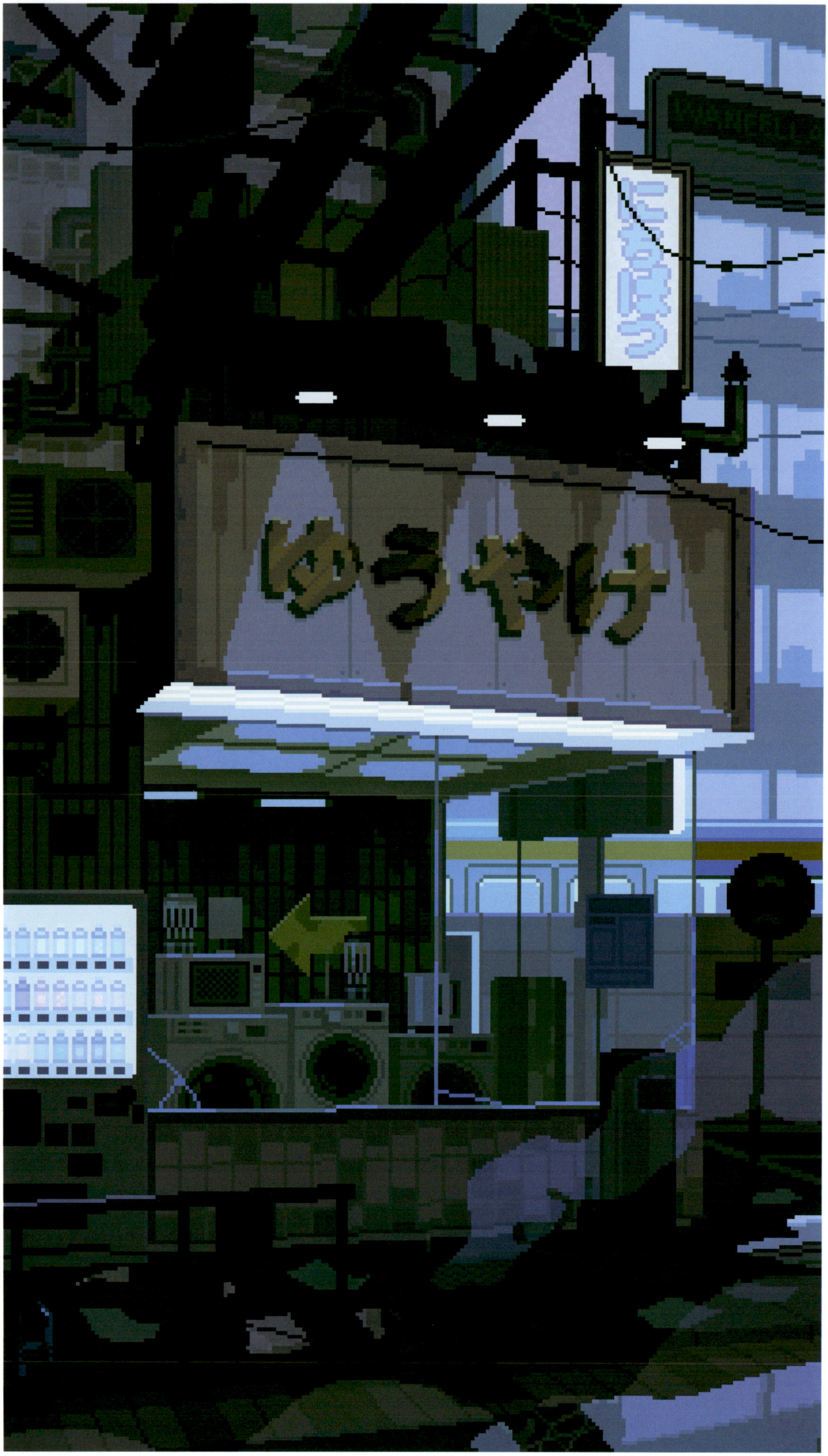
ゆうやけ

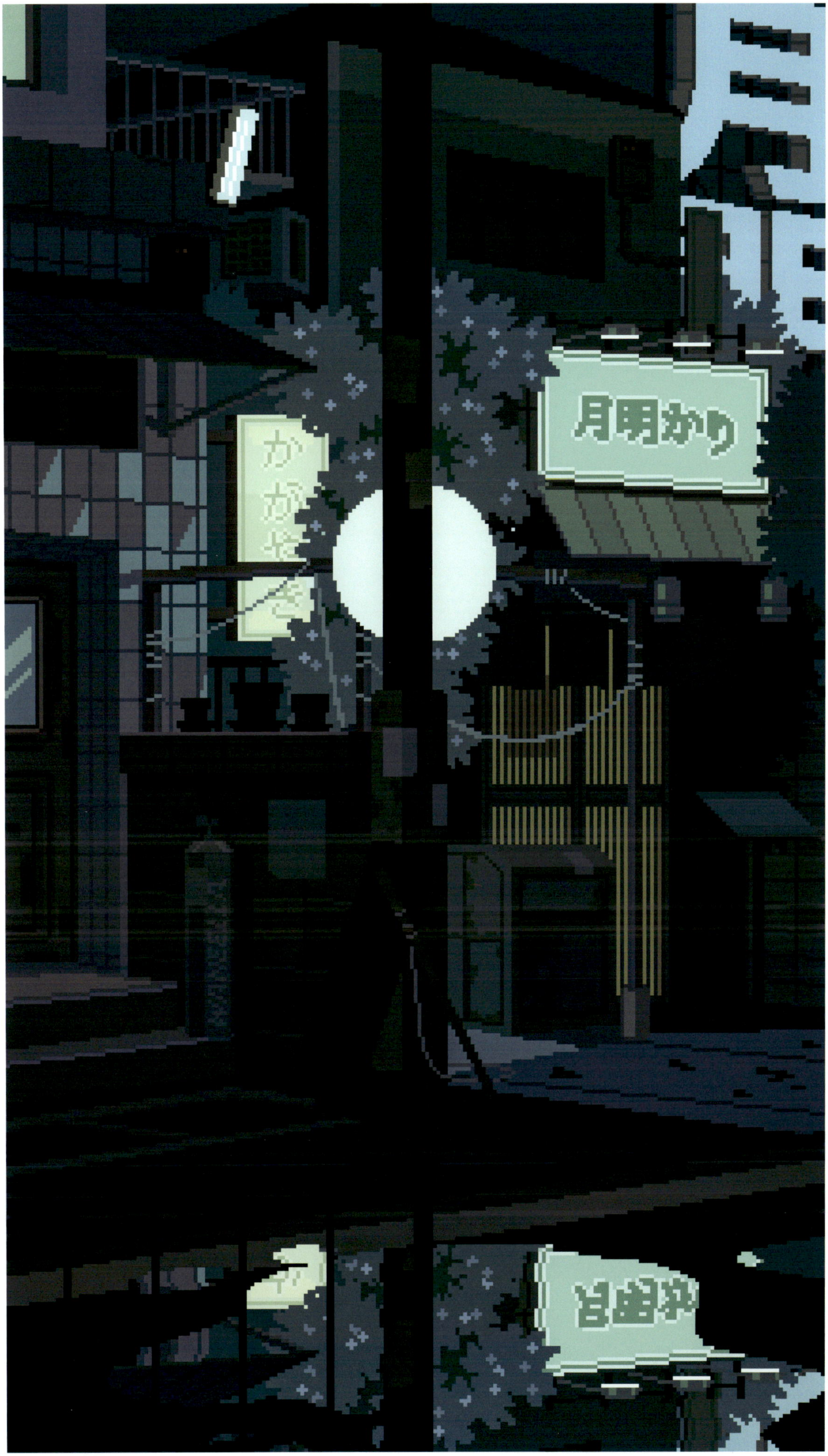
月明かり

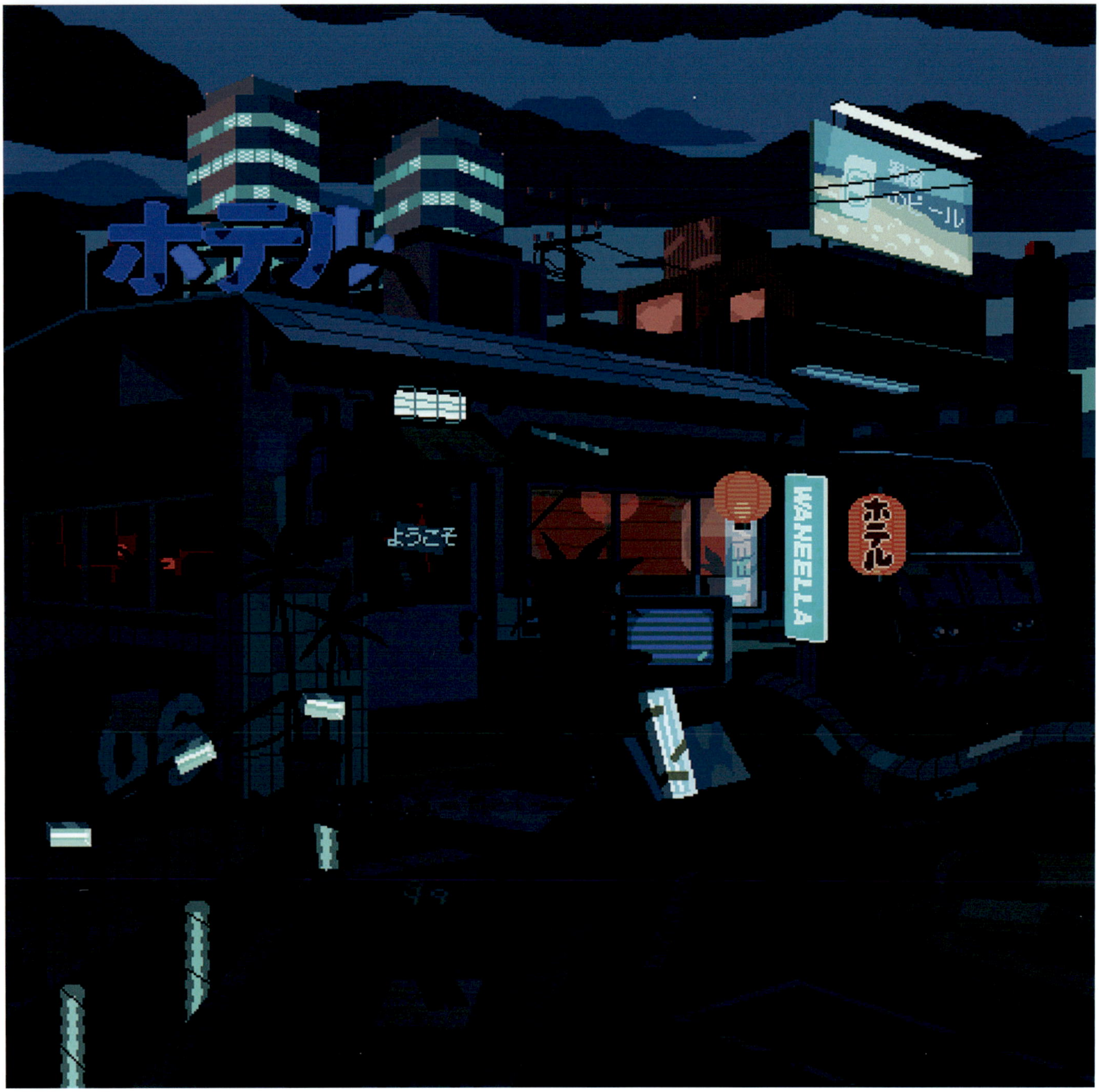

Page 80: *F8ocw2PITC,* 09/06/2018, 216×384px
Page 81: *ehFhfNWpBW,* 28/06/2018, 216×384px
Above: *6USUVRm56F,* 12/06/2018, 480×480px

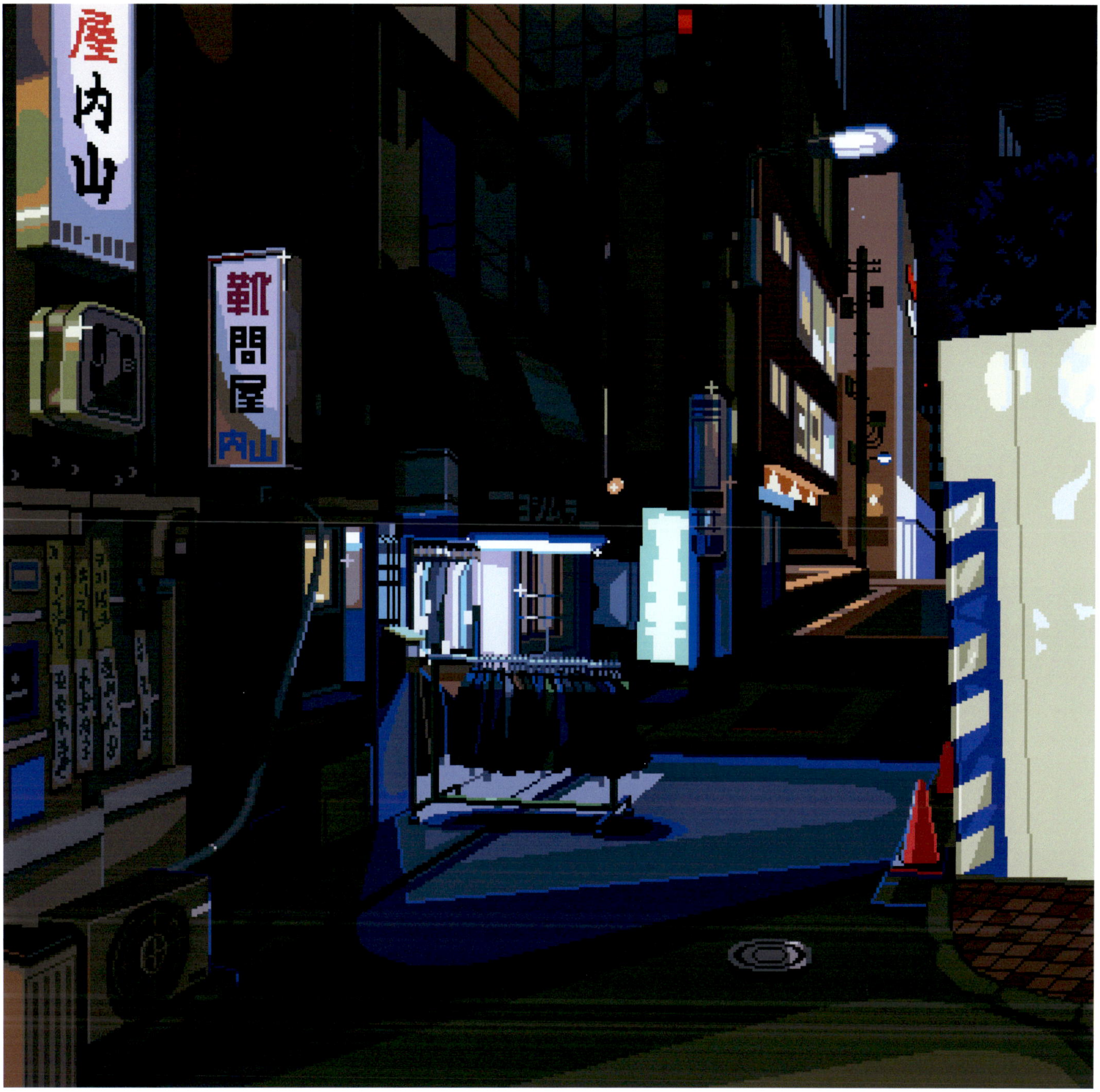

New Moon, 07/08/2019, 400×400px

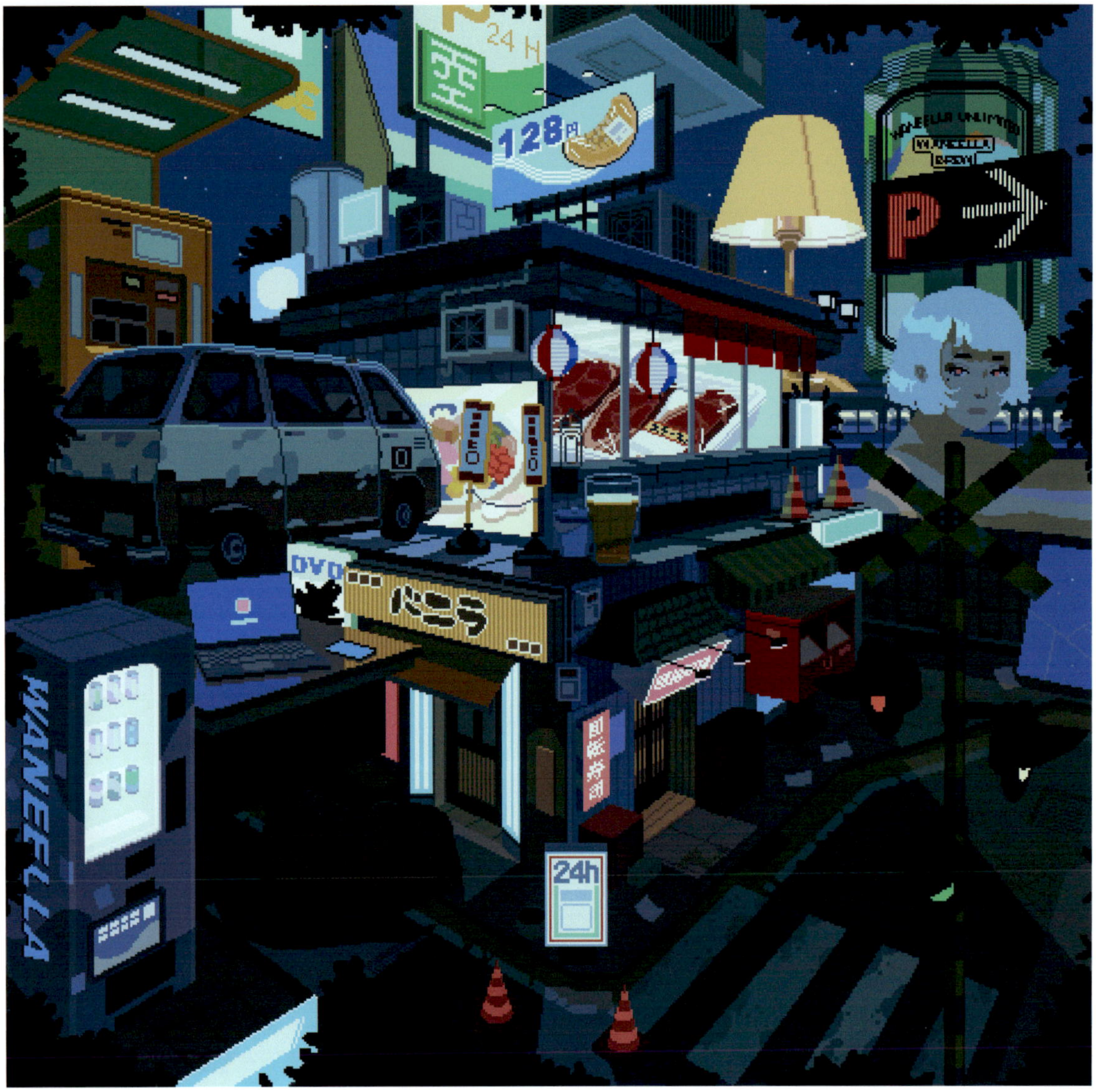

Above: *rARIVxe6GC*, 19/06/2018, 480×480px
Right: *F 7-93*, 25/07/2019, 300×500px

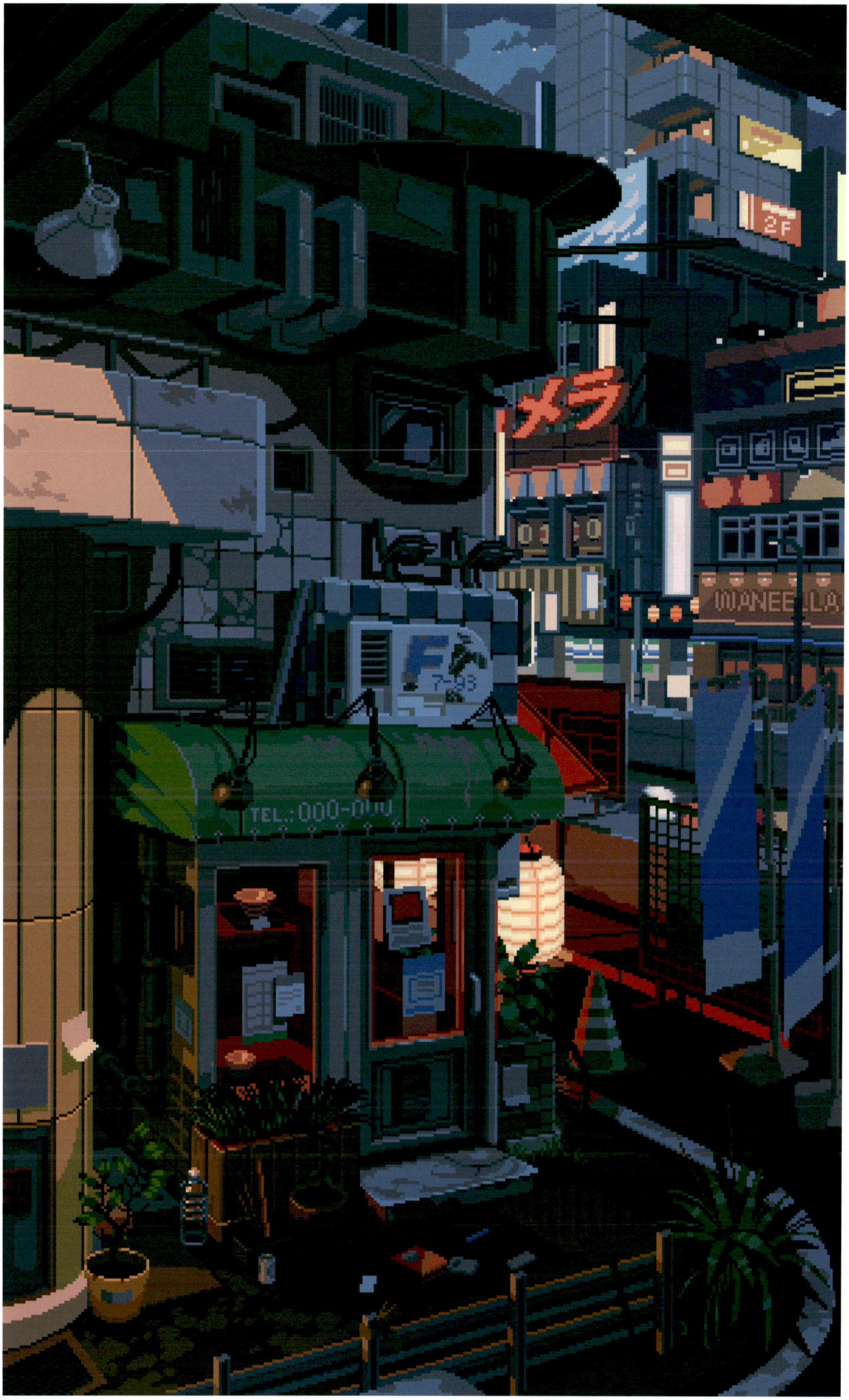

2F
メラ
TEL.: 000-000

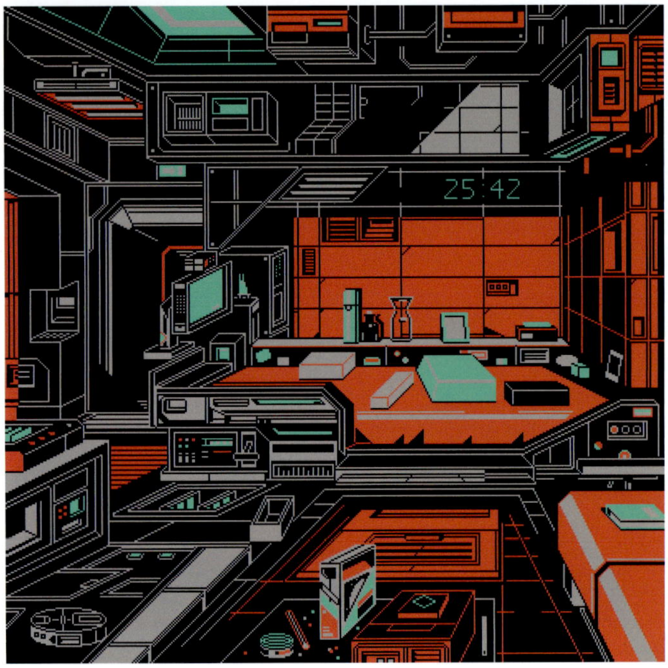

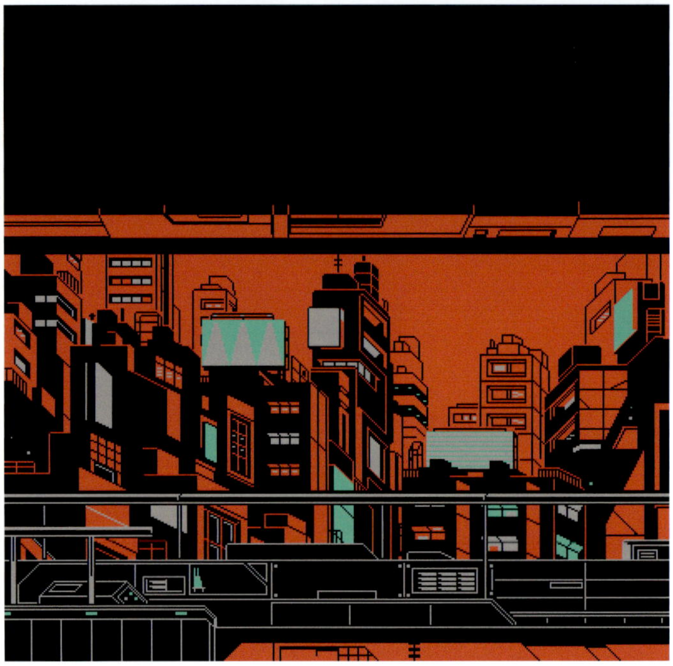

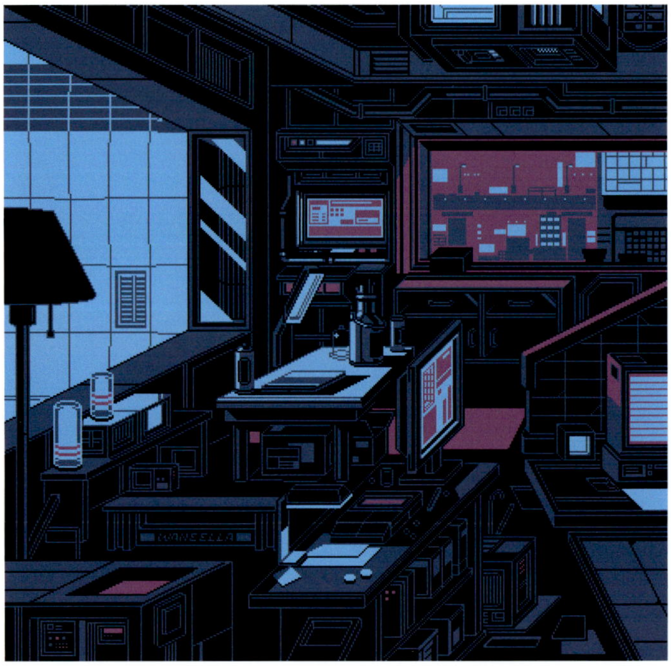

Top left: *Solstice Pt2,* 22/12/2019, 400×400px
Top middle: *Solstice Pt3,* 22/12/2019, 400×400px
Top right: *Solstice Pt1,* 22/12/2019, 400×400px
Bottom left: *Blue Pt1,* 31/12/2019, 400×400px
Bottom middle: *Blue Pt2,* 31/12/2019, 400×400px
Bottom right: *Blue Pt3,* 31/12/2019, 400×400px

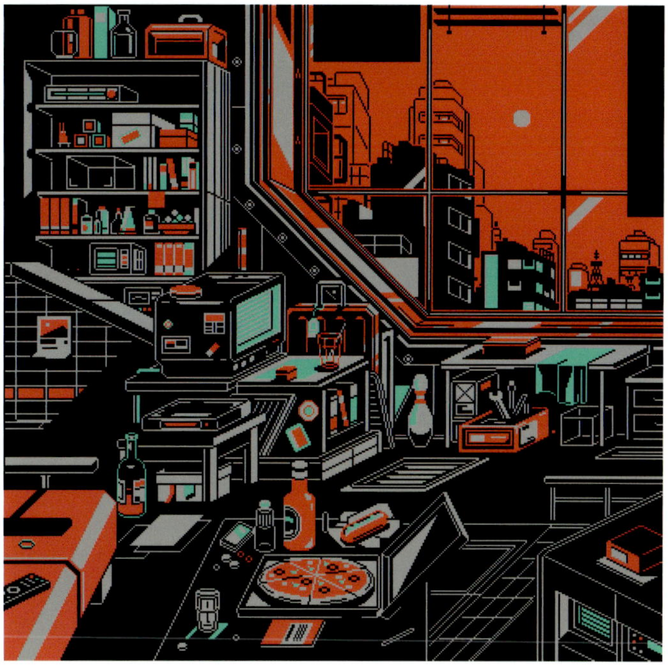

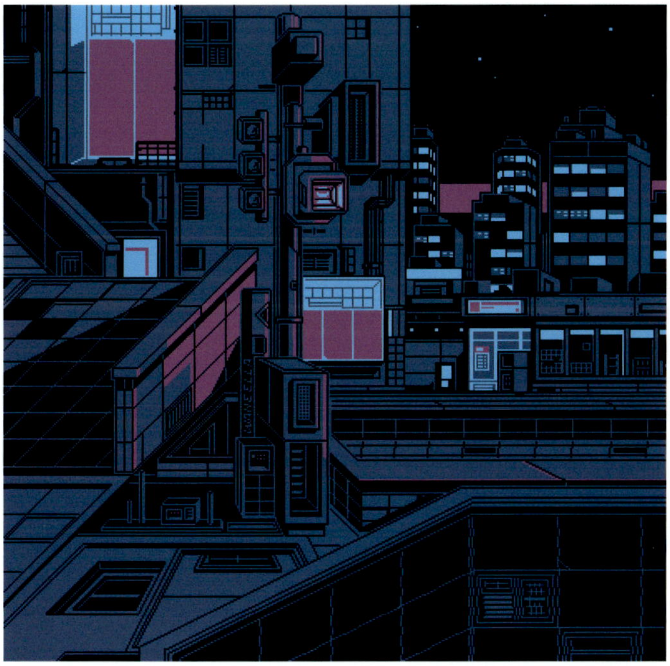

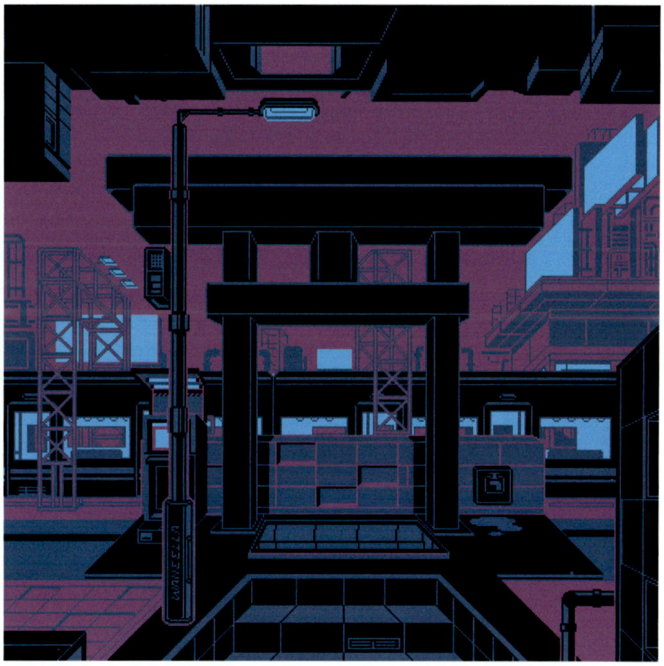

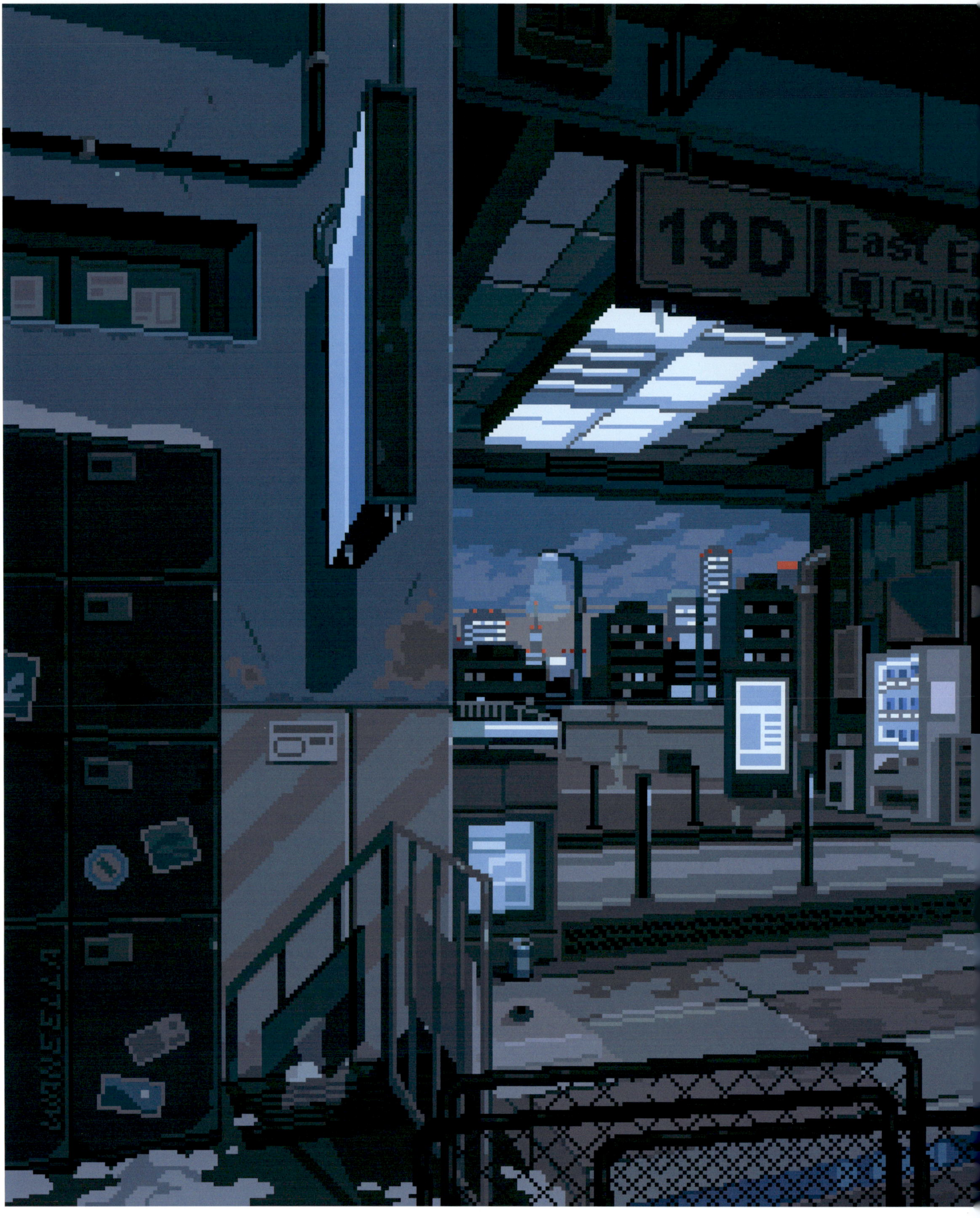

Full Of Hopes, 14/12/2019, 500×300px

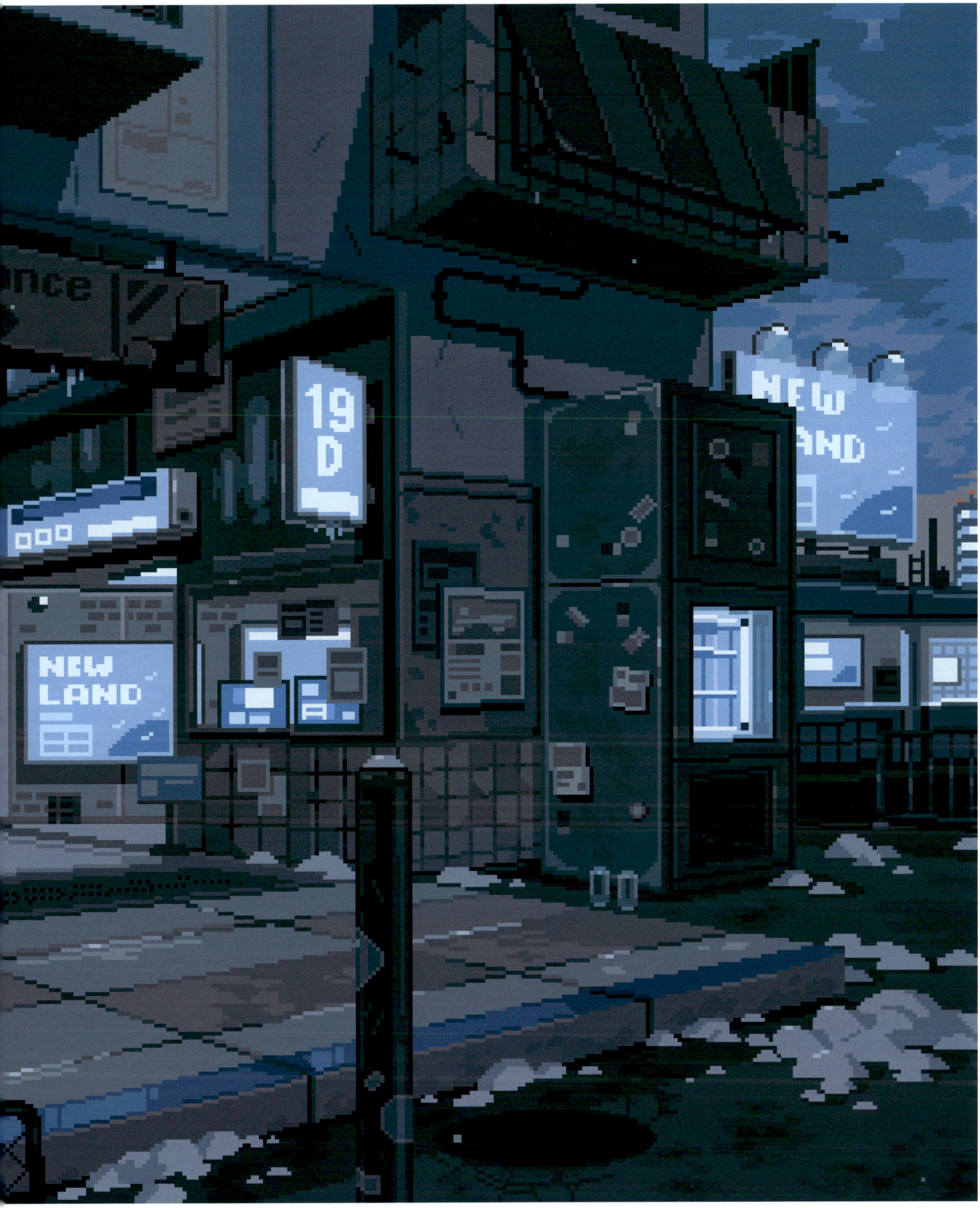
nce
19
D
NEW
LAND
NEW
LAND

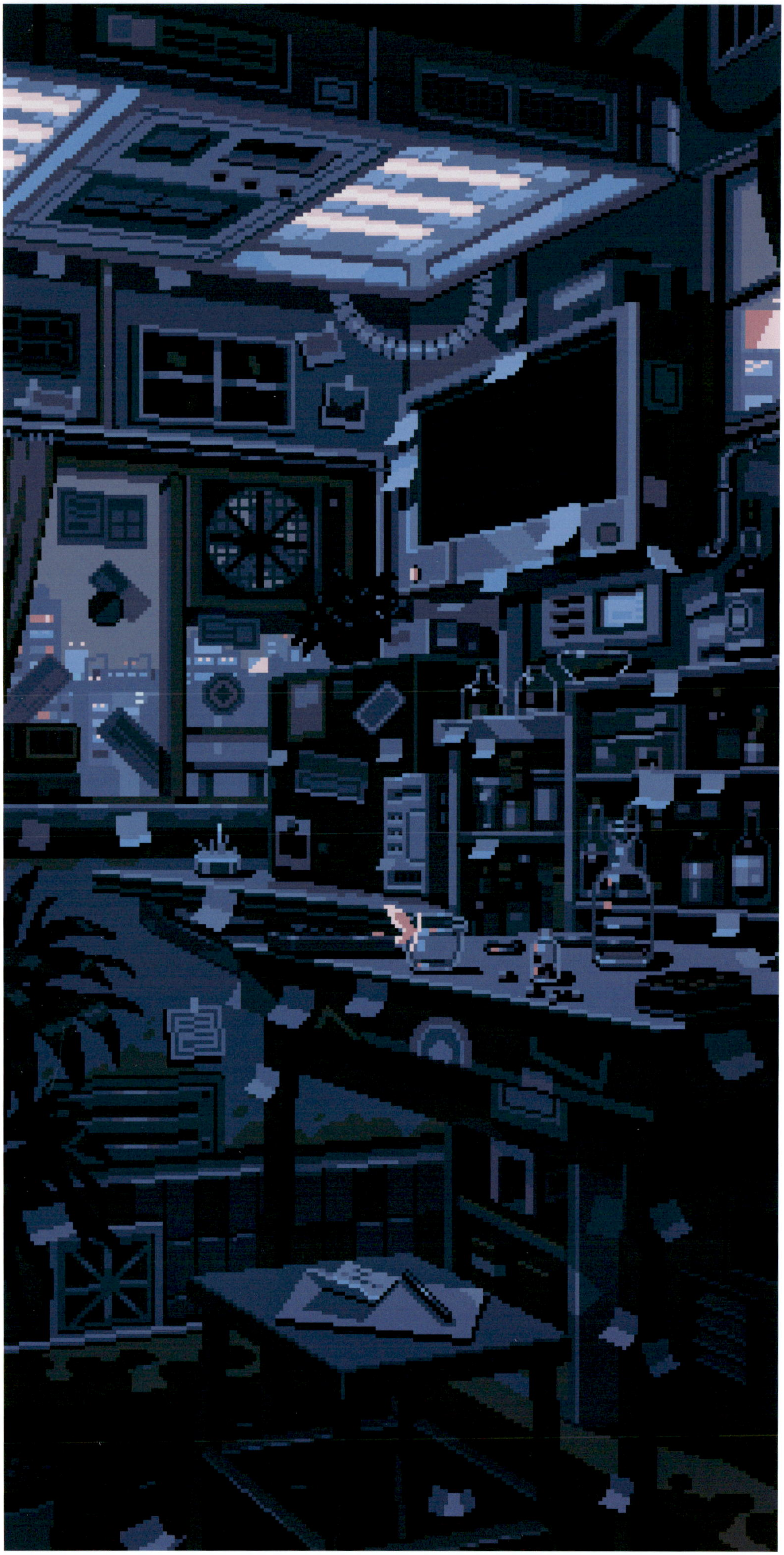

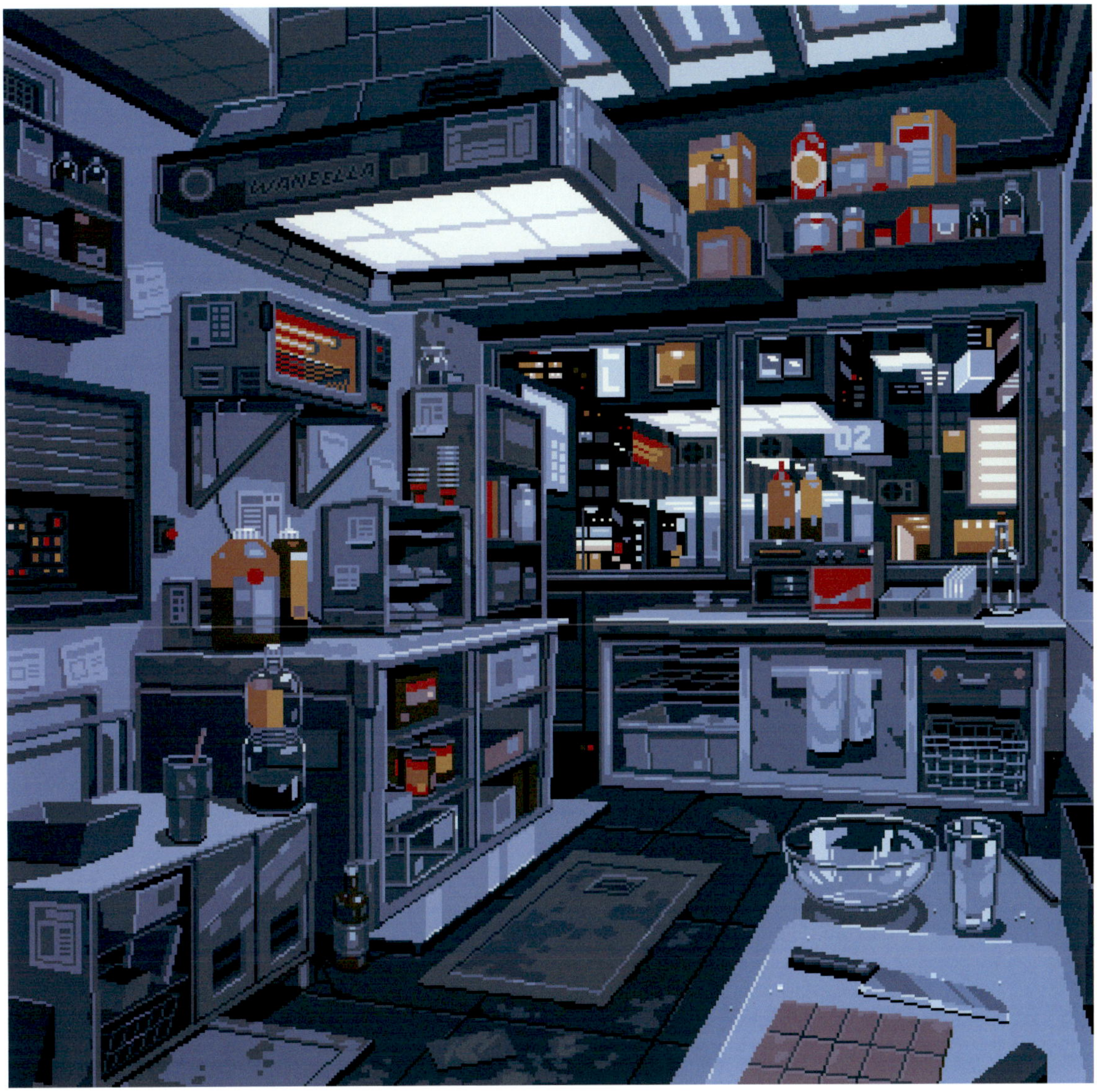

Left: *Memory*, 16/07/2019, 200×400px
Above: *The Last Hour*, 20/06/2019, 400×400px

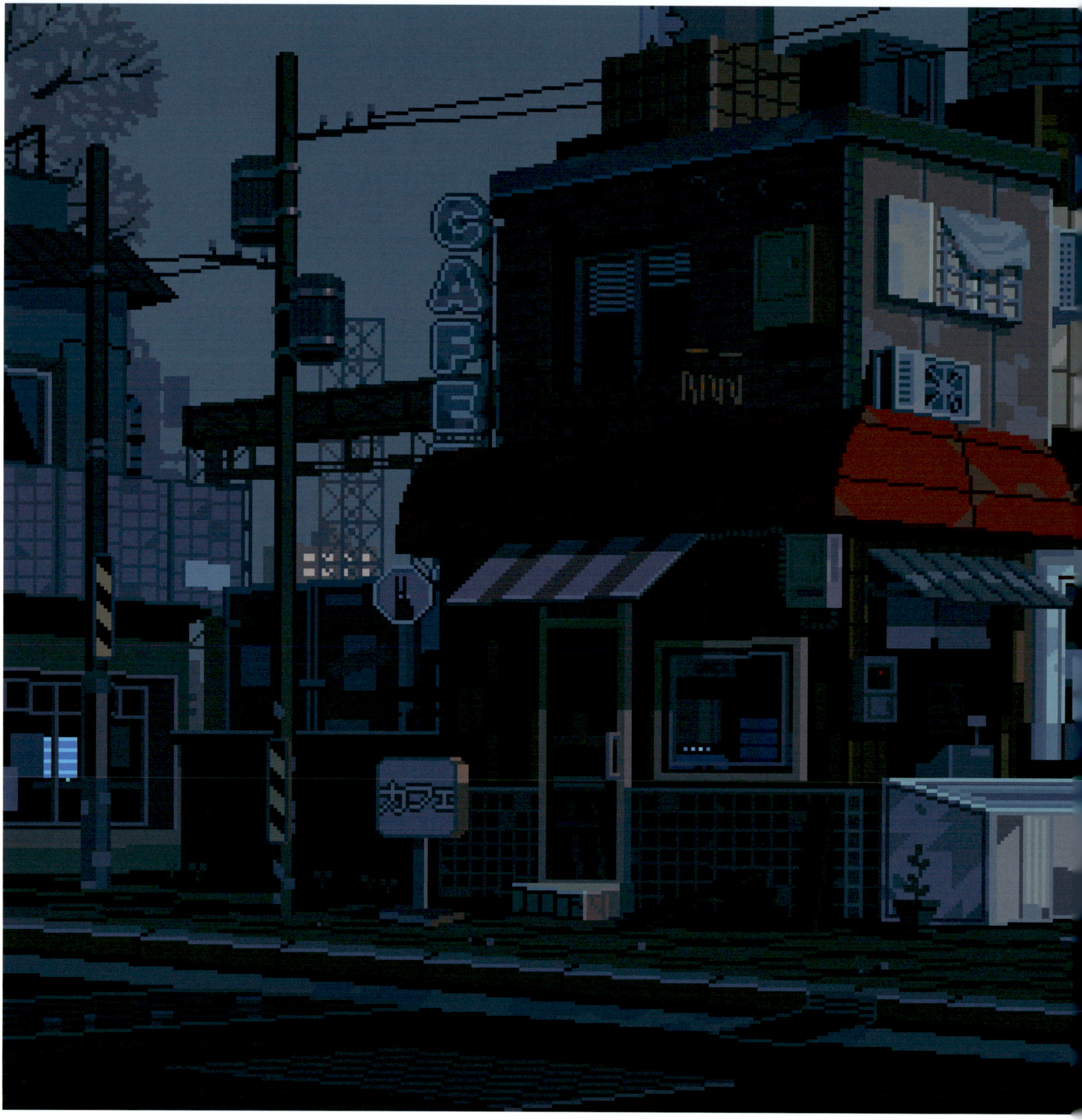

16:32 (Blue version), 25/11/2018, 600×300px

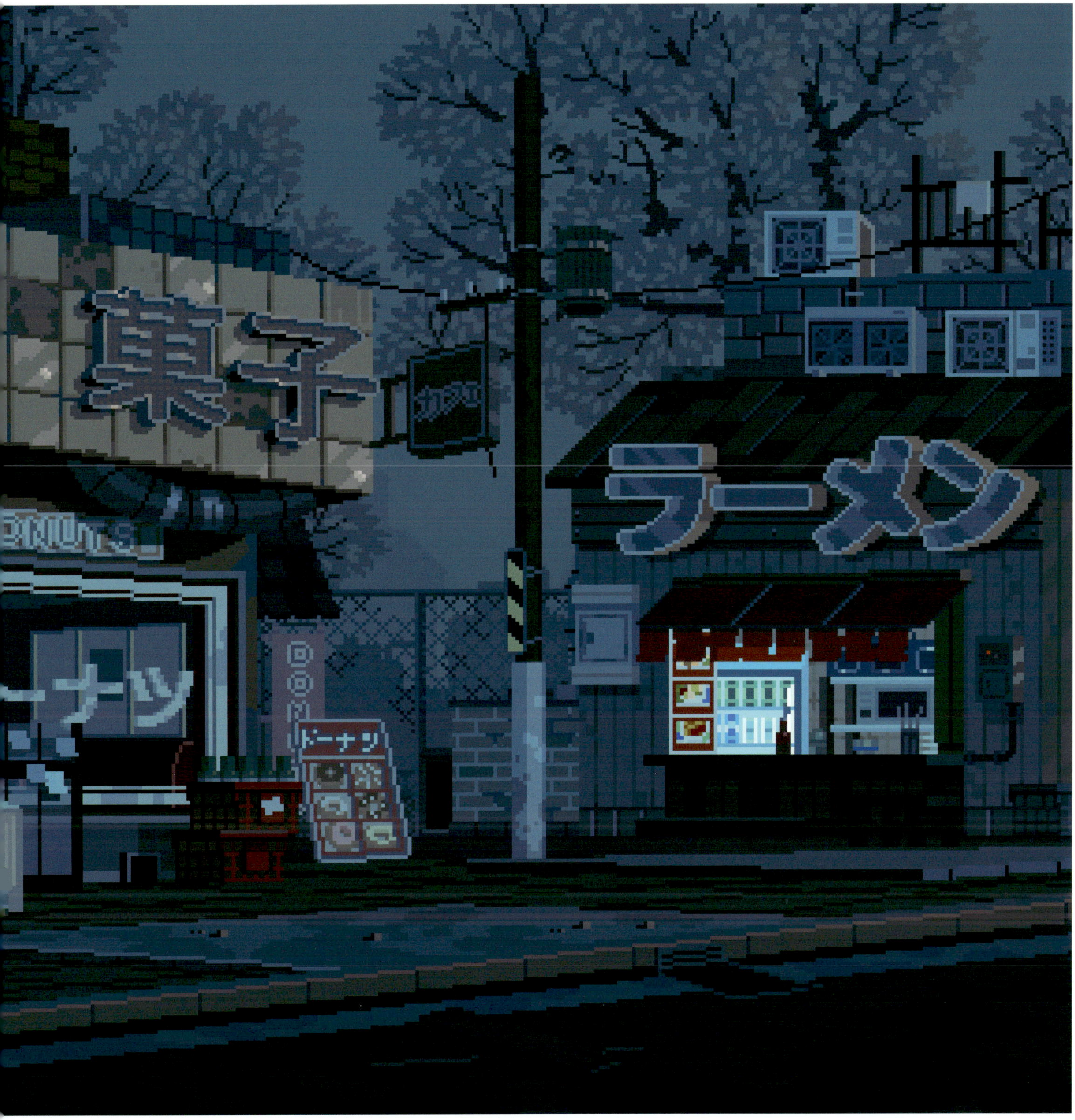
菓子
ラーメン
ドーナツ

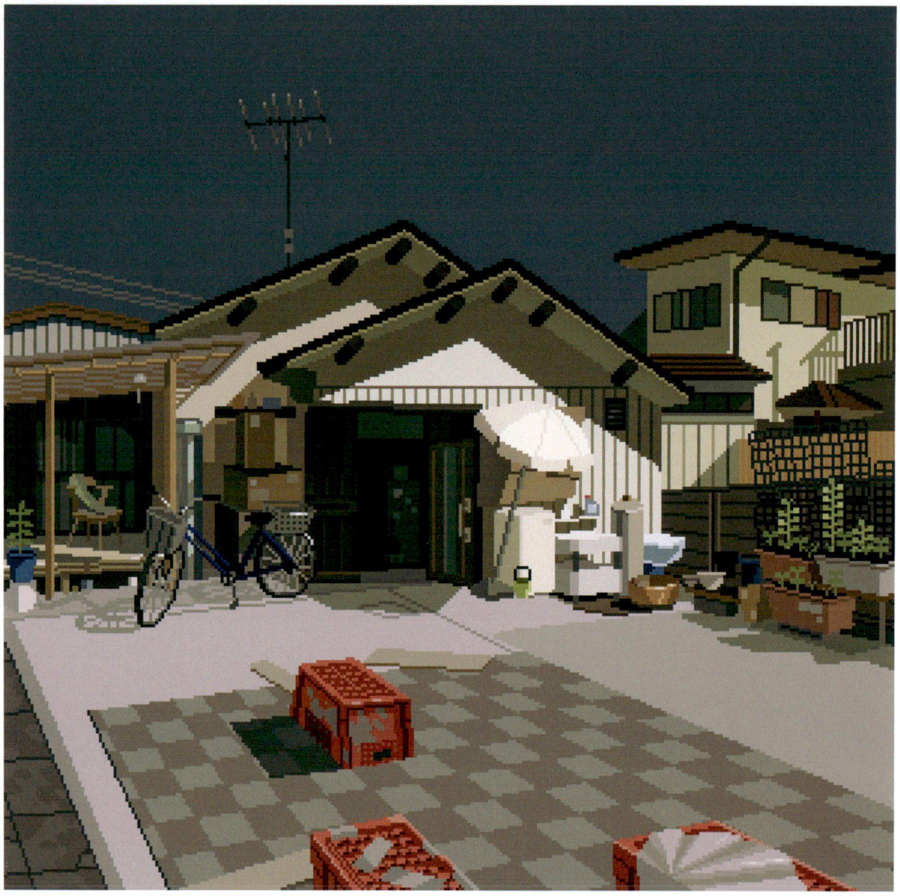

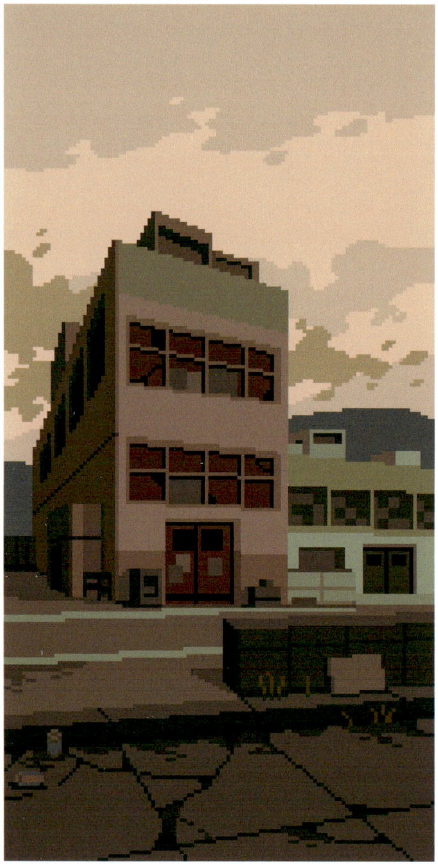

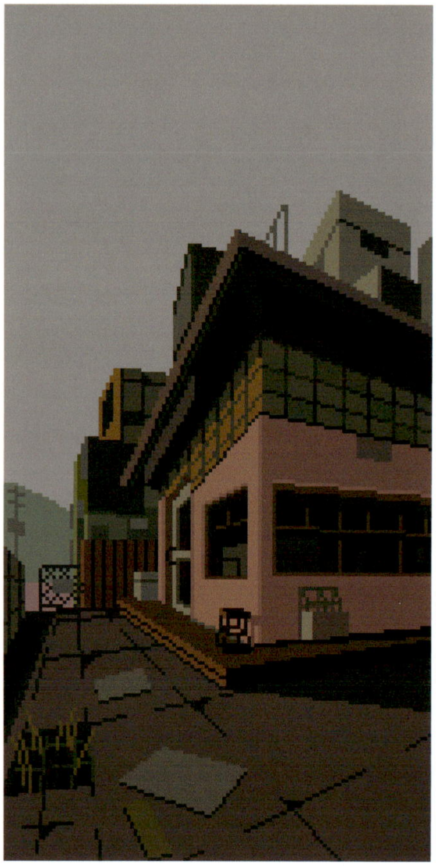

Top: *35.5619289, 139.328367*, 24/12/2018, 300×300px
Above left: *Untitled*, 23/09/2019, 120×240px
Above right: *Untitled*, 22/09/2019, 120×240px

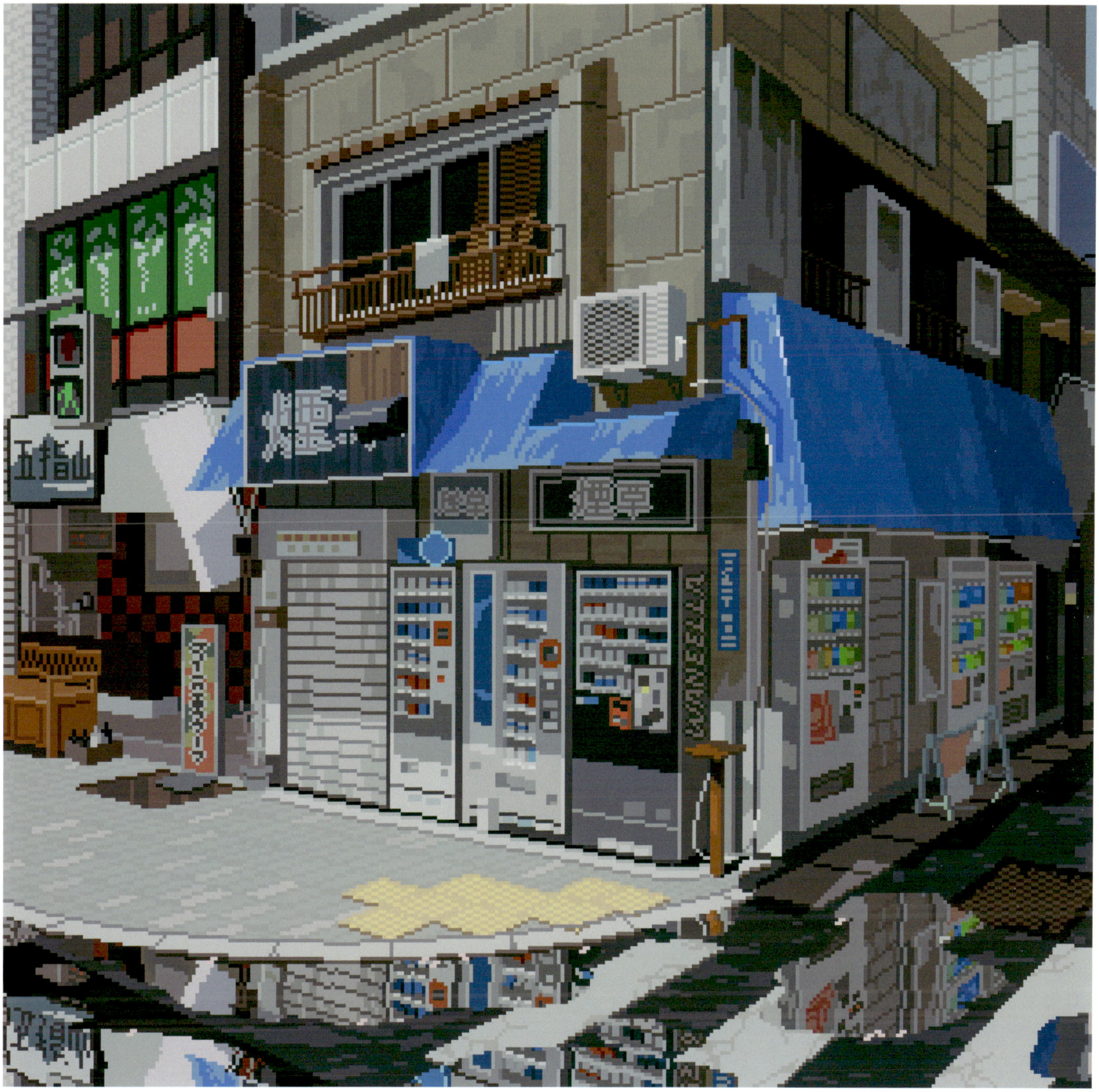

35.6913217, 139.7672178, 27/10/2018, 300×300px

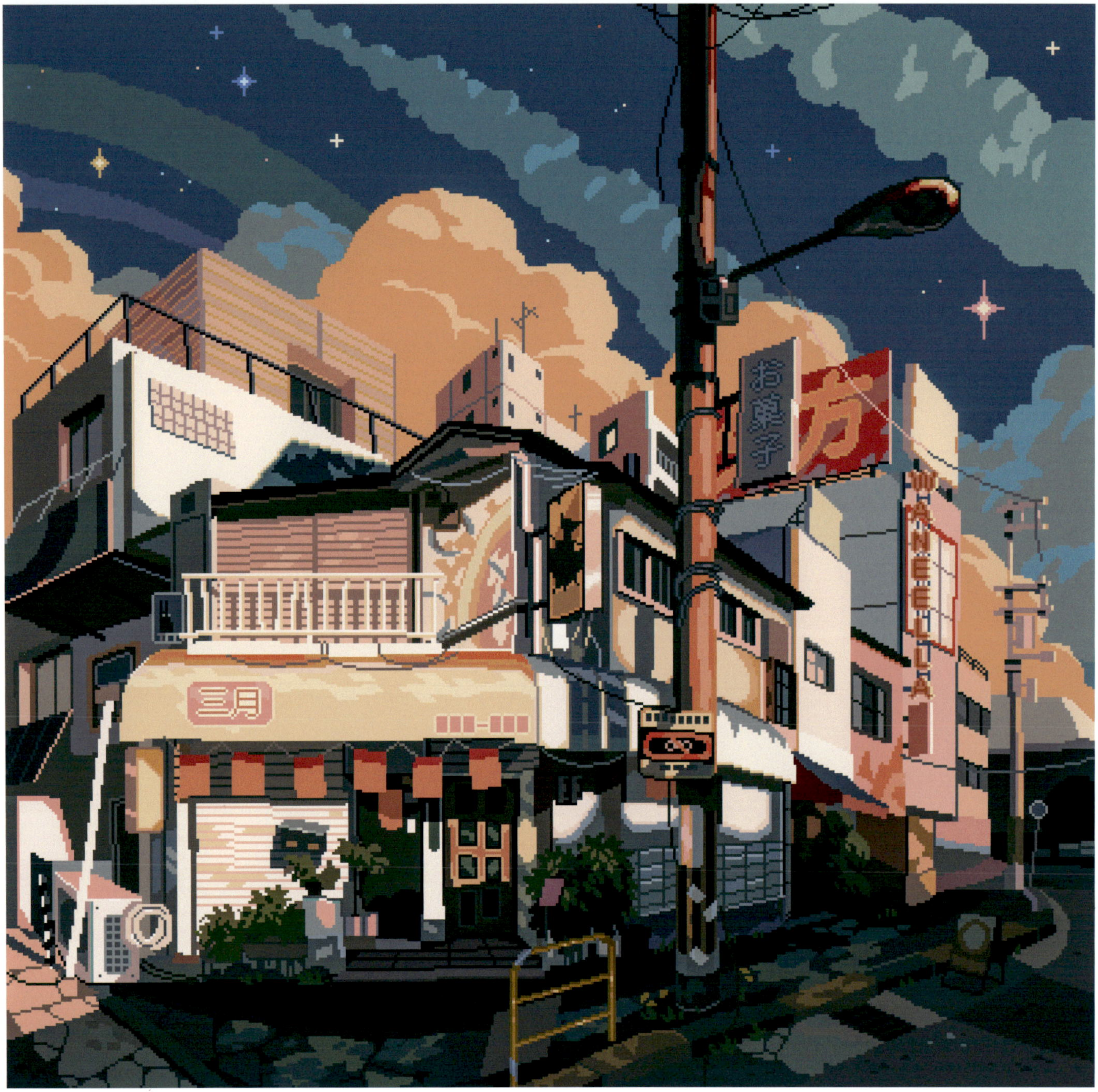

34.6716019, 135.4612272, 21/03/2019, 400×400px

PROCESS

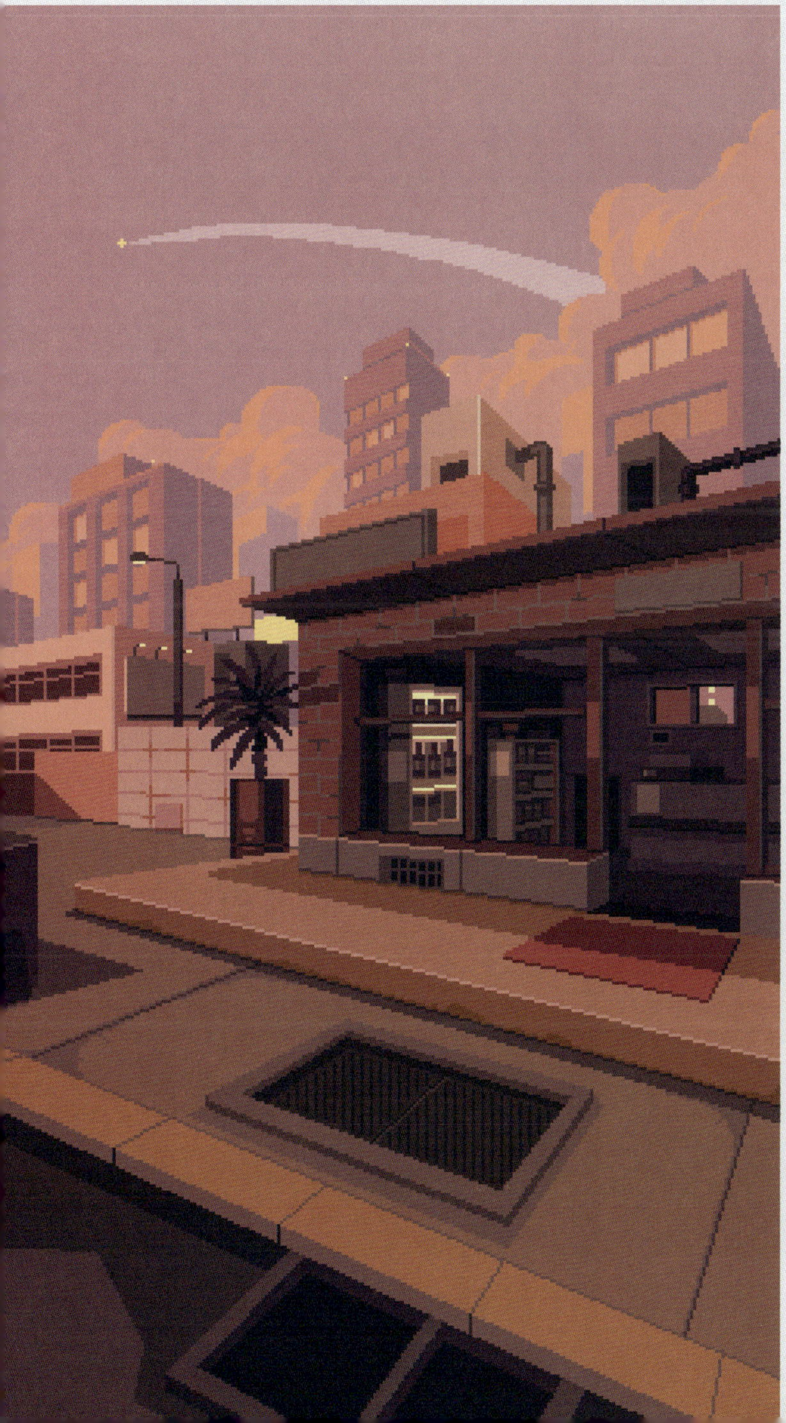

↓ For this image, I first drew a room with the lighting I thought I'd use. It would be the hideaway of a serial killer… or possibly of someone trying to solve a mystery because something bad had happened to them. I sketched the main composition to get a better understanding of what was going on.

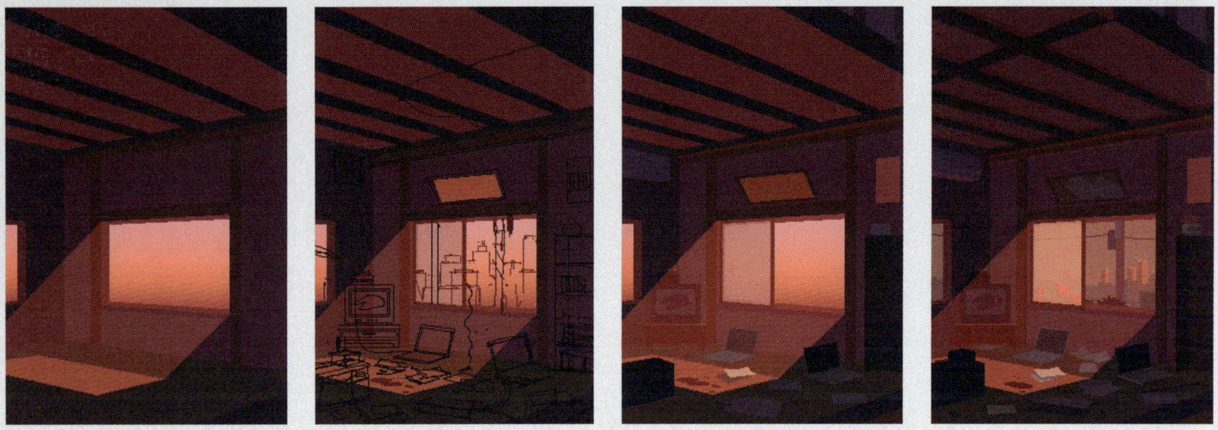

↓ There's a blood stain on the floor – the key to the storytelling. When the rough sketch was done, the easiest next step was to draw all the objects in colour. I rarely know what items I want to include before I start a piece, so I coloured what I already had, then added a bottle, noodle bowls and so on.

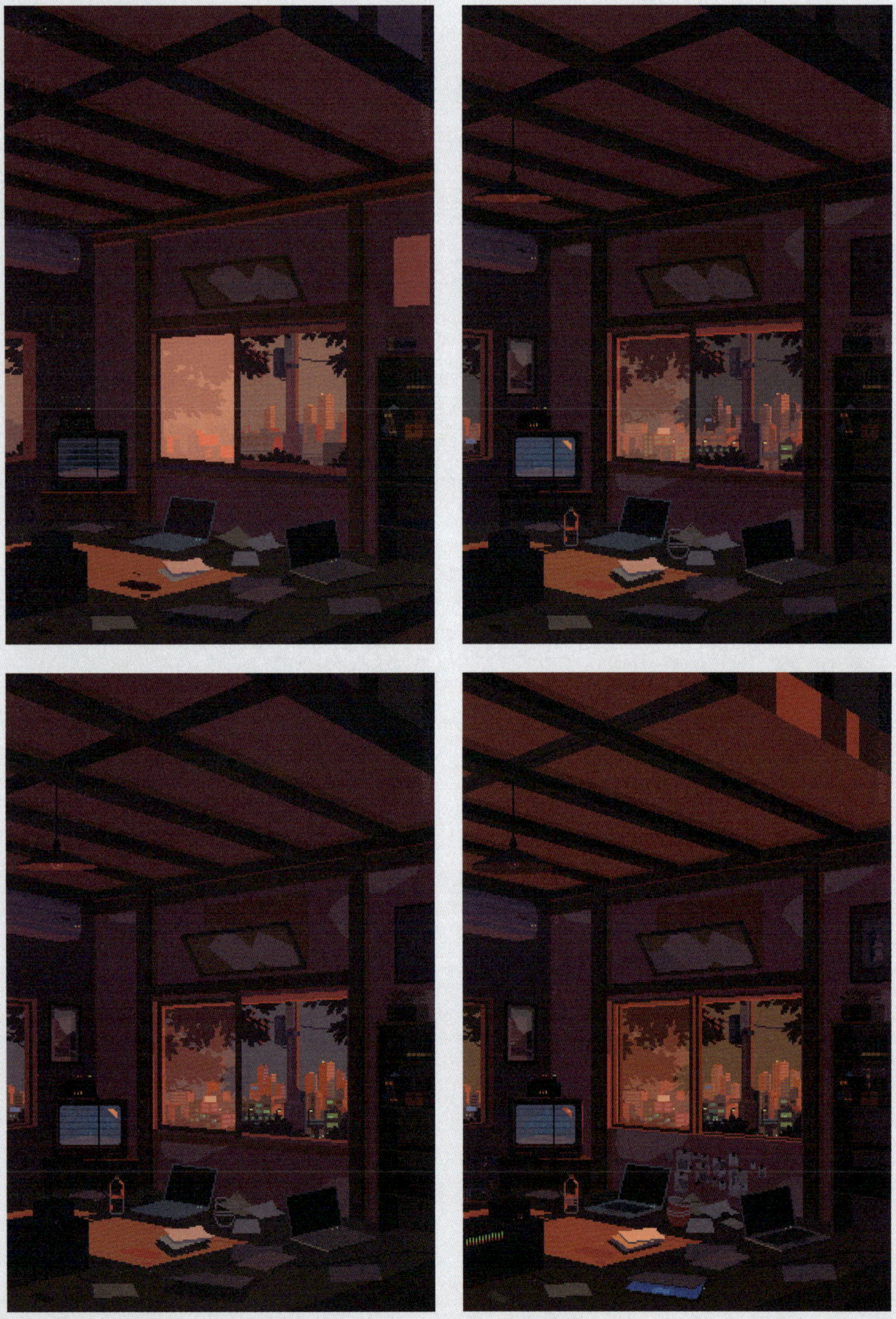

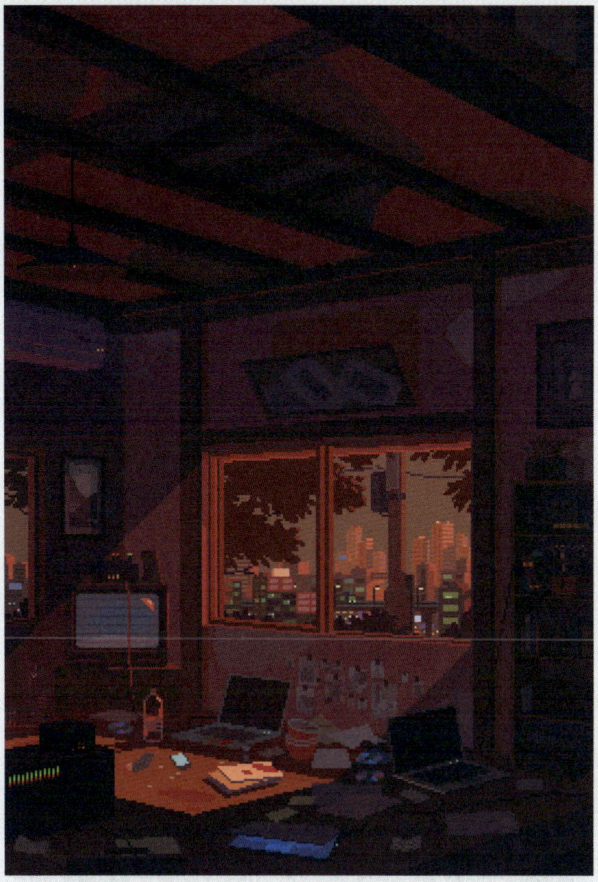
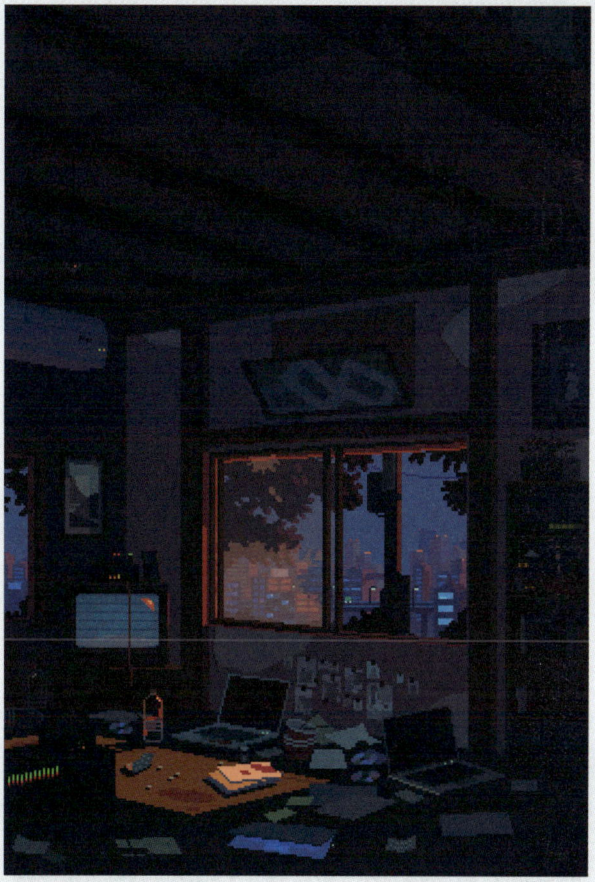

↑ Back when I made this image, I experimented with colour correction a lot. I used Photoshop's Curves tool – allowing changes to colour, brightness, contrast or transparency – which I first discovered as a teenager for editing photos. I really like this approach because it means you can efficiently check other possibilities in order to unlock the image's potential.

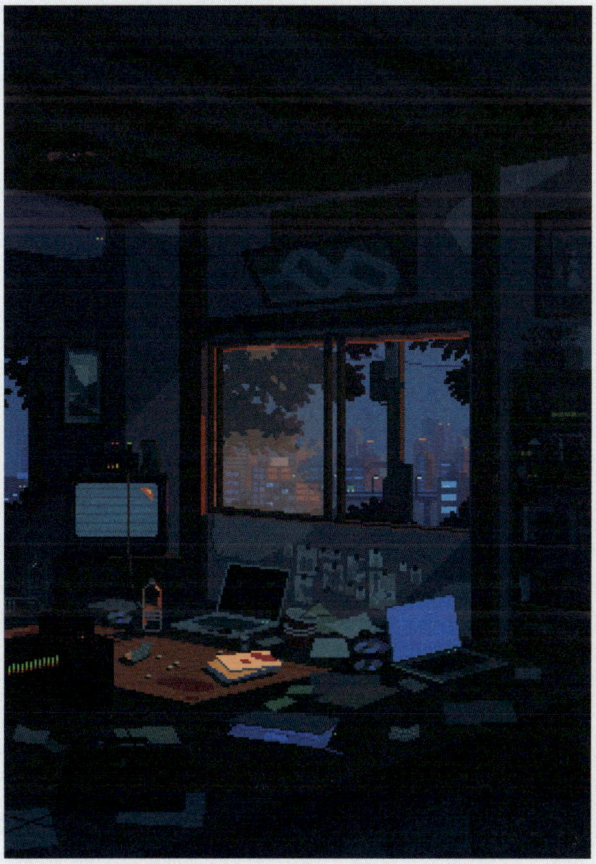
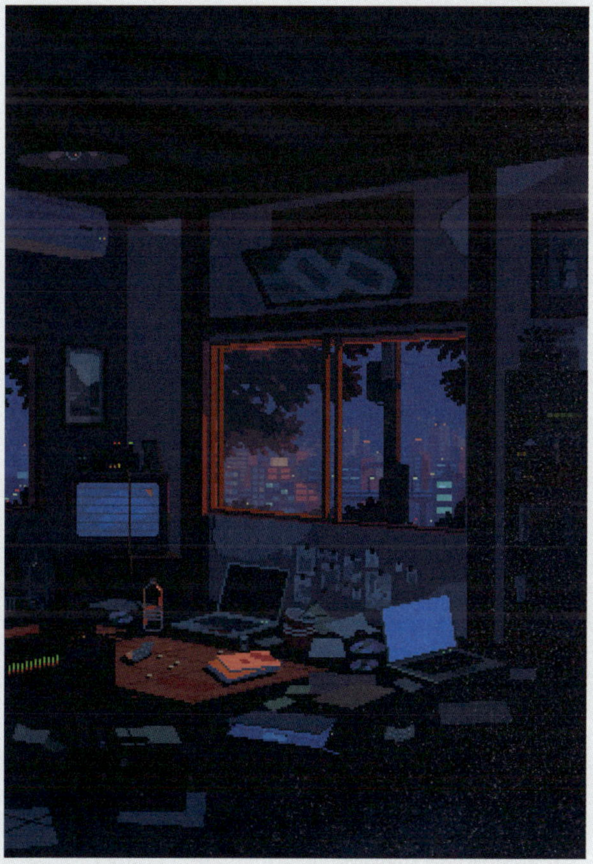

↑ Even though the red and pink sunset colours worked really well, I needed to make the scene simultaneously more dramatic and more serene; less joyful, less bright. This change in tone also helped highlight the main areas and make the illustration more poignant. But I still like the soft sunset version.

↓ I usually start an illustration by setting the perspective grid to get a feeling of the space I'm about to fill. Next, I sketch everything that comes to mind. When drawing cityscapes, it's also useful to choose the sky colour early on, since this will affect the whole drawing.

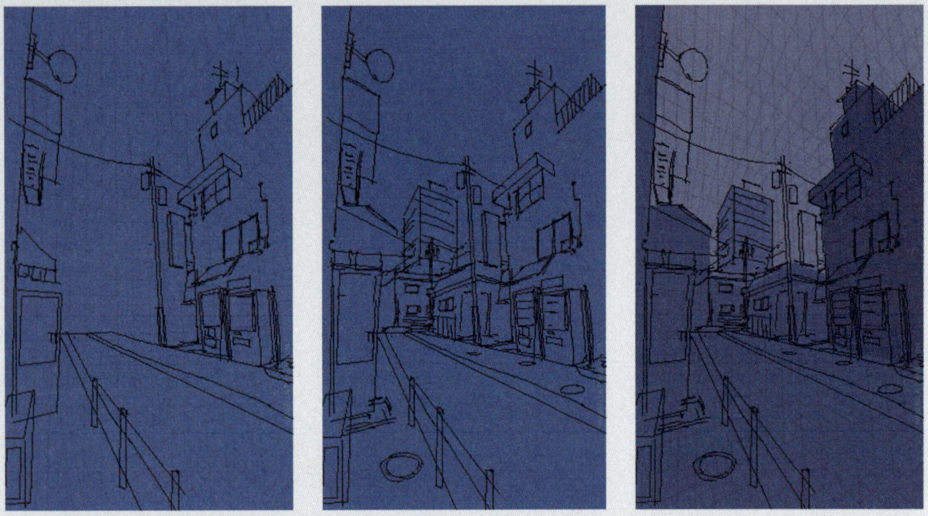

↓ At this stage, I usually start telling myself that if I just colour in all the things I've already sketched, it might be enough to finish the illustration!

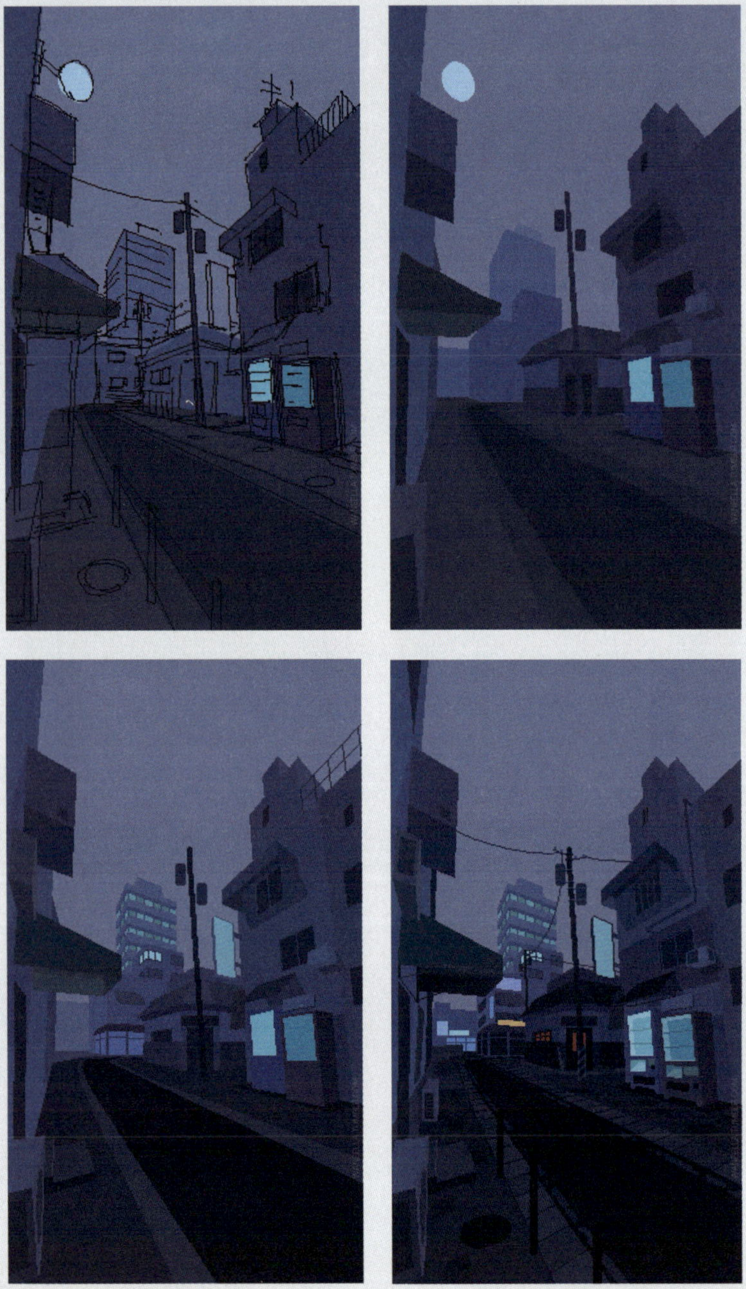

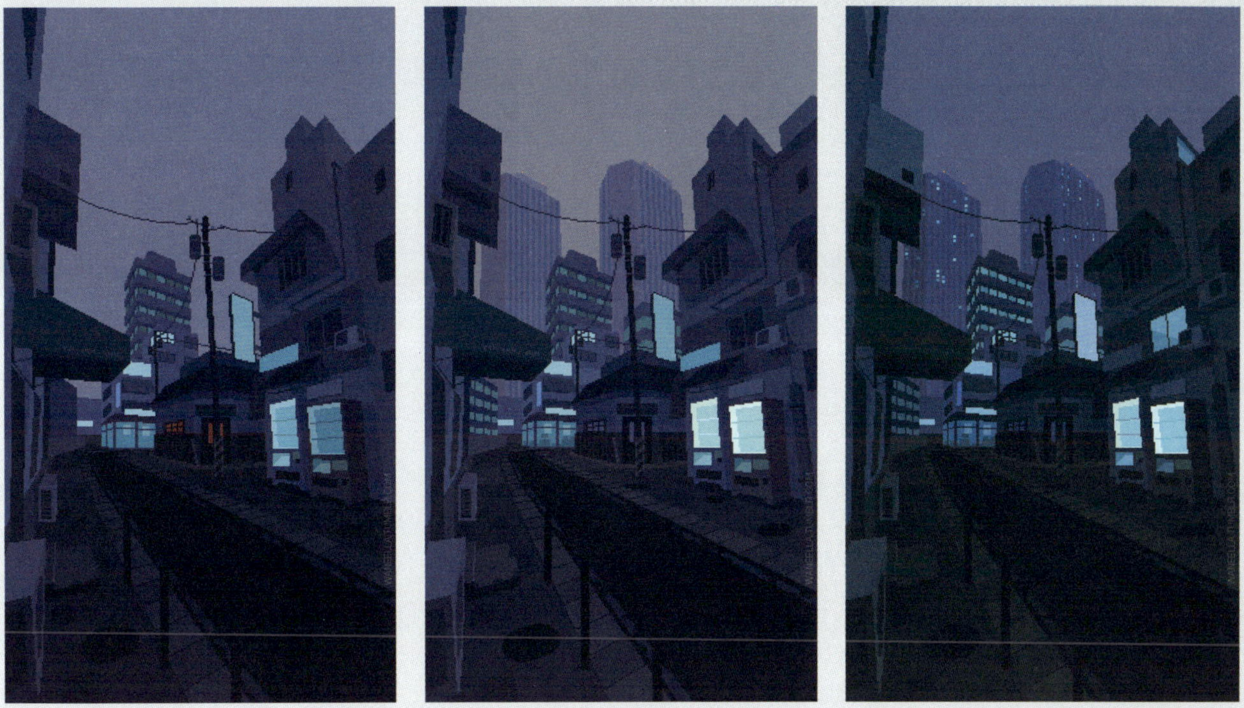

↑ I really wanted to give this illustration the vibe of a small, cozy neighbourhood, surrounded by a huge Tokyo-like megalopolis, but after I'd drawn the two huge office buildings in the background to represent Downtown, I got stuck. I just couldn't find a way to finish this illustration without making it look too monotonously blue!

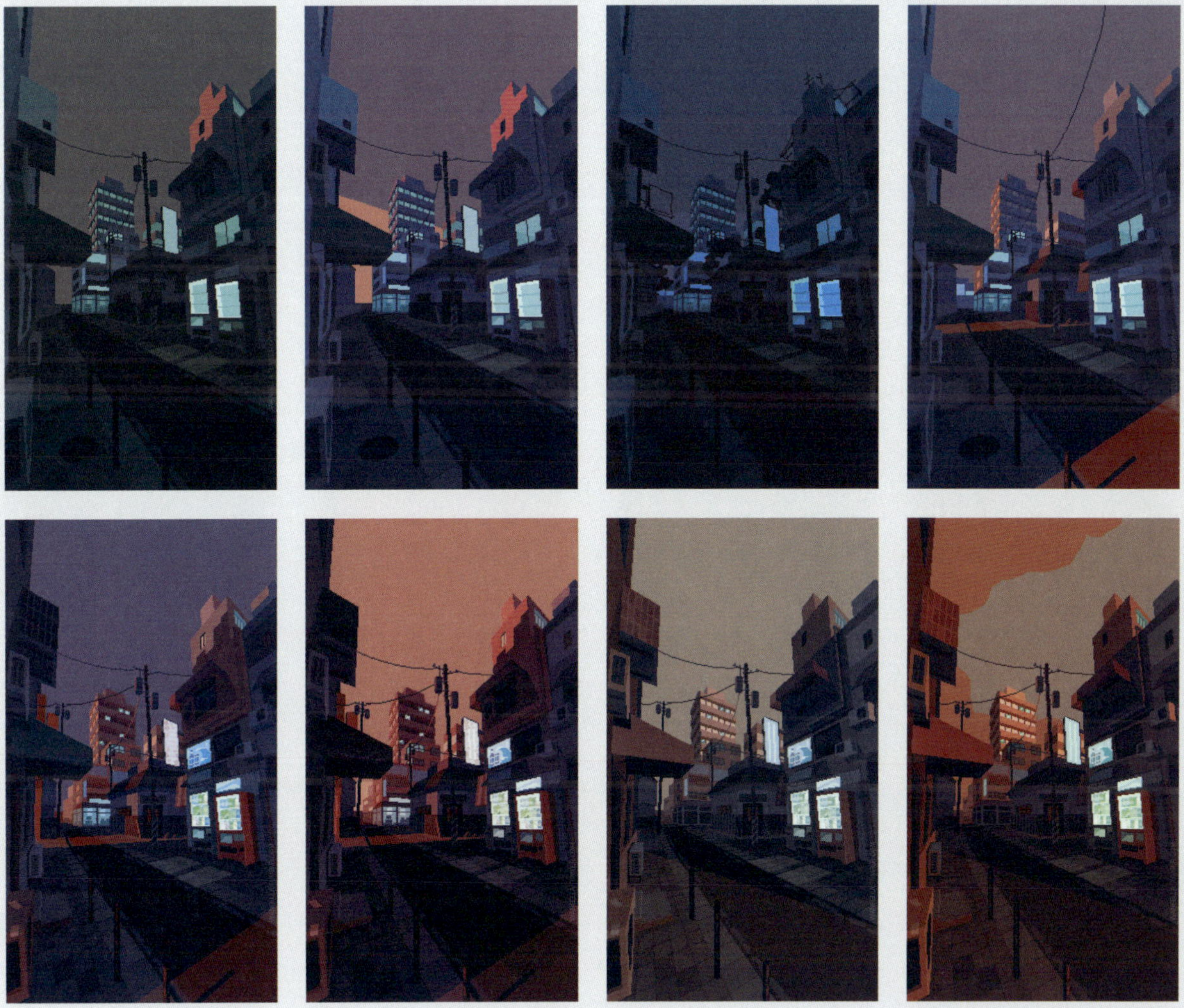

↑ I started to search for ways to escape this trap of my own making. I added evening sunlight falling from one side, then from another. Next, I made the sky a warm peach tone, before reimagining the whole image in autumn colours. Piece by piece, I made elements more vivid, then less contrasting, until I finally began to feel something from the image.

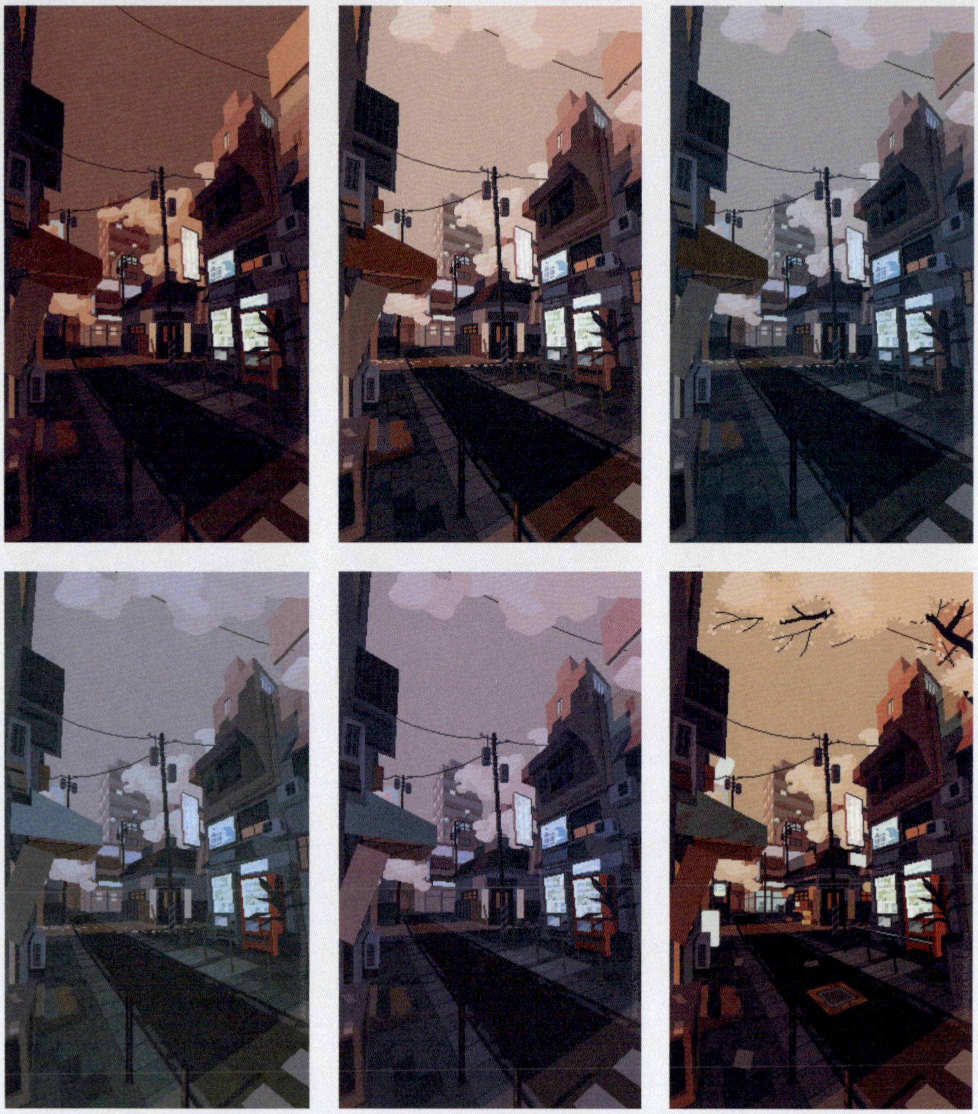

↑ At some point, I understood the need to add some extra elements to the scene in order to make this illustration work – something that would give me a lead in terms of which colours I should be using. This time, the breakthrough came after I had added a blossoming *sakura* tree.

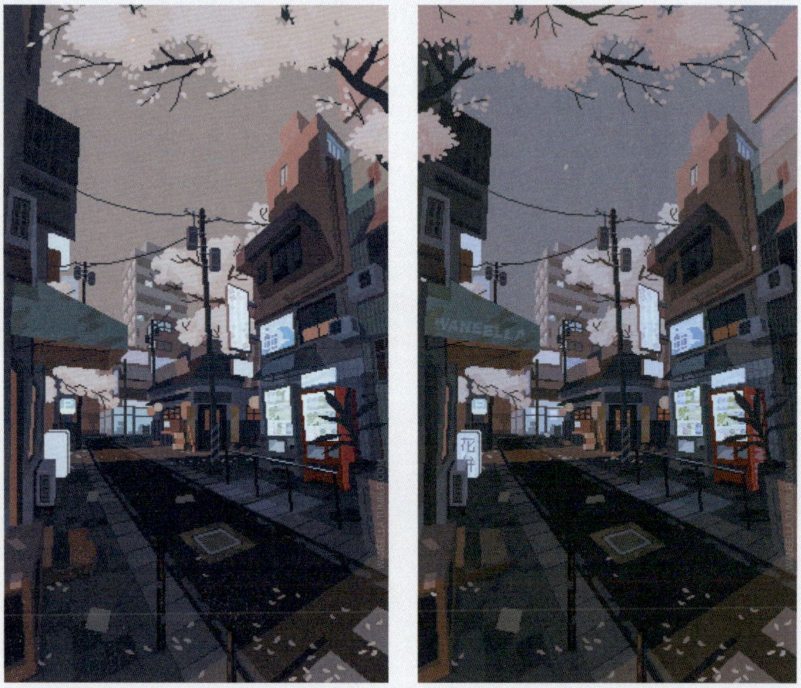

↑ However, I didn't want the scene to look too 'sweet' – I wanted to convey the feeling that it was fading away, like a kind of mirage or dream. I added some petals, and the illustration was complete.

↓ Sometimes I use Google Street View for reference – it's a great way to practice drawing real places! I started this piece in the usual way, setting the perspective grid and making a sketch, before realizing that, since I had the detail of a real-life reference, I could skip much of the drawing and start colouring.

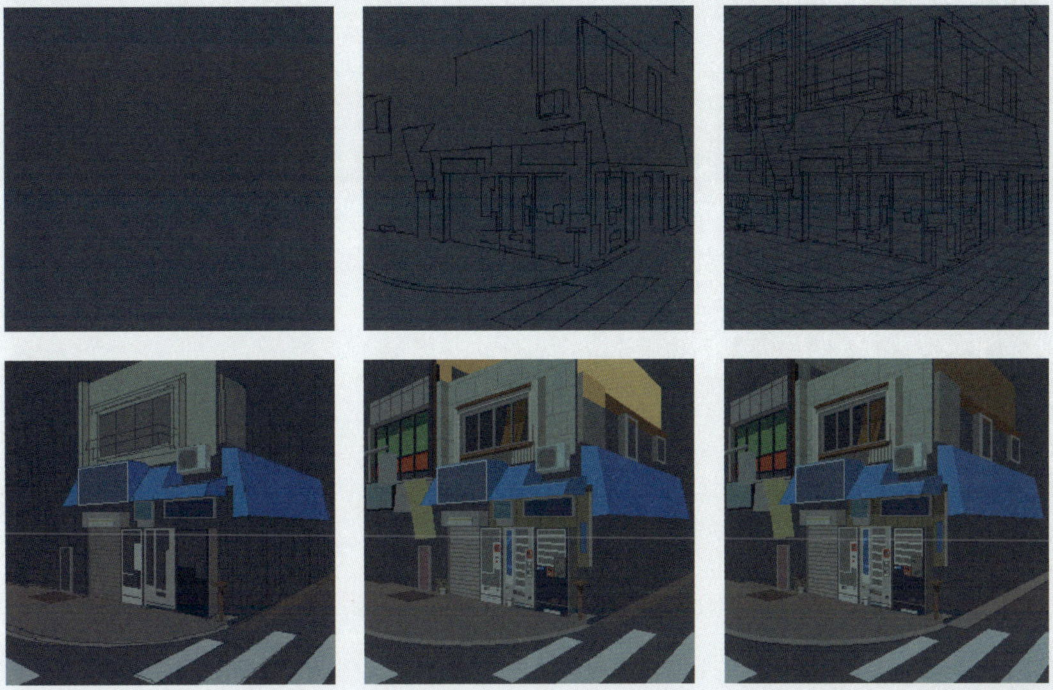

↓ Later on in the process, I started to worry that I was just redrawing an existing place, without adding anything of myself to the illustration. I tried altering the lighting and the time of day – to see if these changes would help get rid of my self-doubt.

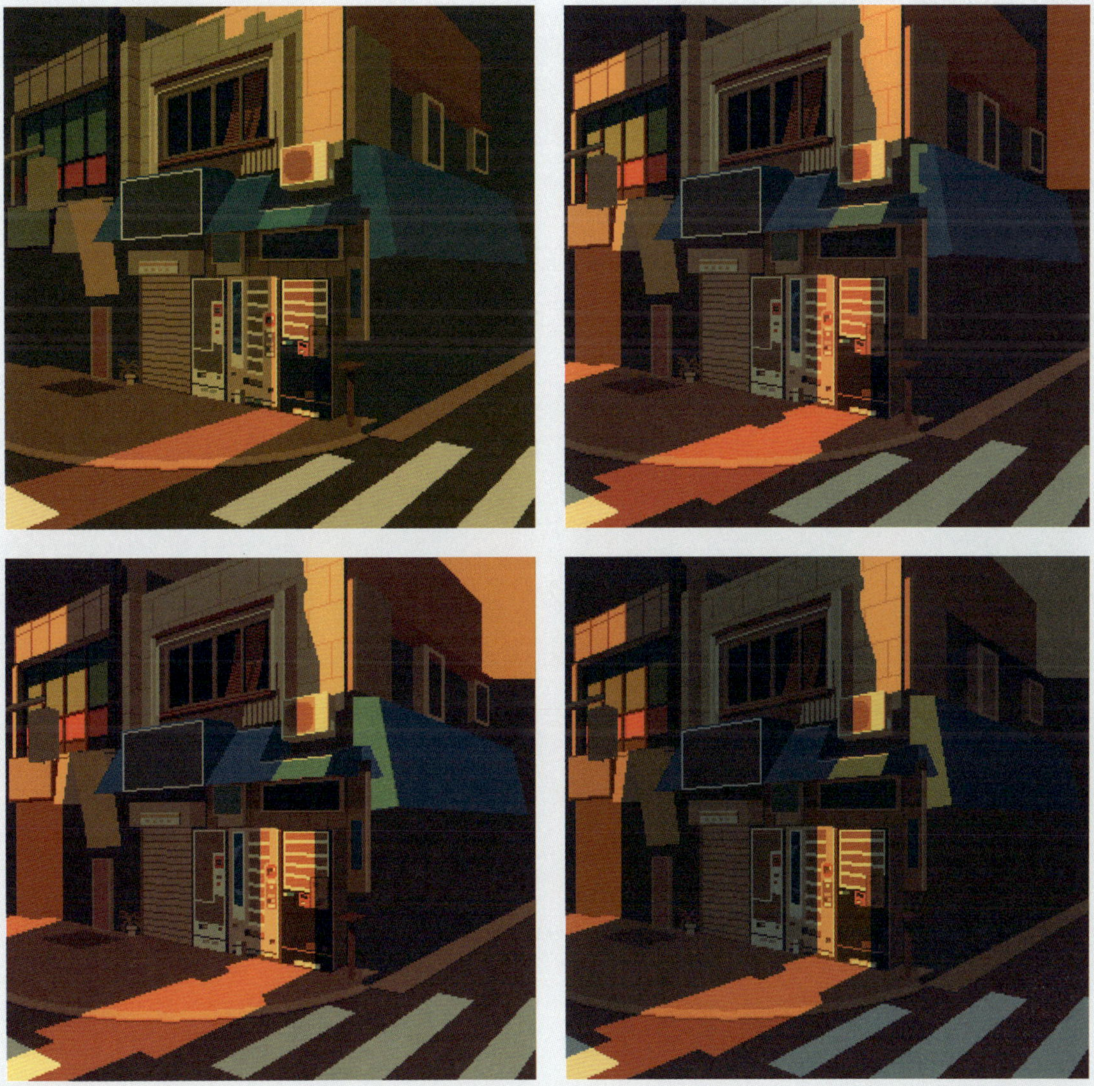

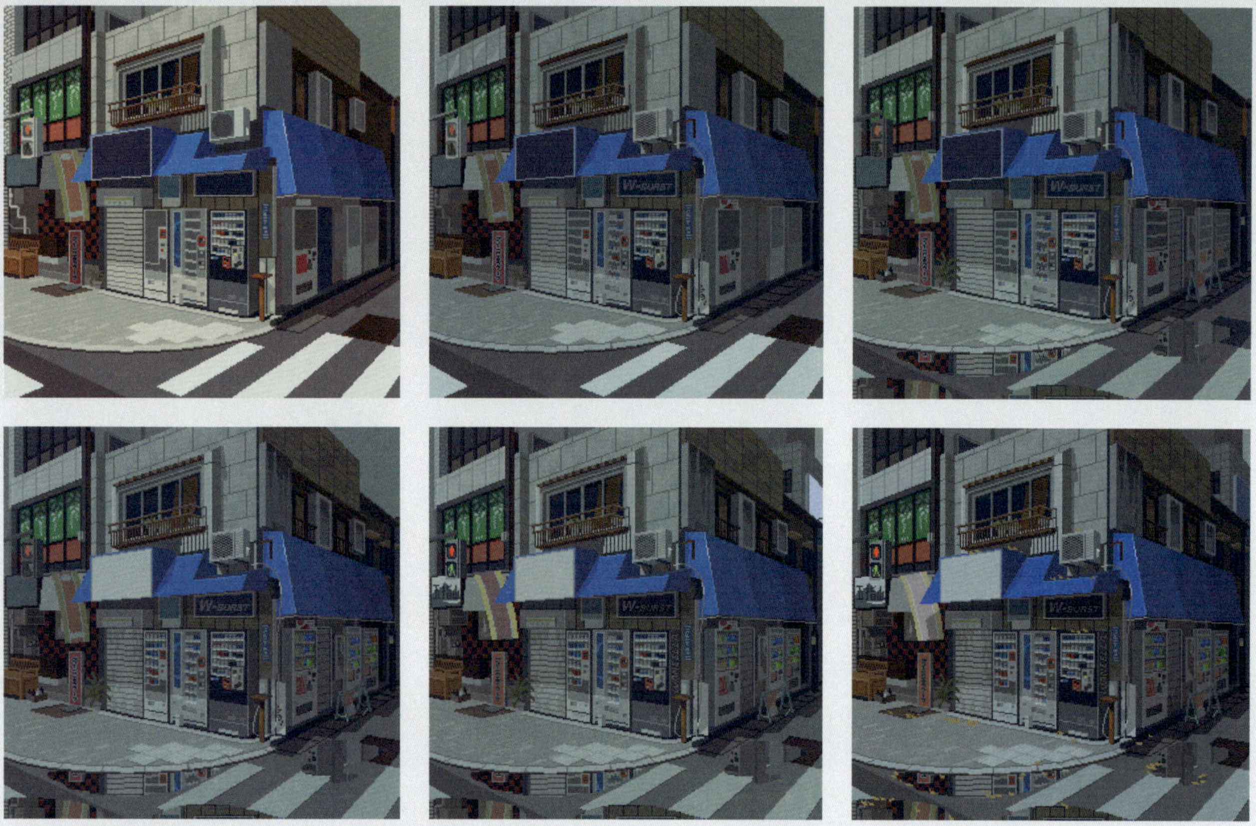

↑ Surprisingly, I decided I liked this corner the way I'd originally drawn it, since I rarely create scenes in daylight and thought it would look fresh and different compared to my other pieces. The only big change I made was to add puddles that I'd later animate, making the image come alive.

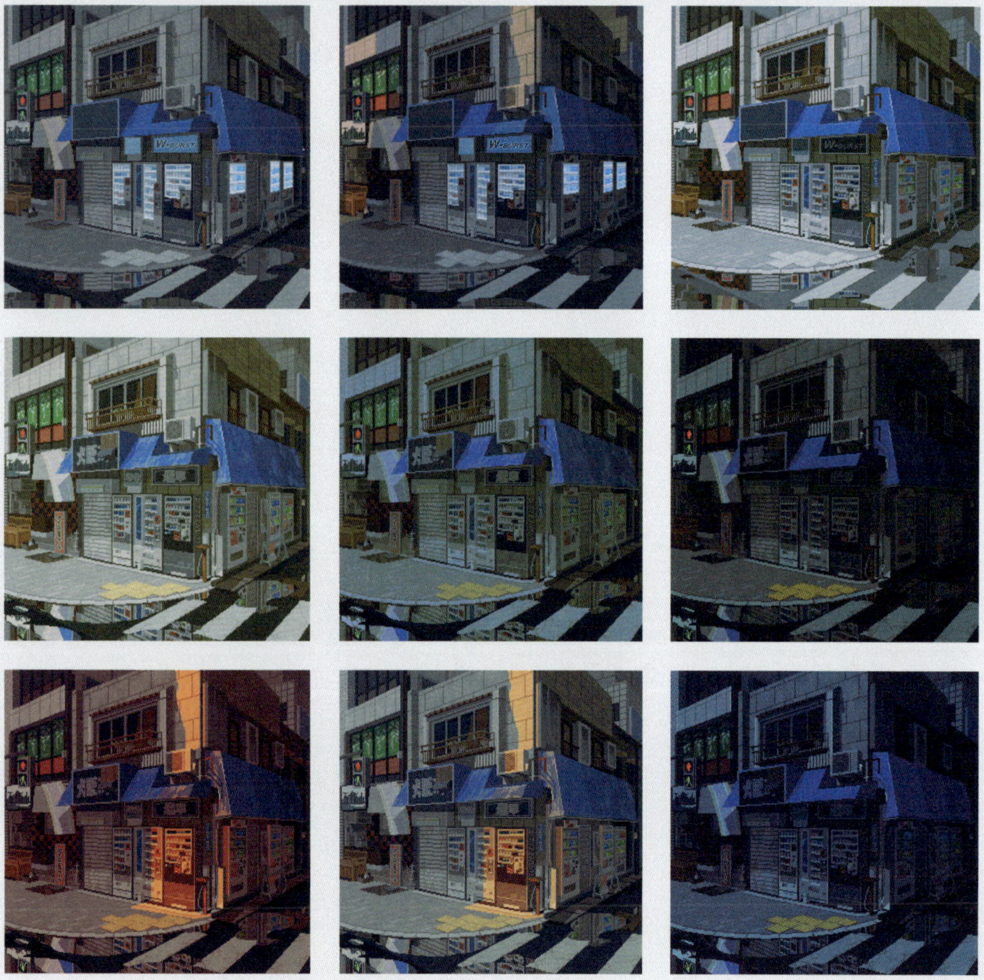

↑ Of course, I still felt the same old insecurities about whether I had made the right decision. So I tried tweaking everything one last time, just in case a better solution revealed itself!

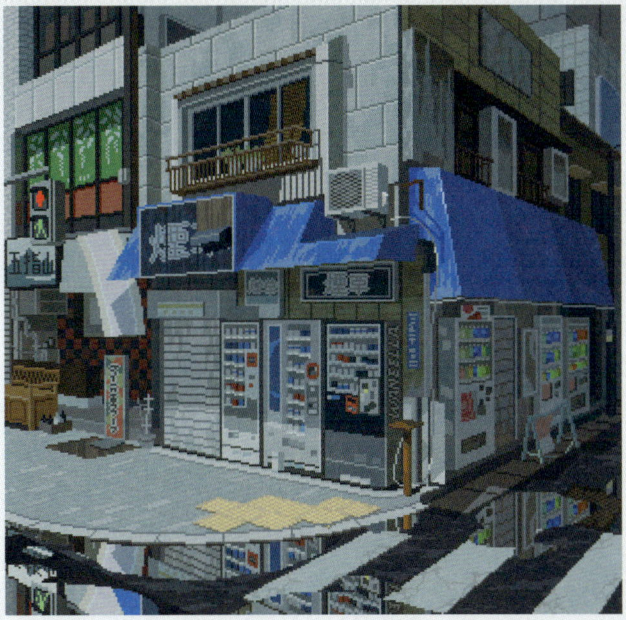

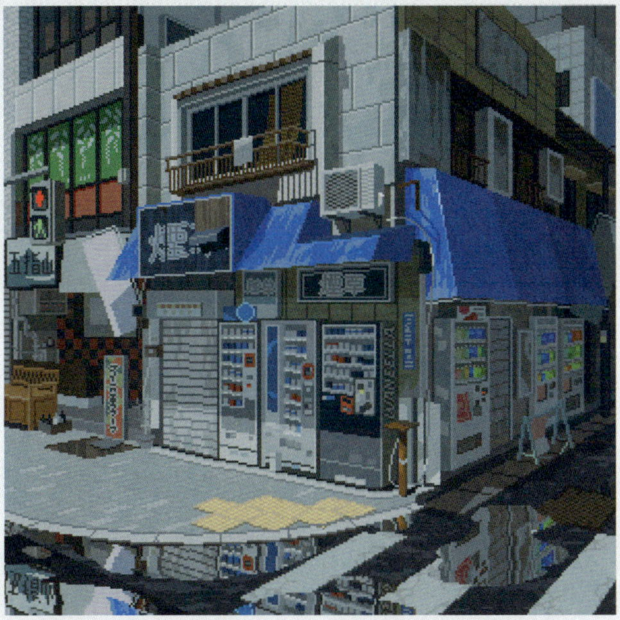

↑ At this stage, I started making the animation, which you can see in these images by the ripples on the puddles. I also changed the shape of the puddle on the right to place it more accurately on the same plane as the road surface.

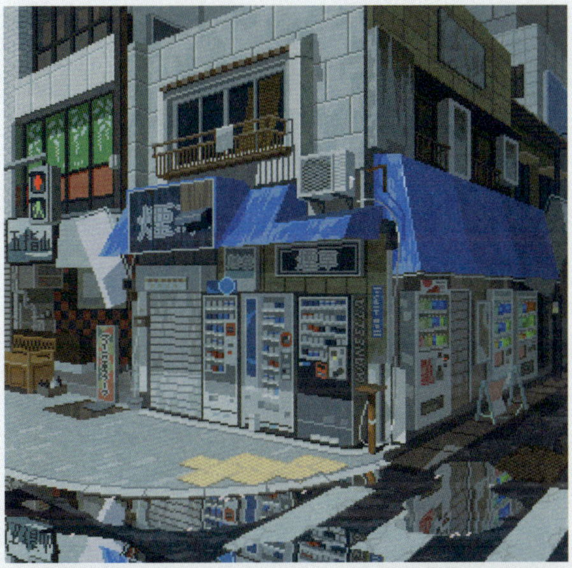

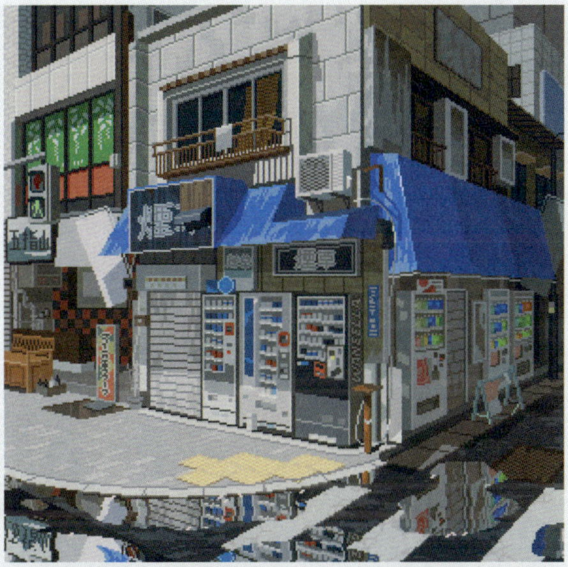

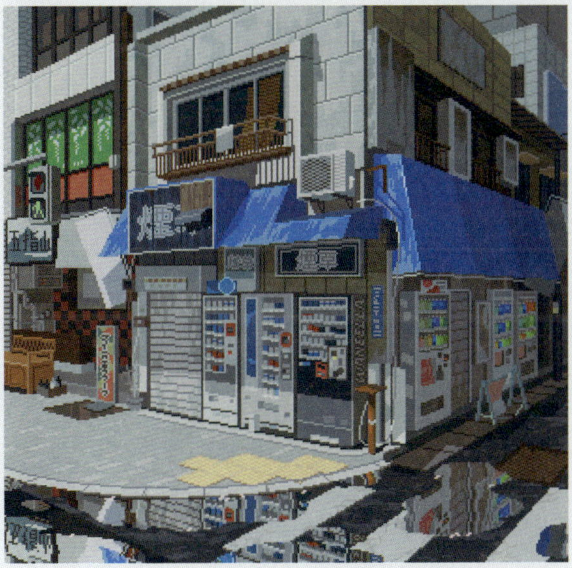

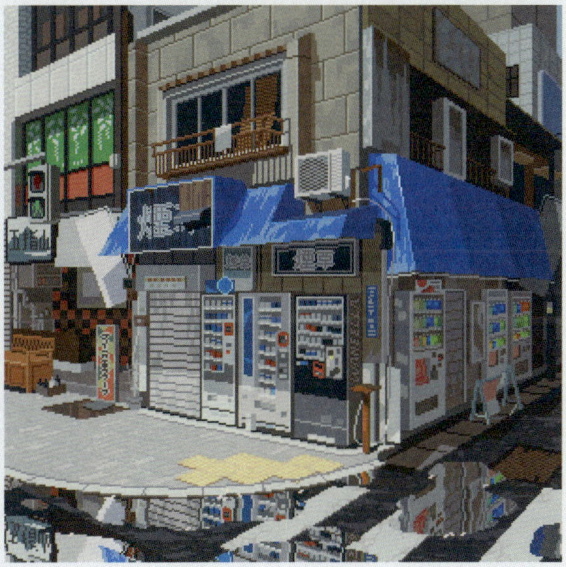

↑ One of the most difficult things for me to determine is the precise moment that each drawing is finished. Here, I wasn't happy with the top part of the right building because it felt too close to the colour of the pavement. When I made that darker and warmer, everything finally fell into place.

↓ Here, I asked my Patreon community to name two random items for me to draw. They chose a pineapple and a telephone. It was a great experiment – I discovered objects I'd never heard of before!

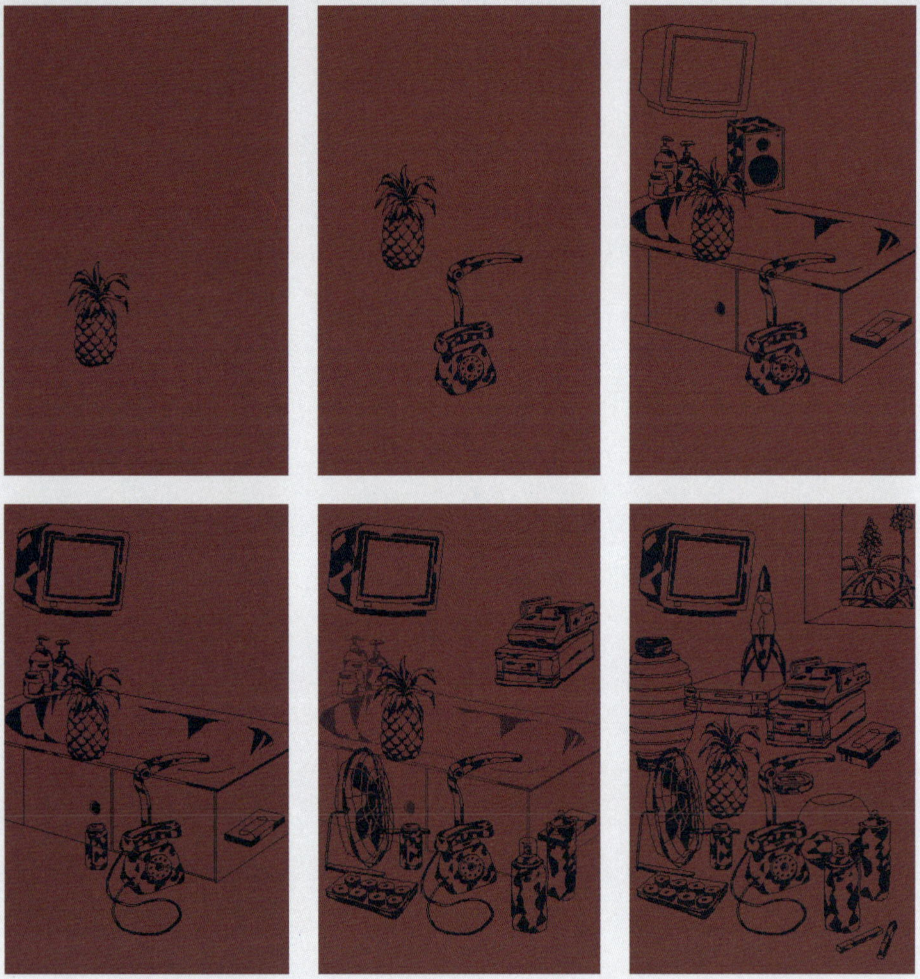

↓ I started with the two objects before even thinking about the setting. I also wanted to retain the line art, so I tried different methods of colouring to see which one worked the best.

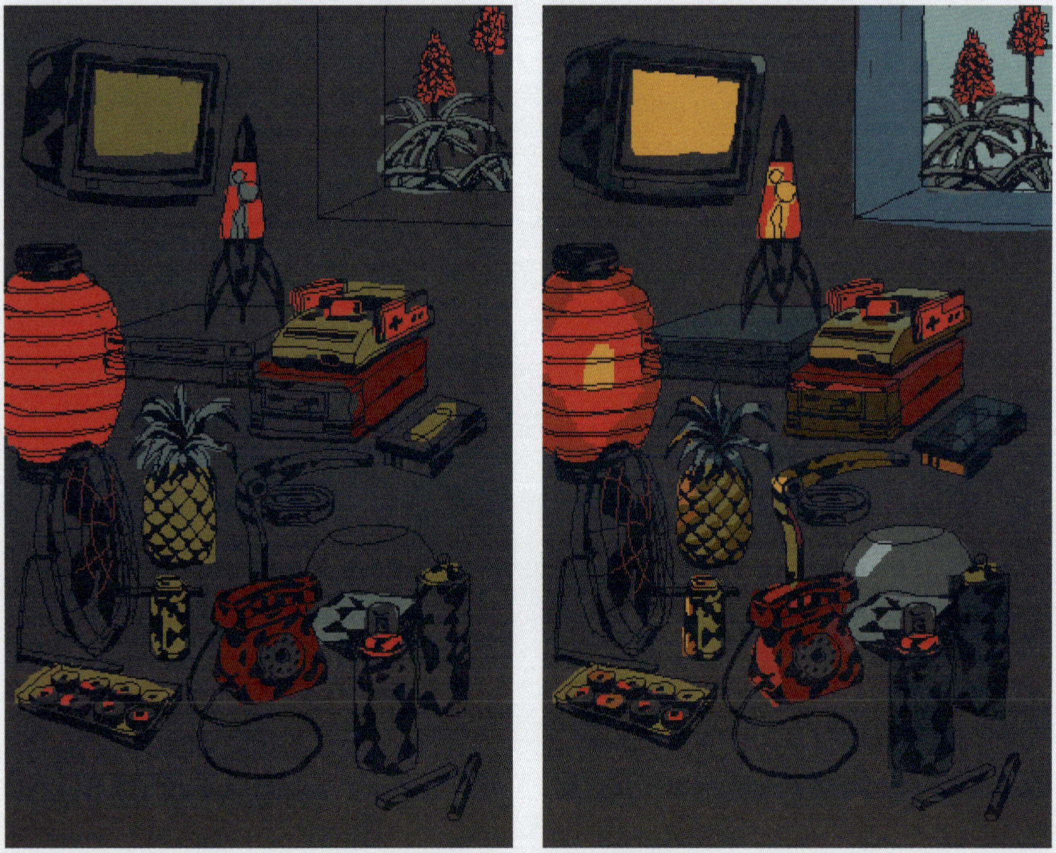

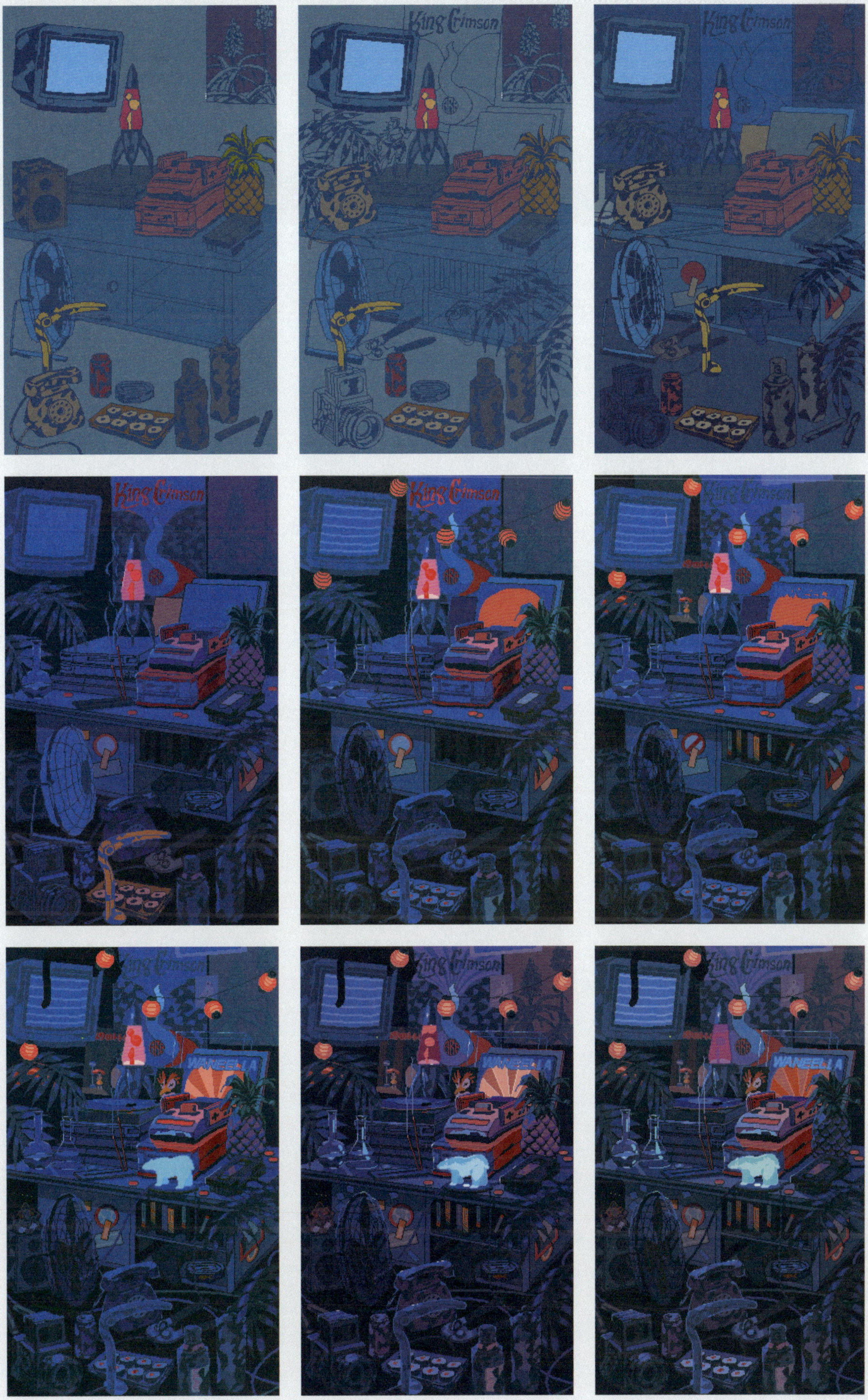

↑ After a few attempts, I understood that the drawing wouldn't feel complete until I made the line art a little less prominant. So I used it as the base for the contour lights, shadows and texture. Another interesting thing about this illustration is that I drew most of the objects on their own separate layers, meaning I was able to rearrange them painlessly once I found the best place for everything to go.

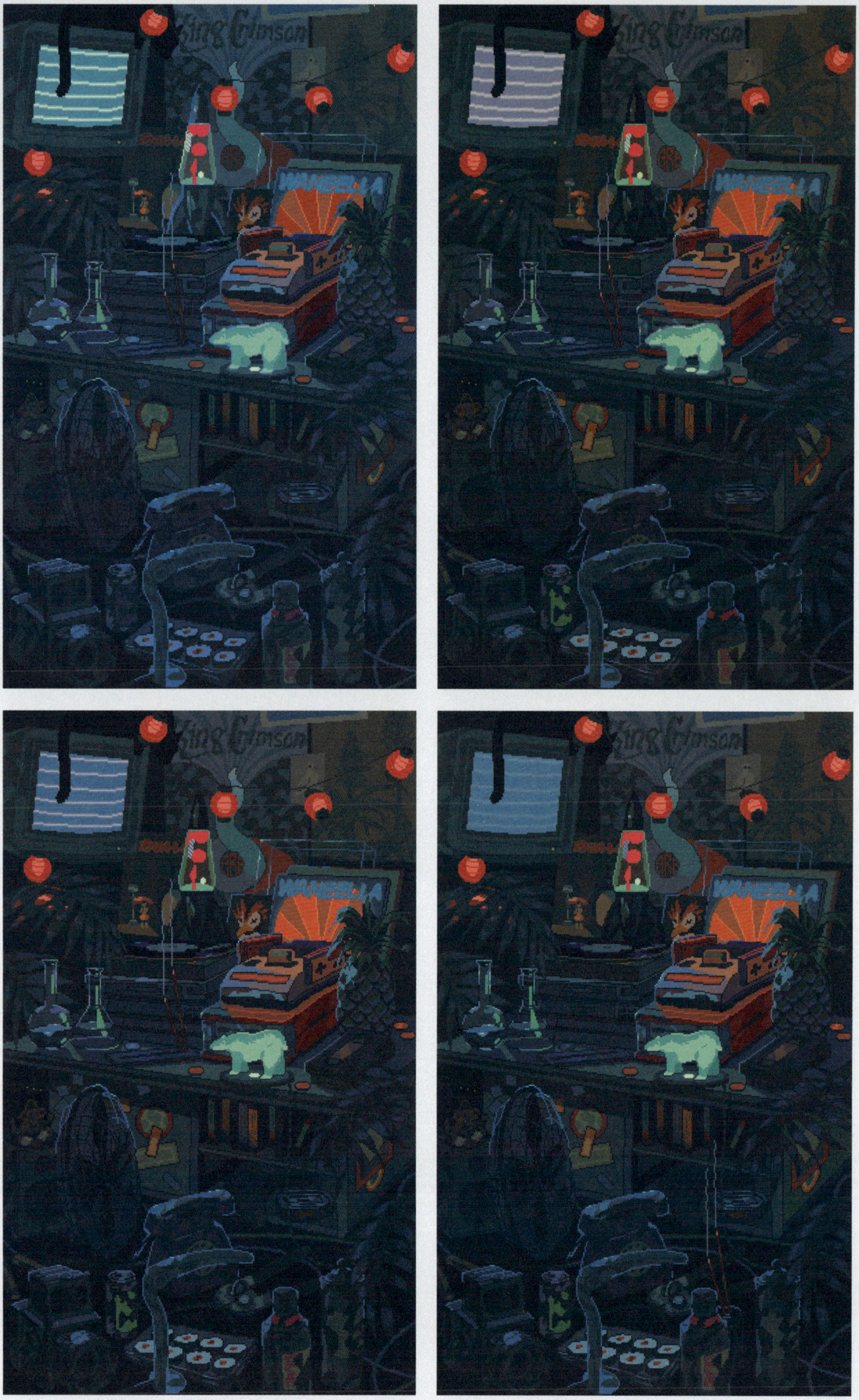

↑ After drawing everything in blue tones, I changed them all to deep greens. Then I thought too much was happening at the top, while the bottom section was boring, even with the animated fan. So I moved the incense sticks to the floor but after I'd posted it online, someone correctly noted that the smoke should be pushed sideways by the fan! I still wonder how I overlooked such an obvious detail.

↓ In this drawing, I continued my career-long quest to incorporate line art within my pixel art. I also wanted to make the scene more lively, which I did by drawing it without an initial perspective-locked sketch. I think it's noticeable that while the perspective is actually very conventional, some of the objects are really crooked due to them being done freestyle. But I was very pleased with the end result.

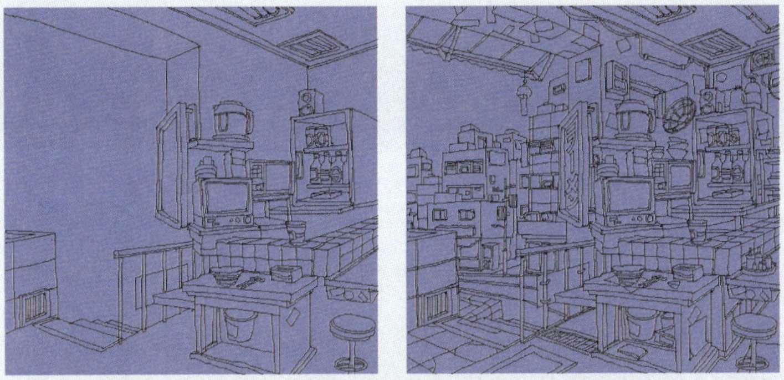

↓ I found it difficult to start colouring this illustration, since I had no clear idea of what the final scene should look like. Still undecided, I filled the scene with contrasting tones and began to try out different colour palettes.

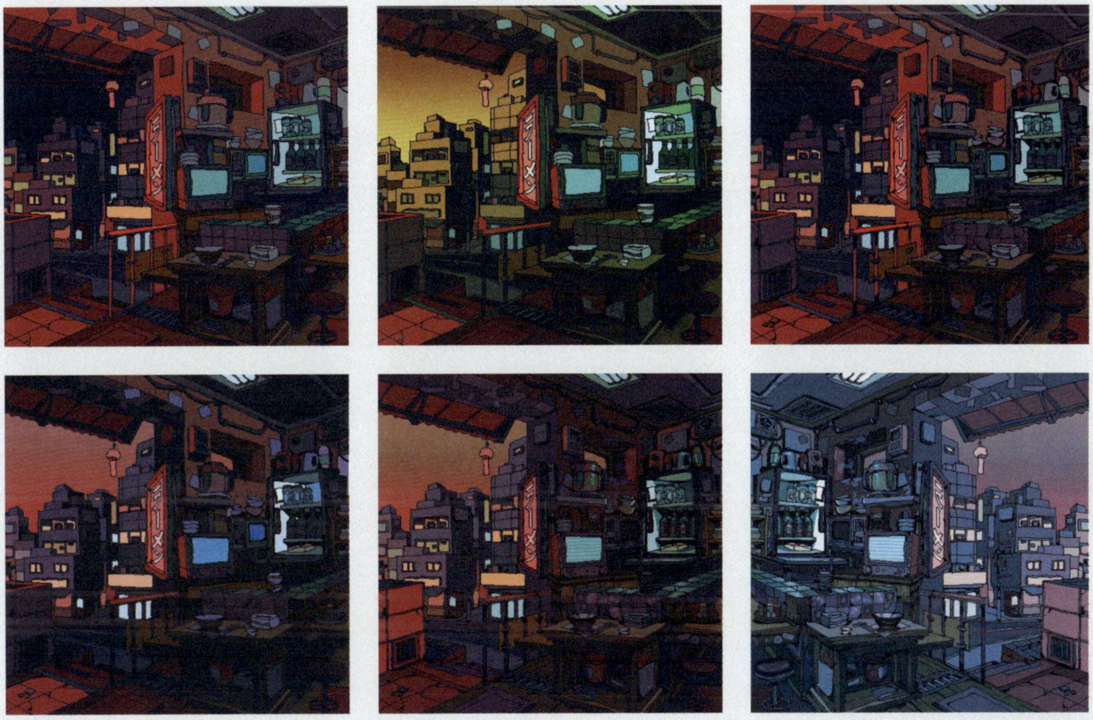

↓ While I was experimenting with all these different colours, I gradually added more detail to the drawing. The process went unexpectedly smoothly; I was both suprised and delighted at how the illustration was slowly revealing itself.

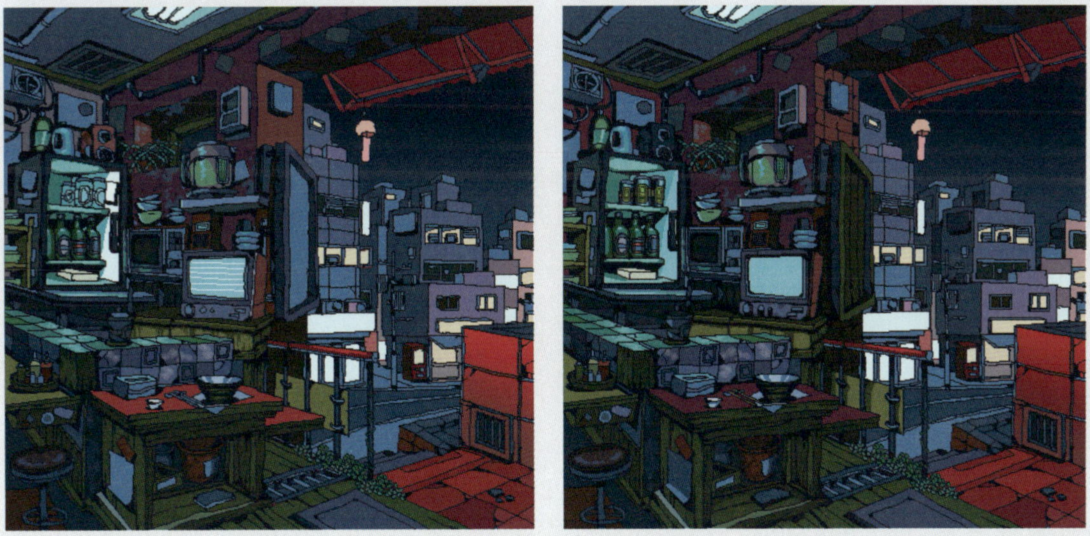

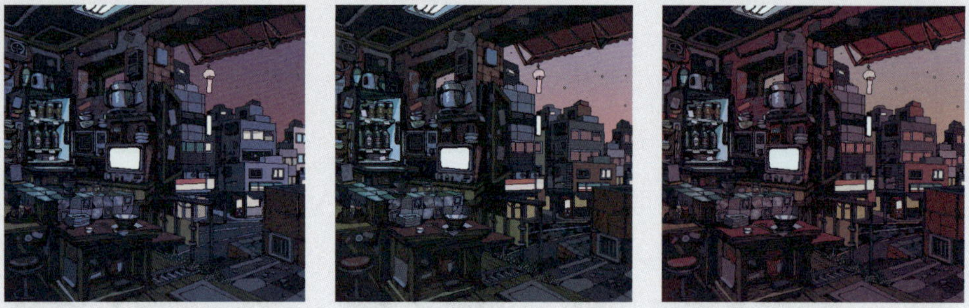

↑ At some stage, I always seem to worry that an illustration has become too dark and monotonous. This time, I tried changing the sky colours to make the mood lighter and more romantic.

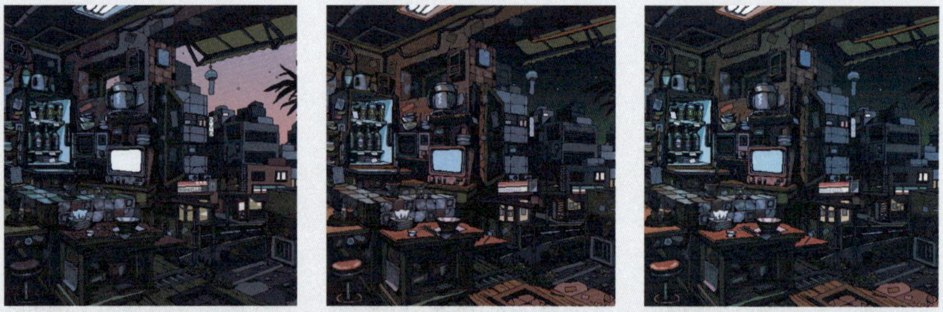

↑ After I had changed the colour of the sky, I reflected that the room looked like a mess. All the surfaces were unrecognizable; the only thing that stood out was the distinct cyan of the TV.

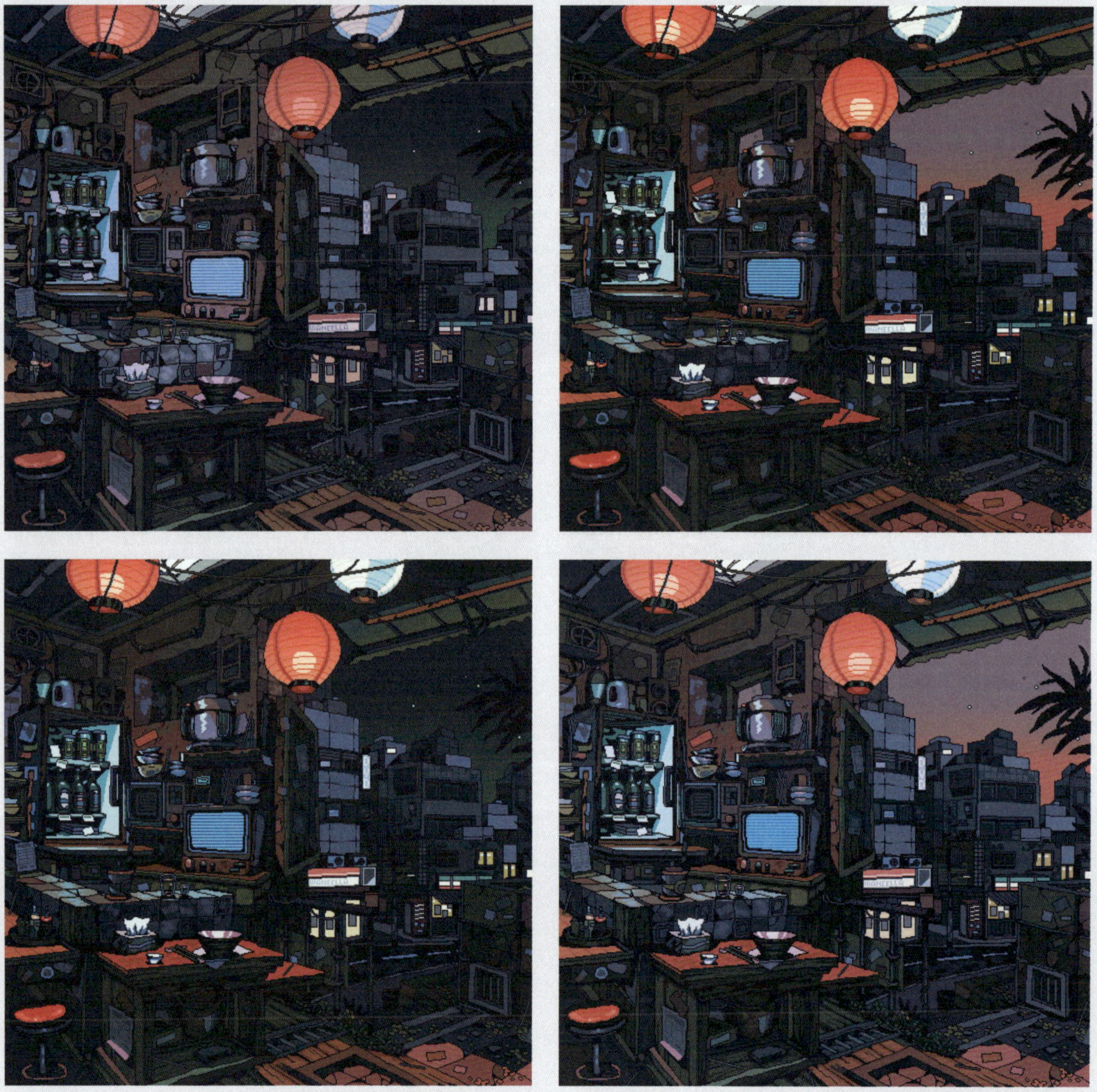

↑ I used red to make the surfaces more noticeable. Since this red light needed a source, I added some paper lanterns above the table. With these small changes, the scene had built itself.

↓ I used a photo I'd taken during a visit to Tokyo as a reference for this illustration, but from the outset, I knew I wanted to try and avoid simply redrawing the scene. Instead, I created a new location, based on the photo, by using some elements from the existing place.

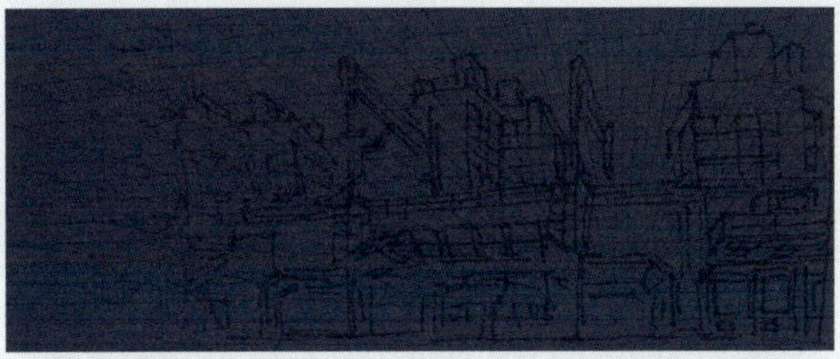

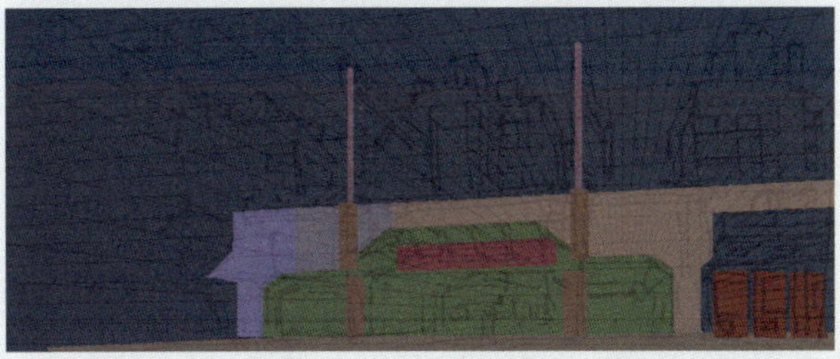

↓ At first, I tried to match the colours from the photo, mainly because I didn't know what I wanted to draw... as usual. When this turned out to be harder than I had imagined, I went my own way.

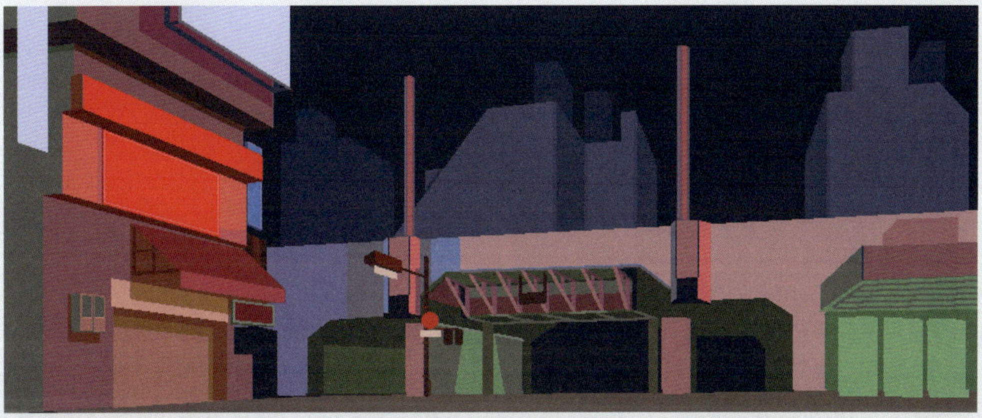

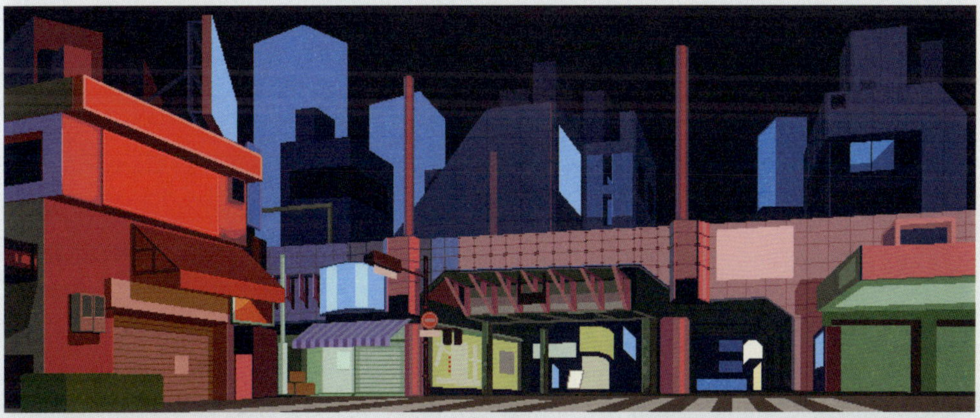

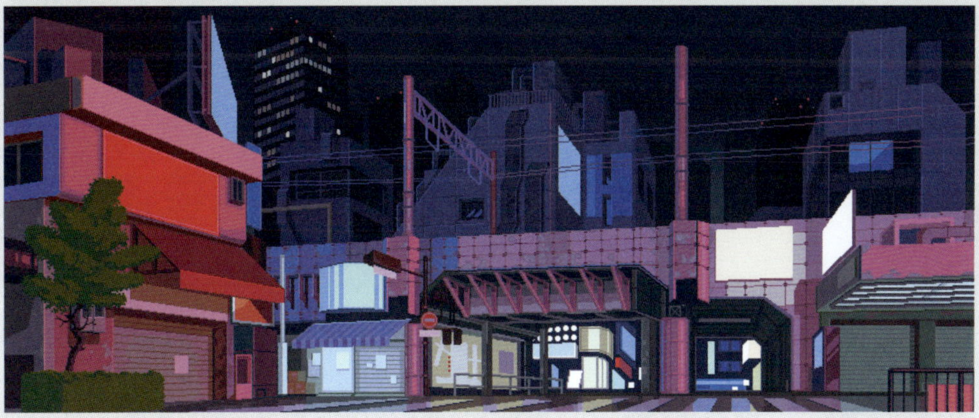

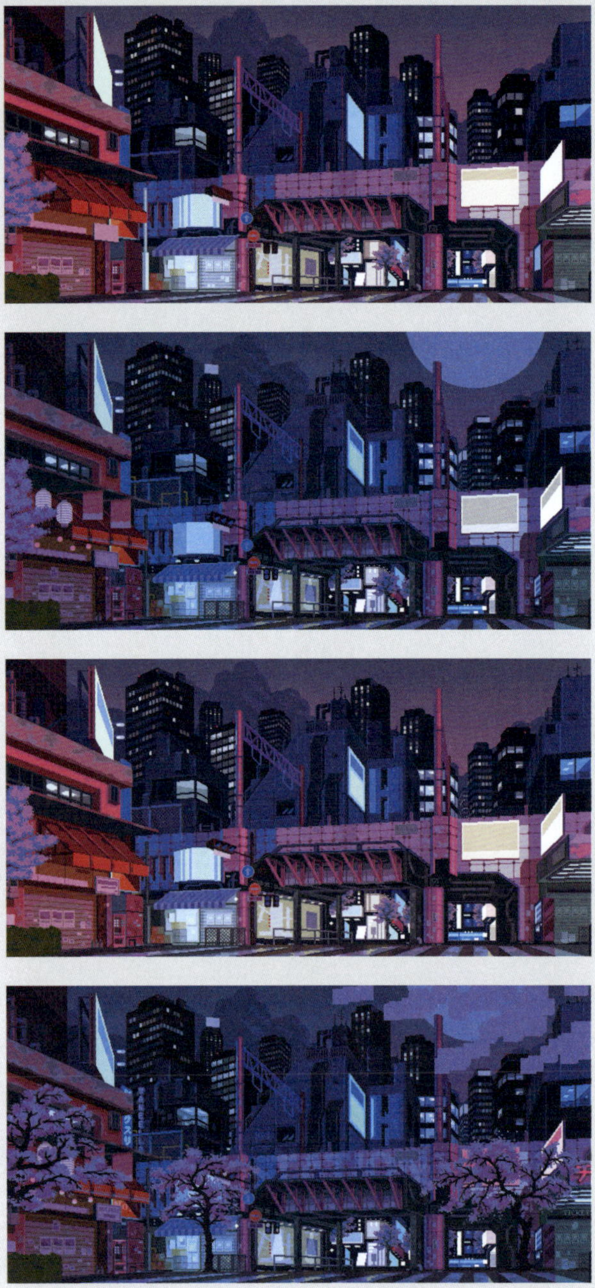

↑ Since the scene is split in half by the bridge, and looks disconnected because of this, I wasn't happy with the overall composition and tried a few different ways to resolve this problem.

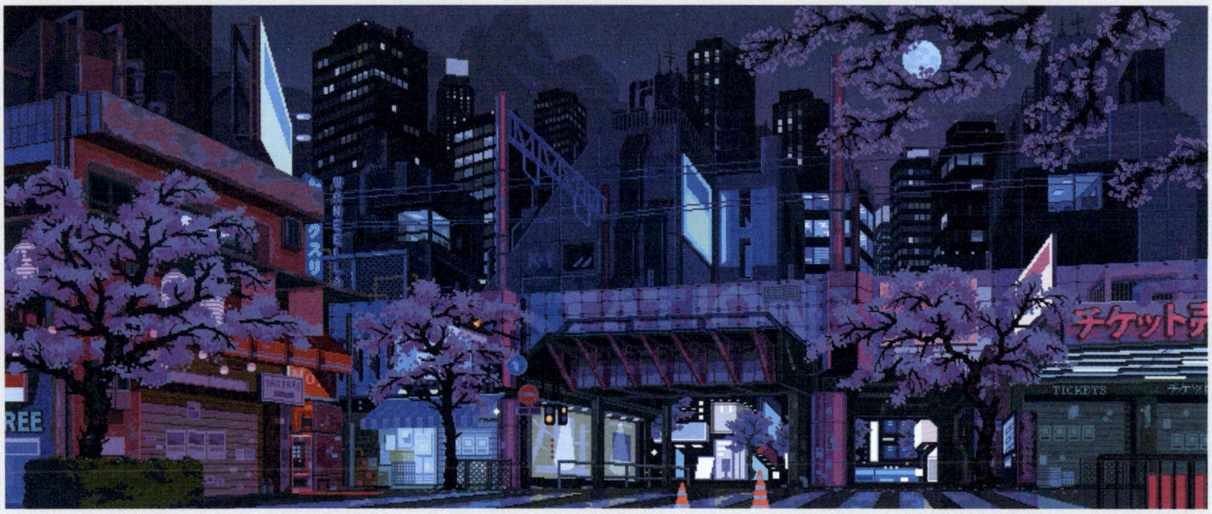

↑ While I liked how the moon looked, I wasn't convinced it should be so unrealistically big. The blossoming tree branches were a great addition, so I had to find a way of combining them with the moon. I found that dark branches, vivid flowers and a small, bright moon created the perfect balance.

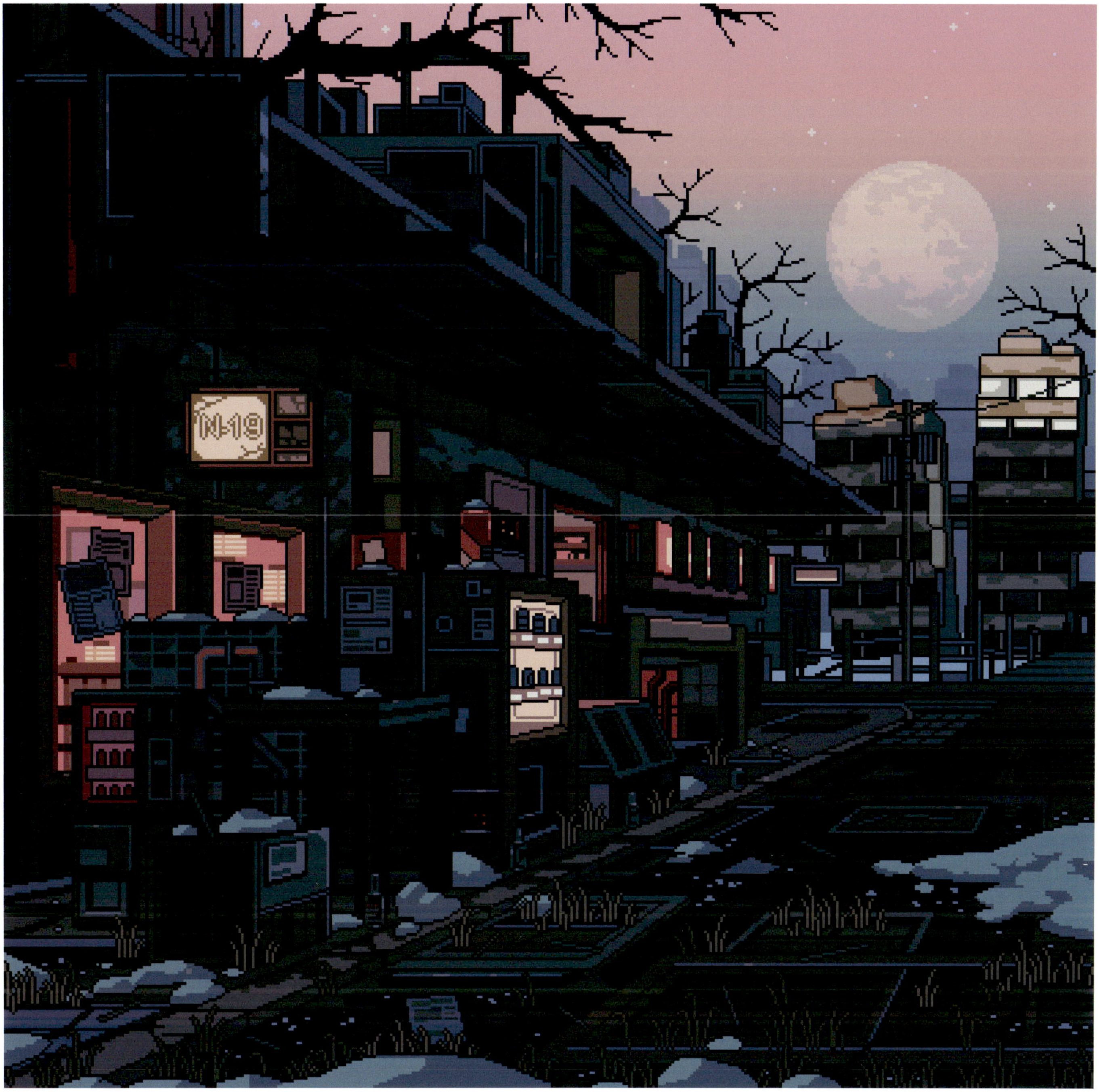

N-19, 16/11/2019, 400×400px

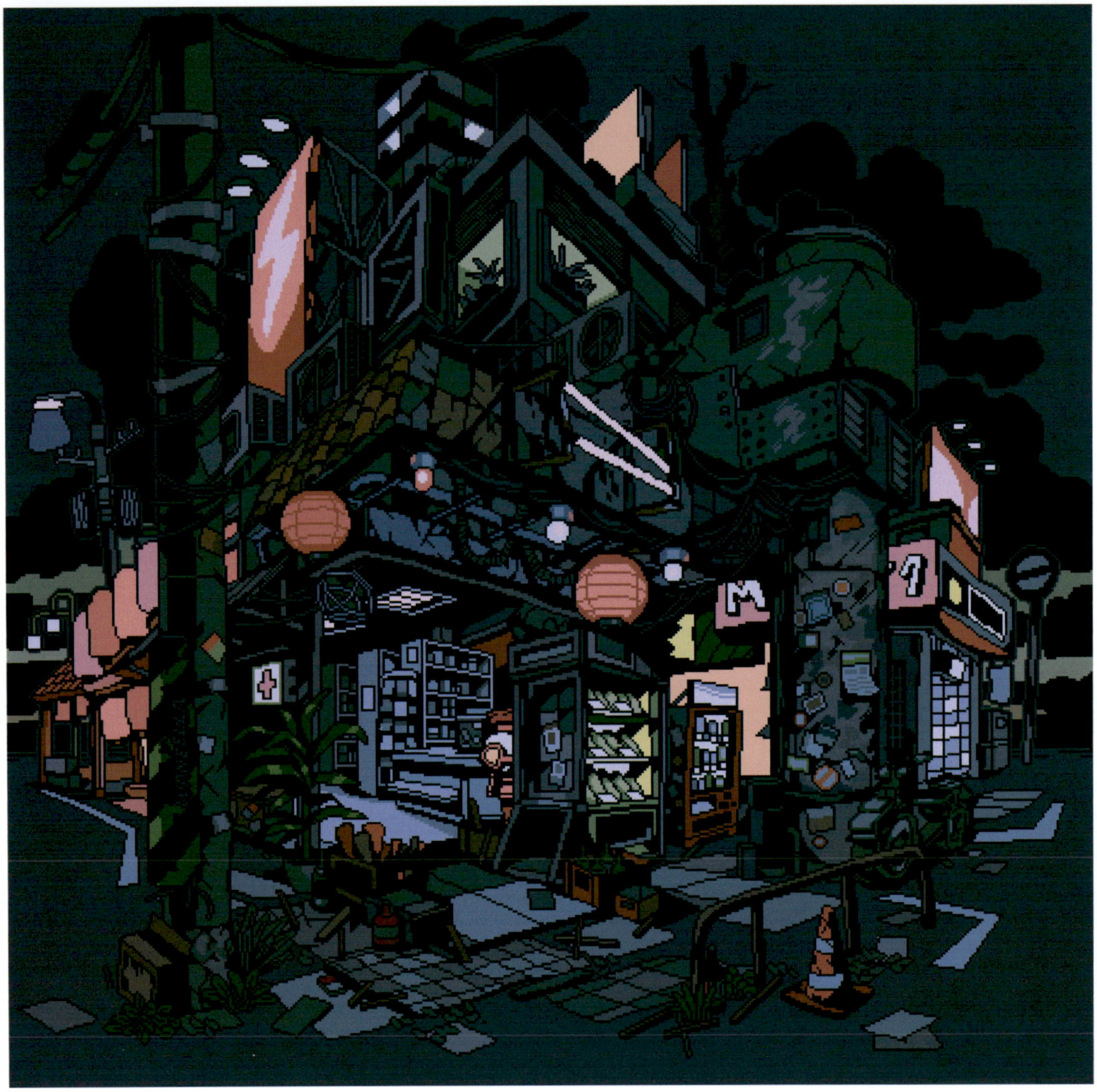

End Of Summer, 19/08/2019, 450×450px

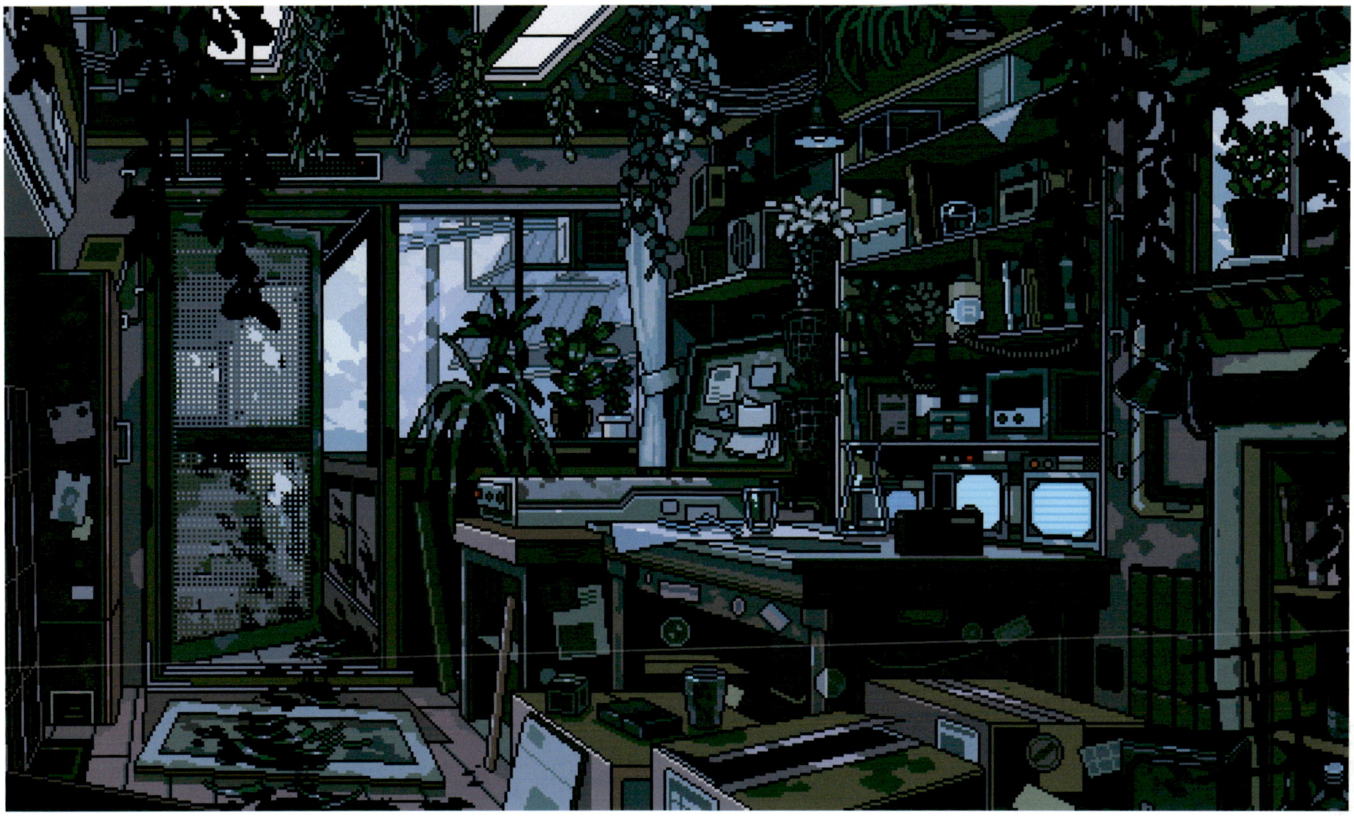

New Specimen, 02/05/2019, 500×300px

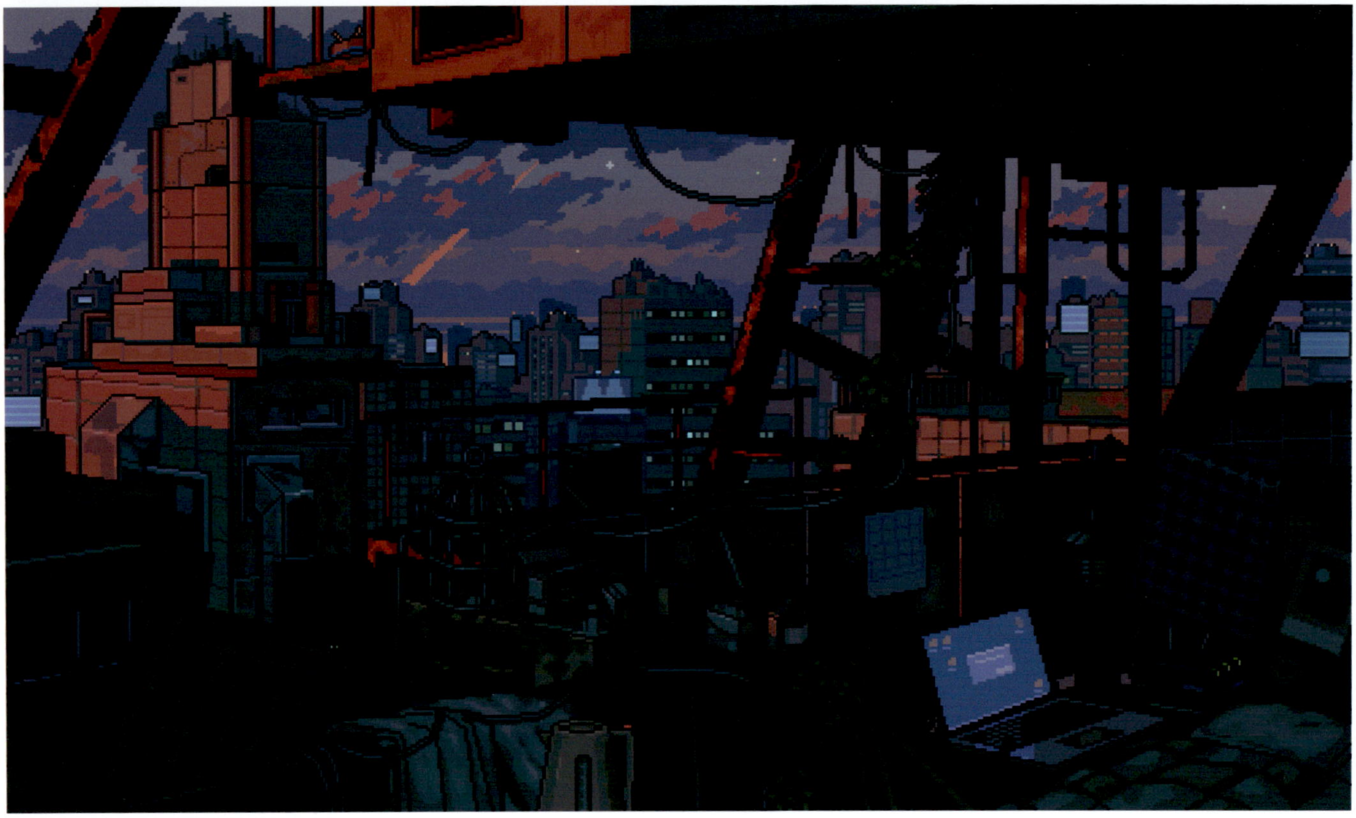

Cell, 18/04/2019, 500×300px

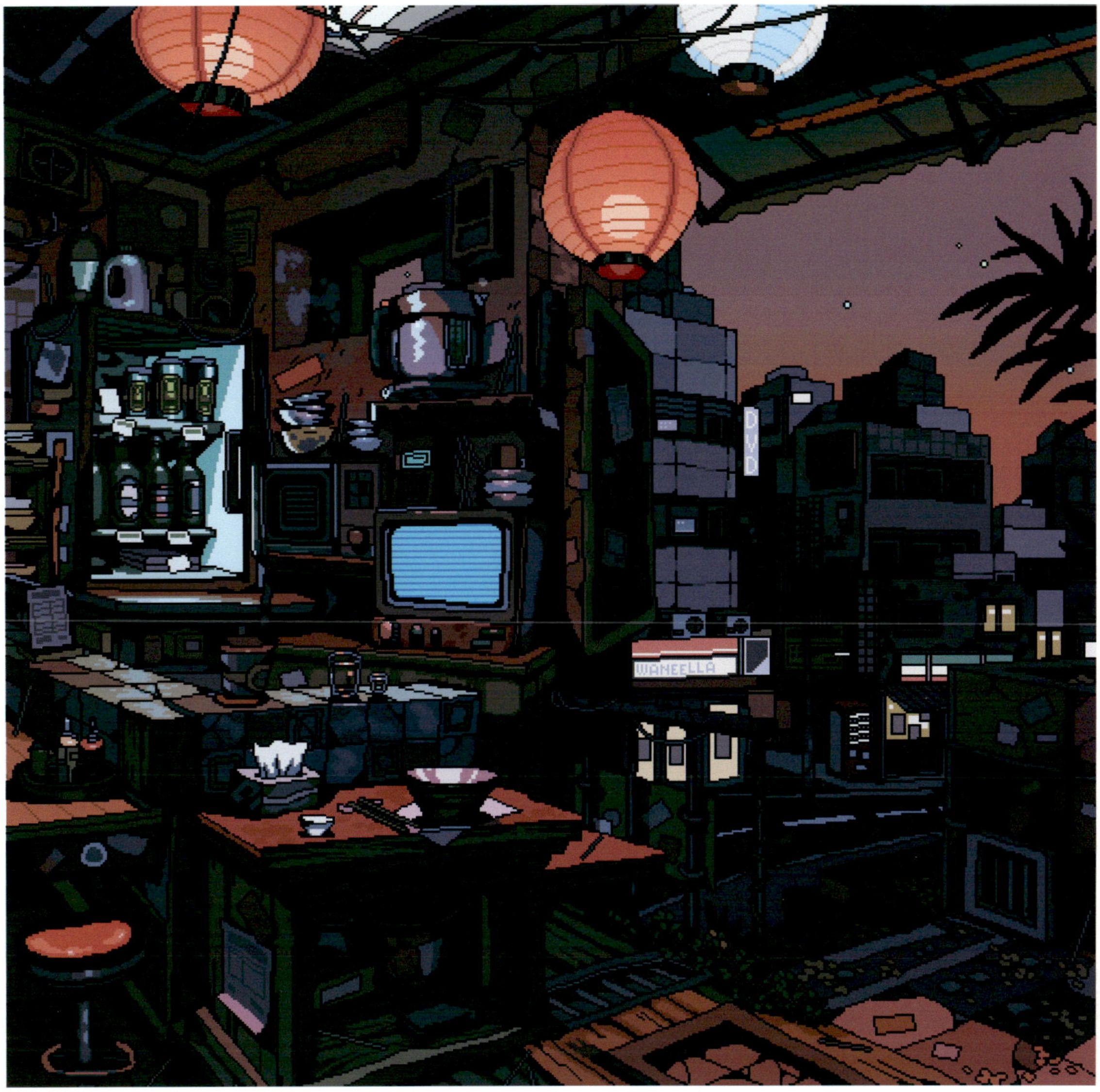

Red Light, 06/09/2019, 500×500px

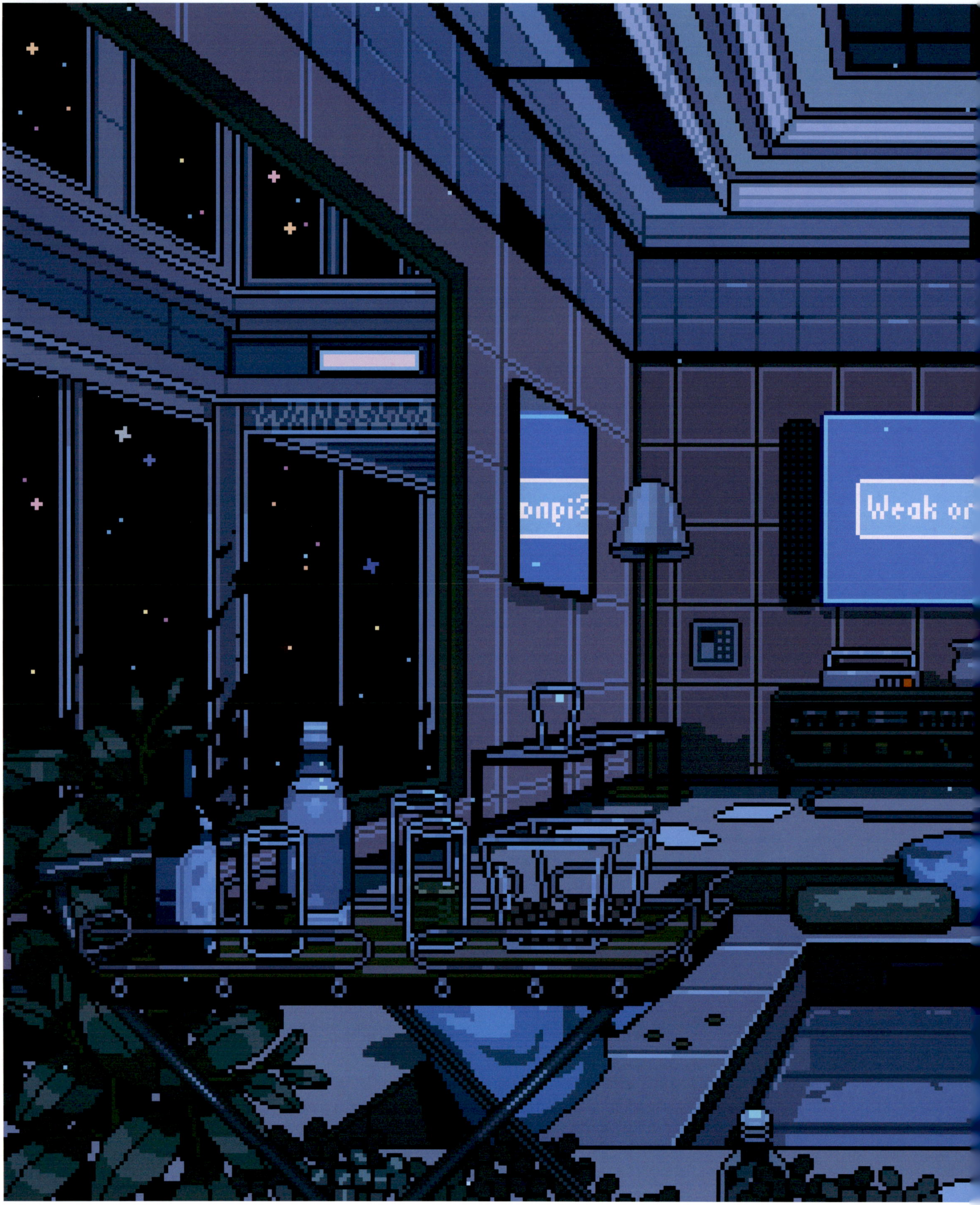

Weak Or No Signal, 11/05/2019, 500×300px

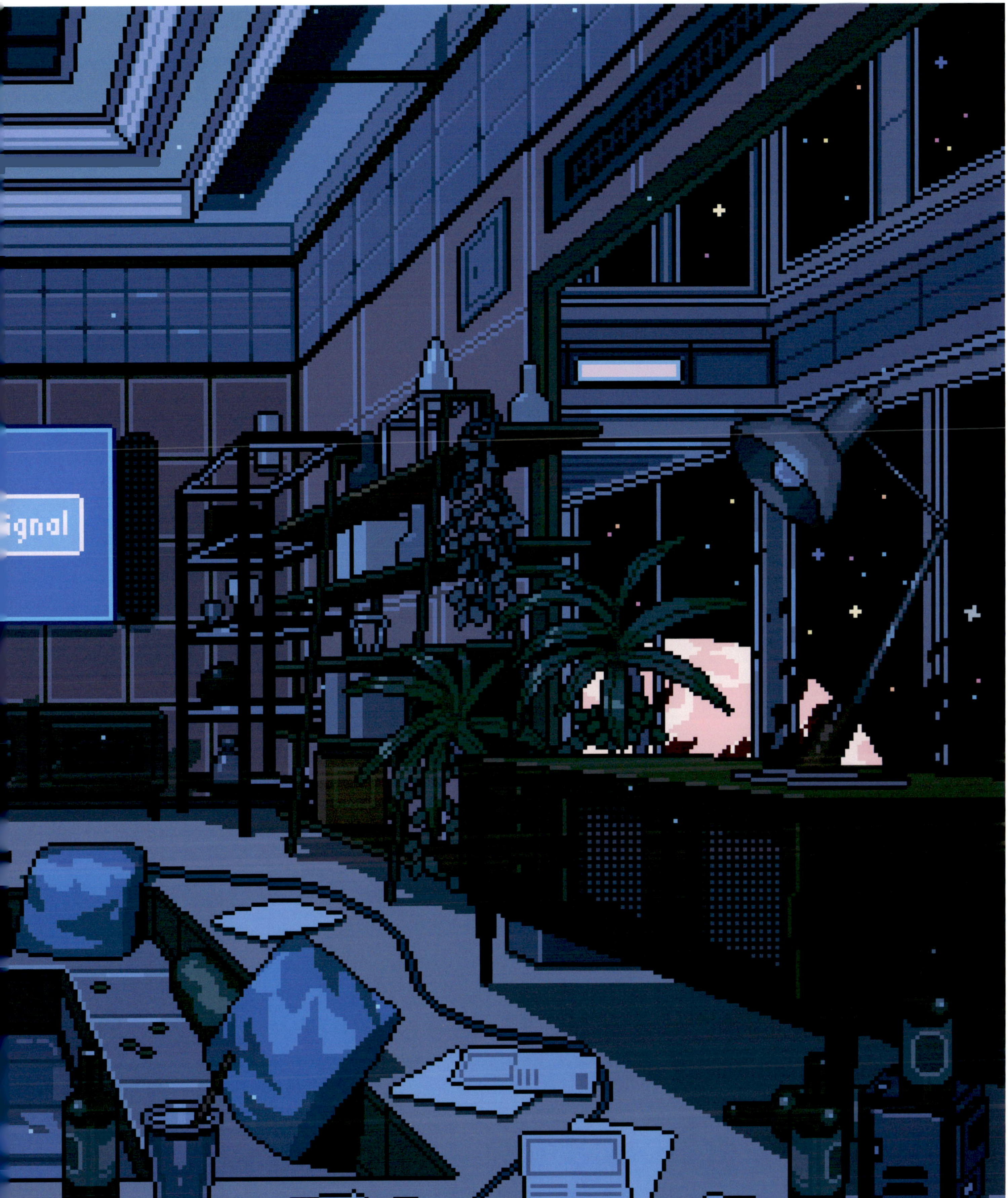
ignal

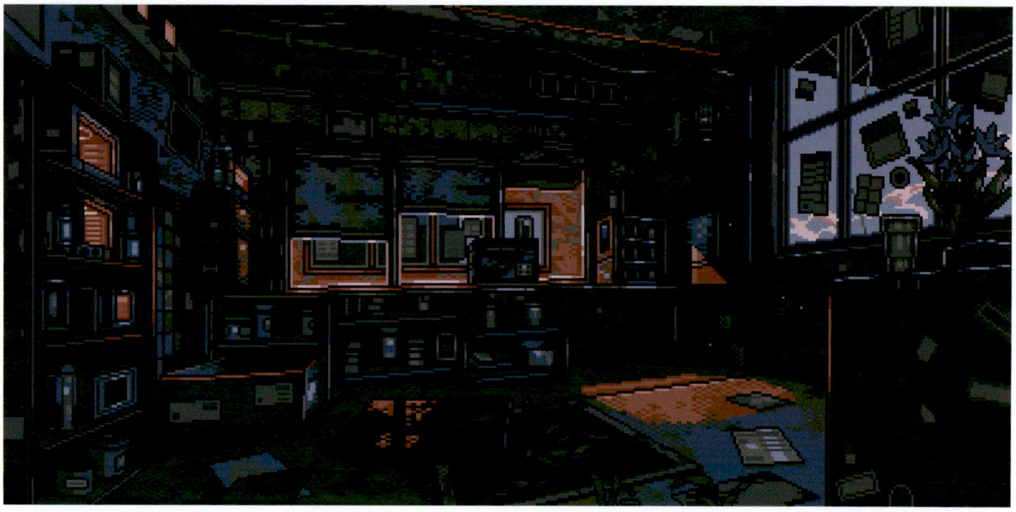

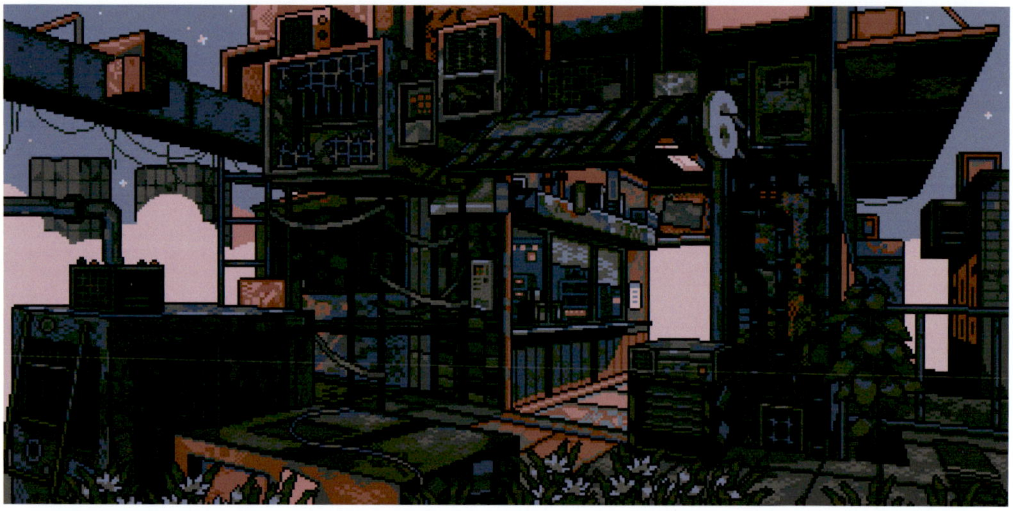

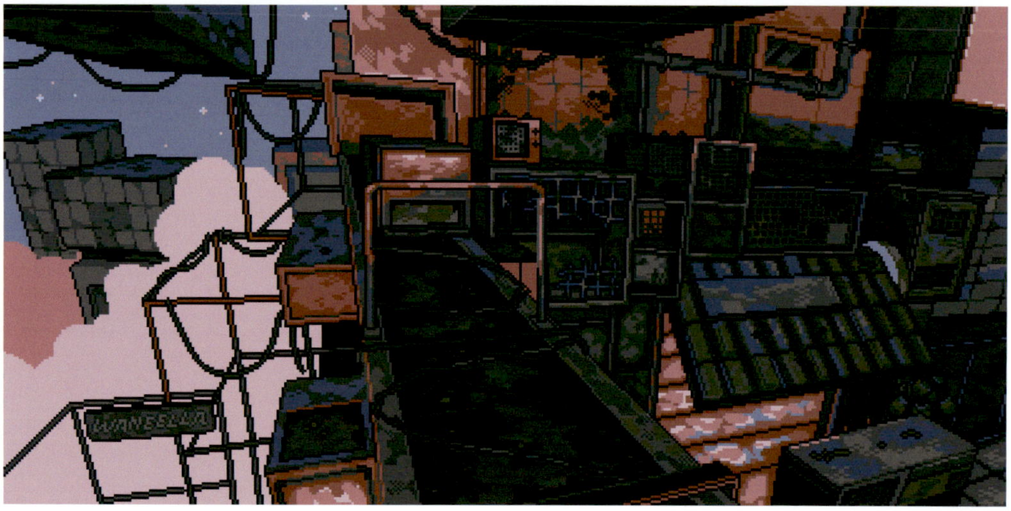

Top: *Satellite Six Pt2*, 13/06/2019, 400×200px
Middle: *Satellite Six Pt1*, 13/06/2019, 400×200px
Above: *Satellite Six Pt3*, 13/06/2019, 400×200px

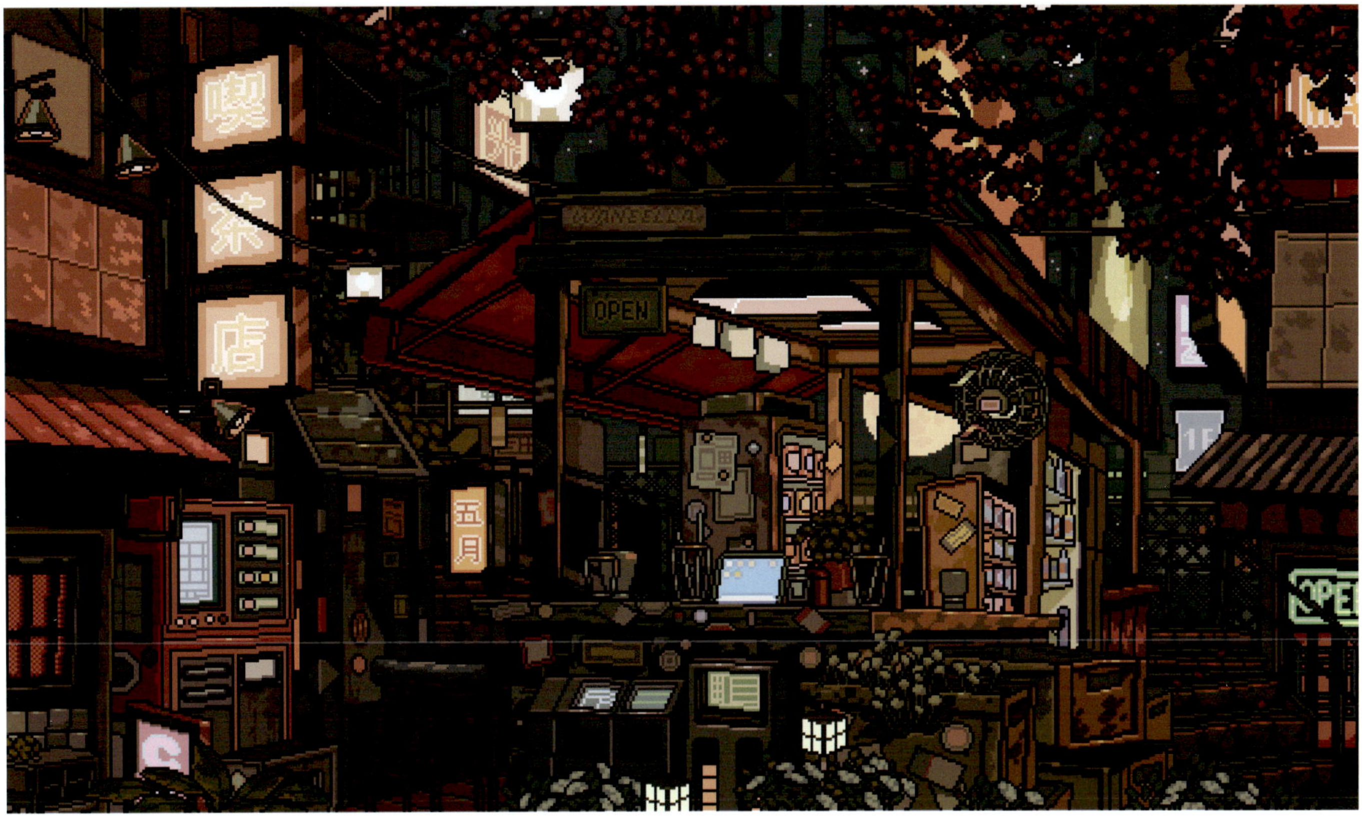

Behind The Station, 24/05/2019, 500×300px

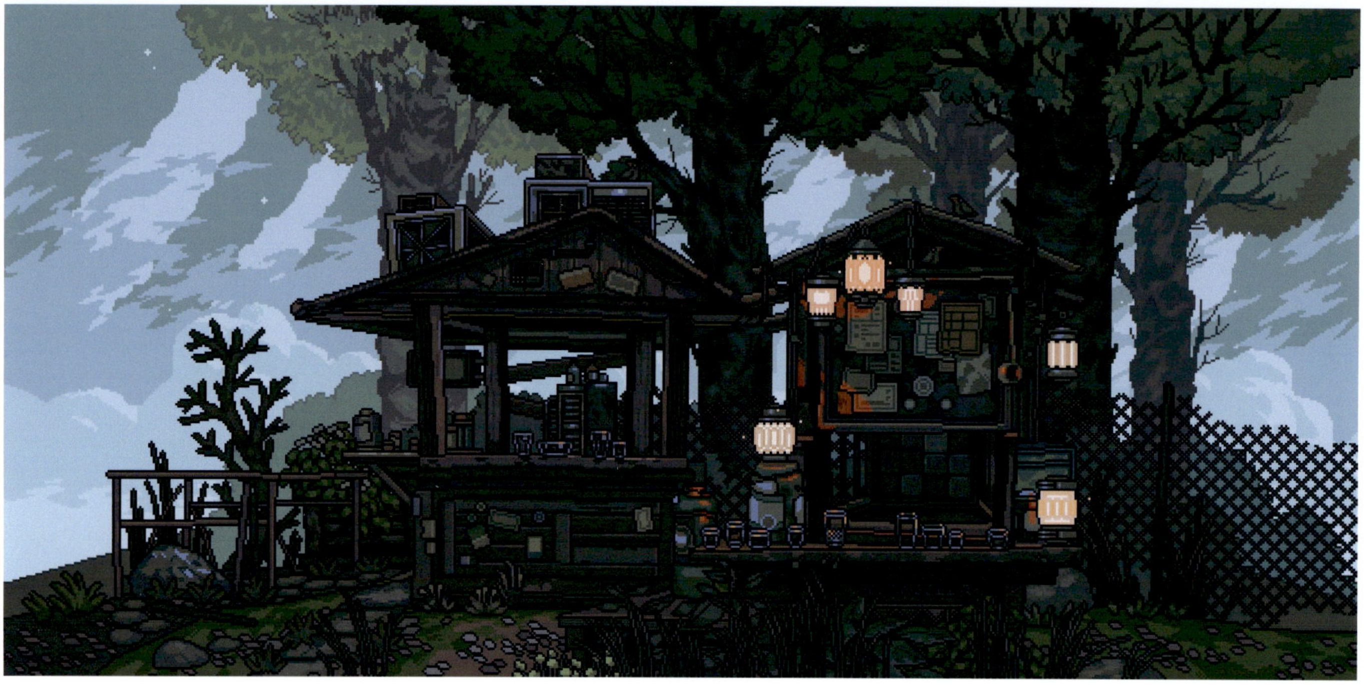

Above: *Birds And Lanterns* (Green version), 31/05/2019, 600×300px
Top right: *35.224191, 138.5668708 Pt1*, 14/03/2019, 400×400px
Right: *35.224191, 138.5668708 Pt2*, 14/03/2019, 400×400px

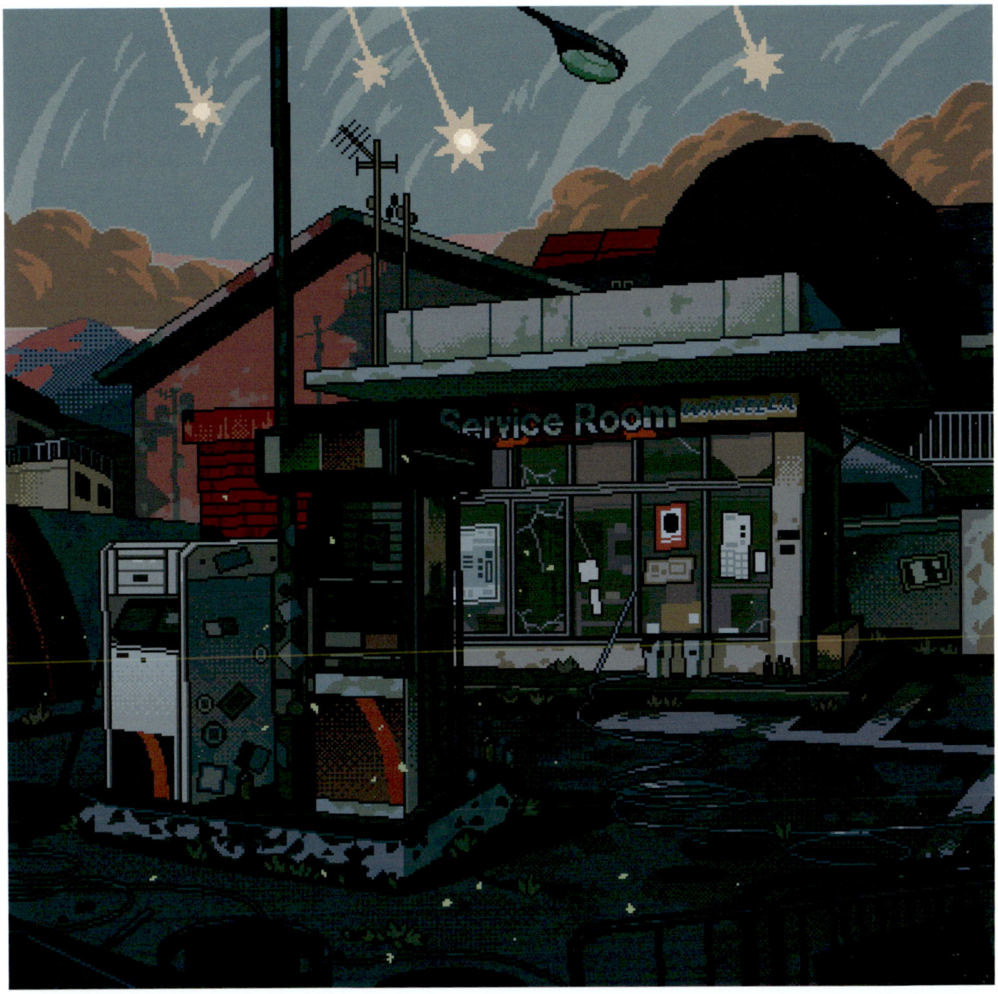
Service Room

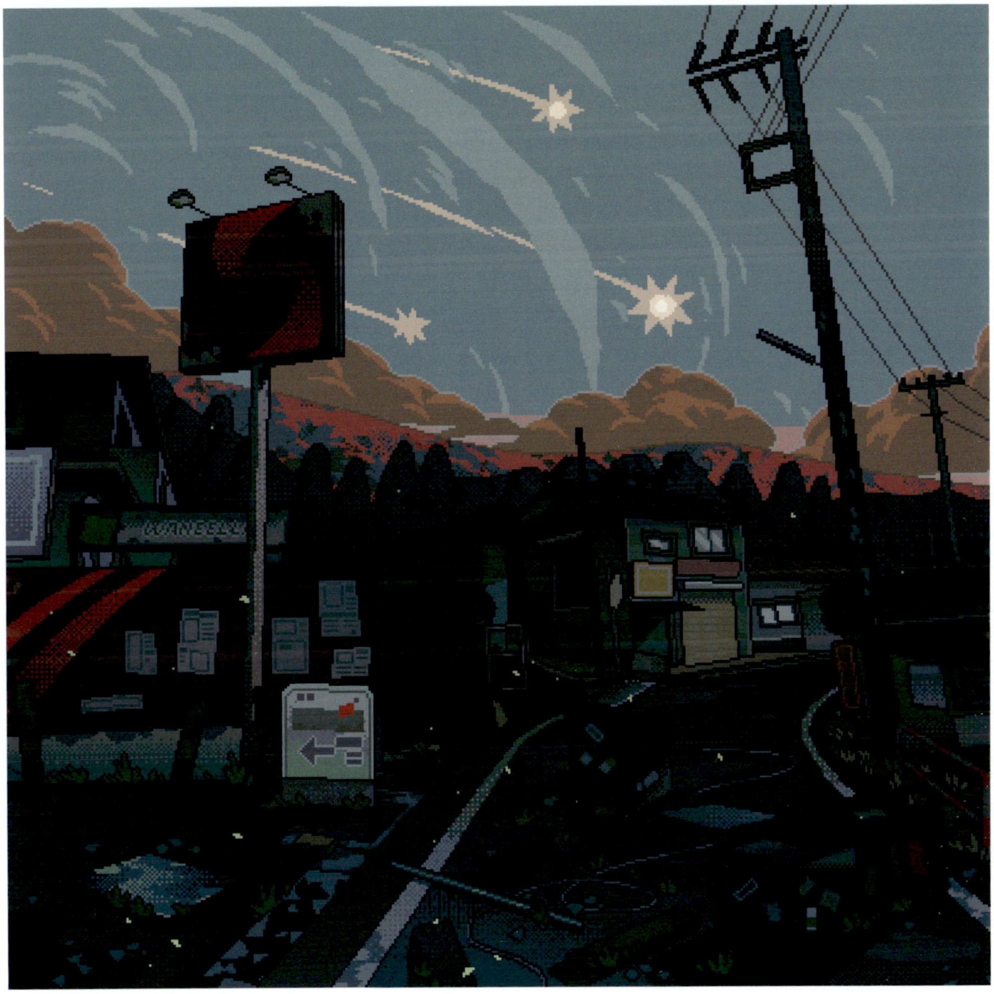

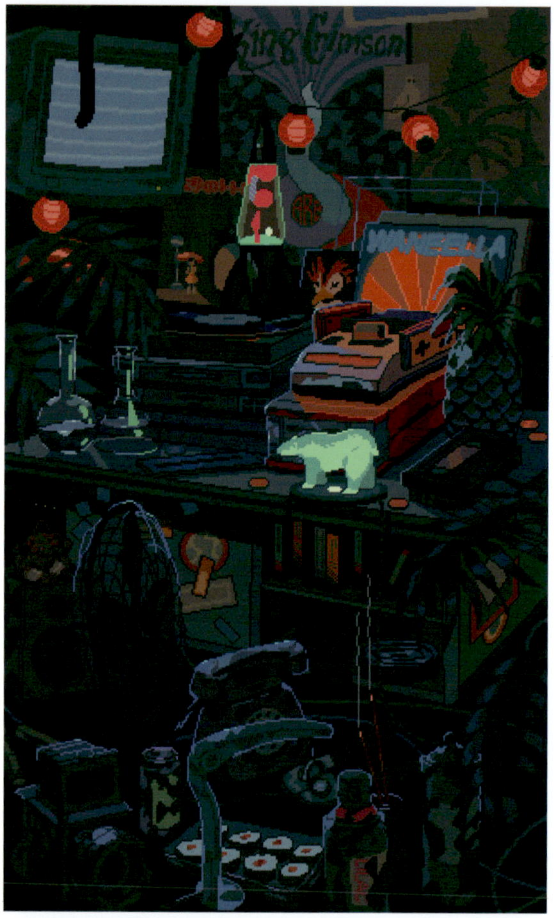

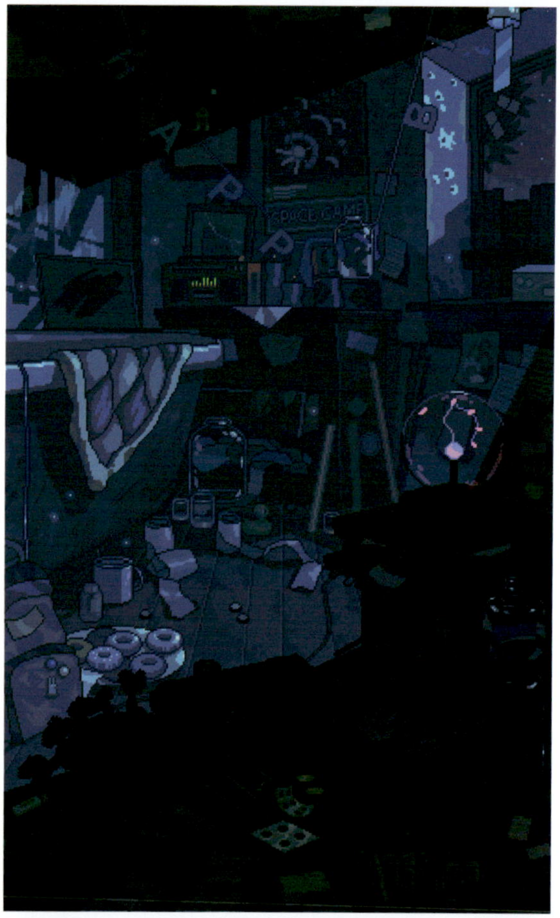

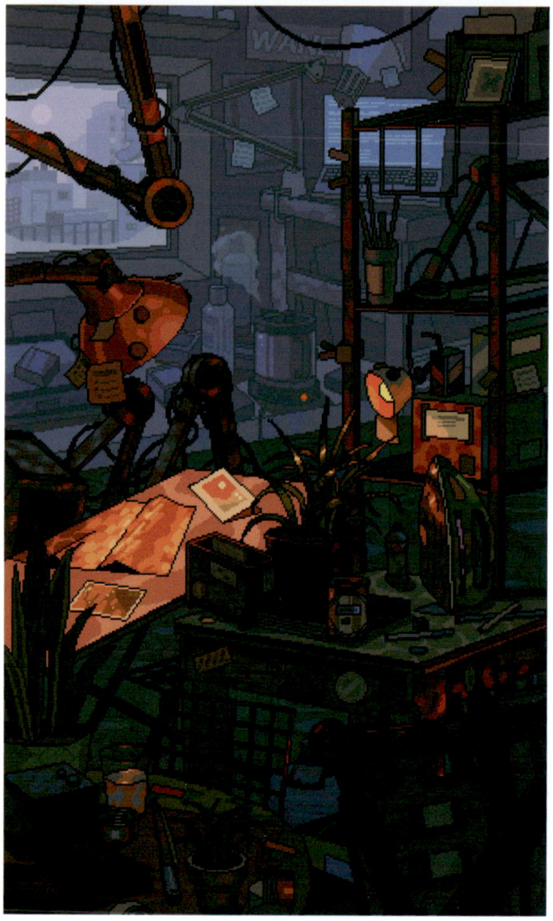

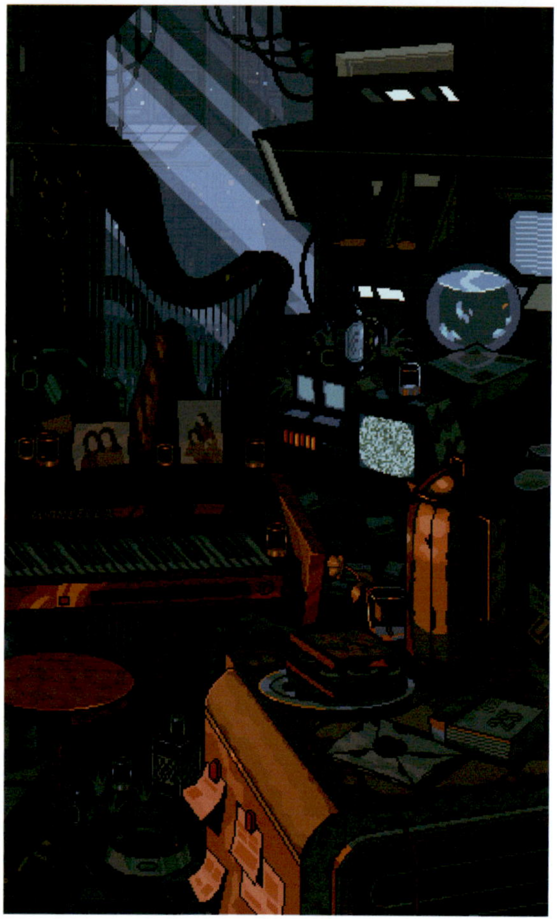

Top left: *01:28*, 24/01/2019, 300×500px
Top right: *02:14*, 20/02/2019, 300×500px
Above left: *06:41*, 15/01/2019, 300×500px
Above right: *23:51*, 05/02/2019, 300×500px

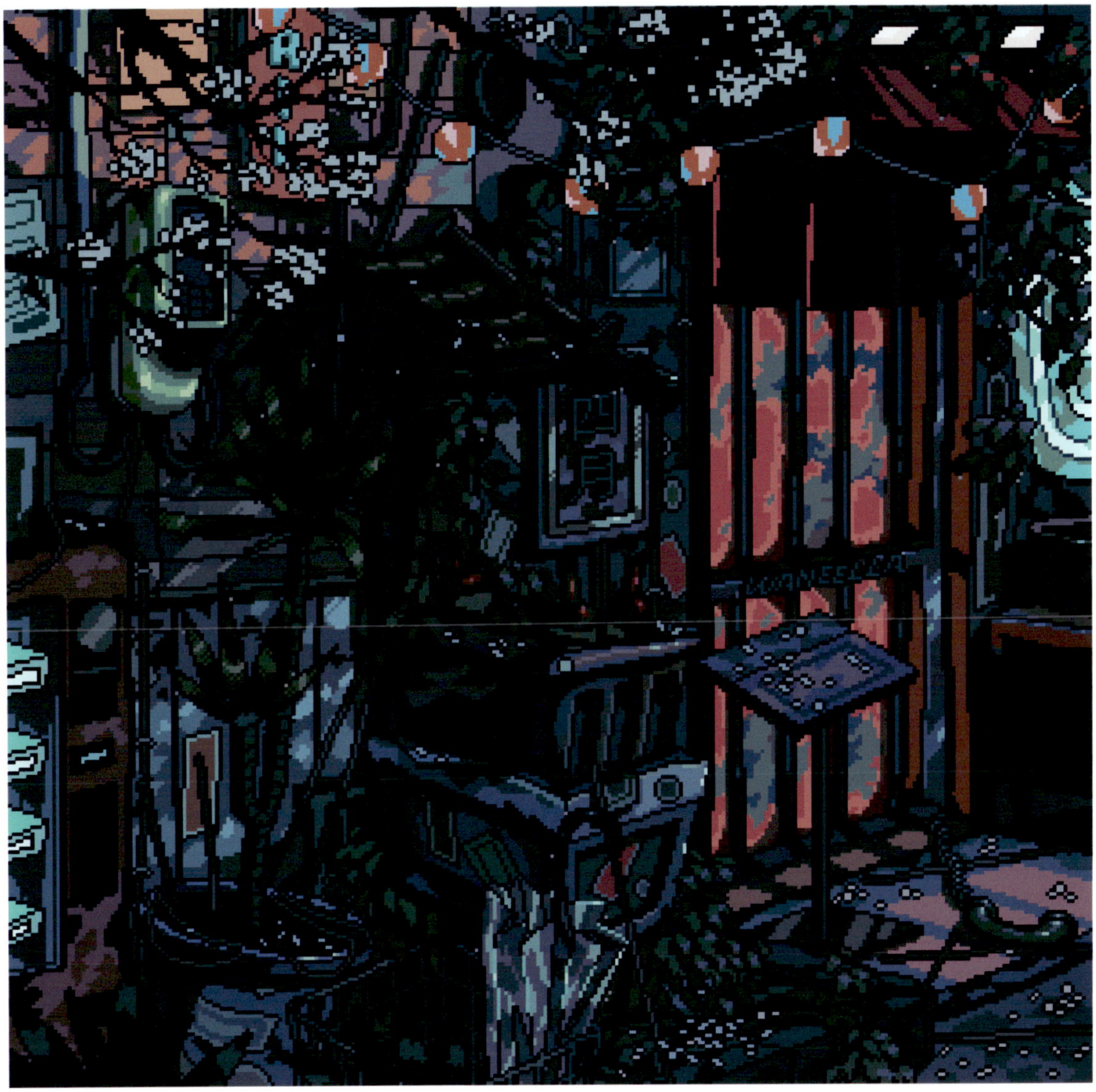

Shine 17, 10/04/2019, 300×300px

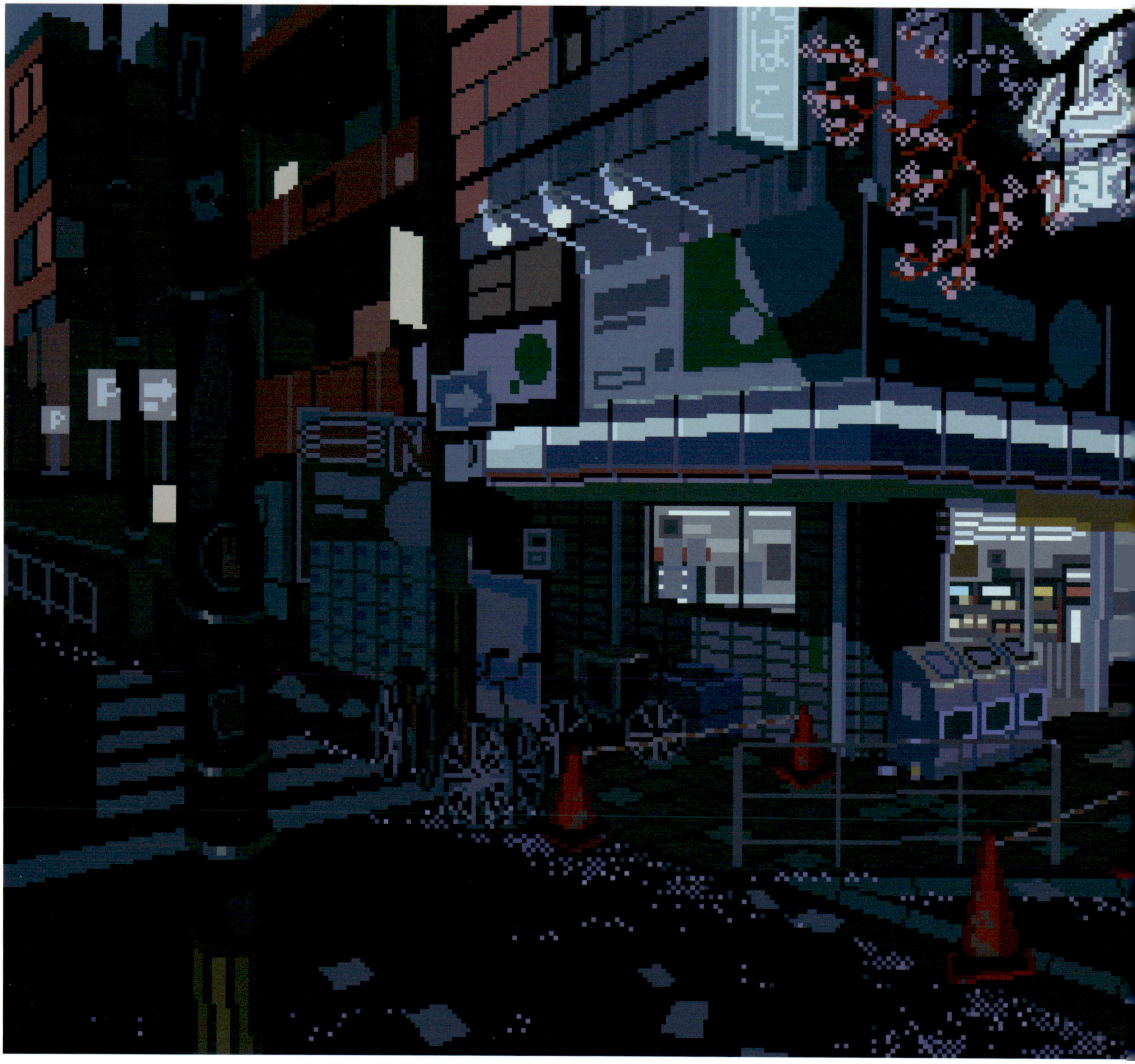

34.6710308, 135.462008, 01/03/2019, 500×227px

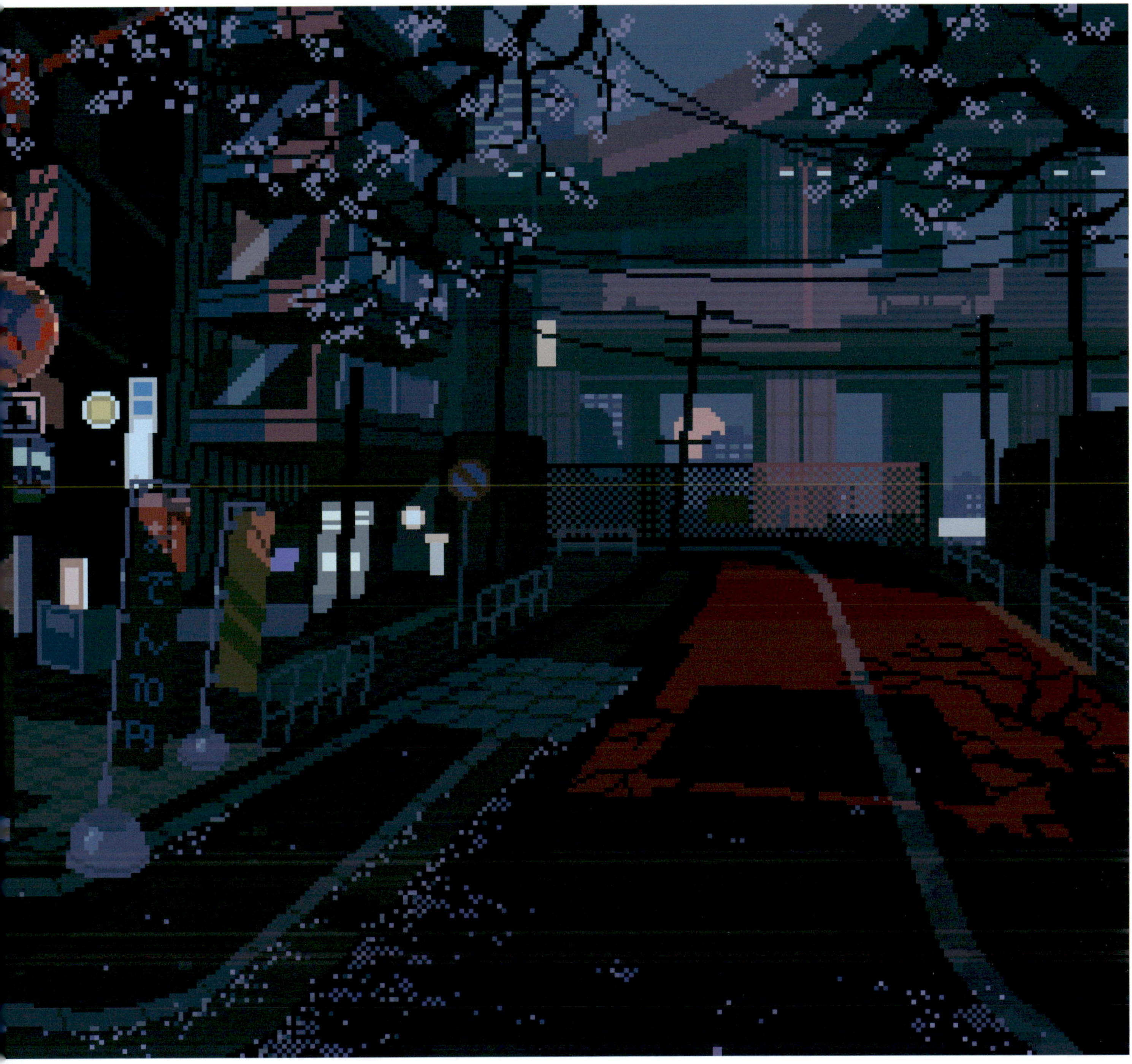

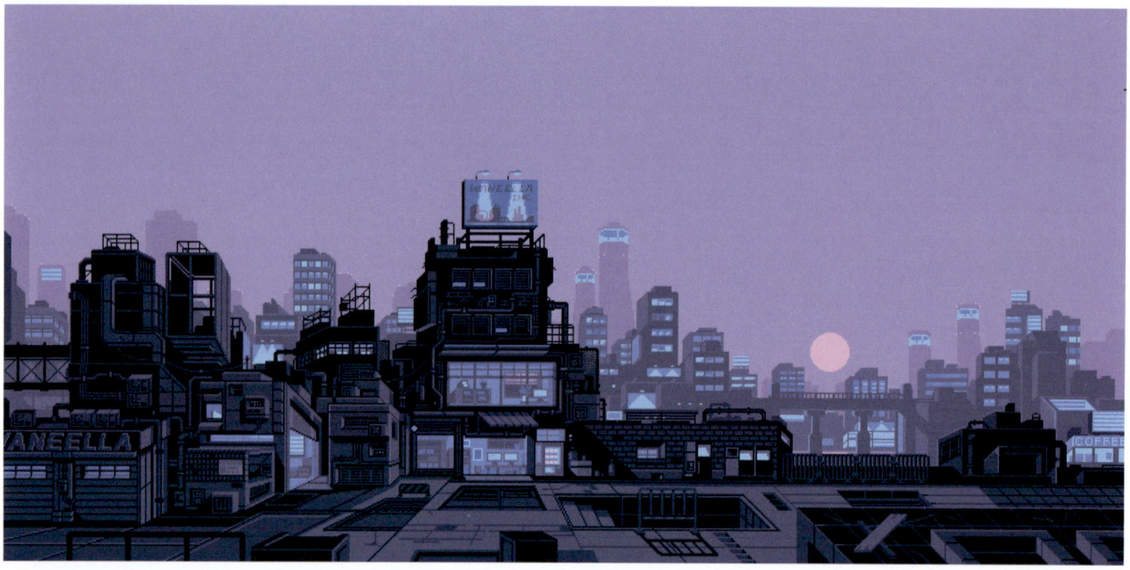

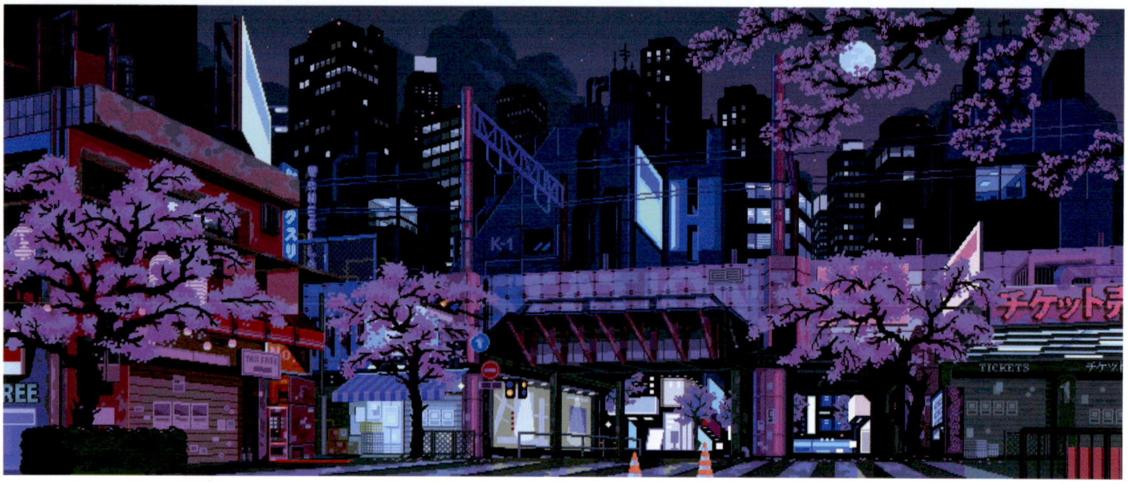

Top: *Dim*, 06/02/2020, 800×400px
Above: *Lull*, 26/03/2020, 845×356px

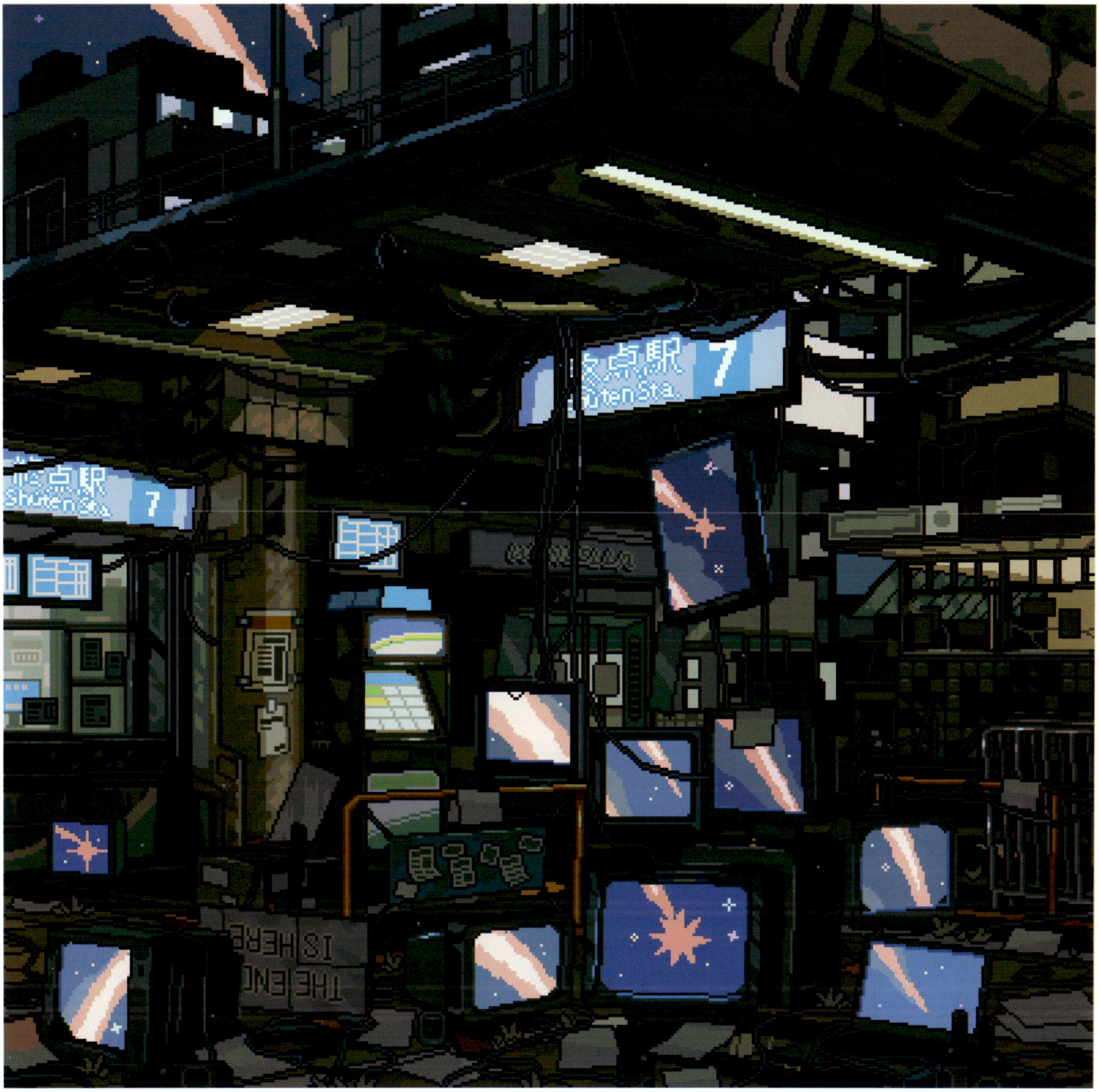

Line 7, 31/03/2019, 400×400px

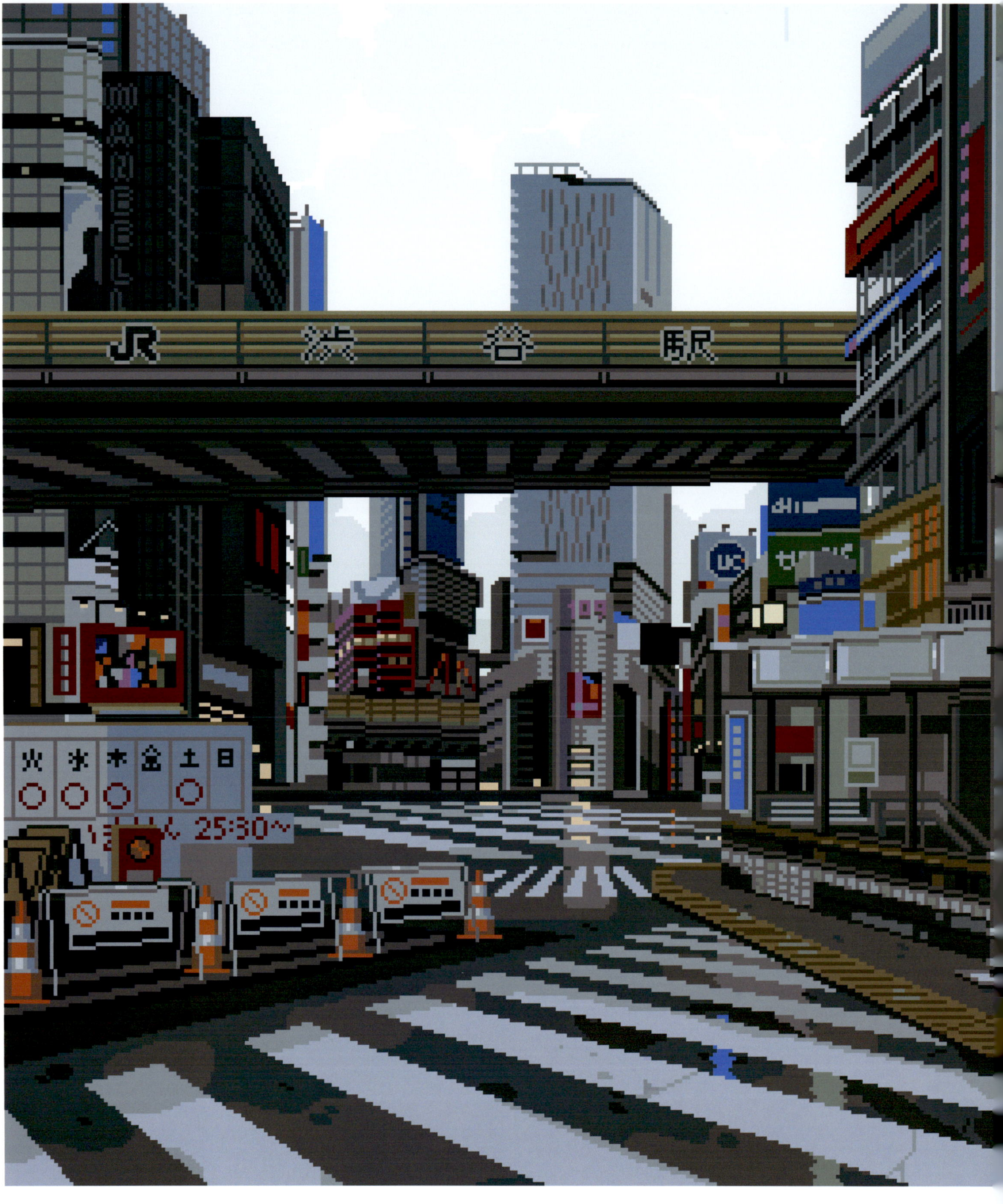

Destination, 29/12/2020, 530×311px

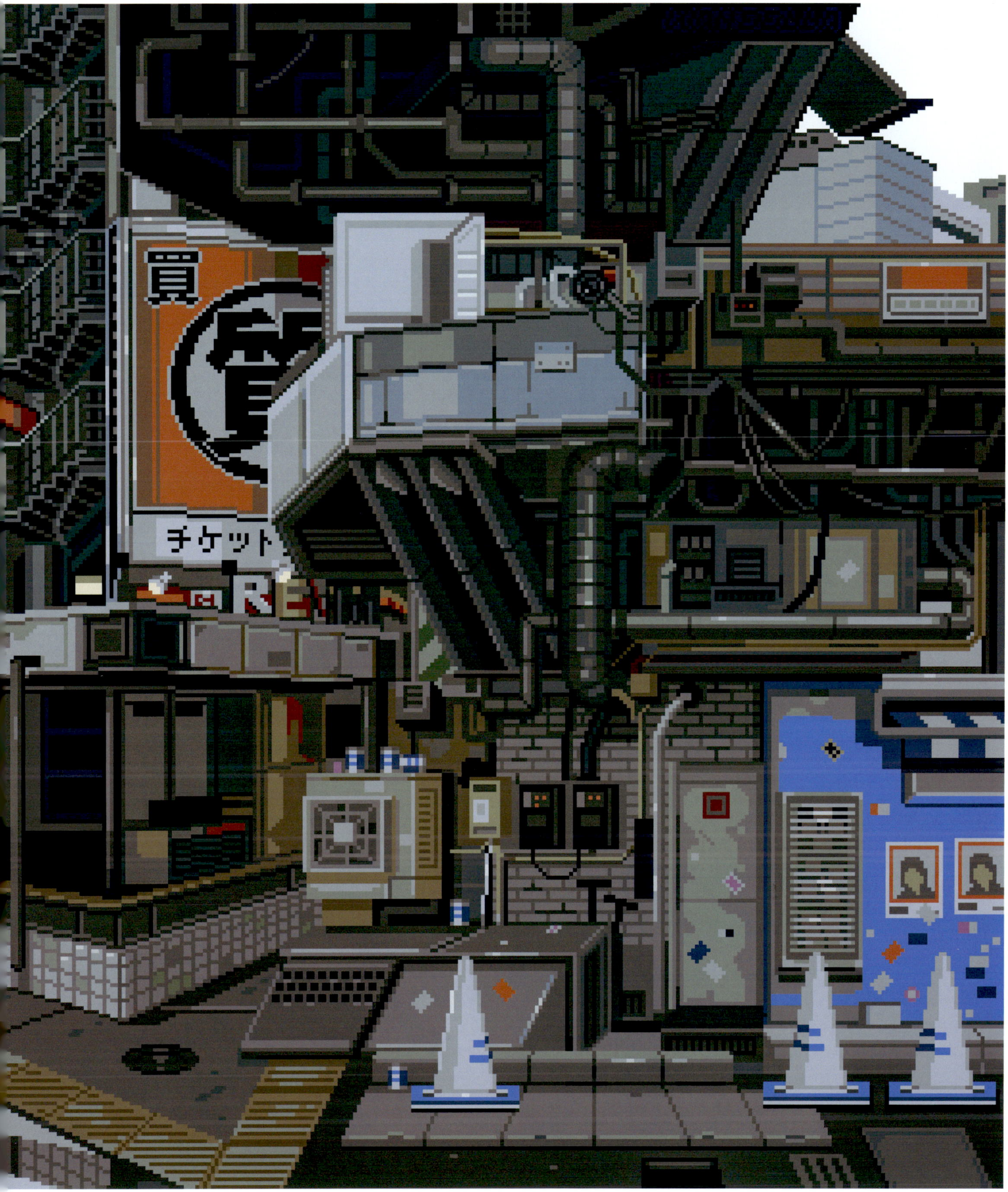
買
チケット

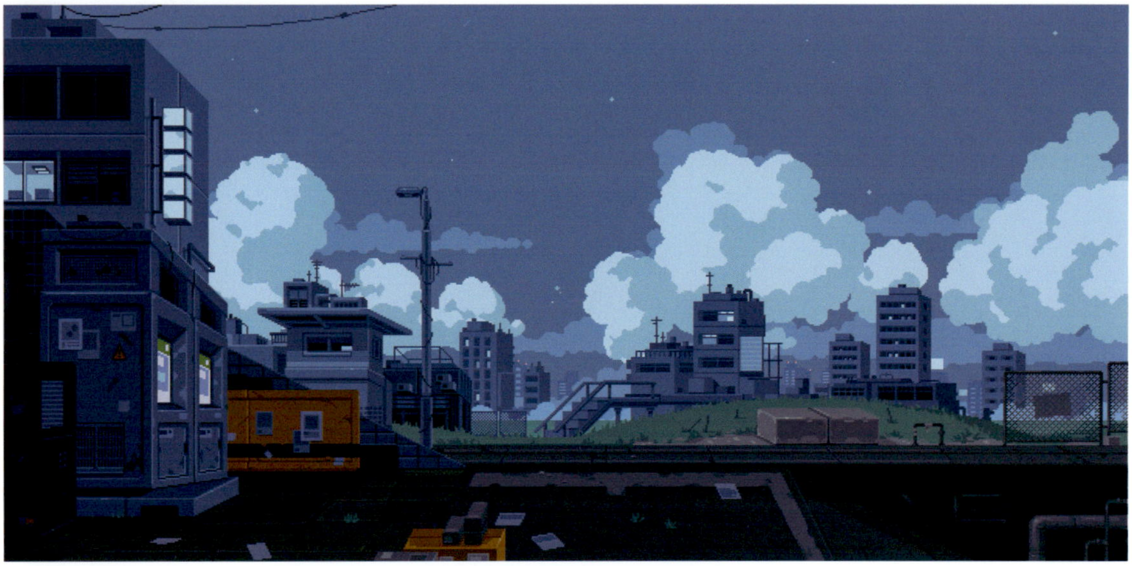

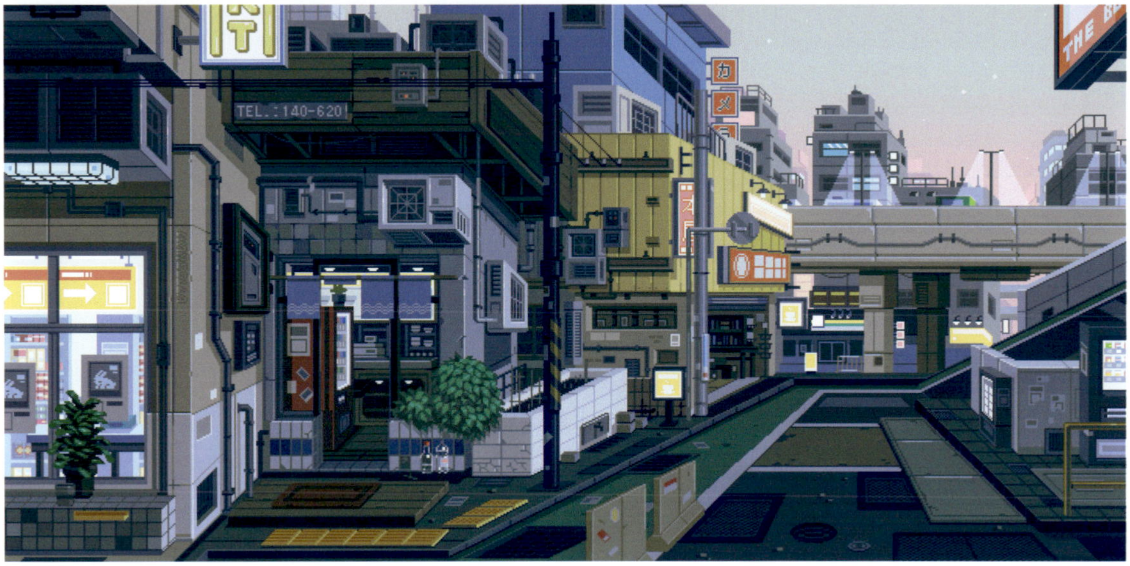

Top: *Maybe We Should Stay Here*, 27/08/2020, 720×360px
Above: *Summer Thoughts*, 16/06/2020, 720×360px

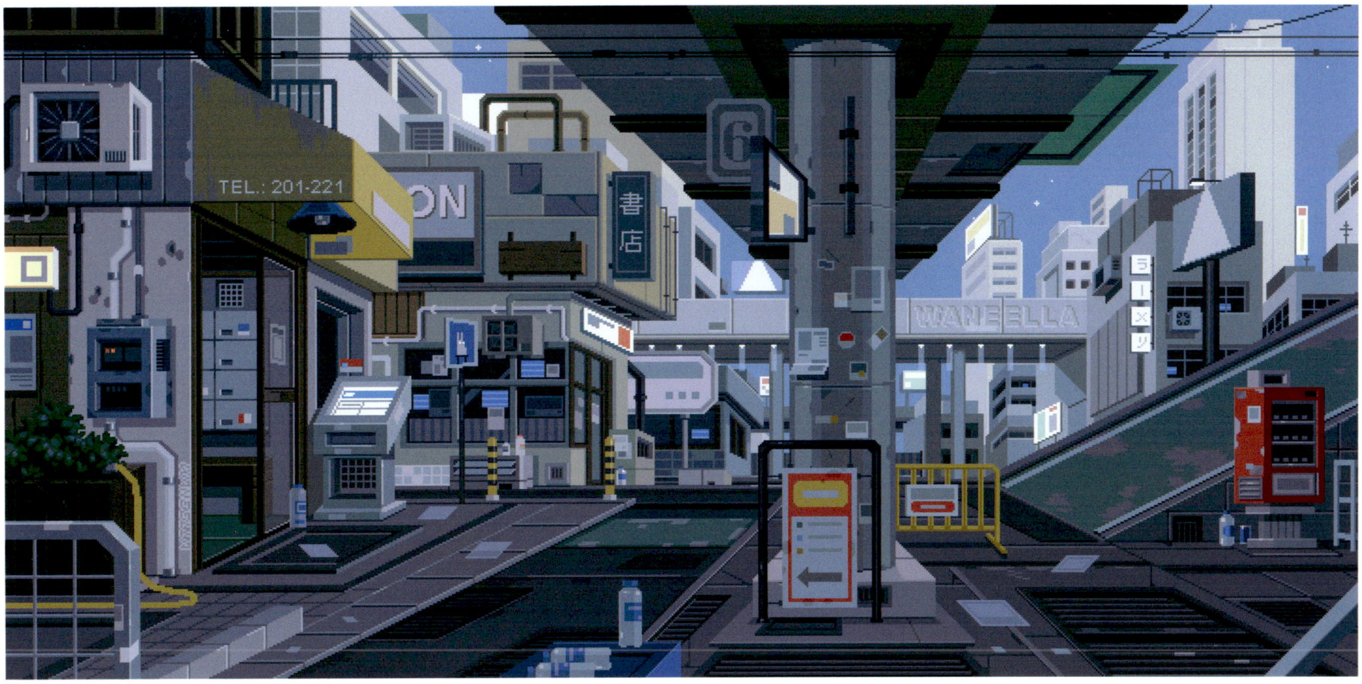

Same Way, 25/12/2020, 720×360px

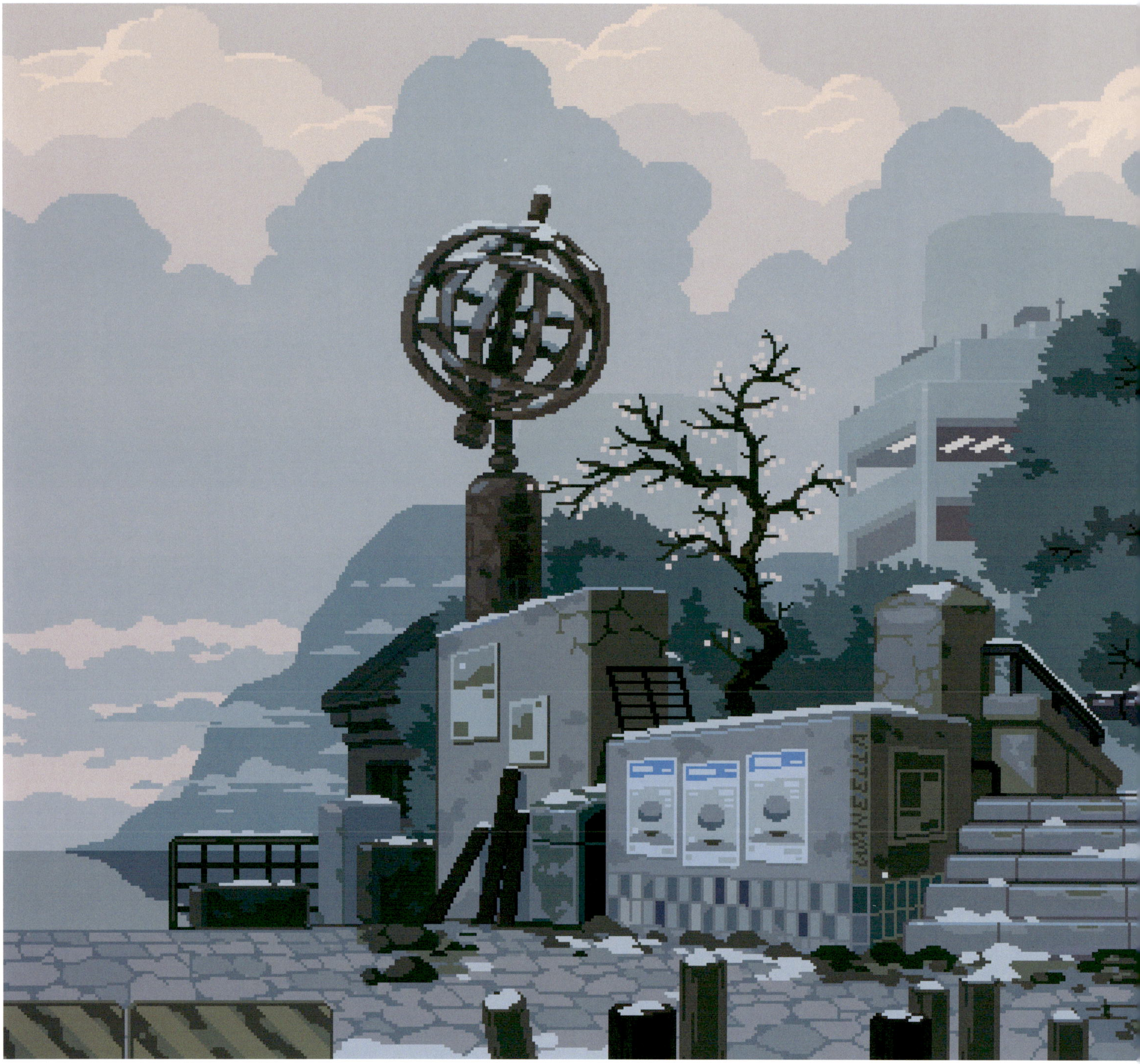

Edge, 03/04/2020, 800×360px

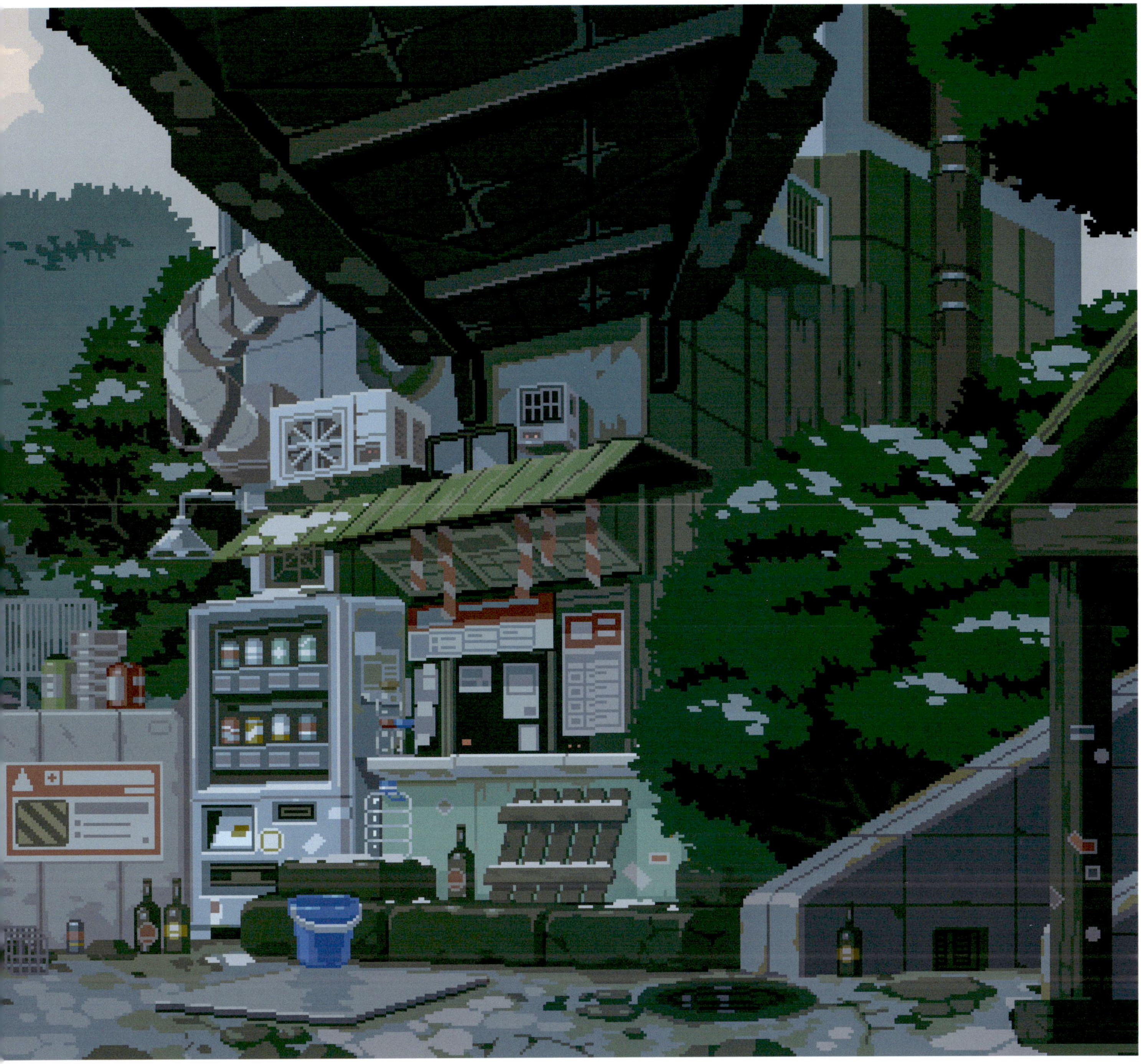

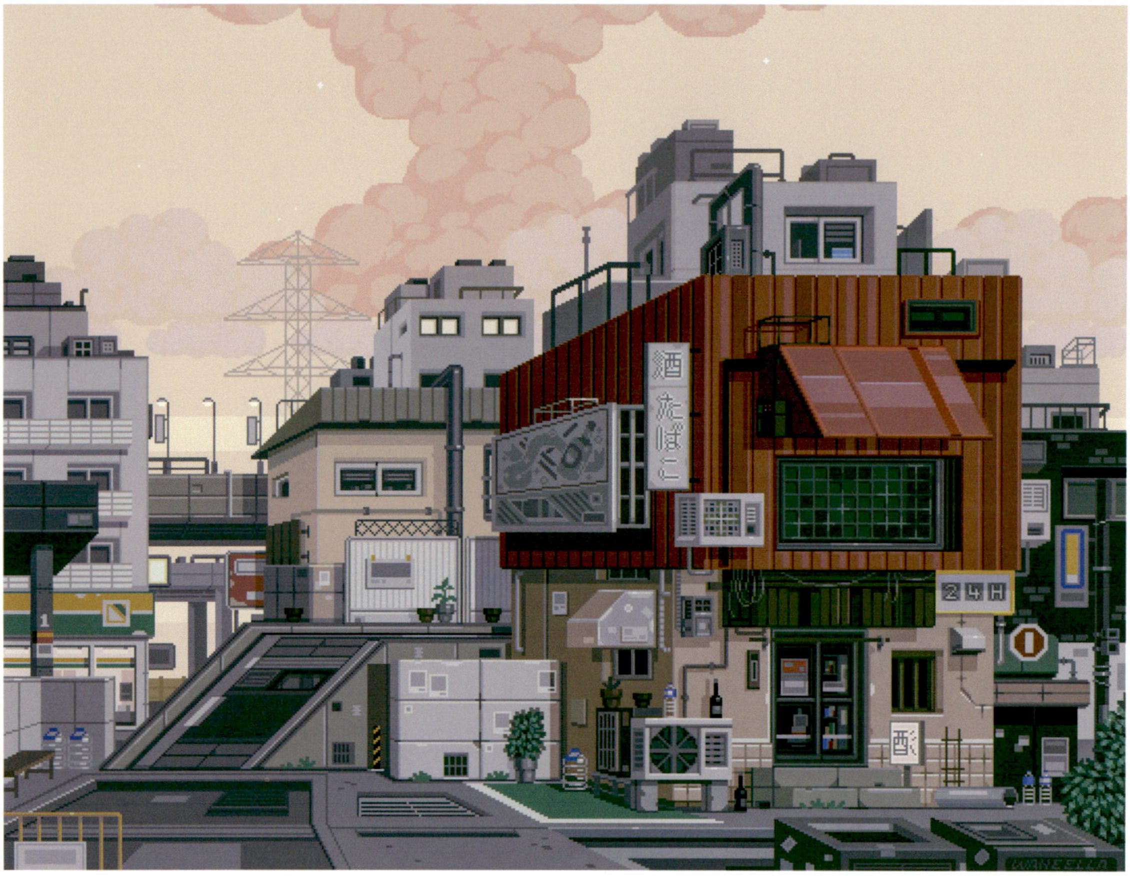

Undertone, 28/06/2020, 540×420px

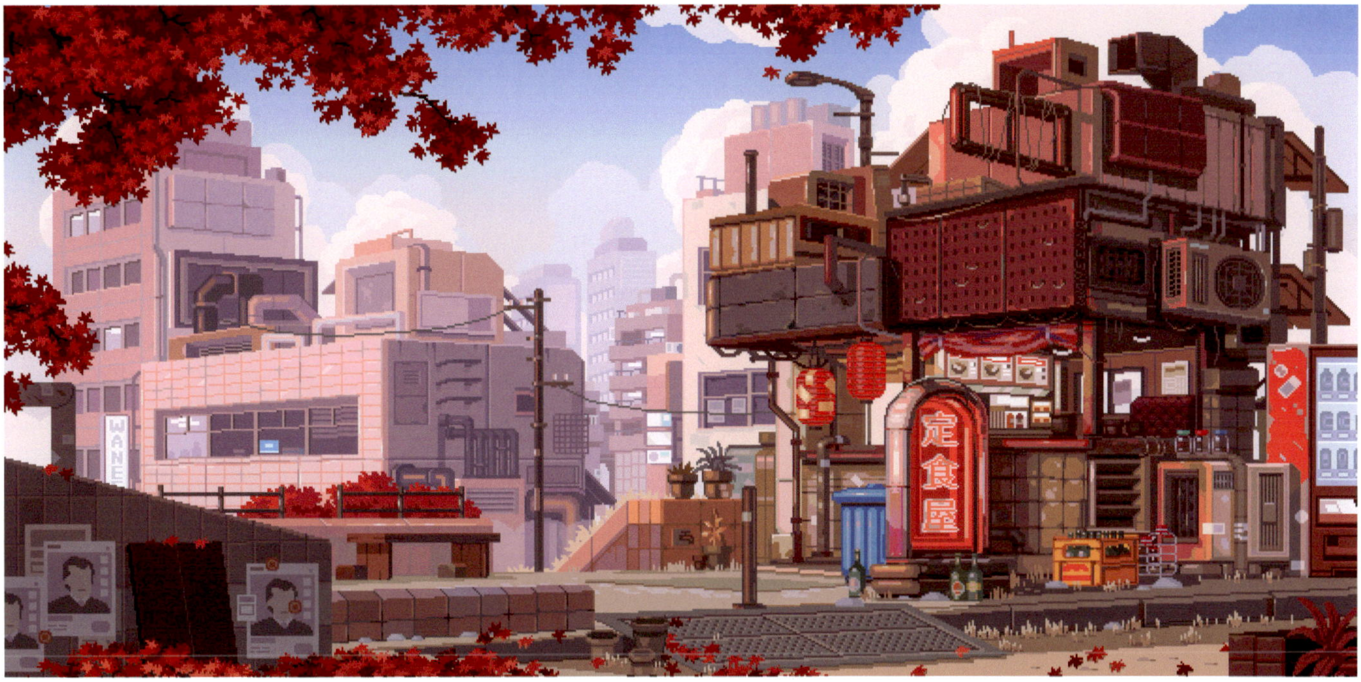

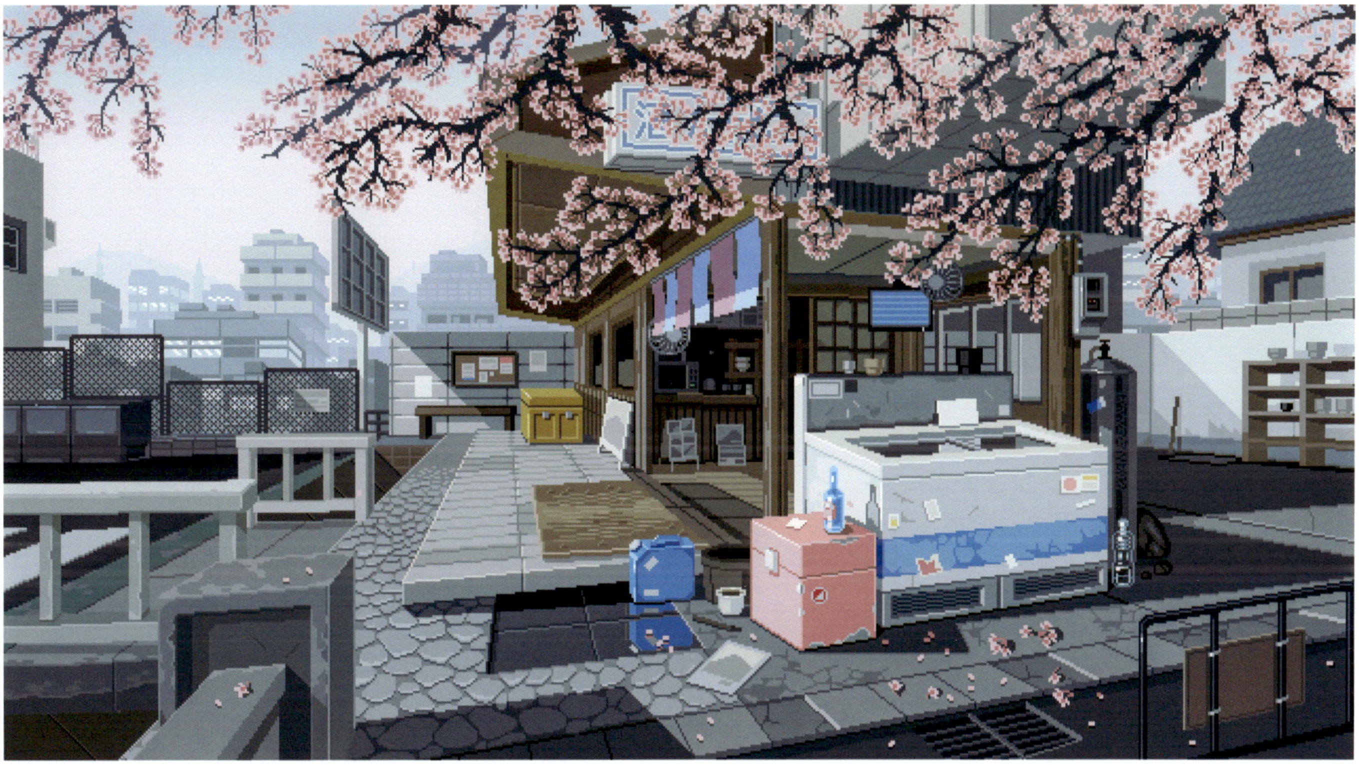

Top: *Zephyr,* 02/05/2020, 720×360px
Above: *Air,* 13/02/2020, 640×360px

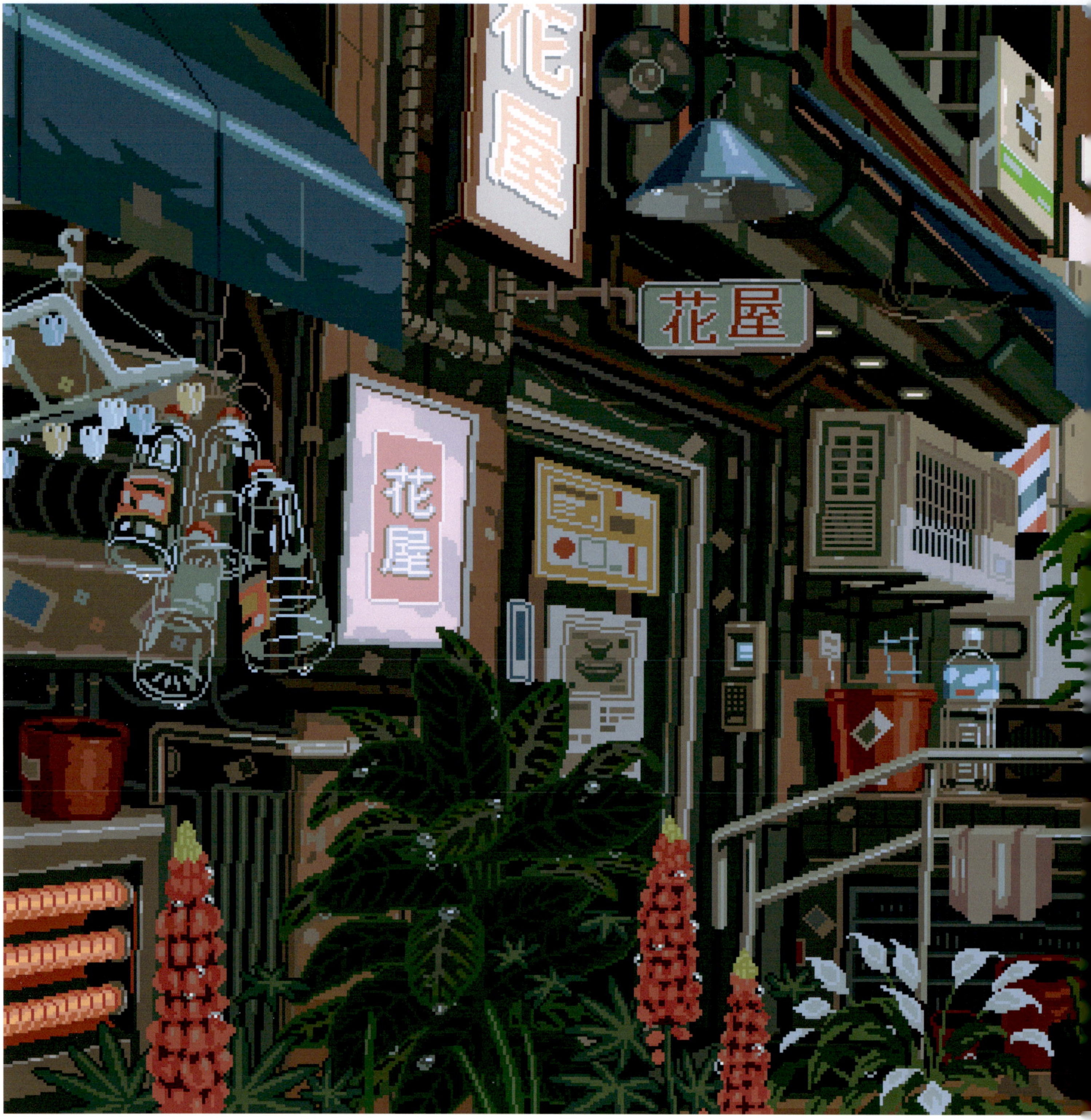

Evening Forecast, 24/05/2020, 720×360px

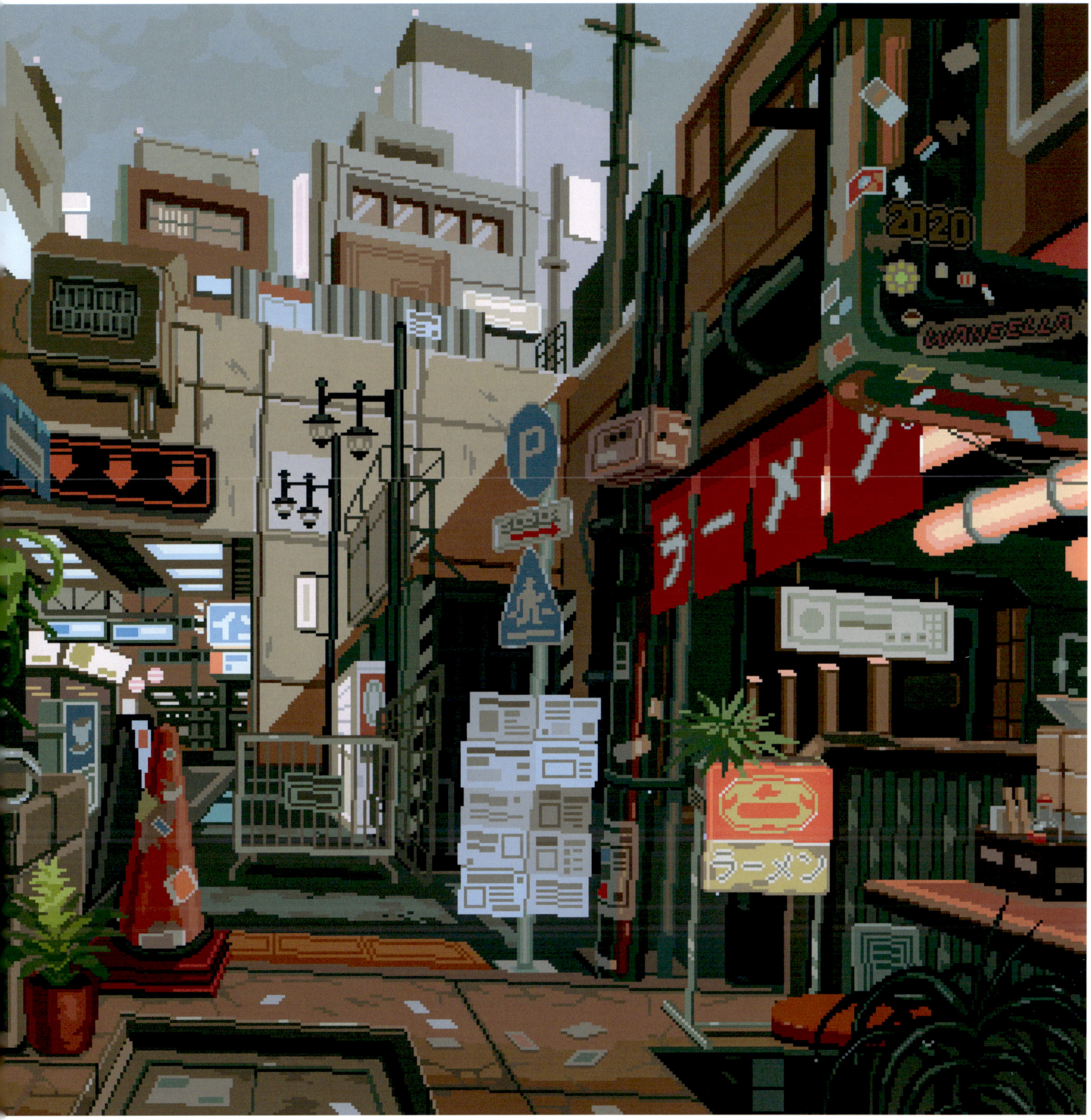
ラーメン
2020
ラーメン

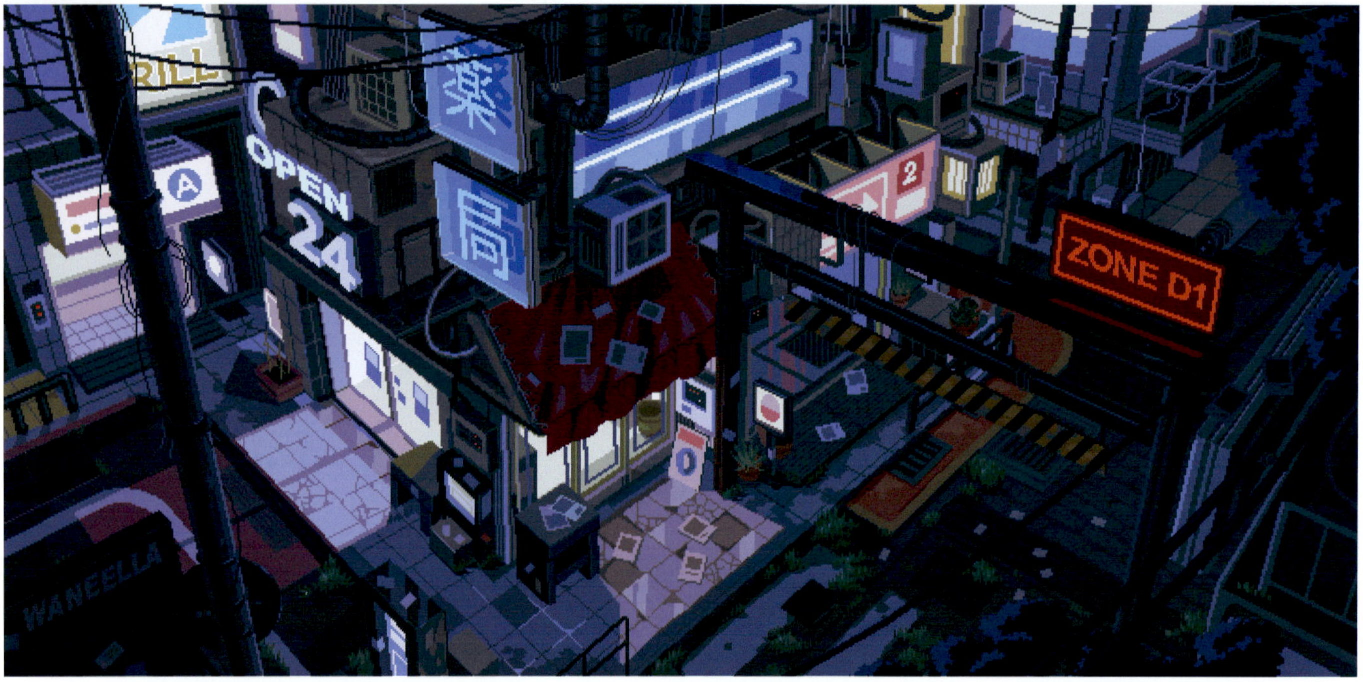

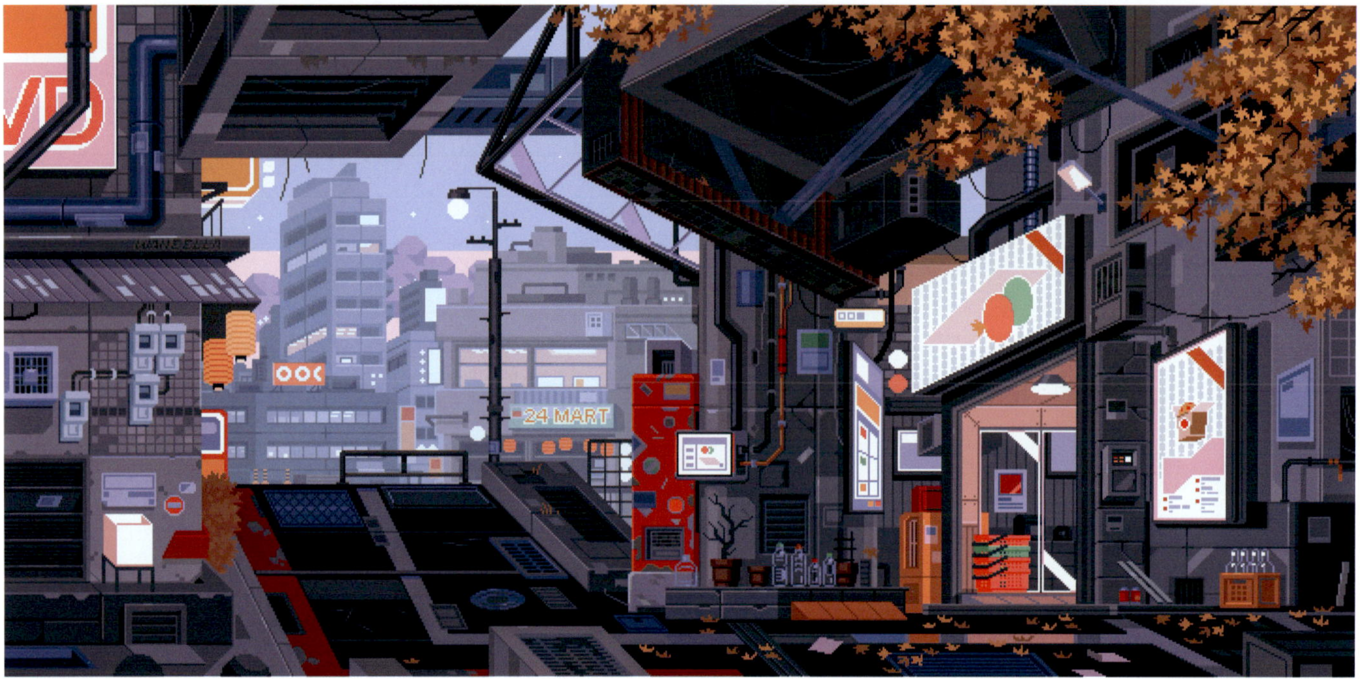

Top: *Pieces*, 13/12/2020, 720×360px
Above: *Circles*, 18/09/2020, 720×360px

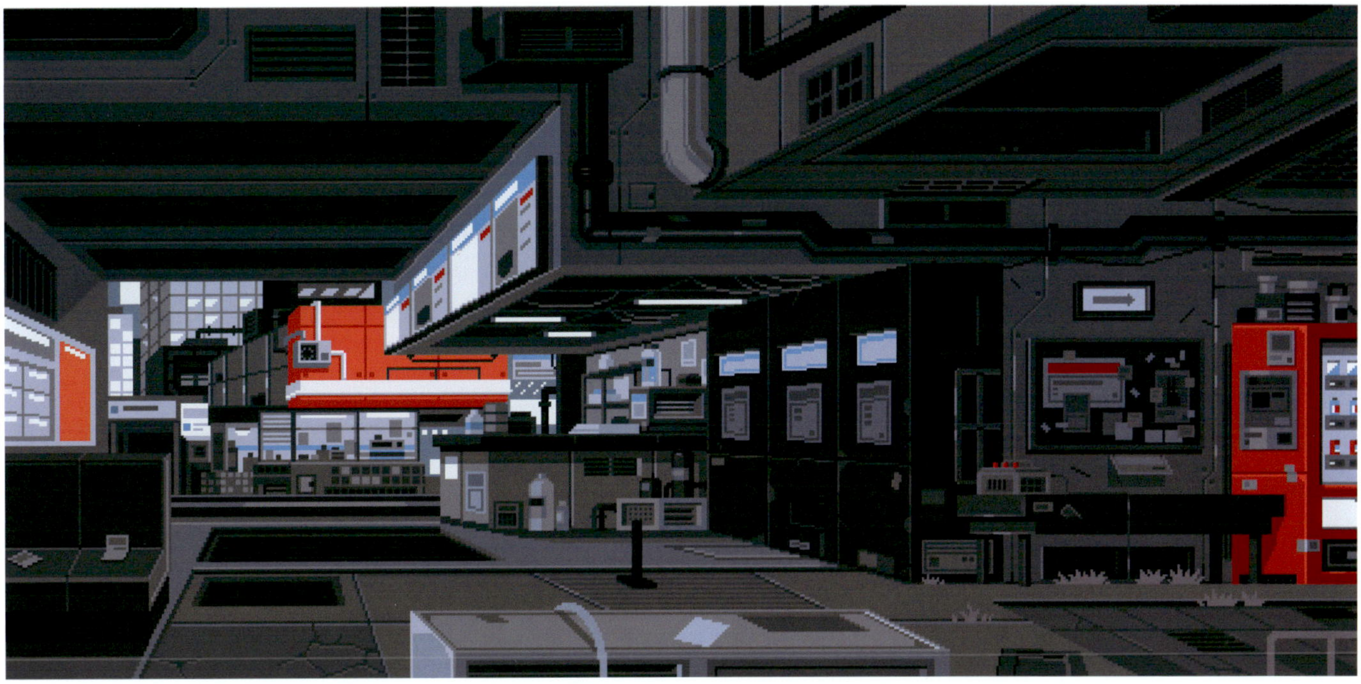

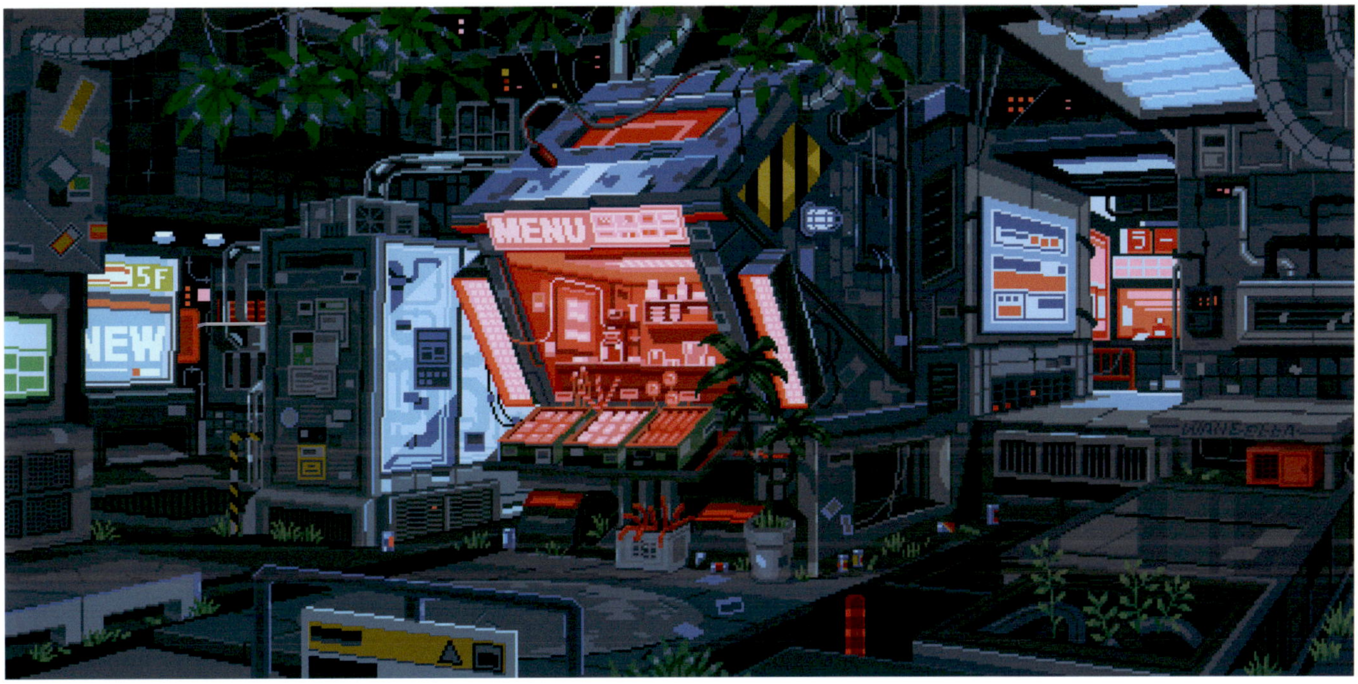

Top: *Untitled*, 26/10/2020, 540×270px
Above: *This One Still Works*, 12/10/2020, 540×270px

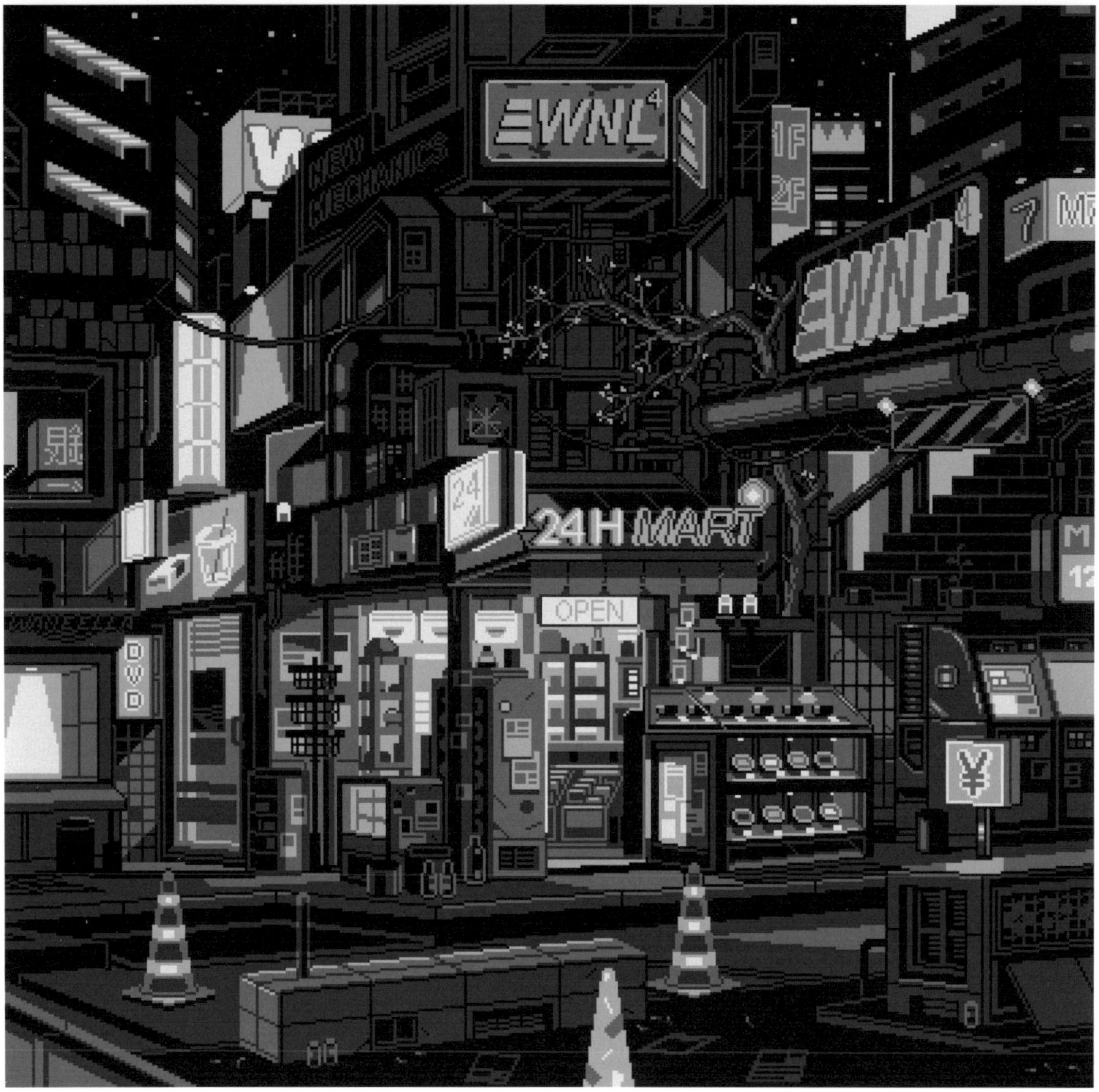

Bloom, 25/01/2020, 400×400px

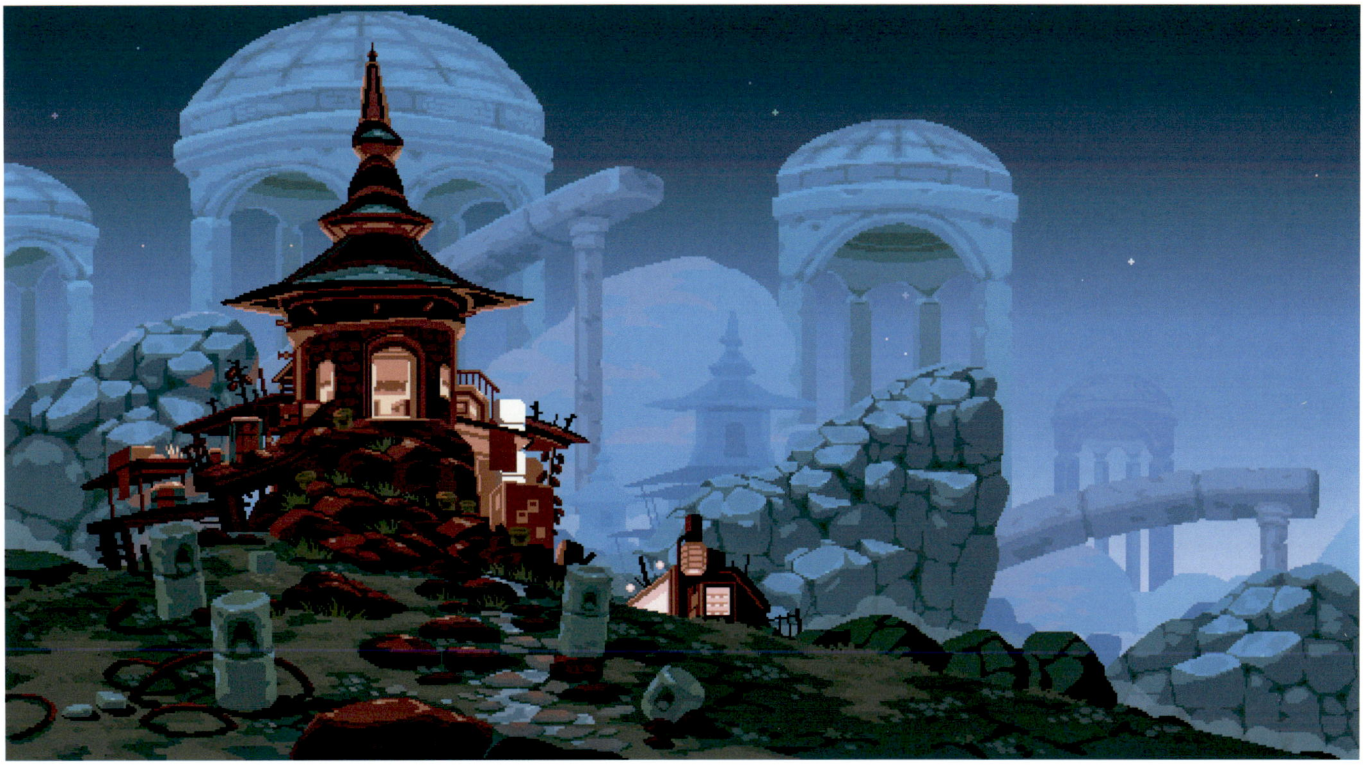

Dawn, 14/03/2020, 640×360px

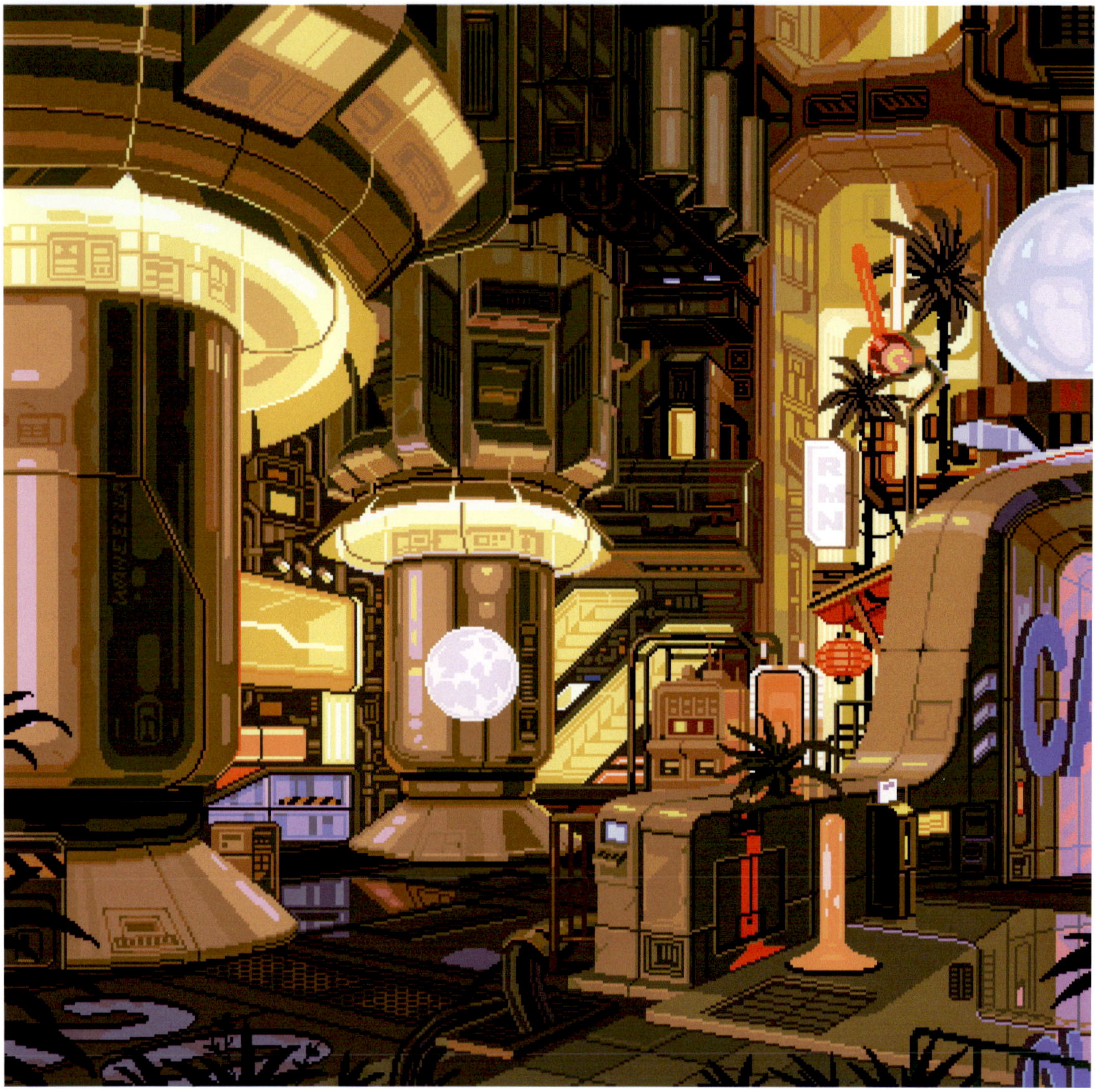

Amber, 18/01/2020, 400×400px

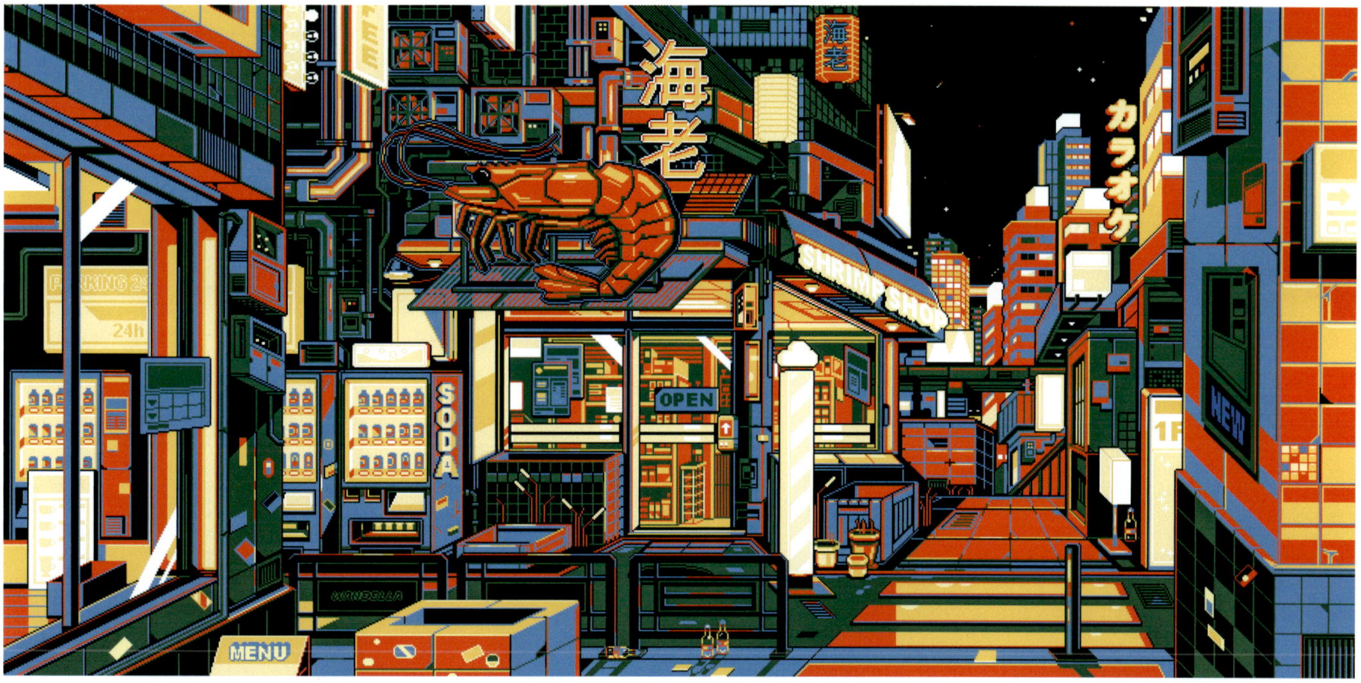

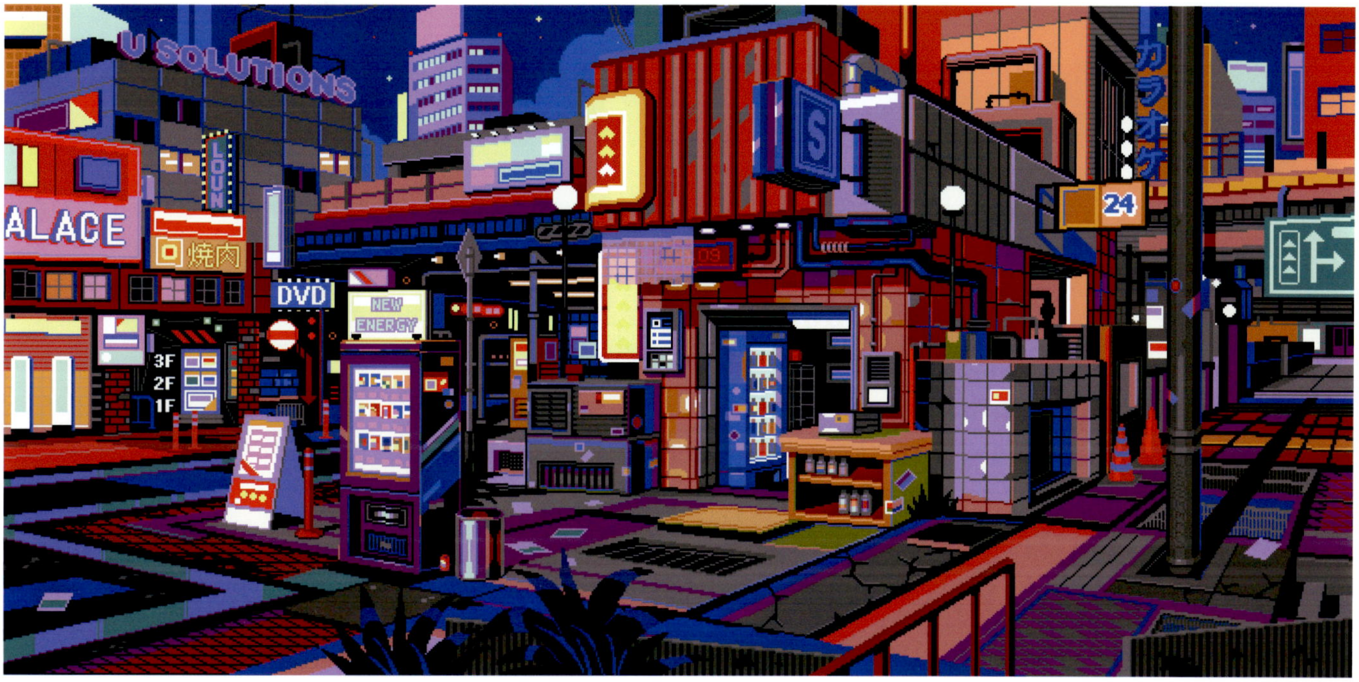

Top: *Lights*, 24/07/2020, 900×540px
Above: *Distorted*, 30/09/2020, 720×360px

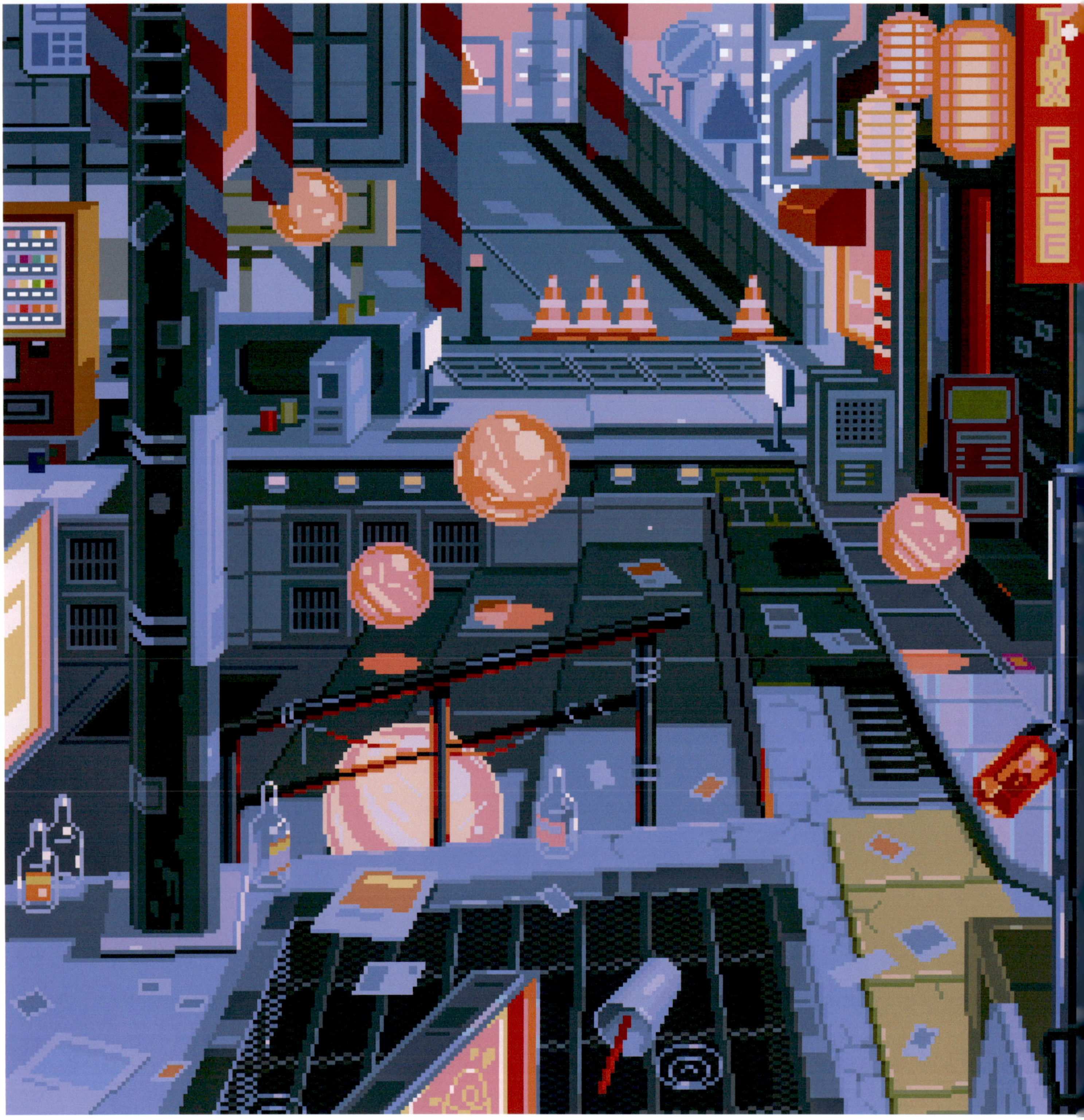

Pearls, 31/05/2020, 540×270px

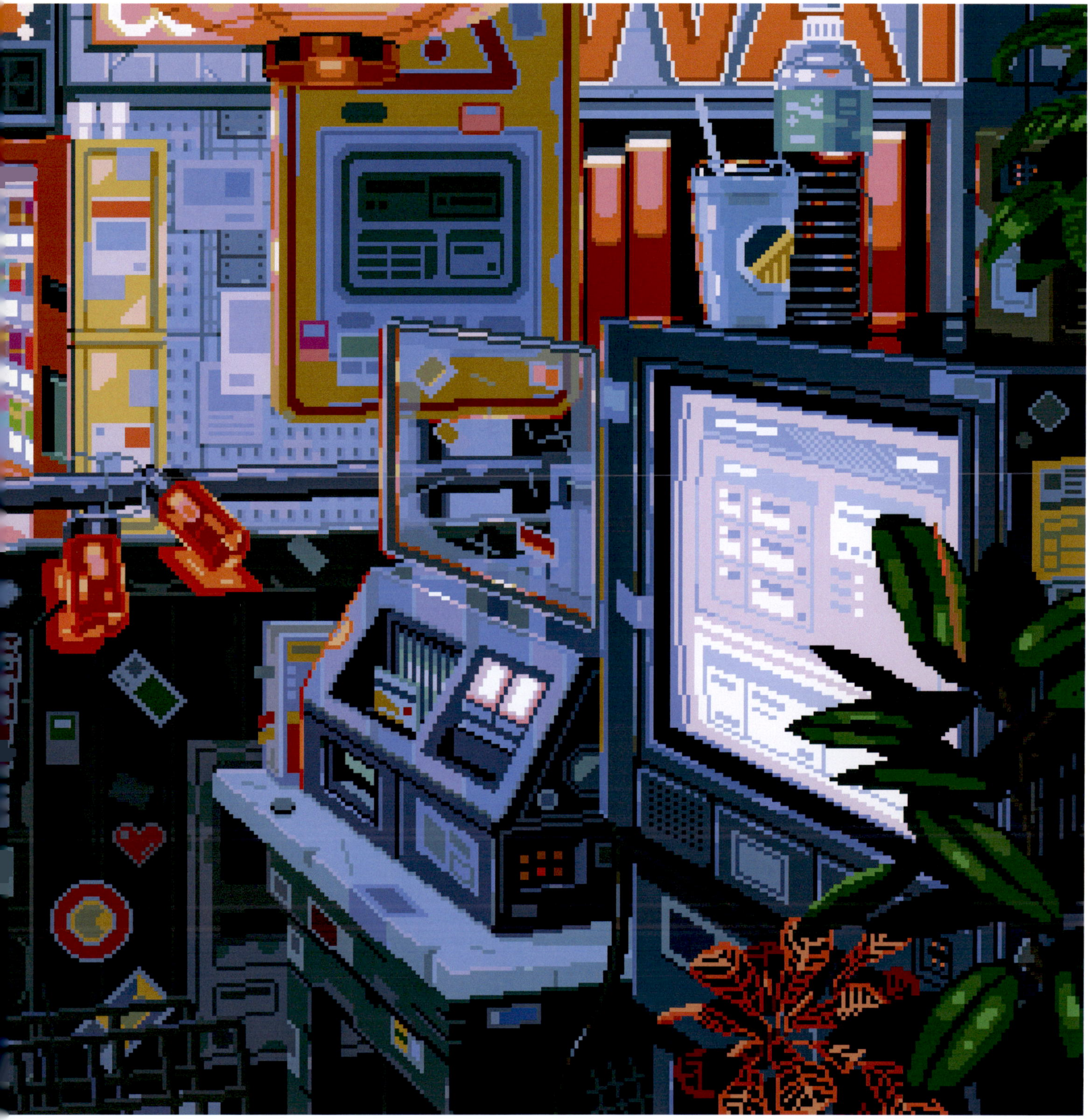

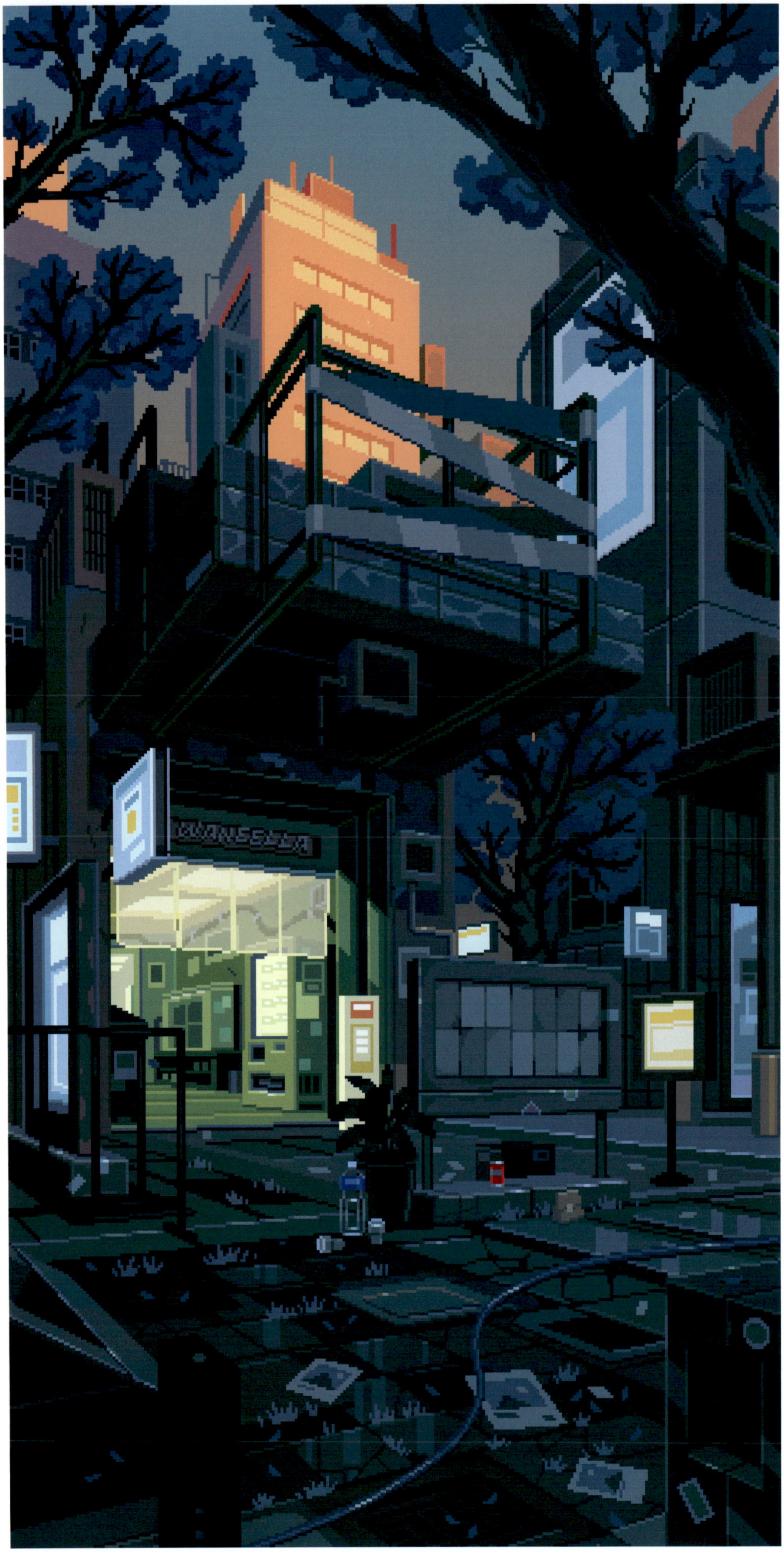

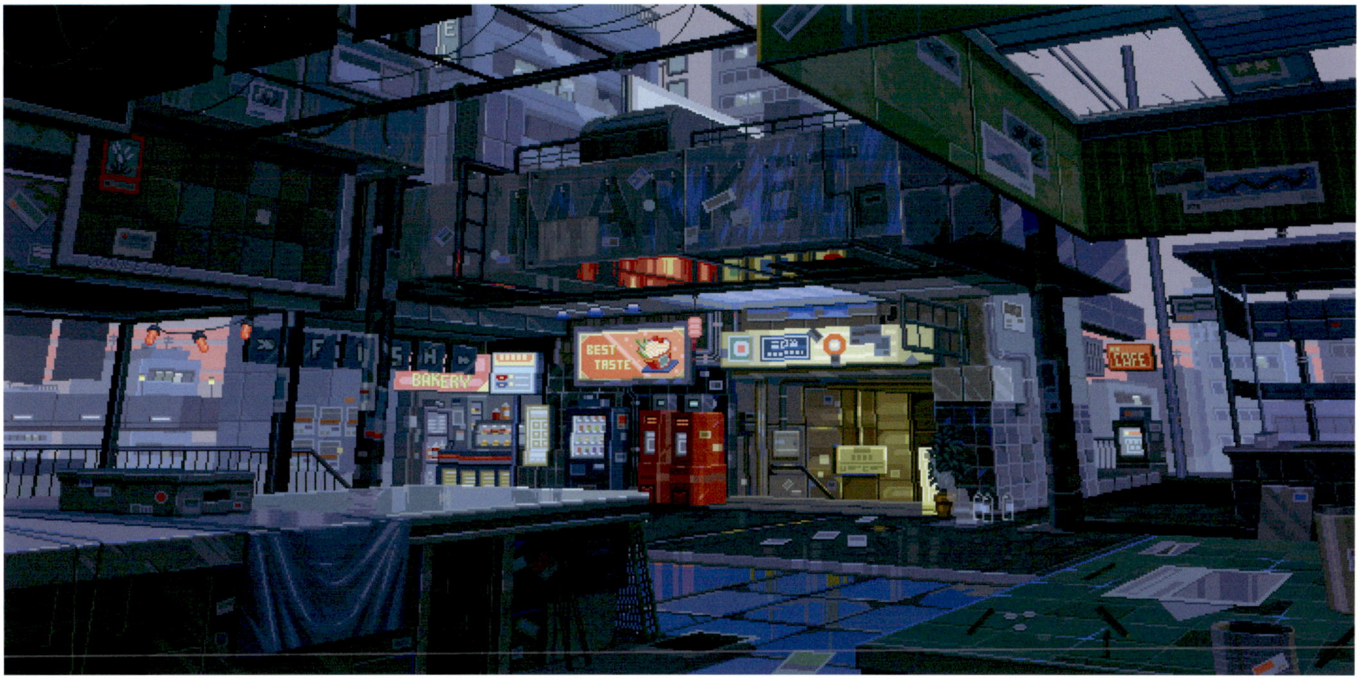

Left: *Evening*, 30/04/2021, 270×540px
Above: *Fragments*, 28/09/2021, 720×360px

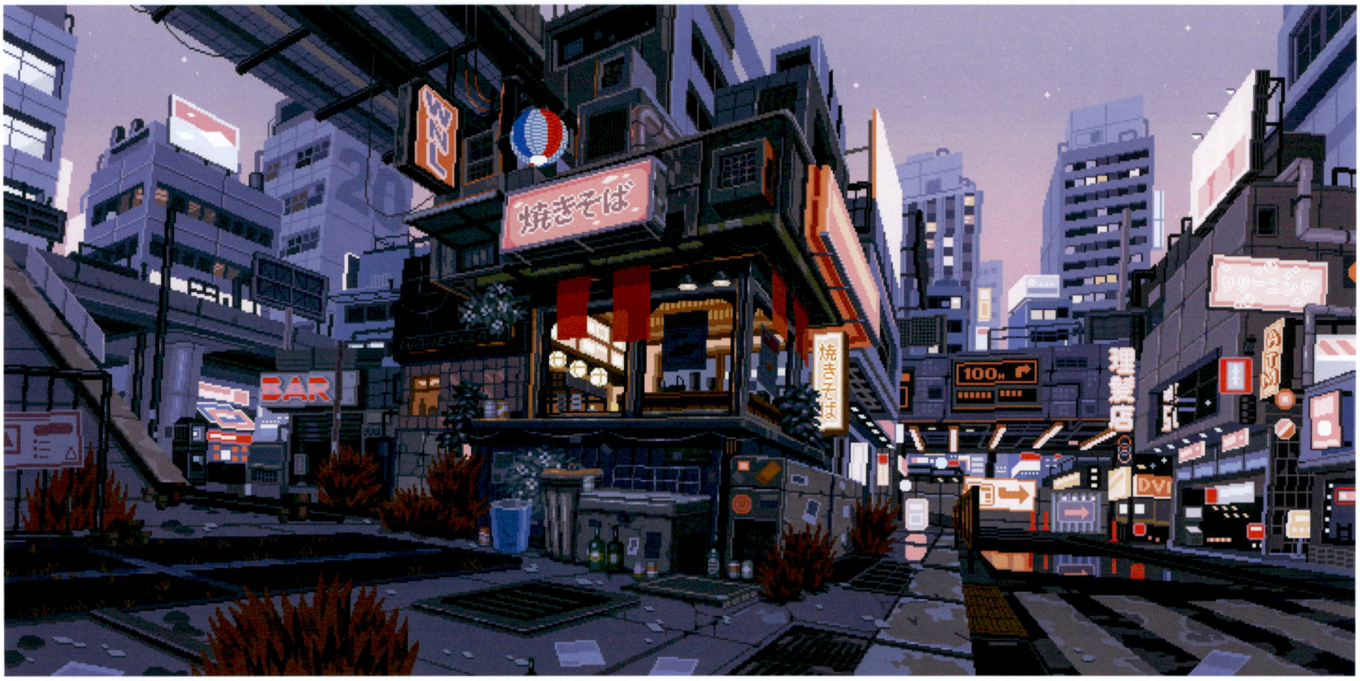

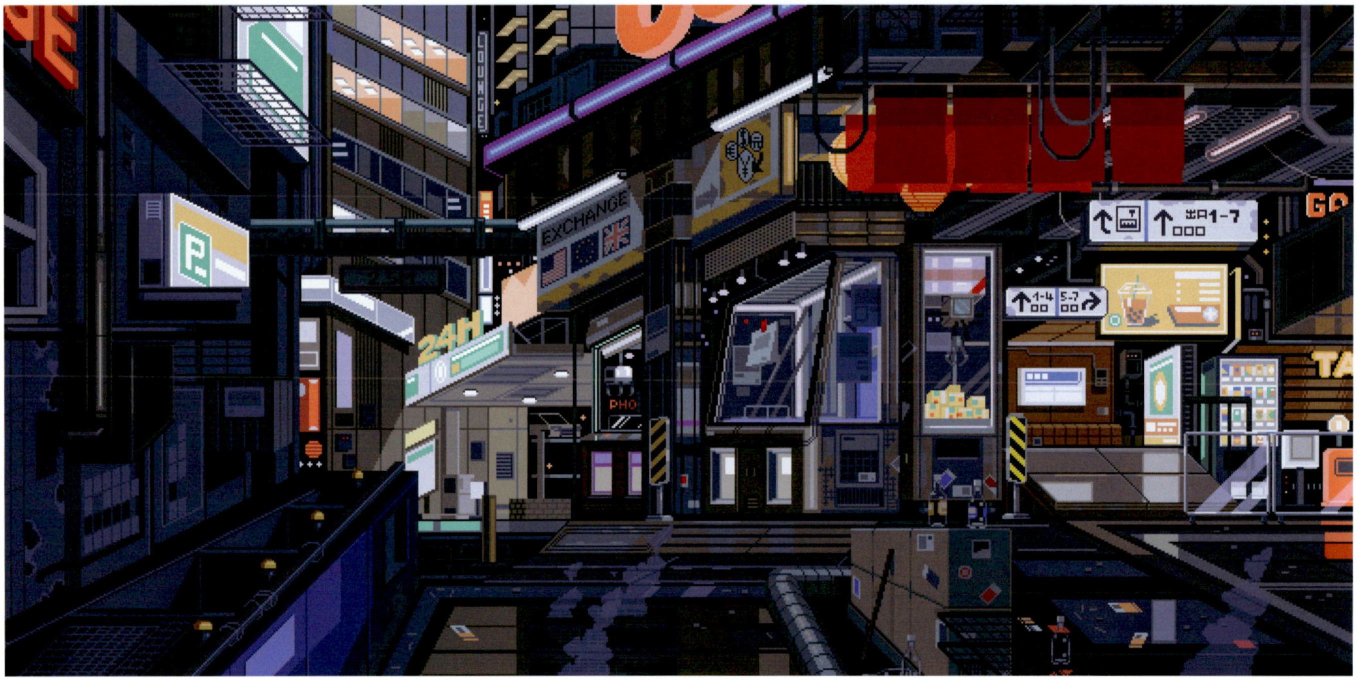

Top: *Abyss*, 15/05/2020, 720×360px
Above: *Night*, 12/06/2021, 720×360px

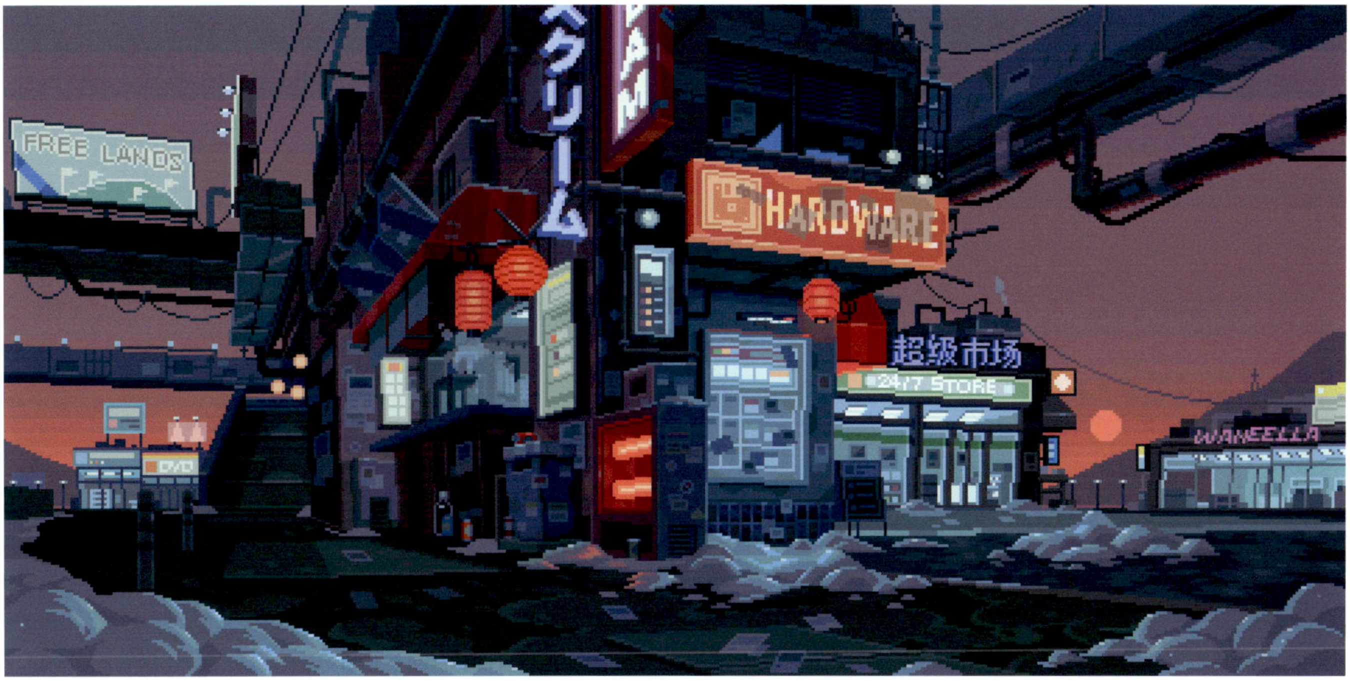

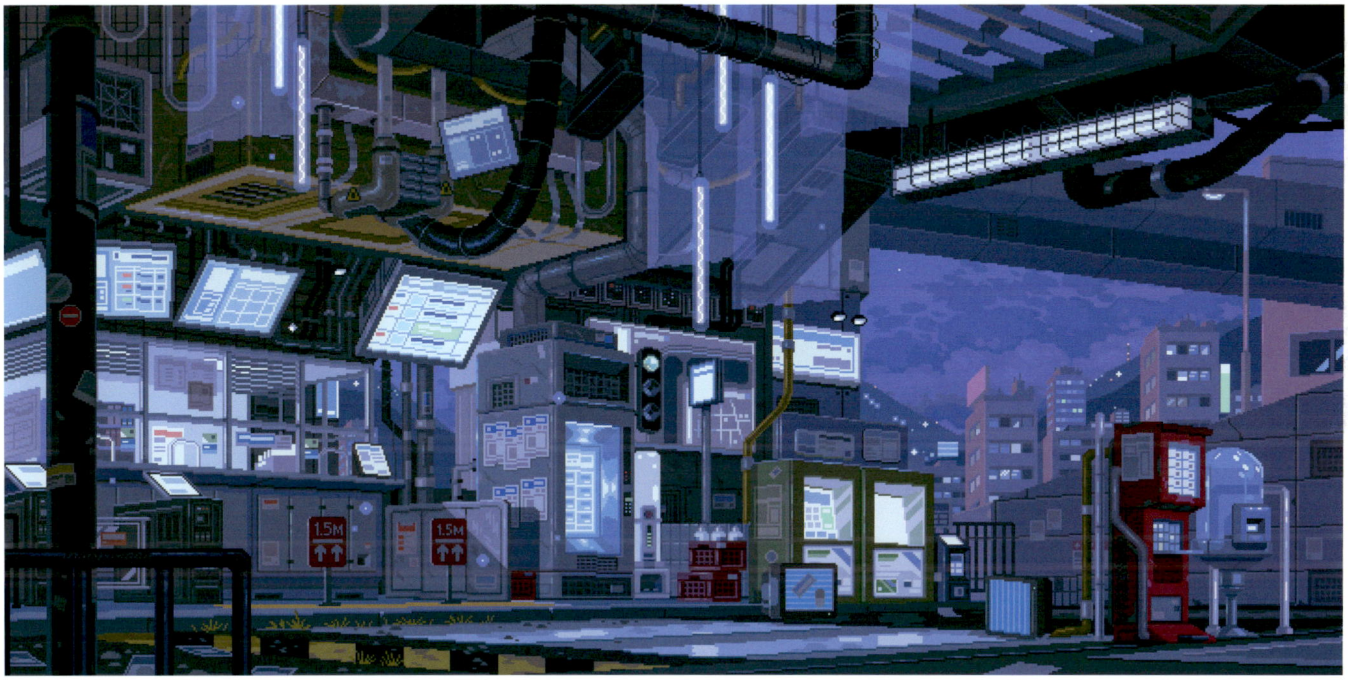

Top: *Faraway Point*, 25/12/2021, 480×240px
Above: *Distance*, 16/04/2020, 720×360px

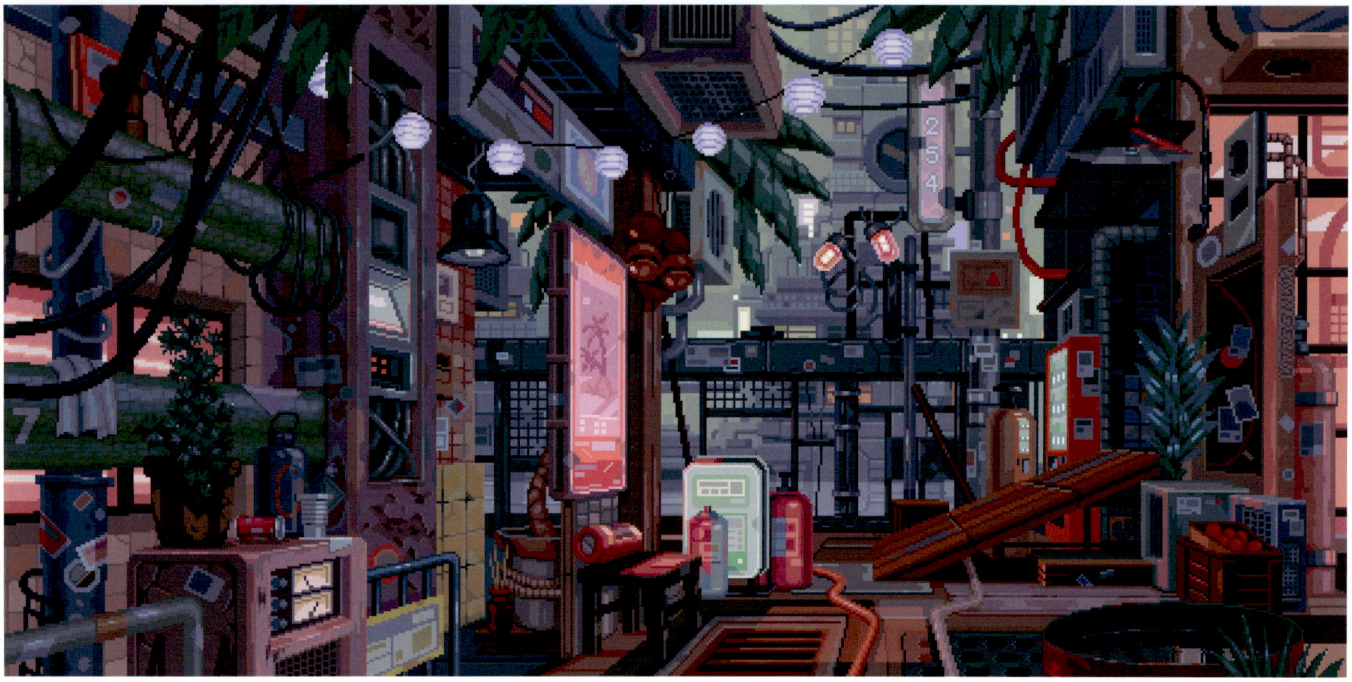

Harbour, 25/04/2021, 560×280px

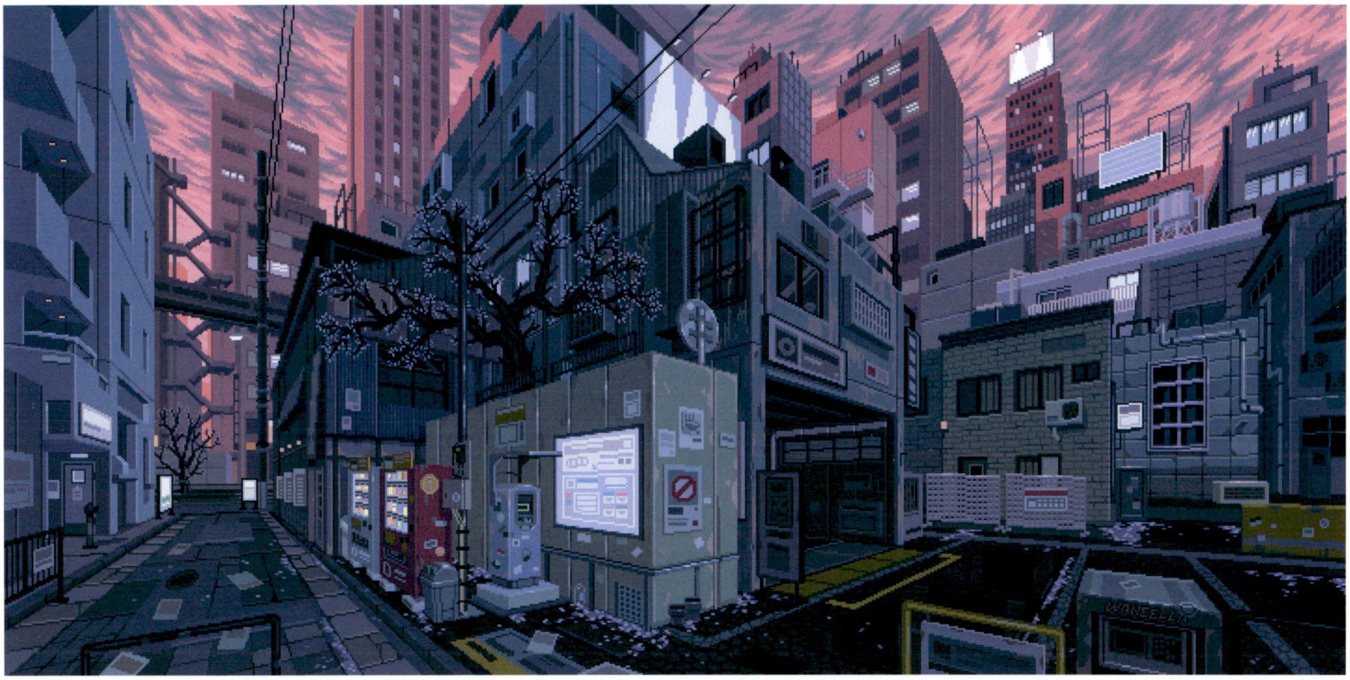

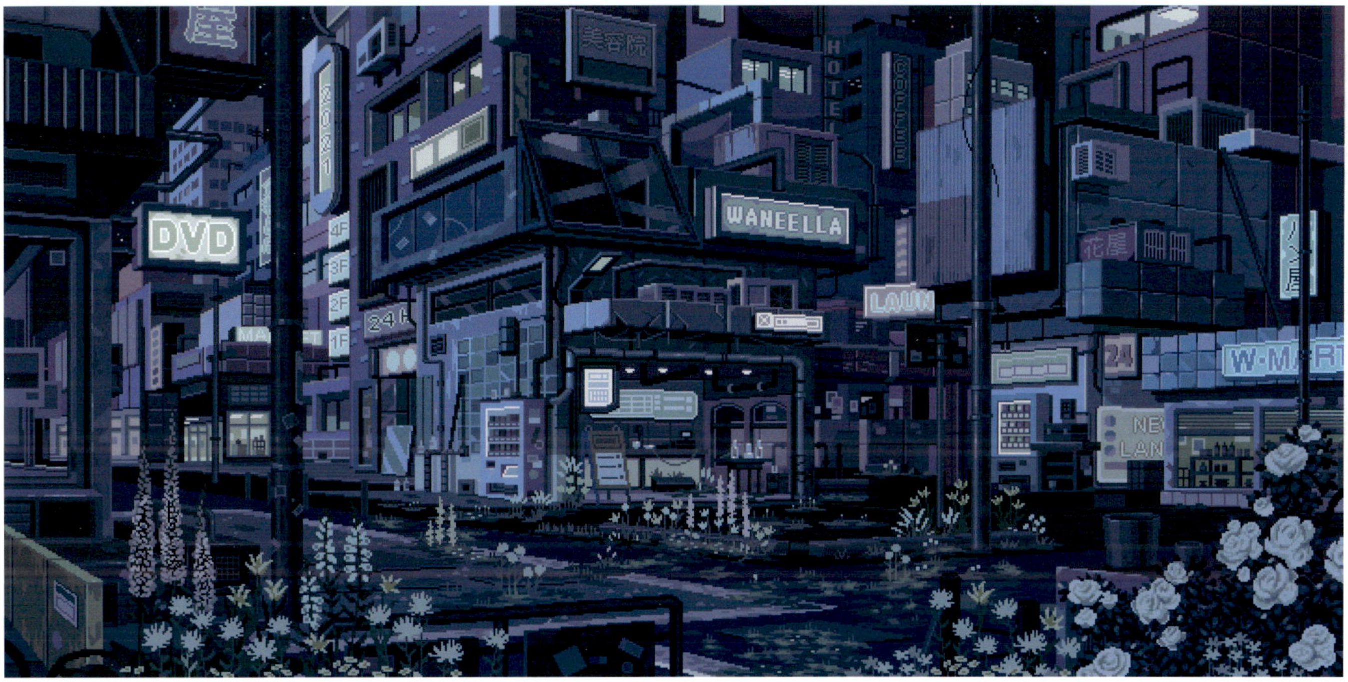

Top: *Empty Spaces*, 22/05/2021, 720×360px
Above: *Stardust*, 25/06/2021, 720×360px

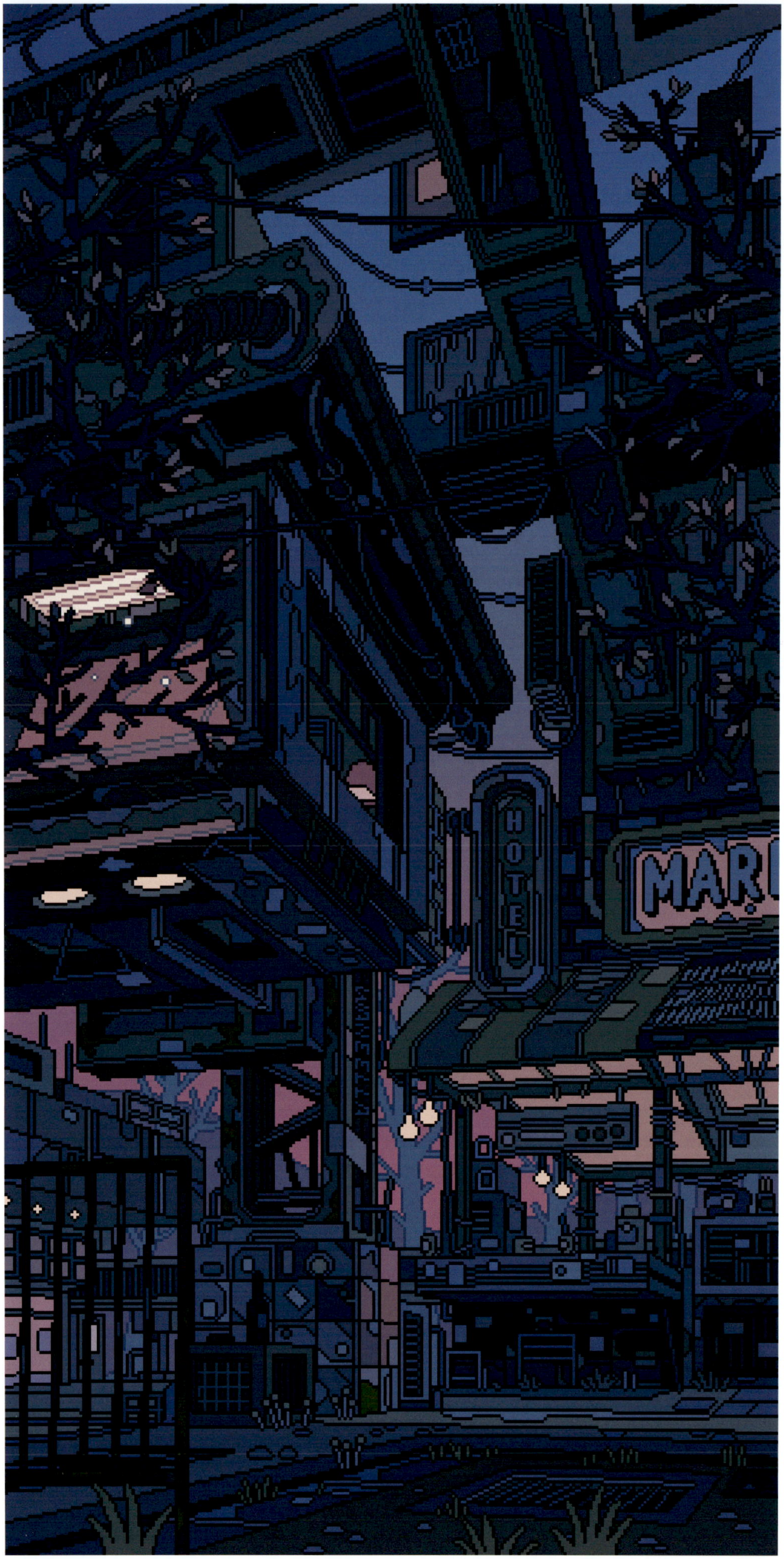
HOTEL
MAR

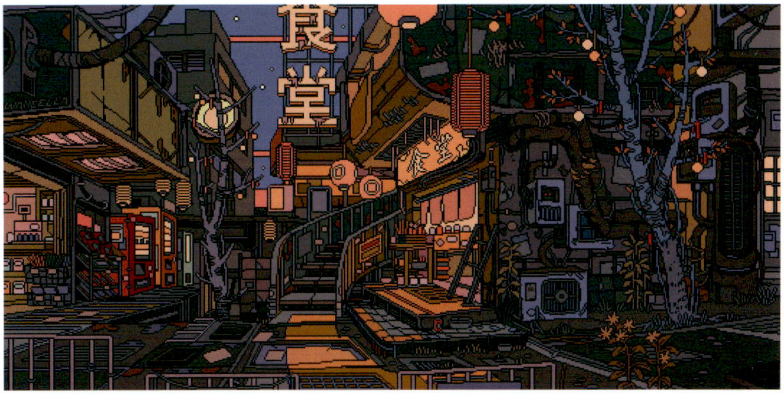

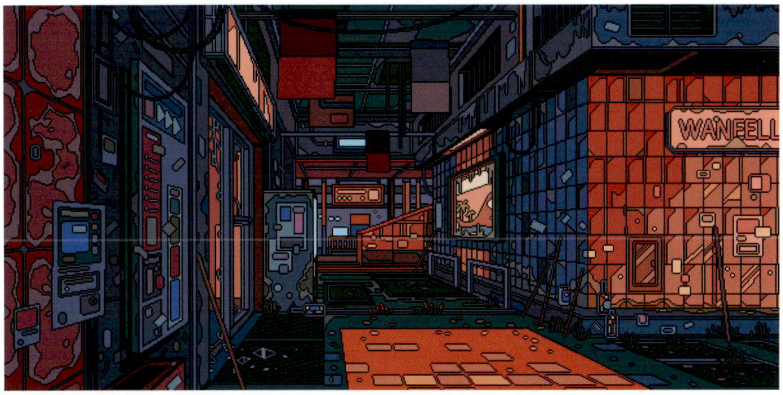

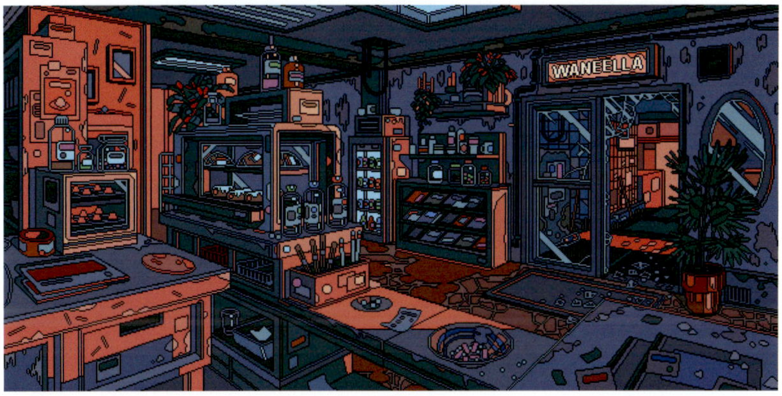

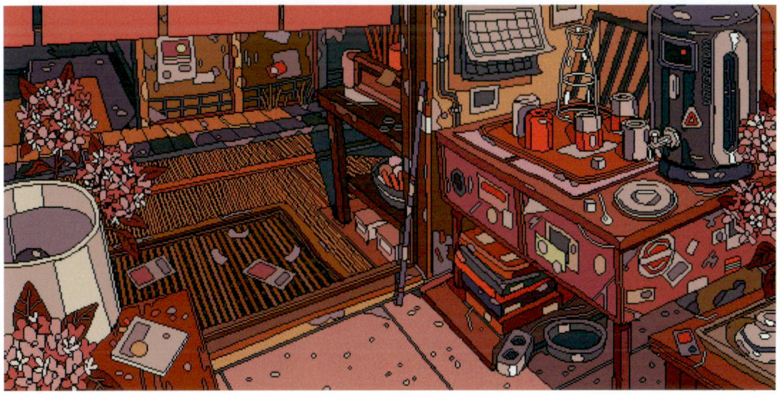

Top: *Looks Like A Nice Place Pt1,* 29/01/2021, 540×270px
Second from top: *Warm Days Pt2,* 10/12/2021, 600×300px
Third from top: *Warm Days Pt1,* 10/12/2021, 600×300px
Above: *Looks Like A Nice Place Pt2,* 29/01/2021, 540×270px
Left: *Southern Outskirts* (Blue version), 21/03/2021, 270×540px

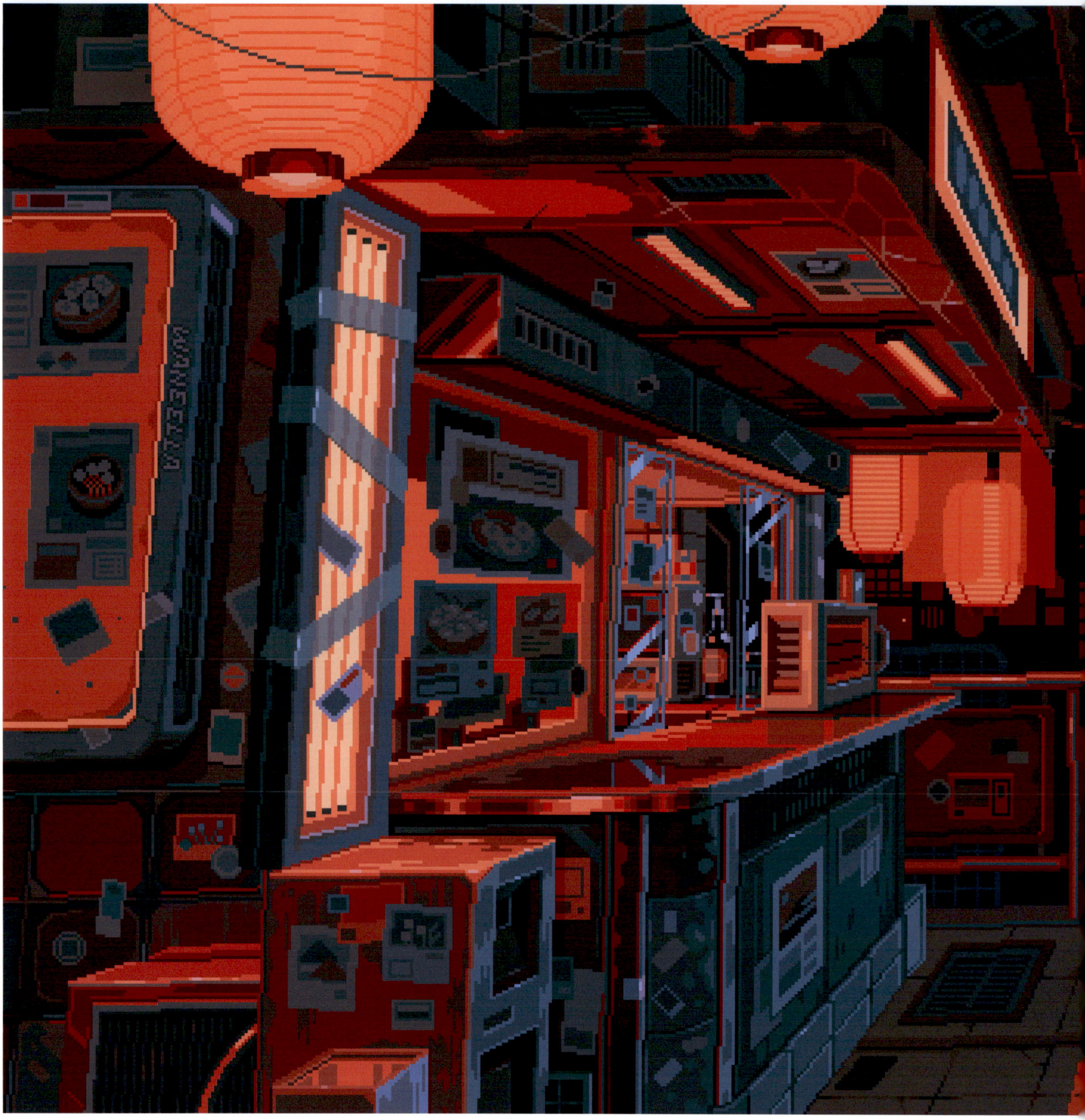

Block R-38, 27/02/2021, 720×360px

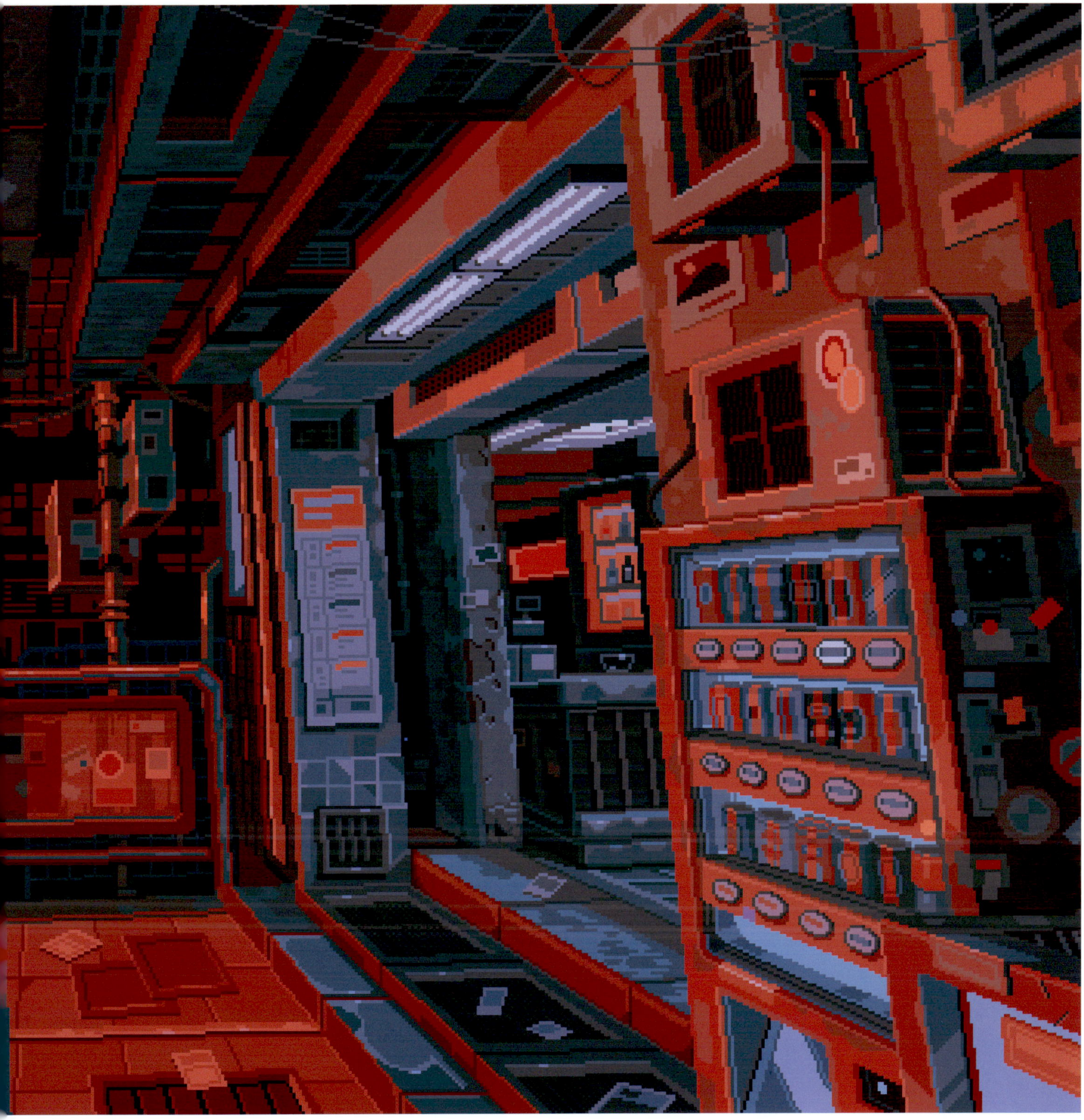

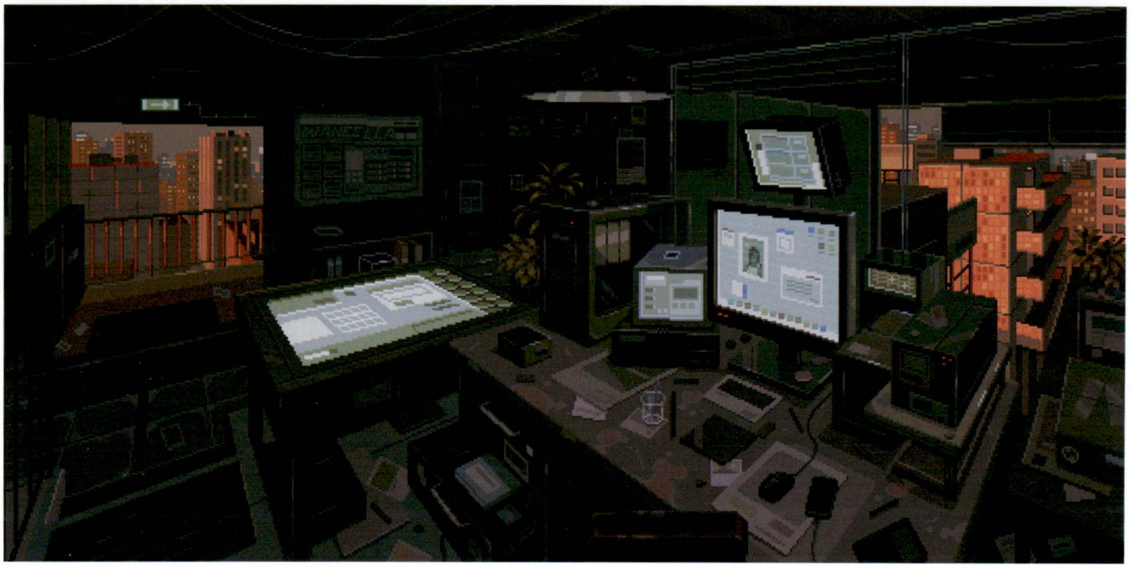

Dark Corners, 26/10/2021, 540×270px

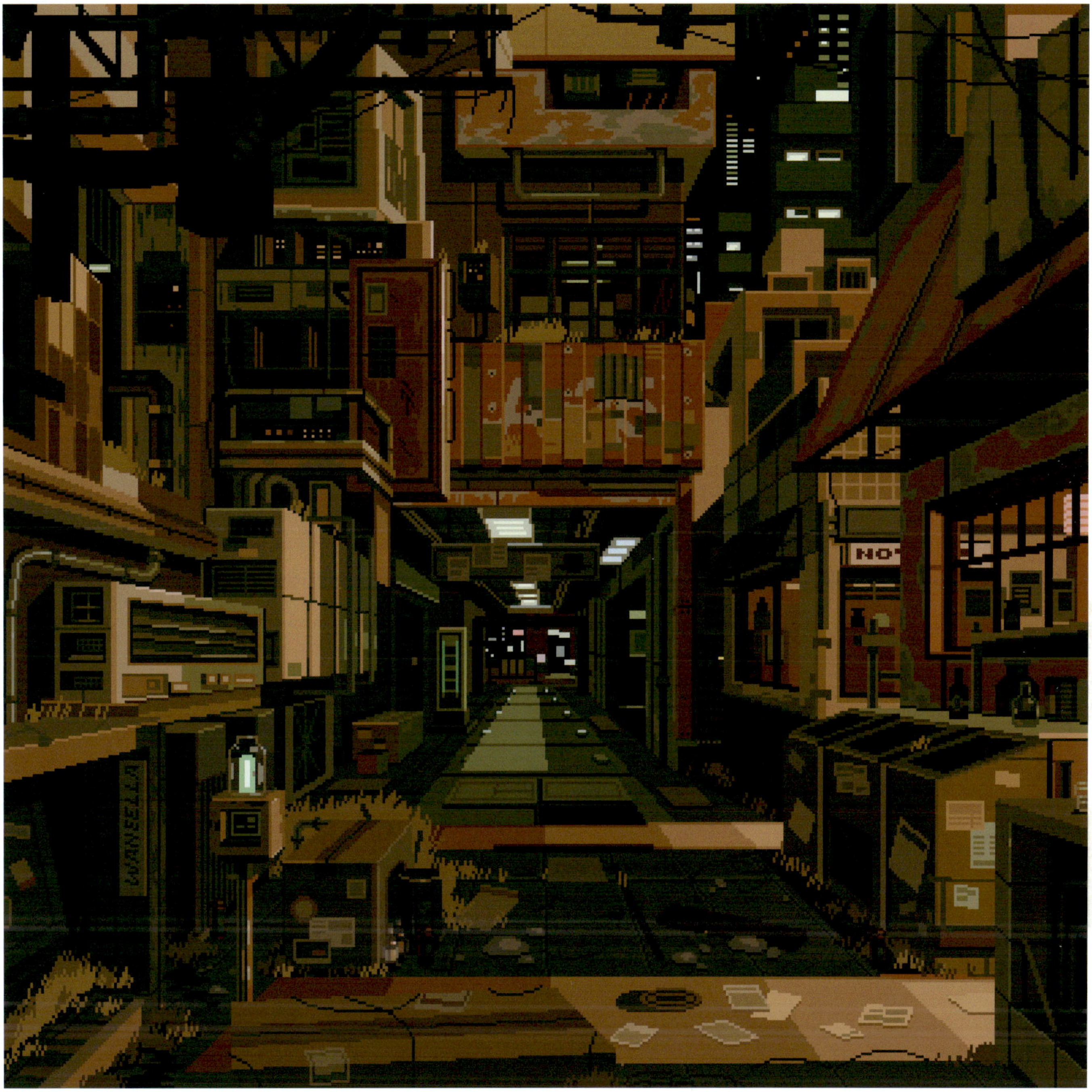

Solar Wind, 25/10/2019, 400×400px

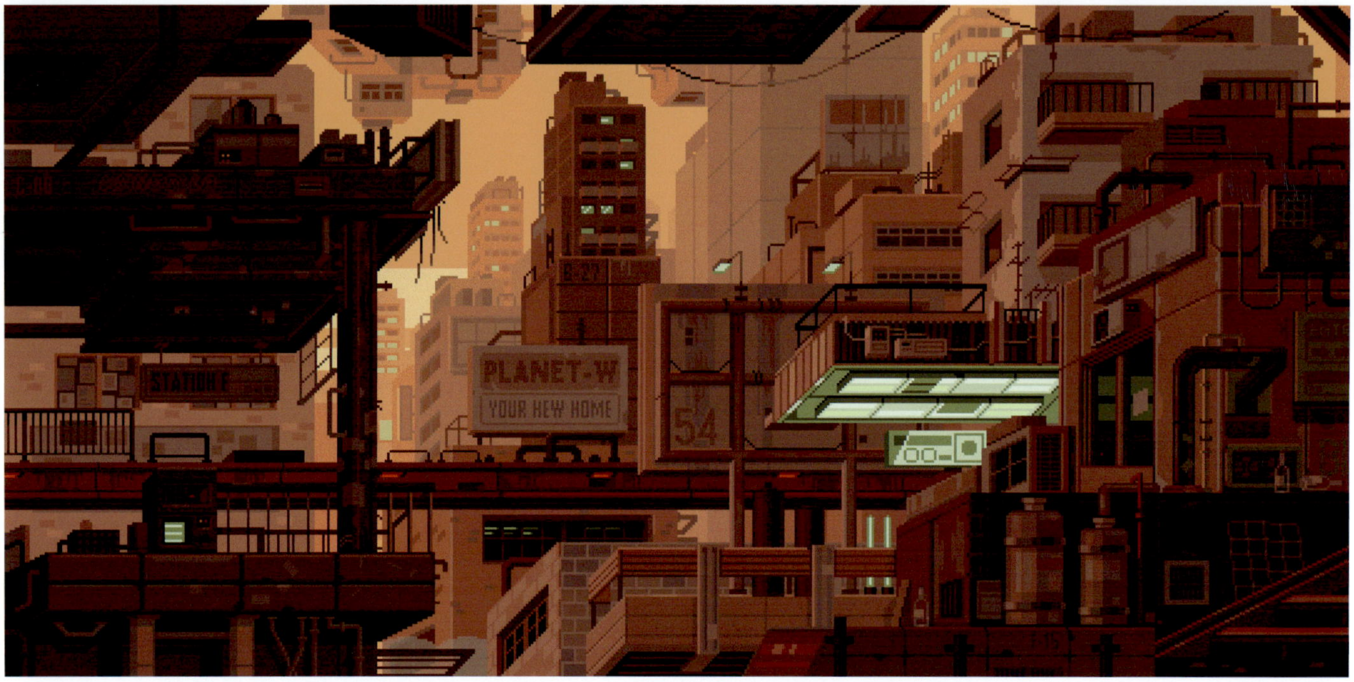

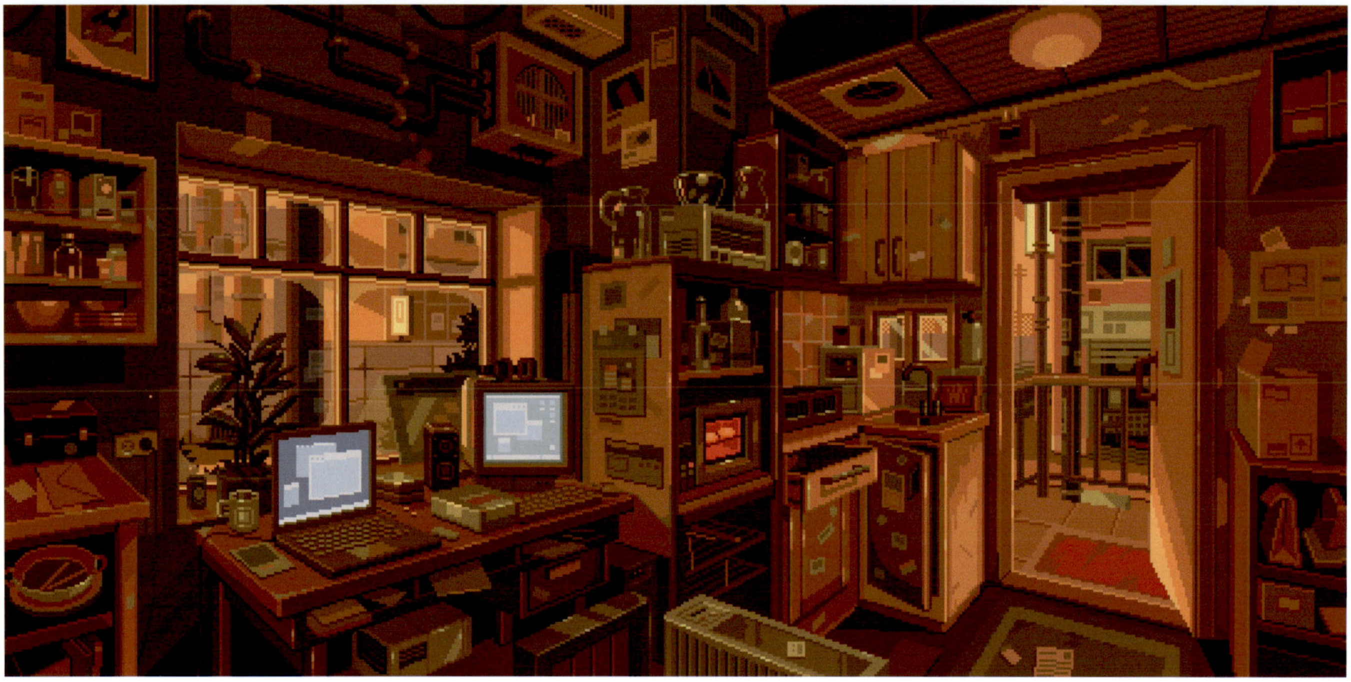

Top: *Old Town,* 13/08/2020, 540×270px
Above: *Heat,* 23/07/2021, 540×270px

PROCESS

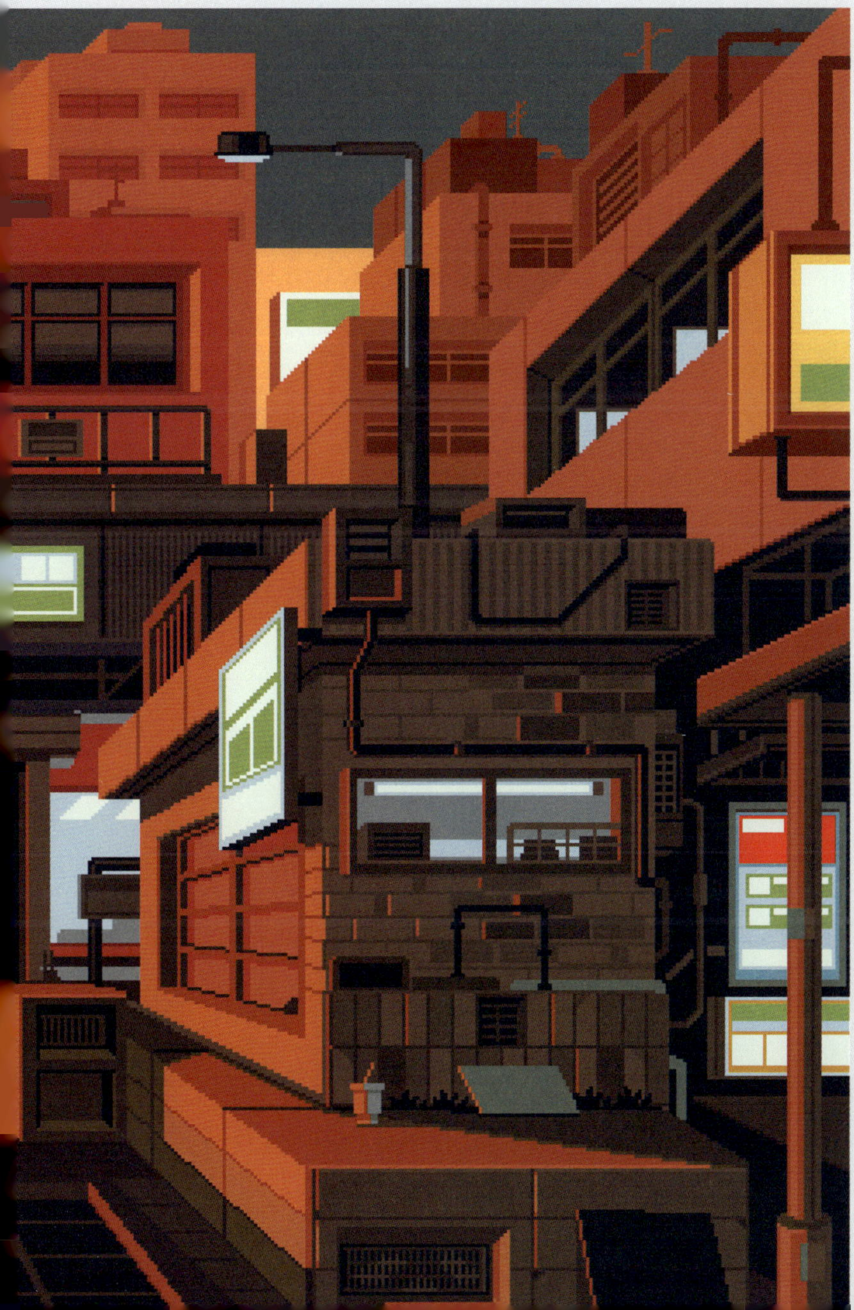

↓ Just before starting this image, I had watched *Initial D* and *Puella Magi Madoka Magica*. Inspired by these films, I knew that I wanted to make something that also featured a retro car.

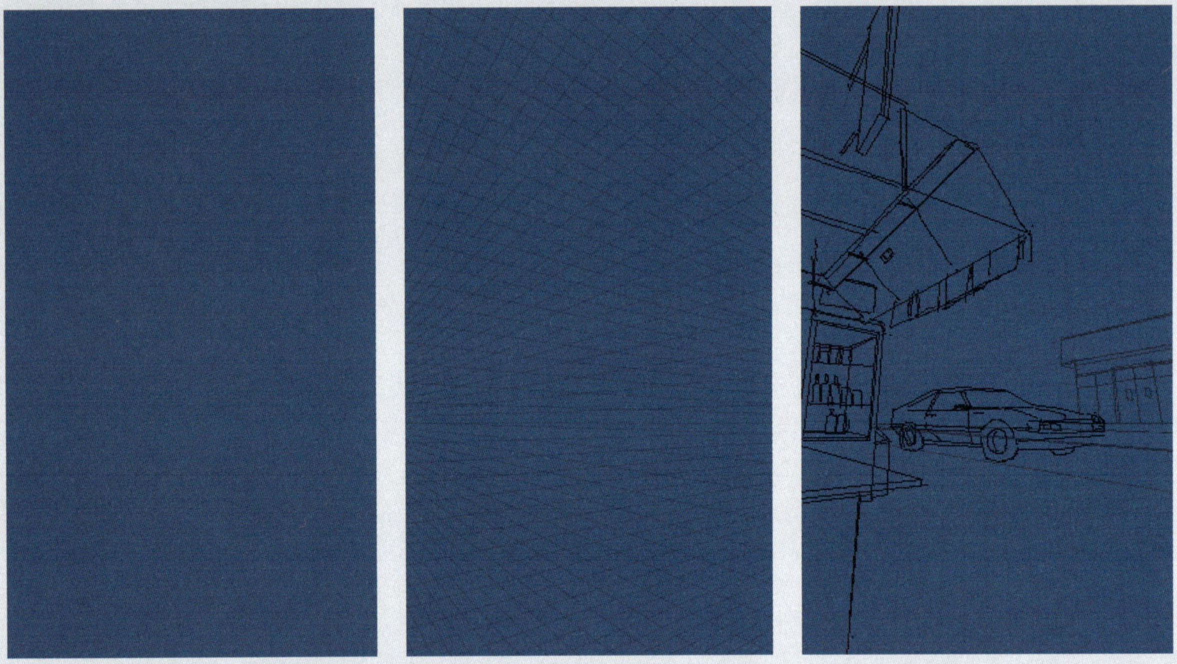

↓ This was one of the rare occasions where I had some idea of what I wanted to draw before starting out. I love the time of day when the sun has dipped below the horizon but the sky isn't yet fully dark – I call it the 'blue hour'. But when I filled out everything with blue, I felt there wasn't enough going on in this illustration, so I started adding different details here and there.

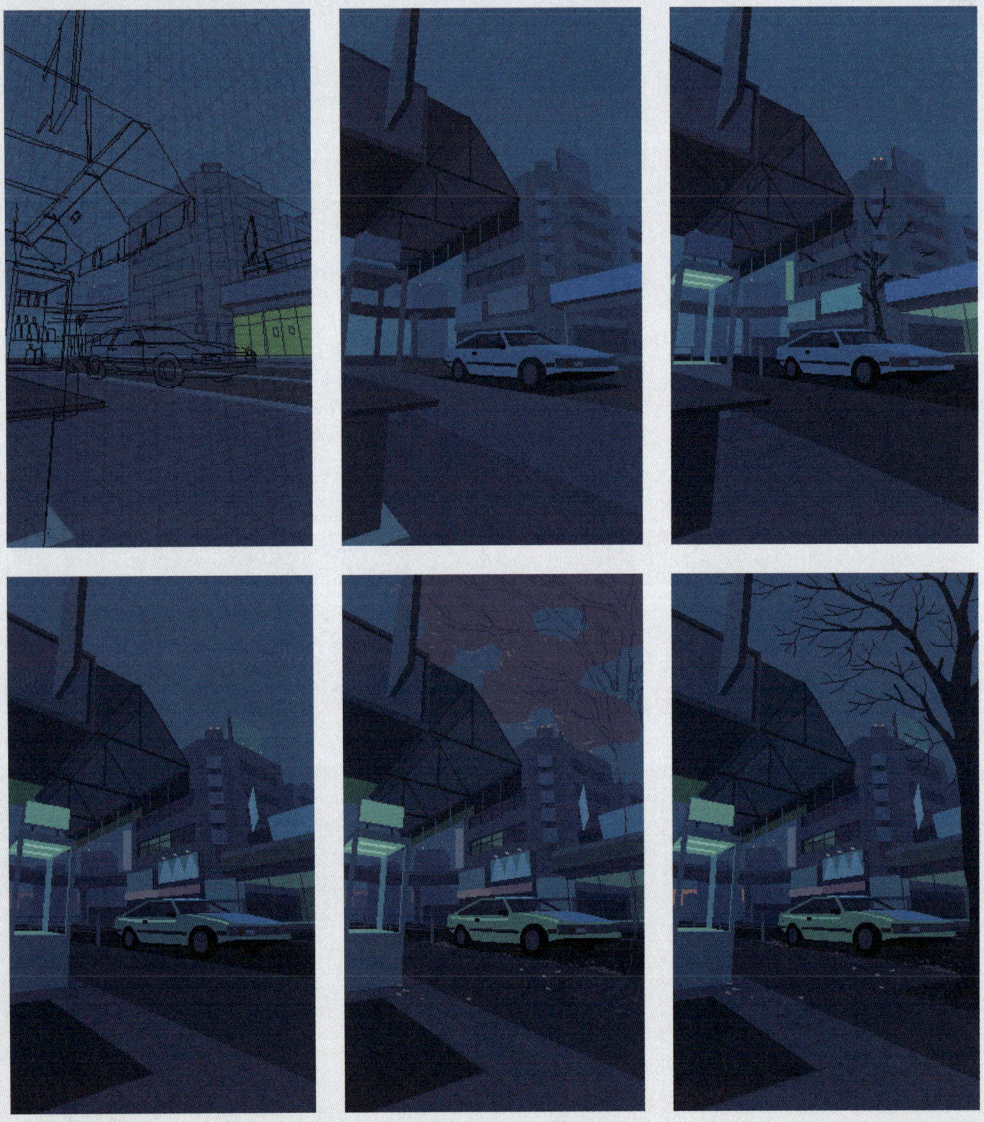

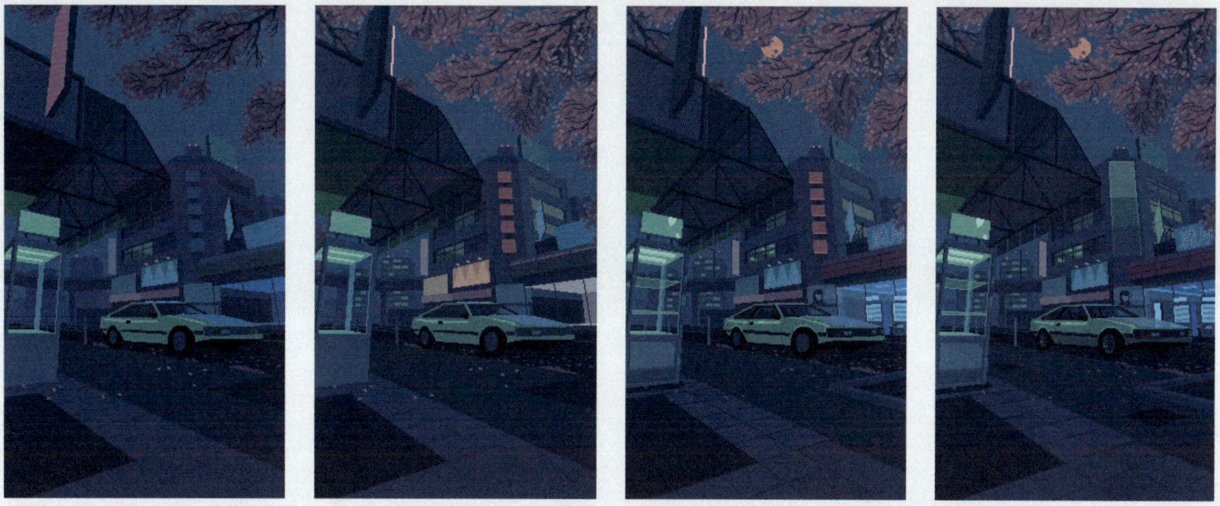

↑ Glowing billboards made a great difference, as did the tree in the foreground. These days, I feel like these additions have become my little shortcut for completing an illustration... when in doubt, add a tree, moon and illuminated signs! This time, however, I wondered whether the moon, high in the sky, was capturing too much attention, so I experimented with placing it in some less obvious positions.

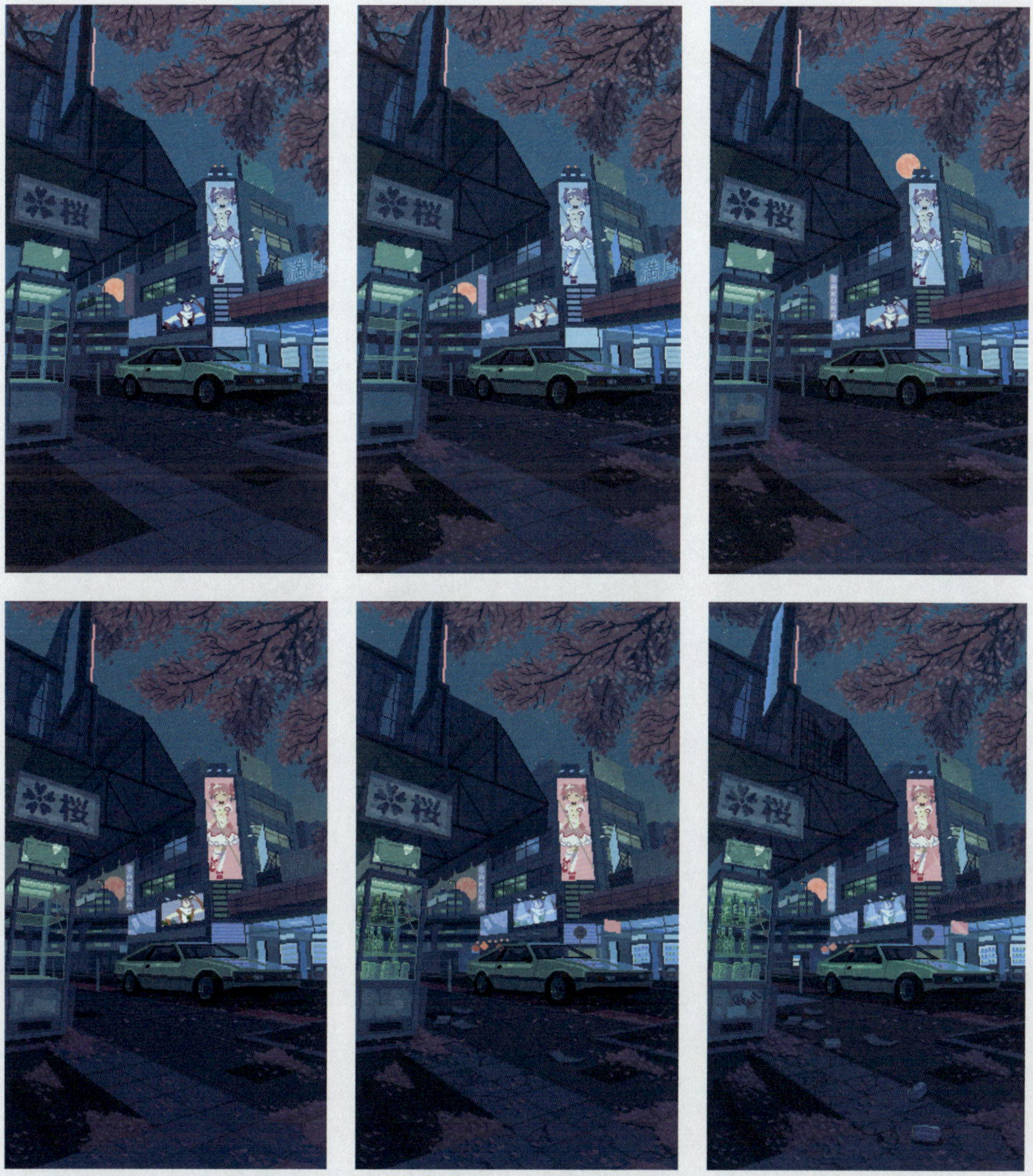

↑ To make the billboards and signs even more prominent, I added characters to them. I'm fond of falling-leaf animations, but in this case I used piles of leaves on the ground instead. When I posted this image on Tumblr, some people instantly recognized the make and model of the car – which was funny, because I hadn't known any details would make it identifiable. I drew it using a reference image.

↓ Recently, I've felt a desire for my illustrations to look more lively, imperfect and even painterly. So, from time to time, I'll start by drawing with blobs of colour rather than sketches, wondering if I'll manage to make something of it. This is one of those attempts. I tried a few compositions but wasn't happy with the results, since everything looked regular and not dynamic enough.

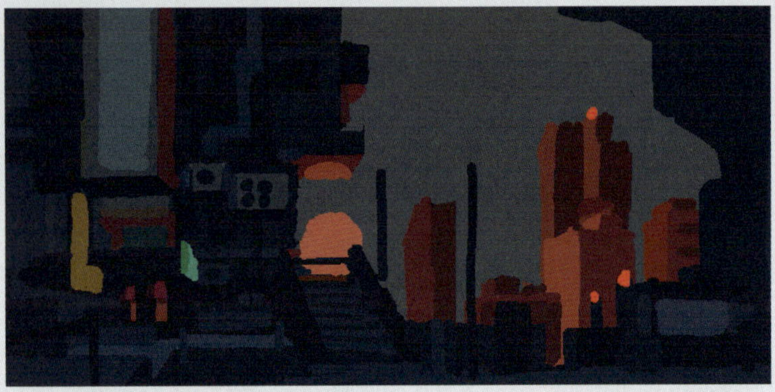

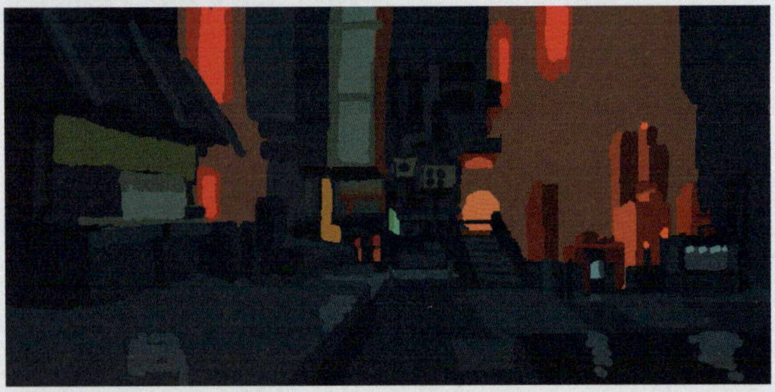

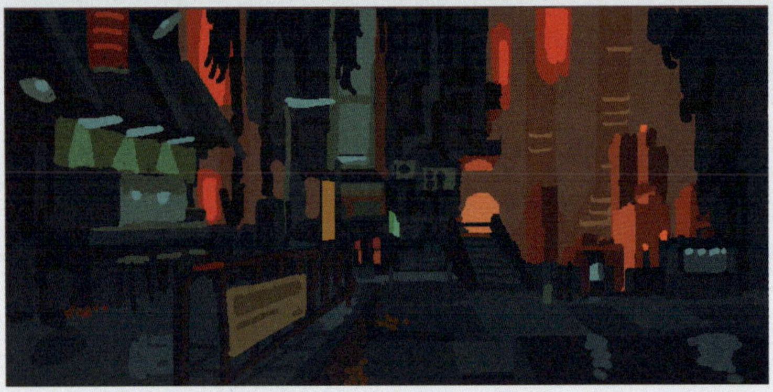

↓ I eventually gave up and used sketches as a colour base, redrawing the composition with smooth, pixel-perfect lines. While these turned out fine, I looked back over my drafts and felt sorry that I hadn't unlocked their potential, so I left this 'correct' variant and returned to the rough version.

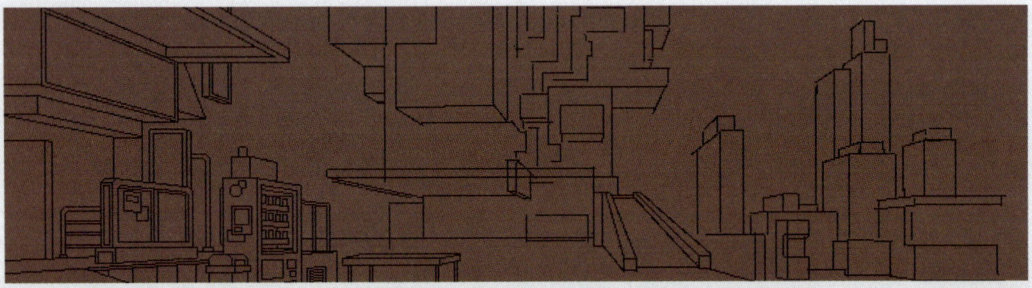

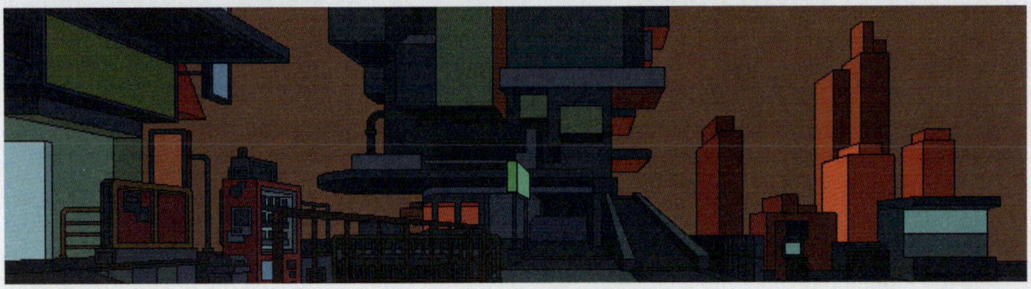

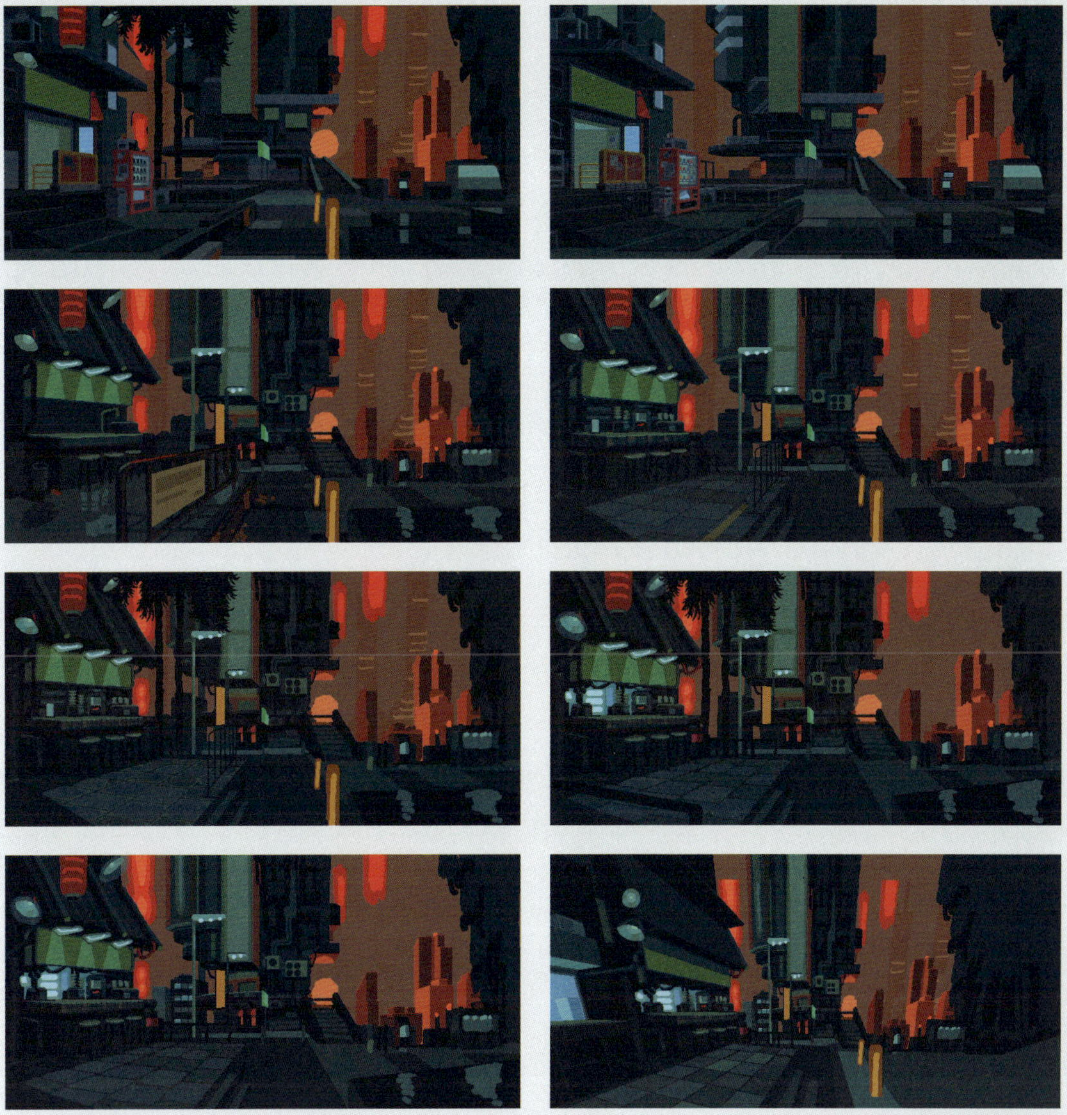

↑ To make this work, I had to use every trick I could think of to close the gap between the reality and my expectations of this illustration. I added some elements that worked, removed others that didn't and even used Photoshop's Liquify tool, which is usually useless for my pixel art.

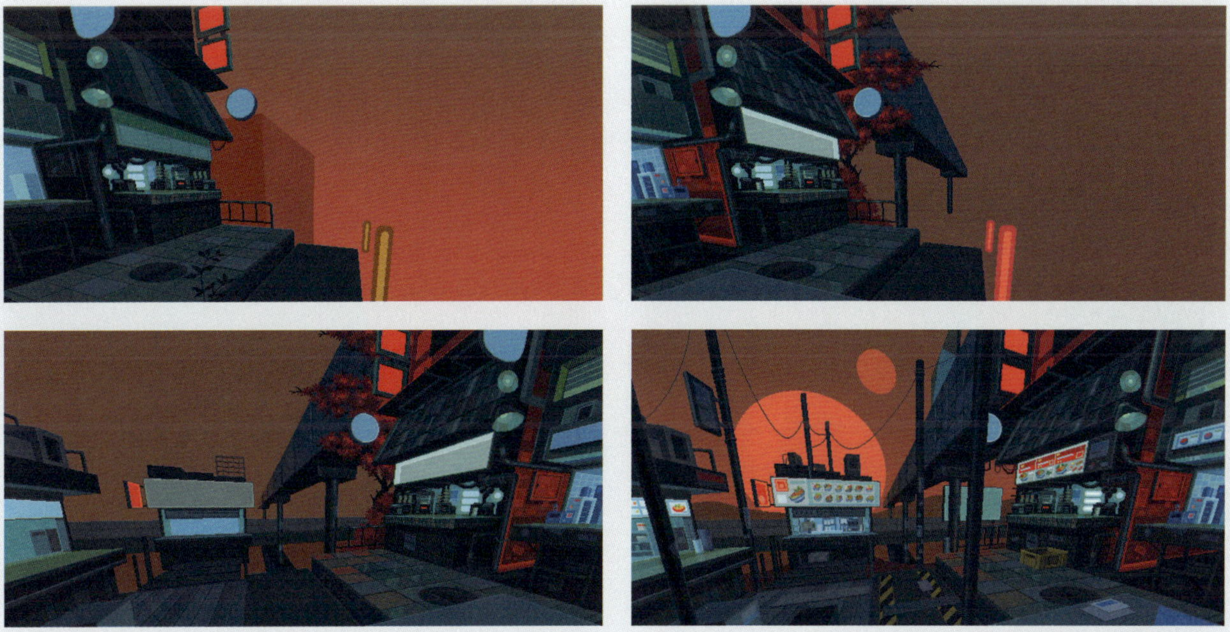

↑ Gradually, the Liquify tool helped me to achieve a perspective so sharp that I could make all the lines smooth and pixel-perfect while still retaining enough motion and life through skewing and distortion. As I redrew each section little by little, I eventually gave up on the centre and right side of the image, concentrating on just the left side.

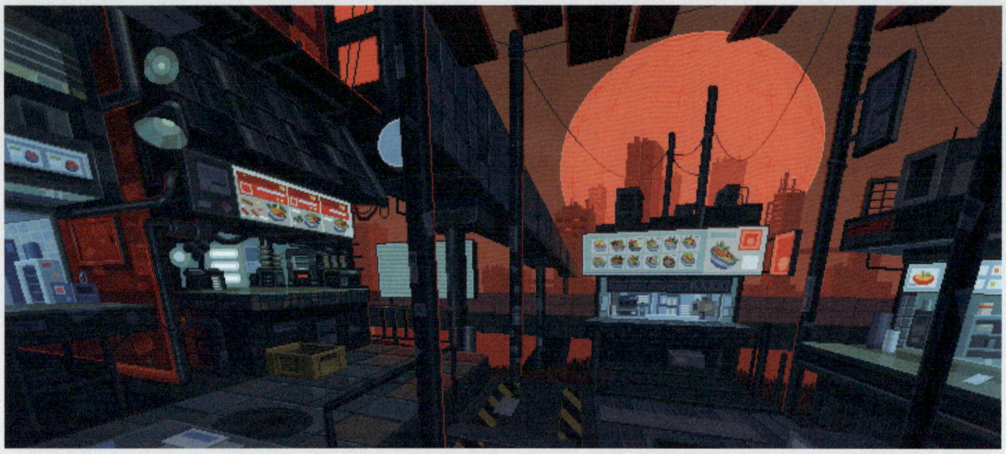

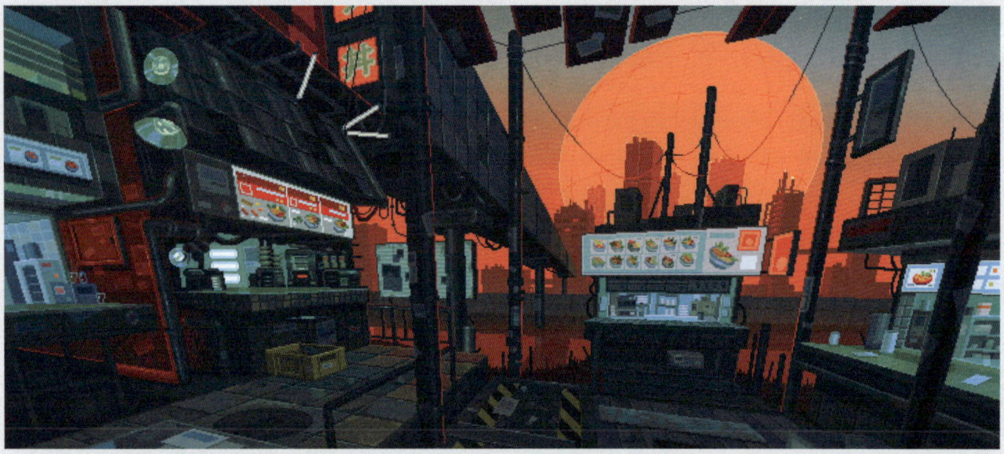

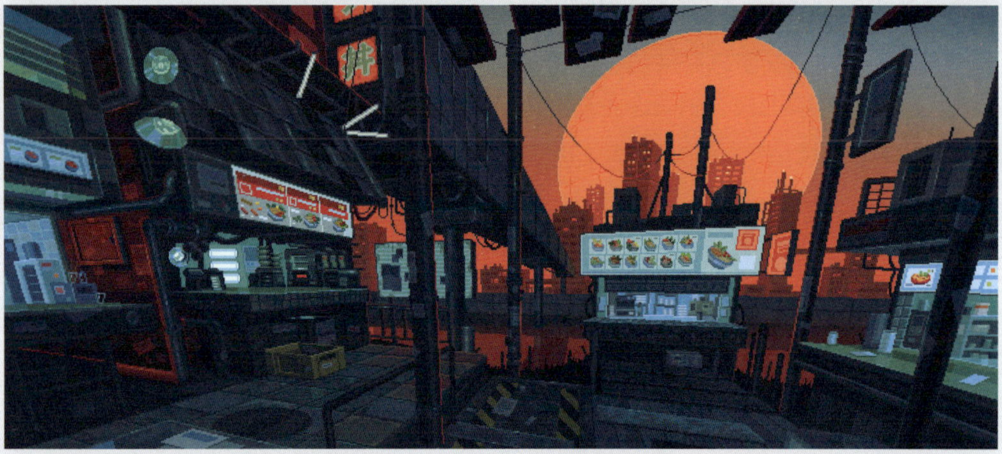

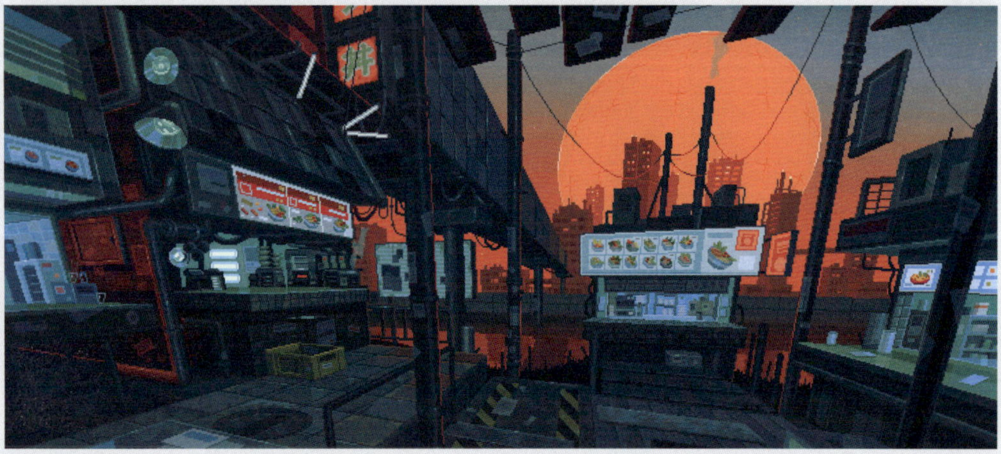

↑ After I'd cropped the image to focus on this section, everything came together quickly. The scene turned into some kind of a harbour – or a city on the water. A big artificial sun worked as the composition's centre, which allowed me to bring the skyscrapers back. I added some small details, textures and reflections, made the animation and suddenly, everything was finished.

↓ This was one of the first times that I drew in Clip Studio Paint, which has an incredible tool where you set a Perspective Ruler for a layer and all the lines align to it. This allows you to draw whole areas in a single move, which is why there's no step between the sketch and the colour - I drew it that fast.

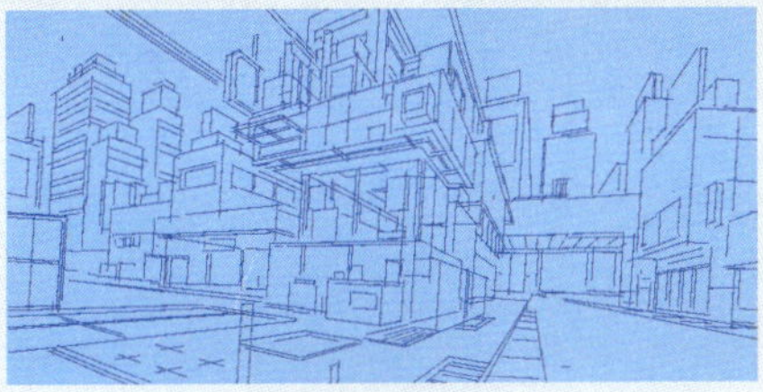

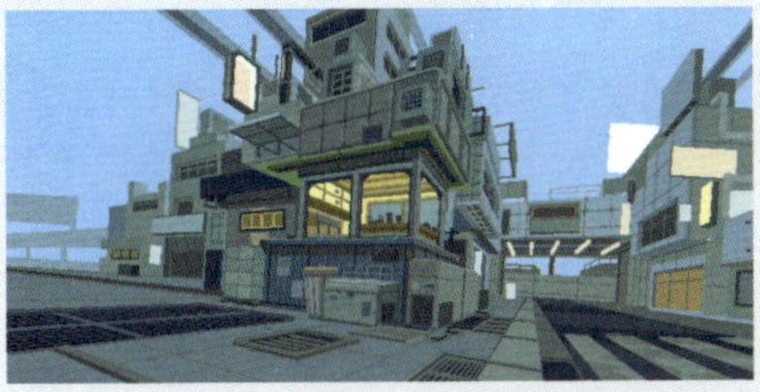

↓ Even though I used this shortcut, I still needed to decide on a location. I initially wanted to place this street somewhere among the mountains, as a contrast to my usual city locations...

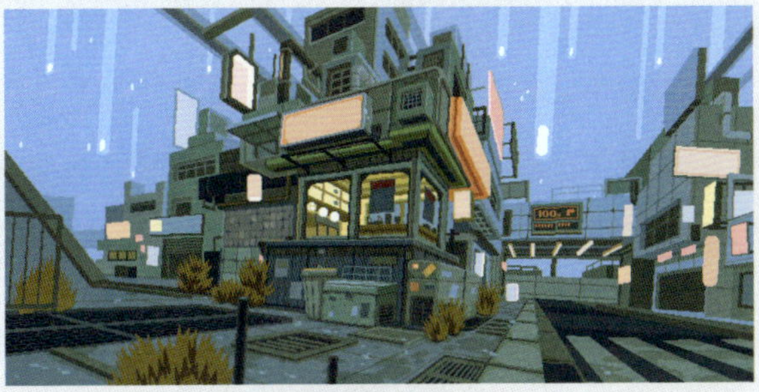

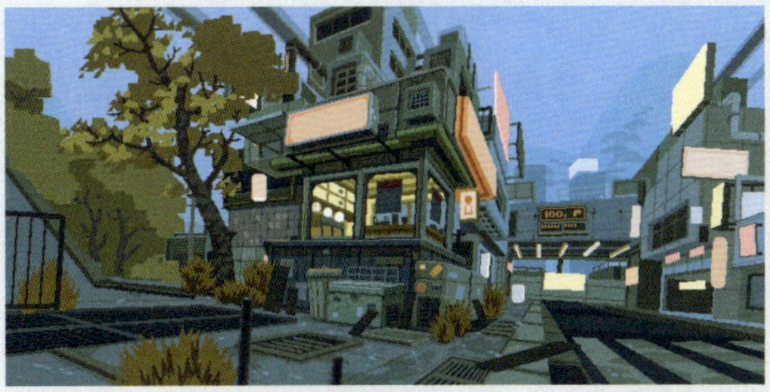

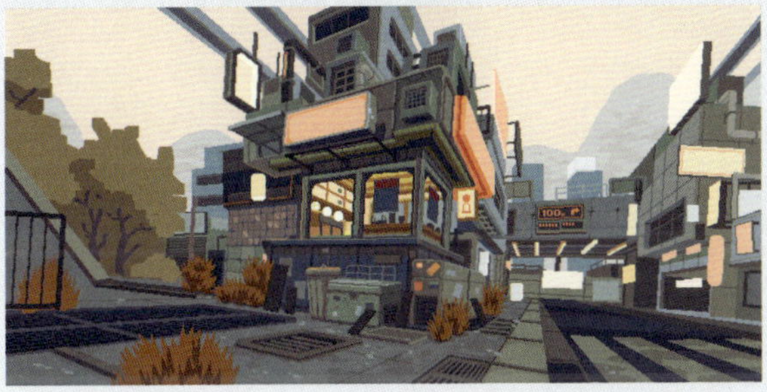

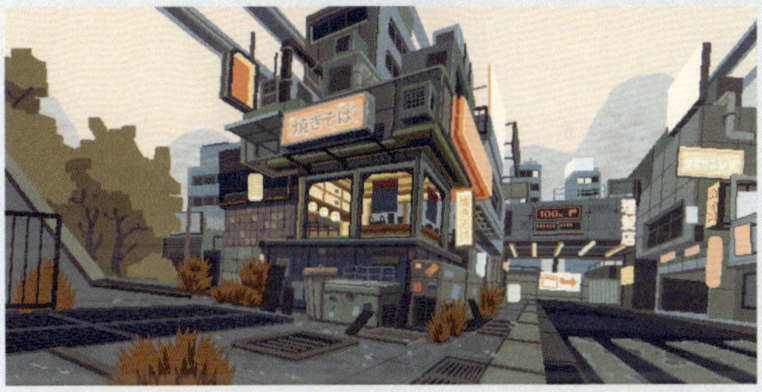

↓ ...But after a few attempts, I realized it was better to stick to the sketch and add the city into the background. When drawing buildings in the distance, there's always a risk of making them so detailed that they start to mix with the foreground. While I tried to avoid that effect, the illustration still started to lack depth, maybe because there wasn't an obvious light source.

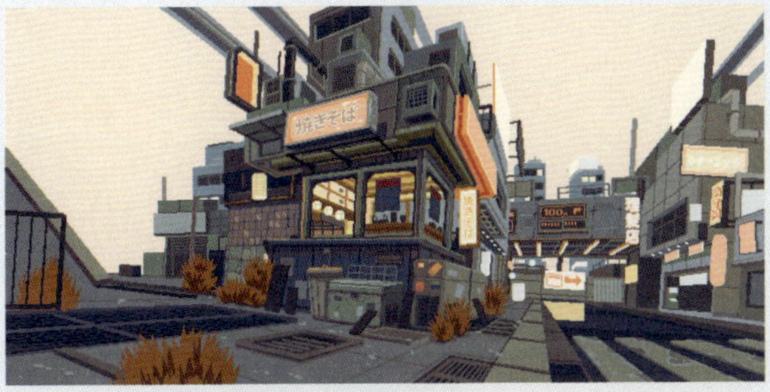

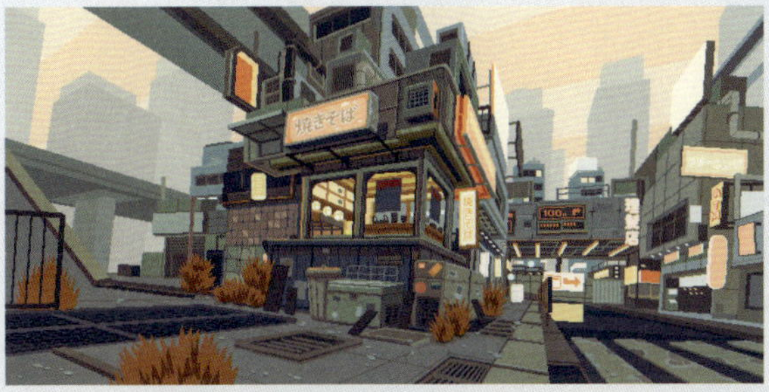

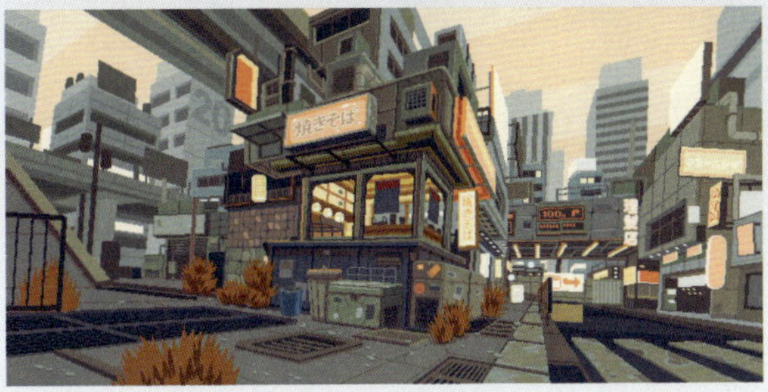

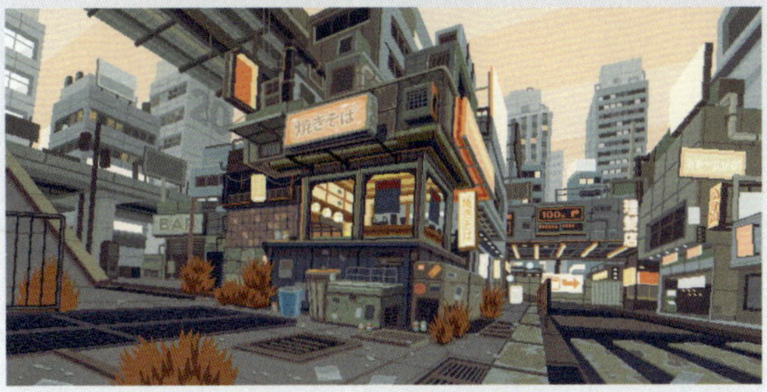

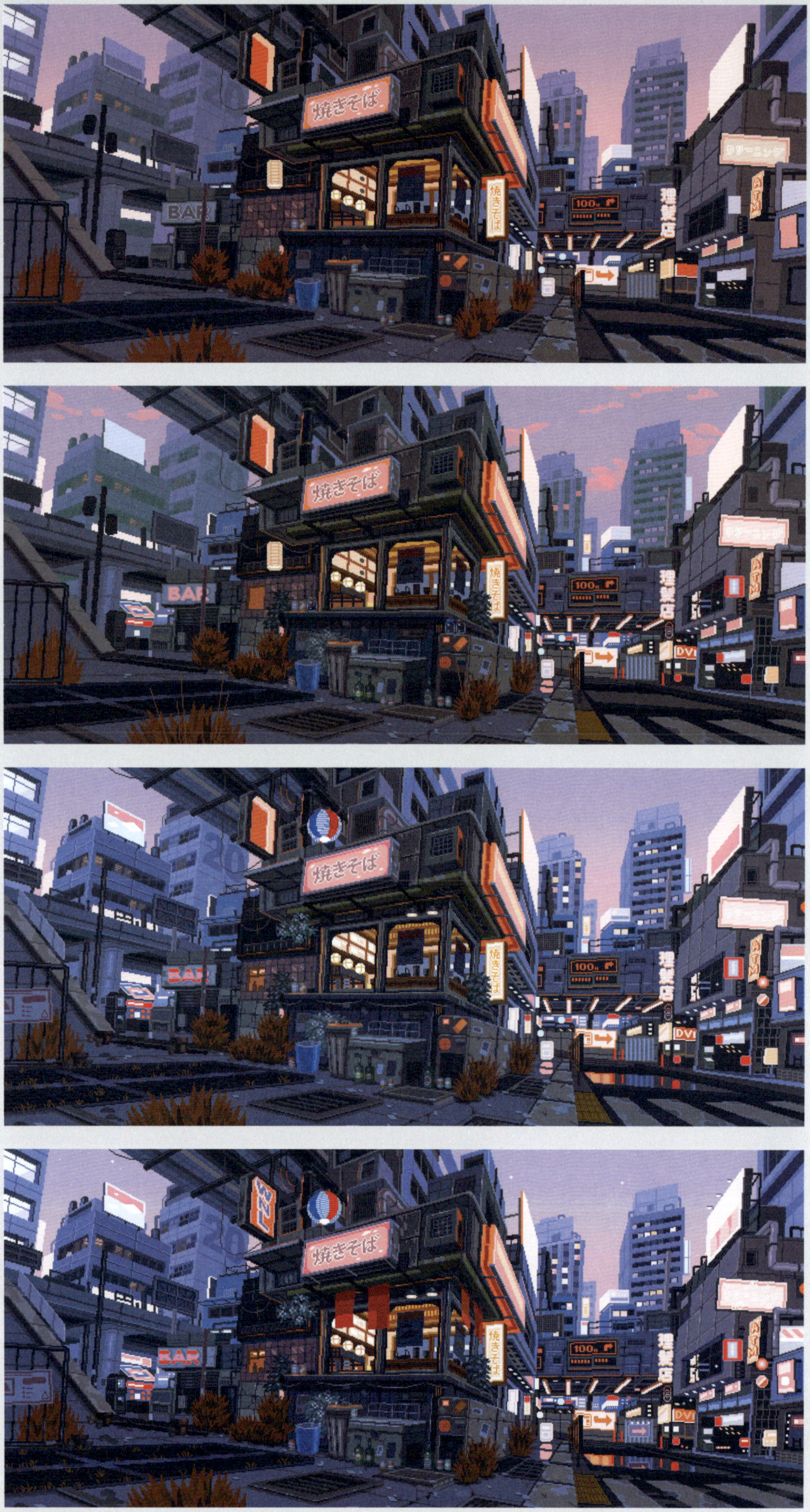

↑ Since adding a new light source would have required corrections to almost everything, I altered the illustration using colour correction and layers with different blending modes. It started to look more vivid, which gave me the idea of adding even more bright colours. I think this approach worked well, with even lit-up buildings in the background now sitting organically among the lights and street signs.

↓ This illustration took me a long time to finish, mainly because I wasn't happy with the initial sketch; but I felt it had potential and that I could definitely work with it.

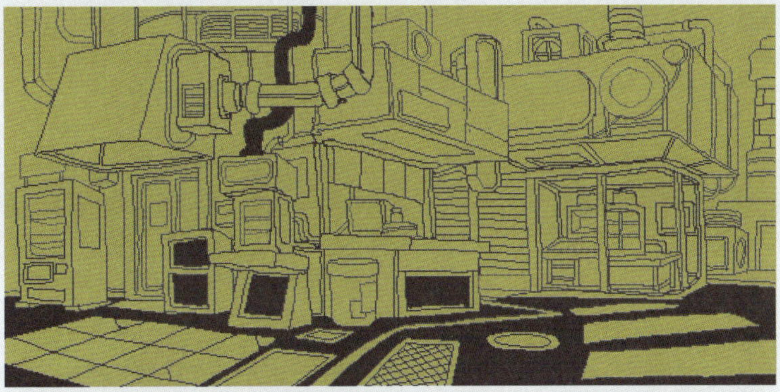

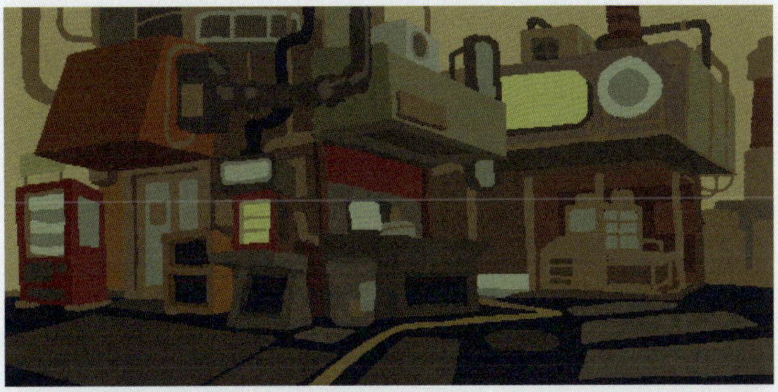

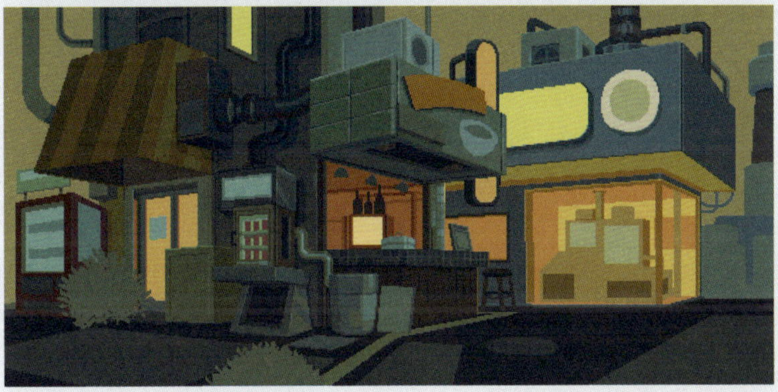

↓ I tried changing the colours and adding different elements until I understood that the problem was that the two shops depicted in the first sketch were too similar in terms of shape and size – so I'd have to choose one. I picked the one on the left before completely redrawing the environment around it.

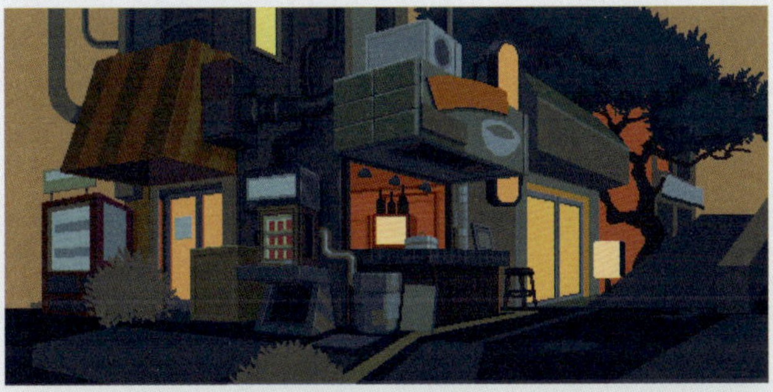

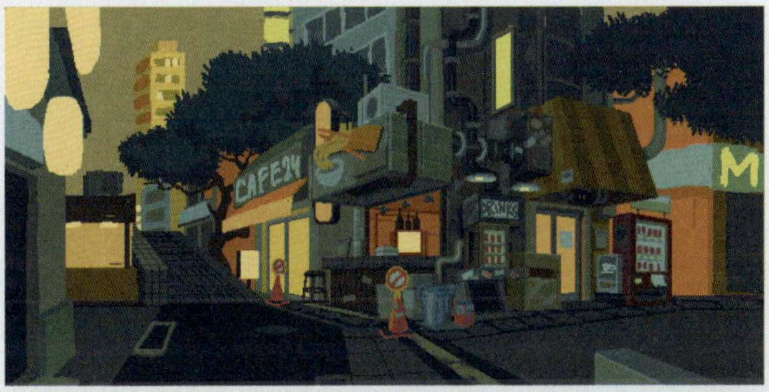

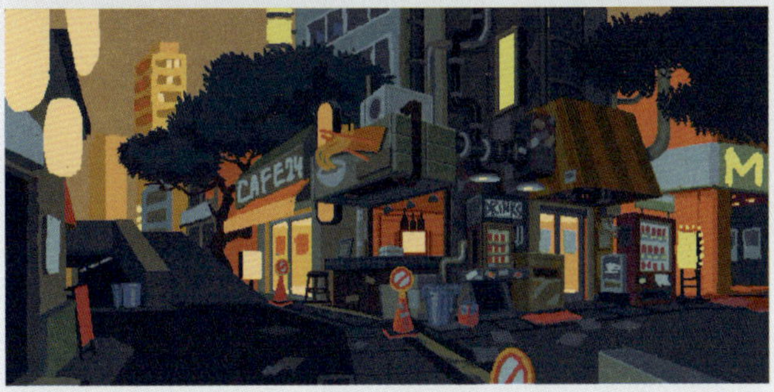

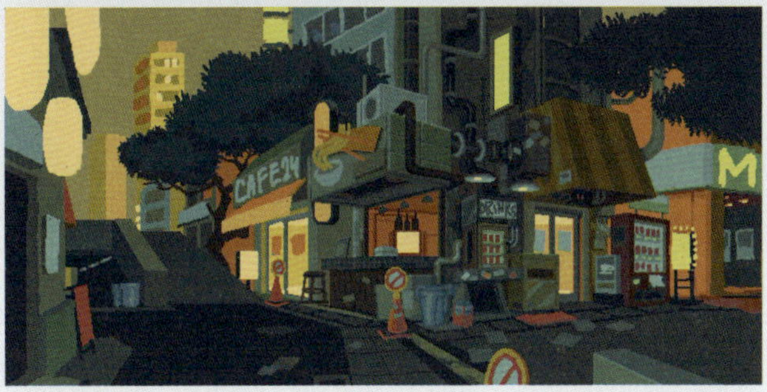

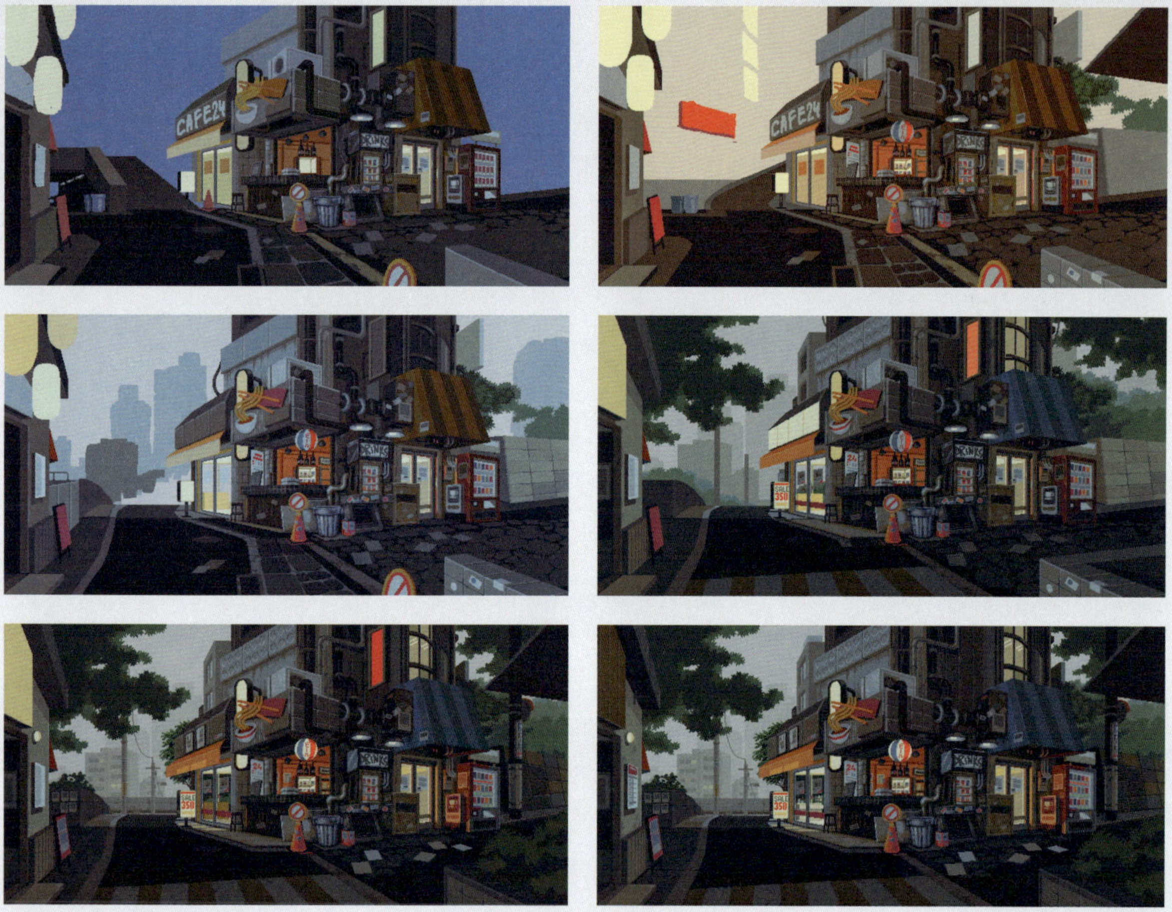

↑ I was worried there were only two main colours in the illustration – green and yellow – so I tried various options in an attempt to add more depth and make the scene look calmer. I eventually found a look that I liked, with overcast skies and a foggy city background. But since I also wanted the neighbourhood to feel cozy, I added some trees and bushes up and down the streets.

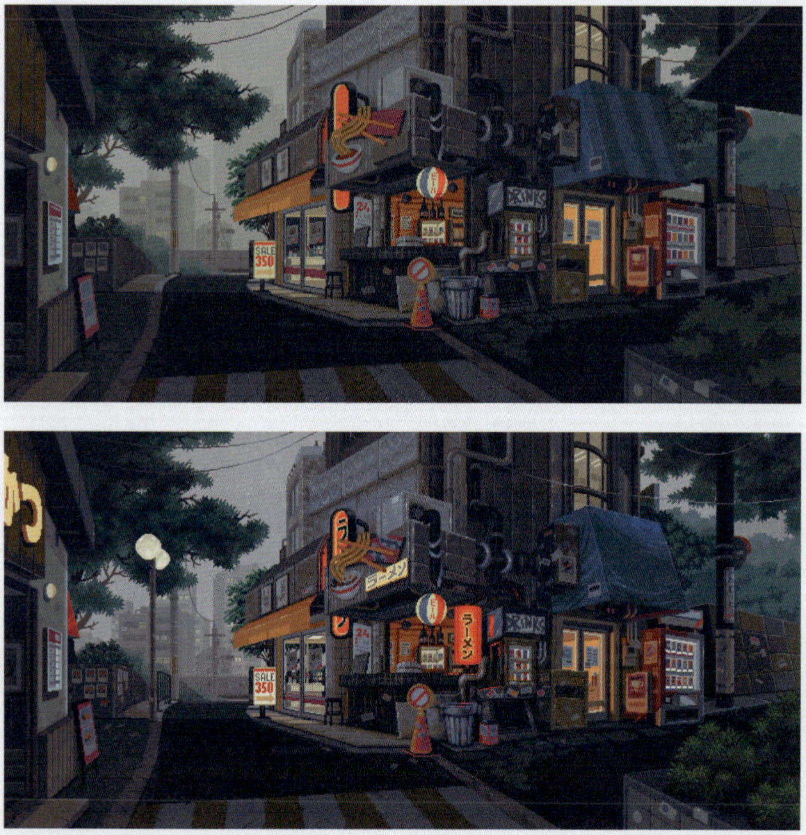

↑ As the final stage, I spent a bit more time on the finer details and textures, while also adding a street light on the left-hand side and the big red lantern in the middle. I'm really happy I continued working on this illustration and didn't give up. I feel like it's one of my best artworks to date.

↓ I started this illustration without a perspective grid because I wanted it to look less rigid and a bit more dynamic. Part way through the sketch, however, I drew a grid to help myself out.

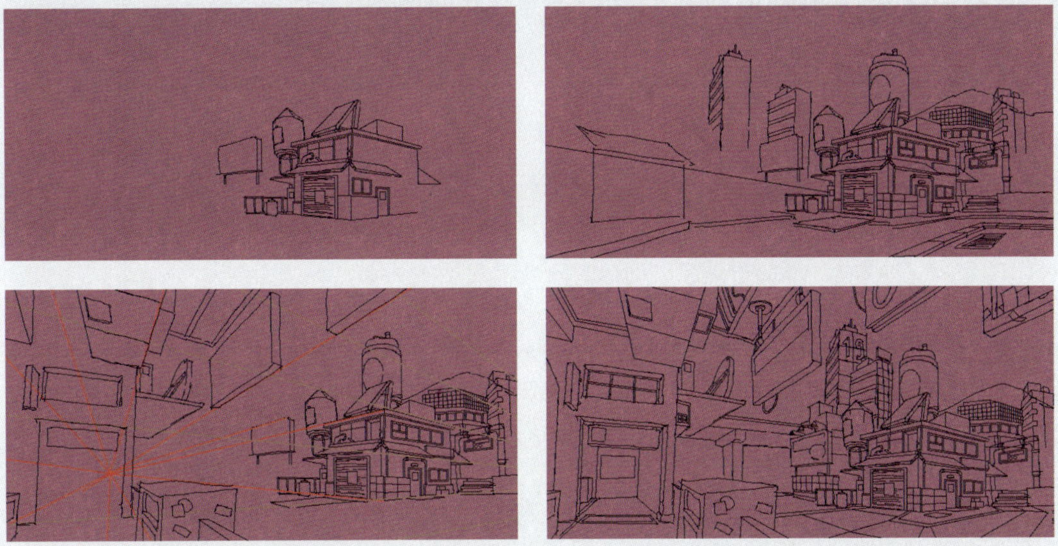

↓ When I came to create this piece, I had been using Perspective Ruler in Clip Studio Paint for some time and was getting the feeling that my work was starting to look too similar. Using such a powerful tool was convenient, especially for dynamic compositions or unusual points of view, but it was starting to become a trap. Here, I tried to move away from this precise perspective to create something new.

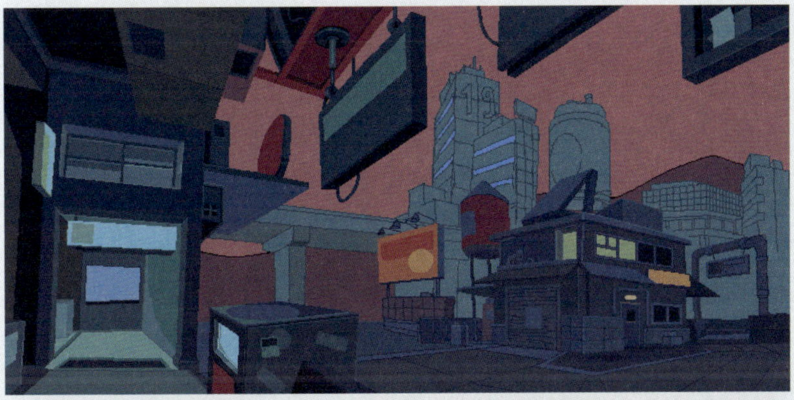

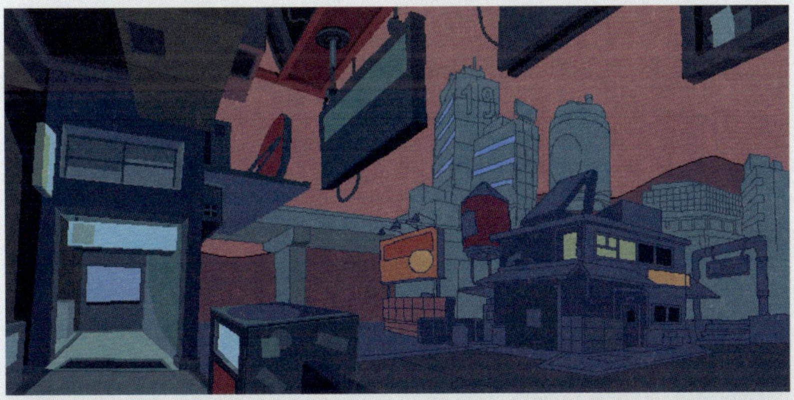

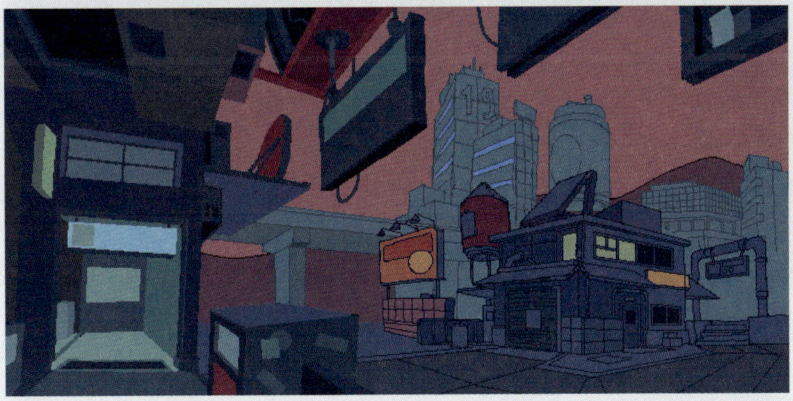

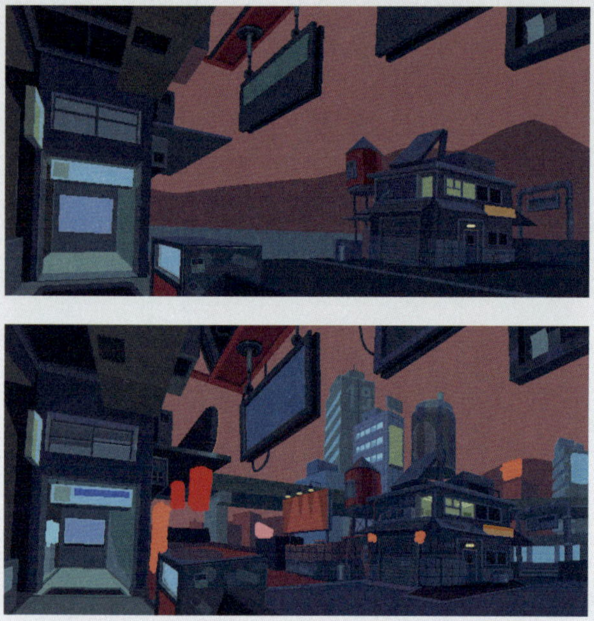

↑ The sketch turned out so well and the process went so smoothly that I started to worry it was too good to be true. I checked that I wasn't overlooking any obvious improvements by tweaking the colours – making them more autumnal – before adding a big tree.

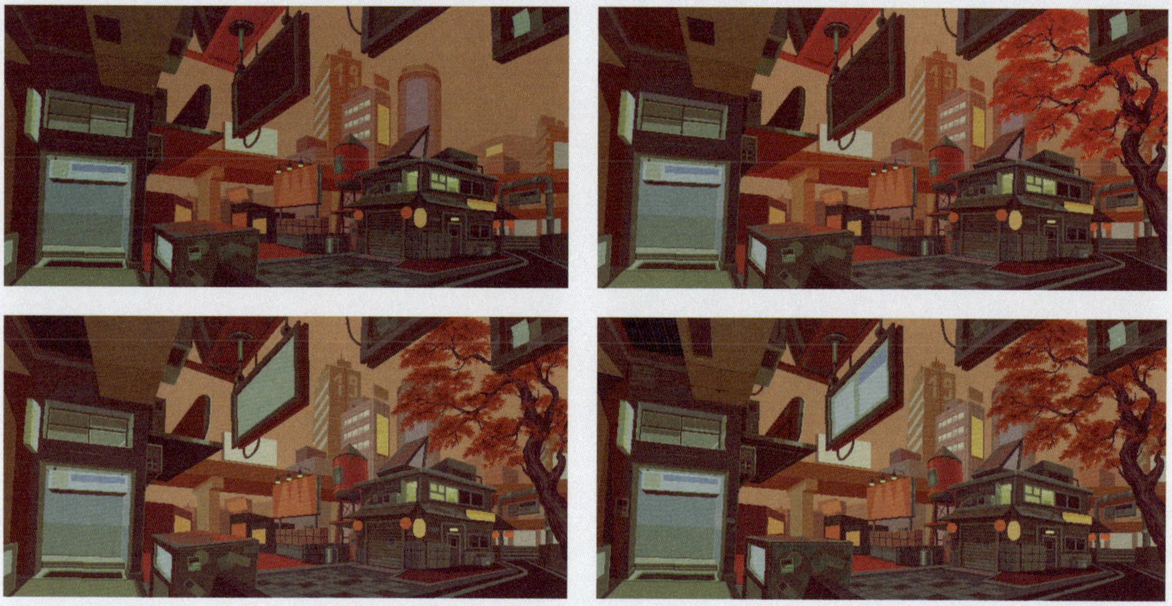

↑ Since the autumnal variant looked quite interesting, I stuck with this palette of reds, oranges and browns. I produce a lot of blue-toned drawings, so I'm always glad when I can break the mould and use a different range of colours.

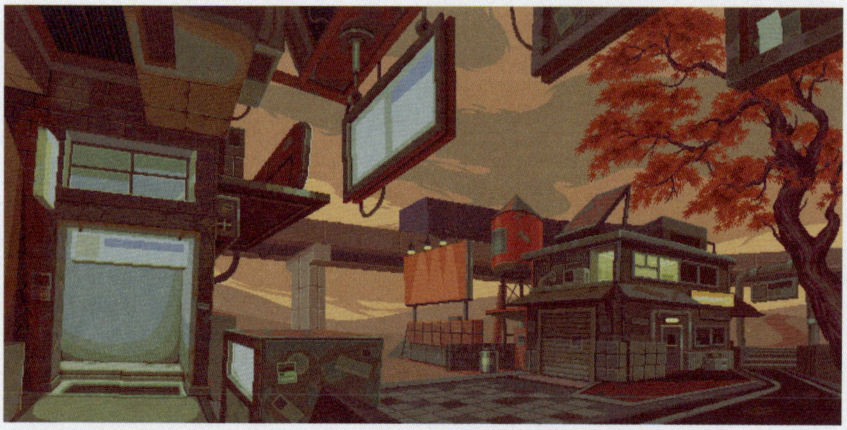

↑ I was very tired when I experimented with this option, in which I removed the background and replaced it with a desert landscape. While I liked the contrast this created, there was simply too much empty space, which needed filling with something – a realization that turned me off this version.

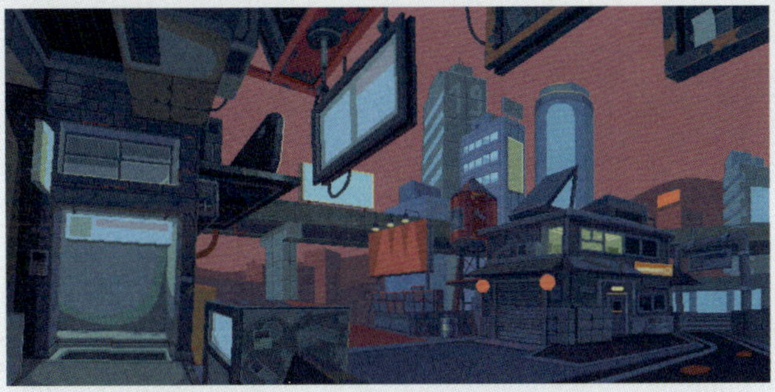

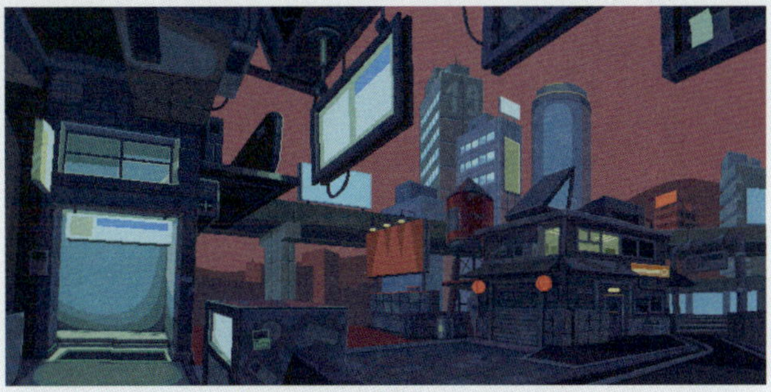

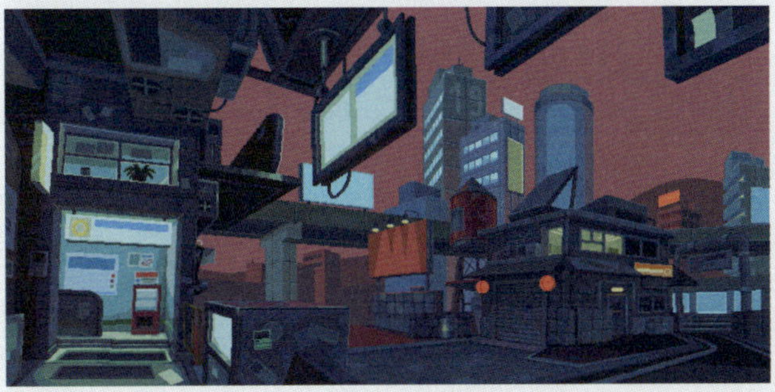

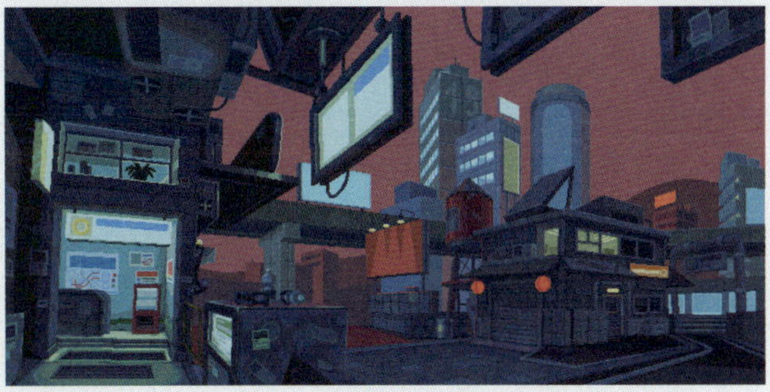

↑ After trying the desert background, I reverted to the initial blue colours. While I had been experimenting with the warmer colours, I'd made some progress on the details. In general, the image looked fresh. So I decided to focus on the foreground, since this is what viewers concentrate on most.

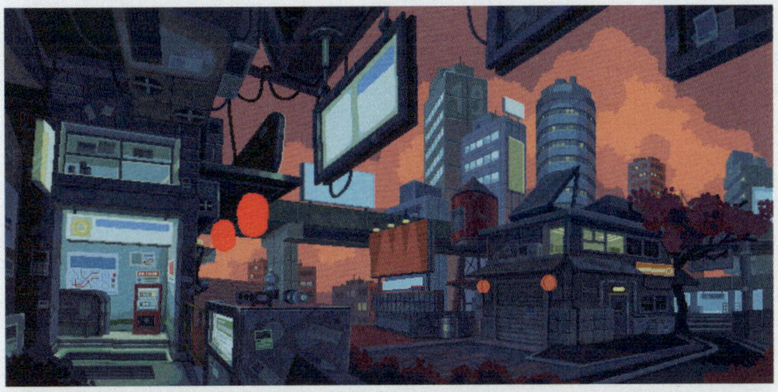

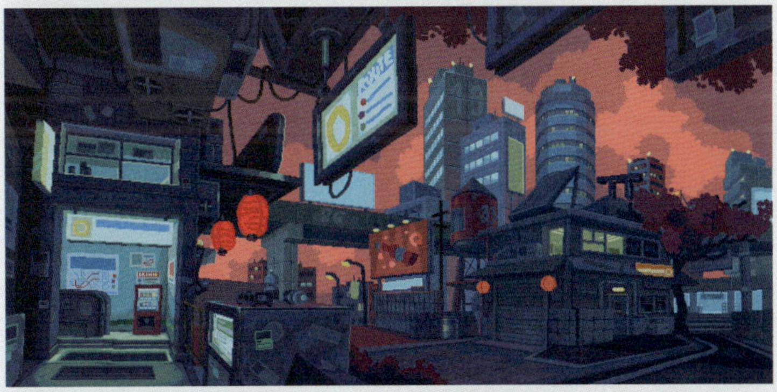

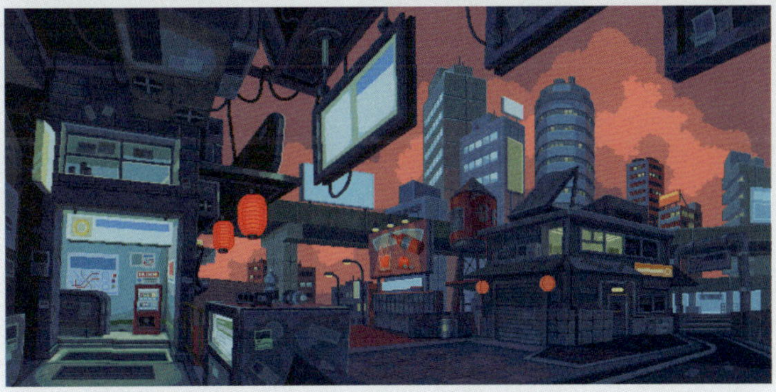

↑ The sky looked boring, so I added some clouds to see if this would solve this problem. I then drew some trees, my tried-and-tested shortcut to finishing off an illustration. While they looked good, I couldn't quite find the right space to place the foliage against the sky.

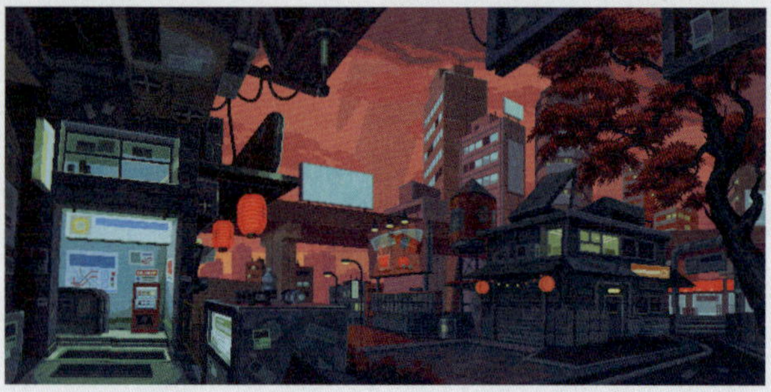

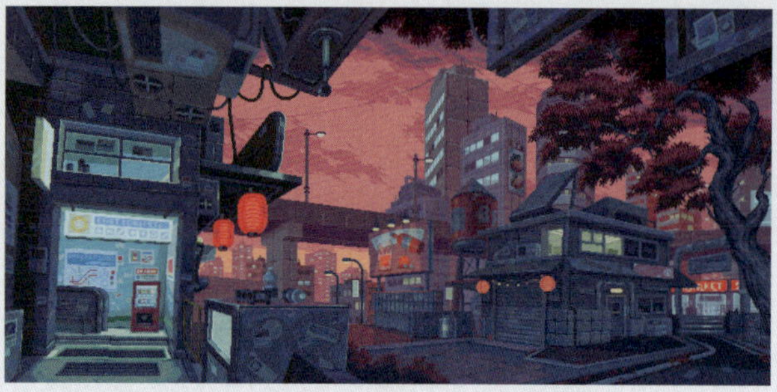

↑ Luckily, I remembered I had already drawn a tree that I thought I could reuse in this version. It looked strange all on its own, so I added an extra branch in the foreground to deepen the perspective. I also changed the clouds, since the tree now eclipsed such a big part of the sky.

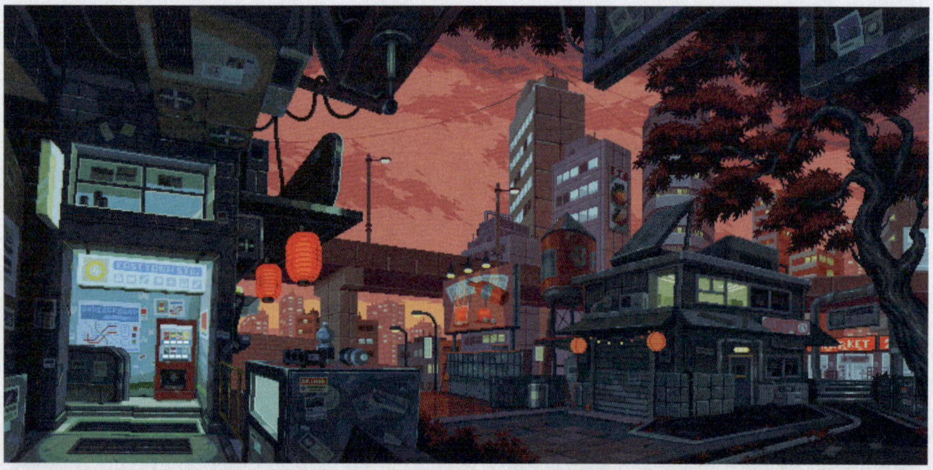

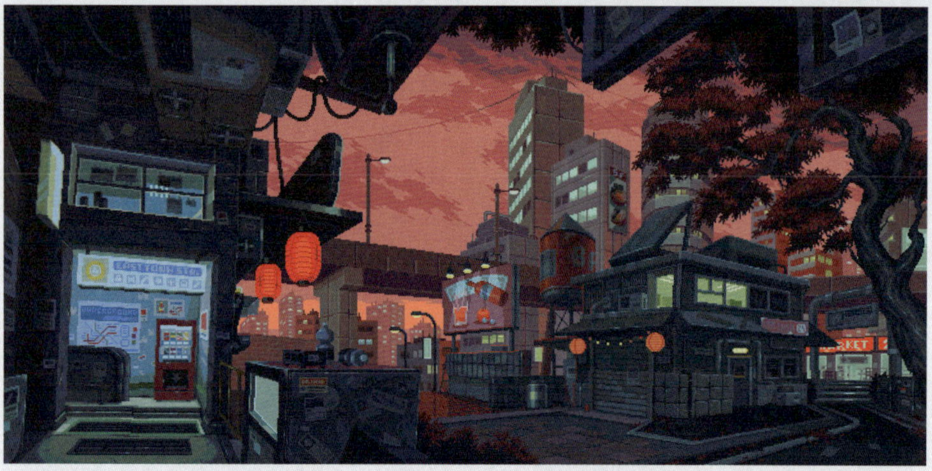

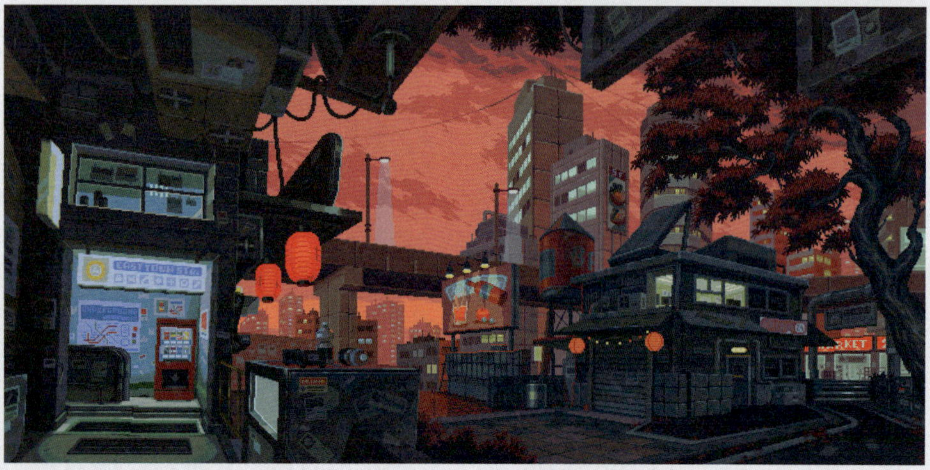

↑ These last stages might look easy because there's very little to do, but I really struggle with finishing a drawing; I usually feel there's something I can improve upon, add or even redraw. I find it difficult to believe it's already good enough. That said, I'm really happy with this result: the image turned out to be vivid and saturated with details. What more could I wish for?

↓ In the sequence below, I couldn't decide whether I should leave the line art or get rid of it. Drawing with line art makes texture, details and shadow so easy that I worry I overload the detail, while illustrating without lines makes lights, shadows and rendering so demanding, I'm anxious I don't add enough.

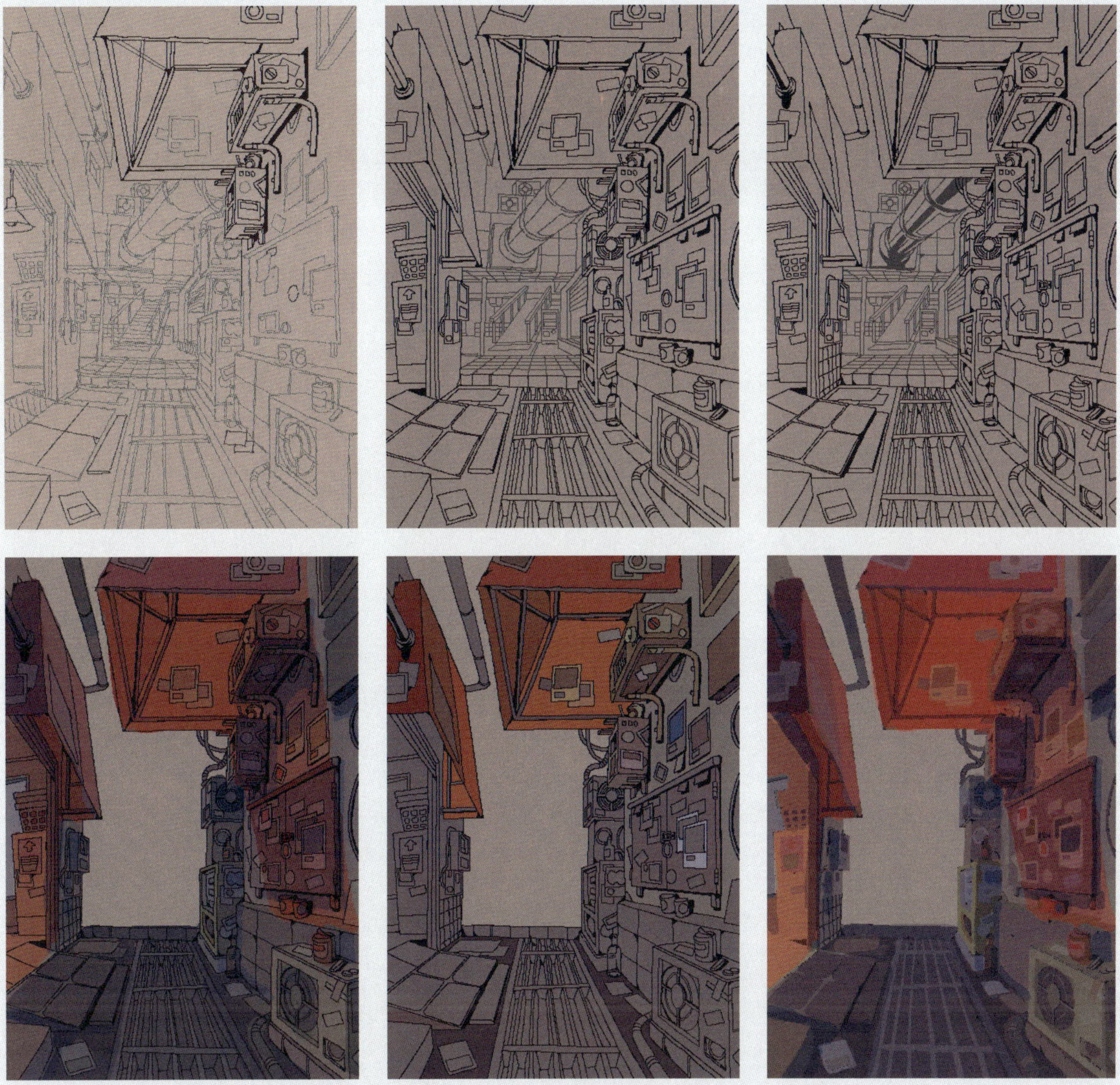

↓ In the end, I decided I didn't have enough willpower to draw all the textures and shapes without lines. So I relaxed and allowed my love of imperfection to take over. I also changed the background composition, turning a long street with pipes into a balcony, with another building across the street.

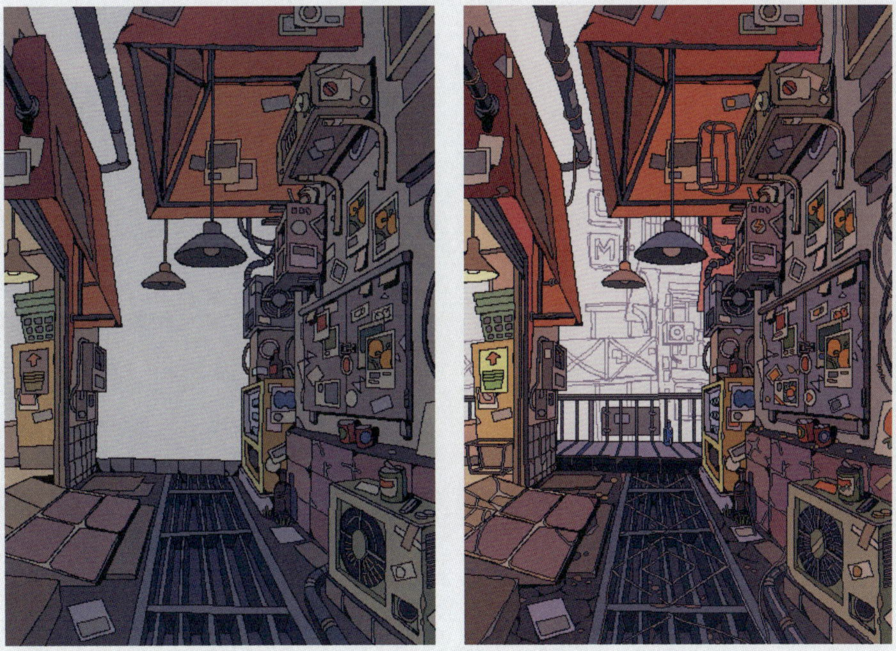

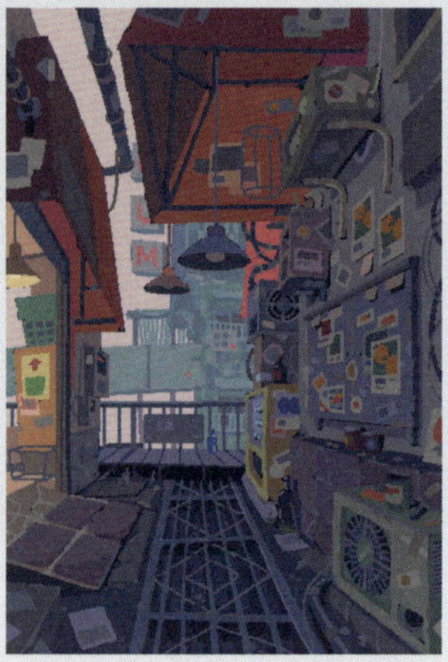
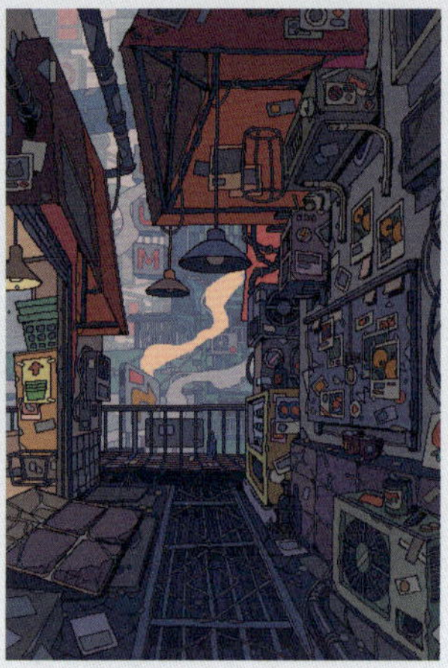

↑ I wasn't immediately satisfied with the end result and briefly thought about returning to the no-line version. But when I saw how broken it looked without the lines, and how much more work I would have to do if I switched them off, I soon reverted to the previous variant.

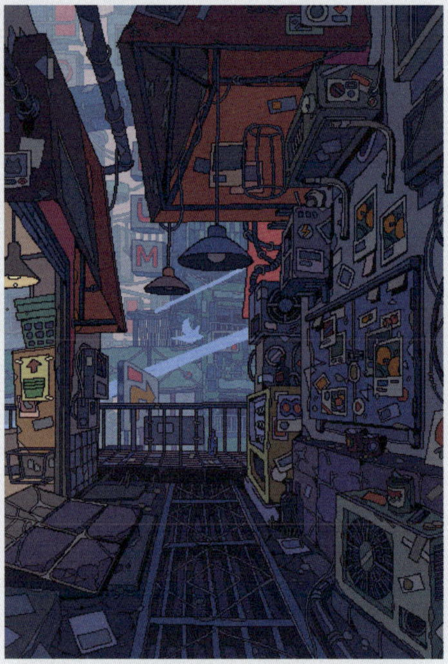
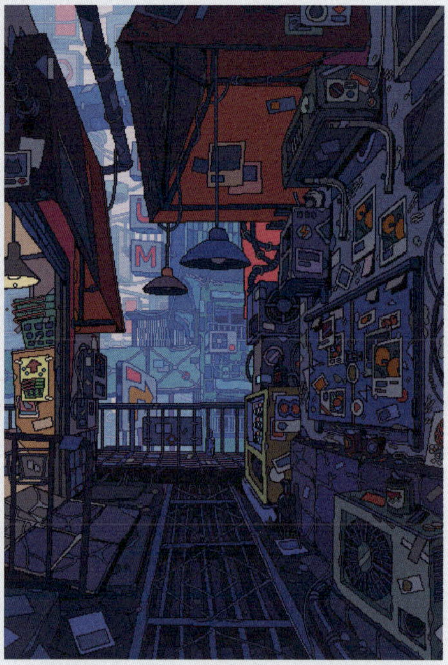
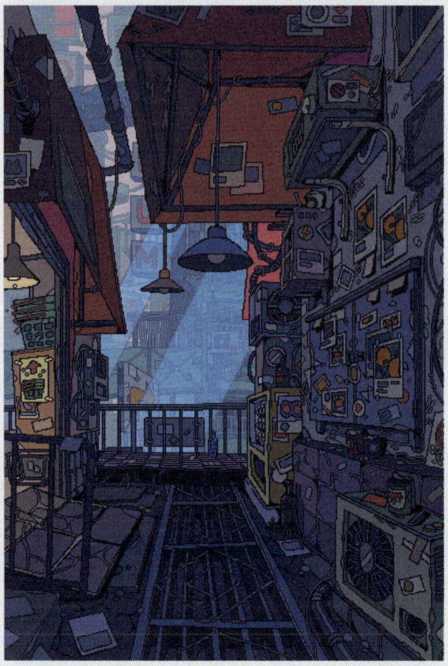
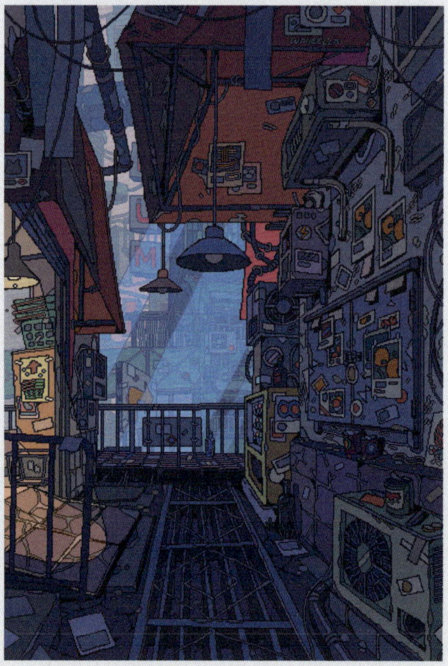

↑ The lines also made animating the image much easier. Without lines, all the lights and shadows on a chosen object would also have to be animated. With lines, where the lights and shadows are already prominent, I was able to keep everything nice and simple, resulting in more noticeable animations.

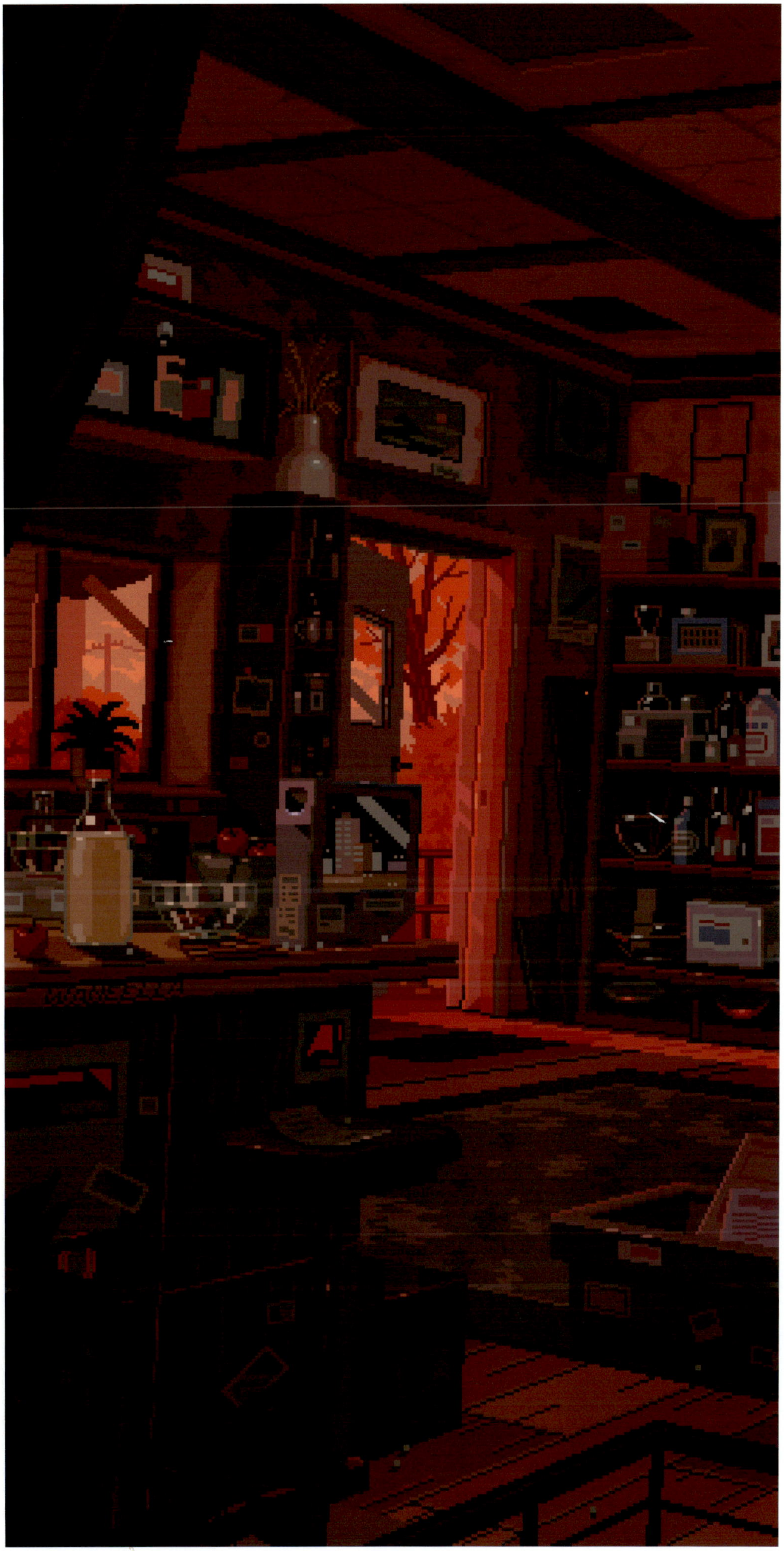

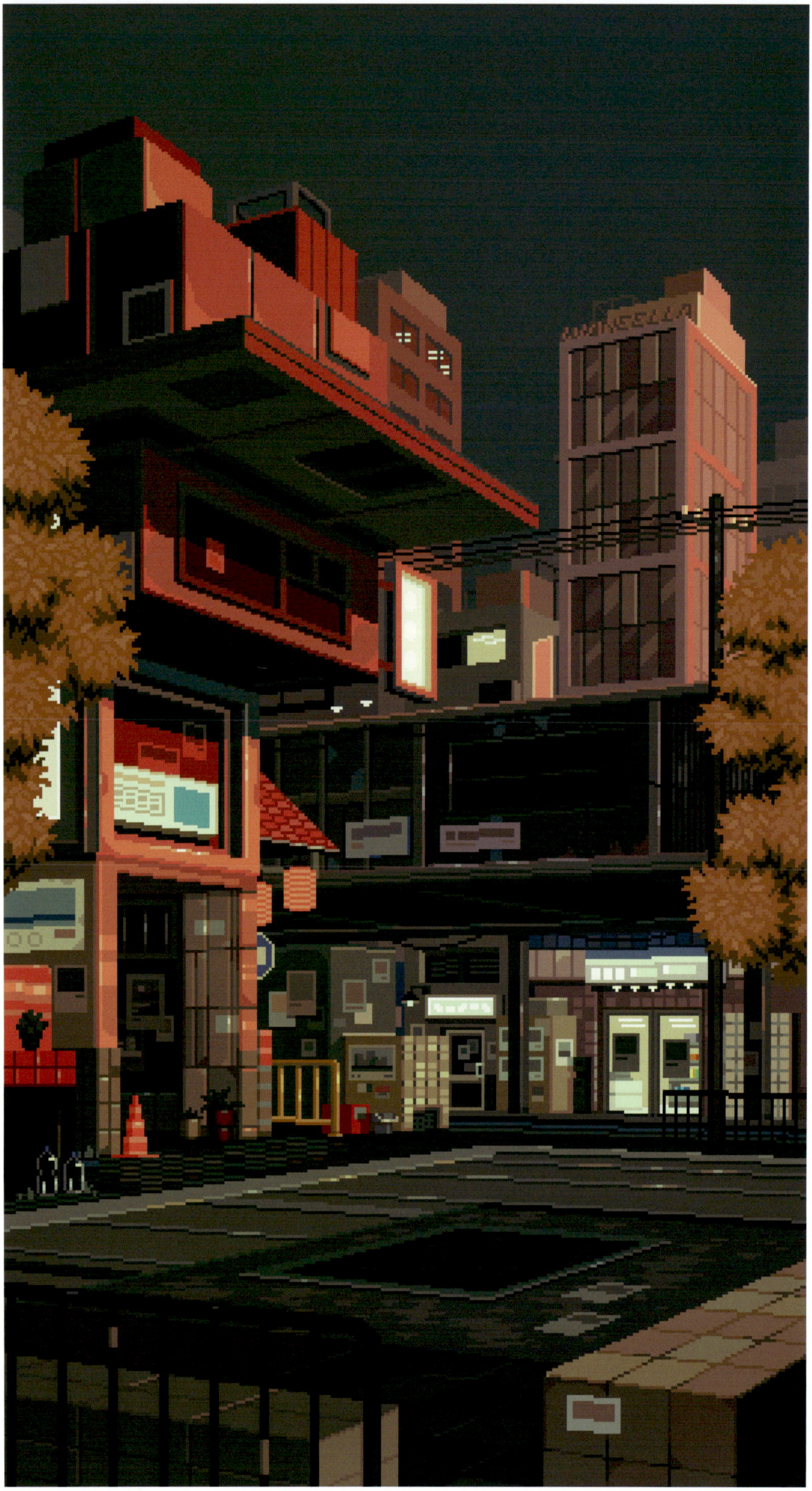

Page 177: *Message*, 01/07/2021, 250×500px
Above: *Blue And Grey* (Grey version), 31/10/2021, 270×500px
Right: *Morning*, 02/08/2021, 250×500px

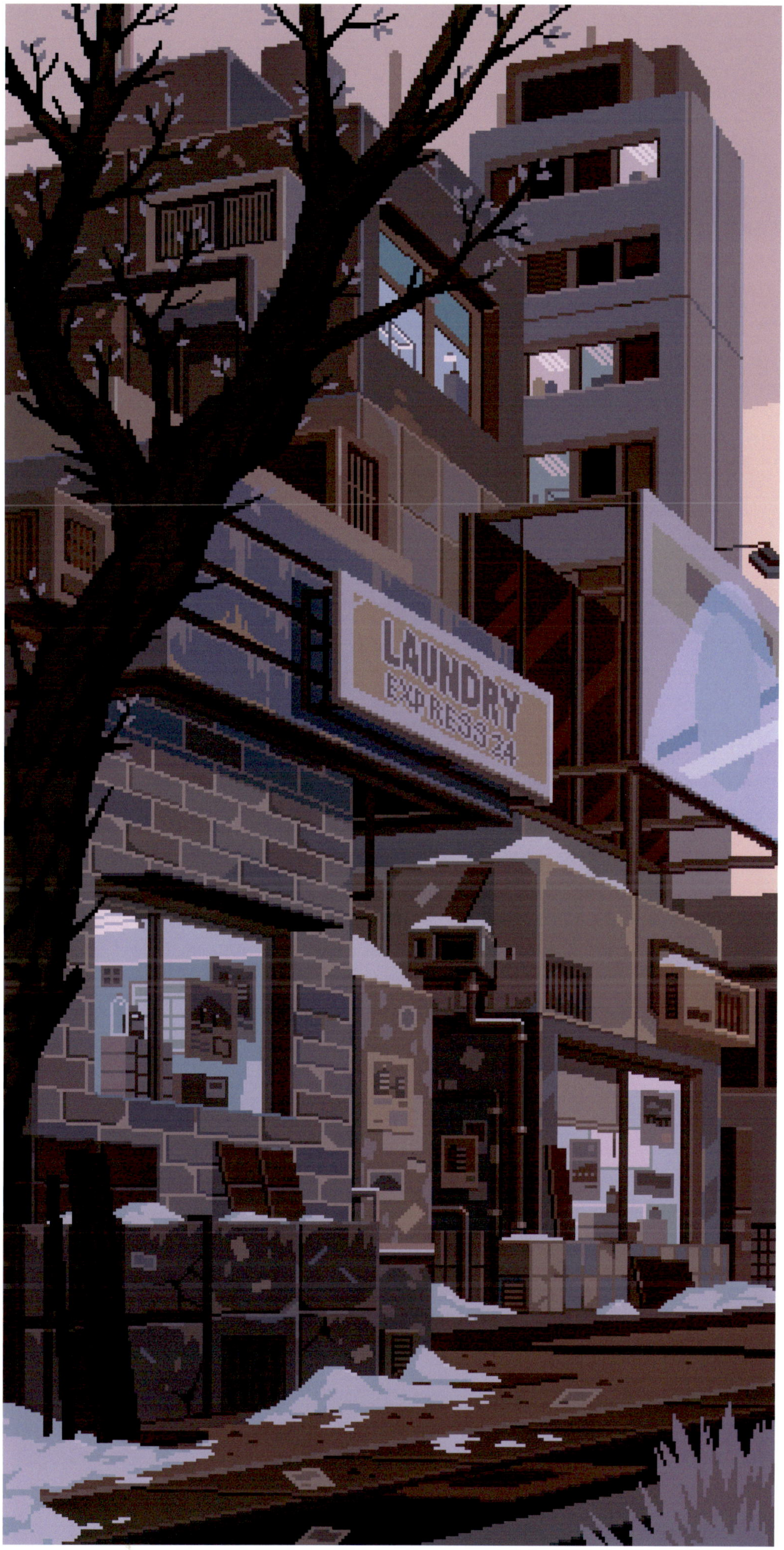
LAUNDRY
EXPRESS 24

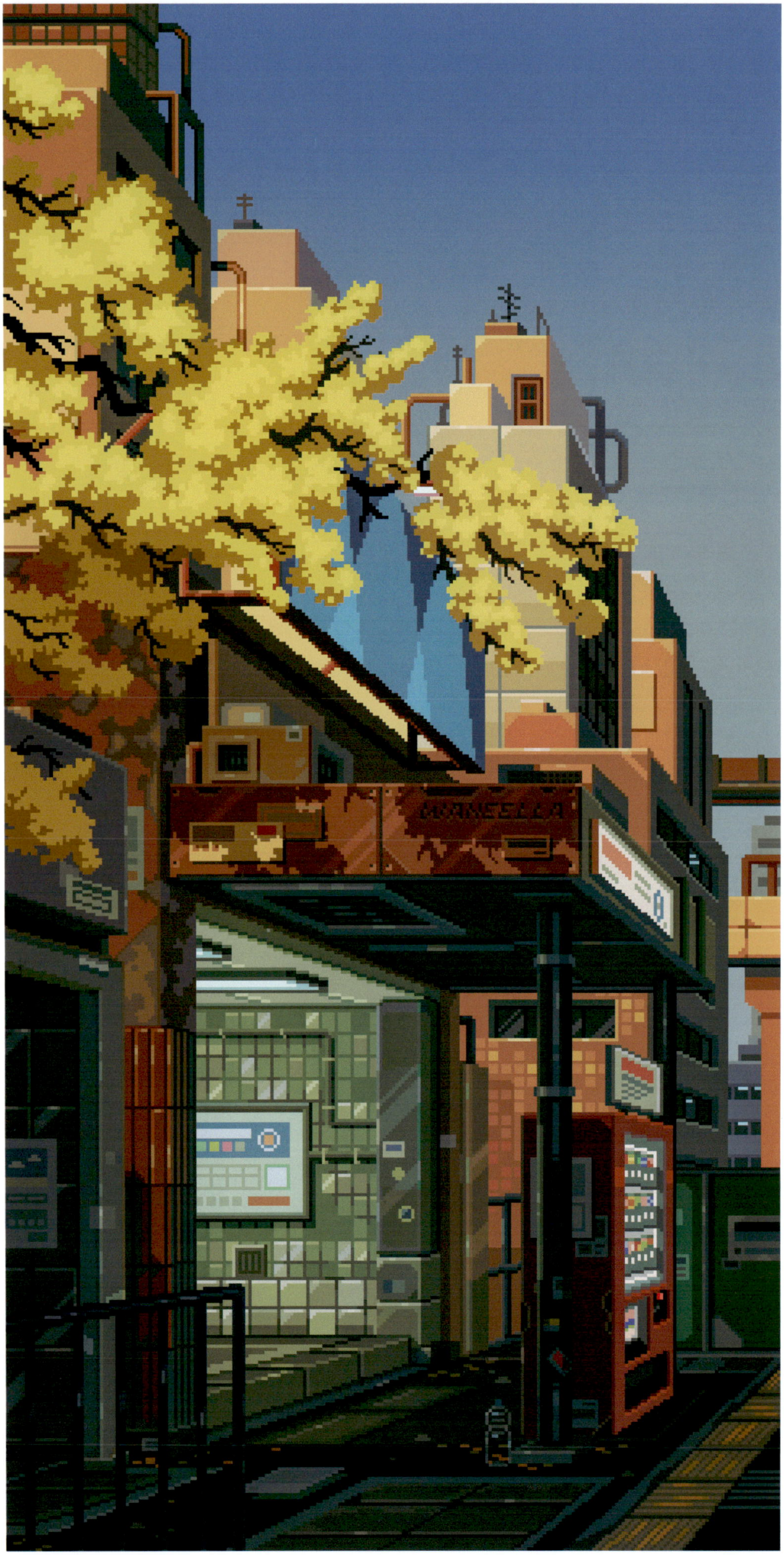

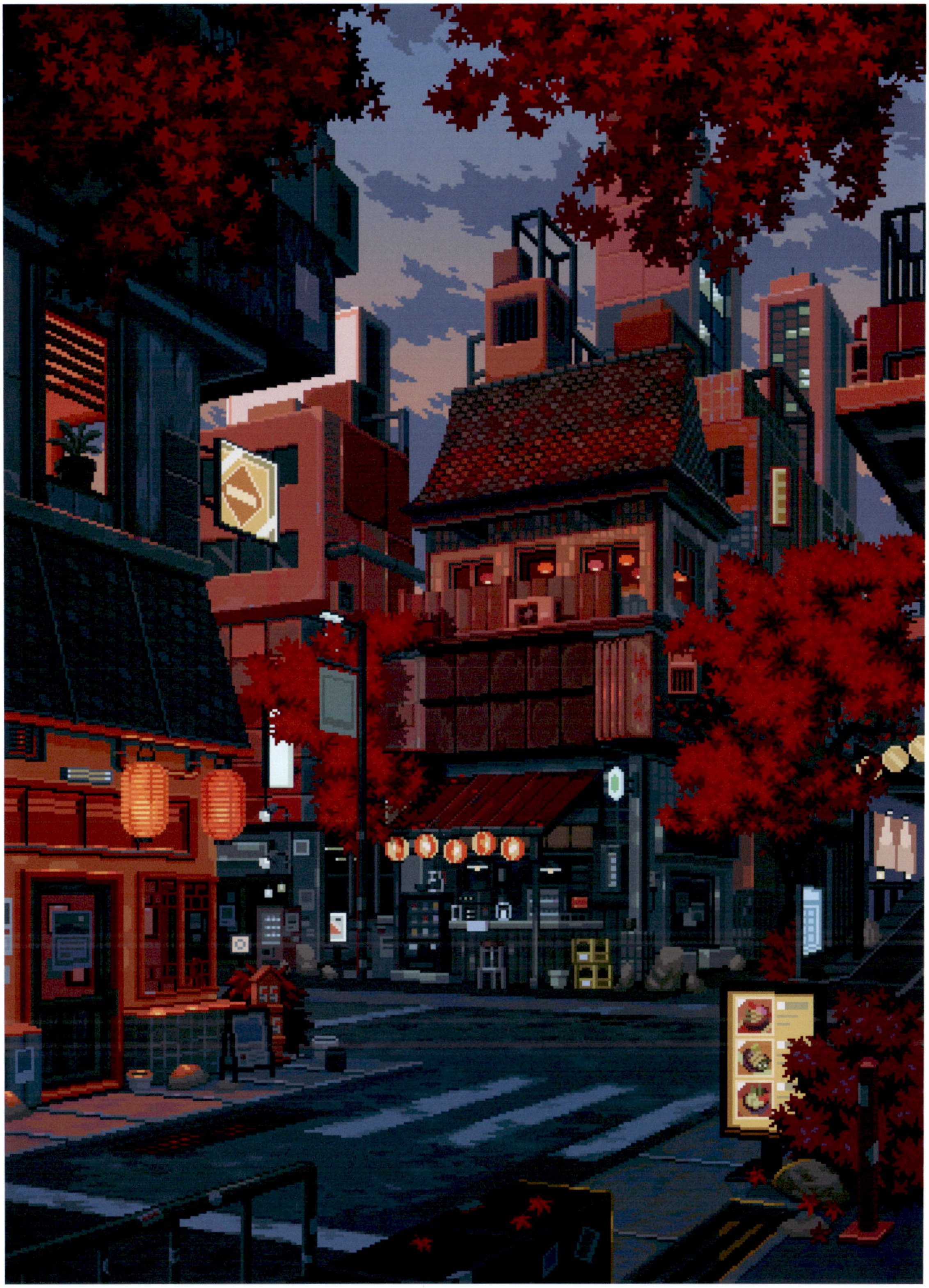

Left: *Yellow*, 20/11/2021, 240×480px
Above: *False Memories*, produced for the Harugo no Mayu Autumn Collection, 03/11/2021, 350×490px

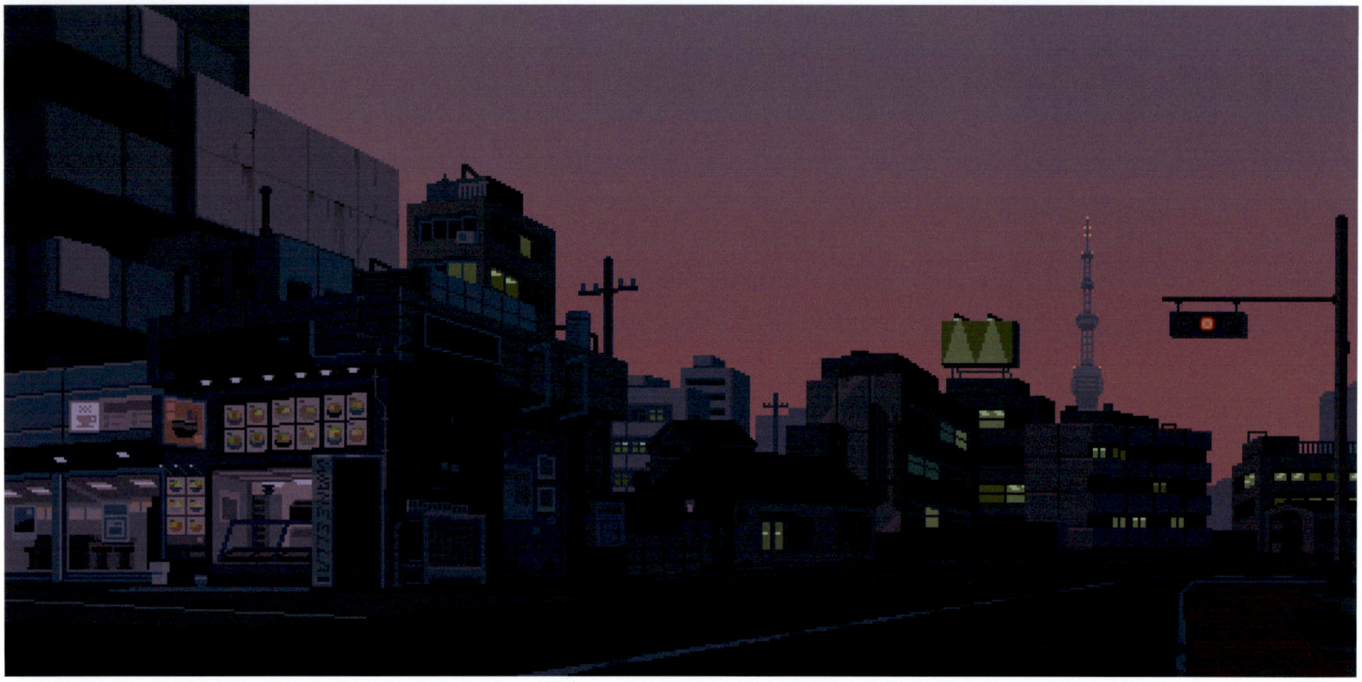

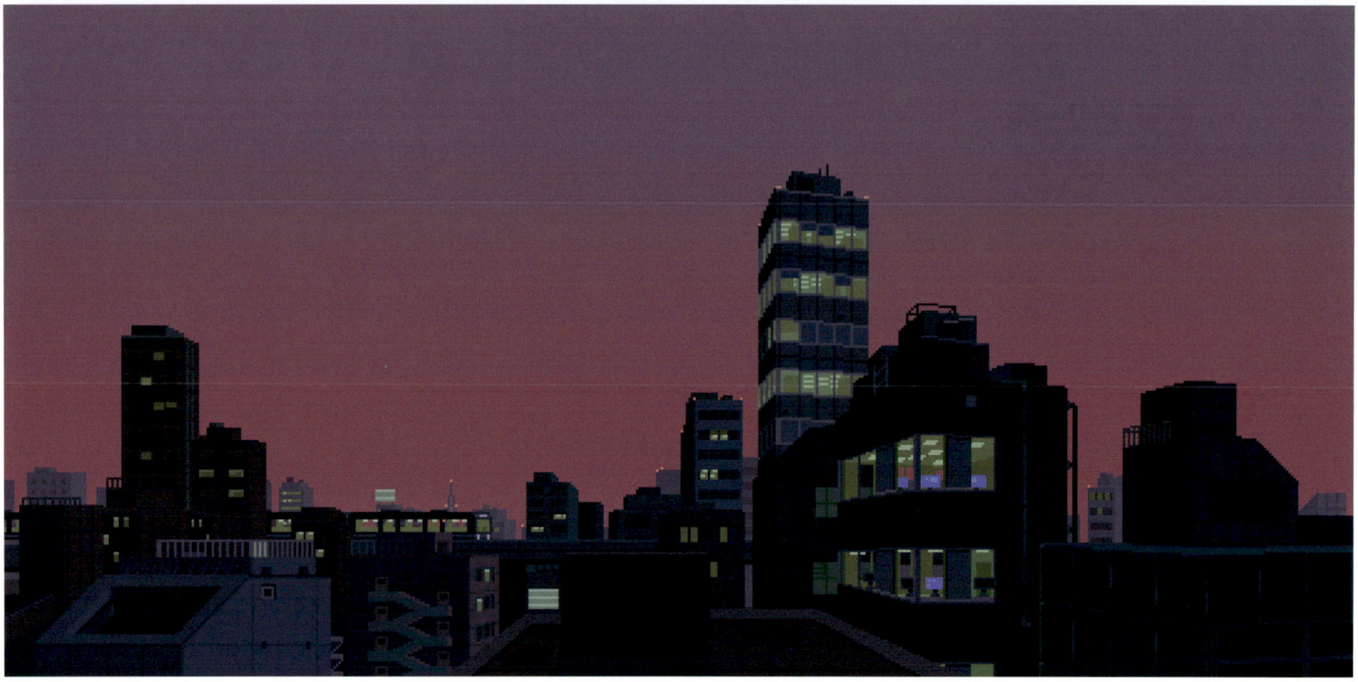

Above: *Horizon (Pt1 & Pt2)*, 14/06/2021, 540×270px
Right: *Stars*, 26/08/2021, 200×400px

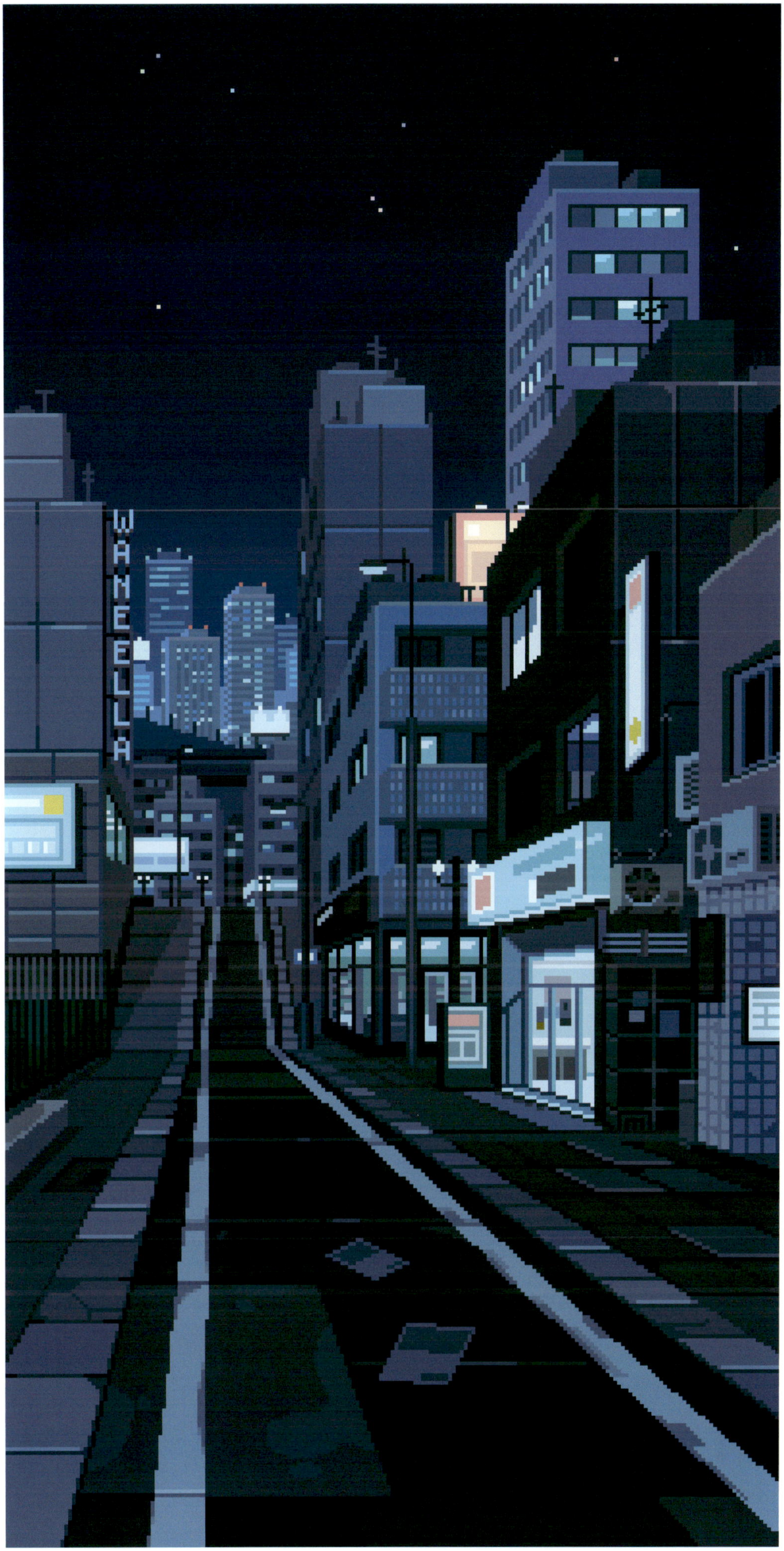
WANEELLA

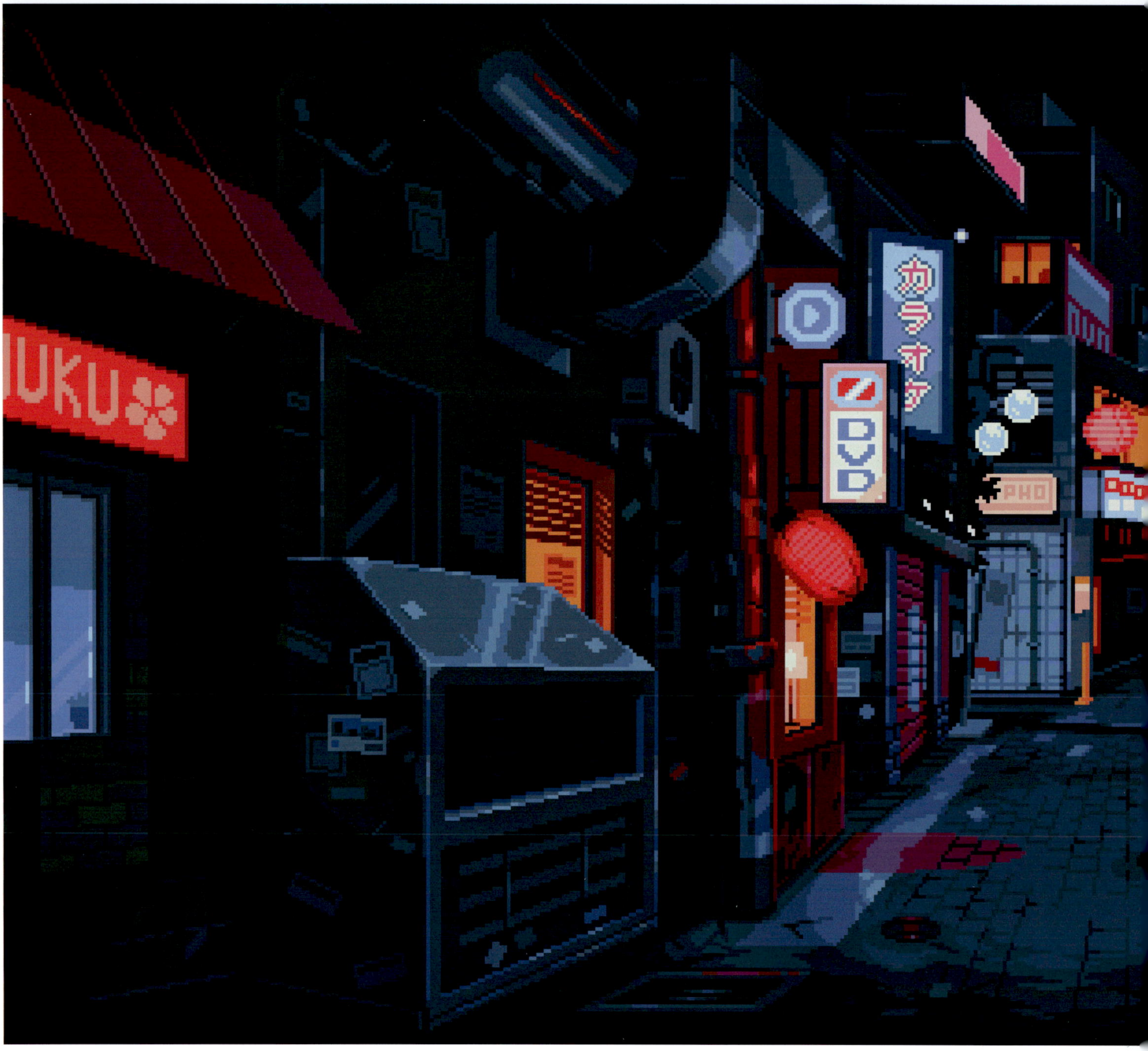

Untitled, created for PressPlayID Harajuku series, 16/11/2022, 638×284px

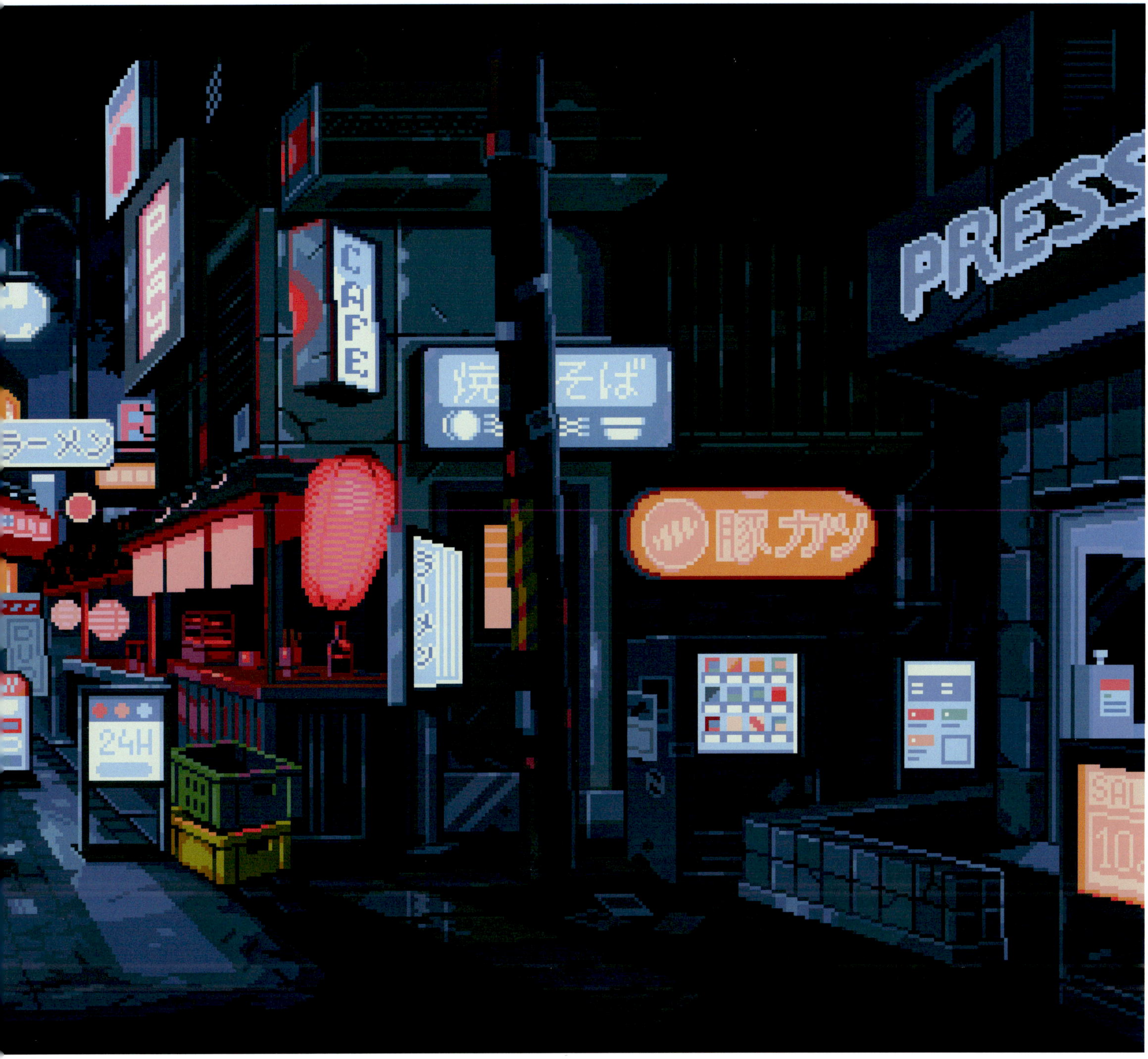
PLAY
CAFE
焼
そば
ラーメン
豚カツ
24H
PRESS

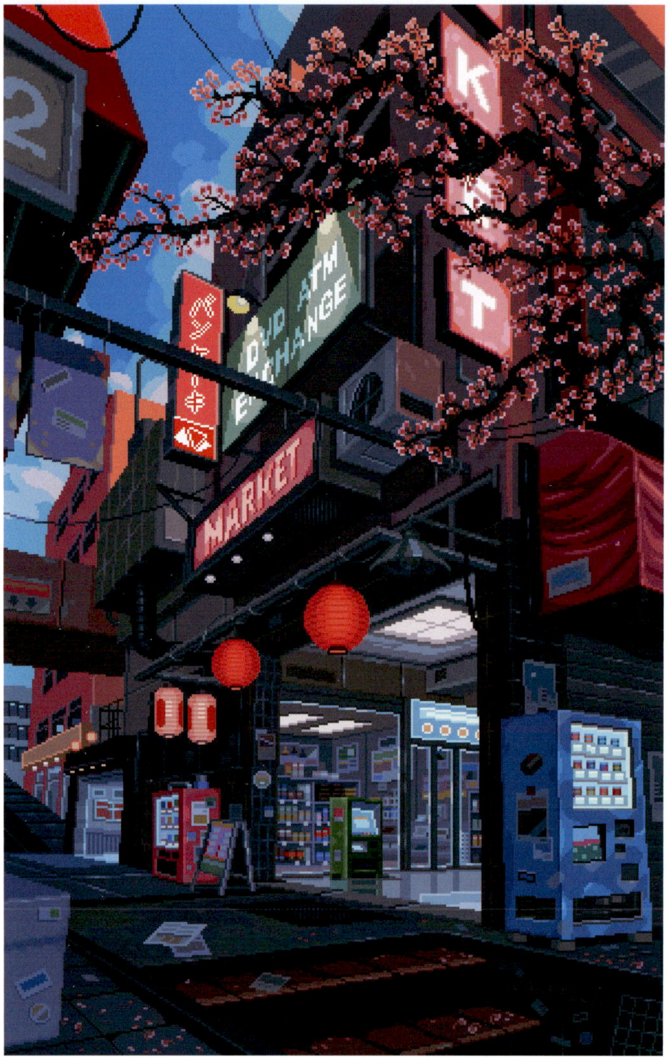

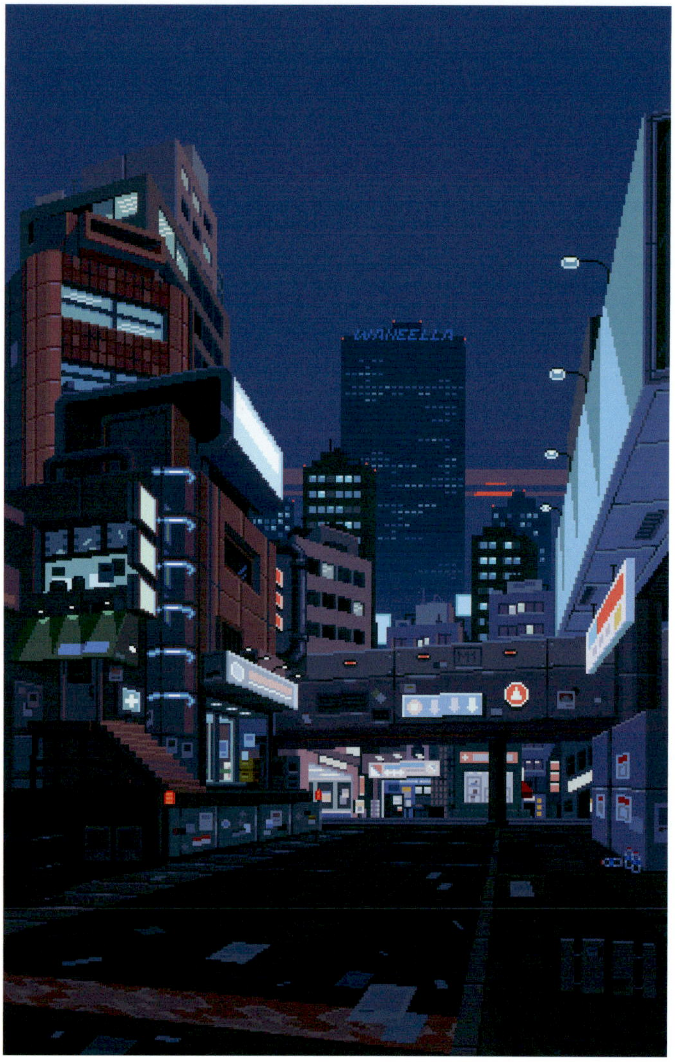

Above: *Dream,* 17/03/2022, 300×480px
Above right: *Sunrise,* 24/07/2022, 300×480px
Right: *December,* 27/11/2022, 240×480px

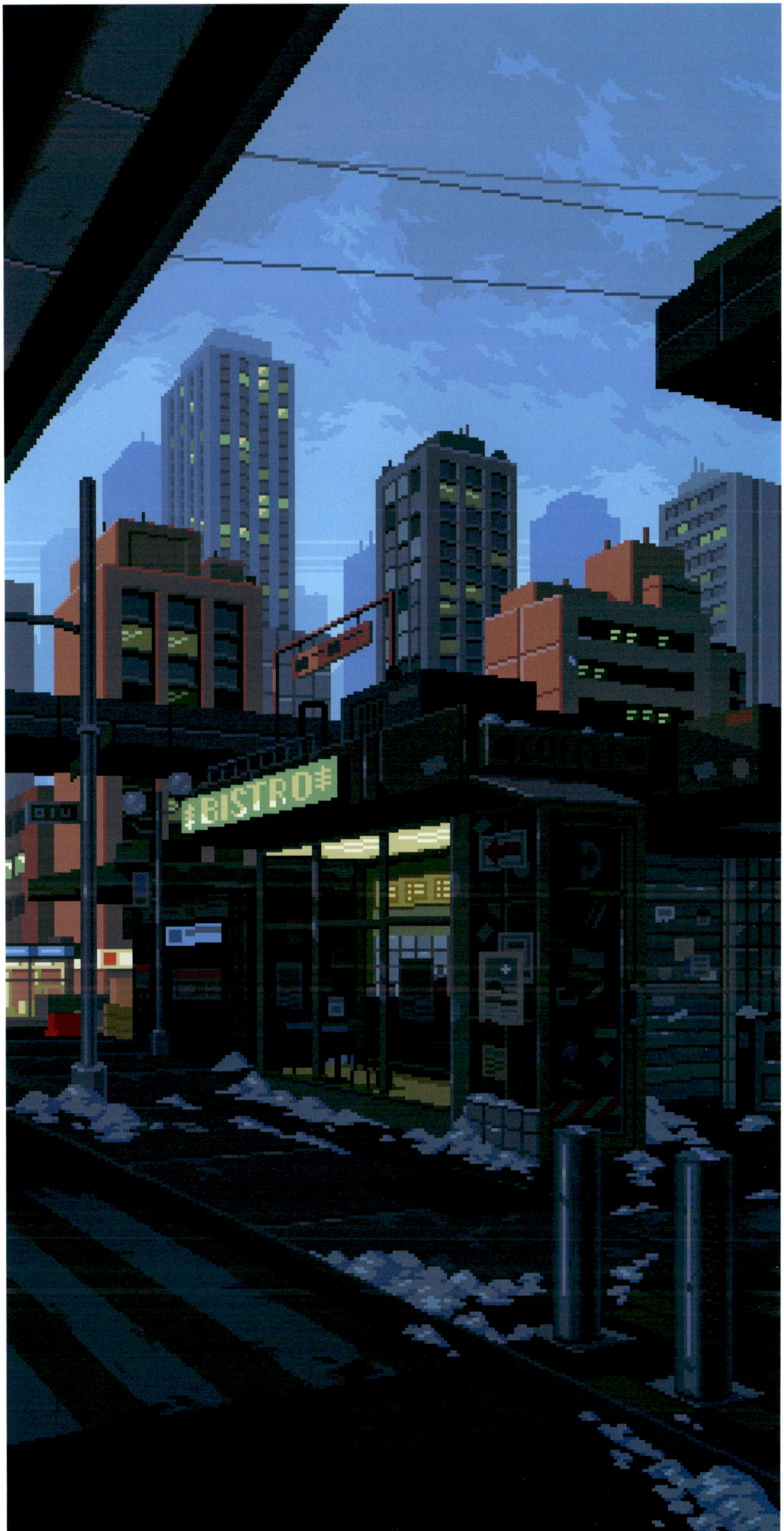
BISTRO

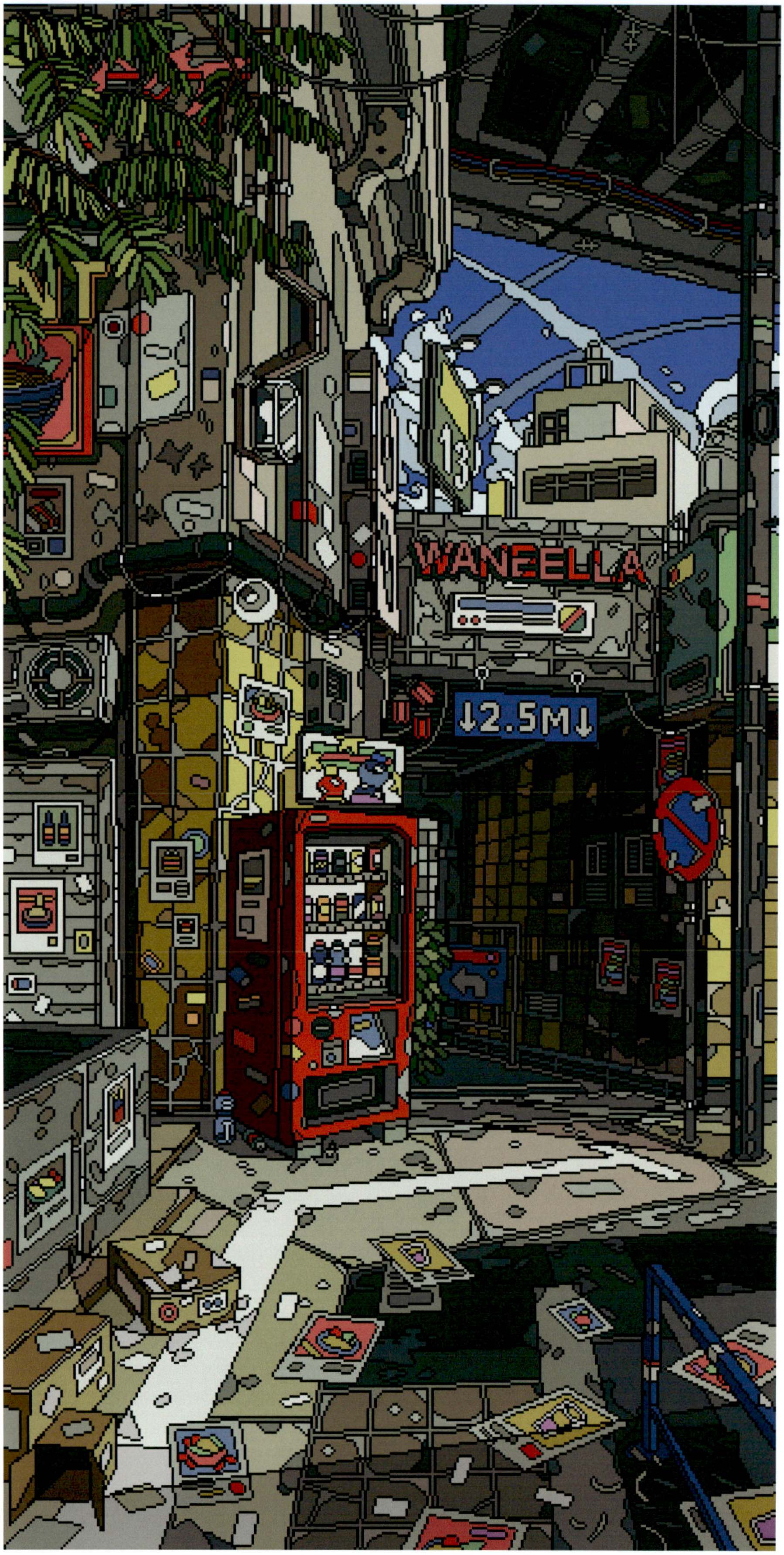

Above: *Breeze*, 28/05/2022, 300×600px
Right: *Silent Night*, 17/05/2022, 240×480px

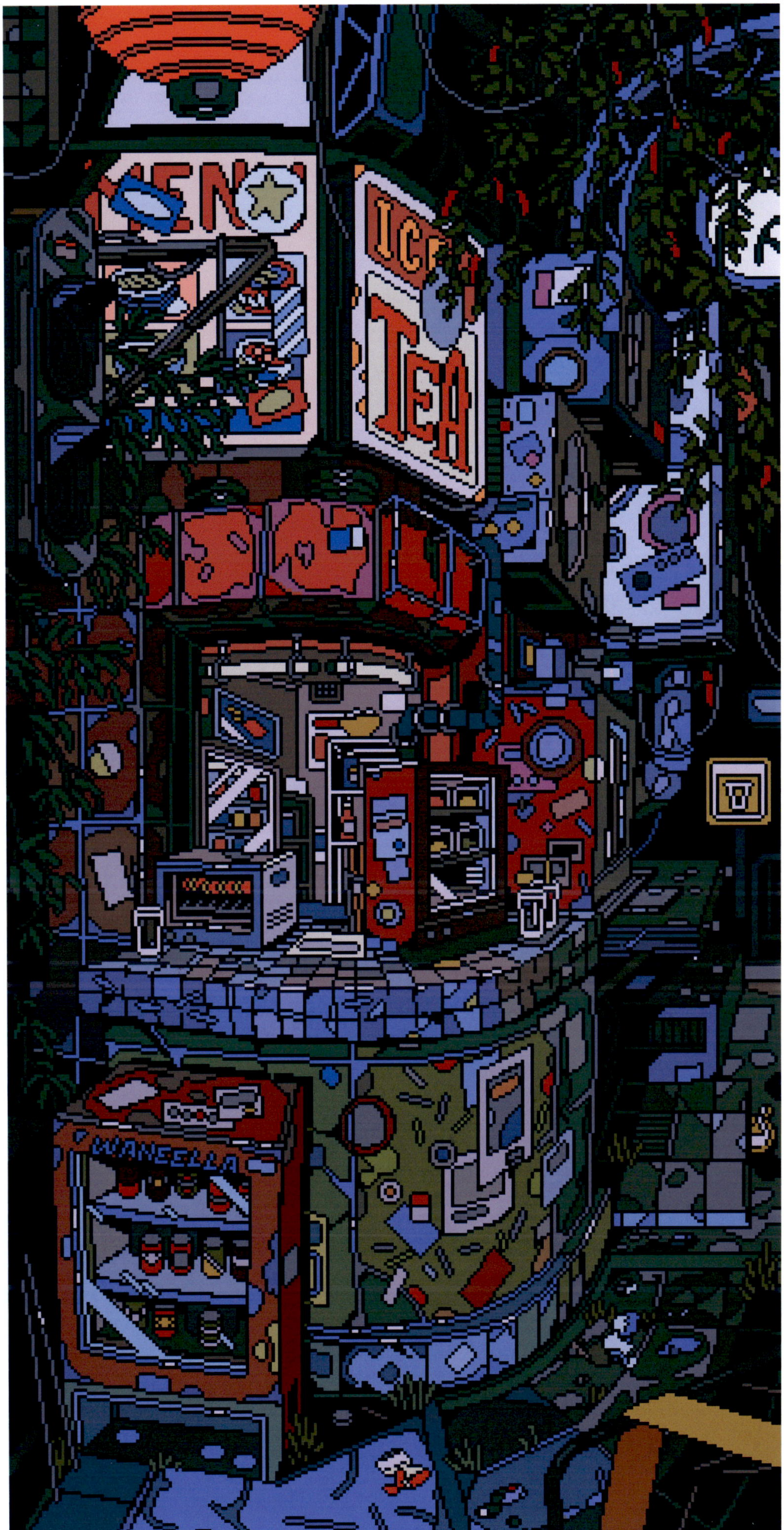
TEA

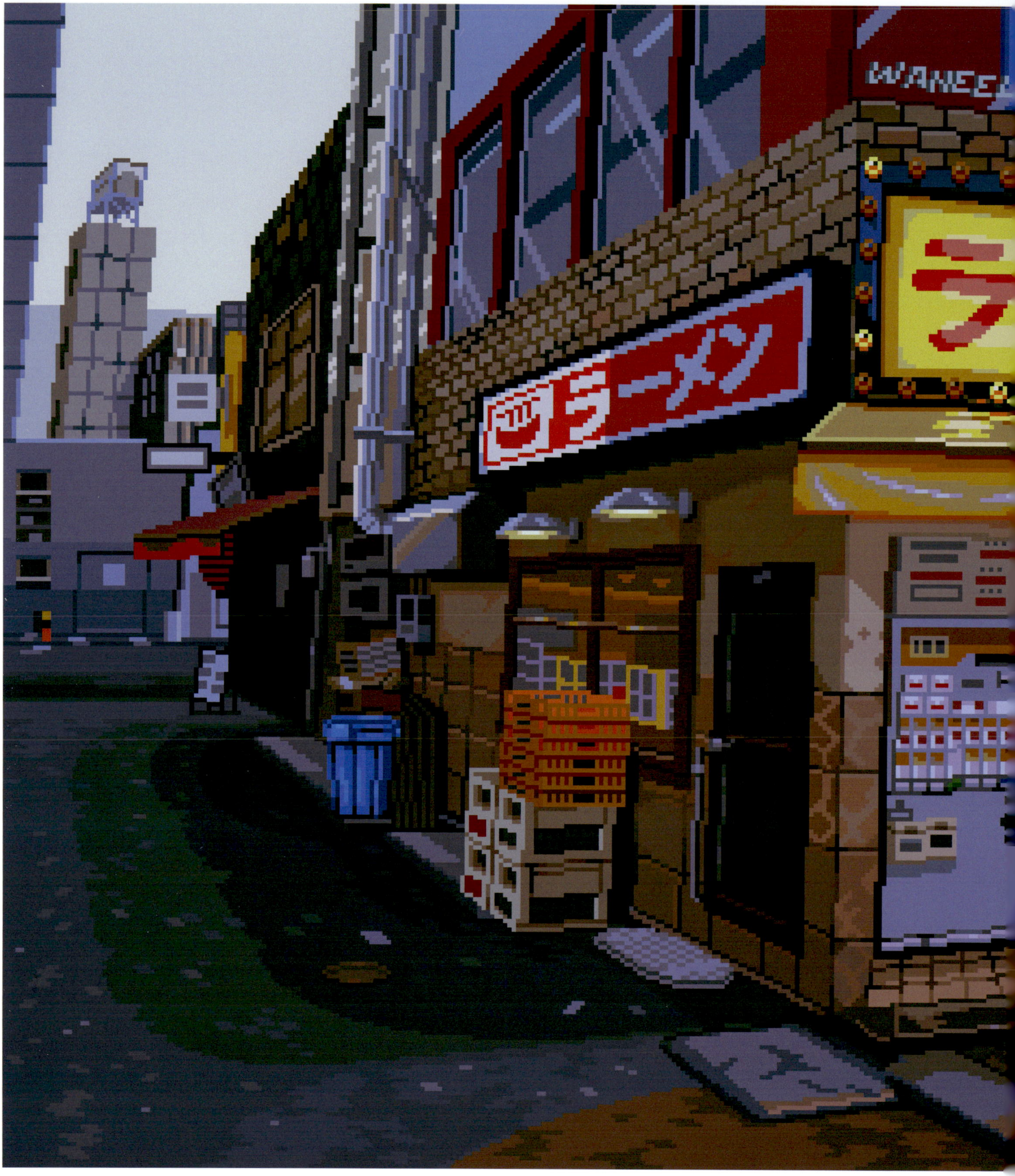

35.6586935, 139.6985097, 27/10/2022, 480×270px

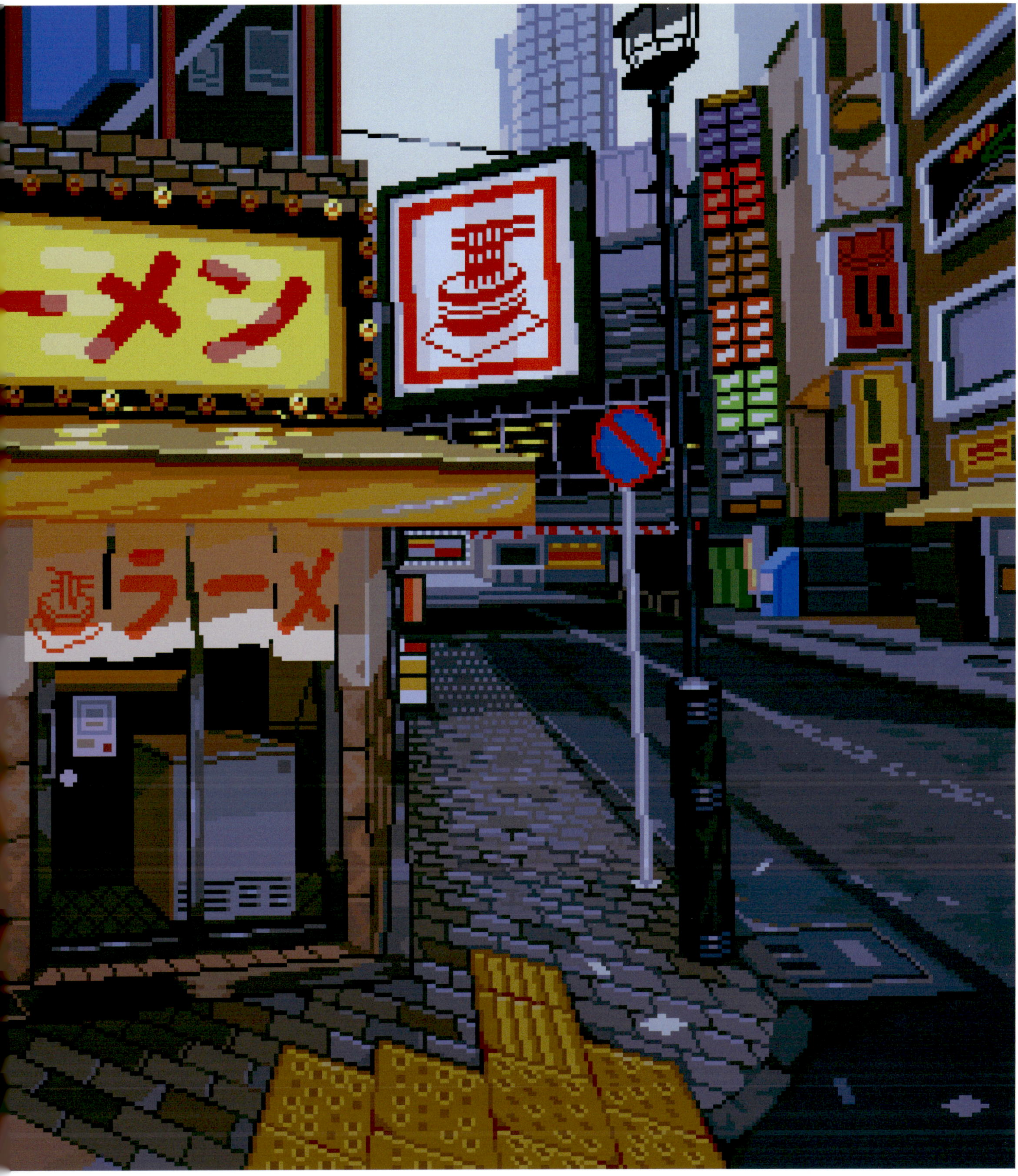
ーメン
ラーメ

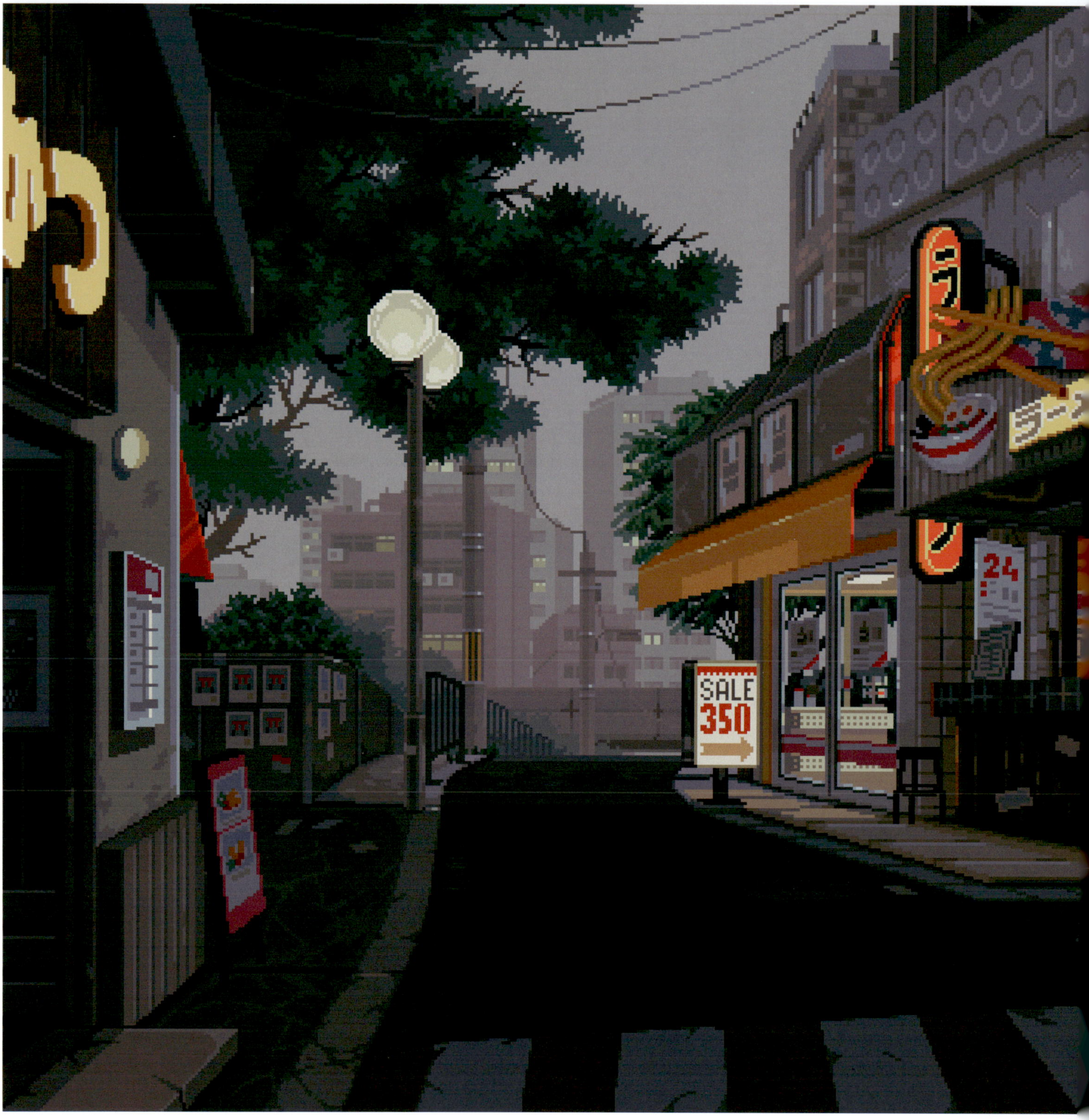

On The Hill, 21/09/2022, 720×360px

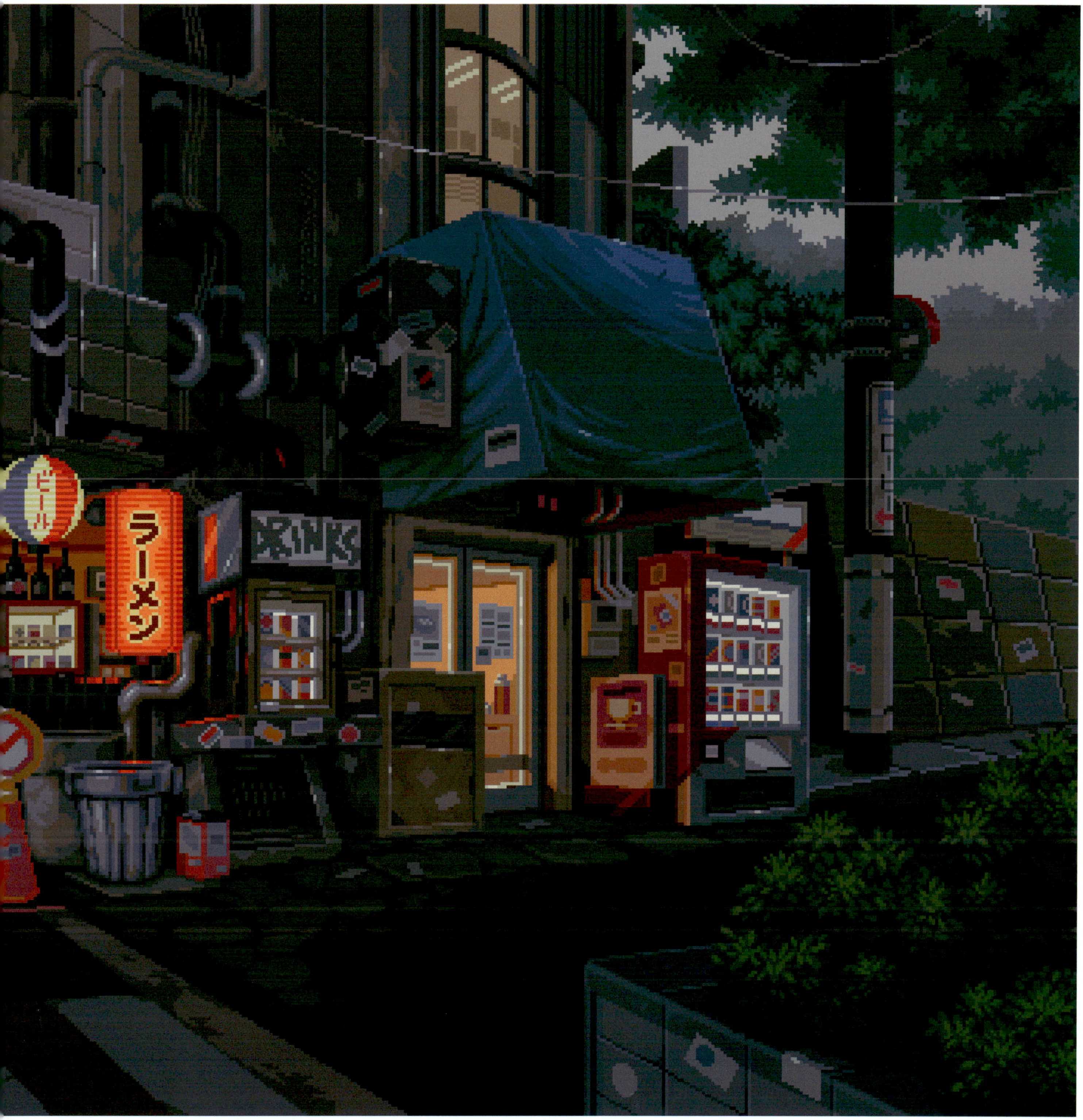
ビール
ラーメン

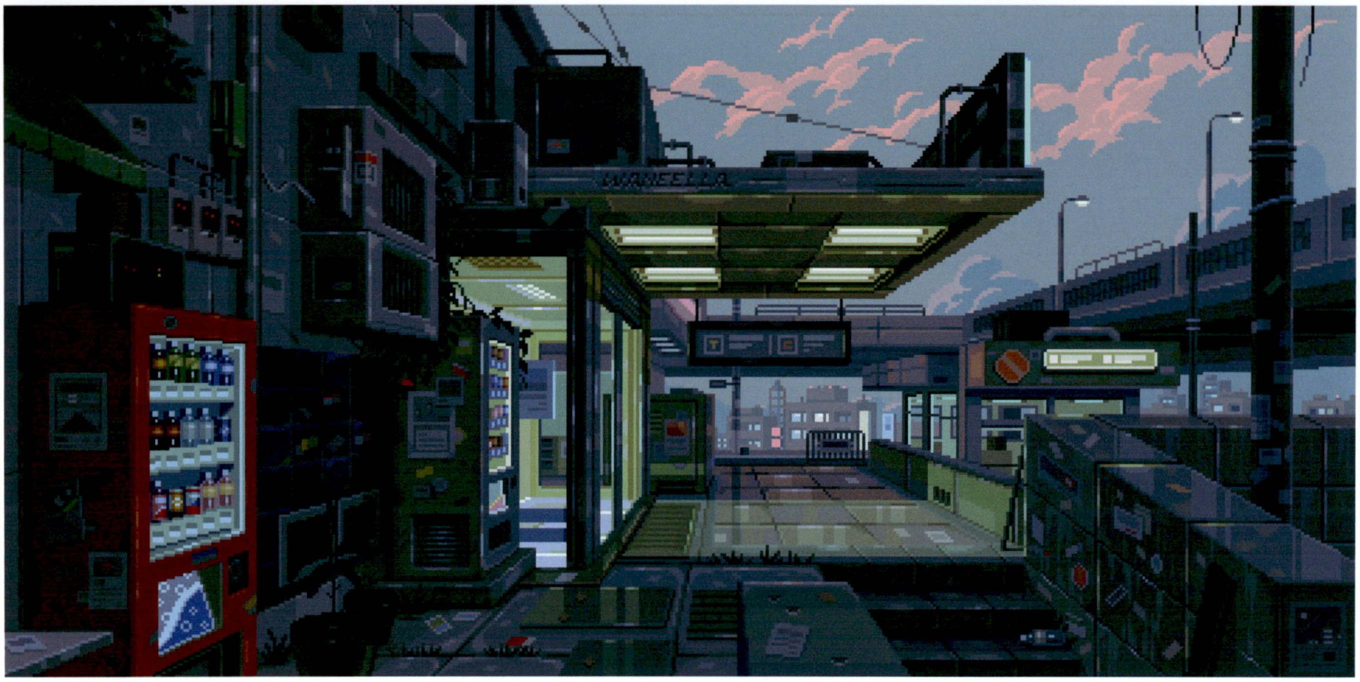

Above: *Return*, 18/02/2022, 480×240px
Right: *Overcast*, 24/08/2022, 350×600px

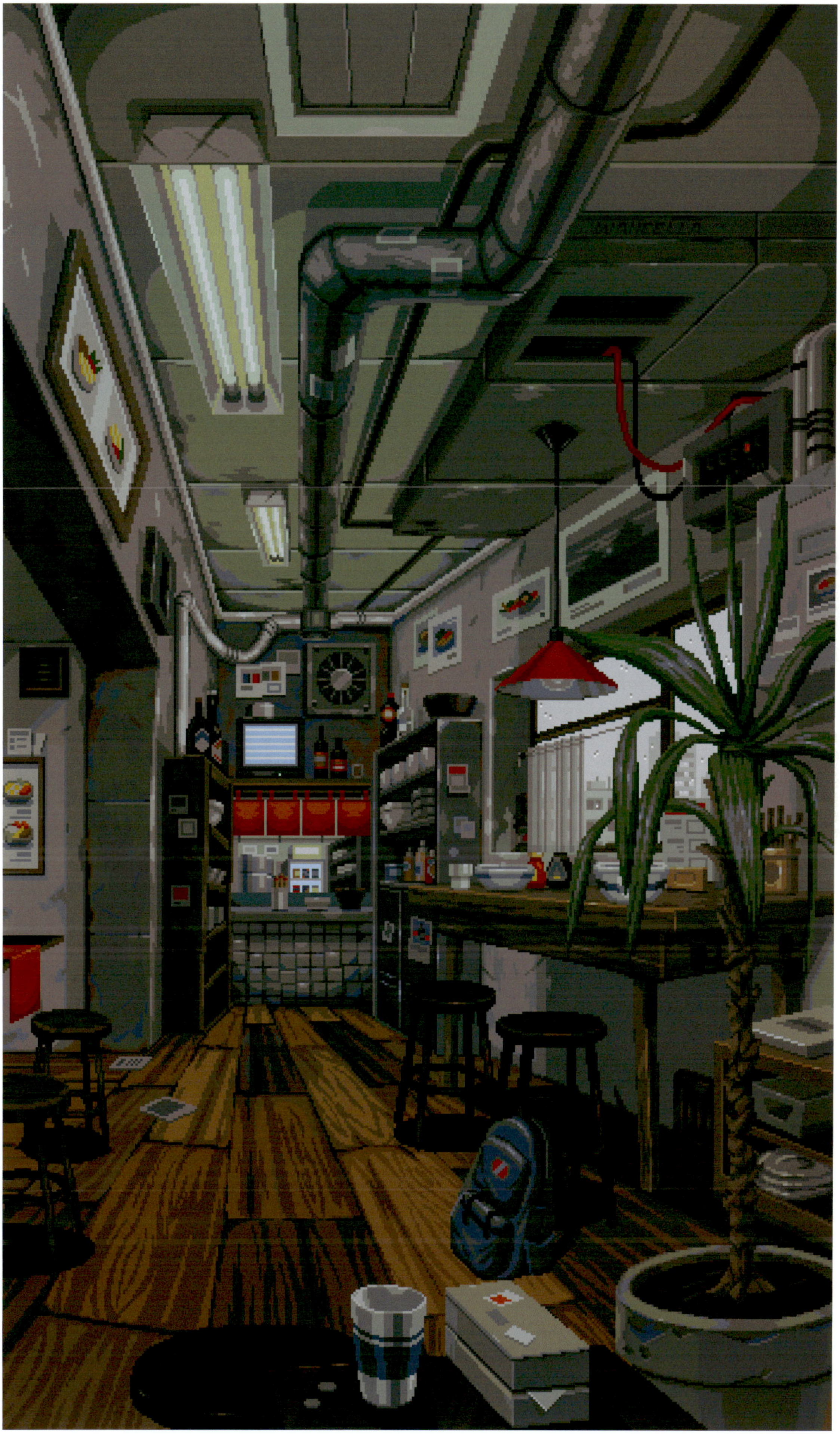

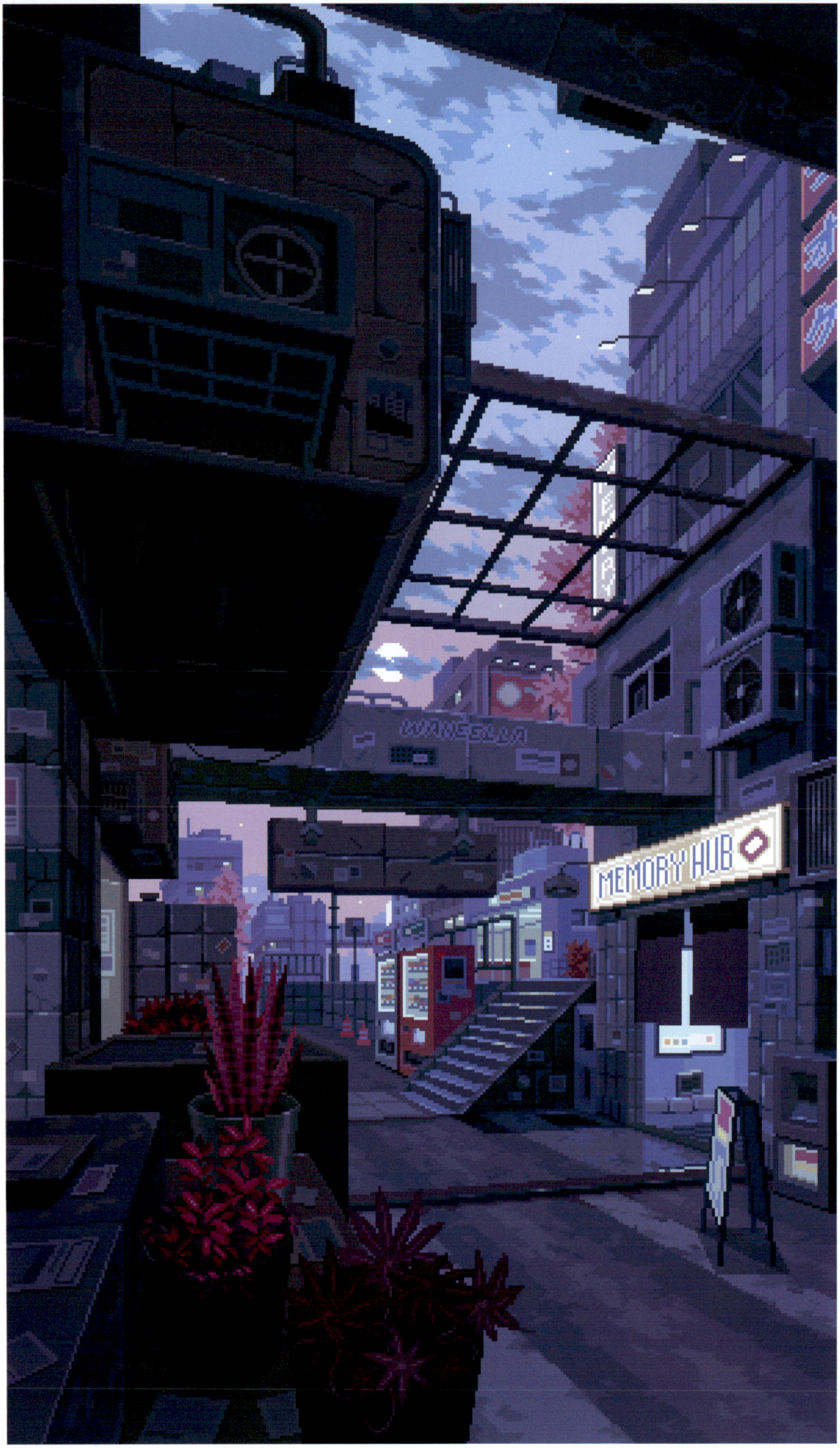

Above: *Infrared*, 22/04/2022, 300×520px
Right: *Hearth*, 22/07/2022, 240×480px

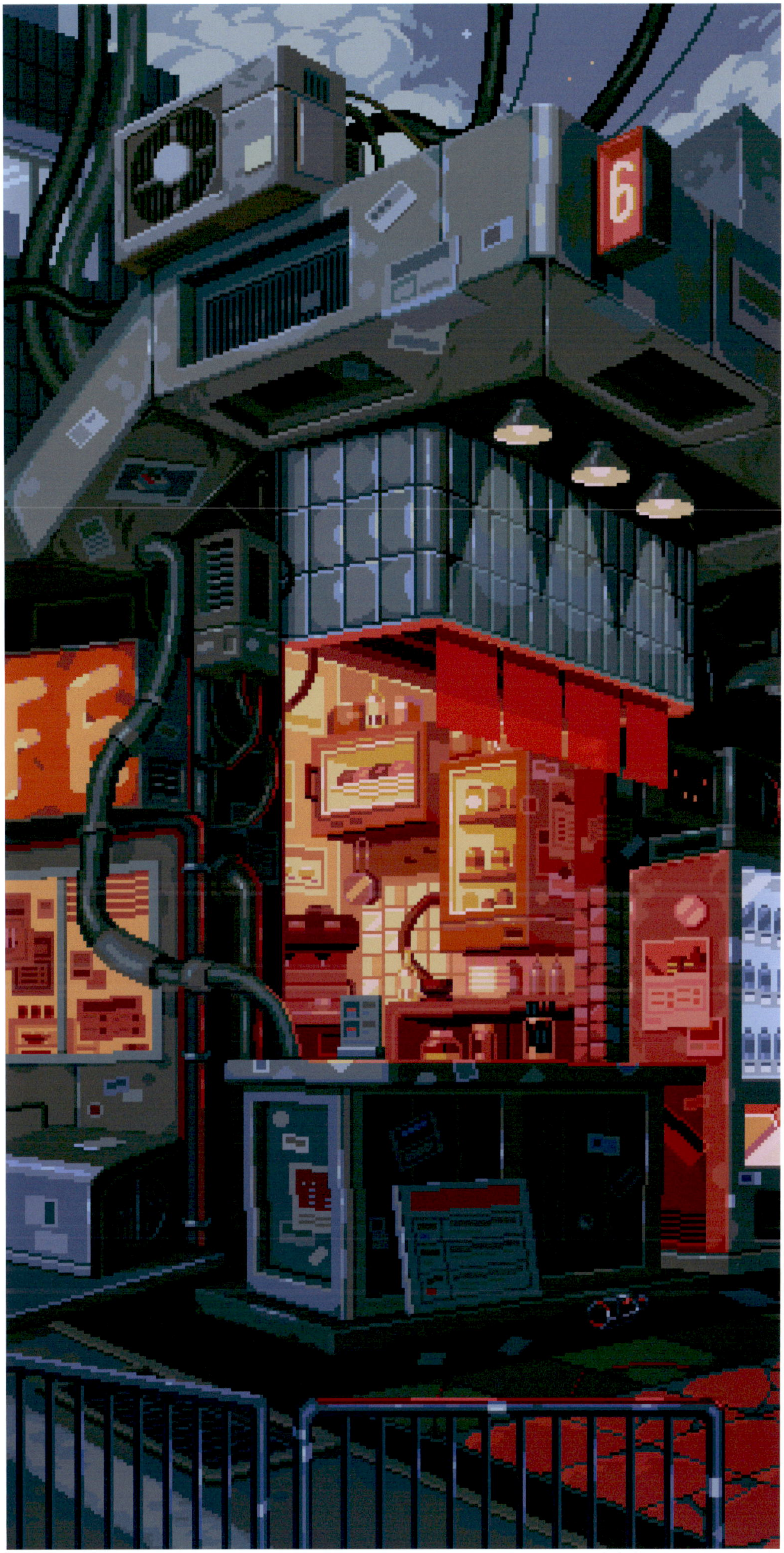
6

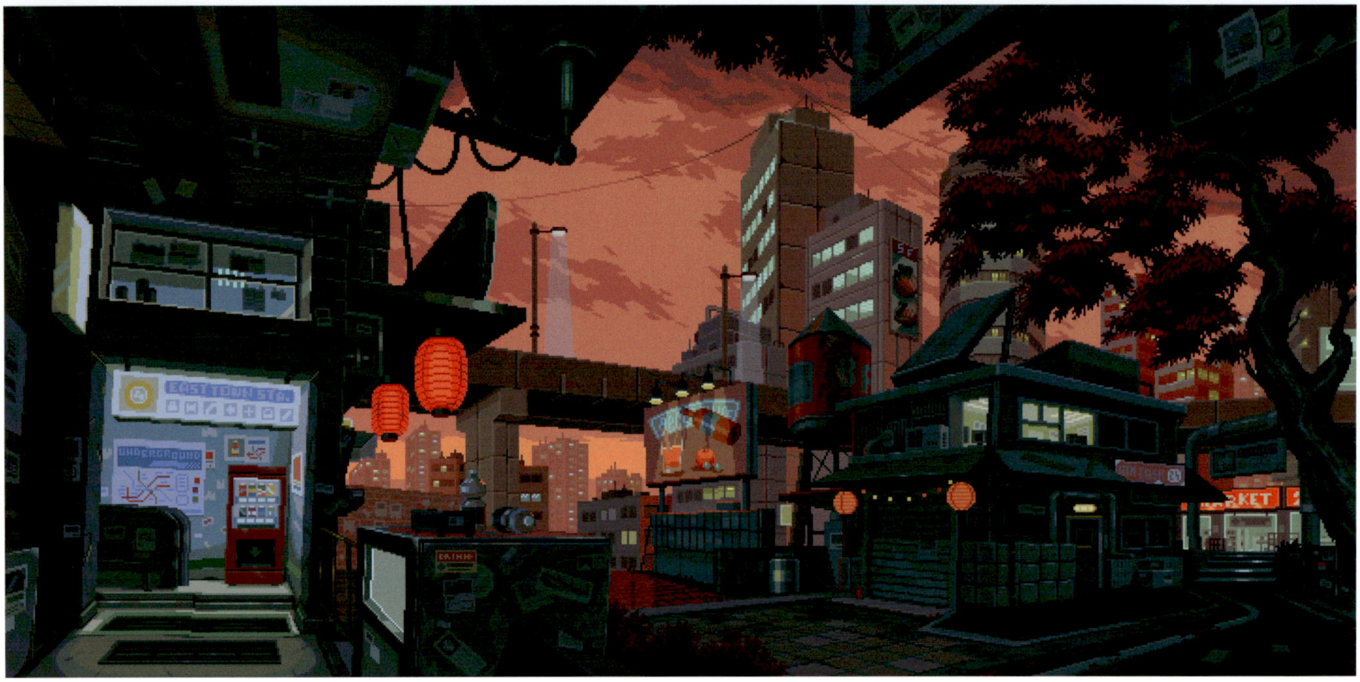

Above: *Rose Waves*, 02/08/2022, 720×360px
Right: *Night Sky*, 09/10/2022, 270×540px

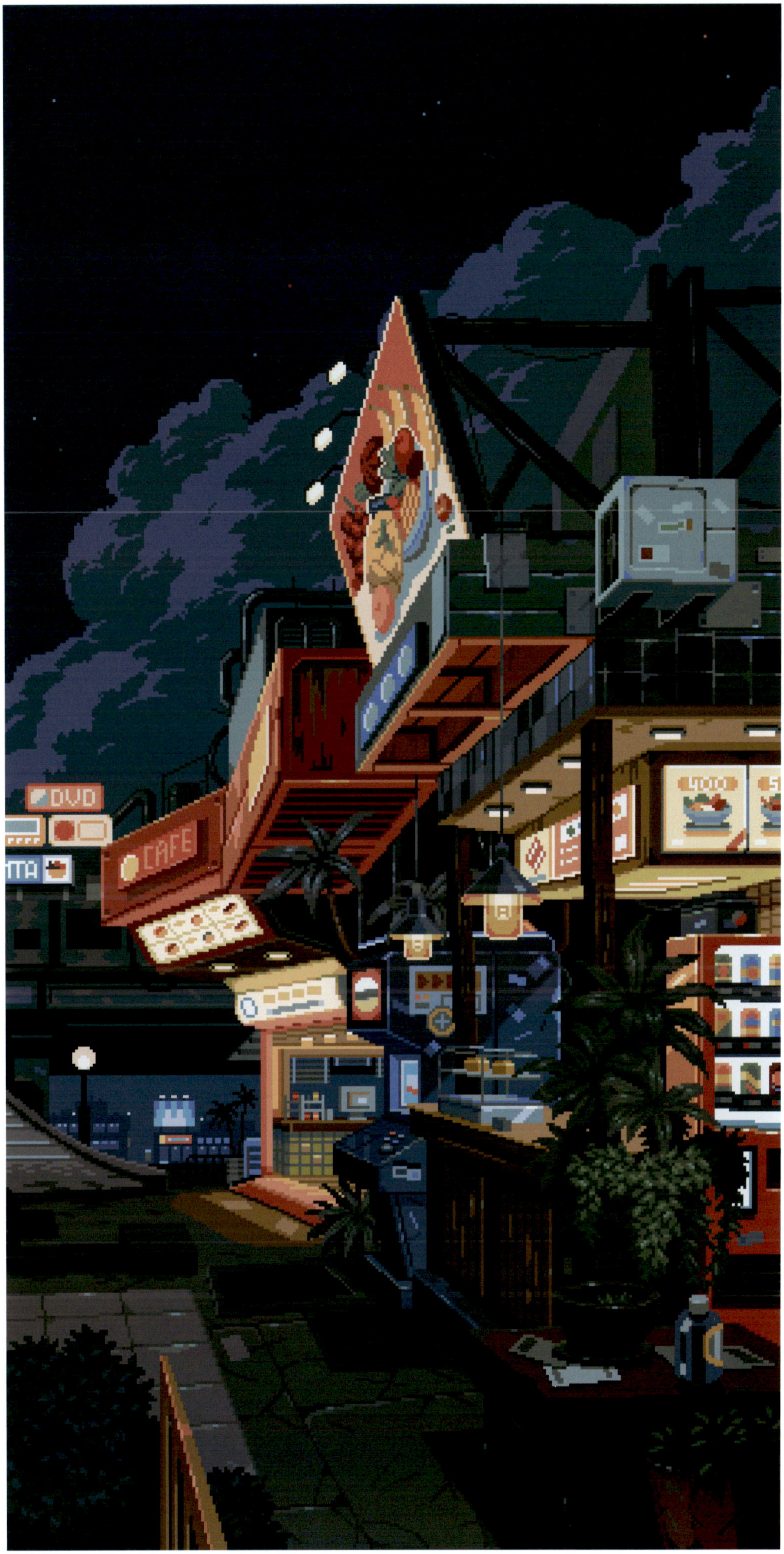
DVD
CAFE

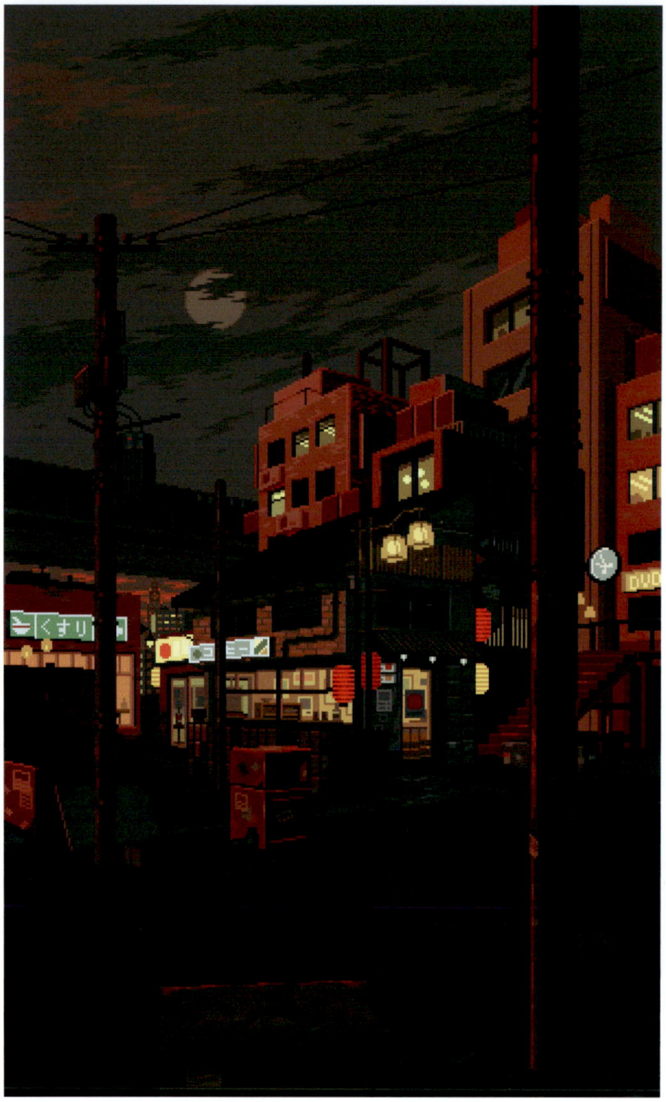

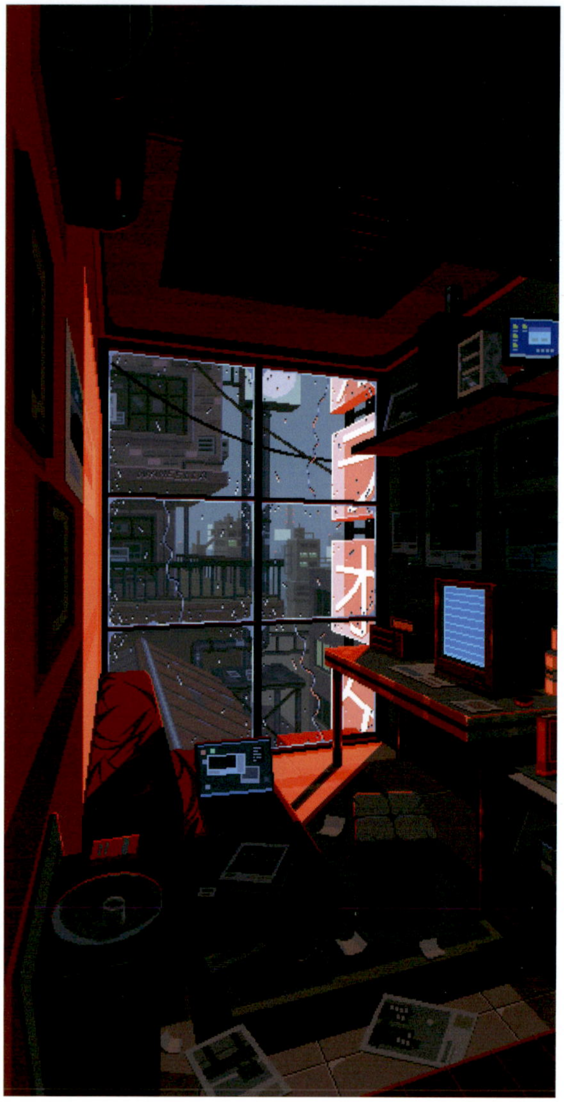

Above: *Pale Moon*, 11/12/2022, 300×500px
Above right: *Rain*, 06/07/2022, 350×700px
Right: *Bored*, 22/05/2023, 216×384px

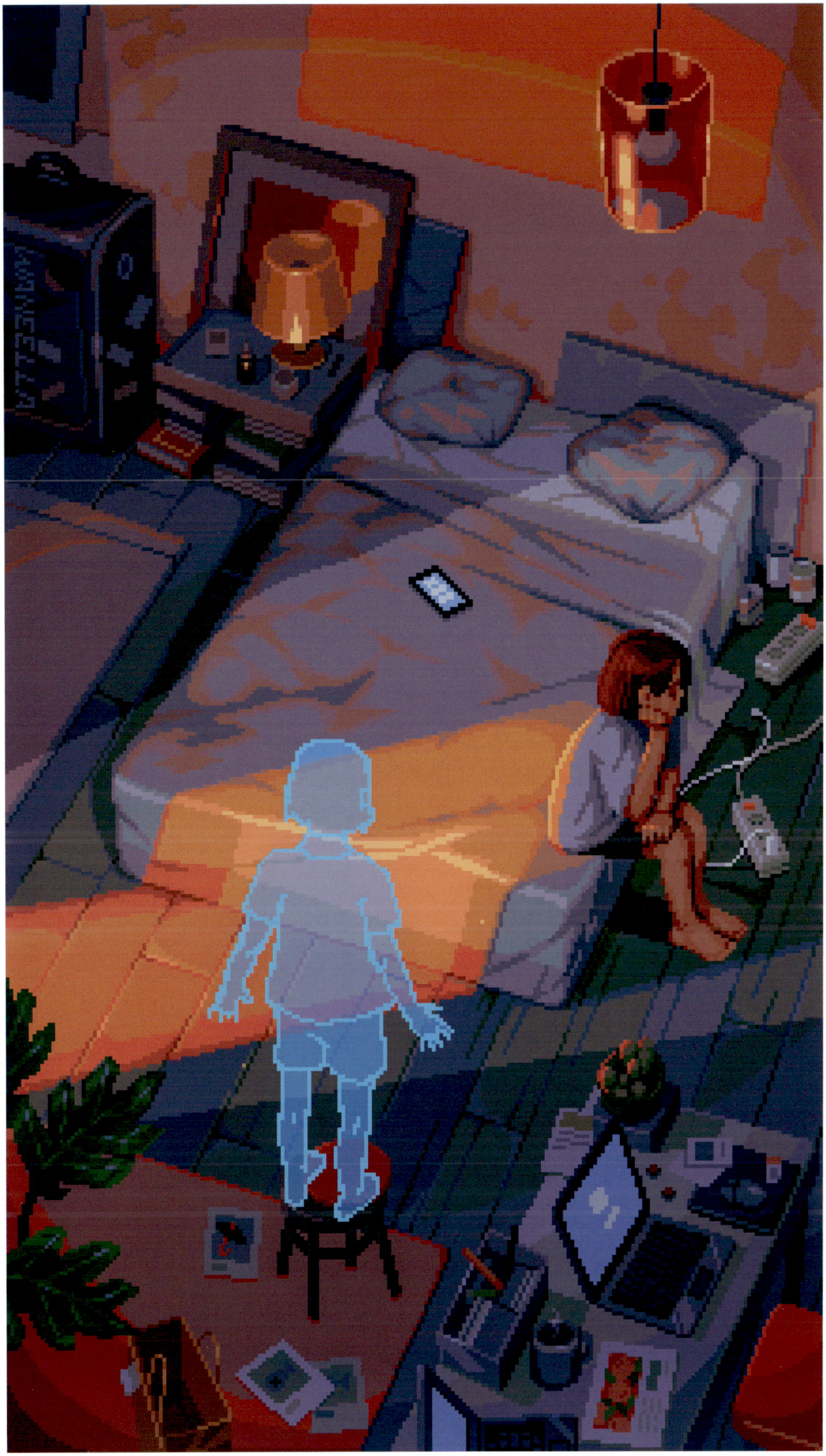

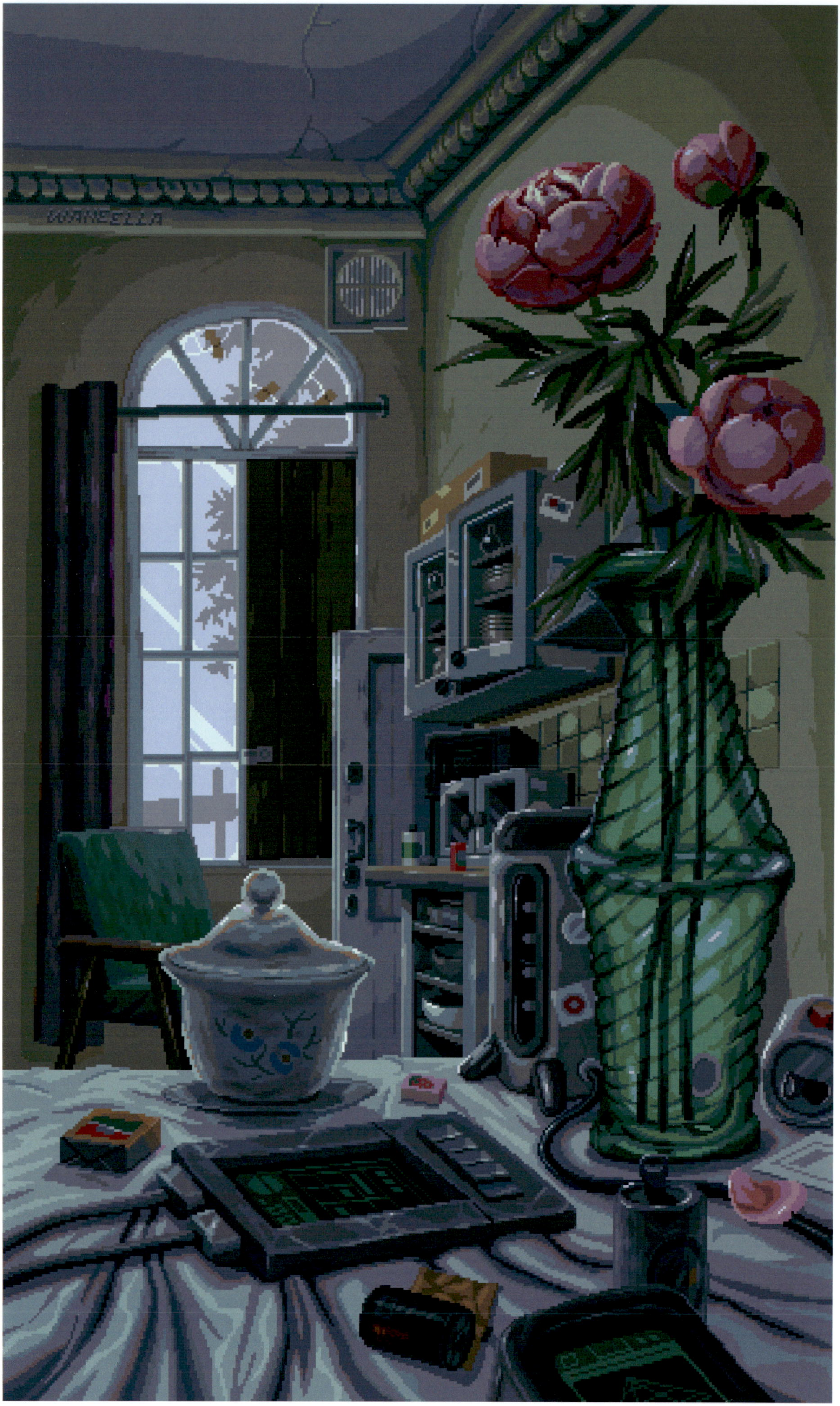
WANEELLA

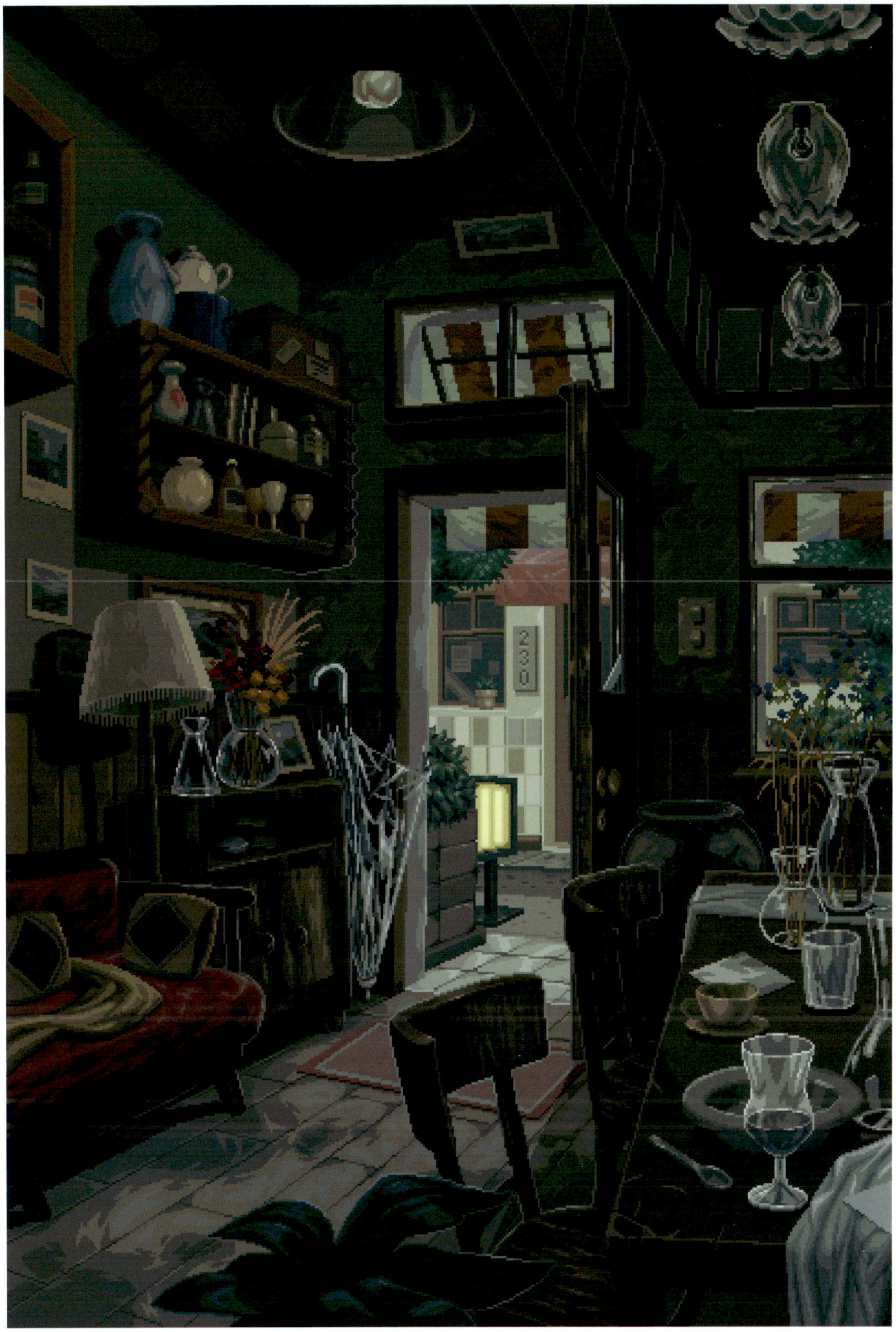

Left: *Leftovers*, 20/05/2023, 320×540px
Above: *Through The Dust*, 28/02/2023, 400×600px

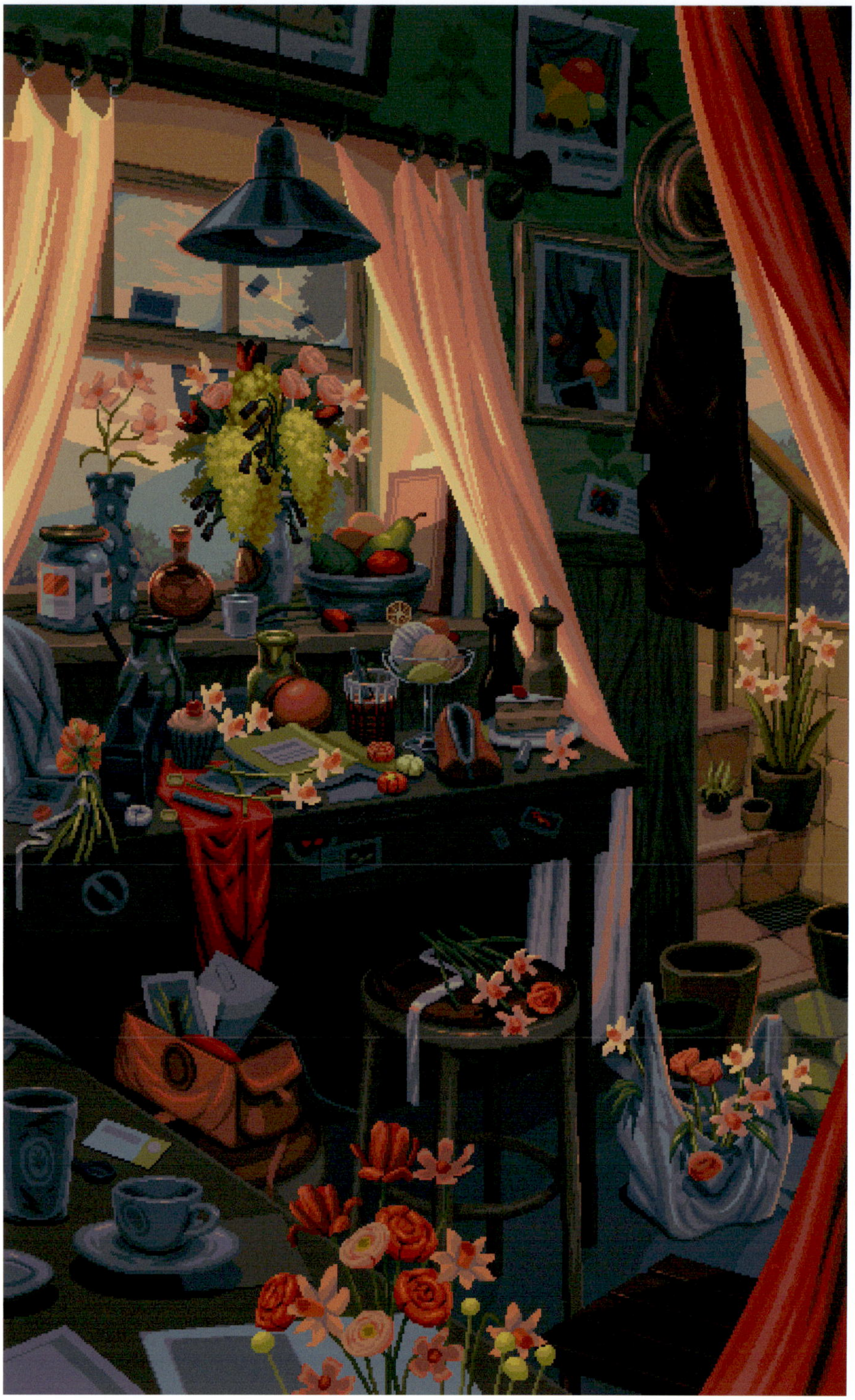

Above: *Golden*, 28/03/2023, 400×660px
Right: *Copper*, 28/09/2023, 180×3200px

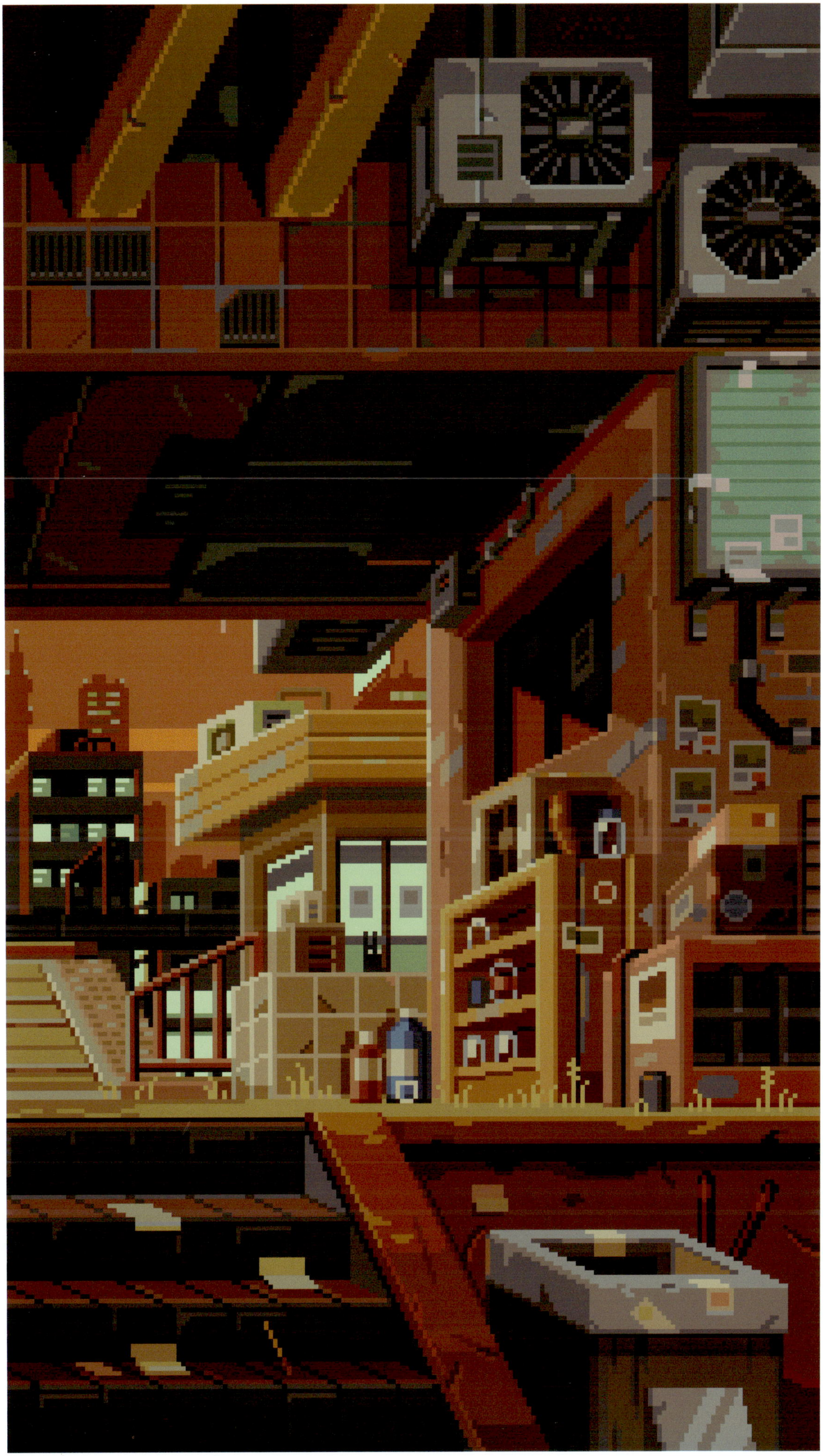

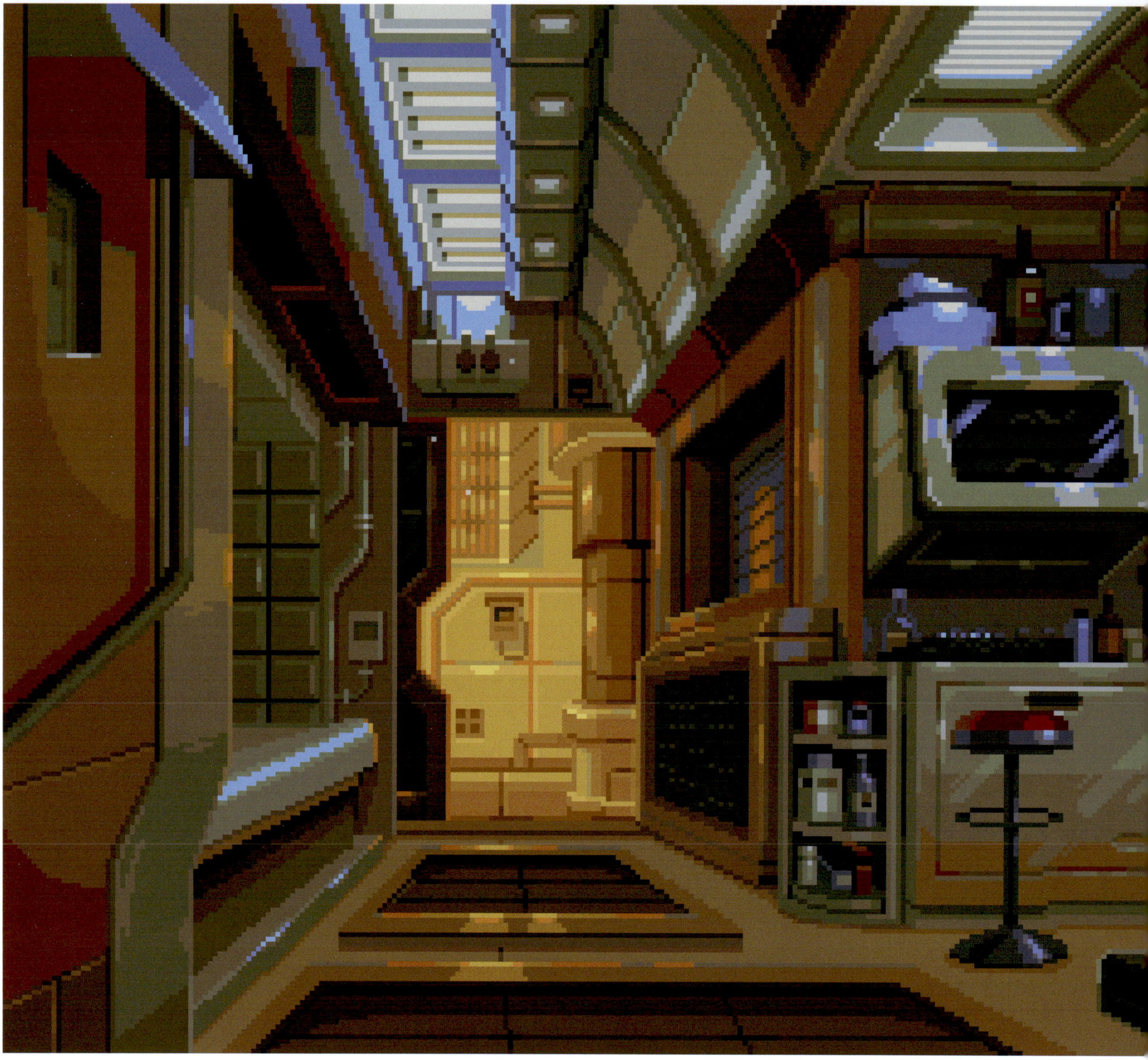

No Sleep Again, 16/08/2023, 486×216px

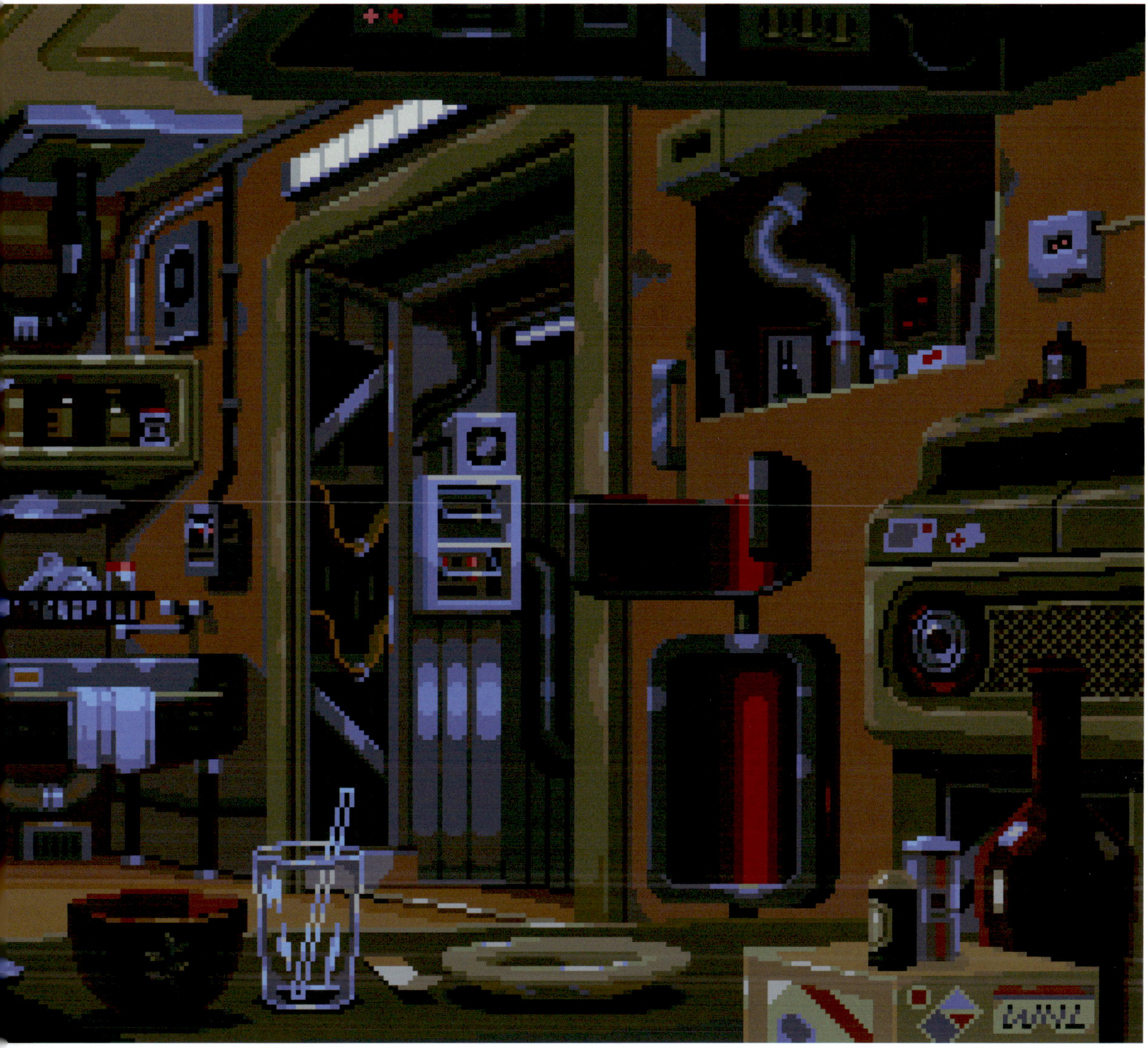

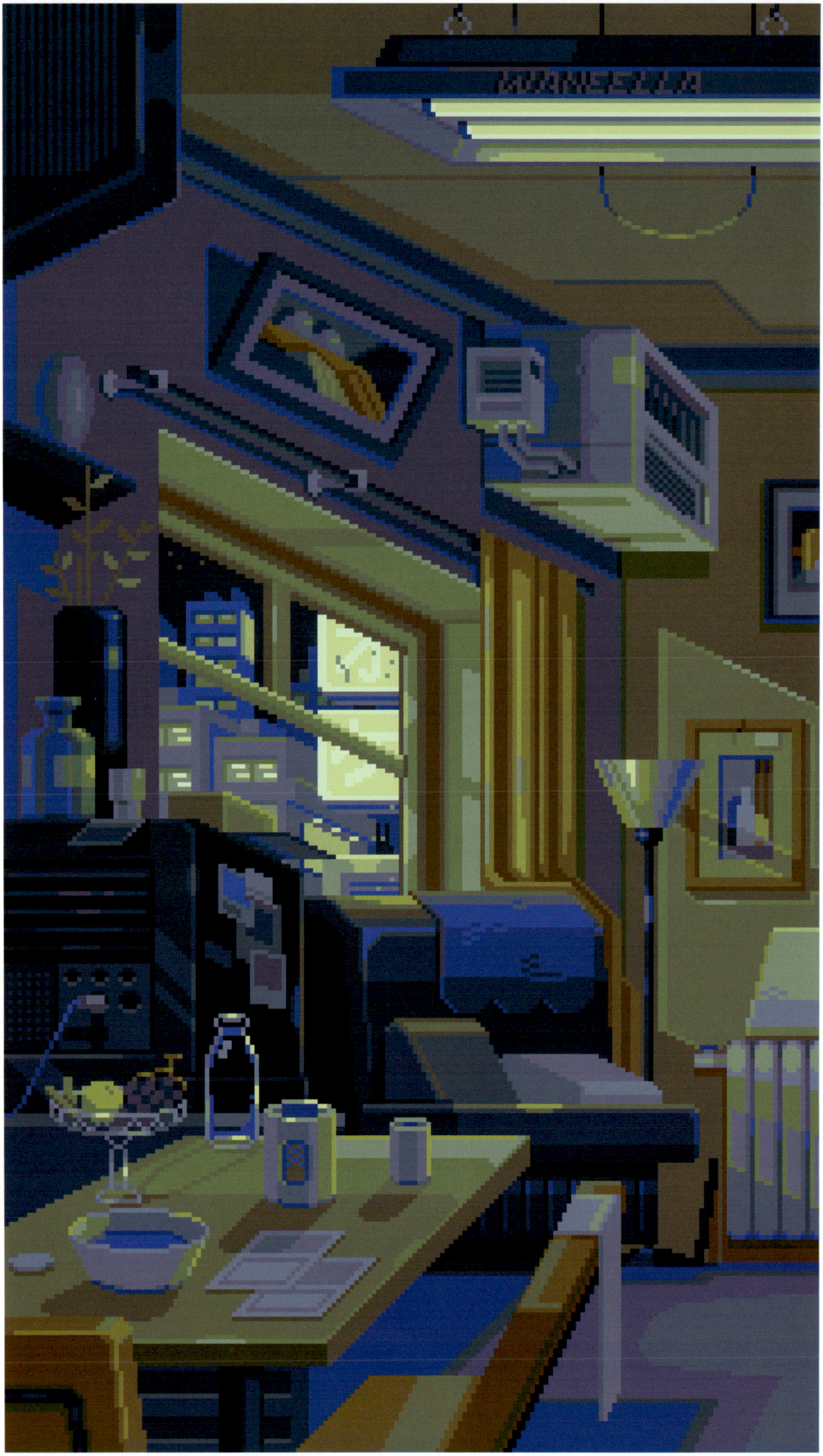

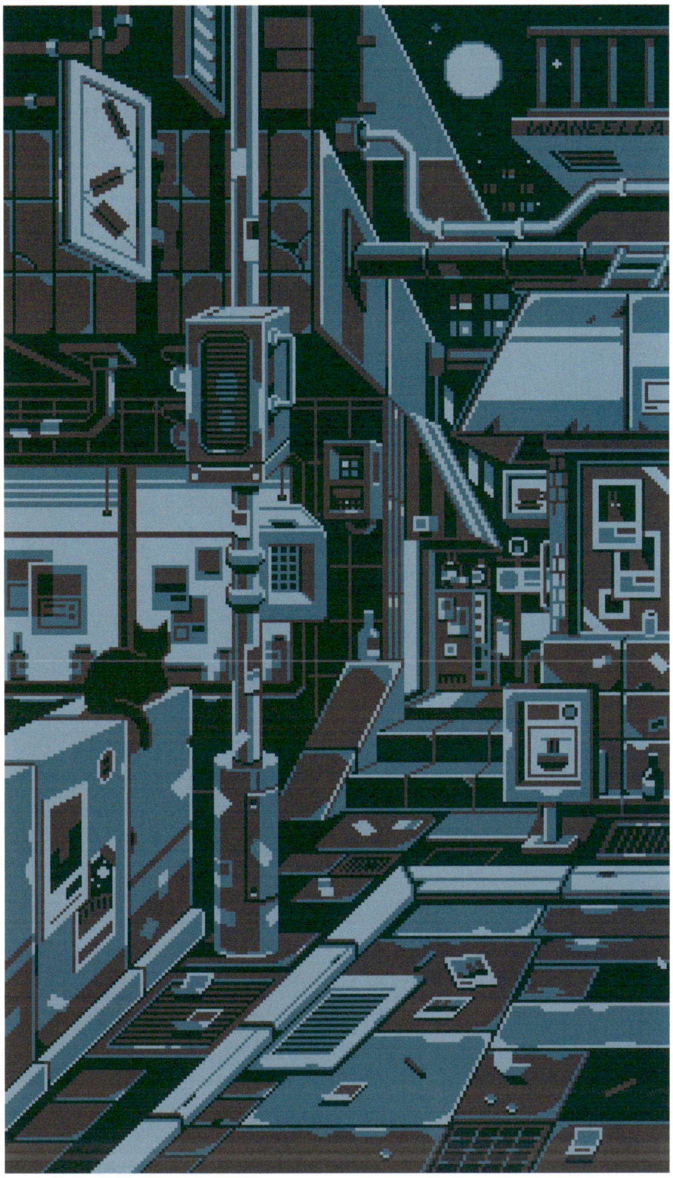

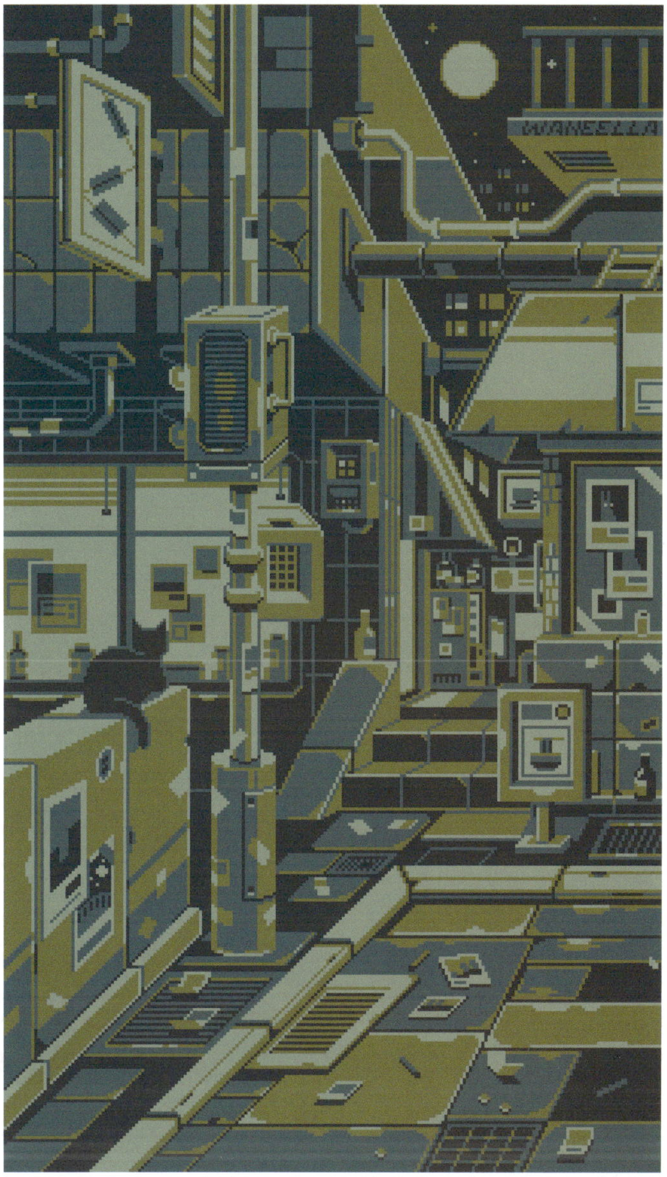

Left: *Still Night*, 17/09/2023, 180×320px
Above: *Let The Moon Shine* (Blue and Grey versions), 24/10/2023, 216×384px

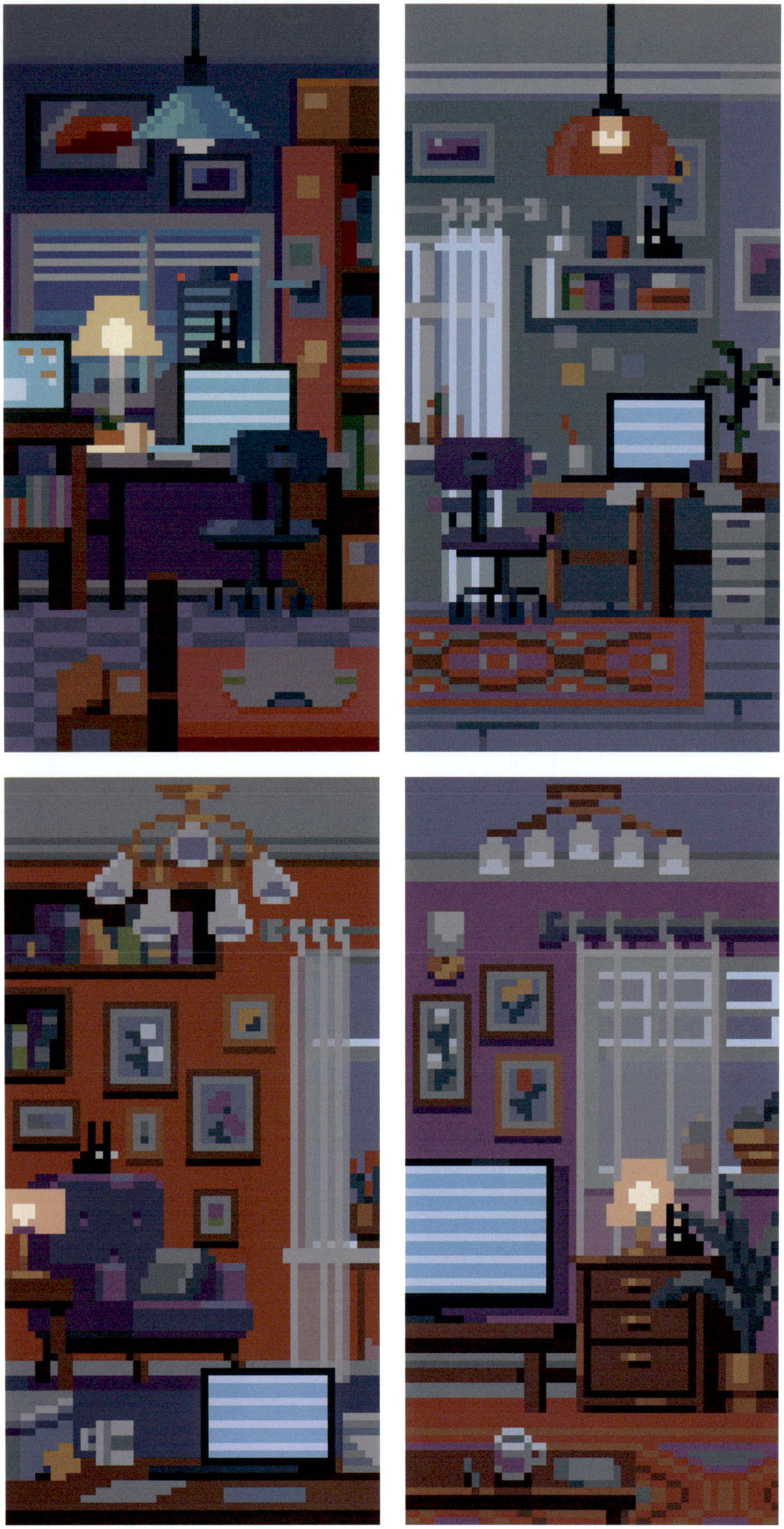

Above: *Tiny Backgrounds*, 08/06/2023, 50×100px
Right: *Light Moments*, 17/02/2023, 160×320px

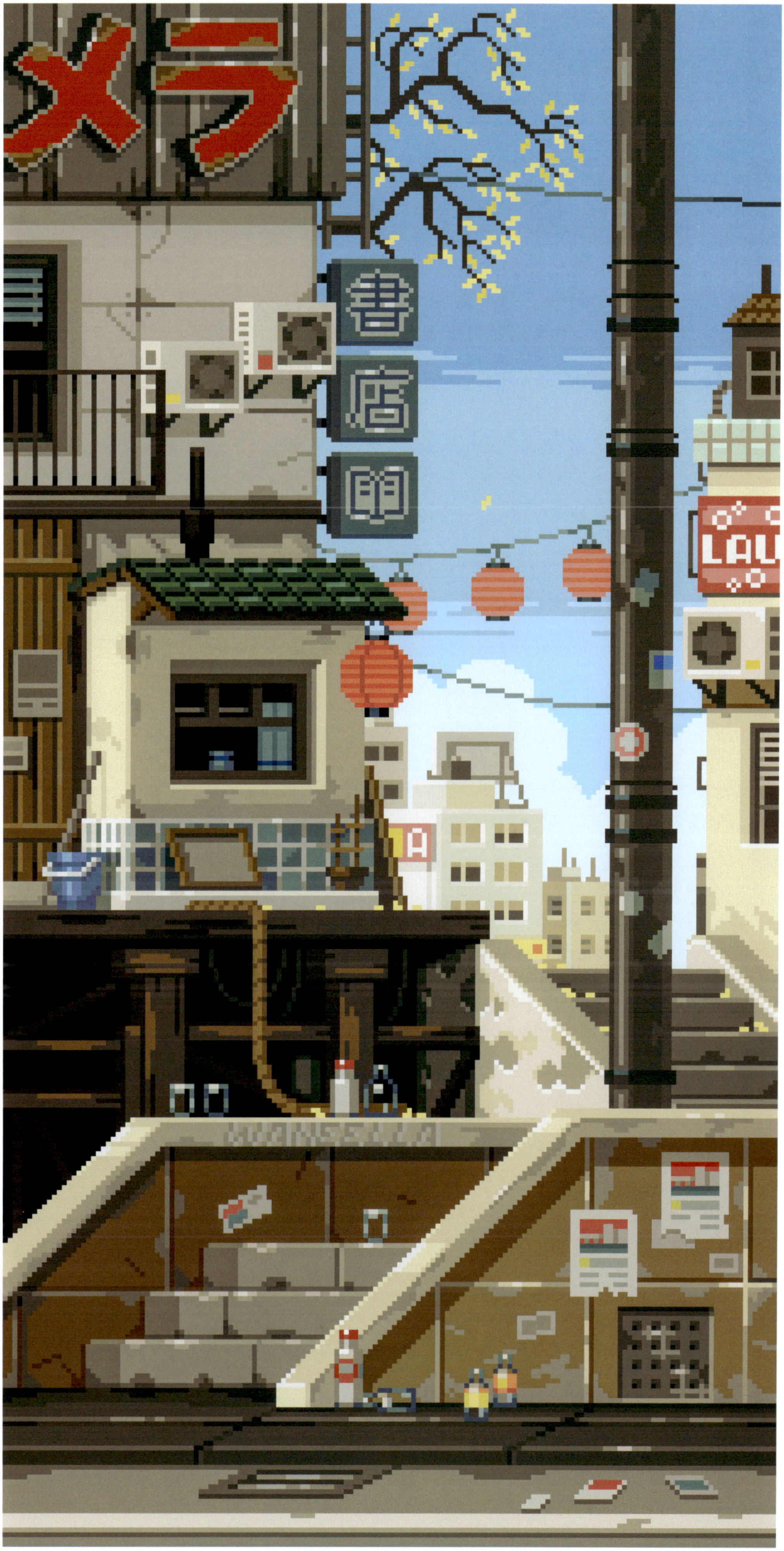
メラ
書
店
LAU

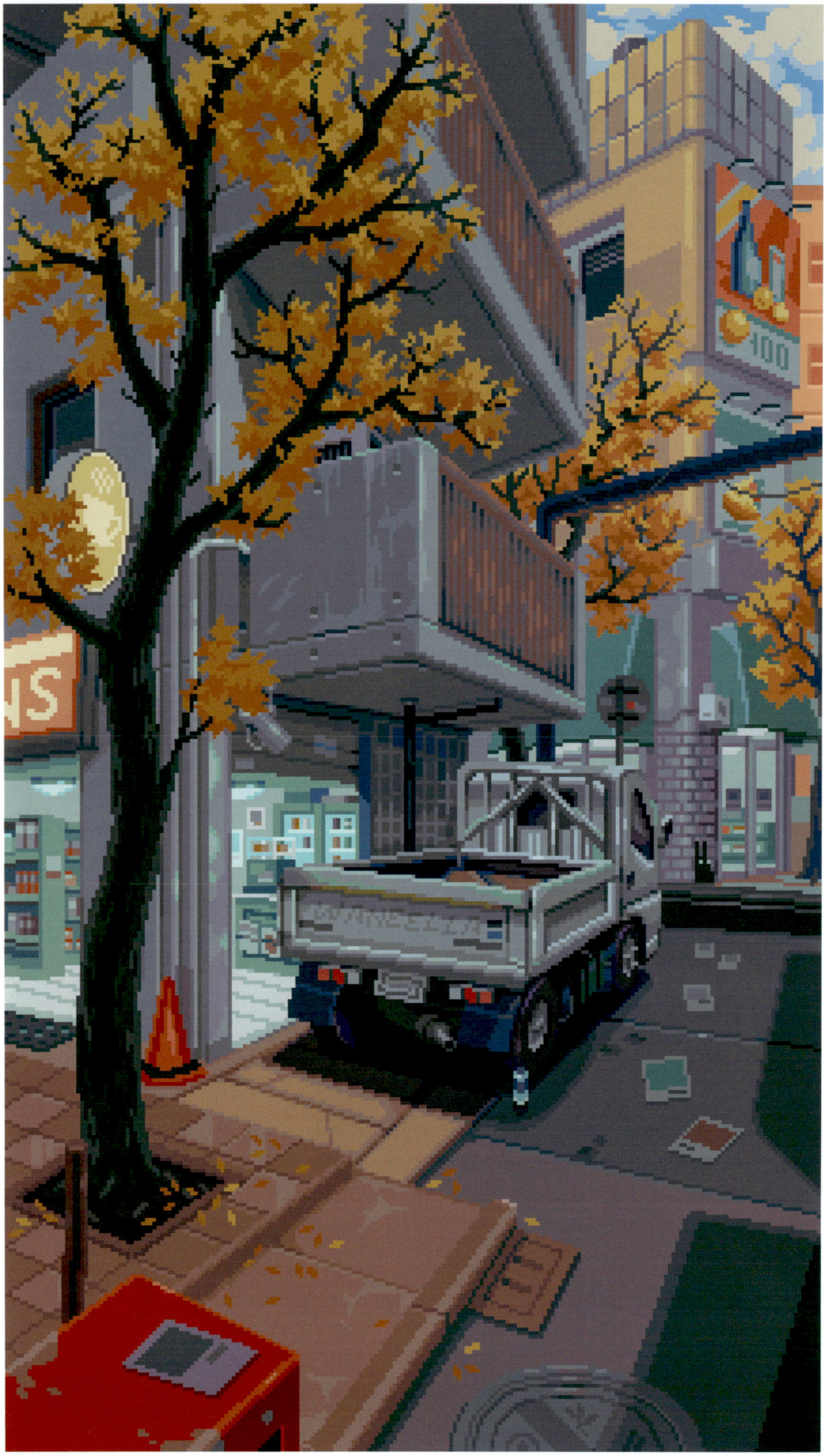

Above: *35.6874285, 139.7270813*, 28/07/2023, 216×384px
Right: *Seashore*, 10/07/2023, 216×384px

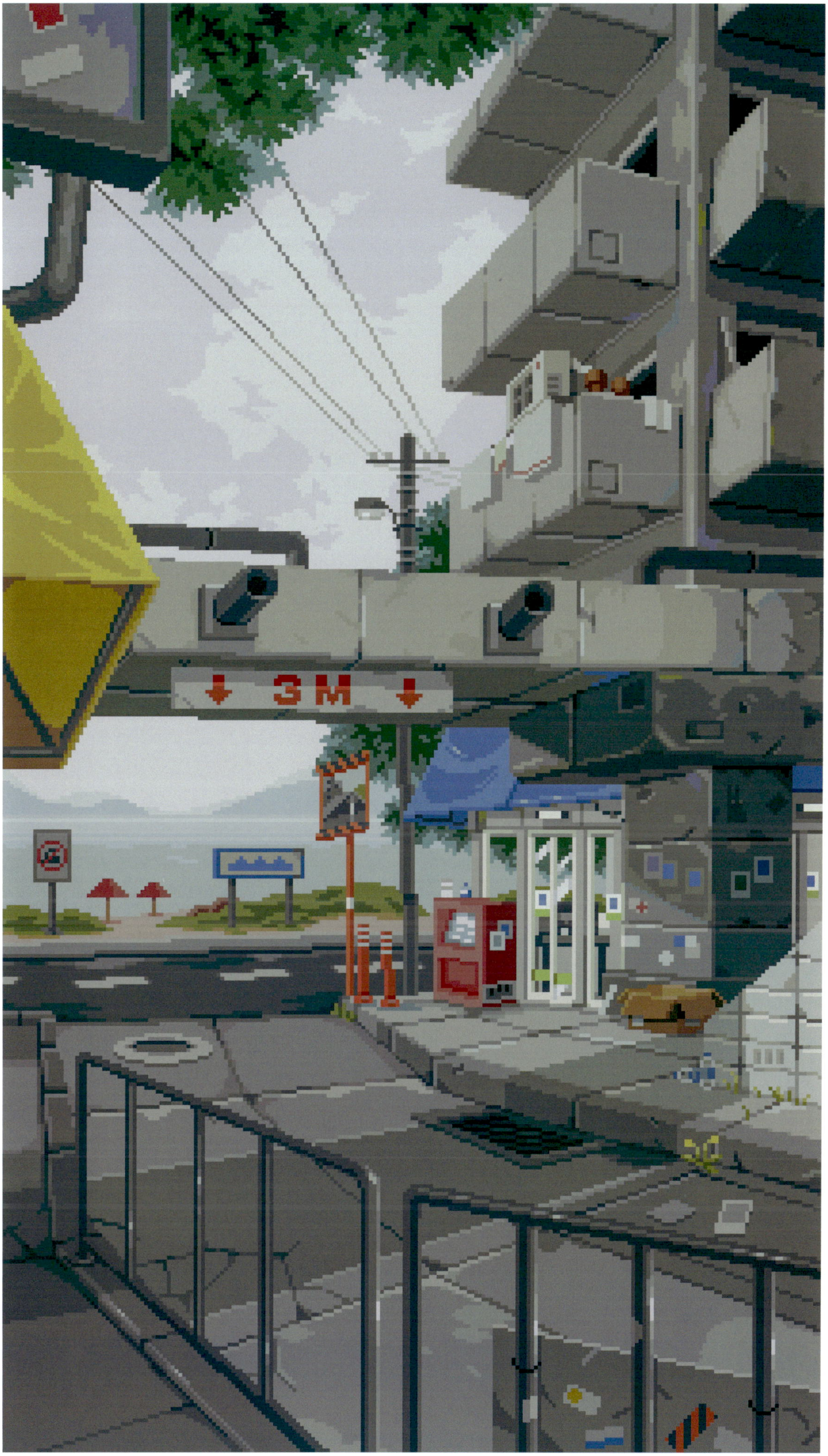
3M

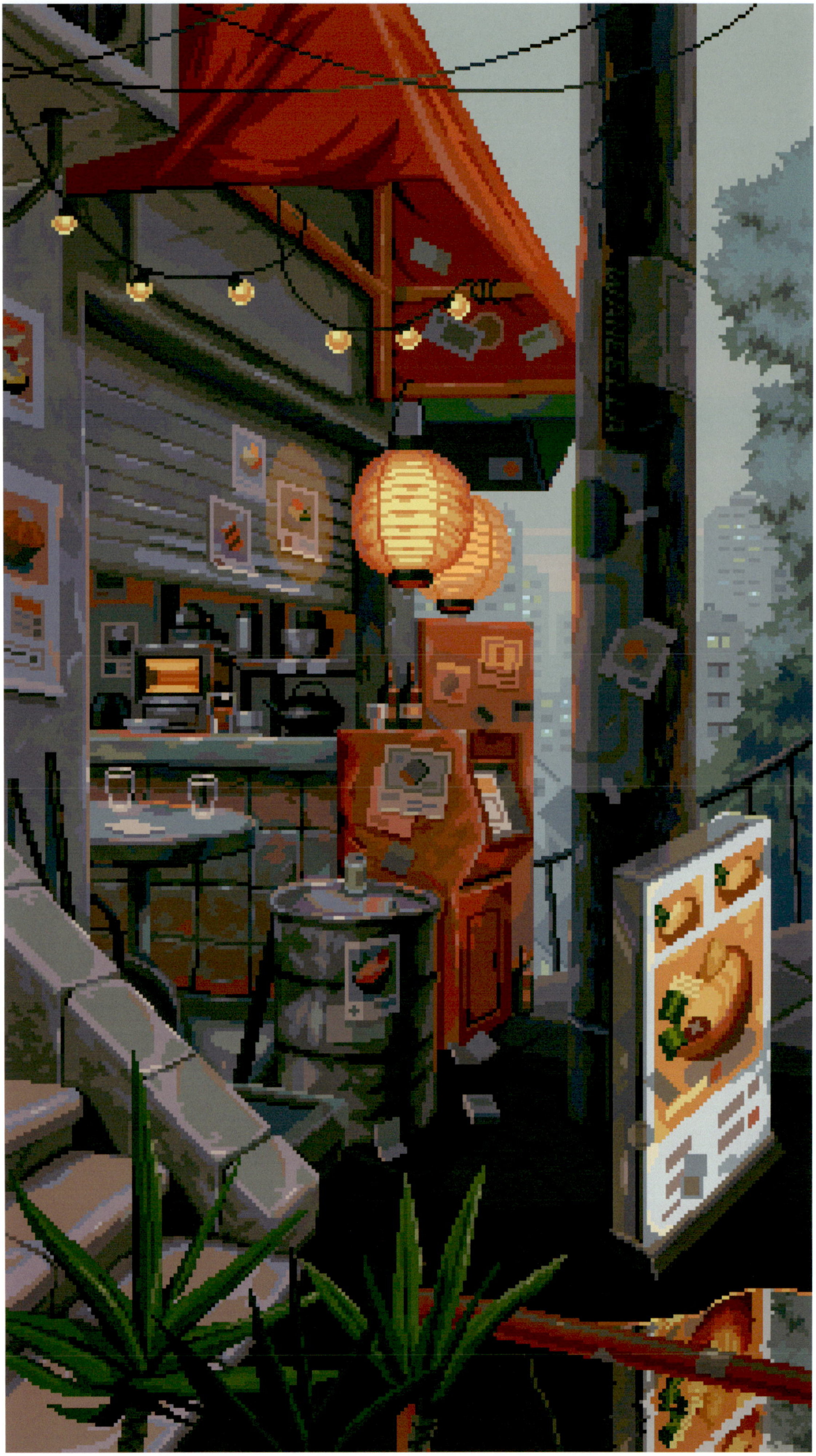

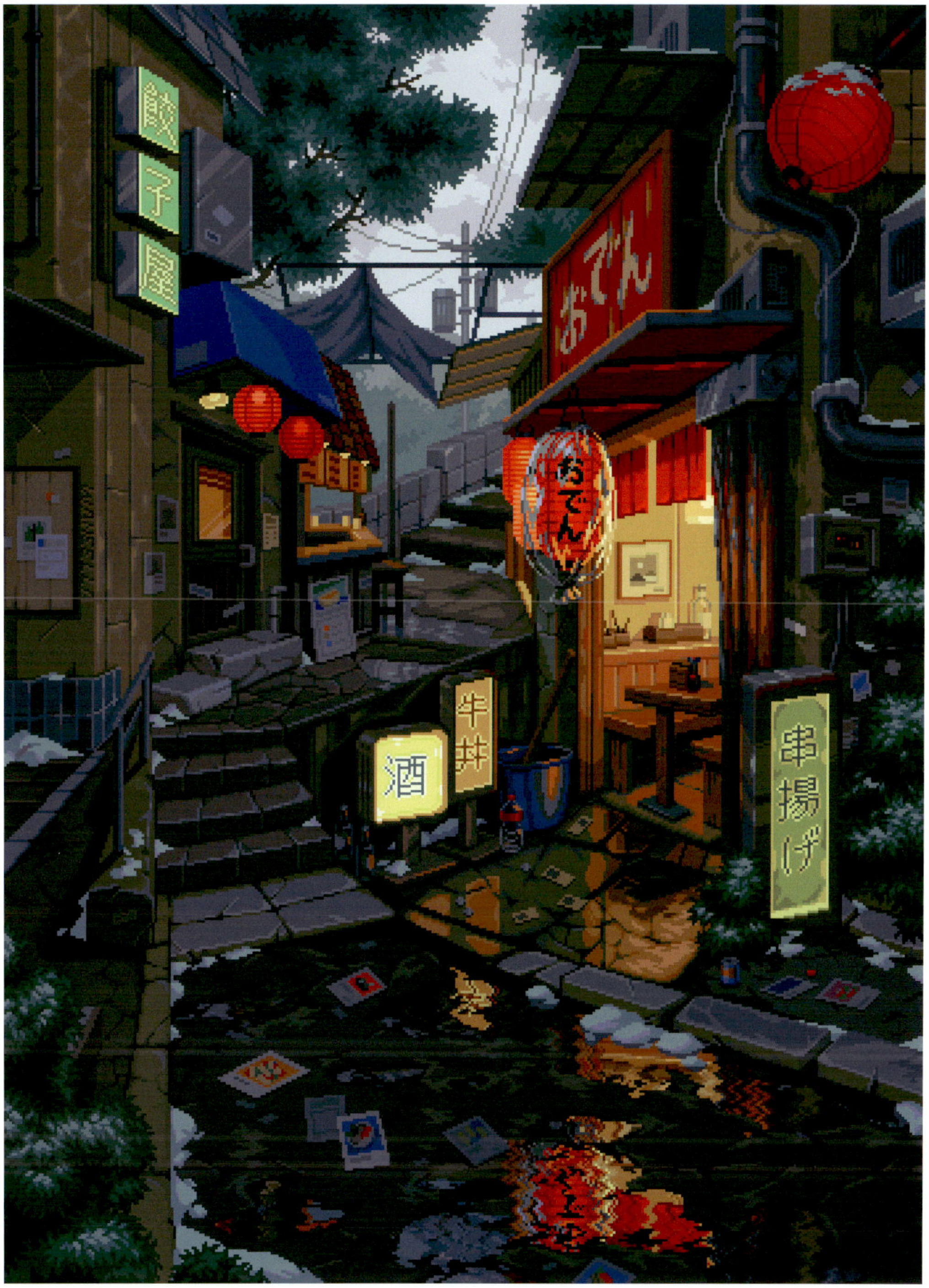

Left: *Before The Rain*, 01/05/2023, 216×389px
Above: *Too Warm For Snow*, produced for the Harugo no Mayu Reflections Collection, 11/01/2023, 350×490px

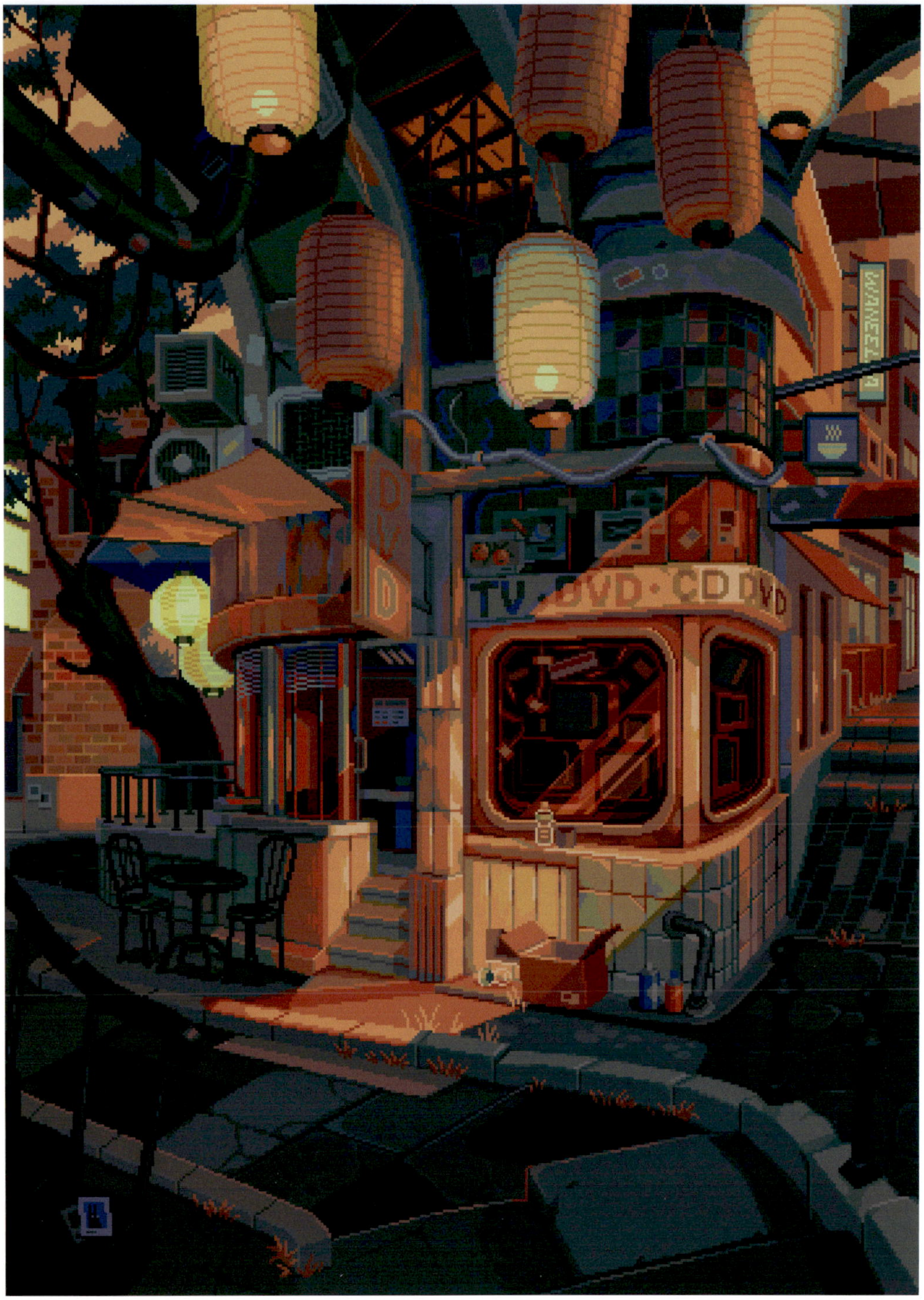

Above: *Closing Hours*, produced for the Harugo no Mayu Day's End Collection, 01/08/2023, 351×497px
Right: *Somewhere Outside*, 12/01/2023, 360×720px

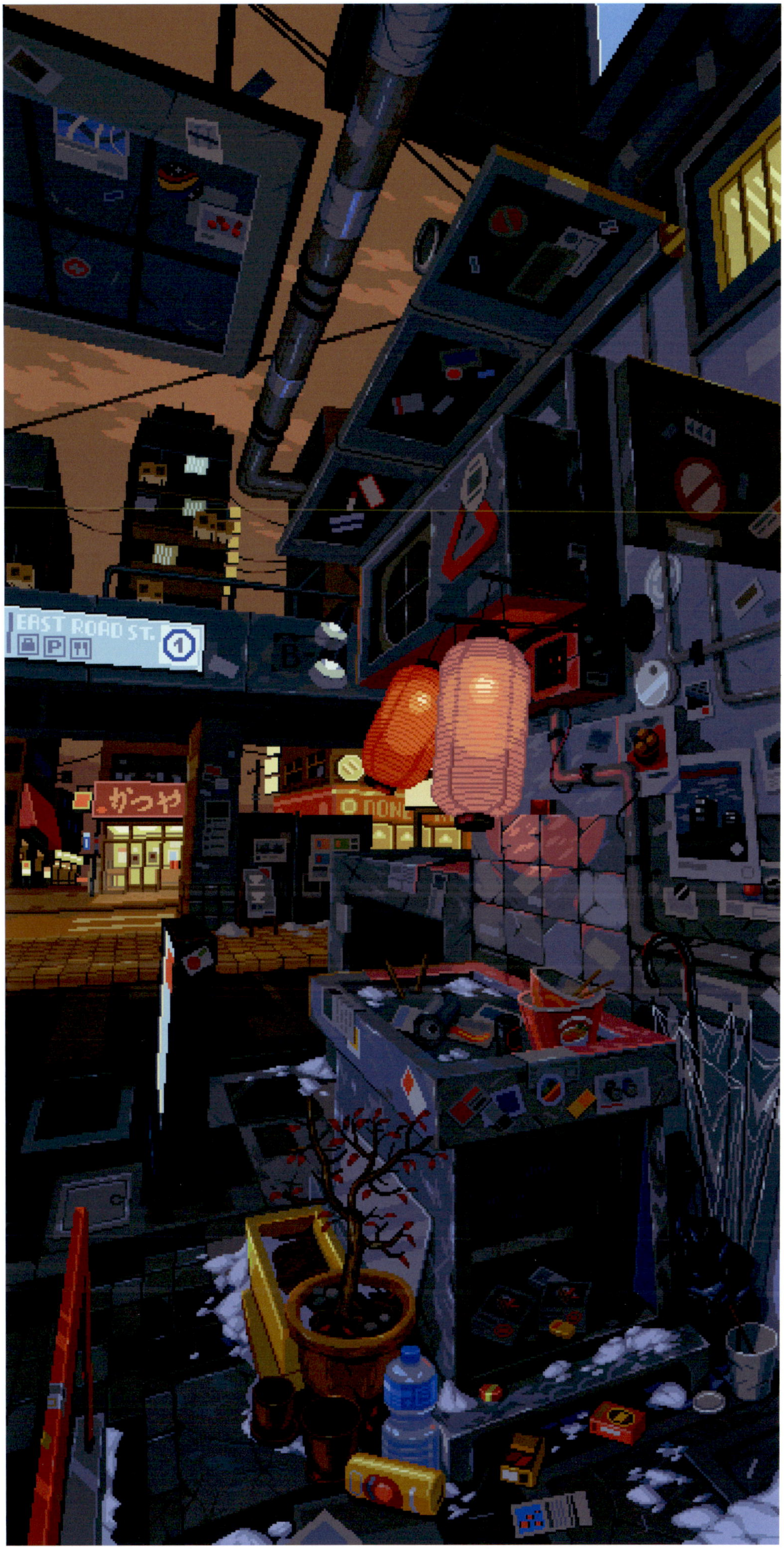
EAST ROAD ST.
P
1
かつや

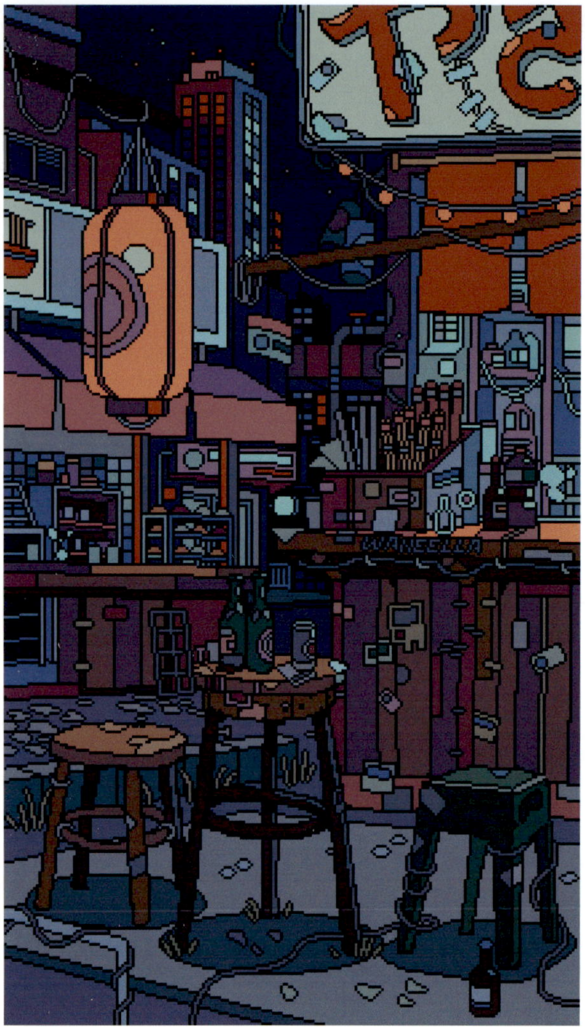

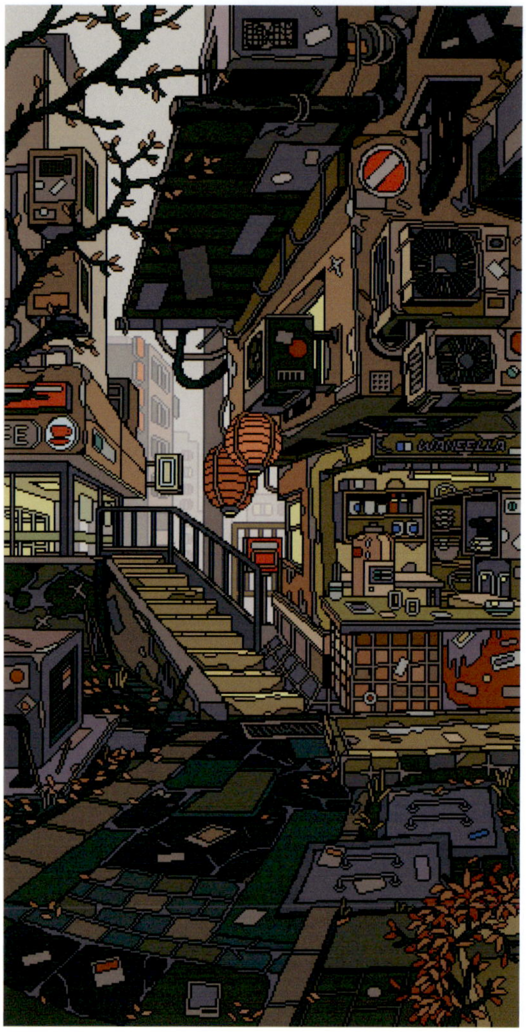

Above: *Purple Fatigue*, 28/08/2023, 216×384px
Above right: *Endless Fall*, 29/06/2023, 270×540px
Right: *Windy Path*, 16/03/2023, 400×600px

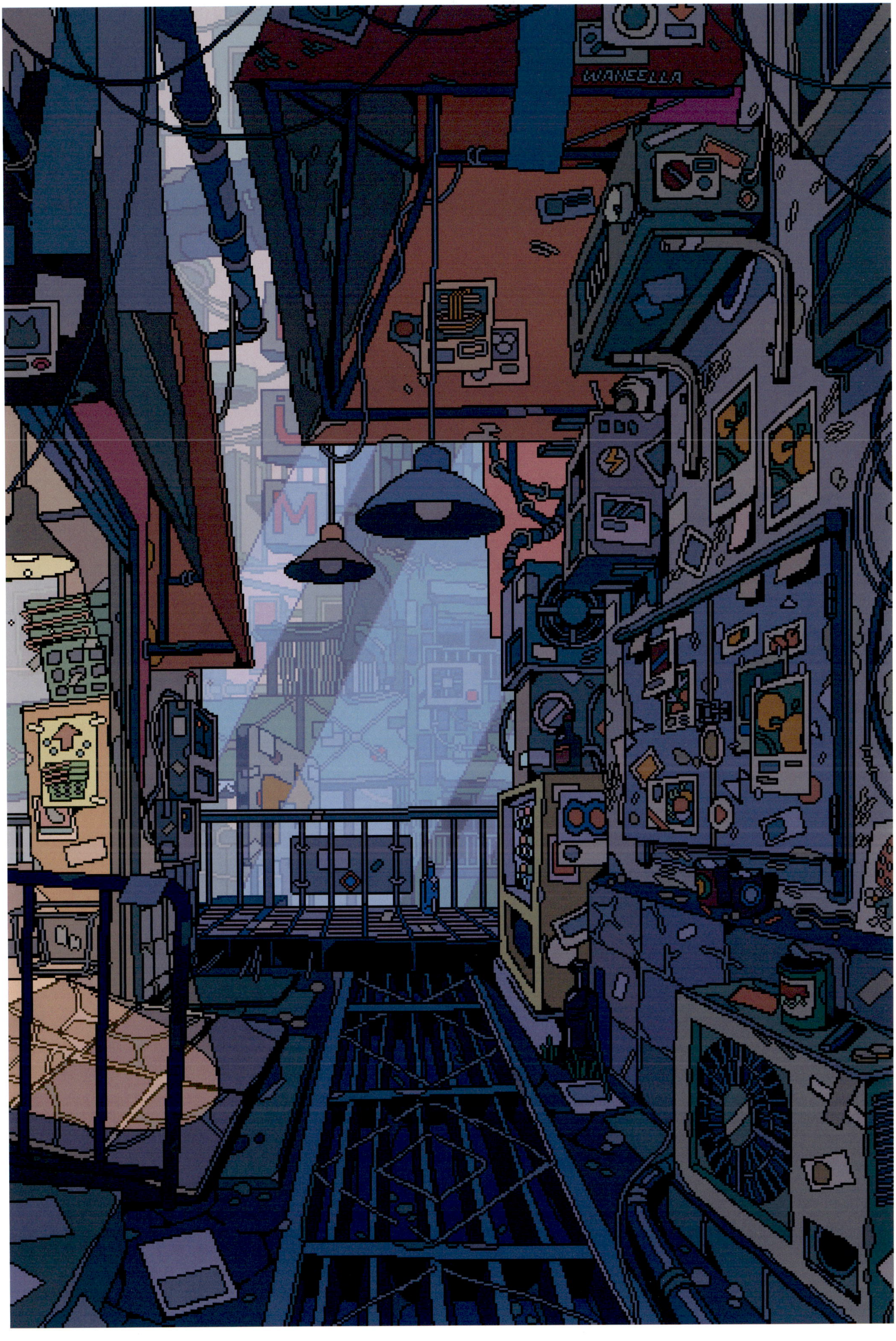

Credits

Pages 25, 29 & 31: Background art for *Pocket Ramble* videogame by Cardboard Robot Games, 2017; Page 28: Background art for *Highrisers* videogame by Solar Powered Games, 2016; Illustration for Desolar twitch. tv / desolar youtube.com / desolarTV, 2016; Pages 30, 32 & 33: Background art for classical music concert *Britain* by Škola Crew, 2017; Page 29: Concept art for an untitled game, 2016; Page 30: *Hosier Lane*, commissioned by Paul Arden, 2019; Page 31: Illustration for Gunship music video; Illustration for *The Tokyoiter* project thetokyoiter.com, 2017; Page 35: Illustration for *198X* videogame by Hi-Bit Studios, 2019; Illustration for *Break The Game* project, courtesy of BREAK THE GAME LLC, 2020; Background art from *River City Girls* videogame, 2018–19, courtesy of WayForward © ARC SYSTEM WORKS; Page 37: Illustration for Steam Autumn Sale 2019 © Valve Corporation 2019; Illustration for *Telescope* single by Tennyson for Ninja Tune, 2019; Illustration for *Telescope* EP by Tennyson for Ninja Tune, 2019; Illustration for *Collapse* single by Tennyson for Ninja Tune, 2019; Page 38: *PAP6xwaneella*, for Pixel Art Park event in Tokyo, 2019; Page 41: Commissioned by Havana for a cancelled game project, 2019; Page 42: Illustration for Rage event by ELEFANT Inc, 2020; Pages 42 & 43: Background art from *River City Girls 2* videogame, 2021, courtesy of WayForward © ARC SYSTEM WORKS; Page 43: Illustration for XPPen by Hanvon Ugee Technology Co Ltd, 2020; *PAP7xwaneella*, for Pixel Art Park event in Tokyo, 2020; Illustration for TourBox by Tourbox Tech Inc, 2021; Background art for *Super IT Friends* by Mike Manor, 2021; Page 46: Background art for *Skeletor vs Eleven* episode of *GEEKED Title Fights*, 2021; Illustration for *The Brusseler* project, 2021; Illustration for *198X* videogame by Hi-Bit Studios, 2021; Illustration for *SANABI* videogame by Wonder Potion, 2021; Page 47: Commissioned by Mattymattykk; *The Jewelled Cypress*, commissioned by Illeos as a gift to trashi3st and Chimera, a FFXIV Free Company, 2022; Illustration for *One More Multiverse* project, 2020; Background art for *Shattered* videogame by Team18K, 2022; *Days Are Getting Shorter*, produced for the Harugo No Mayu Summer Collection, 2021; Page 48: Illustration for Steam Summer Sale 2023 © Valve Corporation 2023; Illustration for Steam Autumn Sale 2023 © Valve Corporation 2023; Commissioned by Doreen Lin, 2021; *Miracles*, illustration for Shanshui Pixel Scenes, 山水像素场景, 2023; Page 181: *False Memories*, produced for the Harugo No Mayu, Autumn Collection, 2021; Page 185: Created for PressPlayID Harajuku series, 2022; Page 215: *Too Warm For Snow*, produced for the Harugo No Mayu Reflections Collection, 2023; Page 216: *Closing Hours*, produced for the Harugo No Mayu, Day's End Collection, 2023.

Acknowledgments

First of all, I would like to thank every person who supported this book's campaign. This publication represents a huge milestone for me, and just a few years ago I could never have imagined that something of this scale would be possible.
Secondly, I want to thank all of my patrons on Patreon – present and past – for supporting me on my artistic journey. Most of the illustrations that are shown in this book were only made because I knew that someone was waiting for them. The artwork that fills these pages simply wouldn't have been made if I didn't have such an amazing community on Patreon.
I would like to thank my family for supporting me in so many ways and for believing in me; for giving me the freedom to do what I want to do. To my mother for helping me bring my ideas to life and encouraging me to find my own way; to my father for his music and for all the support over the years; to my sister for inspiring me to go beyond my comfort zone; to my husband for staying with me at all times. I'm also grateful to all my friends and relatives who didn't let me give up, but instead gifted me so many ideas and opportunities for my growth.
Thank you to every tutor that I met on my journey, and who gave me their knowledge and belief, especially to V.M. Monetov and O.A. Koblova.
A huge thank you to all my clients, who generously granted me permission to print the artworks that I made for them in this book, especially to Desolar, Hamish Campbell, Nico Grupp, Jason Tammemagi, Alexandra Stephanova, Tobias Bjarneby, Luke Pretty, Jane Wagner, Sara Aflageeh, Shunsuke Ishigaki, Jayden Pan, Andrew Joyce, Mattymattykk, Doreen Lin, Paul Arden, Paloma Chen, Illeos, Seunghyeon You, Fabian, Havana, Adam Tierney, Mike Manor, Monoli, Sean Mountain, Team 18K, Jay Shaw, XPPen and The Cardboard Robot Games.
Lastly, thanks to everyone at Thames & Hudson who participated in making this book. Special thanks to Darren Wall for his dedication and the endless support that I received; to Helen Fanthrope and Mytil Ducomet for their incredible patience; and to Cam Winstanley for the warmest words when they were needed the most.
I also want to thank Ikumi Nakamura and Liam Wong for all their help.
This book was made possible by an incredible number of people, and I'm forever grateful to them for turning it into a reality.
Thank you!

Index

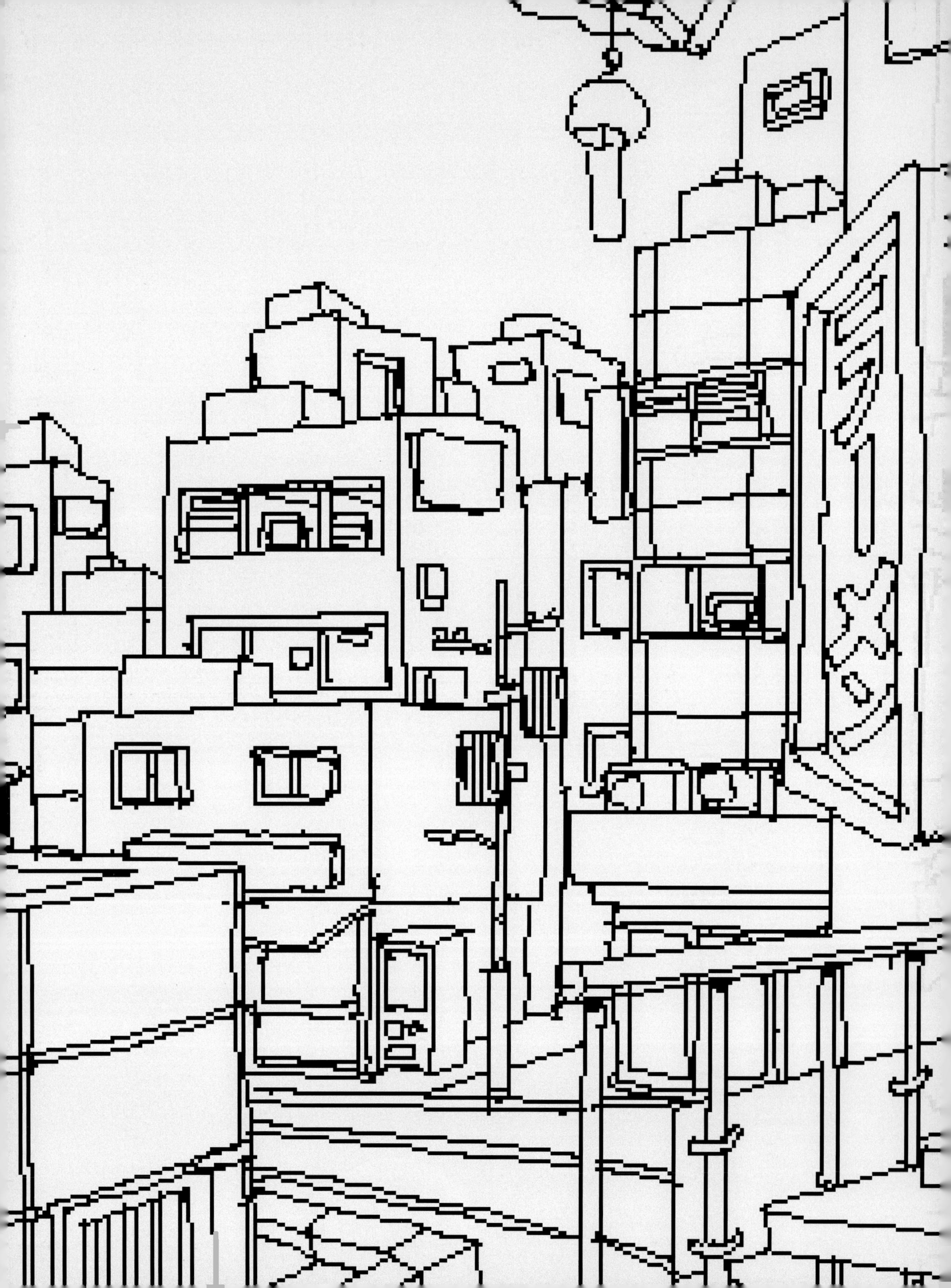

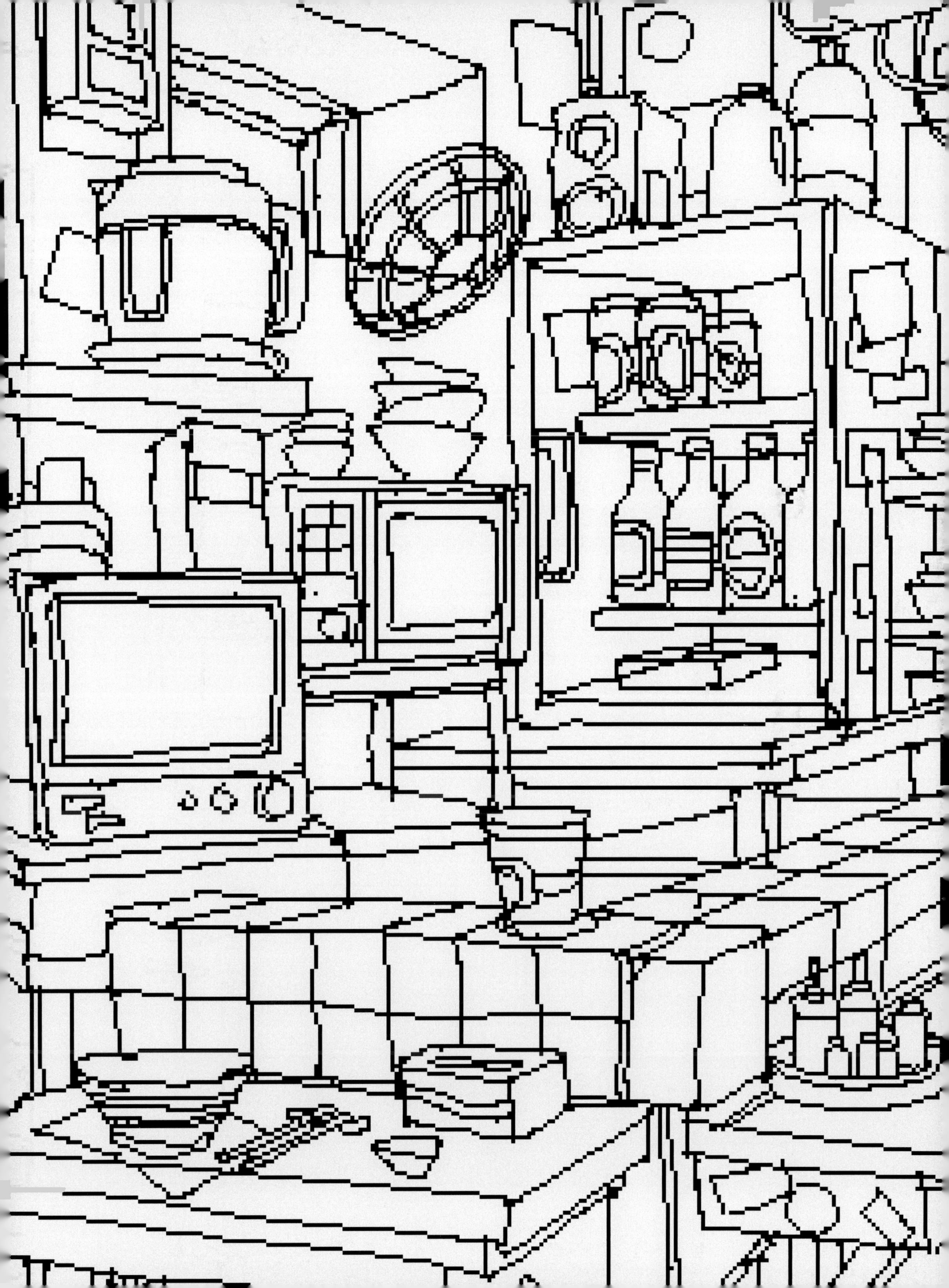

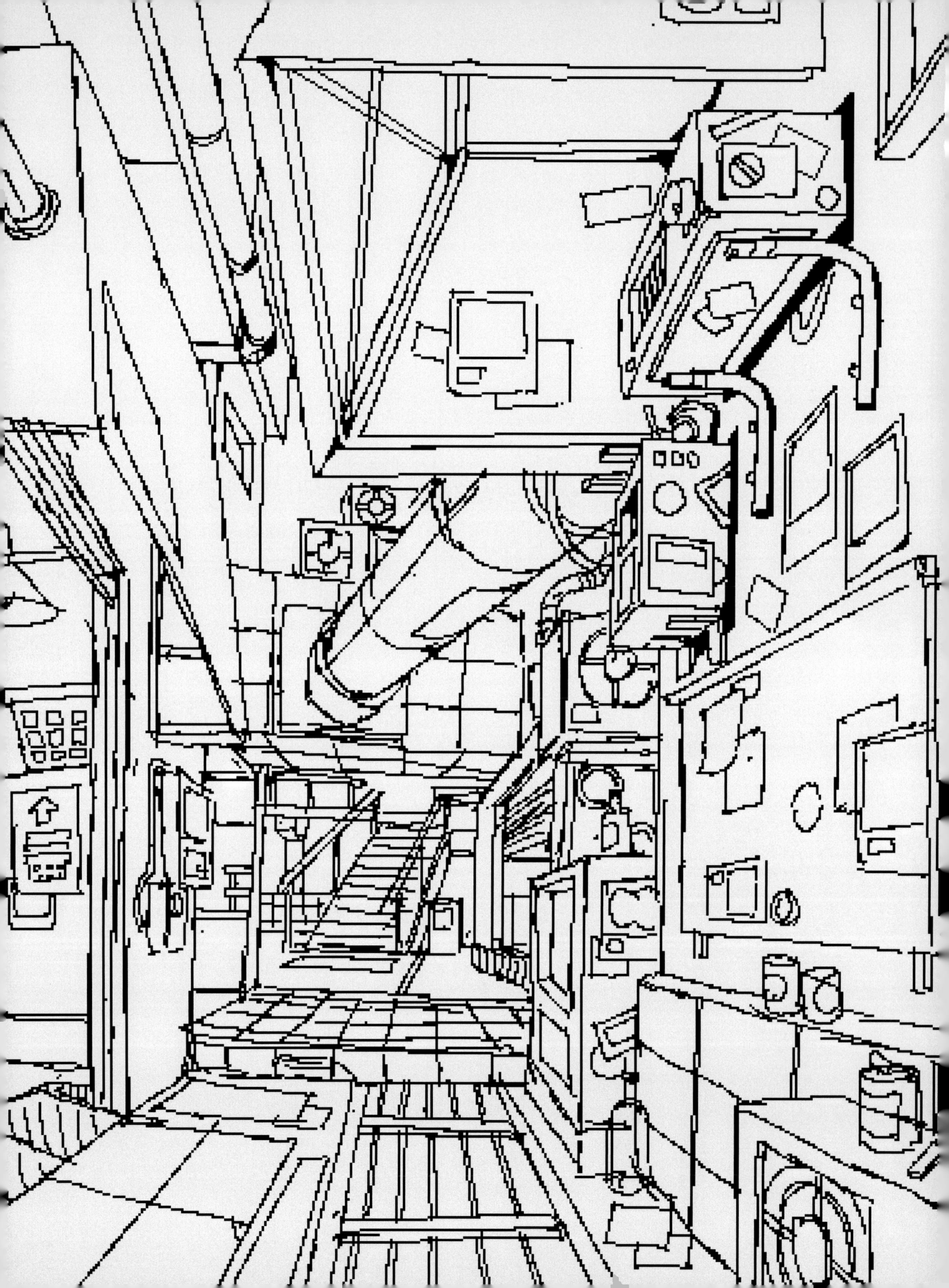